Codex Judaica

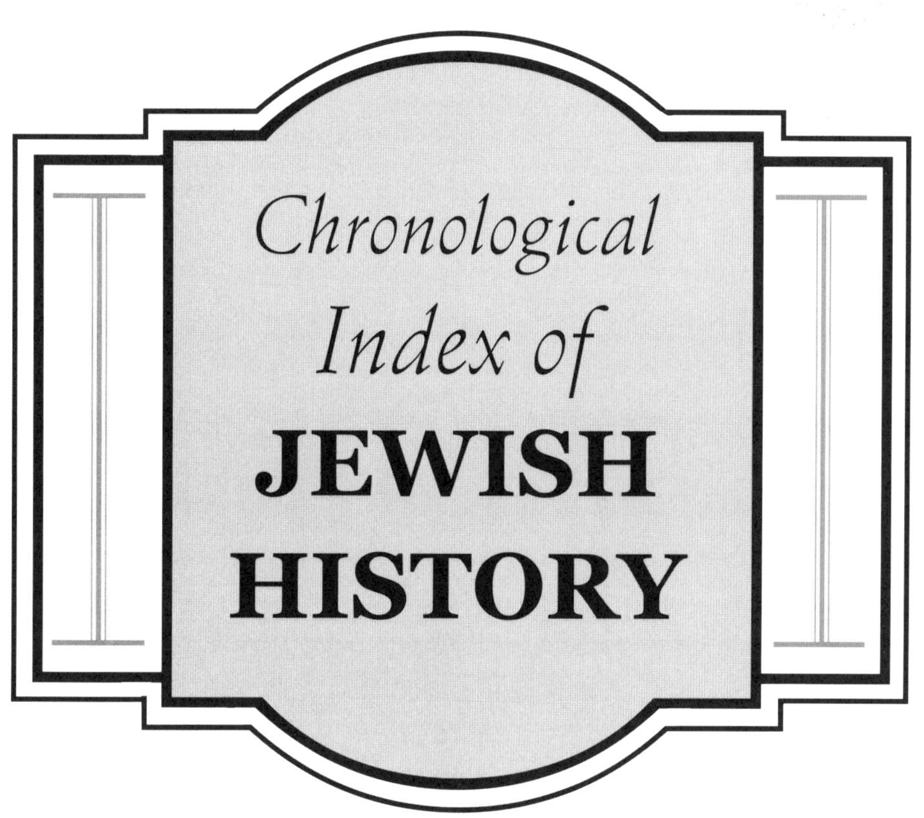

Mattis Kantor

Covering 5,764 Years of Biblical, Talmudic & post-Talmudic History

Zichron Press, New York, 2005
6th Printing, April 2010

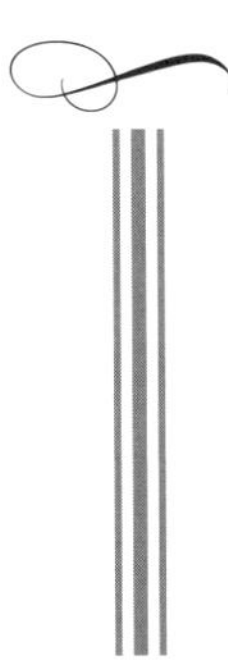

Books by this Author:

- Chassidic INSIGHTS — A Guide for the Entangled I
[1978, 1990, 2003]

- TEN KEYS for Understanding Human Nature — A Guide for the Entangled II
[1994, 2006]

- The Jewish Time Line Encyclopedia
[1989, 1992]

- CODEX JUDAICA *Chronological Index of* JEWISH HISTORY
[2005 - 2016 .... Ten reprints]

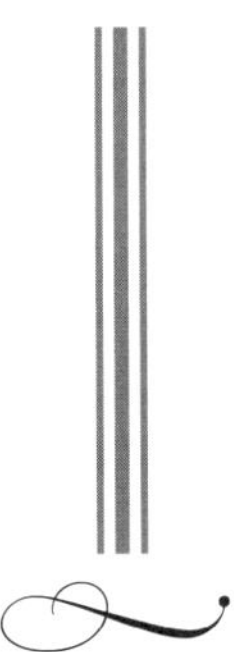

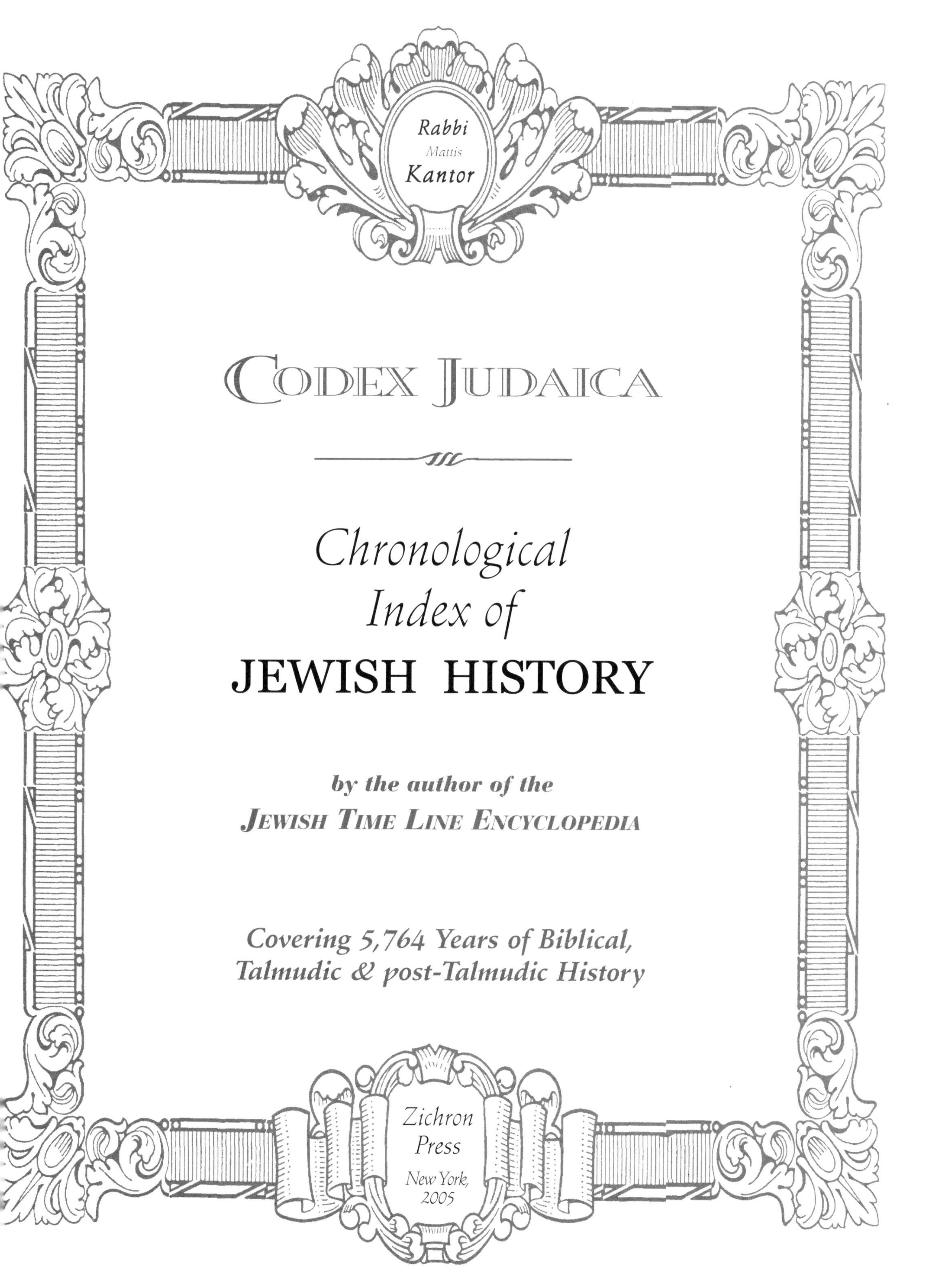

CODEX JUDAICA

Chronological Index of JEWISH HISTORY

by the author of the
JEWISH TIME LINE ENCYCLOPEDIA

Covering 5,764 Years of Biblical, Talmudic & post-Talmudic History

Zichron Press
790 Washington Ave.
Suite 115
Brooklyn, N.Y. 11238
www.codex-judaica.com
zichron.press@eeymail.com

ISBN 0-9670378-3-2

1st printing 2005 - 10th printing 2016

ISBN 978-0--9670378-3-7
90000>
9 780967 037837

זה ספר תולדות אדם
אתם קרואים אדם

בשערי הדורות

מאת הר׳ **יצחק מתתי׳הו קאנטאר** שליט״א
בהר׳ משה פנחס ז״ע

מחבר ספר **בואו שעריו** חלק א׳ וח״ב
(שעדיין לא הובא לבית הדפוס) ובה נכללו ג׳ שערים
שער ההשכלה, שער ההשקפה, ושער העבודה
שכולם כלולים יחד בביאורם עפ״י תורת החסידות
וגם פיעה״ת **בשערי החסידות** אשר כעת
עדיין לא יצא לאור

שנת **תשס״ה** לפ״ק
הדפסה ששית ה׳תש״ע

How to Use this Book.

Browse.

This is an index — an encyclopedia. Although it is written in chronological order, it was not designed to be read from cover to cover.

Readers should turn to a period or year that interests them, and browse on from there. There are also some more specific ways to use this book and benefit from the information in it.

Specific Search.

Use the index to find the item of interest, and read each entry. It is important to use the whole index entry, because although there is cross referencing within the text, those references will not necessarily give a comprehensive listing on the specifics of interest to you. Cross references are displayed in the following levels of priority: *a)* as part of the text; *b)* in parentheses; *c)* in parentheses with a lighter font.

Historical Perspective.

This book was designed to give the researcher or reader a sense of historical perspective.

The book begins with a one page chart — or spectrum — of the various eras of Jewish history, then a timeline of major events, before proceeding with the detailed text, which is also in chronological order.

To gain a proper perspective, it is possible to zero in on an event (or person), and then withdraw back through the broader perspectives to develop a telescoping effect.

This book does not concentrate on biographical detail, but is more concerned with placing events in their proper chronological setting. Entries into any year are in chronological order based on the best information available. Note that any events occurring in the months between Rosh Hashana (the Jewish New Year) and the secular new year (on 1st January), are entered under a new year-heading, with the unchanged secular year in *italics,* as displayed here.

5765 — 2005

5766 — *2005*

Table of Contents

List of Maps

List of Charts

Preface

This book is a digest of the history of Biblical and Talmudic times, post Talmudic scholars (major events in their lives) and events that affected Jewish life in general, until this day. The scope of this book — which places emphasis on the proper sequence of events — is very specific. Events are listed in their year of occurrence unless otherwise indicated — quoting sources until the end of the Talmud era.

Inasmuch as it is an attempt to list — in a clear but very brief manner — all the important information available, presenting it in a style readable to the layman, it has been necessary to omit certain details which would only inject confusion, not clarity.

The chronology of events is based on Biblical and Talmudic sources, and consequently events listed here as having occurred prior to the secular year *one* (1) do not synchronize with the chronology based on other sources *(mainly Persian kings — many with the same names — and the year of their reign, a matter upon which scholars differ in opinions. See 3412/-349)* This book does not attempt to address this issue — that is the scope of an entirely different book.

It is important to note, that the Talmud (and Talmudists) share two fundamental differences with the prevailing attitudes to history.

1) The Talmud maintains that the overall quality of the intellectual and *spiritual* caliber (of man) declines as generations advance, *[Tal.Shab.112b, Eruv.53a / Igg.R.Sher.G.]*; hence Talmud scholars of a particular era (Tekufa) have always maintained a deep and somewhat mystical respect for scholars in preceding era's. *[Tal.B.B.12a, Ramban /See Appendix D]*.

2) The Talmud considers unwritten communication to be superior to written material. In fact written material was viewed as a concession to the lower intellectual standards and abilities of the later generations. *[Tal.Tem.14b, Ket.103b /Rashi B.M.33a / Mmn.Hakd. L'Yad / Hakd.S'MaG]*.

These two 'axioms' deliver a different set of instruments for measuring history, and/or the importance of people and events.

Although — in the presentation of the personalities and events of modern Jewish history — an attempt has been made to use similar perspectives as those used for previ centuries, a number of significant deviations have been made, inasmuch as many of today's notable events and personalities would not have been highlighted in a manner commensurate with their current prominence. Nevertheless, certain events and personalities have been projected into greater importance than their current recognition warrants because — in the opinion of this author —their significance has not yet been felt, or because they will eventually be recognized as having a more lasting nature. Thus the realities of current public acceptance have confined and defined the prominence of certain current events.

The basic purposes of this book are: To present information on traditional Jewish History, in a clear concise and scholarly form; to present this history in a systematic organized manner, so that even the novice can develop a clear sense of perspective.

To achieve these aims, events have been listed with a finely-balanced sense of importance. The importance of an event, for example, may be downgraded (and not headlined) because of the lack of clarity in the exact date. On the other hand, there are personalities (in the Talmud) about whom a relative abundance of biographical detail is available, yet they have not necessarily been given prominence in direct relation to that information. They have been considered in the perspective commensurate to their total impact on Jewish history.

This book emphasizes the chronological placement of events and people, but only deals very briefly with biographical details of personalities. Often more details are given about the less famous than the famous, for it is assumed that the reader has some prior knowledge of the famous, or has access to reliable biographical material elsewhere. It is also considered unlikely that biographic brevity would distort the historical impact of the famous.

In instances of extended or widespread massacres, a total number of casualties is often given, and then instances of specific incidents are chronologically listed. The specifics are not comprehensive, but include only the major incidents, and/or incidents that serve to illustrate the nature of the occurrences. That the accounts of such events come from the traumatized victims and/or onlookers, conflicting reports of detail may often occur.

Many items and "snippets" of information have been enclosed in parentheses ( ) to indicate either *(i)* the secondary importance of the information, or *(ii)* that the documentation of that information is not as sound as the rest of the statement.

Outline

In this book Jewish history is divided into four distinct sections. Each of these sections is subdivided into the various eras (Tekufot), each era being presented as a chapter.

Some eras (Tekufot) are subdivided into a number of subchapters, because of natural historical demarcations, or to reduce excessive length. Nevertheless, in such instances the breaks have been placed at some point of significance.

The timelines are for enhancing the reader's perspective of Jewish history — significant events being highlighted by employing the use of larger and bolder typefaces.

Timeline 1. The Full Spectrum of Jewish History

This is a listing — at the beginning of the book only — of the four major sections into which Jewish history is divided here, and the fifteen era's (Tekufot) with their subdivisions. This is a one page wide-angle view of Jewish History.

Timeline 2. Major Events in Jewish History

This eight (horizontal) page listing — also at the beginning of the book only — adds only the very major and/or familiar events to the previous timeline. With this additional detail, the reader's focus will need to narrow down, although the wide-angle view is still there.

Timeline 3. The Highlights of Jewish History

This thirteen page listing presents more detail yet, and may therefore be somewhat daunting to a reader not very familiar with Jewish history. However— after having read through some of the main text — the reader will find this timeline useful for stepping back and seeing everything within a larger framework. The specific segments of this timeline also appear at the beginning of every Chapter (Tekufa), in similar detail.

THREE TIMELINES

Timeline 1

The Full Spectrum of Jewish History

Three Timelines

The Full Spectrum of Jewish History

SECTION I – THE BEGINNINGS

1. **The New World**
2. **The Forefathers**
3. **Living in Egypt**

SECTION II – THE NATION

4. **Moshe the Leader**
5. **Judges and Early Prophets**
6. **Kings & the First Beit Hamikdash**

SECTION III – RIVERS OF BABYLON, CONVULSIONS IN YEHUDA (JUDEA)

7. **Exile in Babylon**
8. **The Second Beit Hamikdash**
   a. **Anshei Knesset HaGedolah** — ***The Great Council of Sages***
   b. **Greek Cultural Domination**
   c. **Kingdom of Yehuda (Judea)** — ***Dynasty of the Chashmona'im***
   d. **Roman Client Kings & Rulers** — ***The Herodian Dynasty***

9. **The Talmudic Era — The Mishna**
10. **The Talmudic Era — The Gemara**
11. **The Talmudic Academies of Bavel**
    a. **The Rabbanan Savurai**
    b. **The Ge'onim, and Arabic Dominion**

SECTION IV – UNIVERSAL DISPERSION

12. **The Rishonim - Early Scholars**
    a. **Early Rishonim, Tosaphot, and the Crusade Massacres**
    b. **Later Rishonim, Persecutions, and Expulsions**

13. **The Kov'im** — ***The Great Scholars of the Shulchan Aruch & Torah Consolidation***
14. **The Acharonim, Later Scholars**
    a. **Early Achronim and East European Massacre**
    b. **Acharonim and Early Chasidim**
    c. **Later Acharonim, and Changing Society**

15. **The Melaktim & the Current Era**
    a. **The Holocaust**
    b. **The Independent State of Israel**
    c. **The Post—Holocaust Era**

Major Events in Jewish History

Chapter 1

The New World

Jewish Year		Secular Year
1	CREATION OF THE WORLD, AND ADAM & CHAVA (EVE).	**-3760**
687	Metushelach (son of Chanoch) was born.	**-3074**
930	Adam died.	**-2831**
1056	Noah (son of Lemech II) was born.	**-2705**
1558	Shem (son of Noah) was born.	**-2203**
1656	THE GREAT FLOOD COVERED THE EARTH.	**-2105**
1723	Ever (son of Shelach) was born.	**-2038**
1948	Avraham (son of Terach) was born.	**-1813**

Chapter 2

The Forefathers

1948	Avraham (son of Terach) was born.	**-1813**
2018	THE COVENANT (BRIT BEIN HABETARIM) WITH AVRAHAM.	**-1743**
2048	Avraham circumcised himself and Yishmael.	**-1713**
2084	THE AKEDA. YITZCHAK WAS PREPARED TO BE A SACRIFICE.	**-1677**
2108	Yaakov (Jacob) and Eisav (Esau) were born.	**-1653**
2171	Yitzchak blessed Yaakov instead of Eisav.	**-1590**
2216	Yosef was sold.	**-1545**
2229	Yosef became Viceroy of Egypt.	**-1532**
2238	YAAKOV (AND HIS FAMILY) WENT TO EGYPT.	**-1523**

Chapter 3

Living in Egypt

2255	Yaakov died.	**-1506**

2332	The enslavement in Egypt began after Levi died.	**-1429**
2448	THE CHILDREN OF ISRAEL LEFT EGYPT	**-1313**

Chapter 4

Moshe the Leader

2448	THE REVELATION & TORAH ON MOUNT SINAI.	**-1313**
2488	Moshe died.	**-1273**

Chapter 5

Judges & Early Prophets

2488	Bnei Yisrael crossed the Jordan into Canaan.	**-1273**
2516	Yehoshua died.	**-1245**
2533	The rule of Shoftim (Judges) began with Othniel ben Knaz	**-1228**
2654	Devorah became leader.	**-1107**
2694	Gideon became leader.	**-1067**
2779	Yiphtach (HaGil'adi) became leader.	**-982**
2810	Shimshon (Samson) became leader.	**-951**
2830	Eli (HaKohen) became leader.	**-931**
2871	Shmuel became leader.	**-890**

Chapter 6

Kings and the First Beit Hamikdash

2882	Shaul was appointed king.	**-879**
2892	DAVID BECAME KING OF ISRAEL IN YERUSHALAYIM.	-869
2924	Shlomo became king.	-837
2935	THE FIRST BEIT HAMIKDASH WAS COMPLETED	**-827**
2964	SHLOMO DIED AND HIS KINGDOM WAS DIVIDED.	**-797**

3043	Eliyahu went up in a chariot of fire.	**-718**
3142	Yeshayahu (Isaiah) began his prophecies.	**-619**
3187	The first two of the ten tribes were exiled.	**-574**
3195	Another two of the ten tribes were exiled.	**-566**
3205	THE LAST OF THE TEN TRIBES WERE EXILED.	**-556**
3298	Yirmiyahu (Jeremiah) began his prophecies.	**-463**
3319	Yerushalayim was conquered, and Yehoyakim exiled.	**-442**
3327	Yerushalayim conquered again, and Yehoyachin exiled.	**-434**
3332	Yechezk'el (Ezekiel) prophecized in exile.	**-429**
3336	The final Babylonian siege of Yerushalayim	**-425**
3338	THE FIRST BEIT HAMIKDASH WAS DESTROYED.	**-423**

Chapter 7

Exile in Babylon

3389	Daniel read the writing on the wall.	**-372**
3406	MORDECHAI PROCLAIMED THE CELEBRATION OF PURIM.	**-355**
3412	THE SECOND BEIT HAMIKDASH WAS COMPLETED.	**-349**

Chapter 8

The Second Beit Hamikdash

Chapter 8a

Anshei Knesset HaGedola — The Great Council of Sages

3413	Ezra led the second return to Eretz Yisrael.	**-348**
3448	EZRA DIED.	**-313**
3449	The Minyan Shtarot began.	**-313**

Chapter 8b — Greek Cultural Domination.

3515	72 Elders translated the Torah into Greek (Septuagint)	**-246**

3621	The revolt of Mattityahu the Chashmona'i.	-140

Chapter 8c — Kingdom of Yehuda (Judea).
Dynasty of the Chashmona'im.

3622	Yehuda (HaMaccabi) ruled.	-139
3622	The Second Beit Hamikdash was re-dedicated.	-139
3623	CHANUKA WAS DECLARED A FESTIVAL.	-138
3628	Yehuda (HaMaccabi) was killed in battle.	-133
3700	The Romans gained control of Yehuda (Judea).	-61

Chapter 8d — Roman Client Kings & Rulers.
The Herodian Dynasty.

3725	Herod I ruled, killing all the Chashmona'im.	-36
3728	Hillel became leader of the Torah scholars.	-33
3742	Herod I began rebuilding the Second Beit Hamikdash.	-19
3768	HILLEL DIED.	8
3788	The Sanhedrin moved from the Second Beit Hamikdash.	28
3810	Raban Gamliel I (son of Shimon, son of Hillel) died.	50
3826	Vespasian arrived in Yehuda to reassert Roman authority.	66
3829	THE SECOND BEIT HAMIKDASH WAS DESTROYED.	69

Chapter 9

The Talmudic Era — The Mishna

3949	R. YEHUDA HANASSI COMPLETED THE MISHNA AROUND THIS TIME.	189

Chapter 10

The Talmudic Era — The Gemara

3979	Rav Left Eretz Yisrael and settled in Bavel (Babylonia).	219
4119	Hillel II (who established the calendar) became Nassi.	359

4187	R.Ashi died after the compilation of the Gemara.	427
4235	THE TALMUD WAS COMPLETE, WHEN RAVINA II DIED.	**475**

Chapter 11

The Talmudic Academies of Bavel

Chapter 11a — The Rabbanan SAVURAI

Chapter 11b — The GE'ONIM, and Arabic Dominion

4374	JEWS WERE ALLOWED TO RETURN TO YERUSHALAYIM.	**614**
4397	The Arabs conquered Eretz Yisrael.	**637**
4618	R.Amram (who wrote the Siddur) became GAON of Sura.	**858**
4798	R.HAI GAON DIED, AND THE ACADEMIES OF BAVEL DECLINED.	**1038**

Chapter 12

The Rishonim — Early Scholars

Chapter 12a — Early Rishonim, Tosaphot, and the Crusade Massacres.

4856	CRUSADERS (1ST) DESTROYED JEWISH COMMUNITIES.	**1096**
4859	Yerushalayim was captured by the Crusaders.	**1099**
4863	The Rif Died.	1103
4865	RASHI DIED, AND THE ERA OF THE TOSAPHOT BEGAN.	**1105**
4895	THE RAMBAM (MAIMONIDES) WAS BORN.	**1135**
4904	THE FIRST (RECORDED) BLOOD LIBEL TOOK PLACE.	**1144**
4907	Crusaders (2nd) attacked Jewish communities.	**1147**
4948	Jews were allowed to return to Yerushalayim.	**1187**
4950	Jews were massacred in England, in the 3rd Crusade.	**1190**
5002	A massive burning of the Talmud took place in Paris.	**1242**
5030	The Ramban died.	**1270**
5046	The Maharam MeRothenburg was imprisoned.	**1286**
5050	New works advanced the study of KABBALA.	**1290**

5050	THE ERA OF THE TOSAPHOT CONCLUDED AT AROUND THIS TIME.	1290

Chapter 12b — Later Rishonim,
Persecutions, and Expulsions.

5050	All Jews were expelled from England.	1290
5058	The Rindfleisch massacres began.	1298
5109	THE BLACK DEATH MASSACRES SWEPT ACROSS EUROPE.	1349
5151	Jews of Spain were massacred — many became Marranos.	1391
5155	The Final expulsion of Jews from France.	1394
5181	Jews in Austria were massacred in the Wiener Gezera.	1421
5235	THE INVENTION OF PRINTING WAS USED FOR JEWISH BOOKS.	1475
5241	The Inquisition was established in Spain.	1481
5252	ALL JEWS WERE EXPELLED FROM SPAIN AND SICILY.	1492

Chapter 13
The Kov'im*

The Great Scholars of the Shulchan Aruch & Torah Consolidation

5257	All Jews were expelled from Portugal.	1496
5323	The Shulchan Aruch was completed by R.Yosef Karo.	1563
5330	SHULCHAN ARUCH PUBLISHED WITH SUPPLEMENTS OF RAMO.	1570
5332	The Ari'zal died in Tzfat (Safed).	1572
5406	The Shach and Taz (on Shulchan Aruch) were printed.	1646
5408	JEWS WERE MASSACRED BY CHMIELNITZKI'S FORCES.	1648

*See Appendix D

Chapter 14
The Acharonim — Later Scholars.

Chapter 14a, Early Acharonim
and East European Massacres

5433	The Magen Avraham (on Shulchan Aruch) was completed.	1673

5437 Shabbetai Tzvi Died as a Muslim. 1676

5449 The Beit Shmuel (on the Shulchan Aruch) was printed. 1689

5458 The Ba'al Shem Tov was born. 1698

5494 Jews were massacred by the Haidamack bands. 1734

Chapter 14b, Acharonim and Early Chasidim.

5518 The Frankists instigated mass burnings of the Talmud. 1757

5520 The Ba'al Shem Tov died. 1760

5528 Despite resistance the Haidamacks massacre thousands. 1768

5532 The Maggid of Mezeritsch died. 1772

5551 The Pale of Settlement was established in Russia. 1791

5587 Russia began conscripting Jewish children to the army. 1827

Chapter 14c, Later Acharonim and Changing Society.

5641 Many Jews Began Leaving Russia After a Wave of Pogroms. 1881

5665 Many Jews were killed in (official) Russian pogroms. 1905

5674 Over 500,000 Jewish soldiers fought in World War I. 1914

5678 Over 60,000 Jews were killed during Russian Revolution. 1918

5684 Daf HaYomi study cycle commenced. 1923

Chapter 15,

The Melaktim & the Current Era.

Chapter 15a — The Holocaust.

5699 Germany started World War II, and mass killing of Jews. 1939

5701 200,000 Jews were killed at Babi Yar and Ponary. 1941

5702 400,000 Jews of Warsaw were sent to DEATH CAMPS. 1942

5703 The Remaining Jews in Warsaw Staged a Massive Uprising. 1943

5704 300,000 Hungarian Jews were killed in 3 months. 1944

5705	Nazi-Germany was conquered, and World War II ended.	**1945**
5705	6,000,000 JEWS WERE KILLED BY THE NAZIS DURING THE WAR.	**1945**

Chapter 15b — The Independent State of Israel.

5708	THE STATE OF ISRAEL WAS ESTABLISHED IN ERETZ YISRAEL.	**1948**
5708	Eretz Yisrael was invaded by many Arab countries.	**1948**
5709	The "War of Independence" (in Eretz Yisrael) ended.	**1949**
5727	YERUSHALAYIM RE-UNITED UNDER JEWISH RULE, IN SIX-DAY-WAR.	**1967**
5753	A secret agreement signed in Oslo.	**1993**
5754	The Last Lubavitcher Rebbe died.	**1994**

Chapter 15c — The Post—Holocaust Era.

5756	Yitzchak Rabin was assassinated.	1995
5761	TERRORISM AGAINST AMERICA EXPLODES INTO A WORLD WAR (III)	2001

Timeline 3

Highlights of Jewish History

Three Timelines

Chapter 1

The New World

Jewish Year		Secular Year
1	CREATION OF THE WORLD, AND ADAM & CHAVA (EVE).	**-3760**
130	Sheit (Seth son of Adam) was born.	-3631
235	Enosh (son of Sheit) was born.	-3526
325	Keynan (son of Enosh) was born.	-3436
395	Mehalalel (son of Keynan) was born.	-3366
460	Yered (son of Mehalalel) was born.	-3301
622	Chanoch (son of Yered) was born.	-3139
687	**Metushelach (son of Chanoch) was born.**	**-3074**
874	Lemech II (son of Metushelach) was born.	-2887
930	**Adam died.**	**-2831**
1056	**Noah (son of Lemech II) was born.**	**-2705**
1536	Noah began the construction of the ark.	-2225
1556	Yaphet (son of Noah) was born.	-2205
1557	Cham (son of Noah) was born.	-2204
1558	**Shem (son of Noah) was born.**	**-2203**
1656	Metushelach died.	-2105
1656	THE GREAT FLOOD COVERED THE EARTH.	**-2105**
1658	Arpachshad (son of Shem) was born.	-2103
1693	Shelach (son of Arpachshad) born	-2068
1723	**Ever (son of Shelach) was born.**	**-2038**
1757	Peleg (son of Ever) was born.	-2004
1787	Re'u (son of Peleg) was born.	-1974
1819	Serug (son of Re'u) was born.	-1942
1849	Nachor I (son of Serug) was born.	-1912
1878	Terach (son of Nachor I) was born.	-1883
1948	**Avraham (son of Terach) was born.**	**-1813**

Chapter 2

The Forefathers

1948	**Avraham (son of Terach) was born.**	**-1813**
1958	Sarah (daughter of Haran) was born.	-1803
1973	Avraham married Sarah.	-1788
1996	The Dispersion from Bavel after building the tower.	-1765
2000	Terach left Ur Kasdim with his family.	-1761

2006	Noach died.	-1755
2018	**THE COVENANT (BRIT BEIN HABETARIM) WITH AVRAHAM.**	**-1743**
2023	Avraham came to settle in Canaan.	-1738
2034	Yishmael (son of Avraham) was born.	-1727
2048	**Avraham circumcised himself and Yishmael.**	**-1713**
2048	Sdom and Amorrah were destroyed.	-1713
2048	Yitzchak (Isaac) was born.	-1713
2084	**THE AKEDA. YITZCHAK WAS PREPARED TO BE A SACRIFICE.**	**-1677**
2084	Sarah died.	-1677
2108	**Yaakov (Jacob) and Eisav (Esau) were born.**	**-1653**
2123	Avraham died.	-1638
2158	Shem (son of Noach) died.	-1603
2171	**Yitzchak blessed Yaakov instead of Eisav.**	**-1590**
2185	Yaakov went to Charan.	-1576
2187	Ever (great grandson of Shem) died.	-1574
2192	Yaakov married Leah and Rachel.	-1569
2195	Levi (son of Yaakov) was born.	-1566
2199	Yosef (Joseph) was born.	-1562
2205	Yaakov left Charan.	-1556
2208	Binyamin was born.	-1553
2216	**Yosef was sold.**	**-1545**
2228	Yitzchak died.	-1533
2229	**Yosef became Viceroy of Egypt.**	**-1532**
2235	Kehot (son of Levi) was born.	-1526
2238	**YAAKOV (AND HIS FAMILY) WENT TO EGYPT.**	**-1523**

Chapter 3

Living in Egypt

2255	**Yaakov died.**	**-1506**
2309	Yosef died.	-1542
2332	**The enslavement in Egypt began after Levi died.**	**-1429**
2368	Moshe (Moses) was born.	-1393
2406	Yehoshua (Joshua) was born.	-1355
2447	Moshe encountered the burning bush.	-1314
2448	**THE CHILDREN OF ISRAEL LEFT EGYPT**	**-1313**

Chapter 4

Moshe the Leader

Jewish Year		Secular Year
2448	The Children of Israel crossed the reed sea.	-1313
2448	**THE REVELATION & TORAH ON MOUNT SINAI.**	**-1313**
2448	Moshe broke the Tablets.	-1313
2449	Moshe came down Sinai with the second Tablets.	-1312
2449	The Mishkan (Tabernacle) was erected.	-1312
2449	The spies returned from Canaan with bad news.	-1312
2487	Aharon and Miriam died.	-1274
2488	**Moshe died.**	**-1273**

Chapter 5

Judges & Early Prophets

2488	**Bnei Yisrael crossed the Jordan into Canaan.**	**-1273**
2503	The apportionment of Eretz Yisrael was completed.	-1258
2516	**Yehoshua died.**	**-1245**
2533	**The rule of Shoftim (Judges) began with Othniel ben Knaz**	**-1228**
2573	Ehud ben Gerah became leader.	-1188
2654	Shamgar ben Anath died.	-1107
2654	**Devorah became leader.**	**-1107**
2694	**Gideon became leader.**	**-1067**
2734	Avimelech (son of Gideon) became leader.	-1027
2737	Tolah ben Pu'ah became leader.	-1024
2758	Ya'ir HaGil'adi became leader.	-1003
2779	**Yiphtach (HaGil'adi) became leader.**	**-982**
2792	Eylon (HaZevuloni) became leader.	-969
2802	Avdon ben Hillel became leader.	-959
2810	**Shimshon (Samson) became leader.**	**-951**
2830	**Eli (HaKohen) became leader.**	**-931**
2854	David ben Yishai was born.	-907
2871	**Shmuel became leader.**	**-890**

Chapter 6

Kings and the First Beit Hamikdash

Jewish Year		Secular Year
2882	Shaul was appointed king.	**-879**
2884	David became king of Yehuda in Hevron.	-877
2892	DAVID BECAME KING OF ISRAEL IN YERUSHALAYIM.	-869
2924	Shlomo became king.	-837
2928	Building of the Beit Hamikdash commenced.	-833
2935	THE FIRST BEIT HAMIKDASH WAS COMPLETED	**-827**
2964	SHLOMO DIED AND HIS KINGDOM WAS DIVIDED.	**-797**
2964	Rechav'am (son of Shlomo) became king of Yehuda.	-797
2964	Yerav'am ben Nevat became king over Yisrael.	-797
3043	Eliyahu went up in a chariot of fire.	**-718**
3084	Yeho'ash I (Joash) renovated the Beit Hamikdash.	-677
3142	Yeshayahu (Isaiah) began his prophecies.	**-619**
3187	The first two of the ten tribes were exiled.	**-574**
3195	Another two of the ten tribes were exiled.	**-566**
3199	Chizkiyahu (Hezekiah) became king of Yehuda.	-562
3205	THE LAST OF THE TEN TRIBES WERE EXILED.	**-556**
3213	Sancheriv invaded Eretz Yehuda and retreated.	-548
3228	Menasheh (son of Chizkiyahu) became king of Yehuda.	-533
3298	Yirmiyahu (Jeremiah) began his prophecies.	**-463**
3303	Yoshiyahu (Josiah) renovated the Beit Hamikdash.	-458
3319	Yerushalayim was conquered, and Yehoyakim exiled.	**-442**
3321	Yehoyakim burned the Megilla (Eycha) composed by Yirmiyahu.	-440
3327	Yerushalayim conquered again, and Yehoyachin exiled.	**-434**
3331	Yirmiyahu persisted in prophesying calamity.	-430
3332	Yechezk'el (Ezekiel) prophecized in exile.	**-429**
3336	The final Babylonian siege of Yerushalayim	**-425**
3338	The walls of Yerushalayim were penetrated.	-423
3338	The sacrifices ceased in the Beit Hamikdash.	-423
3338	THE FIRST BEIT HAMIKDASH WAS DESTROYED.	**-423**

Chapter 7

Exile in Babylon

Jewish Year		Secular Year
3339	Gedalyah ben Achikam was killed.	-423
3340	Daniel interpreted Nebuchadnetzar's dream.	-421
3352	Yechezk'el prophecized about the future Beit Hamikdash.	-410
3389	**Daniel read the writing on the wall.**	**-372**
3389	Daniel was thrown into the lion's den.	-372
3390	Zerubavel led the return to Eretz Yisrael.	-371
3391	Building of Second Beit Hamikdash commenced, then halted.	-370
3395	Achashverosh II made his great banquet.	-366
3399	Esther was taken to the palace.	-362
3404	Esther took action against Haman's decree.	-357
3406	MORDECHAI PROCLAIMED THE CELEBRATION OF PURIM.	**-355**
3408	Building of the Second Beit Hamikdash was resumed.	-353
3412	THE SECOND BEIT HAMIKDASH WAS COMPLETED.	**-349**

Chapter 8

The Second Beit Hamikdash

Chapter 8a

Anshei Knesset HaGedola — The Great Council of Sages

3413	**Ezra led the second return to Eretz Yisrael.**	**-348**
3426	Nechemyah returned to rebuild walls of Yerushalayim.	**-335**
3448	EZRA DIED.	**-313**
3448	Shimon HaTzadik met Alexander the Great.	**-313**
3449	The Minyan Shtarot began.	**-313**

Chapter 8b — Greek Cultural Domination.

3488	Shimon HaTzadik died.	-273
3515	72 Elders translated the Torah into Greek (Septuagint)	**-246**
3621	The revolt of Mattityahu the Chashmona'i.	**-140**

Chapter 8c — Kingdom of Yehuda (Judea). Dynasty of the Chashmona'im.

3622	Yehuda (HaMaccabi) ruled.	**-139**
3622	The Second Beit Hamikdash was re-dedicated.	**-139**

3623	CHANUKA WAS DECLARED A FESTIVAL.	**-138**
3628	**Yehuda (HaMaccabi) was killed in battle.**	**-133**
3628	Yonatan (son of Mattityahu) ruled.	-133
3634	Shimon (son of Mattityahu) ruled.	-127
3642	Yochanan Hyrkanos (son of Shimon) ruled.	-119
3668	Yehuda Aristoblus (son of Yochanan Hyrkanos) ruled.	-93
3670	Alexander Yannai (son of Yochanan Hyrkanos) ruled.	-91
3688	Shalomit (Queen Salome, wife of Alexander Yannai) ruled.	-73
3696	Aristoblus II (son of Alexander Yannai) ruled.	-65
3700	**The Romans gained control of Yehuda (Judea).**	**-61**
3700	Hyrkanos II (son of Alexander Yannai) ruled.	-61
3721	Antigonus (son of Aristoblus II) ruled.	-40

Chapter 8d — Roman Client Kings & Rulers.
The Herodian Dynasty.

3725	Herod I ruled, killing all the Chashmona'im.	**-36**
3728	**Hillel became leader of the Torah scholars.**	**-33**
3742	**Herod I began rebuilding the Second Beit Hamikdash.**	**-19**
3750	Renovation of the Second Beit Hamikdash was completed.	-11
3761	Archelaus (son of Herod I) ruled.	1
3768	HILLEL DIED.	**8**
3770	Archelaus was deposed by the Roman Emperor.	10
3781	Agrippa I (grandson of Herod I) ruled.	21
3788	The Sanhedrin moved from the Second Beit Hamikdash.	**28**
3804	Agrippa II (son of Agrippa I) ruled.	44
3810	Raban Gamliel I (son of Shimon, son of Hillel) died.	**50**
3826	Vespasian arrived in Yehuda to reassert Roman authority.	**66**
3829	THE SECOND BEIT HAMIKDASH WAS DESTROYED.	**69**

Chapter 9

The Talmudic Era — The Mishna

3834	R.Yochanan ben Zakkai died.	74
3846	Sanhedrin moved from place to place, under R.Gamliel II.	86
3893	Betar fell, and "Bar Kochba's" revolt ended in tragedy.	133
3894	Judaism was banned, and R.Akiva was imprisoned.	134
3949	R.YEHUDA HANASSI COMPLETED THE MISHNA AROUND THIS TIME.	**189**

Chapter 10

The Talmudic Era — The Gemara

Jewish Year		Secular Year
3979	Rav Left Eretz Yisrael and settled in Bavel (Babylonia).	**219**
4007	Shmuel was the Talmudic authority in Bavel.	247
4014	R.Yochanan was the leading Talmudic authority.	254
4050	R.Huna was the leading Talmudic authority.	290
4058	R.Yehuda was the leading Talmudic authority.	298
4060	R.Chisda was the leading Talmudic authority.	300
4069	Rabbah was the leading Talmudic authority.	309
4081	R.Yosef was the leading Talmudic authority.	321
4085	Abayey was the leading Talmudic authority.	325
4098	Rava was the leading Talmudic authority.	338
4119	Hillel II (who established the calendar) became Nassi.	**359**
4152	R.Ashi was the leading Talmudic authority.	392
4187	R.Ashi died after the compilation of the Gemara.	427
4235	THE TALMUD WAS COMPLETE, WHEN RAVINA II DIED.	**475**

Chapter 11

The Talmudic Academies of Bavel

Chapter 11a — The Rabbanan SAVURAI

4311	Mar Zutra proclaimed Jewish self-rule in Babylonia.	551

Chapter 11b — The GE'ONIM, and Arabic Dominion

4349	The Metivta of Pumpedita was reconstituted.	589
4369	The Metivta of Sura was reconstituted.	609
4374	The Persians conquered Eretz Yisrael.	614
4374	JEWS WERE ALLOWED TO RETURN TO YERUSHALAYIM.	**614**
4389	The Byzantine (E.Roman) Empire reconquered Eretz Yisrael.	629
4396	R.Yitzchak was the last GAON of Neharde'a (Firuz-Shabur).	636
4397	The Arabs conquered Eretz Yisrael.	**637**
4405	One of the "TAKKANOT HAGE'ONIM" was enacted at this time.	645
4515	R.Acha(i) Gaon left Bavel (Iraq) for Eretz Yisrael.	755
4519	R.Yehudai became GAON of Sura.	759
4519	The Halachot Gedolot (BaHaG) was written at this time.	759
4548	Another of "TAKKANOT HAGE'ONIM" was enacted at this time.	788

4618	**R.Amram (who wrote the Siddur) became GAON of Sura.**	**858**
4688	Rbnu.Saadya was appointed GAON of Sura.	928
4715	"Four Captives" were ransomed at around this time.	955
4728	R.Sherira became GAON of Pumpedita.	968
4757	R.Hai became (the last) GAON of Pumpedita.	997
4798	**R.HAI GAON DIED, AND THE ACADEMIES OF BAVEL DECLINED.**	**1038**

Chapter 12

The Rishonim — Early Scholars

Chapter 12a — Early Rishonim, Tosaphot, and the Crusade Massacres.

4800	Rbnu.Gershom Me'or HaGola died.	1040
4848	The Rif arrived in Spain (from Morocco).	1088
4856	CRUSADERS (1ST) DESTROYED JEWISH COMMUNITIES.	**1096**
4859	Yerushalayim was captured by the Crusaders.	**1099**
4863	The Rif Died.	1103
4865	RASHI DIED, AND THE ERA OF THE TOSAPHOT BEGAN.	**1105**
4895	THE RAMBAM (MAIMONIDES) WAS BORN.	**1135**
4904	THE FIRST (RECORDED) BLOOD LIBEL TOOK PLACE.	**1144**
4907	Crusaders (2nd) attacked Jewish communities.	**1147**
4907	Rabbenu Tam was captured by the Crusaders.	1147
4908	The Rambam's and the Radak's families left Cordova.	1148
4925	The Rambam visited Eretz Yisrael.	1165
4931	Rabbenu Tam died.	1171
4935	The Rashbam died.	1175
4944	The young son of the Ri was killed.	1184
4948	Jews were allowed to return to Yerushalayim.	**1187**
4949	R.Yaakov D'Orleans was killed in London.	1189
4950	Jews were massacred in England, in the 3rd Crusade.	**1190**
4951	The Radak wrote his commentary.	1191
4954	The Ramban (Nachmanides) was born.	1194
4959	The Ra'avad died.	1198
4965	The Rambam died.	*1204*
4996	Rampaging mobs massacred Jews in France.	1236
5002	A massive burning of the Talmud took place in Paris.	**1242**
5004	Yerushalayim was sacked by Egyptians and Turks.	1244
5012	The Inquisition began to use torture.	1252
5027	The Ramban (left Spain and) settled in Eretz Yisrael.	1267

5030	The Ramban died.	**1270**
5046	The Maharam MeRothenburg was imprisoned.	**1286**
5050	New works advanced the study of KABBALA.	**1290**
5050	THE ERA OF THE TOSAPHOT CONCLUDED AT AROUND THIS TIME.	**1290**

Chapter 12b — Later Rishonim, Persecutions, and Expulsions.

5050	All Jews were expelled from England.	**1290**
5053	The Maharam MeRothenburg died in prison.	1293
5058	The Rindfleisch massacres began.	**1298**
5058	The 'Mordechai' and Hagahot Maimoniyot were killed.	1298
5065	The Rashba placed a limited ban on philosophy.	1305
5065	The Rosh (and his son, the Tur) arrived in Spain.	1305
5066	All Jews were expelled from France.	1306
5070	The Rashba died.	1310
5080	Jews were massacred by the Pastoureaux Crusaders.	1320
5088	The Rosh died.	1327
5096	Jews of Germany were massacred by the Armledder bands.	1336
5098	The Ralbag wrote his commentary on the Bible.	1338
5109	THE BLACK DEATH MASSACRES SWEPT ACROSS EUROPE.	**1349**
5127	The Ran, Rivash, and other scholars in Spain, were imprisoned.	1367
5151	Jews of Spain were massacred — many became Marranos.	**1391**
5151	The Rivash and Rashbatz left Spain.	1391
5155	The Final expulsion of Jews from France.	**1394**
5173	R.Yosef Albo was in a forced debate with Christians.	1413
5181	Jews in Austria were massacred in the Wiener Gezera.	**1421**
5235	THE INVENTION OF PRINTING WAS USED FOR JEWISH BOOKS.	**1475**
5241	The Inquisition was established in Spain.	**1481**
5248	R.Ovadya Bertinura settled in Yerushalayim.	1488
5251	Columbus consulted R.Avraham Zacuto for his travels.	1491
5252	ALL JEWS WERE EXPELLED FROM SPAIN AND SICILY.	**1492**

Chapter 13

The Kov'im *

The Great Scholars of the Shulchan Aruch & Torah Consolidation

5253	R.Yitzchak Abarbanel arrived in Naples, from Spain.	1493
5257	All Jews were expelled from Portugal.	**1496**
5276	The Eyn Yaakov was printed.	1516

5276	The Turks (Ottoman Empire) conquered Eretz Yisrael.	1516
5285	R.Yosef Yoselman saved many Jews during the Peasants War.	1525
5314	A mass burning of Jewish books took place in Rome.	1553
5323	**The Shulchan Aruch was completed by R.Yosef Karo.**	**1563**
5330	**SHULCHAN ARUCH PUBLISHED WITH SUPPLEMENTS OF RAMO.**	1570
5332	**The Ari'zal died in Tzfat (Safed).**	**1572**
5333	The Maharal came to Prague.	1573
5334	The Maharshal died.	1573
5335	R.Yosef Karo died in Tzfat.	1575
5359	The Maharal returned to Prague again.	1599
5374	The Maharsha became Rabbi in Lublin.	1614
5377	The Tosaphot Yom Tov commentary was concluded.	1616
5382	The Shaloh arrived in Eretz Yisrael.	1621
5389	R.Yom Tov Lipman Heller was imprisoned in Prague.	1629
5400	R.Yoel Sirkes, the Bach, died.	1640
5406	**The Shach and Taz (on Shulchan Aruch) were printed.**	**1646**
5408	**JEWS WERE MASSACRED BY CHMIELNITZKI'S FORCES.**	1648

*See Appendix D

Chapter 14

The Acharonim — Later Scholars.

Chapter 14a, Early Acharonim and East European Massacres

5414	The first Jews settled in New Amsterdam (New York).	1654
5415	Many Jews killed in Russian and Swedish invasions of Poland.	1655
5416	Jews were permitted to live in England.	1656
5416	Baruch Spinoza was excommunicated.	1656
5433	**The Magen Avraham (on Shulchan Aruch) was completed.**	**1673**
5437	**SHABBETAI TZVI DIED AS A MUSLIM.**	**1676**
5449	**The Beit Shmuel (on the Shulchan Aruch) was printed.**	**1689**
5458	**THE BA'AL SHEM TOV WAS BORN.**	**1698**
5463	The Pnei Yehoshua's family were killed in an explosion.	1702
5472	The Siftei Chachamim was arrested.	1712
5484	R.Yaakov Culi (Me'am Lo'ez) arrived in Constantinople.	1724
5487	The Mishneh LeMelech died.	1727
5494	**Jews were massacred by the Haidamack bands.**	**1734**

Chapter 14b, Acharonim and Early Chassidim.

5501	The Or HaChayim arrived in Eretz Yisrael.	1741

5507	R.Moshe Chaim Luzzatto (Ramchal) died in Acco (Acre).	1747
5510	R.Yonatan Eybeshutz became Rabbi in Hamburg.	1750
5515	The Noda BiYehuda became Rabbi in Prague.	1754
5518	**The Frankists instigated mass burnings of the Talmud.**	**1757**
5519	Frankists supported blood libel charges in public 'debate'.	1759
5520	**The Ba'al Shem Tov died.**	**1760**
5524	The VA'AD ARBA ARATZOT was discontinued.	1764
5528	**Despite resistance the Haidamacks massacre thousands.**	**1768**
5532	**The Maggid of Mezeritsch died.**	**1772**
5542	R.N. Adler and Chassam Sofer visited the Noda BiYehuda.	1782
5546	R.Elimelech of Lizensk died.	1786
5551	**The Pale of Settlement was established in Russia.**	**1791**
5553	Jews suffered in Reign of Terror of French Revolution.	1793
5558	The Vilna Gaon died.	1797
5559	The Ba'al HaTanya was released from first imprisonment.	1798
5559	Napoleon led an army expedition through Eretz Yisrael.	1799
5566	The Chida (R.Chaim Yosef David Azulai) died.	1806
5566	The Chassam Sofer became Rabbi in Pressburg.	1806
5570	R.Levi Yitzchak of Berditchev died.	1809
5571	R.Nachman of Bratslav died.	1810
5574	R.Akiva Eger became Rabbi in Posen.	1814
5575	Kozhnitzer Maggid and Yehudi of Pershisskha, both died.	1814
5575	Chozeh of Lublin, and R.Mendel of Rymanov, both died.	1815
5579	Anti Jewish (Hep Hep!) riots spread throughout Germany.	1819
5587	**Russia began conscripting Jewish children to the army.**	**1827**
5600	Adm.R.Yisrael of Ruzhin was released from imprisonment.	1840

Chapter 14c, Later Acharonim and Changing Society.

5603	The Tzemach Tzedek of Lubavitch was repeatedly arrested in Russia.	1843
5606	Sir Moshe Montefiore visited Russia to help local Jews.	1846
5609	R.Yisrael Salanter left Vilna.	1848
5611	R.Shimshon Rapha'el Hirsch became Rabbi in Frankfort am Main.	1851
5619	R.Menachem Mendel of Kotzk died.	1859
5624	The Malbim was imprisoned, and then expelled from Rumania.	1864
5626	Chidushei HaRim, Tiferet Shlomo, and Tzemach Tzedek, died.	1866
5633	The Chafetz Chaim was published.	1873
5634	The Minchat Chinuch died.	1874
5638	Petach Tikva agricultural settlement was established.	1878
5641	**MANY JEWS BEGAN LEAVING RUSSIA AFTER A WAVE OF POGROMS.**	**1881**

5646	R.Shlomo Ganzfried (author of Kitzur Shulchan Aruch) died.	1886
5652	R.Chaim (Brisker) became Rabbi in Brisk.	1892
5665	The Sfass Emess died.	1905
5665	**Many Jews were killed in (official) Russian pogroms.**	**1905**
5671	Chazon Ish was published.	1911
5674	**Over 500,000 Jewish soldiers fought in World War I.**	**1914**
5678	**Over 60,000 Jews were killed during Russian Revolution.**	**1918**
5684	**Daf HaYomi study cycle commenced.**	**1923**
5687	The Lubavitcher Rebbe was released from Soviet prison.	1927
5699	Jews were attacked in the Kristallnacht pogroms in Germany.	1938

Chapter 15,

The Melaktim & the Current Era.

Chapter 15a — The Holocaust.

5699	Germany started World War II, and mass killing of Jews.	**1939**
5701	**Nazi-Germany unexpectedly invaded Russia.**	1941
5701	**200,000 Jews were killed at Babi Yar and Ponary.**	**1941**
5702	**400,000 Jews of Warsaw were sent to DEATH CAMPS.**	**1942**
5703	Nazi-Germany experienced massive losses in the battle of Stalingrad.	1943
5703	**THE REMAINING JEWS IN WARSAW STAGED A MASSIVE UPRISING.**	**1943**
5703	Jewish uprisings at Treblinka, Sobibor, and Bialystock.	1943
5703	The Danish people quietly rescued 93% of their Jews to safety.	1943
5704	**300,000 Hungarian Jews were killed in 3 months.**	**1944**
5705	Uprising in Auschwitz DEATH CAMP just before freedom.	1944
5705	**Nazi-Germany was conquered, and World War II ended.**	**1945**
5705	**6,000,000 JEWS WERE KILLED BY THE NAZIS DURING THE WAR.**	**1945**

Chapter 15b — The Independent State of Israel.

5707	Publication of the Talmud Encyclopedia was commenced.	1947
5708	The United Nations divided Eretz Yisrael.	1947
5708	Arabs attacked in Eretz Yisrael, to gain territory.	1947
5708	**THE STATE OF ISRAEL WAS ESTABLISHED IN ERETZ YISRAEL.**	**1948**
5708	**Eretz Yisrael was invaded by many Arab countries.**	**1948**
5709	**The "War of Independence" (in Eretz Yisrael) ended.**	**1949**
5710	All Jews left the ancient Jewish community of Iraq.	1950
5710	Almost all Jews of Yemen emigrated to Eretz Yisrael.	1950
5717	Jewish forces invaded Egypt and conquered the Sinai Desert.	1956

5727	**YERUSHALAYIM RE-UNITED UNDER JEWISH RULE, IN SIX-DAY-WAR.**	**1967**
5734	2,500 Jewish soldiers were killed in the Yom-Kippur-War.	1973
5742	Massive enemy arsenals were discovered in Lebanon.	1982
5753	**A secret agreement signed in Oslo.**	**1993**
5754	**The Last Lubavitcher Rebbe died.**	**1994**

Chapter 15c — The Post-Holocaust Era.

5756	**Yitzchak Rabin was assassinated.**	1995
5760	Court rules that Revisionist Historians are Nazi sympathizers	2000
5761	TERRORISM AGAINST AMERICA EXPLODES INTO A WORLD WAR (III)	2001
5763	Jewish astronaut with Torah scroll in fiery return from space.	2003

THE BEGINNINGS

Section I

Chapter 1

The New World

Section I

Chapter 1

The New World

Jewish Year		Secular Year
1	CREATION OF THE WORLD, AND ADAM & CHAVA (EVE).	**-3760**
130	Sheit (Seth son of Adam) was born.	-3631
235	Enosh (son of Sheit) was born.	-3526
325	Keynan (son of Enosh) was born.	-3436
395	Mehalalel (son of Keynan) was born.	-3366
460	Yered (son of Mehalalel) was born.	-3301
622	Chanoch (son of Yered) was born.	-3139
687	**Metushelach (son of Chanoch) was born.**	**-3074**
874	Lemech II (son of Metushelach) was born.	-2887
930	**Adam died.**	**-2831**
1056	**Noah (son of Lemech II) was born.**	**-2705**
1536	Noah began the construction of the ark.	-2225
1556	Yaphet (son of Noah) was born.	-2205
1557	Cham (son of Noah) was born.	-2204
1558	**Shem (son of Noah) was born.**	**-2203**
1656	Metushelach died.	-2105
1656	THE GREAT FLOOD COVERED THE EARTH.	**-2105**
1658	Arpachshad (son of Shem) was born.	-2103
1693	Shelach (son of Arpachshad) born	-2068
1723	**Ever (son of Shelach) was born.**	**-2038**
1757	Peleg (son of Ever) was born.	-2004
1787	Re'u (son of Peleg) was born.	-1974
1819	Serug (son of Re'u) was born.	-1942
1849	Nachor I (son of Serug) was born.	-1912
1878	Terach (son of Nachor I) was born.	-1883
1948	**Avraham (son of Terach) was born.**	**-1813**

Section I
THE BEGINNINGS

Chapter 1

The New World

The first Chapter (TEKUFA, era) in Jewish history, begins with the Creation of the world, as *mentioned* (but not *described*) in the Bible. The chapter ends with the birth of Avraham where a new and significant chapter begins.

This book assumes that the reader is conversant with the basic text of the CHUMASH (Bible), and therefore reference is made to many events without describing them.

For centuries Jews have counted their beginnings from Biblical creation. At this point in time, science has effectively proven that the earth appears to be very much older than the 5764 years we traditionally count in Jewish history.

Science, however, has not yet proven that it was not initially created to appear that way, and that on the very first day after completion it already appeared to be at an advanced evolutionary stage—a "complete" world, as mentioned in the Talmud *[Chul.60a, Tos, see Mid.Rab.Br.14.7, Ramban Br.5.4]*. A world with a mature man, mature trees, and mature rock formations.

In fact the English philosopher Bertrand Russel has argued that there is nothing, scientific or otherwise, to disprove the following theoretical statement: "*The world was created two days ago.*" Our memories, this book, everything around us would all be part of that creation. The trees would have many rings, to show their apparent age, and old people would have wrinkles and memories, to indicate the many years they appear to have lived.

Frustrating as this argument may be, just the fact that our experience is so real to us, this certainty of our experience is not enough to serve as a logical proof that the world is any older than two days.

Russel was, of course, only presenting an argument in which neither he nor anyone else believes. However, it is an argument that is useful in illustrating the limitations of scientific proof, when such proof is based upon what is essentially a philosophical notion — *that the earth is (or is not) as old as it appears to be.* Or in the words of Albert Einstein (in a letter to a friend), "*The truth is by no means given to us, given to us are the data of our consciousness.*" And measuring that data does naught to providing the truth.

1 -3760

Creation of the World, Adam & Chava (Eve).

The world was created in six days, and upon completion had the appearance of being fully developed and aged. Adam was created as a fully mature man (See opposite page.) *[Tal.Chul.60a, Tos./ Mid.Rab.Br.14.7/Ramban Br.5. 4]*.
The first day of creation was the 25th Elul in the Jewish Year -1, or some call it 0 or 1. Adam and Chava (Eve) were created on the 1st Tishrei *[Mid.Rab. Vay.29/ Pir.Dr.El.8 /RaN.R.H.3a/ Mmn.Hil.Kid.Hach.6.8, Shmitt. 10.2]*.

41 -3720

Kayin and Hevel (Cain and Abel) were born with twin sisters, whom they later married. Kayin lived long (see 1656) and had many children *[Tal.San.58b /Mid.Rab.Br. Br.22.2, Koh.6.3/Rashi Yer.Yev.11.1(61a)]*. Kayin's twin was Kalmana, Hevel's twin was Balbira *[Abarbanel Br.4.1]*.
Some say that all children of the first generations were born as twins *[Sed.Had.]*.
Kayin (Cain) killed Hevel (Abel) in the year 41 *[Mid.Tan.Br.Br.9]*.

130 -3631

Sheit (Seth, son of Adam) was born in 130 *[Bible Br.5.3]*.
Kayin had a son Chanoch (and built a city in his name). He in turn had Irad, who had Mechuyael, who had Metushael, who had Lemech I - similar names to the children of Sheit *[Bible Br.4.17, 18]*.

235 -3526

Enosh (son of Sheit) was born in 235 *[Bible Br.5.6]*.
He was the first to introduce idolatry *[Bible Br.4.26/ Mmn.Hil.A.Z. 1.1]*, some say in 266 *[Pane'ach Raza.q.Sed.Had.]*, and others say after Adam died, in 930 *[Ramban/ Sed.Had.]*. In his lifetime (what appears to have been) a massive tidal wave (tsunami) swept in from the ocean and engulfed a third of the world *[Mid.Tan. Sh. Yit.16, Rab.Br.23.7/ Rashi.Br.6.4]*.

325 -3436

Keynan (son of Enosh) was born in 325 *[Bible Br.5.9]*. Some say that at the age of 40, Keynan ruled wisely over all the people, and that he predicted a flood if they would continue to indulge in immoral behavior (and he engraved this prediction on stone.) *[Yuch.1.1235/ Sed.Had.]*.

395 -3366

Mehalalel (son of Keynan) was born in 395 *[Bible 5.12]*.
Lemech I, the descendant of Kayin, had three sons, Yaval, the first nomadic shepherd; Yuval, who invented musical instruments; and Tuval Kayin, the first to work with metals *[Bible 4.20-22]*. He also had a daughter called Na'ama, see 1554\-2207.

460 -3301

Yered (son of Mehalalel) was born *[Bible Br.5.15]*.

622 -3139

Chanoch (son of Yered) was born in 622 *[Bible Br.5.18]*. Chanoch was a man of high moral standing and was asked to rule over the people (according to some), which he did for 243 years. He (also) waged a war (they say) against the descendants of Kayin, and suggested different diets and life-styles for various geographic locations *[Sef.Hay./Sed.Had.]*.

687 -3074

Metushelach (Methuselah) was born.

Metushelach (son of Chanoch) was born in 687 *[Bible Br.5.21]*. Metushelach who lived for 969 years, was the longest living person (see 1656\-2105) on record *[Bible Br.5.27]*.
Only those recorded in the Bible lived such very long lives, according to some, while others lived natural life-spans *[Mmn.Gd.Ppl.2.47]*.

874 -2887

Lemech II (son of Metushelach) was born *[Bible Br.5.25]*.

930 ~ -2831

Adam died.

Adam died *[Bible Br.5.5]*, and was buried in Ma'arat Hamachpelah at Hevron (Hebron) *[Tal.Eru.53a/ Mid.Rab.Sh.58.4]*.

974 ~ -2787

Na'ama (daughter of Chanoch) was born in 974 *[Sed.Had.]* see 1554\-2207.

987 ~ -2774

Chanoch died *[Bible Br.5.23]*, and (some say) Metushelach his son succeeded him as ruler (see 622\-3139) *[Sef.Hay./Sed.Had.]*.

1042 ~ -2719

Sheit died *[Bible Br.5.8]*, and (some say) he was buried in Arbe'el *[Sed.Had.]*.

1056 ~ -2705

Noah was born.

Noah (son of Lemech II) was born *[Bible Br.5.28,29]*. Some say Lemech II married Ashmua, daughter of his uncle Elishua (the son of Chanoch) and that Noah was named by Metushelach (his paternal grandfather and also, as a son of Chanoch, his maternal great uncle), but (that) his father called him Menachem *[Sef.Hay./ Sed.Had.]*.

1140 ~ -2621

Enosh died *[Bible Br.5.11]*.

1235 ~ -2526

Keynan died *[Bible Br.5.14]*, and (some say) he was buried in the Indian islands *[Yuch.1.1235]*.

1290 ~ -2471

Mehalalel died *[Bible Br.5.17]*.

1422 ~ -2339

Yered died *[Bible Br.5.20]*.

1536 ~ -2225

Noah began the construction of the ark in 1536 *[Bible Br.6.3/Sed.Had.]*. Noah invented agricultural equipment *[Mid.TanBr.Br.11/ Zoh. Br. Br.58b /Rashi Br.5.29]*.

1554 ~ -2207

Noah married Na'ama, (some say) in 1554 *[Sed.Had.]*. There were two women known by the name of Na'ama. One was the daughter of Chanoch (see 974\-2787), the other was the sister of Tuval Kayin (see 395\-3366) (and a descendant of Kayin). There is a difference of opinion as to which one was Noah's wife *[Mid.Rab. Br.23.3/ Rashi Br.4.22, Sif.Chach /Sed. Had.]*.

1556 ~ -2205

Yaphet (son of Noah) was born *[Bible Br.5.32, Rashi]*. One of the sons of Yaphet (see 1651\-2110) was Yavan, *[Bible Br.10.2]*, whom the Greeks were named after. The others were Gomer (see 1787\-1974), Magog, Maday (Mediens), Meshech and Tiras *[Bible Br.10.2]*. Tiras was considered an ancestor of the Persians *[Tal.Yom.10a / Mid. Rab. Br.37.1]*.

1557 ~ -2204

Cham (son of Noah) was born in 1557 *[Sed.Had.]*. One of the sons of Cham (see 1651\-2110) was Kush, after whom the black people of Africa were named; another was Mitzrayim, antecedent of the Egyptians; another was Put, and the fourth was Canaan *[Bible Br.10.6]*.

1558 ~ -2203

Shem was born.

Shem (son of Noah) was born *[Bible Br.11.10]*. The descendants of Shem are still called Semites. Shem was also called MalkiTzedek king of Shalem, a town which was later called YeruShalem (see 2084\ -1677) *[Bible Br.14.18/ Tal.Ned.32b/ Mid.Yal.Br.22.102]*. One of Shem's sons (see 1651\-2110) was Ashur (see 1996\-1765), after whom the Assyrians were named; another was Aram. The others were Lud, Eylam, and Arpachshad (see 1658\-2103) *[Bible Br.10.22]*.

1651 -2110

Lemech II (father of Noah) died *[Bible Br.5.31]*. Some say that construction of the ark was speeded up in this year *[Sef.Hay./Sed.Had.]*. Some say that the three sons of Noah married three daughters of Elyakum the son of Metushelach *[Sef.Hay./Sed.Had.]*.

1656 -2105

The great flood covered the earth.

Metushelach died on the 11th Cheshvan (the 7th day before the flood began) *[Bible Br.7.4/Tal.San.108b]*. Some maintain that Kayin (also) died this year *[Mid.Rab. Sh.31.17]*. If so, he outlived Metushelach by many years. Kayin was killed by his descendant Lemech I (see 130\-3631), who was blind. He had gone hunting with his son, Tuval Kayin, who directed his aim, but mistook Kayin's movement in the distance for an animal. Lemech I was so upset he killed his son in his frenzy *[Rashi Br.4.23]*.
The ark had just been completed in 1656 (see 1536\-2225, 1651\-2110). The great flood began on the 17th Cheshvan *[Bible Br.7.5-7]*. All the people perished in the flood except for Noah and his family. However, Sichon and Og — the giants (see 2487\-1274) — were not affected by the flood *[Mid.Rab.Dev.11.10/Tal.Nid.61a]*.
It rained for forty days and ended on the 28th Kislev. The waters began to recede 150 days later, on the 1st Sivan, and the ark came to rest on the mountain-top on the 17th Sivan. On the 1st Av the mountains appeared out of the water. On the 10th Elul Noah sent the raven, and on the 17th he sent the 1st dove. On the 24th Elul he sent the 2nd dove which returned with a small olive branch, and on the 1st Tishrei he sent the 3rd dove which did not return *[Bible Br.7.17,24; 8.4-14, Rashi/Mid. Rab.Br.33.7]*.

1657 -2104

Noah stayed in the ark (together with all that were with him) until the earth's surface was hard. They came out on the 27th Cheshvan *[Bible Br.8.14]*. They were in the ark for one full (lunar) year and eleven days, the equivalent of one solar year *[Mid.Rab.Br.33.7]*. The ark settled on the mountains of Ararat, in Armenia *[Bible Br.8.4, Targ.Yer./ Yuch.5.2/ Sed.Had.]*. Noah and his sons named the constellations *[Mmn.Hil. Yes.Hat.3.7]*. After the flood, Noah was allowed (in a revelation) to eat meat — which had not been allowed since Adam. He also received a code of seven laws for all humanity to live by *[Bible Br.9.1-7/ Tal.San.59b, 56a]*.

1658 -2103

Arpachshad (son of Shem) was born *[Bible Br. 11.10]*. Canaan once saw his grandfather Noah naked and drunk, and reported this to his father Cham. Cham had been concerned that his father Noah may have more children, so he took this opportunity to castrate him. When Noah realized what had happened, he cursed them both *[Bible Br.9.21-27, Rashi /Tal.San.70a/ Mid.Rab.Bam.10.2/ Rashi Br.9.25]*.

1693 -2068

Shelach (son of Arpachshad) was born *[Bible Br.11.12]*. Some say that Aner and Eshkol, who were allies of Avraham *[Bible Br.14.13, 24]*, were also sons of Arpachshad *[Sef.Hay./Sed.Had.]*.

1723 -2038

Ever was born.

Ever (son of Shelach) was born *[Bible Br.11.14]*. Some say the name "Hebrews" comes from Ever, and others say because Avraham came to Canaan from the other side of the river (Ever HaNahar) *[Mid.Rab.42.8]*.

1757 -2004

Peleg (son of Ever) was born *[Bible Br.11.16]*. Ever had another son, called Yaktan, who in turn had 13 sons. One was called Yovav, and another Avimael (see 2218\-1543) *[Bible Br. 10.25-29]*.

1787 -1974

Re'u (son of Peleg) was born *[Bible Br.11.18]*.
Ashkenaz was born one year before Re'u (1786) *[Tzem.Dav./Sed.Had.]*. He was the son of Gomer who

peoples were named after him *[Tal.Yom.10a/ Mid.Rab.Br.37.1]*. Nimrod, son of Kush (see 1557\-2204), became king in 1788 (according to some) *[Tzem.Dav. / Sed.Had.]*.

1819 -1942

Serug (son of Re'u) was born *[Bible Br.11.20]*.

1849 -1912

Nachor I (son of Serug) was born *[Bible Br.11.22]*.

1878 -1883

Terach (son of Nachor I) was born *[Bible Br.11.24]*.

Chapter 2

The Forefathers

Section I

Chapter 2
The Forefathers

Jewish Year		Secular Year
1948	Avraham (son of Terach) was born.	**-1813**
1958	Sarah (daughter of Haran) was born.	-1803
1973	Avraham married Sarah.	-1788
1996	The Dispersion from Bavel after building the tower.	-1765
2000	Terach left Ur Kasdim with his family.	-1761
2006	Noach died.	-1755
2018	THE COVENANT (BRIT BEIN HABETARIM) WITH AVRAHAM.	**-1743**
2023	Avraham came to settle in Canaan.	-1738
2034	Yishmael (son of Avraham) was born.	-1727
2048	**Avraham circumcised himself and Yishmael.**	**-1713**
2048	Sdom and Amorrah were destroyed.	-1713
2048	Yitzchak (Isaac) was born.	-1713
2084	THE AKEDA. YITZCHAK WAS PREPARED TO BE A SACRIFICE.	**-1677**
2084	Sarah died.	-1677
2108	Yaakov (Jacob) and Eisav (Esau) were born.	**-1653**
2123	Avraham died.	-1638
2158	Shem (son of Noach) died.	-1603
2171	**Yitzchak blessed Yaakov instead of Eisav.**	**-1590**
2185	Yaakov went to Charan.	-1576
2187	Ever (great grandson of Shem) died.	-1574
2192	Yaakov married Leah and Rachel.	-1569
2195	Levi (son of Yaakov) was born.	-1566
2199	Yosef (Joseph) was born.	-1562
2205	Yaakov left Charan.	-1556
2208	Binyamin was born.	-1553
2216	**Yosef was sold.**	**-1545**
2228	Yitzchak died.	-1533
2229	**Yosef became Viceroy of Egypt.**	**-1532**
2235	Kehot (son of Levi) was born.	-1526
2238	YAAKOV (AND HIS FAMILY) WENT TO EGYPT.	**-1523**

Section I
THE BEGINNINGS

Chapter 2

The Forefathers

The second Chapter (Tekufa) in Jewish history begins with the birth of Avraham, covering the period dominated by the forefathers. It ends when Yaakov went to Egypt with all his family.

This book assumes that the reader is conversant with the basic text of the CHUMASH *(Bible), and therefore makes reference to many events without describing them.*

1948 -1813

Avraham was born.

Avraham was born, either in Nissan or in Tishrei *[Bible Br.11.26/ Tal. R.H.10b, 11a]*. (If he was born in Tishrei, it was probably before the 10th (see 2048\-1713).) His father Terach had two other sons, Nachor II and Haran. After Avraham was born in the city of Kutha *(in Aram)*, Terach moved eastward to Ur Kasdim where Haran was born. Nachor II had remained in the land of Aram *[Bible Br.11.31; 24.10/ Bachya Br.11.28/ Sed. Had.]*. Avraham's mother was Amathla'a the daughter of Karnevu *[Tal.B.B.91a]*. Haran, who was from a different wife, died before his father Terach *[Bible Br. 11.27, 28; 20.12, Rashi]*.

1958 -1803

Sarah was born.

Sarah, (daughter of Haran), was also known as Yiska; she was Lot's younger sister and Avraham's niece *[Bible Br.11.27-29/ Tal.Meg.14a / Sef.Hay./ Sed.Had.]*.

Avraham was hidden by his father Terach for the first ten years of his life, because astrologers had warned Nimrod (the king) that this child would become powerful *[Tal.B.B.91a/Sef.Hay./ Sed.Had.]*. He came out of hiding (with his mother) this year at the age of 10. Some say that she took him to Noah and Shem, where he spent many years learning from them *[Sef.Hay./ Sed.Had.]*. He had already refused to believe in idols at the age of three. See 1996\-1765 *[Tal.Ned.32a / Kes.Mish. Hil.A.Z.. 1.3]*.

1973 -1788

Avraham married Sarah *[Mid.Yal.Br.15.78 / Sed.Had.]*.

1996 -1765

Dispersion from Bavel after building the tower.

Construction of Tower of Bavel abruptly ended in 1996 *[Mid. Yal.D.H.I 1073]*. Until this time, some say, all the people had spoken one common language besides their own *[Tal.Yer. Meg. 1.9/Mid.Tan. Dev.2/ Tor.Tem.Br.11.1]*. Ashur had left the country because he did not approve of the tower construction (which was led by Nimrod), and he established the towns of Ninveh, Rechovot, and Kalach *[Bible Br.10.11/Mid. Rab. Br.37.4]*. Some say that Avraham recognized the concept of one G-d in this year *[Mid.Rab.Br.64.4/Sed.Had.]*, and others say eight years earlier, when he was 40 *[Mmn.Yad Hil.A.Z.1.3, Hag.Mm., Kes.Mish]*. See 1958\-1803. Peleg died *[Mid.Yal.1073]* and Chevron *(Hebron)* was built during this year *[R.Saadya.q.Sed.Had.]*.

1997 -1764

Terach's father, Nachor I, died *[Bible Br.11.25]* before his own grandfather Re'u (see 2026\-1735) and while Noah their common ancestor was still alive (see 2006\-1755). See 2158/-1603.

2000 -1761

Some say that Terach left Ur Kasdim with his family (see 1948\-1813) in this year *[Sef.Hay./ Sed.Had.]*. Avraham had destroyed the idols of Terach, which had aroused the anger of Nimrod (the king) (see 1958\-1803), who subsequently sought to destroy Avraham in a furnace. Avraham was miraculously saved, and Terach decided to leave the country *[Mid.Rab.Br.38.13/Sef.Hay./ Sed.Had.]*. Terach planned to settle in Canaan, but stopped on the way and settled in Charan, see 1948\-1813 *[Bible Br.11.31]*.

Some say that Terach had another wife, Pelilah, in his old age (see 1948\-1813), and had a son called Tzova, who had a son called Aram, who had a daughter called Machalat (see 2218\-1543) *[Sef.Hay./ Sed.Had.2075, 2083]*.

2006 -1755

Noah died *[Bible Br.9.29]*. In the year 2008 the people of Sdom and Amorrah rebelled against Kedarla'omer (a king), and thirteen years later, in 2021, he returned to subjugate them in the war of the five kings against four. See 2018\-1743 *[Bible Br.14.4/Tos.Ber.7b]*.

2018 -1743

The Covenant (BRIT BEIN HABETARIM) made with Avraham.

Avraham had lived in Charan for three years (see 2000\-1761) before he went on to Canaan, the original destination, in the year 2003. It was during this stay in Canaan that the ceremony of The Covenant *(BRIT BEIN HABETARIM)* took place on the 15th Nissan 2018 (see 2023\-1738). Avraham went back to Charan, after the BRIT, and stayed there for as long as five years. If it was a full five years, then the war between four and the five kings must have been in 2023, after he returned to Canaan, see 2006\-1755 *[Mech.Sh.12.40, Rashi/ Sed.Ol./ Tos. Ber.7b, Shab.10b./Mrsha. Meg.9a/Sed.Had.]*.

2023 -1738

Avraham came to settle in Canaan.

When Avraham came to Canaan (see 2018\-1743), the local (Canaanite) people were speaking HEBREW, whilst he spoke Aramaic *[Ramban Br.45.12 Manscpt.Ed.]*. There was a famine in Canaan this year *[Bible Br.12.4, 10]*, and Avraham went to Egypt, where, on the 15th Nissan, he had trouble over the abduction of Sarah, his wife *[Bible Br.12.10, Rashi/Mid.Yal. Br.12.68]*. Some say that the BRIT BEIN HABETARIM *(the Covenant)* was this year (or slightly later) *[Bible Br.15.1-9/Mid.Rab.Br. 46.2/Rashi Br.15.1; 21.1]*. However this raises many questions *[Mech.Sh.12.40]*, see 2018\-1743, 2448\-1313. Avraham wandered through the land (for a few months) before he settled *[Bible Br.12.8,9]*.

2026 -1735

Re'u (son of Peleg) died *[Bible Br.11.21]*.

2034 -1727

Avraham married his second wife, Hagar, who was the daughter of Pharaoh *[Mid.Yal.Br.12.68, Rashi Br.16.1, 3]*, and Yishmael their son, was born in 2034 *[Bible Br.16.16]*. Some say that Avraham was the first person to have white hair, others say he was the first to grow a beard *[Tal. B.M.87a, Mrsha/ Mid.Rab.Br.65.9, Yef.To.q.O.Hat.4.1556]*.

2048 -1714

Avraham and Yishmael circumcised.

Avraham circumcised himself and his son Yishmael, on the 10th Tishrei *[Bible Br.17.24/Mid.Y.16.80]*. Yishmael was 13 years old. Avraham was 99 years old, and his 100th birthday was in the following Nissan or Tishrei (see 1948\-1813) *[Sed.Had.]*. Some say the circumcision took place on the 13th Nissan *[Mid.Rab.Br.50.12]*. In an earlier revelation, Avraham and Sarah had their names changed (from Avram and Sarai). On the third day after the circumcision, three angels predicted that Yitzchak would be born within a year *[Bible Br.17.5,15; 18.10/Tal.B.M.86b]*.

Sdom and Amorrah were destroyed. Lot's wife, Irith, looked back at the destruction of Sdom, because her 2 married daughters were left behind *[Bible Br.18.16; 19.1, 13, 24/Mid.Yal. Br.19.84/ B.Turim Br.19.26]*. Being isolated in a cave, Lot's two rescued daughters believed that the whole world was destroyed, and therefore conceived two children from him, Mo'av and Ben Ami (Amon) *[Bible Br. 19.31, 37, 38]*. Avraham moved to the land of Plishtim in this year, and had trouble with Avimelech, the king, over the abduction of his wife *[Bible Br.20.1, 2]*. He lived there for 26 years *[Rashi Br.21.34]*.

2048 -1713

Yitzchak (Isaac) was born.

Yitzchak was born on the 15th Nissan in this year, which was a Jewish leap year *[Tal.R.H.11a]*. Accordingly, Yitzchak would have been born in the 7th month of pregnancy (from Tishrei, see 10th Tishrei 2048/-1714). Avraham made a banquet to celebrate Yitzchak's becoming "developed" (some say at eight days old (his circumcision day), others say at age 2 or 13). He invited (some say) all the great people (Shem, Ever, Avimelech king of the Plishtim) and also his father, Terach, and brother, Nachor II, who both came from Charan for the occasion *[Bible Br.21.8/Mid.Rab.53.10, Mat.Keh./Sed.Had.]*.

2049 -1712

Serug (grandfather of Terach) died (after his son Nachor I, see 1997\-1764) *[Bible Br.11.23]*.

Nachor II (son of Terach) married Milka his niece, the daughter of Haran (see 1958\-1803), and they had many sons. One was called Utz and another Betuel. Among the children of Betuel was a son called Lavan and a daughter called Rivka *(Rebecca)* *[Bible Br.22.20-23]*.

Iyov *(Job)* was the son of Utz, according to some *[Mid.Rab.Br. 57.4/ Yal.Reuv.q. Sed.Had./ IbnEz.Iyov.1.1 Eych.4.21]*, or he was Utz, according to others [Mid.Yal.Bam.766]. There were a number of people called Utz [Bible Br.10.23, 36.28]. There are some who say Iyov married Dinah the daughter of Yaakov [Mid.RabBr.57.4/ Yer.Sot.5.6p20] and others say Iyov lived many years later (see 2449\-1312 9th Av) [Tal. B.B.15b/Sed.Had.] and he lived in the land of Utz [Iyov 1.1, Metz.Dav].

2061 -1700

Avraham sent Yishmael and his mother away in 2061 [Mid.Rab.Br.53.13, Mat.Keh.]. Yishmael married two wives (one after the other), who (some say) were called Meriva (or Assiya) and Fatima (or Malchut), and he eventually settled in the land of Plishtim near his father [Pir.Dr.El.29/ Mid.Yal. Br.95,/ Sef.Hay./ Sed. Had. 2061, 2088].

Eliezer, the servant of Avraham, was a descendant of Canaan [Mid.Rab.Br.59.9]. Some say he was the son of Nimrod (the nephew of Canaan, see 1557\-2204, 1787\-1974) [Mid.Yal.Br.109/ Me'am Lo'ez Br.24.2], others say he had been the servant of Nimrod [Pir.Dr.El.16].

2083 -1678

Terach died [Bible Br.11.32].

2084 -1677

The Akeda. Yitzchak was Prepared To Be a Sacrifice.

Yitzchak was still 36 years old or just 37, depending on the day in Nissan that the Akeda took place (see Nissan 2048\-1713) [Mid.Rab. Br.55.4, Sh.15.11/ Sed.Had.]. Avraham named the place of the Akeda "Yir'eh", and this was added to its previous name "Shalem" (see 1558\-2203), hence the name "Yerushalayim" [Bible Br.22.14/ Mid.Rab.Br.56, Yal.Br. 22.102/Tos.Tan.16a]. Sarah heard that Avraham had taken Yitzchak to offer him as a sacrifice, and she travelled to search for them. When she reached Hevron *(Hebron)*, she was informed that he had not been sacrificed. The good news was too overwhelming for her, and she died [Bible Br.23.1, 2, Rashi/Mid.Rab.Br.58.5, Vay. 20.2/ Sed.Had.]. Avraham negotiated the purchase of the Ma'arat Hamachpela in Kiryat Arba (see 930\-2831), near Hevron, and he buried her there [Bible Br.23.19,20].

Yitzchak married Rivka (see 2049\-1712) shortly thereafter. Some say that Rivka was then 10 years old [Sef.Hay./Sed.Had.].

Some say that Nachor II (brother of Avraham) died at around this time, and that Avimelech, king of the Plishtim, also died, and his son Benmelech was made king and renamed Avimelech, as was the custom [Sef.Hay./Sed.Had.].

2096 -1665

Arpachshad (son of Shem) died [Bible 11.13].

Avraham married another wife by the name of Keturah (some say in the year 2088), and they had six sons. One of them was called Midyan, and the others were Zimran, Yakshan, Medan, Yishbak and Shuach [Bible Br.25.1,2/Sef.Hay./ Sed.Had.]. Some say that Keturah was actually Hagar, who had changed her name, others say she was a descendant of Yaphet, whereas Hagar was a descendant of Cham and Sarah a descendant of Shem [Mid.Rab. Br.61.4, Tan.9, Yal.Iyov.904/ Pir.Dr.El.29/ RashBam Br.25.1, IbnEz./ Ramban Br.25.6].

2108 -1653

Yaakov *(Jacob)* and Eisav were born [Bible Br.25.26].

2123 -1638

Avraham died.

On the day Avraham died (some say in Tevet [Sed.Had]), Eisav came home tired (because he had killed someone). It was on that day that he sold his rights, as the firstborn, to Yaakov [Bible Br.25.7/ Tal.B.B.16b]. Some say it was Nimrod (who was out hunting) that Eisav killed [Mid.Rab.Br.65.16/Sef.Hay./ Sed.Had.].

At this time Yitzchak moved to the land of Plishtim, and had difficulties with Avimelech the king (see 2084\-1677), over his wife Rivka [Bible Br.26.6-10].

2126 -1635

Shelach (grandson of Shem) died [Bible Br.11.15].

2158 -1603

Shem died [Bible Br.11.11]. He had outlived eight out of the next nine generations of his descendants (except for Ever (see 2187\-1574)) and they were: his son Arpachshad *(see 2096\-1655)*, Shelach *(see 2126\-1635)*, Peleg *(see 1996\-1765)*,

Re'u *(see 2026\-1735)*, Serug *(see 2049\-1712)*, Nachor I *(see 1997\-1764)*, Terach *(see 2083\-1678)*, and Avraham *(see 2123\-1638)*.
In 2148 Eisav had married Yehudit (daughter of Be'eri), and Basmat (daughter of Eylon), both Chitites (descendants of Canaan) *[Bible Br.26.34 / Sed.Had.]*.

2171 -1590

Yitzchak blessed Yaakov instead of Eisav.

Yitzchak blessed Yaakov on the 15th Nissan *(the first day of Pesach)*, and Yaakov had to leave Be'er Sheva because Eisav was angry — he felt that these special blessings were stolen *(perhaps the origin of children 'stealing' the Afikoman at the seder [author])*. *[Bible Br.27.42-44/Pir.Dr.El./Rashi Br.27.9]*. He spent fourteen years studying with Ever before he went to Charan (see 2185\-1576).
Yishmael died in this year, just before Eisav married his daughter Machalat *[Bible Br.28.9, Rashi/Tal. Meg.17a]*.

2185 -1576

Yaakov (at the age of 77 *[Rashi Br.25.26]*) arrived in Charan (see 2171\-1590), and it was at this stage that he had the dream of the ladder *[Bible Br.28.12, Rashi 28.9]*.

2187 -1574

Ever (great grandson of Shem) died (see 2171\-1590) *[Bible Br.11.17]*.

2192 -1569

Yaakov had to work for seven years in Charan before he married Lavan's daughters (in 2192) — Rachel one week after Leah. He also married Zilpah and Bilhah *[Bible Br. 29.23-30/Rashi Br.28.9]*. Some say that Rachel and Leah were the same age, or even twins, except that Rachel was physically much smaller. *[Sed.Ol.2/ Or.Hach.Br.29.16]*
Lavan — Yaakov's second cousin (see 2049\-1712) — had no sons until after Yaakov arrived *[Rashi Br.30.27]*, even though he was at least 100 at that time (see 2185\-1576) *[Rashi Br.28.9, 25.26, 35.29]*.
Some say that it was in 2191 *[Sef.Hay./ Sed.Had.]* that Eisav married Ahalivamah (officially) the daughter of Anah, who was the son of Tzivon, a descendant of Canaan. Actually Ahalivamah was the (illegitimate) daughter of Tzivon (her grandfather), and even her (official) father was Tzivon's illegitimate son. (Tzivon had previously had an illegitimate son (called Anah) from his own mother. He then had Ahalivamah from this son (Anah's) wife) *[Bible Br.36.2, Rashi]*.

2195 -1566

Levi was born on the 16th Nissan *[Bible Sh.6.16/Mid. Yal.Sh.1]*.
Reuven, the oldest son of Yaakov, was born on the 14th Kislev. Shimon was born on the (21st or) 28th Tevet, Yehuda on the 15th Sivan, Yissachar on the 10th Av, Zevulun on the 7th Tishrei, Dan on the 9th Elul, Naftali on the 5th Tishrei, Gad on the 10th Cheshvan, Asher on the 20th Shvat *[Mid.Yal.Sh.1/Bachya Sh.1.6]*. (Yosef *(Joseph)*, see 2199\-1562, Binyamin, see 2208\-1553).
Some say Dinah was a twin of Zevulun *[Ibn Ezra Br.30.21]*.

2199 -1562

Yosef *(Joseph)* was born on the 1st Tammuz *[Mid.Yal.Sh.1]*.

2205 -1556

Yaakov left Charan.

Lavan chased Yaakov when he left Charan *[Bible Br.31.23, 38]*, and (some say) he also sent messengers to Eisav to stir up his anger at Yaakov (see 2171\-1590) *[Sef.Hay./Sed.Had.]*. Yaakov's subsequent confrontation with Eisav (on his return to Canaan) was on the 9th Av *[Rashal Br.Vayish.q.Sed.Had.]*. Yaakov was given the extra name of Yisrael *(Israel)* in a revelation *[Bible Br.33.29; 35.10]*.
Dinah, who was captured (in Canaan) by Sh'chem, became pregnant, some say, and had a daughter called Osnat. Yaakov sent Osnat away because her uncles did not treat her kindly. She was adopted by Potiphera in Egypt (see 2229\-1533) *[Mid.Yal.Br.34.134]*.

2208 -1553

Binyamin was born on the 11th Cheshvan

[Mid.Yal.Sh.1, Rab. Bam.14], and his mother, Rachel, who died at his birth, was buried in Beit Lechem [Bible Br.35.18,19]. Rivka had died around 2207 [Rashi Br.33.17; 35.8].

Yaakov and his sons had a number of battles with the local Canaanites, who attacked them because of what they did to the city of Sh'chem [Rashi Br.48.22/ Ramban Br.34.13/ Bachya Br.35.6/ Sef.Hay./ Sed.Had.].

2216  -1545

Yosef was sold.

Yosef spent his first year in Egypt as a servant of Potiphar before he was placed in the dungeon for 12 years, because of the wife of Potiphar, who (some say) was called Zuleicha [Bible Br. 39.1-23, 41.14, 46 / Mid.Rab.Sh.7.1, Bam.15.12/ Sef.Hay./Sed.Had.].

Leah died this year [Mid.Yal. Br.34.135/ Sed.Had.2214].

Reuven (some say) married Elyoram the daughter of Chivi (the Canaanite) [Sef.Hay./Sed. Had.].

Eisav had many children, and Eliphaz, his son, had an illegitimate daughter called Timna, (from the wife of Seyir). Eliphaz then had a son from his daughter Timna, who was called Amalek [Bible Br.36.12, Rashi, Ramban/ Mid. Tan. VaYeshev].

2218 -1543

The Twelve sons of Yaakov married (according to some [Sef. Hay./Sed.Had.]):-

❖ Reuven, see 2216\-1545. ❖ Yehuda married Eilat, the daughter of Shua. ❖ Levi married Adina, the daughter of Yovav *(see 1757\-2004)*, and ❖ Yissachar married her sister Arida. ❖ Dan married Aphlala, daughter of Chamudan the Moabite, ❖ Gad married Utzit, daughter of Amoram *(son of Utz, son of Nachor II, see 2049\-1712)*, and ❖ Naftali married her sister Merimat. ❖ Asher married Edon the daughter of Aphlal, who was the son of Hadad, the son of Yishmael, and after she died childless he married Hadura the daughter of Avimael *(see 1757\-2004)*, who had a girl, Serach, from her previous husband (Malkiel son of Eylam, see 1558\-2203) [Ramban Bam.26.46, Targ. Yon.]. ❖ Zevulun married Merusha, the granddaughter of Midyan *(see 2096\-1665)*. ❖ Binyamin married Machalat, the daughter of Aram, in 2218, *(see 2000\-1761)*.

2228 -1533

Yitzchak died [Bible Br.35.28].

2229 -1533

Yosef became Viceroy of Egypt.

Yosef was released from prison on the 1st of Tishrei *(Rosh Hashana)*, and was thirty years old when he appeared before Pharaoh and was appointed [Bible Br.41.46/ Tal.R.H.11a]. Yosef married Osnat, his niece, the adopted daughter of Potiphera (see 2205\-1556) [Mid.Yal. Br.34. 134]. Pharaoh gave him the Egyptian name of Tzaphnat Pane'ach [Bible Br.41.45].

Some say that graduates of a special school *(university)* in Khartoum were the Khartumim who acted as Pharaoh's advisers [Pirush (Inyaney) Chalom Par'oh Br.41.8].

2235 -1526

The seven years of plenty came to an end and the famine began [Tal.Toseph.Sot.10.3].

Kehot (ben Levi) was born [Ralbag q.Sed.Had.] when Levi was 40.

Menasheh and Ephrayim (Yosef's sons), were born before the famine years [Bible Br.41.50].

2238 -1523

Yaakov (and his family) went to Egypt.

Yocheved, the daughter of Levi, was born as Yaakov and his family were entering Egypt [Bible Br.47.9/ Tal.B.B. 123b].

Yaakov was never told that his sons had sold Yosef and he thought that those who had found him as lost had sold him [Ramban Br.45.27].

Chapter 3

Living in Egypt

Section I

Chapter 3

Living in Egypt

Jewish Year		Secular Year
2255	Yaakov died.	**-1506**
2309	Yosef died.	-1542
2332	The enslavement in Egypt began after Levi died.	**-1429**
2368	Moshe (Moses) was born.	-1393
2406	Yehoshua (Joshua) was born.	-1355
2447	Moshe encountered the burning bush.	-1314
2448	THE CHILDREN OF ISRAEL LEFT EGYPT	**-1313**

Section I
THE BEGINNINGS

Chapter 3

Living in Egypt

The third chapter (Tekufa) in Jewish history begins when the children of Yaakov (Yisrael), came to settle in a foreign land.
It ends when the Children of Israel left as a nation, to a great new future, under the leadership of Moshe.

This book assumes that the reader is conversant with the basic text of the CHUMASH (Bible), and therefore makes reference to many events without describing them.

2255 -1506

Yaakov died.

After living in Egypt for 18 years Yaakov died, and he was taken to Canaan to be buried. Eisav attempted to stop Yaakov's sons from burying him in Ma'arat Hamachpela. In the ensuing fight, Chushim the son of Dan, killed Eisav, and Yaakov was buried on the 15th Tishrei *[Bible Br.47.28/Tal. Sot.13a/Sed.Had.]*.
Amram (ben Kehot) was born before the death of Yaakov *[Tal.B.B.121b, Rashbam]*. He married Yocheved, (see 2238\-1523), who was 22 when Yaakov died. Yaakov could have told her what he heard from Avraham, who heard from Noah, who heard from Lemech II, who heard from Adam.

2309 -1452

Yosef died.

Yosef died on Shabbat afternoon *[Bible Br.50.26/ Zoh.Sh.156a]*. He was the first of the brothers to die (see 2332\-1429) *[Tal.Ber.55a]*. All the sons of Yaakov (according to some) died on the same day of the same month, in which they were born, see 2195\-1566 *[Siddur Yavetz]*.

2332 -1429

The enslavement in Egypt after Levi died.

Levi died on the 16th of Nissan and the enslavement process of the Children of Israel *(Bnei Yisrael)* began in Egypt. He was the last of the brothers to die (see 2309\-1452) *[Bible Sh.6.16, Rashi / Mid.Yal. Sh.1/ Sed.Ol.3]*.
Yaakov had appointed Levi as the guardian of all the knowledge and tradition that he had received from his father Yitzchak, who had in turn received it from Avraham. The children of Levi continued this tradition *[Mmn.Hil.Av.Z.1.3]*.

2361 -1400

Miriam (the daughter of Amram) was born *[Sed.Ol.3/ Sed.Had]*.

2365 -1396

Aharon was born *[Bible Sh.7.7, Bam.33.39]*.

2368 -1393

Moshe (Moses) was born.

Moshe was born on the 7th Adar *[Bible Sh.7.7/ Tal.Kid.38a]*. His father (Amram) called him Chaver, but Kehot, his grandfather (who died this year), called him Avigdor *[Mid.Yal.Sh.2.166/ Ralbag/ Sed.Had.]*.
Moshe was placed at the river on the 6th Sivan *[Tal.Sot.12b]*. His mother, Yocheved, could tell him things that she heard of (dating back to creation) at no greater distance than 6th (reliable) word of mouth (see 2255\-1506).

2406 -1355

Yehoshua *(Joshua)* was born *[Yuch.1/ Tzem.Dav.]*.
Amram (Moshe's father) died before 2392, and Achiyah Hashiloni (see 2964\-797) was born before Amram died *[Tal.B.B.121b]*.

2410 -1351

Kalev (ben Yefuneh) was born *[Bible Ysh. 14.10]*. Yefuneh was Chetzron, the son of Peretz ben Yehuda *[Bible D.H.I 2.9/ Tal.Sot. 11b]*.
Moshe had killed the cruel Egyptian about two years earlier, in 2408 *[Mid.Rab.Br.100.10]*.

2418 1343

The children of Yisrael *(Israel)* knew of (the prediction of) a 400 year duration to their exile *[Bible Br.15.13]*. The descendants of Ephrayim made a calculation, with a commencing date of 2018, the year of the Brit Bein HaBetarim (when the exile was first mentioned), and they decided that the time had already come. They managed to leave Egypt, but many then perished in their unsuccessful attempt to reach Canaan (under the leadership of Gon) *[Bible D.H.I 7.21/Tal.San. 92b/ Mid.Yal.Sh.227, D.H.I 7.1077/ Pir.Dr.El.48/ Sed.Had.]*.

2447 -1314

Moshe encountered the burning bush.

Moshe had a revelation in the burning bush on the 15th Nissan, and exactly one year passed until the Exodus from Egypt.

The plagues commenced on the 1st Av, and continued consecutively, on the first of each month, until the last plague, which was on the eve of the 15th Nissan 2448 *[Mid.Yal. Sh.4.176/ Bachya Sh.10.5]*.

2448 -1314

Bnei Yisrael were free from slave labor, from the 1st Tishrei 2448 *[Tal.R.H.11b, Tos.]*.
In Nissan, Bnei Yisrael were told that in commemoration of their redemption, Nissan would in future be considered the 1st month (instead of Tishrei) when reckoning years by the month *[Bible Sh.12.2, Ramban]*.

2448 -1313

The Children of Israel (Yisrael) left Egypt.

The Children of Israel *(Yisrael)* who left Egypt on the 15th Nissan, were 600,000 men of draftable age (20-60). In normal demographic extensions, this would add up to a total population of approximately 2,000,000 people.
This exodus from Egypt was exactly 430 years after the Brit Bein HaBetarim in 2018, and exactly 400 years after Yitzchak was born, see 2418\-1343 *[Bible Br.15.13, Sh.12.40, 41, Mech.]*.
Many Egyptians (some say 40,000) left with them, including many Khartumim (see 2229\-1553) *[Bible Sh.12.38/ Mid.Tan.Sh.19/ Zoh.2.191a]*. These people (who were referred to as Erev Rav) are not mentioned again *[Bible Sh.32.33]* and they do not formally appear in any future countings, although other incidents are attributed to them (see Tammuz 2448\-1313).

[2448\-1313 is continued in Section II, Chapter 4.] 

THE NATION

Section II

Chapter 4

Moshe the Leader

Section II

Chapter 4
Moshe the Leader

Jewish Year		Secular Year
2448	The Children of Israel crossed the reed sea.	-1313
2448	**THE REVELATION & TORAH ON MOUNT SINAI.**	**-1313**
2448	Moshe broke the Tablets.	-1313
2449	Moshe came down Sinai with the second Tablets.	-1312
2449	The Mishkan (Tabernacle) was erected.	-1312
2449	The spies returned from Canaan with bad news.	-1312
2487	Aharon and Miriam died.	-1274
2488	**Moshe died.**	**-1273**

Section II
THE NATION

Chapter 4

Moshe the Leader

The fourth Chapter (Tekufa) of Jewish history
is distinct from all the others, in that it
(a) covers only forty years and (b) is named after a person.
The events of this 40–year period were significant enough
to stand as a chapter on their own,
and the leadership of Moshe (Rabbenu) was so great
that the events that occurred during his rule
comprise a separate chapter in the history of the people.
The chapter begins when Bnei Yisrael left Egypt,
and ends with the death of Moshe
and the imminent entry of the
Children of Israel into the holy Land of Israel.

This book assumes that the reader is conversant with the basic text of the CHUMASH *(Bible), and therefore makes reference to many events without describing them.*

[2448\-1313 is continued from chapter 3.]

2448 -1313

Bnei Yisrael crossed the reed sea.

Pharaoh sent observers to supervise the immediate return of Bnei Yisrael after the three days of freedom they had requested. These supervisors returned to Pharaoh on the fourth day to report that Bnei Yisrael had no intention of returning. The Egyptians pursued them on the fifth and the sixth days, and on that night (entering the seventh day, the 21st **Nissan**) Bnei Yisrael crossed the sea *[Tal.Sot.12b/ Mech./ Sed.Ol./Rashi Sh.14.5]*.

Bnei Yisrael arrived at Marah on the 23rd **Nissan**, where, through a miracle, the water became sweet and drinkable *[Bible Shm.15.22]*. Bnei Yisrael received ten laws there, including the law of Shabbat *[Tal.San.56b]*. It was only seven days later (on the 1st day of **Iyar**), when someone transgressed the law of Shabbat, by removing trees and collecting wood *[Bible Bam.15.32, Rashi/ Sifri/ Mid.Yal. Bam.15.749/ Tal. Shab.96b, Yer.San.5.1]*.

Bnei Yisrael arrived in the desert of Sinn on the 15th **Iyar**, and the morning after their arrival the Mann (Manna) came down for the first time *[Bible Sh.16.1, 7, 13/Tal.Kid.38a]*. It was then that Moshe instituted the first blessing for Birkat HaMazon *(Grace After Meals)* *[Tal.Ber.48b]*.

The Revelation & Torah on Mount Sinai.

Bnei Yisrael arrived in the desert of Sinai on the 1st **Sivan** *[Bible Sh.19.1/Tal.Shab.86b]*. On the 5th **Sivan** Moshe built an altar *[Bible Sh.24.4, Rashi]*; the Torah was given in a revelation on Sinai on the 6th; and on the 7th Moshe went up on the mountain for forty days *[Bible Dev.9.9/Tal. Shab.86b, Tan.28b/ Sed.Ol./ Tos.B.K.82a/Sed.Had.]*.

Moshe broke the Tablets.

Bnei Yisrael had calculated he would come down on the fortieth day, the 16th **Tammuz**, and when he did not appear, they thought he had died, and they made the golden calf. The Erev Rav were the instigators (according to many), and (some say) two Khartumim among them were the leaders *[Bible Sh.32.1/ Tal.Shab.89a/ Mid.Rab. Bam.15.21, Tan. Sh.19]*. Moshe came down from the mountain — and broke the Tablets — on the 17th. He went up Mount Sinai again on the next day (18th **Tammuz**), and he remained there for another forty days. He came down on the 29th **Av**, and went up once again on the 30th of **Av**, for yet another forty days *[Bible Sh.32.15/ Tal.Shab.89a/ Mid.Rab. Bam.15.21] Sed.Ol./Rashi Dev.9.18/ Tos.B.K.82a/ Sed.Had.]*.

2449 -1313

Moshe came down with the second Tablets.

Moshe placed the 2nd tablets in a special ark, when he brought them down on the 10th **Tishrei** (Yom Kippur). They were later transferred to the Holy Ark — which was a chest with an opening lid — built by Betzalel (the great grandson of Kalev) *[Bible Sh.40.20, Rashi, Dev.10.1-5, Rashi 10.1, D.H.I 2.19/ Sed.Ol./Rashi Sh.18.13]*.

On the very next day (the 11th **Tishrei**) Bnei Yisrael began donating gifts for the building of the Mishkan *(Tabernacle)* *[Mid.Rab.Sh.51.4, Tan.Sh.Pek.11/ Sed.Ol.]*.

It was on this day that Moshe sat — in court — to hear cases, and pass judgement, and he was advised, by his father in law Yitro, to institute a judicial system *[Bible Sh.18.13,19, Rashi]*.

2449 -1312

The Mishkan (Tabernacle) was erected.

Some say the Mishkan was completed on the 25th **Kislev**, others say on the 1st **Adar** *[Mid.Tan.Sh.Pek.11, Pesikta Rab.6.5]*. It was initially erected on the 23rd **Adar**, the services and sacrifices were performed, and it was then dismantled, and in this manner erected daily for seven days, until it was permanently erected, on the 1st **Nissan**, Rosh Chodesh, the day that Nadav and Avihu — two of Aharon's sons — died. The daily sacrifices and contributions brought by the leaders (of the twelve tribes) commenced — with Nachshon ben Aminadav of the tribe of Yehuda — on that day (and were even brought on Shabbat, see 2935 \ -827) *[Bible Sh.40:17, Bam.7.48/ Tal.Shab.87b/ Mid.Rab. Vay.20.12, Bam.12.15, Tan.Nasso(7.48)/ Sed.Ol./ Rashi Vay.9.1]*. (Nachshon died later in this year *[Mid.Yal.Shof.42.3]*.)

On that day, the ritually impure *(tme'im)* were relocated *[Rashi Bam.5.2]*, which means that Aharon was already functioning as a Kohen earlier, and was deciding cases of *tzara'as (skin disorders)*.

On the 2nd **Nissan**, Moshe prepared the sacri-

fice of the first PARA ADUMA *(Red Heifer)* *[Bible Bam.19.2/ Sed.Ol.]*. The PESACH sacrifice — the first after the Exodus from Egypt — was brought on the 14th **Nissan** *[Bible Bam. 9.1,2]*.
Moshe was instructed to count Bnei Yisrael on the 1st **Iyar** *[Bible Bam.1.1]*. Those who could not bring their Pesach sacrifice on time, because of their ritual impurity, brought it on the 14th **Iyar** *[Bible Bam.9.11]*. Eldad and Medad (see 2516\-1245) became prophets at the end of **Iyar** *[Calculated from:- Tal. Tan.29a, Bible Bam.11.26; 33.16; 33.19, Rashi]*.

The spies returned with bad news.

Moshe sent the spies on the 29th **Sivan**, and they returned, with bad news, on the 8th **Av**. That night (9th **Av**), Bnei Yisrael bemoaned their plight, and were condemned to spend forty years in the desert *[Bible Bam.14/Tal.Tan.29a/ Sed.Ol.]*. Neither the women, the young, nor the old (under 20 and over 60) died as a result of this *[Tal.B.B.121b/Rashi Bam.26.64]*.
Iyov, see 2049\-1712, died just before the journey of the spies *[Tal.B.B.15a/ Mid.Yal. Br.Lech.16/ Rashi Bam.14.9]*.
The rebellion of Korach took place soon thereafter *[Bible Bam.16/Sed.Ol.8]*.
Besides this event, the Bible does not describe any events that may have taken place, from the return of the spies until the death of Miriam (see 2487/-1274), but it does list the 20 places at which Bnei Yisrael stayed, during those 38 years. The first 19 of these years were spent in Kadesh Barne'a, where they were encamped when the spies had been sent
[Bible Dev.1.46, Rashi, Rashi Dev.2.16-17/ Tzem.Dav./ Sed.Had.].

2487 -1274

Aharon and Miriam died.

Miriam died on the 10th **Nissan** *[Bible Bam.20.1/ Tzem.Dav./Sed.Had.2488]*.
Aharon died on the 1st **Av**, and he was succeeded as KOHEN GADOL *(High Priest)* by his son Elazar *[Bible Bam.20.23-29, 33.38]*.
At this stage Bnei Yisrael had the various wars mentioned in the Bible, including the incident with Balak, king of Mo'av, and Bil'am the sorcerer. They conquered (and settled) the eastern bank of the Jordan River, including the territories of the giants, Sichon and Og (see 1656\-2105), who were killed in battle *[Bible Bam.22.2-21; 24.10-14; 21.21-35]*.

2488 -1273

Moshe Died.

Moshe began reviewing the Torah with Bnei Yisrael on the 1st **Shvat**, and finished on the 6th **Adar** *[Bible Dev.1.3/ Mid.Yal. Ysh.1/ Sed.Ol.]*. On Shabbat, the 7th **Adar**, he gathered all of Bnei Yisrael once again, and entered them into a covenant. He prepared them for his imminent death by reciting the SHIRA *(poem)* of Ha'azinu and by blessing them. He then went up to the peak of Mount N'vo, and saw the promised land *[Bible Dev.32.1; 33.1; 34.1/Tal. Kid.38a/Mid.Yal. Ysh.1/ Zoh.Sh.156a]*. Before he died he had completed the writing of the CHUMASH *(Bible)* *[Bible Dev.31.24-26/ Tal.B.B.15a]*.

[2488\-1273 is continued in chapter 5.]

Chapter 5

Shoftim
Judges & Early Prophets

Section II

Chapter 5
Shoftim — Judges & Early Prophets

Jewish Year		Secular Year
2488	**Bnei Yisrael crossed the Jordan into Canaan.**	**-1273**
2503	The apportionment of Eretz Yisrael was completed.	-1258
2516	**Yehoshua died.**	**-1245**
2533	**The rule of Shoftim (Judges) began with Othniel ben Knaz**	**-1228**
2573	Ehud ben Gerah became leader.	-1188
2654	Shamgar ben Anath died.	-1107
2654	**Devorah became leader.**	**-1107**
2694	**Gideon became leader.**	**-1067**
2734	Avimelech (son of Gideon) became leader.	-1027
2737	Tolah ben Pu'ah became leader.	-1024
2758	Ya'ir HaGil'adi became leader.	-1003
2779	**Yiphtach (HaGil'adi) became leader.**	**-982**
2792	Eylon (HaZevuloni) became leader.	-969
2802	Avdon ben Hillel became leader.	-959
2810	**Shimshon (Samson) became leader.**	**-951**
2830	**Eli (HaKohen) became leader.**	**-931**
2854	David ben Yishai was born.	-907
2871	**Shmuel became leader.**	**-890**

Section II
THE NATION

Chapter 5

Shoftim – Judges & Early Prophets

The fifth Chapter (Tekufa) in Jewish history
begins when Bnei Yisrael entered
the promised land of Canaan,
and ends with the appointment of the first king,
which indicates that there was a significant
strengthening of political self perception.

This book assumes that the reader is familiar with some of the basic events mentioned in the T'NACH (Bible) and therefore makes reference to many events without describing them.

[2488\-1273 is continued from chapter 4.]

2488 -1273

Bnei Yisrael crossed the Jordan into Canaan.

Bnei Yisrael mourned the death of Moshe for thirty days, (until the 7th **Nissan**) during which time Yehoshua had sent the two spies, Pinchas (ben Elazar) and Kalev (see 2516\-1245) *[Rashi Ysh.2.1/ Mid.Tan.Bam.Shl.1, Yal.Ysh.2.9]*. Rachav, the woman who assisted them (in Yericho), converted and later married Yehoshua *[Tal.Meg.14b, Zev.116b]*.

For three days Bnei Yisrael prepared themselves for the westward journey into the promised land, and they crossed the Jordan River on the 10th **Nissan** *[Bible Ysh.4.19]*. Those of Bnei Yisrael who had not been circumcised in the desert, did so under Yehoshua's guidance, on the 11th **Nissan** *[Tal.Yev.71b]*.

On the 14th **Nissan** they made the Pesach sacrifice. The Mann *(Manna)* had stopped (coming down) from the day of Moshe's death — supplies lasted until the 16th **Nissan**, when local grain became available *[Bible Ysh.5.9-12/Tal. Kid.38a]*. Yehoshua then instituted the 2nd blessing in Birkat HaMazon (grace after meals) *(see 15th Iyar 2448\-1313)* *[Tal.Ber.48b]*.

Bnei Yisrael erected the Mishkan at Gilgal (as well as erecting the 12 stones they took from the Jordan), before the 7 day "siege" of the city of Yericho, which commenced on the 22nd **Nissan** *[Bible Ysh.4.5/Sed.Ol.11/Sed.Had./D.YbY]*.

2495 -1266

Bnei Yisrael ended their conquests *[Tal.Zev.118b]* in which Yehoshua conquered the thirty-one kings who did not accept his terms *[Bible Ysh.12.24/ Tal.Yer. Shvi.6.1.16b/Mmn.Hil.Mel. 6.5, Kes.Mish, Radvaz]*. Many other kings had maintained palaces in this land *[Med.Rab. Shm.32, Tan.Mishp.17, Yal.Mishl.964, Sifri /Rashi Dev.33.17]*.

Some of the Canaanites took the option offered by Yehoshua and left the country — some migrated to Allemani, a Franco-German dukedom *[Tal.Yer. Shevii.6.?/ Ibn Ezra Ovad.1.20/ Rashi Dev.3.9/ Mmn.Hil.Mel.6.5, Radvaz]*. Shovach, king of Armenia, and other rulers established contact with Yehoshua *[Yuch.5.10]*.

Elazar and Yehoshua began the task of apportioning the land (including that which was not yet conquered) *[Bible Ysh.14.1]*.

2503 -1258

Apportionment of Eretz Yisrael was completed.

With the apportionment completed, the Mishkan was moved from Gilgal and erected at Shilo, with stone walls replacing the original wooden beams. *[Bible Ysh.18.1/Tal.Zev.112b, 118b]*.

The counting for the seven year Shmitta cycles (and the fiftieth year as Yovel), commenced in 2503 *[Tal.Erch. 12b/ Sed.Ol. 11/ Mmn. Hil. Shmitt.10.2]*.

The tribes of Reuven, Gad, and half of Menasheh returned to their families (east of the Jordan), and expressed concern (over the possibility of) being disenfranchised from the rest of Bnei Yisrael *[Bible Ysh.22]*.

2516 -1245

Yehoshua died.

Yehoshua completed the writing of Sefer Yehoshua before he died on 26th Nissan *[Tal.B.B.14b/ TBY.O.C.580.1/Yuch.1]*. The last passage cites the death of Elazar, which was around this time *[Bible Ysh.24.33/ Mid. Yal. Ysh.24.35]*.

After Yehoshua, leadership was assumed by the ZEKEINIM *(Elders)* *[Bible Ysh.24.31, Shof.2.7]* with Kalev included as the main figure *[Tal.Naz.56b]*. Other notables were Pinchas (as Kohen Gadol, succeeding his father Elazar), Eldad and Medad (see Iyar 2449\-1312) *[Mid.Rab.Bam.3.7/ Yuch.1]*. The leadership of the ZEKEINIM lasted for 17 years, until 2533 *[Sed.Ol./ Yuch.1/ TBY. O.C.580.1]*.

2533 -1228

The rule of the Shoftim began.

The last of the ZEKEINIM *(Elders)* died on the 5th Shvat, and Othniel ben Knaz became leader of Bnei Yisrael for forty years *[Bible Shof.3.11/ Sed.Ol./ Yuch.1/ TBY.O.C.580]*. He was the first of 15 consecutive leaders called SHOFTIM *(Judges)*, whose leadership lasted for almost 350 years, until the first king was appointed *(see 2882\-879)*. Othniel — also called Yavetz *[Tal.Tem.16a]* — was Kalev's half brother (and he married Kalev's daughter) *[Bible Shof.1.13/Tal. Sot.11b, Tem.16a]*.

For eight years Kushan Rishatayim, king of Aram Naharayim, dominated Bnei Yisrael, until Othniel overpowered him *[Bible Shof.3.8,9]*.

2573 -1188

It was during the rule of Othniel, that Michah (see 2964\-797) had made his idol (*Pessel Michah*, (see 2870\-891)), and that the controversy with the tribe of Binyamin (about the Pilegesh BeGiv'a) took place *[Bible Shof.17-21/ Mid.Yal. Shof.68/ Sed.Ol. 12/ Rashi Shof.17.1, Radak]*. One hundred people from

the tribe of Binyamin (consequently) settled in Europe (according to some) in Italy and Germany *[Rashi Shof.20.45]*.
Othniel died in 2573, and Ehud ben Gerah — from the tribe of Binyamin — became leader (SHOFET, *Judge*) for eighty years *[Bible Shof. 3.15; 3.30/Sed.Ol./Yuch.1]*.
For eighteen years Bnei Yisrael were dominated by Eglon, king of Mo'av, until Ehud (after eleven years of rule) gained entry to his palace and killed him *[Bible Shof.3.14-25/Mid.Yal. Shof. 42.3/Sed. Ol.12]*.

2654 -1107

Devorah became leader.

Shamgar ben Anath (a Kohen) — a SHOFET — ruled during the last years of Ehud's (eighty year) rule *[Bible Shof. 3.31/Mid.Yal.Shof.42.3/Tzem.Dav./Sed.Had.]*. They both died in 2654 *[Tol.Am.Ol.1.41]*. Some maintain that Shamgar was after Ehud, as it appears in the Bible *[Radak Shof. 4.1]*.
After Ehud and Shamgar, Devorah (the prophetess) ruled for forty years *[Bible Shof.5.31/Sed.Ol./Yuch.1]*, together with her husband, Barak (ben Avinoam), who was also known as Lapidut *[Shof..4.4, Radak, Ralbag/ T.D.B.E.9/ Mid.Yal. 42]*. For twenty years of her rule, Bnei Yisrael were dominated by Yavin king of Canaan, and Sisra, his general, until she and Barak waged war against them *[Bible Shof.4/ Mid.Yal.Shof. 42.3/Sed.Ol.12]*.
Although Devorah was considered one of the SHOFTIM (*Judges*), some say she never actually acted as a judge on legal matters on her own, and that either she judged because of her prophecies or she instructed the judges during her rule *[Tos.Nid.50a]*.

2694 -1067

Devorah died, and Gideon became leader.

After Devorah died in 2694, Gideon (ben Yo'ash, from the tribe of Menasheh) was leader (SHOFET, *JUDGE*) for forty years *[Bible Shof.8.28/Sed.Ol./Yuch.1]*. He is also referred to as Yerubaal, because (at night on the 15th Nissan) he destroyed an altar used for the worship of the Baal idol *[Bible Shof.6.27, 32, / Mid.Yal.62]*.
For seven years of his rule, Bnei Yisrael were dominated and harassed by the people of Midyan until Gideon overpowered them in a surprise night attack *[Bible Shof. 6.2-6; 7.19, 8.11, 28/ Ralbag Shof. 8.28/ Sed. Had.]*.

2734 -1027

Avimelech succeeded his father Gideon as SHOFET in 2734, and he ruled for three years *[Bible Shof.9.22/Sed.Ol./Yuch.1]*.

2737 -1024

Tolah (ben Pu'ah, from the tribe of Yissachar) succeeded Avimelech, and ruled for twenty-three years *[Bible Shof.10.1,2/ Sed.Ol.]*.

2758 -1003

Ya'ir HaGil'adi (from the tribe of Menasheh) became a SHOFET in 2758, and he ruled for twenty two years *[Bible Shof.10.3/ Sed.Ol./ Yuch.1]*. The beginning and the end of his leadership, actually overlapped with that of Tolah and Yiphtach *[Yuch.1]*.
The eighteen year domination and harassment of Bnei Yisrael at the hands of the people of Amon, started during Yair's rule, in 2764 (see 2779\-982) *[Bible Shof.10.8/Sed.Ol.]*.

2779 -982

Eli (the Kohen) was born in 2772, *[Tzem.Dav./ Sed.Had.]*, and Yiphtach HaGil'adi became SHOFET for six years, in 2779 *[Bible Shof.12.7/Sed.Ol./Yuch.1]*.
The domination and harassment by the people of Amon ended in 2782, (see 2758\-1003), when Yiphtach overpowered them in battle.
Although Yiphtach ranked lowest among the SHOFTIM, he was nevertheless a prophet *[Bible Shof.11.32,33/ Tal.R.H.25b/ Mid.Rab. Vay.37.3, Yal.Shof.67, 68]*.

2785 -976

Ivtzan, also called Bo'az, succeeded Yiphtach in 2785, and he ruled for seven years *[Bible Shof.12.8, 9/ Tal.B.B.91a/Yuch.1]*. He married Ruth in his later years *[Tal.B.B.91a]*.
Bo'az was the son of Sal'mon the son of Nachshon ben Aminadav. Aminadav was the son of Ram, who was the son of Chetzron, who was the son of Peretz, the son of Yehuda *[Bible Rut.4.18-20]*.

2792 -969

Eylon HaZevuloni (from the tribe of Zevulun) succeeded Ivtzan as SHOFET in 2792, and he ruled for ten years *[Bible Shof.12.11/ Yuch.1]*.

2802 -959

Avdon ben Hillel HaPir'atoni, who was from the tribe of Ephrayim, succeeded Eylon, and

SHOFTIM
JUDGES AND EARLY PROPHETS

2488	YEHOSHUA (Joshua)	**-1273**
2516	ZEKEINIM (Elders)	**-1245**

2533	SHOFTIM (Judges)	**-1228**
2533	Othniel ben Knaz	-1228
2573	Ehud ben Gerah	-1188
2654	Shamgar *died.	-1107
265	**Devorah**	**-1107**
269	**Gideon**	**-1067**
2734	Avimelech	-1027
2737	Tolah ben Pu'ah	-1024
2758	Ya'ir HaGil'adi	-1003
2779	**Yiphtach**	**-982**
2792	Eylon HaZevuloni	-969
2802	Avdon ben Hillel	-959
281	**Shimshon (Samson)**	**-951**
283	**Eli (HaKohen)**	**-931**
2871	**Shmuel**	**-890**

** All others listed at beginning of rule.*

ruled for eight years *[Bible Shof.12.13-15/Yuch.1]*.

2810 -951

Shimshon (Samson) became leader.

Shimshon (ben Mano'ach, from the tribe of Dan) succeeded Avdon, and he ruled for twenty years (see 2830\-931) *[Bible Shof.16.31/ Yuch.1]*. His mother, Tzal'lephunit, was told that he should be a NAZIR *[Bible Shof.13.3-5/ Tal.B.B. 91a/Bam.Rab.10.5]*. He was famous for his great physical strength despite the fact that he was lame in both legs *[Tal.San.105a, Sot.10a/Med Yal.Shof.13.69]*. He was the wisest of the wise in his generation, and for twenty years after his death, the Plishtim were subdued, until they were certain that he had no sons who had inherited his strength *[Tal.Sot.10a, R.H.25b, Yer./Sed. Had./Mid.Yal. Shof. 16.71/Mrsha.Sot.10a (2) (5)]*.

2830 -931

Eli HaKohen became leader.

Eli ruled as a SHOFET for forty years and he also succeeded Pinchas as Kohen Gadol *(see 2516\-1245)* *[Bible Shm.I 4.18/Yuch.1/ Mmn. Hakd.L'Yad]*. He was a descendant of Ithamar, the son of Aharon *[Rashi Shm.I 2.30]*.

Shmuel was born.

On the very day that Eli became leader, Chanah *(Hannah)* came to Shilo and prayed for a son (Shmuel) who was born in the same year *[Sed.Ol. 13/Rashi Naz.5a, Shm.I 1.9, 22]*. Both she and her husband Elkana were prophets *[Tal.Meg.14a, Rashi/Sed.Ol.20/ Mid.Rab.Bam.10.5]*.
Shimshon (see 2810\-951) died in the year 2831 *[Tzem.Dav./Sed.Had.]*.

2854 -907

David (ben Yishai) was born.

David, who was born in 2854 *[Tzem.Dav./Sed.Had.]*, was the son of Yishai, who was the son of Oved, the son of Bo'az (see 2785\-976) and Ruth *[Bible Rut.4.20]*. Ruth was the daughter or granddaughter of Eglon, king of Mo'av (see 2573\-1188), who was a descendent of Balak (see 2487\-1274) *[Tal. San. 105b, Sot.47a, Hor.10b, Naz.23b]*.

2870 -891

Eli died on the 10th Iyar (some say 2871) *[TBY. O.C.590.1/ Tzem.Dav./ Sed.Had]*, upon learning (from Shaul) that the Holy Ark had been captured by the Plishtim, and that his two sons were killed in battle *[Bible Shm. I 4.18/ Mid. Yal.Shof.4.102/Rashi Shm.I 4.12/Sed. Had.]*. *(This was the only occasion in which this Holy Ark was taken out to battle [Rashi Bible Dev. 10.1/ Radak Shm.I 4.4/Metz.Dav. Shm.I 4.7].)*
On the day that Eli died, the Mishkan was destroyed *[Tal.Zev.118b]*.
Pessel Michah (see 2573\-1188) was worshipped by some, until this time *[Bible Shof.18.31, Rashi 17.1]*.

2871 -890

Shmuel became leader.

Shmuel, who had already gained acceptance as a leader during the life of Eli, succeeded him as SHOFET in 2781 *[Bible Shm.I 4.1/Radak Shof.18.1/ Tzem.Dav./Sed.Had.]*.
The Mishkan was reconstructed at Nov, (see 2870\-891) *[Tal. Zev.118b/Sed.Ol.13]*. The Holy Ark was in the hands of the Plishtim for seven months, until they returned it to Beit Shemesh *[Bible Shm.I 6.1,15]*. It was then brought by Bnei Yisrael to the house of Avinadav at Kiryat Ye'arim, where it remained for twenty years, even though the Mishkan was at Nov *[Bible Shm.I 7.1-2]*.

2881 -880

Shmuel, at a later stage in his life, had appointed his two sons — Yoel and Aviyah — as leaders, but they were not following his ways. Then in 2881 Bnei Yisrael asked Shmuel to appoint a king like all nations, and he did not immediately approve of the idea *[Bible Shm.I 8.1-7/ Tal.Naz. 5a, Tem.14b.]*. Shmuel himself was considered a leader without peer amongst the prophets *[Mid. Shochar Tov 90.4]*.

Chapter 6

Kings & the First Beit Hamikdash

Section II

Chapter 6

Kings and the First Beit Hamikdash

Jewish Year		Secular Year
2882	Shaul was appointed king.	**-879**
2884	David became king of Yehuda in Hevron.	-877
2892	DAVID BECAME KING OF ISRAEL IN YERUSHALAYIM.	-869
2924	Shlomo became king.	-837
2928	Building of the Beit Hamikdash commenced.	-833
2935	THE FIRST BEIT HAMIKDASH WAS COMPLETED	**-827**
2964	SHLOMO DIED AND HIS KINGDOM WAS DIVIDED.	**-797**
2964	Rechav'am (son of Shlomo) became king of Yehuda.	-797
2964	Yerav'am ben Nevat became king over Yisrael.	-797
3043	Eliyahu went up in a chariot of fire.	**-718**
3084	Yeho'ash I (Joash) renovated the Beit Hamikdash.	-677
3142	Yeshayahu (Isaiah) began his prophecies.	**-619**
3187	The first two of the ten tribes were exiled.	**-574**
3195	Another two of the ten tribes were exiled.	**-566**
3199	Chizkiyahu (Hezekiah) became king of Yehuda.	-562
3205	THE LAST OF THE TEN TRIBES WERE EXILED.	**-556**
3213	Sancheriv invaded Eretz Yehuda and retreated.	-548
3228	Menasheh (son of Chizkiyahu) became king of Yehuda.	-533
3298	Yirmiyahu (Jeremiah) began his prophecies.	**-463**
3303	Yoshiyahu (Josiah) renovated the Beit Hamikdash.	-458
3319	Yerushalayim was conquered, and Yehoyakim exiled.	**-442**
3321	Yehoyakim burned the Megilla (Eycha) composed by Yirmiyahu.	-440
3327	Yerushalayim conquered again, and Yehoyachin exiled.	**-434**
3331	Yirmiyahu persisted in prophesying calamity.	-430
3332	Yechezk'el (Ezekiel) prophecized in exile.	**-429**
3336	The final Babylonian siege of Yerushalayim	**-425**
3338	The walls of Yerushalayim were penetrated.	-423
3338	The sacrifices ceased in the Beit Hamikdash.	-423
3338	THE FIRST BEIT HAMIKDASH WAS DESTROYED.	**-423**

Section II

THE NATION

Chapter 6

Kings & the First Beit Hamikdash

The sixth Chapter (Tekufa) in Jewish history begins when the first king was appointed, and ends when the last king was dethroned, and the First Beit Hamikdash was destroyed.

This book assumes that the reader is familiar with the major occurrences described in the T'NACH (Bible), and therefore makes reference to many events and people without describing them.
However, the events occurring at the end of this chapter, are scattered among many places in the T'NACH (Bible), (notably in MELACHIM/Kings, Divrei HAYAMIM/Chronicles, and YIRMIYAHU/Jeremiah), and therefore required a more detailed mention in this book.

Kings of Yehuda

Rechav'am	2964
Aviyah	2981
Assa	2983
Yehoshaphat	3024
Yehoram II	3047
Achazyahu II	3055
Athalya Ruled	3056
Yeho'ash I	3061
Amatzya	3100
Uziyahu	3115
Yotam	3167
Achaz	3183
Chizkiyahu	3199
Menasheh	3228
Amon	3283
Yoshiyahu	3285
Yeho'achaz II	3316
Yehoyakim	3316
Yehoyachin	3327
Tzidkiyahu	3327

Kings of Yisrael

Yerav'am I	2964
Nadav	2985
Ba'asha	2986
Elah	3009
Zimri	3010
Omri	3010
Ach'av	3021
Achazyahu I	3041
Yehoram I	3043
Yehu	3055
Yeho'achaz I	3083
Yeho'ash II	3098
Yerav'am II	3115
Zecharyahu	3153
Shalom	3154
Menachem	3154
Pekachya	3164
Pekach	3166
Hoshea	3187

Shaul	2882
David (limited rule)	2884
Ish Boshet (limited rule)	2889
David	2892
Shlomo	2924

All Biblical Kings

Kings of Yehuda		Kings of Yisrael
Rechav'am	2964	
	2964	Yerav'am I
Aviyah	2981	
Assa	2983	
	2985	Nadav
	2986	Ba'asha
	3009	Elah
	3010	Zimri
	3010	Omri
	3021	Ach'av
Yehoshaphat	3024	
	3041	Achazyahu I
	3043	Yehoram I
Yehoram II	3047	
Achazyahu II	3055	
	3055	Yehu
Athalya Ruled	3056	
Yeho'ash I	3061	
	3083	Yeho'achaz I
	3098	Yeho'ash II
Amatzya	3100	
Uziyahu	3115	
	3115	Yerav'am II
	3153	Zecharyahu
	3154	Shalom
	3154	Menachem
	3164	Pekachya
	3166	Pekach
Yotam	3167	
Achaz	3183	
	3187	Hoshea
Chizkiyahu	3199	
Menasheh	3228	
Amon	3283	
Yoshiyahu	3285	
Yeho'achaz II	3316	
Yehoyakim	3316	
Yehoyachin	3327	
Tzidkiyahu	3327	

2882 -879

Shaul was appointed king.

Shaul (ben Kish), who was from the tribe of Binyamin, was the first of forty three kings who reigned — some concurrently — for a total of 456 years, until the destruction of the first Beit Hamikdash (see 3338\-423).
He had been anointed by Shmuel in 2881 *[Bible Shm.I 10.1/Tal.Tem.14b]*, and was appointed in 2882 *[Tzem.Dav./Sed.Had.]*. Although he was chosen because he was a very outstanding person *[Bible Shm.I 9.2; 10.24]*, he nevertheless had to prove himself — in the successful battle against Nachash the Amoni — before he was universally accepted *[Bible Shm.I 11.11-14]*.

2883 -878

When Shaul did not completely fulfill his duties, Shmuel sought another lineage for future kings *[Bible Shm.I 13.13,14; 15.17, 23,26,28]*. This was done discreetly in order not to arouse the anger of Shaul *[Bible Shm.I 16.2]*. Shmuel anointed David (ben Yishai, see 2854\-907), in 2883 *[Sed.Had.]*. He was the seventh of eight brothers *[Bible Shm.I 16.10; 17.12 D.H.I 2.15, Rashi, Radak]*.
When David killed Golyath *(Goliath)*, he received all the praise, and Shaul had to give him his daughter (Michal) for that feat, as he had promised. Shaul then developed a jealousy towards David *[Bible Shm.I 17.25; 18.6-8, 27-29]*.

2884 -877

Shmuel aged early and died on the 28th Iyar 2884, four months before Shaul *[Tal.Tan.5b; Rashi Shm.I 1.22, 12.2, Tem.15a/ TBY. O.C. 580.1/ Sed.Had.]*. He had transformed his leadership role into that of prophet only — in his later years — and gave the political leadership to others. (His sons, then Shaul, and then he appointed David).
Shmuel wrote the books of Shoftim, Ruth, and Shmuel *[Tal.B.B.15a]*.
After the death of Shmuel, David married Avigayil, the widow of Naval *[Bible Shm.I 25.1-2, 40-42]*.
In the last part of his life, Shaul was obsessed with his jealousy of David (his son-in-law), who was also his son Yehonatan's best friend, and he hunted him all over the country. Gad, the prophet, assisted David with advice, when he was evading Shaul *[Bible Shm.I 19-24; 26; 22.5]*.
Avner was Shaul's general, and Do'eg Ha'adomi was the Av Beit Din *(Chief Justice)* *[Bible Shm.I 17.55; 21.8, Rashi]*.
When Shaul saw his three sons killed in a losing battle against the Plishtim, he attempted to take his own life *[Bible Shm.I 31.2-6; II 1.6-9/Tzem.Dav./ Sed.Had.]*.

David became king in Hevron.

David was thirty years old when he became king, in Hevron, upon the death of Shaul, and he ruled over his own tribe of Yehuda. His reign, in this limited form, lasted for seven and one half years *[Bible Shm.II 2.4, 11/Metz.Dav. Mel.I 2.11/ Tzem.Dav./ Sed. Had.]*.
The Mishkan at Nov was destroyed in this year (when Shmuel died), and was rebuilt at Giv'on. The Holy Ark was still at Kiryat Ye'arim until 2892 (see 2871\-890) *[Tal.Zev. 118b/ Tzem.Dav./ Sed.Had.]*.

2892 -869

David became king of Israel in Yerushalayim.

From 2884 until 2889 no one had ruled over all of Bnei Yisrael (see 2884\-877). In 2889, Avner appointed Ish Boshet (son of Shaul) as king of Bnei Yisrael, and he ruled for 2 years. Six months after Ish Boshet was assassinated, which David avenged, all of Bnei Yisrael accepted David as their king *[Bible Shm.II 2.8-10; 4.7; 5.1-3/Rashi San.20a/Tzem.Dav./Sed. Had.]*.
David captured the fortress of the people of Yevussi, within Yerushalayim, and called it Ir *(City of)* David *[Bible Shm.II 5.7, 9;]*.
During the festive procession accompanying the Holy Ark to the new Ir David (in 2892), Uzah (ben Avinadav, see 2871\-890) humiliated the Ark and died. David then left it with Oved Edom Hagiti (the Levi) for three months, before continuing to Yerushalayim *[Bible Shm.II 6.6-7, 10-11/D.H.I 26.4,5/Tal.Sot.35a/Tzem. Dav.]*.
David instituted a 3rd blessing in Birkat HaMazon *(Grace After Meals)*, (see 2488\-1273) *[Tal.Ber.48b/ Kes.Mish. Hil. Ber. 2.1]*.
Natan the prophet told David that his son (not he) would build the Beit Hamikdash *[Bible D.H.I 17.1-15]*.

2912 -849

The incident with David and Bat Sheva (the daughter of Eliyam ben Achitofel) was on the 24th Elul, after Uriyah, her husband had given

her a conditional divorce on the 7th Sivan. David was forgiven on the 10th Tishrei (Yom Kippur) *[Bible Shm.II 11.3-4 /Tal.Shab.56a, Tos./ MidYal.Shm.II.151/ Zoh.Ber.Hakd.8a/Radak. Shm. II 17.3/Sed.Had.]*. Shlomo was born in 2912, and was their second son. The first son had died *[Bible Shm.II 11.5; 12.18,24/Tal.San.69b/ Tzem.Dav./ Sed.Had.]*.
The incident with Amnon (David's son) and Tamar (his stepdaughter) occurred in 2913 *[Bible Shm.II 13/Radak Shm.II 13.1/ Tzem.Dav.]*.

2921 -840

Avshalom (David's son) fled to Geshur in 2915, after he took revenge on his half brother Amnon (for the incident with Tamar, see 2912\-849). He then returned to Yerushalayim for two years, before going to Hevron and declaring himself king in 2921 (with the support of David's former advisor, Achitofel (see 2912\-849)). Avshalom died at the hands of Yo'av (David's general and nephew), and his men, when he was caught in a tree by the hair of his head *[Bible Shm.II 13.28,38; 14.28; 15.9-12; 18.9,14,15, D.H.I 2.16/Rashi Radak Shm.II 18.9/ Tal.Naz.5a, Tos./Tzem. Dav./Sed.Had.]*.
Sheva ben Bichri also attempted a rebellion against David and was killed *[Bible Shm.II 20.1,22]*.

2924 -837

David died and Shlomo became king.

Towards the end of his rule, David counted Bnei Yisrael, and there were 1.3 million men of draftable age, which translates into more than 5 million people (see 2448\-1313) *[Bible Shm.II 24.9, Radak; D.H.I 21.5, 6, Rashi 5]*.
In the last days of David's life Adoniyahu (his spoiled son) proclaimed himself king, with the backing of Yo'av, (see 2921\-840). Natan the prophet advised Bat Sheva to inform David of this, and to remind him of his promise that Shlomo (her son) would become king. David subsequently dispatched Tzadok (Kohen Gadol), Natan (the prophet), and Benayahu (an important figure), to publicly anoint Shlomo, (who was only 12 years old). When word of this spread, everyone deserted Adoniyahu *[Bible Mel.I 1.5-49; Ralbag Mel.I 1.38/Sifri/ Sed.Had.]*.
David died (in Ir David) on Shabbat afternoon of Shavu'ot (which some say was on the 7th Sivan that year) *[Bible Mel.I 2.10/ Tal.Shab.30b, Yer.Chag.2.3/ Zoh.Sh.Ter. 156a/Tos.Chag.17a/ Rashal Vay.q.Sed.Had./ Lik. Sich. 8.22. Note 8]*.
He wrote Tehillim *(Psalms)*, which include some verses by ten elders *[Tal. B.B.14b-15a, Rashi; Pes.117a]*.

2928 -833

Building of the Beit Hamikdash commenced.

David had prepared many of the supplies needed for building the Beit Hamikdash, and he also gave Shlomo instructions *[Bible D.H.I 22]*. Building began in Iyar, and Hiram, king of Tzur *(Tyre)*, who was friendly with David, helped supply wood from Lebanon *[Bible Shm.II 5.11, Mel.I 5.24; 6.1, 37]*.
The components of the Mishkan — made by Moshe in the desert — were buried under the Beit Hamikdash *[Tal.Sot.9a/ Mid. Rab.Br.42.3]*.
Shlomo added to the 3rd blessing in Birkat HaMazon *(Grace After Meals)* (see 2892\-869) *[Tal.Ber.48b/ Kes.Mish.Hil.Ber.2.1]*.

2935 -827

The First Beit Hamikdash was completed.

On the 7th Tishrei, Shlomo gathered all of Bnei Yisrael to honor the entry of the Holy Ark into the new Beit Hamikdash. The extensive celebrations — including feasting, even on Yom Kippur, see 2449 \ -1312 — lasted for seven days, and they then celebrated Sukkot *[Bible Mel.I 8.1-6, 65; D.H.II 5; 7.9/ Tal. M.K.9a, Shab.30a]*. The finishing touches to the new building were completed in Cheshvan *[Bible Mel.I 6.38, Ralbag; D.H.II 7.10, 11]*.
Shlomo was a disciple of Shim'i but he had cursed David during Avshalom's uprising. Shlomo cunningly found grounds to have him killed. Shlomo subsequently married the daughter of Pharaoh *[Bible Mel.I 2.8-9, Radak; 37-46/ Mid. Rab.Bam. 10.3/Sed.Had.]*.

2948 -813

Hiram the king of Tzur *(Tyre)* (see 2928\-833), gave Shlomo gifts of silver and wood supplies, and then they exchanged gifts of complete cities *[Bible Mel.I 9/ Tzem.Dav./Sed.Had.]*.

2964 -797

Shlomo died, and his kingdom was divided.

Shlomo had composed Mishli *(Proverbs)*, Kohelet *(Ecclesiastes)*, and at the end of his life, Shir Hashirim *(Song of Songs)* *[Rashi B.B.14b, Tos., Mrsha.15a]*.
When Yerav'am ben Nevat had criticized Shlomo for his wrongdoing, Achiyah Hashiloni — who

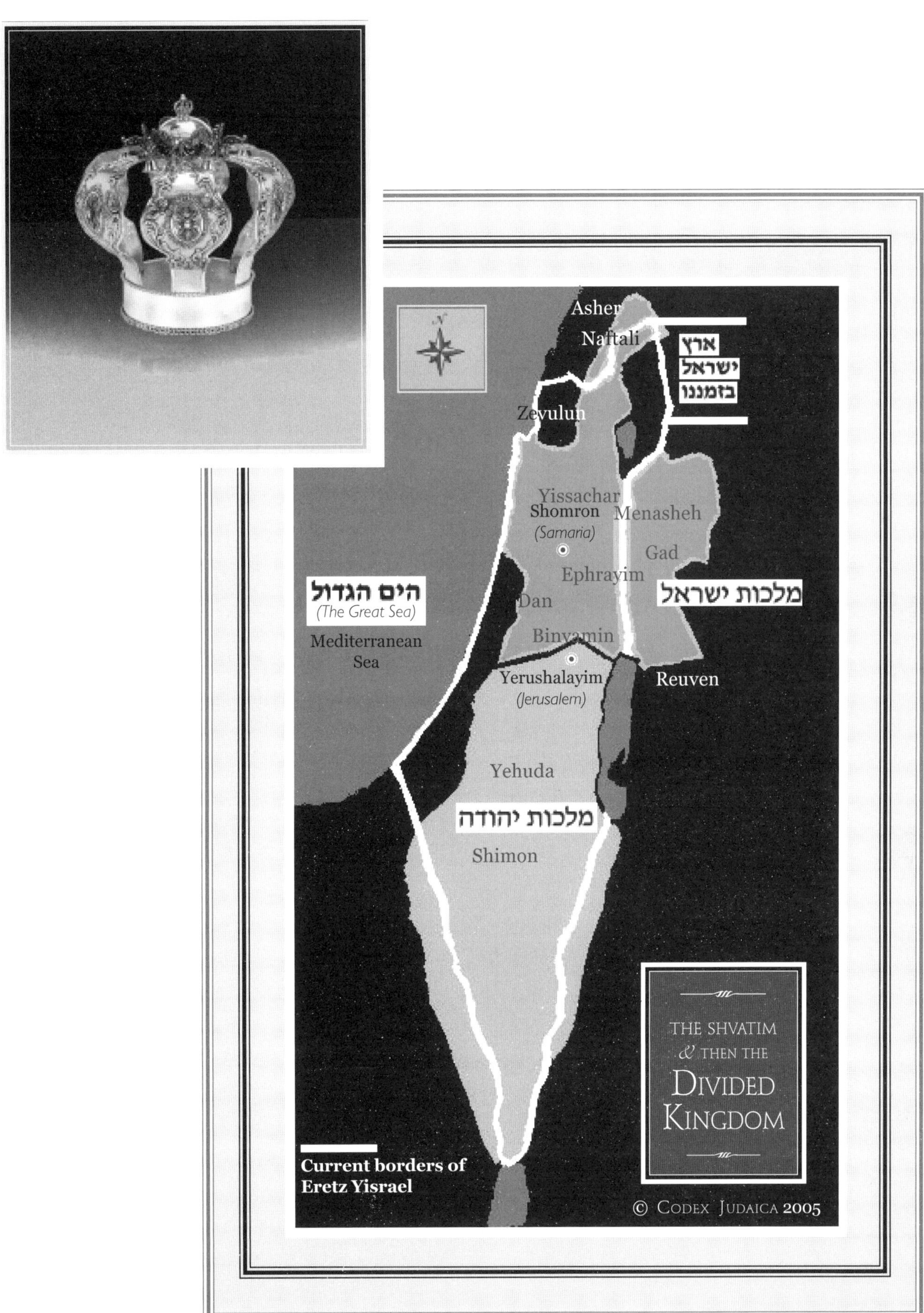
Asher
Naftali
ארץ
ישראל
בזמננו
Zevulun
Yissachar
Shomron
(Samaria)
Menasheh
Gad
Ephrayim
הים הגדול
(The Great Sea)
Mediterranean
Sea
Dan
מלכות ישראל
Binyamin
Yerushalayim
(Jerusalem)
Reuven
Yehuda
מלכות יהודה
Shimon
THE SHVATIM
& THEN THE
DIVIDED
KINGDOM
Current borders of
Eretz Yisrael
© CODEX JUDAICA 2005

was already Eliyahu's *(Elijah's)* mentor at that stage — prophesied that Yerav'am would be king of ten tribes *[Bible Mel.I 11.26, Rashi; 31/Yuch.1/Sed.Had.]*.
Shlomo died and Rechav'am was to be his successor. He rejected the advice of the older advisers (the elders), and accepted the advice of his friends, when he informed Bnei Yisrael that he would rule with a stronger hand than his father Shlomo. Bnei Yisrael then turned to Yerav'am I to be their king, and he reigned in the north *[Bible Mel.I 12.8,14,19/Tzem.Dav./ Sed.Had.]*.
Rechav'am subsequently ruled over the tribes of Yehuda and Binyamin, in Yerushalayim (the south), for seventeen years *[Bible Mel.I 14.21/ Tzem.Dav./ Sed.Had.]*.
Yerav'am's father, Nevat, was also identified as Michah (see 2573\-1188) and Sheva (ben Bichri) (see 2921\-840) *[Tal.San. 101b, Mrsha/Radak Mel.I 11.26]*.
For three years, Bnei Yisrael were making visits to the Beit Hamikdash in Yerushalayim, thus strengthening the rule of Rechav'am *[Bible D.H.II 11.16,17]*. Yerav'am I made two golden calves, for Bnei Yisrael to worship, one in the north and one in the south. He then set up border guards, on the 23rd Sivan, to prevent them from going to the Beit Hamikdash, in order to retain their loyalty to him *[Bible Mel.I 11.28/ TBY.O.C. 580.1]*.

2969 -792

Shishak, king of Egypt, invaded Yerushalayim, and took treasures from the Beit Hamikdash and from the palace *[Bible Mel.I 14.25, 26/Tzem.Dav./Sed.Had.]*.

2981 -780

Rechav'am was succeeded by his son Aviyah, (Aviyam), who battled constantly with Yerav'am I, king of Yisrael *[Bible Mel.I 15.1,7, D.H.II 13.2, 14-19/ Tzem.Dav./Sed. Had.]*.

2983 -778

Assa succeeded his father Aviyah as king of Yehuda in 2983, but unlike his father and grandfather, he was a righteous person, similar to his ancestor David. Peace reigned between Yehuda and Yisrael for the first ten years of his rule (see 2993\-768) *[Bible Mel.I 15.8-11, 16, 32; Metz.Dav.16; D.H.II 14.5/Tzem.Dav./ Sed. Had.]*.

2985 -776

Ido, who had been a prophet since the time of Shlomo, criticized Yerav'am I. He was subsequently killed by a lion *[Bible Mel.I 13.1-4, 24/Rashi 13.1/ Sed.Had.]*.
Yerav'am I sent his wife to (secretly) consult Achiyah Hashiloni, about the sickness of his (rebellious) son Aviyah (who often went to the Beit Hamikdash, see 2964\-797). Achiyah Hashiloni prophesied to her that Yerav'am I's dynasty would not last long (see 2986\-775) *[Bible Mel.I 14.1-10/Tal.M.K.28b]*.
Yerav'am I was succeeded by his son Nadav as king of Yisrael in 2985 *[Bible Mel.I 14.20/Tzem. Dav./Sed.Had.]*.

2986 -775

Ba'asha ben Achiyah, from the tribe of Yissachar, assassinated Nadav and the whole family of Yerav'am I in 2986 (see 2985\-776), and proclaimed himself king of Yisrael *[Bible Mel.I 15.27-30/ Tzem.Dav./ Sed.Had.]*. He continued to maintain Yerav'am's golden calves for worship *[Bible Mel.I 15.34; 16.2]*.

2993 -768

Ba'asha king of Yisrael waged a battle against Assa king of Yehuda (see 2983\-778) *[Bible Mel.I 15.32/ Tzem.Dav./ Sed. Had.]*.

2998 -763

The largest battle recorded in the Bible took place when Zerach HaKushi invaded Eretz Yehuda with over one million troops, and was defeated by Assa *[Bible D.H.II 14.8/ Tzem. Dav./Sed.Had.]*.

3009 -752

Elah succeeded his father Ba'asha as king of Yisrael, in 3009 *[Bible Mel.I 16.6/Tzem.Dav./Sed.Had.]*.
Yehu ben Chanani prophesied to Elah — as he had to Ba'asha — that their dynasty would not last long because they followed in the ways of Yerav'am I *[Bible Mel.I 16.1,7]*.

3010 -751

Zimri was a (cruel) servant in the palace of Elah. He killed Elah the king of Yisrael and all his family in 3010 (see 3009\-752), and pronounced himself as king *[Bible Mel.I 16.9,15/Radak 16.9/ Tzem. Dav./ Sed.Had.]*.

When the people heard that Zimri had killed Elah, and made himself king, they countered by proclaiming Omri, a general, as king. Omri led an attack on the palace and the trapped Zimri — who had been king for seven days — set the palace alight, and perished in the flames. Nevertheless, part of Yisrael did not accept Omri, but followed Tivni (ben Ginat) for more than 4 years — until he was killed in 3014 — and they all then accepted Omri as king *[Bible Mel.I 16.16-24, Rashi 16.22, 23/ Mid.Yal.Mel.I 15/ Sed.Ol./ Tzem. Dav./ Sed.Had.]*.
Omri built up Shomron as the capital of the kingdom of Yisrael, in 3020 *[Bible Mel.I 16.24/ Tzem. Dav./ Sed.Had.]*.

3021 -740

Ach'av succeeded his father Omri as king of Yisrael, in 3021 *[Tzem.Dav./ Sed.Had.]*. He and his wife Izevel (Jezebel) turned further from the way of the Torah than had all the preceding kings *[Bible Mel.I 16.30; 21.25]*, and they were almost successful in their attempt to kill all the prophets *[Bible Mel.I 18.4]*.
Eliyahu had publicly refuted the priests of the Ba'al (on Mount Carmel) and killed them. Izevel then sought to kill Eliyahu despite the fact that he had just predicted the end of a three year drought *[Bible Mel.I 18.19-44; 19.2*.
Ovadya, a wealthy convert from Edom, became a prophet when he rescued 100 prophets from Ach'av by hiding them in caves and spending all his money to support them *[Bible Mel.I 18.4/ Tal. San.39b/ Mid. Rab.Sh. 31.4]*.

3024 -737

Assa (king of Yehuda) — whose legs were stricken with illness in 3022 — died in 3024, and he was succeeded by his son Yehoshaphat *[Bible Mel.I 15.23, D.H.II 16.12/ Tzem.Dav./Sed.Had.]*.
Yehoshaphat, who had great respect for Torah scholars, followed in his father's ways (see 2983\-778) *[Bible Mel.I 22.43]*.
In 3027, he sent messengers throughout Yehuda, (Ovadya and Michiyahu were among them), to teach his people *[Bible D.H.II 17.7-9/ Tal.Mak.24a/ Tzem.Dav./Sed.Had.]*.

3041 -720

When Eliyahu had prophesied to Ach'av (see 3021\-740) that his dynasty would be wiped out (because Izevel had Navot killed for his vineyard), Ach'av had shown remorse *[Bible Mel.I 21.29]*.
Michiyahu ben Yimla, the prophet (see 3024\-737), had assisted Ach'av in the war against Ben Haddad I, king of Aram, up until the point where Ach'av — in victory — treated Ben Haddad I like a brother. In the final battle, in 3041 — after a 3-year pause — Ach'av was killed as Michiyahu had predicted, and his son Achazyahu I succeeded him as king of Yisrael *[Bible Mel.I 20.13,22,25,32,42; 22.17,27; Rashi 20.13/ Tzem.Dav./Sed.Had.]*.

3043 -718

Eliyahu went up in a chariot of fire.

Achazyahu I was seriously injured when he fell from the attic balcony in 3043, two years after he succeeded his father as king of Yisrael.
Shortly before Eliyahu went up in a chariot of fire — leaving Elisha behind — he conveyed a prophecy to Achazyahu I that he would not recover *[Bible Mel.II 1; 2.11; Radak 1.1/Sed.Ol.17/Tzem.Dav./Sed.Had.]*.
Achazyahu I was succeeded (in 3043) by his brother Yehoram I, because he had no sons *[Bible Mel.II 1.17]*.

3047 -714

Yehoram II became king of Yehuda in 3047 two years before his father Yehoshaphat died *[Sed.Ol.17/ Rashi Mel.II 8.16/ Tzem.Dav./Sed.Had.]*. He was married to Athalya (the daughter of Ach'av, king of Yisrael) *[Bible Mel.II 8.18]*. Yehoram II originally conducted his affairs in the proper manner, but he later strayed severely, by following the ways of his father-in-law, Ach'av *[Bible Mel.II 8.27, D.H.II 21.6/Tal.Hor.11b]*.

3055 -706

Achazyahu II became king of Yehuda in 3055, when his father Yehoram II became very sick — as was prophesied in the letter sent to him by Eliyahu. Yehoram II died a year later, at the age of 40 *[Bible D.H.II 21.12-20/Rashi Mel.II 9.29/Tzem.Dav./Sed.Had.]*.
Elisha had prophesied to Yehu (son of Yehoshaphat, son of Nimshi) that he would become king. Yehu ben Nimshi (as he was called) rebelled against Yehoram I king of Yisrael (in 3055), and killed him, Izevel and all the remaining family of Ach'av (see 3056\-705). (The fulfillment of the prophecy of Eliyahu (see 3041\-720) had been

delayed for a generation, because Ach'av had shown remorse.) Yehu pronounced himself king, and he cunningly stamped out the Ba'al worship that Ach'av had introduced *[Bible Mel.I 21.29; II 9; 10/Tzem.Dav./Sed.Had.]*.

3056 -705

In the rebellion against Yehoram I king of Yisrael (see 3055\-706), Yehu also killed Achazyahu II king of Yehuda. Athalya (Achazyahu's mother, see 3047\-714), then killed almost all the rest of the royal family (of the House of David), and made herself queen in 3056. However, Yehosheva managed to save a baby nephew (the son of her brother Achazyahu II) from (its grandmother) Athalya. Yehosheva, who was the wife of Yehoyada the Kohen Gadol (see 3098\-663), hid this year-old boy (Yeho'ash I) in the Beit Hamikdash, where he remained for six years *[Bible Mel.II 9.27; 11.1-3/Sed.Had.]*.

3061 -700

After hiding the boy Yeho'ash I in the Beit Hamikdash for six years (see 3056\-705), Yehoyada (the Kohen Gadol) made him king of Yehuda in 3061, and in the process, Athalya was killed *[Bible Mel.II 11.4-16, D.H.II 23/Tzem.Dav./ Sed.Had.]*.

3083 -678

Yeho'achaz I succeeded his father Yehu, as king of Yisrael. Yona, who had been Elisha's messenger to anoint Yehu (see 3055\-706), prophesied that his dynasty would last for four generations *[Bible Mel.II 9.1, Rashi, 10.30, Rashi, 35]*.
The kingdom of Yisrael was dominated by Chaza'el the king of Aram and his son Ben Haddad II for most of the reign of Yeho'achaz I, until they were ousted later by Yeho'ash II his son (see 3098\-663) *[Bible Mel.II 13.3-5, Radak, Mel.II 13.17-25/ Tzem.Dav./ Sed.Had.]*.

3084 -677

Yeho'ash I renovated the Beit Hamikdash.

Approximately 155 years after Shlomo had begun building the Beit Hamikdash, Yeho'ash considered it necessary to strengthen and redecorate the structure *[Bible Mel.II 12.6,7/Sed.Ol.18/ Tzem.Dav./ Sed. Had.]*.

3098 -663

Yeho'ash II succeeded his father Yeho'achaz I as king of Yisrael in 3098 *[Bible Mel.II 13.9, 10/Tzem.Dav./ Sed.Had.]*. Elisha and his disciple, Yehoyada Kohen Gadol (see 3061\-700), both died in this year *[Bible Mel.II 13.14/Mid.Yal.Naso.q.Sed.Had./ Yuch.1/Sed.Had.]*.
Yeho'ash I had respected Yehoyada, and followed his advice (see 3061/-700). However, after Yehoyada's death, Yeho'ash I allowed himself to be idolized — because he had lived in the Beit Hamikdash for six years (see 3056\-705) — and he subsequently strayed from his previous ways *[Bible D.H.II 24.17, Radak/Mid.Rab.Sh.8.2]*.

3100 -661

Zecharyah ben Yehoyada had succeeded his father as Kohen Gadol (see 3098\-663), but he was killed on the orders of Yeho'ash I (king of Yehuda) on Yom Kippur, (which was also Shabbat). Yeho'ash I was killed in bed, by his servants, as a consequence of that incident *[Bible D.H.II 24.21,22,25/Mid.Rab. Eych.2.4]*.
Amatzya succeeded his father Yeho'ash I, although he had already ruled for one year during his fathers life. He overpowered Edom in 3112, and then instigated a battle with Yeho'ash II (king of Yisrael), and lost *[Bible Mel.II 14.1,7-13/ Sed.Ol.18/Tzem.Dav./Sed.Had.]*.

3115 -646

Yerav'am II became king of Yisrael in 3115, three years before his father Yeho'ash II died *[Rashi Mel.II 15.8/Tzem.Dav./ Sed. Had.]*, and he extended the borders of Eretz Yisrael, as had been prophesied by Yona (see 3083\-678) *[Bible Mel.II 14.25]*. He later attempted to banish Amos the prophet (see 3142\-619) because of his prophecy that his dynasty would not last *[Bible Amos 7.10-17, Rashi]*.
When he was sixteen years old Uziyahu (son of Amatzya) was taken as king of Yehuda after a rebellion against his father in 3115 (see 3130\-631). Uziyahu, who was also called Azaryah, continued to rule for the fifteen years that his father was still alive *[Bible Mel.II 14.19; 15.1, D.H.II 26.1/ Rashi Mel.II 15.8/ Tzem.Dav./Sed.Had.]*.

3130 -631

After the rebellion against him, Amatzya king of Yehuda (see 3115\-646) fled to exile, where he was killed fifteen years later (in 3130), during his son Uziyahu's rule *[Bible Mel.II 14.19/Rashi Mel.II 15.8]*. Uziyahu captured and rebuilt the city of Eilat, after the death of his father *[Bible Mel.II 14.22]*.

3142 -619

Yeshayahu (Isaiah) began his prophecies.

Amos had begun his prophecies in 3140 (see 3115\-646), and Hoshea had prophesied before him *[Rashi Hosh.1.2, Amos 1.1/Tal.B.B.14b]*.

When in 3142 Uziyahu attempted to perform the incense burning sacrifice in the Beit Hamikdash — a function reserved specifically for Kohanim — he was struck with leprosy and was seriously incapacitated *[Bible Mel.II 15.5, D.H.II 26.16-21/Sed.Ol. 19]*.

At that time — on that day — Yeshayahu made his first prophecy *[Targ.Yon.Yesh.6.1, Rashi 1.1/Mid.Tan.Tzav 13]*. Amotz, the father of Yeshayahu, was a brother of Amatzya (see 3100\-661) *[Tal.Meg.10b]*.

3153 -608

Zecharyahu succeeded his father Yerav'am II as king of Yisrael, but he only ruled for six months, see 3154/-607. *[Bible Mel.II 15.8]*.

3154 -607

Shalom ben Yavesh rebelled against Zecharyahu — and killed him publicly — in 3154, thus fulfilling the prophecy of Yona (see 3083\-678). Shalom declared himself king of Yisrael *[Bible Mel.II 15.10-13/Tzem.Dav./Sed.Had.]*.

Menachem ben Gadi rebelled against Shalom after he ruled for only one month, and forcefully established his own rule *[Bible Mel.II 15.14,16]*.

Phul, king of Ashur *(Assyria)*, invaded Eretz Yisrael, and Menachem paid a very large sum for him to withdraw his forces *[Bible Mel.II 15.19,20]*.

3164 -597

Pekachya succeeded his father Menachem as king of Yisrael *[Mel.II 15.23/Tzem.Dav./ Sed.Had.]*.

3166 -595

Pekach ben Remalyahu, the general, rebelled against Pekachya, and became king of Yisrael in 3166 *[Bible Mel.II 15.25/ Tzem.Dav./Sed.Had.]*.

3167 -594

Yotam succeeded his father Uziyahu as king of Yehuda in 3167 *[Bible Mel.II 15.32/Tzem.Dav./Sed.Had.]*.

Michah began his prophecies during the reign of Yotam; and at that time there were four major prophets — Hoshea, Yeshayahu, Amos and Michah (see 3142\-619) *[Bible Yesh.1.1, Hosh.1.1, Mich.1.1/Tal.Pes.87a]*.

3183 -578

At the end of Yotam's rule (see 3167\-594), the kingdom of Yehuda had protracted battles against Retzin, king of Aram, and against Pekach, king of Yisrael (see 3187\-574) *[Bible Mel.II 15.37,38, Rashi, Radak, Ralbag]*.

Achaz succeeded his father Yotam (in 3183), but did not follow in the ways of King David at all. He tampered with the sanctity of the Beit Hamikdash, and curtailed the study of Torah *[Bible Mel.II 16.2-18/ Tal.San.103b, Maharsha/ Tzem.Dav./ Sed.Had.]*.

3187 -574

First two of the ten tribes were exiled.

Achaz (king of Yehuda) had arranged — by way of a bribe — that Tiglath Pil'esser. king of Ashur *(Assyria)*, should help him in his protracted war against Aram, and against Pekach (king of Yisrael) *[Bible Mel.II 16.7,8]*.

It was at the end of the reign of Pekach (in 3187) that Tiglath Pil'esser invaded Eretz Yisrael, conquered territory, and expelled the tribes of Gad, Reuven, and half of Menasheh *(see 2503\-1258)* *[Bible Mel.II 15.29, Ralbag, D.H.I 5.26/Mid.Rab.Eycha Petichta 5/ Rashi Mel.II 17.1/Tzem.Dav. /Sed. Had.]*.

When the tribe of Hoshea ben Elah was expelled (the tribe of Reuven), he rebelled against Pekach, and became king of Yisrael *[Bible Mel.II 15.30/Sed.Had.]*. He was the last king of Yisrael, but in reality merely the local representative of the king of Ashur until he rebelled against him (see 3195\-566) *[Bible Mel.II 17.3,4, Ralbag 17.1]*. On the 15th Av he removed the border guards *(see 2964\-797)*, and thus became the only king of Yisrael to allow his people to go to the Beit Hamikdash *[Tal.Git.88a, Tan.30b-31a]*.

3195 -566

Another two of the ten tribes were exiled.

Hoshea ben Elah king of Yisrael, rebelled (in 3195) against Shalmanessar king of Ashur *(Assyria)*, who retaliated by expelling the tribes of Zevulun and Naftali from Eretz Yisrael *[Bible Mel.II 17.4-6/Mid.Rab.Eycha Petichta 5/Rashi Mel.II 17.1/ Tzem.Dav./Sed.Had.]*.

3199 -562

Chizkiyahu (Hezekiah) became king of Yehuda.

Chizkiyahu succeeded his father Achaz in 3199, and he subsequently was (one of) the most righteous of all the kings of Yehuda (some say more than King David). He took care to ensure that all the people were well educated in the laws of the Torah, and he refused to be dominated by the king of Ashur *(Assyria)*, as his father was (see 3187\-574). He also repelled the Plishtim from Eretz Yehuda *[Bible Mel.II 18.1, Rashi, 5, Radak, Ralbag 7,8/ Tal. San.94b/Tzem.Dav./Sed.Had.]*.

Chizkiyahu and his peers — who continued after him — recorded the books of Yeshayahu, Mishli *(Proverbs)*, Shir Hashirim *(Song of Songs)*, and Kohelet *(Ecclesiastes)* (see 2964\-797) *[Tal.B.B.15a, Rashi, Tos., Maharsha]*.

3205 -556

The last of the ten tribes were exiled.

Shalmanessar invaded Eretz Yisrael in 3202 (see 3187\-574, 3195\-566), and by 3205 had completely conquered it, and destroyed the capital, Shomron (see 3010\-751). He then expelled the remainder of the ten tribes *[Bible Mel.II 18.9-11; 17.6, Radak 17.24, Rashi 17.1/ Tzem.Dav./Sed.Had.]*.

The king of Ashur *(Assyria)* resettled peoples from other conquests around Shomron. The people of Kutha (see 1948\-1813) and Bavel *(Babylonia)* were among them. When these peoples — the Kuthim — were (later) attacked by lions, they saw it as an omen, and requested to be taught the religion of the land, which they did not then fully accept (although some say they subsequently did, and then rejected it again at a later stage) (see 4046\286) *[Bible Mel.II 17.25,33/Tal.San.85b, Rashi, Kid.75b, Min.42a, Rashi, Tos/Tos.Suk.8b]*.

3213 -548

Sancheriv invaded Eretz Yehuda, and retreated.

Sancheriv king of Ashur *(Assyria)*, was expanding his empire. He resettled all the peoples of his conquests (see 3205\-556). He invaded Eretz Yehuda, and approached Yerushalayim. Chizkiyahu was terminally ill at the time, but was informed by Yeshayahu that he would live for a further fifteen years *[Bible Mel.II 18.13, 19.35-37, 20.1-6; Yesh.37.38/ Sed.Ol.23/ Tal. San.96a, Ber.28a/Tzem.Dav./Sed.Had.]*.

When Yeshayahu insisted that Chizkiyahu marry and have children, Chizkiyahu married Yeshayahu's daughter *[Tal.Ber. 10a, Hag.Bach]*.

On the third day of his illness, Chizkiyahu recuperated, as Yeshayahu had prophesied. On that night (15th Nissan), when Bnei Yehuda were celebrating with their Pesach sacrifices, Sancheriv miraculously — and hastily — withdrew. On his return home, he was killed by his sons, while worshipping his idol (a board from Noah's ark) *[Bible Mel.II 19.35-37; 20.1-11, Yesh.37.38/ Sed.Ol.23/Tal.San. 96a/ Mid.Rab.Sh.18.5/ Tzem.Dav./ Sed.Had.]*.

Sancheriv left some Egyptian prisoners in Eretz Yehuda in his hasty withdrawal. They subsequently converted, and returned to Egypt *[Tal.Min.109b/Rashi Yesh.19.18]*.

3228 -533

When Chizkiyahu had befriended a delegation of well-wishers from Bavel *(Babylonia)*, Yeshayahu prophesied about the exile of his descendants in that country *[Bible Mel.II 20.12-18]*.

Menasheh (son of Chizkiyahu) became king.

Menasheh succeeded his father Chizkiyahu as king of Yehuda in 3228, and initially he was the worst of all the kings of Yehuda. He placed a statue in the Beit Hamikdash on the 17th Tammuz *[Bible Mel.II 21.2-7/Tal.San.103b, Tan 26b, Rashi, Yer.Tan.4.5(23b)/ TBY.O.C.549/ Tzem. Dav./ Sed.Had.]*. He killed Yeshayahu (his grandfather, see 3213\-548) *[Tal.Yev.49b]*, and was warned by the prophets Nachum and Chabakuk that his deeds would cause the destruction of Yehuda *[Bible Mel.II 21.10-14, Rashi/Mid.Yal.Chab.1]*.

3283 -478

Menasheh's reign was the longest of both Yehuda and Yisrael. He was captured by the armies of Ashur *(Assyria)* in 3250, and taken to Bavel *(Babylonia)* for a while, and there he changed his ways *[Bible D.H.II 33.11,12/Sed.Ol.24/Tal.San.103a/T.D.B.E. 19]*.

Amon succeeded his father Menasheh in 3283. He conducted his affairs in a very bad way, and was killed by his servants, who were subsequently killed by the people. The people then turned to

Yoshiyahu *(Josiah)* his son and proclaimed him king (see 3285\-476) *[Bible Mel.II 21.21-24]*.

3285 -476

Yoshiyahu *(Josiah)* the son of Amon was only eight years old when he was proclaimed king of Yehuda in 3285 (see 3283\-478). *(Bible Mel.II 22.1/ Tzem.Dav./ Sed.Had.]*. He began to follow in the ways of King David in earnest in 3293, and in 3297 he began cleansing Yehuda of idol worship, a program that he intensified after the prophecy of Chuldah (see 3303\-458) *[Bible D.H.II 34.3/Radak Mel.II 23.4, Ralbag 23.25/Tzem.Dav./Sed.Had.]*.

3298 -463

Yirmiyahu (Jeremiah) began his prophecies.

Yirmiyahu ben Chilkiyahu HaKohen (who, some say, was Chilkiyahu the Kohen Gadol, see 3303\-458), began his prophecies in 3298 *[Bible Yir.1.1, Radak/Tos.B.K.16b/Sed.Had.]*.

In 3302 Yirmiyahu returned some of the people of the ten tribes from their exile, to live under the rule of Yoshiyahu *[Tal.Erch.12b, 33a, Tos./Rashi Mel.II 23.22, San.110a/Sed.Had.]*.

Tzephanya, a descendent of Chizkiyahu, was also prophesying during the reign of Yoshiyahu *[Bible Tze.1.1]*.

3303 -458

Yoshiyahu renovated the Beit Hamikdash.

In 3303 Yoshiyahu began renovations of the Beit Hamikdash, (218 years after Yeho'ash I, see 3084\-677). Chilkiyahu, the Kohen Gadol, found a Sefer Torah which had been hidden during the period when Achaz would have probably destroyed it (see 3183\-578). Yoshiyahu consulted Chuldah, the prophetess (wife of Shalum ben Tikva), and she confirmed (see 3285\-476) that there was significance in the fact that the scroll was opened to the dire predictions of exile *[Bible Mel.II 22.4,5,13-15, D.H.II 34.8/ Rashi Mel.II 22.8/Tzem.Dav./Sed.Had.]*.

3316 -445

Yoshiyahu had been concerned about the numerous prophecies of destruction — of the Beit Hamikdash — and he consequently buried the Holy Ark (and other holy items), in an underground chamber built by Shlomo *[Bible D.H.II 35.3 Metz.Dav./Tal.Cri.5b, Yom.52b, Hor.12a/ Mmn.Hil. B.Hab.4.1]*.

N'cho, Pharaoh of Egypt, was passing his armies through Eretz Yehuda in 3316 on his way to war with Ashur *(Assyria)*. Yoshiyahu went out against him and was killed. The people of Yehuda anointed Yeho'achaz II (his younger son) as king. After he had served for three months, Pharaoh N'cho took him into captivity (where he eventually died) *[Bible Mel.II 23.29-34/Tzem.Dav./ Sed.Had]*. Then Pharaoh N'cho appointed Elyakim — an older son of Yoshiyahu — as the king, and renamed him Yehoyakim *[Bible Mel.II 23.34]*.

In 3317 — because of the prevailing uncertainties — Yehoyakim appointed his son Yehoyachin (who was also called Yechanya) to rule after him *[Bible D.H.II 36.9, Mel.II 24.8, Radak]*.

3319 -442

Yerushalayim conquered, Yehoyakim exiled.

In 3318, Nebuchadnetzar the king of Bavel *(Babylonia)* — who was a very short man — rebelled against the king of Ashur *(Assyria)* who dominated Bavel (see 3205\-556). In 3319 he invaded Eretz Yehuda and conquered Yerushalayim, plundered the Beit Hamikdash, and expelled Yehoyakim the king to Bavel *(Babylonia)*, together with Daniel — who was 15 — Chananyah Misha'el, and Azaryah, (among others). He returned Yehoyakim to rule — under his dominion — over Yehuda which Yehoyakim did for three years *[Bible Dan.1.1-6, Ibn Ezra 1.4/ Tal. Erch.12a/ Mid.Yal.Dan.4 (1062)/ T.D.B.E.Rab.31 (29?)/ Radak Mel.II 24.1/ Tzem.Dav./ Sed.Had.]*.

3321 -440

Yehoyakim burned the Megilla (Eycha) composed by Yirmiyahu.

Yirmiyahu persistently prophesied about an imminent calamity unless the people changed. In 3320 he documented such a prophecy in a Megilla called Eycha *(Lamentations)* and distributed it through Baruch ben Neriyah — his disciple — because he himself was imprisoned by Yehoyakim. The people proclaimed a fast because of the serious message it conveyed, but Yehoyakim heard it read, tore it, then threw it into the fire, on the 28th Kislev *[Bible Yir.36.5,9,10,22,23; 45.1, Rashi 36.5; 37.4/see IbnEz Eych.1.1/ TBY.O.C.580.1/ Tzem.Dav./Sed.Had.]*.

3327 -434

Yerushalayim conquered again, and Yehoyachin exiled.

Uriyahu the prophet fled to Egypt after prophesying about imminent disaster. Yehoyakim had him returned, and killed him *[Bible Yir.26.20-23]*.

Yehoyakim rebelled against Nebuchadnetzar in 3323, and four years later (in 3327) he was defeated on the battle field. He died while being led in prisoners' chains *[Bible Mel.II 24.1,2, Radak, D.H.II 36.6 Radak/ Mid.Yal.Mel.II 24/Ibn Ez.Dan.1.4/Tzem.Dav./ Sed.Had.]*.

Yehoyachin then succeeded his father Yehoyakim (see 3316\-445) as king of Yehuda. However he only ruled for three months (and ten days) before Nebuchadnetzar had Yerushalayim laid under siege for the second time, and Yehoyachin surrendered peacefully. Nebuchadnetzar plundered the Beit Hamikdash (again) and the palace, and he took the leaders of the people, including Yehoyachin, Yechezk'el (the prophet) and Mordechai *(who may yet have been a youth, see 3331\-430)*, to Bavel *(Babylonia)* *[Bible Mel.II 24.8-16, D.H.II 36.9,10, Yech.1.1,2, Est.2.6]*.

Nebuchadnetzar appointed Tzidkiyahu king of Yehuda (some say after turning him back from the exile), and made him ruler of his surrounding conquests *[Bible Mel.II 24.17, Yir.27.3, Rashi/Sed.Had.]*.

Tzidkiyahu (whose name was also Matanya, and Shalum, until Nebuchadnetzar changed it) was the third son of Yoshiyahu to be king, and was an uncle to Yehoyachin, whom he succeeded. He was the last king of the House of David *[Bible Mel.II 24.17, D.H.I 3.15, D.H.II 36.10, Rashi/Tal.Git.5b/Tzem.Dav./ Sed.Had.]*.

At this time, Nebuchadnetzar was training the intelligent young exiles in Bavel *(Babylonia)* (see 3319\-442) for (civic) leadership. Daniel and his friends were among them, who agreed to only eat certain vegetables and water *[Bible Dan.1.1-6,12]*.

3331 -430

Yirmiyahu persisted in prophesying calamity.

Yirmiyahu, who was released from prison by Tzidkiyahu, continuously prophesied about an imminent destruction *[Bible Yir.37.4, Rashi, 28.1]*. In Av 3331, he debated with Chananyah ben Azur, who had prophesied that Nebuchadnetzar and his armies would soon leave Eretz Yehuda. Yirmiyahu exclaimed that he too, wished it be so, but that unless the people changed, there would be disaster. He also prophesied that Chananyah would die that year, which he did *[Bible Yir.28/Mid.Yal.Yir.28]*.

3332 -429

Yechezk'el (Ezekiel) prophesied in exile.

Yechezk'el's first recorded prophecy — on the 5th Tammuz 3332 — did not pertain to Yerushalayim. However, on the 5th Elul 3333, he prophesied about its imminent destruction *[Bible Yech.1.1-3, Rashi; 8.1, Radak, 8.18; 9.4-10; 11.4-11; 12.8-11, 17-20]*.

On the 10th Av 3334, he was consulted by the elders who were struggling to find meaning in their religious life in exile *[Bible Yech.20.1, Rashi]*. Yirmiyahu also addressed that uncertainty, by sending a letter telling the people not to return, but to settle down to a normal life for seventy years *[Bible Yir.29.1-11/Mmn.Pir.Mish. Hakd.-Begin. (2nd)]*.

3336 -425

The final Babylonian siege of Yerushalayim.

Tzidkiyahu rebelled against Nebuchadnetzar, who then returned to Yerushalayim to recapture it in on 10th Tevet 3336 *[Bible Mel.II 24.20; 25.1/Yech.24.1,2/Tzem.Dav./Sed. Had.]*. Many people had taken refuge in (the fortified city) Yerushalayim before the siege, and food had become extremely scarce *[Bible Yir. 8.14; 52.6; Eycha 1.11/ T.D.B.E.30]*. The army of Yehuda, inside the walls of Yerushalayim, had inflicted heavy casualties on the Babylonian army outside *[Mid.Yal.Eycha 1009]*.

3337 -424

Yirmiyahu was accused of treason — because his prophecies were demoralizing — and Yir'iyah (the grandson of Chananyah, see 3331\-430) falsely testified that he had seen him conspiring with the enemy. Some ministers had Yirmiyahu lowered into a dungeon, but Tzidkiyahu saved him, and locked him in a courtyard prison. He continued to prophesy, about exile — and future return — about the destruction of Yerushalayim, and about how the Egyptians —who were on their way to assist — would soon withdraw *[Bible Yir. 32.1-2; 33.1-7; 37.7,13; 38.1-6,10,13,17-18/Mid.Yal.Yir.28]*.

Yirmiyahu had cursed the day he was born (which was the 9th Av), because he despised being a prophet witness of doom for the land and the people that he loved *[Bible Yir.11.14; 15.10; 20.14-18/ Mid.Yal.Yir.36/ Sed.Had.3298]*.

3338 -423

The First Beit Hamikdash was destroyed.

The attack on Yerushalayim was led by Nebuzradan, one of Nebuchadnetzar's ministers *[Bible Mel.II 25.8,9]*, and on the 9th Tammuz the walls of Yerushalayim were penetrated *[Bible Yir.52.6-7/ Tzem.Dav./ Sed.Had.]*. On the 17th Tammuz sacrifices ceased in the Beit Hamikdash *[Tal.Erch.11b]*.

Tzidkiyahu attempted to escape via an eighteen-mile-long tunnel, but was captured by some enemy troops, who, while chasing a deer, saw him coming out at Yericho. He was taken to Nebuchadnetzar, who was encamped in Rivlah *(Antioch) [Bible Mel.II 25.3-7, Rashi 25.4/ Tal.Eruv.61b/ Mid.Rab.Bam.2.9, Yal.Mel.251.25 / Rashi Yech.11.10]*.

On Friday the 7th Av, the enemy entered the Beit Hamikdash, where they feasted and vandalized until late in the 9th, when they set the structure afire. The fires burned for 24 hours *[Bible Mel.II 25.8, Yir.52.13/ Tal.Tan.29a]*.

The conquering armies confiscated the archives of Yehuda, including the writings of Shlomo, and took them for the scholars of Babylonia *[Kuz.1.63; 2.66, Otz.Nechm./ Mmn.Gd.Ppl.1.71/ Tor.HaOl.3.7]*.

In Eretz Yehuda there remained only a small number of YEHUDIM *(Jews)* — as they were now called, instead of IVRIM *(Hebrews)* (see 3390\-371) *[Rashi Est.2.5/ see Bible Mel.II 26, 28; Yir.43.9, 52.28,30; Dan.3.12/ Onk.Sh.2.6 etc.]*. Many had died of hunger and disease during the siege, vast numbers were killed by enemy troops, and many were taken to exile in Bavel *(Babylonia)*. *[Bible Mel.II 25.11-13, Yir.52. 15,16,30, Yech.5.2,12 / Tal.Git. 57b, 58a, San.96b/ Sed. Had.5380-3]*. Others fled to what was later known as France, Germany and Spain *[Ovad.1.20, Rashi, IbnEz.]*.

[3338\-423 is continued in chapter 7.] 

RIVERS OF BABYLON, CONVULSIONS IN YEHUDA (JUDEA)

Section III

[Turkey]
Ninveh
[Kurdish Mountains]
Tigris
[Syria]
[Iran]
(Persia)
Euphrates
Pumpedita
Baghdad
Nehardea
Ctesiphon
Jordan
Machoza
Babylon
Sura
Basra
Bavel
(Babylonia)
Iraq
Bavel
(Babylonia)
[Iraq]
[Kuwait]
Persian Gulf
[Saudi Arabia]
© Codex Judaica 2005

Chapter 7

Exile in Babylon

Section III

Chapter 7

Exile in Babylon

Jewish Year		Secular Year
3339	Gedalyah ben Achikam was killed.	-423
3340	Daniel interpreted Nebuchadnetzar's dream.	-421
3352	Yechezk'el prophecized about the future Beit Hamikdash.	-410
3389	**Daniel read the writing on the wall.**	**-372**
3389	Daniel was thrown into the lion's den.	-372
3390	Zerubavel led the return to Eretz Yisrael.	-371
3391	Building of Second Beit Hamikdash commenced, then halted.	-370
3395	Achashverosh II made his great banquet.	-366
3399	Esther was taken to the palace.	-362
3404	Esther took action against Haman's decree.	-357
3406	MORDECHAI PROCLAIMED THE CELEBRATION OF PURIM.	**-355**
3408	Building of the Second Beit Hamikdash was resumed.	-353
3412	THE SECOND BEIT HAMIKDASH WAS COMPLETED.	**-349**

Section III
RIVERS OF BABYLON, CONVULSIONS IN YEHUDA (JUDEA)

Chapter 7

Exile in Babylon

The seventh Chapter (Tekufa) in Jewish history begins with the destruction of the first Beit Hamikdash, and the forced exile to Bavel *(Babylonia)*. The people were called Jews, at this stage, (rather than Children of Israel).

The chapter ends when some Jews returned to live in Eretz Yisrael and the Second Beit Hamikdash was erected.

[3338\-423 is continued from chapter 6.]

3338 -423

Nebuchadnetzar issued a command (to his people) to take care of Yirmiyahu. He was released from the courtyard jailhouse (see 3337\-424), but insisted on chaining himself to the people being led into exile. However, he then decided to remain in Eretz Yisrael rather than live a privileged life in Bavel *(Babylonia)*, as he had been promised *[Bible Yir.39.11-14; 40.1,4; Rashi/ Mid.Yal. Teh.137/Rashi Meg.13a]*. Gedalyah ben Achikam, who was appointed ruler, instructed the people who were left in Eretz Yisrael to live peacefully with the new circumstances *[Bible Mel.II 25.22,24]*.

3339 -423

Gedalyah ben Achikam was killed.

Yishmael ben Netanya — a descendant of King David, whose mother was a descendant of a non-Jewish royal family — was incited by Ba'aliss the king of Amon, that he should be ruling, not Gedalyah *[Bible Yir.40.14, Metz.Dav., MetzTz/ Tal.Meg.15a, Yer.Hor.3.8 / Radak Yir.41.1]*. Yochanan ben Kareyach then warned Gedalyah of a plot. Gedalyah, because of his honesty, did not believe he was being deceived by Yishmael, but while they sat together at dinner on the 2nd Tishrei, Yishmael killed him *[Bible Yir.40.14; 41.1-2, Radak/ TBY.O.C.549]*.
Subsequently Yishmael killed Gedalyah's local supporters as well as the Babylonian troops who were in the vicinity. He then began leading the remaining people to Amon. When Yochanan, who was a leader of some stray troops, heard what Yishmael had done, he pursued Yishmael, who escaped with a handful of people. Yochanan, afraid that the Babylonians would seek retaliation, led the people — including Yirmiyahu — to Egypt. This was against the advice of Yirmiyahu (whom he had initially consulted) *[Bible Yir. 41; 42; 43]*. According to some, Plato had discussions with Yirmiyahu in Egypt *[Tor.HaOl.1.1 q. Sed.Had.3300]*.
All the children of Tzidkiyahu were killed in his presence in the north at Rivlah *(Antioch)* (see 3338\-423) — then he was blinded, on the 7th Cheshvan, and led in chains into exile *[Bible Mel.II 25.7/TBY. O.C.580.1]*.
Serayah — the KOHEN GADOL — a descendent of Pinchas (ben Elazar), was also one of those killed at Rivlah *[Bible Mel.II 25.18-21, Radak, Ralbag; Ez.7.1-5, Metz.Dav.7.1]*.

3339 -422

On the 5th Tevet a messenger came, to inform Yechezk'el, and the other Jews (YEHUDIM) who were already in Bavel *(Babylonia)* (see 3319\-442, 3327\-434) that Yerushalayim was conquered (and the Beit Hamikdash had been destroyed) *[Bible Yech.33.21-22, Metz.Dav.]*.
The Jews being led to exile after the destruction were not led directly to Bavel, but were diverted in different directions. Thus, despite their continuous march, they arrived in Bavel much later *[Mid.Rab.Br.82.10, Eycha 2.4, Yal. Teh.137/ Rashi Tze.2.8]*. Many then died when they drank the water of the Euphrates *[Mid.Yal. Teh.137]*.
On the 1st Adar Yechezk'el prophesied about the fall of Egypt *[Bible Yech.32.1, Radak]*.

3340 -421

Daniel interpreted Nebuchadnetzar's dream.

Nebuchadnetzar asked Daniel to remind him of the dream he had just had, as well as to interpret it; and he subsequently wanted to idolize him, for having been successful in both. However, he rewarded him with a powerful position instead *[Bible Dan.2.1-5, 46,48, Rashi Dan.2.1, 46/ Sed.Ol.25/Mid.Yal. Dan. 1060.2]*.
On the 10th Tishrei (Yom Kippur), Chananyah, Misha'el, and Azaryah, who were given positions of power at Daniel's request, refused to bow down to Nebuchadnetzar's new idol, but were miraculously saved from the fire into which they were thrown. On that day, also in Bavel *(Babylonia)* Yechezk'el prophesied about the dry bones *[Bible Dan. 2.49, 3.12-27, Yech.37 / Tal.San.92b / Mid. Yal. Sh.Hsh.7.9]*.

3342 -419

Tzur *(Tyre)* was conquered by Nebuchadnetzar, and those Jews who had taken refuge in Tzur — and also in Amon and Mo'av — were now also taken to Bavel *(Babylonia)* *[Bible Yir.52.30, Rashi]*.
Normal life continued in exile (see 3332/ -429), and eventually some Jews became very wealthy and influential. They settled in many cities, including Hutzal and Neharde'a — where they built notable synagogues — and also in Tel Aviv. They also excelled in the study of Torah (in Aramaic) *[Bible Yech.3.15/ Tal.B.K. 80a, Meg.29a, Git.6a/ Rashi B.K.80a/ Tos.B.K.80a, Git.6a, Yev. 115a/T.D.B.E.Rab.5, 23/ Igg.R.Sher.Gaon/ Mmn.Hil.Nizk. Mam. 5.8]*. As they integrated among other peoples, the use of Hebrew as a language began to decline *[Mmn.Hil.Tfi.1.4]*.

3346 -415

Egypt was conquered by Nebuchadnetzar, and Yirmiyahu and Baruch ben Neriyah were taken to Bavel *(Babylonia)* with the few survivors of those who had gone to Egypt in 3339 *[Bible Yir.44.28, Radak; 44.30 Metz.Dav/Sed.Ol.26]*. The whole region was totally desolate, having been conquered by Nebuchadnetzar, who sacked and looted, but did not seriously concern himself with dominion (over conquests) *[Bible Chab.1.9, Metz.Dav.]*. None of the populace surrounding Eretz Yisrael and Yehuda were successful in settling the country *[Ramban Vay.26.32]*.

3352 -410

Yechezk'el prophesied about the future Beit Hamikdash.

This prophecy occurred on the 10th Tishrei (Yom Kippur) (see 3340\-421) *[Bible Yech.40.1; 43.10-11, Rashi 43.11, Radak 43.10/Mmn.Hil.Mel.4.8, Radvaz, Hil.Mas.Hakrbn.2.14, Lech.Mish.]*.
Yirmiyahu wrote the books of Melachim I & II *(Kings I & II)* and Yirmiyahu — also Megillat Eycha *(Lamentations)* (see 3321\-440) — before he died *[Tal.B.B.15a]*.
Nebuchadnetzar had experienced another dream, which Daniel interpreted to mean that Nebuchadnetzar would be struck with insanity for seven years, and live with animals in the wilderness. In his fear of this, he had followed Daniel's advice and distributed provisions for the needy Jews in Bavel *(Babylonia)* for a period of 12 months *[Bible Dan.4/ Tal.Sot.20b-21a, Rashi]*. The seven years would have been at around this time.

3364 -397

Ehvil M'rudach was not eager to succeed (his father) Nebuchadnetzar's rule upon his death on the 25th Adar, because previously he had succeeded him, when Nebuchadnetzar had disappeared for seven years into the wilderness (see 3352\-410), and when he had suddenly reappeared, he punished his son for his relatively benevolent rule. This time he waited two days to confirm that he had truly died *[Bible Mel.II 25.27, Rashi, Radak, Ralbag, Metz.Dav.; Yir.52.31, Dan.4.30, Metz. Dav./ Mid.Rab.Vay.18.2, Yal.Chab.1. 562, Yal.Dan.2. 1059]*.
Ehvil M'rudach released Yechanya (Yehoyachin) and his uncle (the blind) Tzidkiyahu from prison, on the 27th Adar, but Tzidkiyahu — the last ruler of the House of David — died on the same day *[Bible Mel.II 25.27/Tal.M.K.28b/Mid.Yal. Yir.34, Dan.2.1059]*. Yechanya was treated with respect for the rest of his life *[Bible Mel.II 25.30, Yir.52.31]*.

3386 -375

Daniel's first prophetic dream predicted the fall of Bavel *(Babylonia)* and the rise of other nations to central power *[Bible Dan.7, ibn Ezra 7.1]*.
Ehvil M'rudach died in this year, and Belshatzar, his son, became king *[Sed.Ol.29]*. His style of rule was similar to his grandfather, Nebuchadnetzar (see 3364\-397) *[Tal.Meg.11a/ Mid.Yal.Dan.4]*.

3389 -372

Daniel read the writing on the wall.

Daniel had again dreamed (see 3386\-375) of the future power centers of the world (and a mystical number of 2,300 was given to him). He did not disclose his dreams clearly — as a prophet would disclose prophecies — and although he was shaken and ill for a number of days, he nevertheless continued his palace duties without interruption *[Bible Dan.8.14, 20-24, 27, Rashi / Metz.Dav. 8.27]*.
Bavel *(Babylonia)* had been invaded by Darius I *(Daryavesh I, son of Achashverosh I, king of Media)* in alliance with his son-in-law Cyrus *(Coresh, king of Persia)*, but their initial attack had been repelled *[Rashi Dan.5.1; 9.1]*.
Belshatzar made a banquet the evening after repelling the invasion, and in his drunken euphoria he brought out the vessels of the Beit Hamikdash — captured by Nebuchadnetzar — and they guzzled in them. A hand appeared and wrote a cryptic message on the wall of the palace hall, which no one — not even the Jews — could read. It was in Aramaic, in a calligraphic style (ASHURIT) only used for very holy writings, and had not been seen or used since Yoshiyahu had buried the ark (and Moshe's Torah scroll) (see 3316\-445). The message, as decoded by Daniel — who read vertical lines instead of horizontal — predicted the imminent fall of Bavel *[Bible Dan.5., Rashi, Metz.Dav/Rashi San.22a]*. On that night, the Mediens (under Darius I), and the Persians (under Cyrus), returned for battle, and in the ensuing confusion, Belshatzar was killed by his own troops *[Bible Dan.5.30/Mid.Rab.Sh.Hsh.3.4.2]*. Darius I then became king of the empire, and Babylonia ceased to be the center of power *[Bible Dan.6.1]*.

Daniel was thrown into the lion's den.

Daniel was one of the three Viceroys appointed by Darius I to oversee the kingdom, and he excelled in his statesmanship, and became the most prominent of them. This led to jealousy and intrigue, in which Darius I was maneuvered into proclaiming that for thirty days no one was permitted to address any formal requests, for anything at all, except to the king. Daniel (predictably) continued his daily prayers — which was a breech of the decree — and was consequently sent to a lions' den (on the 15th Nissan), from which he miraculously emerged untouched, to the relief of Darius I *[Bible Dan.6]*.

3390 -371

Zerubavel led the return to Eretz Yisrael.

Darius I was killed in battle, after ruling for one year *[Rashi Dan.6.29]*. Cyrus — his son-in-law — became king, and the power of the empire (see 3389\-372) moved to Persia. Daniel appointed Zerubavel to succeed him in his position — as well as appointing others to important positions— and then withdrew from public life *[Ibn.Ez.Est.2.9/ Metz.Dav.Dan.1.21 6.29]*.

Cyrus immediately encouraged the Jews of Bavel *(Babylonia)* to return to Eretz Yisrael and to rebuild the Beit Hamikdash *[Bible D.H.II 36.22,23, Ez.1.1-4]*. Over 40,000 people returned with Zerubavel — who was of the royal family — including Yehoshua (the Kohen, a nephew of Ezra), Nechemyah, and Mordechai, but the majority remained behind (see 3413\-348) *[Bible Ez.2.64, 65/ Mid.Tan.Sh.Tetz.13/ Rashi D.H.I 5.41 / Ibn Ez.Cha.1.1/ Tal. Kid.69b, Rashi/ Ran. Meg.1b]*.

More than a quarter of those who returned to Eretz Yisrael with Zerubavel were from tribes other than Yehuda and Binyamin *[Sed.Ol./Rashi Ez.2.64/ Metz.Dav.Nech.11.4]*.

3391 -370

Building of Second Beit Hamikdash commenced, then halted.

Yehoshua (the Kohen) and Zerubavel (the leader) began building the altar, when the people gathered in (the desolate) Yerushalayim after they had arrived *[Bible Ez.3.1-3/Ibn Ez.Cha.1.1/ Rashi Kid.69b]*. Although the foundation stones of the Second Beit Hamikdash were not yet laid, they began the daily sacrifice services on Rosh Hashana, 3391 *[Bible Ez. 3.1-6/Tal.Zev.62a]*. Zerubavel and Yehoshua — now the KOHEN GADOL — organized the construction of the Beit Hamikdash, which commenced in Iyar. They also organized a choir of Levi'im *(Levites)* to sing — as was the practice, during services in the Beit Hamikdash — while the building progressed *[Bible Ez.3.8,10]*.

The local residents, who were Kuthim *(Samaritans)* (see 3205\-556), asked to help, but were not allowed. They subsequently disrupted the rebuilding, and tried to persuade Cyrus to withdraw his authorization to build. The construction ground to a halt, and the Kuthim actively sought to have the ban continued (see 3395\-366) *[Bible Ez.4; Rashi 4.1,7; Metz.Dav.4.1/Rashi Meg.16a]*.

3392 -369

Daniel, who was still a Viceroy of the empire, was on the bank of the river Chidekel with the prophets Chagay, Zecharyah and Malachi (Ezra), when he was overcome — on the 24th Nissan — by another mystical vision (which they did not see) *[Bible Dan.6.29; 10; 11; 12/Tal.Meg.15a]*. In this vision he was given two mystical numbers (1,290 and 1,335) *[Bible Dan.12.11,12]*. Chagay and Zecharyah went to Eretz Yisrael (see 3408\-353, 3412\-349). Malachi (Ezra) went later (see 3413\-348).

3395 -366

Achashverosh II made his great banquet.

Achashverosh II — who was not of royal descent — became king of the empire in 3392, after the death of Cyrus. He maintained and confirmed the moratorium on building the Beit Hamikdash, after being contacted by the Kuthim (see 3391\-370) *[Bible Ez.4.6/Tal.Meg.11a, Rashi 16a!, 11a/Sed.Ol./Rashi Est.9.10]*. In the third year of his reign he made an elaborate banquet, at which he had his wife Vashti — the daughter of Belshatzar — killed for not obeying his humiliating orders *[Bible Est.1/ Tal.Meg.11b/Mid.Yal.Est.1.1049/ Sed.Ol.24,28/ Sed.Had.]*.

3399 -362

Esther was taken to the palace.

Esther (Hadassa), who was 40 when taken to the palace in Tevet (some say she was older yet), realized that there must be some special purpose to her life, once she was selected *[Bible Est.2.7,16/Mid.Rab.Est.6.6, Br.39.13/ Sed.Had.]*.

Mordechai — a prophet — had come to Bavel *(Babylonia)* three times: the first time with Yehoyachin (see 3327\-434); the second, after the destruction of the 1st Beit Hamikdash; and the third time, probably with Nechemyah (see 3426\-335) after work on the Second Beit Hamikdash was halted in 3391

[Bible Est.2.5,6, Ez.2.2/ Tal.Meg.13a, 15a, Rashi 13a/ Mid.Yal.Est.1053].

3404 -357

Esther took action against Haman's decree.

The decree to exterminate the Jews was issued by the king, on the 13th Nissan, at the instigation of Haman — the prime minister — and Mordechai communicated the contents of the decree to Esther, through Daniel (Hatach), who — although retired — still had access to the palace *[Bible Est.3.8; 4.5-10/ Tal. Meg.15a]*. At Esther's request, the Jews of Shushan fasted on the 13th, 14th and 15th Nissan (even though the 15th was Pesach) *[Bible Est.4.15-17/ Tal.Meg.15a/ Mid.Rab.Est.8.7, Yal.4, Pir.Dr.El.53]*.
On the last day of the fast — 15th Nissan (Pesach) — Esther approached Achashverosh II in his chambers, invited him and Haman to dinner that evening. She then invited them again for the next evening. At this second dinner, she finally revealed that she was Jewish, and was clandestinely keeping to her religion. She pleaded the case for her people, with Achashverosh II, Haman was disgraced and consequently hanged, and Esther then attempted to have the decree withdrawn (see 3405\-356) *[Bible Est.2.20; 5.1-8; 7.1-10/ Tal.Meg.13a/ Mid.Yal.1053]*.

3405 -356

Achashverosh II was unwilling to send out proclamations withdrawing Haman's decree (some say he was restricted by law from doing so), but he permitted Mordechai and Esther to send out supplementary proclamations, which they did on the 23rd Sivan 3404 *[Bible Est.8.8,9 / Rashi/ IbnEz]*. These new proclamations, in the name of the king, authorized the Jews to fight anyone who attempted to implement the previous decree *[Bible Est.8.10-13]*.
Consequently, on the 13th (and 14th) of Adar 3405, the Jews had to fight those sought to do them harm, although many non-Jews were impressed with their stand and converted to Judaism. On the 14th — and 15th — the Jews rejoiced in their relief (see 3406\-355) *[Bible Est.8.17; 9.1-5,17,18]*.

3406 -355

Mordechai proclaimed the celebration of Purim.

After the 15th Adar 3405, Mordechai wrote and distributed an account of events in the Book of Esther, in which he also declared the celebration of Purim. In 3406 — the same year that Achashverosh II died — Esther and Mordechai sent out reminders about the forthcoming celebration of Purim *[Bible Est.9.20-23,29, Rashi]*. The ANSHEI KNESSET HAGDOLA (see 3426\-335, 3448\-313) accepted Mordechai's proclamations *[Tal.B.B.15a]*, and he became a statesman in the palace, which eventually diminished his influence in theseJewish scholarly circles *[Tal.Meg.16b/Rashi Est.10.3]*.

3408 -353

Building of the Second Beit Hamikdash was resumed.

The prophets Chagay and Zecharyah prophesied, and conveyed the message of the prophecy to Zerubavel and Yehoshua, (on the 1st Elul), that they should not to be concerned with previous obstructions to rebuilding the Beit Hamikdash. They then also involved themselves in the independent resumption of construction. On the 24th Elul preparations had begun, and on the 24th Kislev building resumed. Later in 3408, Darius II (Daryavesh II, the son of Esther and Achashverosh II, who succeeded his father in 3406) formally allowed the building of the Second Beit Hamikdash to continue — this was seventy years after the destruction of the first *[Bible Cha.1.1,2,15; 2.18, Rashi; Ez.5, Rashi 1-2; Ez.6/ Mid.Rab.Est. 8.3/ Sed.Had.]*.

3412 -349

The Second Beit Hamikdash was completed.

On the 4th Kislev 3410, Zecharyah had prophesied — in Eretz Yisrael — that there was no longer any need to mourn the destruction of the First Beit Hamikdash (even in Bavel) *[Bible Zech.7.1-7; 8.19, Rashi 7.2, Radak 7.5]*.
The Second Beit Hamikdash was completed on the 3rd Adar 3412 *[Bible Ez.6.15]* and stood for 420 years (from 3408-9) until destroyed by the Romans (see 3829/69) *[Tal.Erch.12:]*. *[Secular history documents a different chronology for Persian kings and accordingly requires a much greater span of time for its standing, see Preface.]*
The king of Persia insisted that an engraving of the city of Shushan be placed in the Beit Hamikdash, as a clear indication of who had authorized the structure to be erected. The picture was placed on the eastern gate, which was consequently called Sha'ar Shushan *[Tal.Min. 98a, Rashi, Mido.1.3, Mmn.Pir.Mish]*.

Chapter 8

The Second Beit Hamikdash

Section III

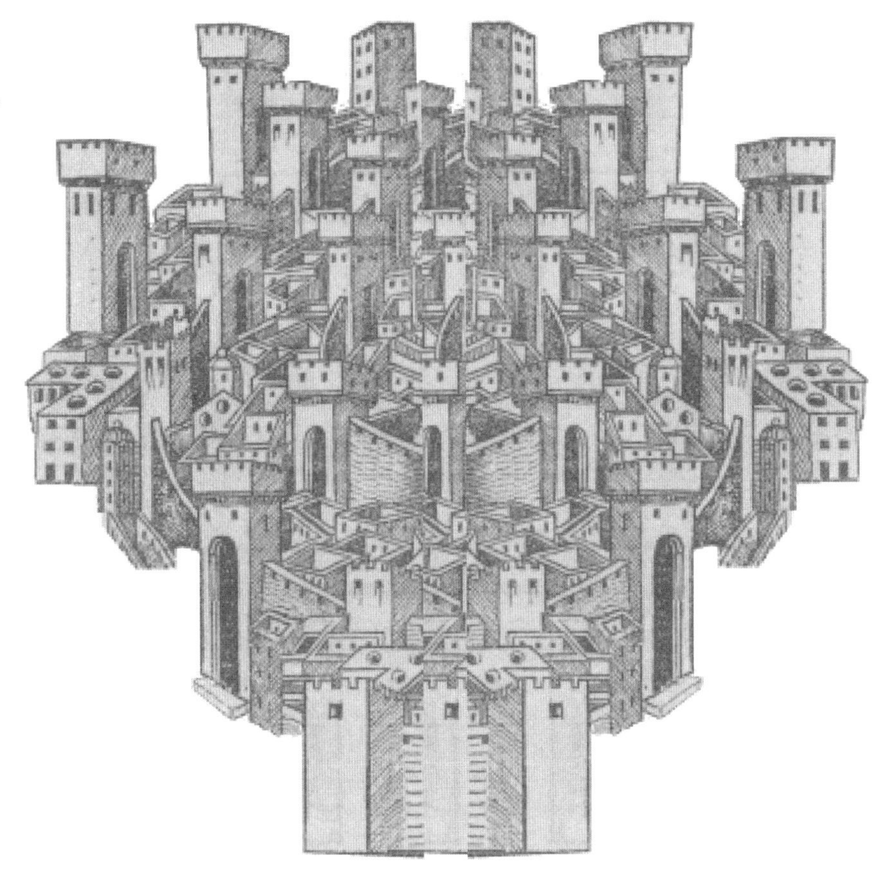

Section III

RIVERS OF BABYLON
CONVULSIONS IN YEHUDA (JUDEA)

Chapter 8

The Second Beit Hamikdash

The eighth Chapter (Tekufa) in Jewish history covers the convulsive life of Jews in Eretz Yisrael — which was reduced in size to Eretz Yehuda (Judea) — under almost continuous pressure from within and without.

This Chapter has four distinct eras.
(1) At the outset the dominating force in Eretz Yehuda (Judea) was the new Beit Hamikdash and the remaining elders of the Great Council — Anshei Knesset HaGedola.
(2) After the conquests of Alexander the Great, Greek culture rose to the fore.
(3) The rebellion of the Chashmona'im led to a period of Jewish monarchy.
(4) Once Rome spread its influence into the land, they imposed their own rulers (not necessarily Jewish) on the land of Judea.

This chapter ends with the destruction of the second Beit Hamikdash, when the Jewish people suffered a severe blow to their national standing.

Chapter 8
The Second Beit Hamikdash

Jewish Year		Secular Year
	Chapter 8a	
	Anshei Knesset HaGedola — The Great Council of Sages	
3412	THE SECOND BEIT HAMIKDASH WAS COMPLETED.	**-349**
3413	Ezra led the second return to Eretz Yisrael.	**-348**
3426	Nechemyah returned to rebuild walls of Yerushalayim.	**-335**
3448	EZRA DIED.	**-313**
3448	Shimon HaTzadik met Alexander the Great.	**-313**
3449	The Minyan Shtarot began.	**-313**
	Chapter 8b — Greek Cultural Domination.	
3488	Shimon HaTzadik died.	-273
3515	72 Elders translated the Torah into Greek (Septuagint).	**-246**
3621	The revolt of Mattityahu the Chashmona'i.	**-140**
	Chapter 8c — Kingdom of Yehuda (Judea).	
	Dynasty of the Chashmona'im.	
3622	Yehuda (HaMaccabi) ruled.	**-139**
3622	The Second Beit Hamikdash was re-dedicated.	**-139**
3623	CHANUKA WAS DECLARED A FESTIVAL.	**-138**
3628	Yehuda (HaMaccabi) was killed in battle.	**-133**
3628	Yonatan (son of Mattityahu) ruled.	**-133**
3634	Shimon (son of Mattityahu) ruled.	**-127**
3642	Yochanan Hyrkanos (son of Shimon) ruled.	**-119**

Jewish Year		Secular Year
3668	Yehuda Aristoblus (son of Yochanan Hyrkanos) ruled.	-93
3670	Alexander Yannai (son of Yochanan Hyrkanos) ruled.	-91
3688	Shalomit (Queen Salome, wife of Alexander Yannai) ruled.	-73
3696	Aristoblus II (son of Alexander Yannai) ruled.	-65
3700	**The Romans gained control of Yehuda (Judea).**	**-61**
3700	Hyrkanos II (son of Alexander Yannai) ruled.	**-61**
3721	Antigonus (son of Aristoblus II) ruled.	**-40**

Chapter 8d — Roman Client Kings & Rulers.

The Herodian Dynasty.

3725	Herod I ruled, killing all the Chashmona'im.	**-36**
3728	Hillel became leader of the Torah scholars.	**-33**
3742	Herod I began rebuilding the Second Beit Hamikdash.	**-19**
3750	Renovation of the Second Beit Hamikdash was completed.	-11
3761	Archelaus (son of Herod I) ruled.	1
3768	HILLEL DIED.	**8**
3770	Archelaus was deposed by the Roman Emperor.	10
3781	Agrippa I (grandson of Herod I) ruled.	21
3788	The Sanhedrin moved from the Second Beit Hamikdash.	**28**
3804	Agrippa II (son of Agrippa I) ruled.	44
3810	Raban Gamliel I (son of Shimon, son of Hillel) died.	**50**
3826	Vespasian arrived in Yehuda to reassert Roman authority.	**66**
3829	THE SECOND BEIT HAMIKDASH WAS DESTROYED.	**69**

Chapter 8a
Anshei Knesset HaGedola — The Great Council of Sages

3413 -348

Ezra led the second return to Eretz Yisrael.

When the Second Beit Hamikdash was completed, Baruch ben Neriyah was too old and weak to make the journey to Eretz Yisrael. His disciple Ezra — the son of Serayah (see 3339\-423) — did not leave Bavel *(Babylonia)* until the next year, after his death *[Bible Ez.7.1-7/Tal.Meg.16b, R.H.3b/ Mmn.Hakd. L'Yad]*.

Ezra was the head of the Sanhedrin, known as ANSHEI KNESSET HAGDOLA (see 3426\-335, 3406\-355), and this court went to Eretz Yisrael with him *[Rashi B.B.8a, 15a/Mmn.Hakd.L'Yad]*.

Ezra emphasized clarification of family lineage (in Bavel and in Eretz Yisrael), and he arrived in Yerushalayim on the 1st Av. He came to Eretz Yisrael with only a small group of Jews, compared to the numbers that came in the first return with Zerubavel. The majority of Jews — including great Torah scholars — remained in Bavel (see 3390\-371), primarily because of the harsh conditions prevailing in Eretz Yisrael *[Bible Ez.7.9, 8/Tal.Yom.9b, Suk.20a, Rashi/RaN.Meg.1b/SMaG Hakd.]*.

Ezra officially gave the months Babylonian names (Nissan, Iyar, etc., instead of 1st month, 2nd, etc.), as a form of commemoration of the exile that had been (see 2447\-1314) *[Tal.Kid.69a-b, Rashi 69b, Yev.86b, Yer.R.H.1.2/ Tos.R.H.7a/Ramban Sh.12.2]*.

3414 -347

After praying and fasting for a period of time — over the prevailing laxity in religious observance — Ezra addressed a three-day assembly of all the Jews on the 20th Kislev, and they accepted his proclamation to be firmer in their adherence to their religious practices. They set up courts, which sat on the 1st Tevet, to investigate and assess the intermarriage problem. On the 1st Nissan they reported that (only) 17 Kohanim, and 96 others, had taken non Jewish wives *[Bible Ez.10, 9]*.

Ezra made the second Para Aduma *(Red Heifer)* (see 2449\-1312) *[Tal.Par.3.5]*.

The Jews of Eretz Yisrael still referred to themselves as Bnei HaGola *(exiles)* living in Eretz Yisrael *[Bible Ez.4.1, 6..19, 8.35, 10.7,16]*.

3426 -335

Nechemyah returned to rebuild walls of Yerushalayim.

Nechemyah had returned to Babylonia and became an important minister to Darius II. He received disturbing reports on conditions in Eretz Yisrael, and particularly on the security problem in Yerushalayim — whose wall had not been repaired since the destruction in 3338. In Nissan he gained the support of the king to go to Yerushalayim and rebuild the walls. During this reconstruction they had to keep continuous guard units against their enemies, the Kuthim *(Samaritans)* *[Bible Nech.1.1-3; 2.1,5-8,10, 19; 3.10, 4.1,2,10-17]*.

After the walls were completed (on the 25th **Elul**) and the gates were fitted (on the 7th **Iyar**), they celebrated with two concurrent parades led by Ezra and Nechemyah *[Bible Nech. 6.15; 12.27-42/Tal. Shev.15b]*.

The gates of Yerushalayim were opened at certain times only, because many houses were still uninhabited, and the Kuthim had continued their antagonism (see 3391\-370, 3395\-366) *[Bible Nech.7.1-4]*. Ezra and the ANSHEI KNESSET HAGDOLA excommunicated the Kuthim *(Samaritans, from Shomron, see 3205\-556, 4046\286)* *[Mid.Yal. Mel.II 17, Pir.Dr.El.38]*.

The 120 elders of the ANSHEI KNESSET HAGDOLA — 80 of them were prophets — included Ezra (Malachi, see 3392\-369) as head, Zecharyah, Chagay, Daniel, Chananyah, Misha'el, Azaryah, Nechemyah, Mordechai, Zerubavel, and Shimon HaTzadik *[Tal. Meg.17b, Av.1.1, Yer.Ber.2.4 17a, Yer.Meg.1.5 6b/Rashi B.B. 15a, Chul.139b/Mmn.Hakd.L'Yad]*. They instituted, among other things, (see 3406\-355, 3413\-348, 3448\-313) daily prayer, the Shmona Esrei *(18)* blessings of prayer, Kiddush, Havdala, and the regular individual blessings *[Tal.Ber.33a-b, 26b, Rashi, Meg.17b/ Mmn.Hil.Tfi.1.3,4]*.

3438 -323

Nechemyah was recalled to Bavel *(Babylonia)*, by Darius II *[Bible Nech.13.6]*, and before returning, he had repopulated the city of Yerushalayim, although the numbers still remained very small *[Bible Nech.7.4, Metz.Dav; 11.1-2]*.

When he went back to Eretz Yisrael — the 3rd time (see 3426\-335) — after a short absence, he set out to correct the worsening religious and security situations. He also induced the wealthy to support the poor *[Bible Nech.5, 9.1, 10.30, 13.9,15-25]*.
The Jewish birthrate was very high at this time — and for a number of generations later — exponentially increasing the population of Eretz Yisrael *[Mid.Rab.Sh.Hash.1.16.3, Eycha 1.2]*.

3448 -313

Ezra died.

Ezra died on the 9th Tevet; Chagay and Zecharyah had also died, and Nechemyah had again returned to Bavel *(Babylonia)* (see 3438\-323) where he died. This marked the end of prophecy *[Tal.San. 11a, Yom.9a/Yuch.1.14/ Kuz.3.39,65,67/ Yuch.1/ Mag.Av.O.C.580.6]*.
Ezra the scribe — and the head of the ANSHEI KNESSET HAGDOLA — had officially publicized (published) all 24 books of the TORAH *(Bible)* (some had been unavailable) in accurate original holy writing (see 3389\-372). He clarified every detailed letter, and incorporated the last prophets as well *[Tal.B.B.15a Rashi, San.22a, Rashi, Av.Dr.Nat.1.4, Rashi Shab.6b/Mid.Tan.Sh.Besh.16]*.
Alexander (the Macedonian), who conquered Persia (see 3390\-371), sought to extend the empire. All the archives of Yehuda *(Judea)*, originally confiscated by the Babylonians (see 3338\-423) were transferred to Alexander, and to Aristotle his mentor *[Tal.A.Z.9a/Kuz.1.63, Otz.Nech.; 2.66/Tor.HaOl.3.7/ Tzem.Dav./Sed.Had.]*.

Shimon HaTzadik met Alexander the Great.

The Kuthim *(Samaritans)* (see 3426\-335) received Alexander's permission to destroy the Beit Hamikdash, by describing it as a symbol of rebellion against the empire *[Tal.Yom.69a]*. Shimon HaTzadik, the last of the ANSHEI KNESSET HAGDOLA, was chosen to meet Alexander, and seek relief *[Tal.Av.1.1, Mach.Vit./Mmn.Hak.L'Yad/Dor.Har.1.197]*. When he went out to meet Alexander on the 25th Tevet, adorned in the garments of the Kohen Gadol, Alexander jumped off his horse and bowed to him, explaining to his surprised (and angry) generals that he often had visions of a similar man leading him into battle. Alexander withdrew his support of the destructive plans of the Kuthim after visiting the Beit Hamikdash, and seeing the services conducted there *[Tal.Yom. 69a, A.Z.9a/Yuch.1.13]*. The Kuthim *(Samaritans)* later built their own temple on Mount Gerizim *[Yuch.1.14/Sed.Had.]*.
Canaanite and Yishmaelite tribes made representations to Alexander, claiming the territory of Eretz Yisrael. Geviha *(the hunchback)* successfully argued the Jewish case on the 24th Nissan *[Tal.San.91a/Mid.Rab.Br.60.7]*.
Alexander, a Macedonian, was raised in the culture of his neighboring Greek city-states. He spread this culture wherever he went, and after his conquest of the Middle East, Greek letters *(Alpha, Beta, etc.)* were used — as symbols for identification purposes — in the Beit Hamikdash (see 3515 \ -246) *[Tal.Shek. 3.2, Riv'van]*.

3449 -313

The Minyan Shtarot began.

Alexander requested that a statue of him be placed in the Beit Hamikdash. Shimon HaTzadik explained how disagreeable this would be to Jewish religious feelings, and suggested that the Jews would bestow an even greater honor on him, by naming all the male Kohanim born in that year "Alexander". They would also accept that year (of his conquest of the empire), as the first year of counting — Year 1 — in all legal documents. This system, called Minyan Shtarot, commenced on the 1st Tishrei 3449, and was still in use 1,500 years later, when its use began to decrease, although it was not formally discontinued until more than 300 years later (see 5277\1517) *[Tal.Yom.69a, A.Z.9a, Rashi/Sed.Ol. 30/Mmn.Hil.Kid.Hach.11.16, Hil.Gir.1.27/Yuch.1.13/ Dor.Har.1.109]*.

Chapter 8b
Greek Cultural Domination

3454 -307

Alexander died and his kingdom was divided among four of his generals, who ruled over separate (warring) states. Eretz Yisrael was geographically caught between two of them, the Egyptians — ruled by a dynasty of kings, most of whom were called Ptolemy — and the Syrians — whose kings were (mostly) called Seleucius, Antiochus, and Demetrius. There were many wars between these two Greek cultured states, and Eretz Yisrael was usually dominated by one or the other [Rashi Dan.11.4-17].

The Ptolemy who reigned after Alexander's death attempted (unsuccessfully) to have the Torah translated by five scholars (see 3515\-246) [Tal.Sof.1.7, 8/Tzem.Dav.2.3454, 3484]. He also exiled over 100,000 Jews to Egypt [Yuch.5.154/ Tzem.Dav./Sed.Had.], and Alexandria began to flourish as a Jewish center [Tal.Suk.51b, Hag.R.B.Rans., Yer.Suk.5.2/ Yuch.1.13].

3488 -273

Shimon HaTzadik died.

Shimon HaTzadik was Kohen Gadol for 40 years — and Av *(Head)* of the Sanhedrin. If (as some say) he directly succeeded Ezra [Mmn.Hakd.L'Yad], then he died in 3488. If (as others say) he succeeded his father Chonyo I, who in turn succeeded his father Ido [Yuch.5.154], then he may have died after 3488 [Tal.Yom.9a/Dor.Har.1.197,199]. Antigonus (Ish Socho) succeeded him as Av *(Head)* of the Sanhedrin [Tal.Av.1.3/Dor.Har.1.199].

Shimon HaTzadik's son Chonyo II left for Egypt (see 3454\-307) after a dispute out of jealousy (with his brother Shim'i, who became Kohen Gadol) and he built an altar — for sacrifices — in Egypt [Tal. Min.109b, Mmn.Pir.Mi./Tol.Am.Ol. 2.394].

Yehoshua ben Sira — who was still young at this time — praised Shimon HaTzadik at the end of his book, *Ben Sira*, (although he only called him Shimon the Kohen Gadol, see 3580\-181). This book was not accepted as a Torah writing, although the Talmud quotes phrases from it in a number of places [Tal. San.100b, Rashi/ Toseph.Yad.2.5/ Sed.Had.3298/ Dor.Har.1.193].

3515 -246

72 Elders translated the Torah into Greek (Septuagint).

In this second attempt to have the Torah translated (see 3454\-307), seventy-two great Torah scholars were gathered by the ruling Ptolemy, sequestered separately, and forced to translate the Torah into Greek. They produced seventy-two synchronized translations — including identical changes in thirteen places — on the 8th Tevet [Tal.Sof.1.7,8, Meg.9a/TBY.O.C.580.1/Tzem.Dav./ Tol.Am.Ol. 2.397]. Versions — published later — are believed not to be true to the original [Sed.Had.]. Greek became a significant second language among Jews (see 3448\-313 end) as a result of the translation [Mmn.Pir.Mi.Meg.17a/Tos.Y.T.Shek.5.3].

3530 -231

Antigonus Ish Socho had died by this time, and Yosef (Yosee) ben Yochanan — his disciple — had been appointed Av *(Head)* of the Sanhedrin [Tal.Av.1.4/Dor.Har.1.173, 199].

The misinterpretation of Antigonus' teachings — by two of his students (Tzadok and Baytuss) — were further amplified by their disciples, and eventually developed into a movement called Tzedukim *(Sadducees)*, of which the Baytussim were a faction. Josephus (a sympathizer of theirs) described them [Ant.18.1.4] as a secularist movement, believing only in the here and now [Tal.R.H.22b, Av.Dr.Nat.5.2 /Dor.Har.2.361-3,372, 400,413,419-21,479].

3550 -211

Chonyo II — who had returned from Egypt (see 3488\-273) to become Kohen Gadol — was petty and tight fisted. He refused to hand over the taxes payable to Egypt. Yosef ben Tuviyah then volunteered — to the ruling Ptolemy — to collect the taxes (for a commission), and his proposal was accepted. This averted a crisis, but established him as the powerful (ruthless and wealthy) leader of an organized class of collaborating tax collectors, who filled the power vacuum created by a

weak Kohen Gadol *[Yuch.5.6.155/Dor.Har.1.171, 184]*.
In order to redeem some of the leadership that was lost by the office of the Kohen Gadol (who had also been responsible for such civil matters as tax collection) through this default, the Sanhedrin created the higher position of Nassi *(President)* of the Sanhedrin, and appointed another of Antigonus' disciples, Yosef (Yosee) ben Yo'ezer to fill it. This was the first such combined leadership, Yosef ben Yochanan as the Av *(Head)* of the Sanhedrin, and — above him — Yosef ben Yo'ezer as the Nassi *[Tal.Av.1.4/ Mmn.Sef.Mitz.316, Hil.San.1.3/Dor.Har.1.199, 200]*.

3570 -191

Yosef ben Yochanan had died, and conditions in Eretz Yisrael were influenced by such forces as the tax collectors (see 3550\-211), the Tzedukim *(Sadducees)* (see 3530\-231), the Hellenists (who promoted acceptance of 'progressive' Greek culture), and the Kuthim *(Samaritans)*. These groups shared a common antagonism to the majority of the Jews — who maintained a close adherence to the laws and traditions of the TORAH, under the guidance of the Sanhedrin — who were later called Perushim *(Pharisees)* *[Yuch.5.6.156/Dor.Har. 2.362-5,Note(3)]*.

3580 -181

At around this time (some say), there emerged a cult called Essenes, who (mostly) lived in secluded agricultural communes. Many in this elitist group did not marry and have families, because they considered that to be too materialistic. According to Josephus *[Ant.18.1.3, 5]* (a sympathizer *[Vita 2.]*), their sacrifices were not accepted in the Beit Hamikdash because they had different laws of purity. There were similarities (of intensity) between the customs of the Essenes and those of the Kuthim *(Samaritans)* *[Tal.Ber.47b/Yuch.5.6.157/ Sed.Had.3460]*.
Chonyo II had died around this time, and his son Shimon II became Kohen Gadol. People began referring to the first Shimon as Shimon HaTzadik, to distinguish between him and his grandson, as they were both named Shimon ben Chonyo Kohen Gadol *[Dor.Har.1.181, 195]*.

3600 -161

Eretz Yisrael was dominated by the Syrians at this time (see 3454\-307). Shimon II had died, and his son Chonyo III had become Kohen Gadol. He reduced the political power of the Hellenists and of the tax collectors (the descendants of Yosef ben Tuviyah, see 3550\-211). Both these groups differed essentially only in the emphasis of their collaboration and identification with the ruling powers (Syrian Greeks) *[Dor.Har.1.176, 184, 186; 2.393]*.

3610 -151

In collaboration with the ruling Antiochus of that time, (Yeshua) Jason, a Hellenist, replaced his brother Chonyo III as Kohen Gadol. Chonyo III subsequently went to Egypt and built a temple for the altar of Chonyo II his grandfather (see 3488\-273), which stood for over 300 years *[Tal.Meg.10a/ Tos.Zev.119a(Zu)/Yuch.5.156/ Tol.Am.Ol.2.404]*.
The Hellenists, in collaboration with the Syrian Greeks, conducted a harsh program to eliminate Jewish religious observance, in Eretz Yisrael *[Dor.Har.2.375]*. Menelaus — who excelled in cultural collaboration — replaced Jason as Kohen Gadol, and actively involved the Syrians, to increase the religious persecution and desecration *[Dor.Har.2.374-6]*. At first they disallowed certain sacrifices to be brought to the Beit Hamikdash, but when they gained a more strategic foothold in Yerushalayim itself, they completely stopped the holy services. Apustomus, one of the Syrian leaders, burned a Sefer Torah on the 17th Tammuz *[Tal.Tan.26b, Rashi, 28a, Mrsha]*.
The Syrian (Greeks) then enforced severe penalties for Jews who kept the religious laws of the Torah, especially Shabbat, Mila *(circumcision)* and marriage *[Tal.Ket.3b, San.32b]*. There were many incidents of death and destruction. Miriam (some say Chanah) and her seven sons were brutally killed *[Tal. Git.57b/Mid.Rab.Eych.1.50, Haradal/ Yuch.1.14/ Tzem.Dav.]*.
Yosef ben Yo'ezer had been killed. Yehoshua ben Perachya and Nitai Ha'arbeli became — respectively — Nassi *(President)* and Av *(Head)* of the Sanhedrin *[Tal.Av.1.6/Mid.Rab.Br. 65.22/Dor.Har.1.160]*.
At this time the Jews in Bavel *(Babylonia)* *(see 3342\-419, 3413\-348,)* were living peacefully, free from the troubles that tormented the Jews of Eretz Yisrael, and they had scholarly leadership and direction. The Jews in Egypt *(see 3454\-307)* were thriving, but not in Torah scholarship, even though they had established their own Sanhedrin *[Tal.Ket.25a, Min.110a, Mrsha, Suk.51b, Rashi, Tos./ Mid.Tan.Br.Noach 3/Yuch.5.156/Sed.Had./ Dor.Har. 1.101-2]*.

3621 -140

The revolt of Mattityahu the Chashmona'i.

After years of physical and spiritual destruction in Eretz Yisrael, Mattityahu — the aging son of Yochanan — and his five sons (Yochanan, Shimon, Yehuda, Elazar, and Yonatan) staged a local rebellion in Modi'in, when the Syrian (Greek) authority came to initiate his daughter before her marriage. The revolt quickly spread under his leadership *[Meg.Tan.6/Yuch.1.14/ Tzem.Dav./ Sed.Had.]*.

Some say the revolt of the Chashmona'im was in 3590 — this is inconsistent with the Talmud [See Appendix A] *[A.Z.9a/Tzem.Dav.3590, 3621/Sed.Had.]*.

Chapter 8c

Kingdom of Yehuda (Judea) – Dynasty of the Chashmona'im

3622 -139

Yehuda (HaMaccabi) ruled.

After a year of leadership, and many successful battles against the Syrians (Greeks), Mattityahu died, and his son Yehuda became leader *[Tal.A.Z.9a/ Mid.Rab.Sh.15.6/Sed.Ol./ Yuch.1.14/ Tzem.Dav./ Sed.Had./ Ramban Br.49.10]*. The small band of fighters had grown into a national movement, and they gained control of the Beit Hamikdash, which they entered on the 25th Kislev (some say the 24th) *[Tal.Shab.21b/ Targ. Sh.Hash. 6.9/Mmn.Hil.Chan.3.2/ Meiri Shab.21b (Jer.p25)]*.

The 2nd Beit Hamikdash was re-dedicated.

The Beit Hamikdash had remained unused, misused, and desecrated for years. Many of the sacred items and utensils needed repair or replacement. Most of the holy utensils were ritually impure, and there were no ritually pure supplies stored away for the services — the most difficult of them to obtain was oil. However, a small container of oil was found — only sufficient for one day — and it miraculously burned for eight festive days in a makeshift Menora *[Tal.Shab.21b, Min.89a, A.Z.43a, Rashi, 52b/Meg.Tan.2, 9/ Rashi.Sh.27.21]*.

Yochanan (ben Mattityahu) became Kohen Gadol [See Appendix B] *[Tal.R.H.18b/Mmn.Hakd.Pir.Mi.Zer.Chap.4,6,7/ Roke'ach 225/Levush Hil.Chan.670]*. Yehudit, his daughter, infiltrated the enemy camp, and killed their leader *[Tal.Shab.23a, Rashi/Mid.q.RaN Shab.10a(23a)/ Shilt.Gib. Mord. 456.2/KolBo Chan.44 p.3c/ Ramo O.C.670.2]*.

3623 -138

Chanuka was declared a festival.

Yochanan Kohen Gadol composed the "Al HaNissim" prayer *[Roke'ach 225/KolBo 44p4b, 122p926]*. Together with his peers, the leaders of the Sanhedrin (Yehoshua ben Perachya and Nitai Ha'arbeli), he was responsible for the festival of Chanuka *[Roke'ach225/Levush Hil.Chan.670]*, and its declaration *[Tal. Shab.21b/ Mmn.Hil.Chan.3.3/Hak.Pir.Mi.chap.4, 7]*.

The Chashmona'im won many successive victories, and those days were set aside and celebrated (as commemorative days) for some time, without any specific laws or customs *[Tal. R.H.19b/ Meg.Tan.2,6,9,12]*.

3628 -133

Yehuda (HaMaccabi) was killed in battle.

The Chashmona'im had to fight many battles, even after their initial victories in 3621-3622; in one of those battles, Elazar was crushed by an elephant, and (later) Yehuda was killed. Yehuda had made friendly contacts with the Romans, who were already building an empire, and saw it useful to have allies in the strategic Middle East *[Targ.Sh.Hash. 6.8,9/Ramban.Br.32.4; 49.10/Yuch.1.14/ Tzem.Dav./ Sed.Had.]*.

Four months after Yehuda was killed in battle, his brother Yonatan became ruler of Yehuda (Judea). His was a relatively peaceful reign over what was now called the Kingdom of Yehuda (Judea) *[Tzem.Dav./Sed.Had.]*.

Yochanan Kohen Gadol, his brother [see Appendix B], had sent delegations all over the country to inquire about religious practices, and to implement many adjustments *[Tal.Sot.47a, 48a, Par.3.5]*.

Jews from Egypt (see 3610\-151) came to the Beit Hamikdash for festivals, and the visiting Egyptian artisans helped extend the skills used there *[Tal. Yom.38a, 61a,b]*.

The Chashmona'im became well established, the Sanhedrin exercised its powers, and the Tzedukim could no longer be overt atheists (for fear of the penalties). They therefore claimed to adhere (only) to the Written Law of the Bible, which was available to these second and third generation secularists/Hellenists/Tzedukim in Greek (see 3515\-246) — the only language most of them knew. Their interpretations of the Written Law were free and varied, and some say that this was the beginning of a sect called Kra'im *(Karaites)* (see 4523\763) *[Mmn. Pir.Mi.Av.1.3, Hil.Mam.3.3/ Yuch.1.14/ Tzem.Dav.4515/ Dor.Har. 2.361-364, 387, 413]*.

3634 -127

Yonatan was killed in battle, and he was succeeded as ruler of the kingdom of Yehuda by his brother Shimon in 3634 *[Ramban Br.49.10/ Yuch.1.14/Tzem.Dav./Sed.Had.]*.
The Perushim (see 3570\-191) who had remained in Eretz Yisrael during the many years of strife (before the revolt of the Chashmona'im), had been impoverished by the continuous persecutions, whereas the collaborating secularists/ Hellenists/Tzedukim, many of whom were descendants of Yosef ben Tuviyah and his tax collecting agents, retained their wealth, and upper class status *[Tal.Av.Dr.Nat.5.2/ Dor.Har.2.391]*.

3642 -119

Shimon the ruler had lived a wealthy life style and 'out-classed' the wealthy secularists (see 3634\-127)). He was killed by his son in law, or a Ptolemy from Egypt. Some say this was one and the same person. His two older sons were also killed, but his son Yochanan Hyrkanos (also called Yannai I) escaped and became ruler of Yehuda (Judea) *[Tos.Yom.18a/Yuch.5.6.156/ Tzem.Dav./ Sed.Had./ Dor.Har.2.392/Tol.Am.Ol.2.409]*.
Yochanan Hyrkanos also became Kohen Gadol, probably directly after his uncle, Yochanan Kohen Gadol, which some say was in 3628 *[Tzem.Dav.3668]*. He attempted to avenge his father's death, but was restrained by a threat to kill his mother, who was killed anyway. He conquered territories and forced some Judaism on the conquered peoples; he fought battles against the south (Egypt) and the north (Syria). He opened the grave of King David and took some gold that was buried there, which he used to encourage the Antiochus of that time to leave Eretz Yehuda (Judea) *[Yuch.5.156/ Tzem.Dav./ Sed.Had./ Dor.Har.2.392-3]*.

3648 -113

In 3648 the Romans took a dominant stand in their ties with Yehuda (Judea) (see 3628\-133) *[Tal.A.Z.8b]*. Nevertheless, because of the successful battles of Yochanan Hyrkanos (see 3642\-119), there was peace and prosperity in the expanded kingdom of Yehuda. Yochanan Hyrkanos (Yannai I) invaded Shomron, the capital of the Kuthim *(Samaritans)*, and destroyed their temple on Mount Gerizim (see 3448\-313) *[Yuch.1.14/Tzem.Dav./Sed.Had.]*. On his return from a successful battle, he made a banquet to which he also invited Tzedukim, with whom he had maintained cordial relations. One of them stirred his suspicions — delicately questioning how genuine the allegiance of the Perushim could be (due to his dual role as Kohen Gadol and ruler), and when (subsequently) one of the older Perushim inelegantly criticized him, Yochanan Hyrkanos was infuriated. The Tzedukim incited him to have the (scholarly leaders of the) Perushim killed, a challenge he eventually accepted *[Tal.Kid.66a, Mrsha/ Dor.Har.2.391]*.

3668 -93

Yochanan Hyrkanos himself became a Tzeduki in his later years, after the incident at the banquet (see 3648\-113). He had killed most of the Torah scholars, except that Yehoshua ben Perachya fled to Egypt, and Shimon ben Shatach was hidden by his sister Shalomit (Salome I), who was the daughter in law of Yochanan Hyrkanos (see 3670\-91) *[Tal.Kid.66a,Ber.29a, 48a, Ches.San.107b/ Mag.Av.2.4/Sed.Had./Dor.Har.2.460, 476]*. After he died, in 3668 *[Tzem.Dav.]*, or 3666 *[Yuch.5.156]*, his son Yehuda Aristoblus succeeded him as ruler of Yehuda (Judea), instead of his wife (as he had wished) *[Dor.Har.2.454]*. Yehuda Aristoblus, also a Tzeduki, demeaned the role of Kohen Gadol by appointing the highest bidder to that honorable position. Thus (with their money, see 3634\-127) the Tzedukim gained control of the key political and religious positions of power, and appointed members of their own families to other important positions *[Tal.Yom.8b, Mmn.Pir.Mi.18a, Pes.57a/ Mid.Rab.Vay.21.9]*.
The power oriented Yehuda Aristoblus jailed his brother Alexander Yannai, and also his mother (who died in prison), but favored his younger brother Antigonus, whom he later killed (because of a suspected revolt) *[Tzem.Dav./Dor.Har.2.454-7]*.

3670 -91

After he killed his younger brother Antigonus

(see 3668\-93), the sick Yehuda Aristoblus did not live long. He had no children. His brother, Alexander Yannai (also a Tzeduki), was released from imprisonment (see 3668\-93) and succeeded him *[Tzem.Dav./Sed.Had.]*. Some say that Shalomit was originally the wife of Yehuda Aristoblus, and because they had no children, she released Alexander Yannai (from prison), married him (*Yibum*), and made him king of Yehuda (Judea) *[Bible Dev.25.5-10/Dor.Har.2.460]*.

Shalomit (Salome I) arranged for her brother Shimon ben Shatach to be appointed to the Sanhedrin, which by that time was completely dominated by Tzedukim. He excelled over the others in scholarship, and by careful strategy was able to replace them (one by one) with his disciples (see 3680\-81) *[Meg.Tan.10]*.

3671 ≈ -90

Yeshua ben Sitda, a student of Yehoshua ben Perachya, was rejected because of his undesirable behavior. He was (later) accused of idol worship and witchcraft, and punished accordingly by the Sanhedrin *[Tal.Ches.San. 43a, 67a, 107b/ Yuch.1.16]*. Some (manuscript) versions of the Talmud refer to him as Yeshu HaNotzri *(the Nazarene)*, and relate events (mostly of his death) which bear similarities to those surrounding Jesus (see 3790\30) *[Tal.Ches.San.43a, 67a, 103a, A.Z.17a, Ber.17b/ Toseph.Shab. 11.15, Chul.2.6-end]*. Many say (or imply) that this was in fact Jesus (despite the lack of chronological synchronization, see 3790\30) *[Mmn.Igg.Teman(end)/Sef.Hak.q.Sed.Had./ Ramban Mil. Vik.22/ Yuch.1.16/Sed.Had.3560, 3671, 3707, 3724, 3761]*. Those opinions that claim they are not the same person *[Me'iri Sot.47a, (p.115 Jer. 1947), Hak.L'Avot (p.28, Jer. 1964)]*, could be supported by the references in the Talmud which appear to be contradictory in the chronological placement of Yeshu *[Tal.Ches.A.Z.17a/ Toseph.Chul2.6-end/Mid.Rab. Koh.1.8#3]*. Accordingly, events surrounding an earlier Yeshu may have later been used (or confused) to describe a later one. The history of Jesus (see 3790\30) is shrouded in mystery; his historical prominence is not reflected in the writings of his time, and references to the early history of the church were often influenced by pressures brought to bear (see 5023\1263).

3680 ≈ -81

Yehoshua ben Gamlah was appointed Kohen Gadol (after his wealthy wife, Martha (Miriam)

Kings & Rulers of the Chashmona'im Dynasty

	Jewish Year	Secular Year
Yehuda HaMaccabi	3622	-139
Yonatan	3628	-127
Shimon	3634	-127
Yochanan Hyrkanos	3642	-119
Yehuda Aristoblus	3668	-93
Alexander Yannai	3670	-91
Shalomit	3688	-73
Aristoblus II	3696	-65
Hyrkanos II	3700	-61
Antigonus	3721	-40

bat Baytuss paid an appropriate amount (see 3668\-93) to Alexander Yannai). Later (in concert with Shimon ben Shatach) he helped establish a national Torah educational system *[Tal.B.B.21a, Yev.61a, Tos., Yom.18a, Tos.,/Tal.Yer.Yom.5.1, Ket.8.11/Meg.Tan.12/ Mid.Rab.Eych.1.47/Yuch.1.15]*.
Shimon ben Shatach covertly sent a message to (his mentor) Yehoshua ben Perachya to return from Egypt (see 3668\-93) *[Tal. Ches.San.107b/ Dor.Har.2.469]*. He cleverly convinced Alexander Yannai to contribute to the expenses of the (poor peoples') sacrifices *[Tal.Yer.Naz.5.3/Mid.Rab.Br.91.3]*. He also managed to have him appear before the Sanhedrin over a charge of murder being brought against a servant of his. The resultant confrontation of power (in the court) highlighted the need to establish the subsequent law that a king should not participate in court proceedings *[Tal.San.19a]*.
Alexander Yannai had a confrontation with the Perushim, after someone threw an Etrog at him, some say accidentally, during the Sukkot services (others say he ridiculed the services) in the Beit Hamikdash. He killed many of the Torah scholars, although some managed to escape and others fled the country *[Tal.Suk.48b/ Meg.Tan.12/Yuch.1.14/ Tzem.Dav./ Dor.Har.2.480-2]*.
Choni Ham'agel, a great Torah scholar of this time, managed to remain prominent, yet survive *[Tal.Tan.23a, Yer.Tan.3.9/ Mmn.Hakd.Mi.Zer. Chap.4, 7]*.

3686 -75

The people rebelled against Alexander Yannai (see 3680\-81) and fought open battles against him for six years during which at least 50,000 people were killed. He gruesomely killed 800 men and their families. When he was sick and dying he expressed his regrets; nevertheless his wife Shalomit (Salome I) considered retiring herself (and their two young sons) into private life, and discontinuing the dynasty (of the Chashmona'im) *[Dor.Har.2.484-92, 504-5]*.

3688 -73

Shalomit (Salome I), also called Shalminin *[Meg.Tan.10]* and Shel Tzion *[Shab.16b/Sed.Had.3670]*, succeeded her husband (see 3686\-75) as ruler of Yehuda (Judea). She was advised by him (before he died on the 7th Kislev) to rule until their sons (Hyrkanos II, and Aristoblus II) were older, and also to associate with the Perushim because they could be trusted, and would allow the dynasty (of the Chashmona'im) to continue *[Tal.Sot.22b, Rashi/Meg.Tan.9 per Dor.Har. 2.678-9, 503-5/ Tzem.Dav./Sed.Had.]*. She appointed Hyrkanos over matters of the Beit Hamikdash, and Aristoblus (a Tzeduki) as a regional governor, away from Yerushalayim *[Tzem.Dav.]*.
Yehoshua ben Perachya and Nitai Ha'arbeli had died, Shimon ben Shatach had convinced Yehuda ben Tabbai to return from Egypt, and subsequently they became leaders of the Sanhedrin, as Nassi (president) and Av (head) *[Tal.Yer.San. 6.6/ Dor.Har.2.470, 475-6]*. During the peaceful years of Shalomit's rule, they made special judgments to reassert the authority of religious law *[Tal.San.45b, 46a, Mak.5b, Chag.16b/Tzem.Dav.]*. Shimon ben Shatach guided Todos *(Theodus)*, a leader of the Roman Jewish community *[Tal.Ber. 19a, Pes.53a, Rashi]*.

3696 -65

Before his mother Shalomit died, Aristoblus II had begun wielding power with the army under his control. When she died, he took control of Yehuda *(Judea)*, after a civil war with his brother Hyrkanos II that lasted for three months (until the elders made peace) *[Tal.Sot.49b, Rashi/ Yuch.5.156/Tzem.Dav./Sed.Had./Dor.Har.2.518-20]*.
Under his rule the Tzedukim regained political power (see 3688\-73) *[Dor.Har.2.538]*.
Shimon ben Shatach and Yehuda ben Tabbai had already died, and Shem'aya and Avtalyon (descendants of converts, and of Sancheriv) became the leaders of the Sanhedrin *[Tal.Av 1.9, Git.57b, San.97b/ Yuch.1.17/Dor.Har. 1.71]*. Hillel — a Babylonian disciple — had once almost frozen to death while standing at the window of their joint-school of study *(Beit Midrash)* in his eagerness to learn *[Tal.Yom. 35b/Dor.Har.1.50]*.

3700 -61

The Romans gained control of Yehuda (Judea).

Hyrkanos II (stirred by Antipater, a Roman sympathizer, who was his friend and adviser) regretted having given the rule to his brother Aristoblus II (see 3696\-65). He waged a bitter civil war to become ruler, and both brothers attempted to involve Pompey, whose Roman legions had been in the region for some time already. Pompey grasped the opportunity to exercise power and installed Hyrkanos II (who was weaker brother) as king, with Antipater as his minister *[Tal.Min.64b, Sot.49b, Rashi/Rashi Sh.Hash.6.12, Rashi San.97b/Yuch.5.156/ Tzem.Dav./Sed.Had./Dor.Har.1.1; 2.146]*. Aristoblus II was led in captivity to Rome (which had already conquered and controlled a vast empire). Antipater (a schemer of Idumean descent, who married a non Jewish Idumean wife) was in effective control of Yehuda *(Judea)* through his friend Hyrkanos II. They were sympathetic to the Perushim (due to political considerations), which meant that Torah scholarship could flourish, as it had under the rule of Shalomit (Salome I), the mother of Hyrkanos II (see 3688\-73) *[Tzem.Dav./Sed.Had./ Dor.Har.2.544-6]*.

3714 -47

R.Yochanan ben Zakkai was born in 3714 (see 3834\74), during the reign of Julius Caesar, who respected Hyrkanos II *[Tal.R.H.31b/Tzem.Dav./Sed.Had.]*.

3715 -46

Shem'aya and Avtalyon had died, and Alexander II (a son of Aristoblus II) had rebelled against the Roman installation of his uncle Hyrkanos II as king instead of his father (see 3700\-61). He was defeated with Roman assistance, who — at the request of Antipater — also increased the powers of Hyrkanos II to include all civil matters. These had previously been administered through the Sanhedrin in the Beit Hamikdash court *[Tal.Sot.48a, Yer.Sot. 9.11/Dor.Har.1.36, 55, 59, 61-63, 70]*.

No appointment was made to replace Shem'aya or Avtalyon (as head of the Sanhedrin). The respected Family of Beteira were temporarily given the leadership responsibilities *[Tal.Pes.66a, B.M.85a/ Yuch.1.18/ Dor.Har.1.76]*.

Shamai, who had been a respected member of the high court, established his own school of study (Beit Midrash) *[Dor.Har.1.76]*. Admon and Chanan were (independently) famous judges (for their rulings) in two of the numerous lower courts *[Tal.Ket.104b-105a/Mmn.Hakd.Mi.Zer.4]*. Hyrkanos II reluctantly succumbed to the public pressure to have Herod (the son of his friend Antipater) brought to a trial court for participating in the willful slaying of a group of Jewish nationalists who had rebelled against the Roman occupation forces. Herod arrogantly (and threateningly) appeared with some of his (armed) soldiers, and only through the brave admonition of Shamai did the court proceedings continue. Hyrkanos II arranged, however, that the trial be postponed, and Herod escaped *[Tzem.Dav./Sed.Had.3724/Dor.Har.1.46; 2.626-7, 630, 735]*.

Roman Emperors

Republic	
{-52} — {-49}	Pompey
{-49} — {-44}	Julius Caesar
{-44} — {-31}	Marc Antony
Empire	
{-27} — 14	Augustus (Octavian)
14 — 37	Tiberius
37 — 41	Caligula (Gaius)
41 — 54	Claudius
54 — 68	Nero
68	Galba
69	Otho
69	Vitellius
69 — 79	Vespasian
79 — 81	Titus
81 — 96	Domitian
96 — 98	Nerva
98 — 117	Trajan
117 — 138	Hadrian
138 — 161	Antoninus Pius
161 — 180	Marcus Aurelius Antoninus

3721 -40

Antigonus, another son of Aristoblus II (see 3715\-46), engaged the help of the king of Partha *(Persia)* — a successful warrior against the Romans — to conquer Yerushalayim and remove his uncle Hyrkanos II from his Roman-sponsored power. The attack succeeded and Hyrkanos II was taken to Partha as a captive. He was later released to lead the Jews living in his Persian kingdom which included Bavel *(Babylonia)*; and the Romans later returned to remove Antigonus (the last of the Chashmona'im dynasty), and reassert their control over Yehuda *(Judea)* (see 3725\-36) *[Tzem.Dav./Sed.Had.]*.

Chapter 8d
Roman Client Kings & Rulers – Herodian Dynasty

3725 -36

Herod I ruled, killing all the Chashmona'im.

The emperor Augustus sent his Roman legions to forcefully install Herod I (see 3715\-46) as ruler of Yehuda *(Judea)* in 3725 (see 3721\-40) *[Sed.Ol./Tal.A.Z.9a/Tzem.Dav./ Sed.Had.]*.

Herod I realized that he would not be accepted because of his ancestry (see 3700\-61) and because of his ruthlessness (see 3715\-46), so he proceeded to kill all the family of the Chashmona'im, including (eventually) his own wife Miriam — daughter of Alexander II (see 3715\-46) — and their children. He even encouraged Hyrkanos II to return, from exile, to Yerushalayim (see 3721\-40), only to kill him, thus eliminating all of the Chashmona'im *[Tal.B.B.3b/Yuch.5.156/Tzem.Dav./ Sed. Had.]*.

3727 -34

For two years Herod I terrorized the Jews into accepting his reign (see 3725\-36). He restructured the country — building fortresses such as Massada — with the apparent intention of creating a secular kingdom in which the Jews would only be a part. Cities built with monies collected from Jews, he populated with non-Jews. On the completion of Caesaria he made a great celebration. He had apparently intended that this would be his new capital — instead of Yerushalayim — but was thwarted by the Romans, who suspected the strategic significance of his ambitions *[Dor.Har.1.9-18]*.

3729 -32

Hillel became leader of the Torah scholars.

Hillel (see 3696\-65) who was a descendant of King David *[Tal.Ket.62b]*, had returned to Bavel *(Babylonia)*, but came to Eretz Yisrael in 3729 for Pesach. He was the only scholar to know a specific law relating to the Pesach of that year. The Family of Beteira (see 3715\-46) stepped aside, and Hillel was appointed leader of the scholars. He later became the Nassi *(President)* of the Sanhedrin — with Shamai as Av *(Head)* — an office he elevated during the decline of the office of Kohen Gadol (see 3668\-93, 3550\-211, 3781\21) *[Tal.Shab. 15a, Pes.66a, Suk.20a, Chag.16a, Rashi, Yom.Mish.1.6]*.

Hillel opened his own Beit Midrash — separate from Shamai's (see 3715\-46) — a departure from the previous tradition of combined schools (see 3696\-65). He did not wish to prematurely arouse the suspicions of Herod I that the central Sanhedrin was to re-emerge as a powerful and united voice under his leadership. In this manner Hillel quietly ushered in a new era, the era of the TANNA'IM (1st generation Talmudists) *[Tal.Suk.20a/Dor.Har.1.76, 77, 144; 2.548, 672]*. Herod I (later) respected Hillel *[Dor.Har.1.44]*.

3742 -19

Herod I began rebuilding the 2nd Beit Hamikdash.

When Herod presented the idea of rebuilding the second Beit Hamikdash — which was in bad disrepair after 334 years — the Jews were wary of this uncharacteristic suggestion (see 3727\-34), even though it had been raised by one of the TANNA'IM, Bava ben Buta (who, although being blinded, had survived Herod's massacre of TANNA'IM). The Jews feared that Herod was actually scheming to demolish it without ever rebuilding. Some say that this reconstruction was in fact a maneuver to mislead the Romans about his strategic ambitions in the region (see 3727\-34) *[Tal.B.B.3b-4a/ Tzem.Dav./ Sed.Had./ Dor.Har.1.18-20]*.

3750 -11

Renovation of the 2nd Beit Hamikdash completed.

The magnificent structure of Herod's Beit Hamikdash, completed in 3750, included gold taken from the grave of King David (see 3642\-119) *[Tal.B.B.4a, Suk.51b/ Yuch.5.156/Tzem.Dav./Sed.Had.]*. Herod I placed a religiously offensive (Roman) golden eagle above the entry to the Beit Hamikdash (see 3760\-1). Some say that due to Herod's cruel disdainful treatment of the Jews (see 3725\-36, 3742\-19, 3760\-1, 3761\1), they became second-rate citizens in the eyes of the Romans; and the international perception of the Jew irreversibly declined *[Dor.Har.1.27, 30, 35, 36; 2.673-8; 3.41]*.

Nessi'im
Presidents of the Sanhedrin

	Jewish Year	Secular Year
Yosef (Yosee) ben Yo'ezer	*see* 3550	-211
Yehoshua ben Perachya	*see* 3610	-151
Shimon ben Shatach	*see* 3688	-73
Hillel	*see* 3729	-32
Shimon (ben Hillel)	*see* 3769	8
Rbn.Gamliel I (ben Shimon)	*see* 3769	8
R.Shimon ben Gamliel I	*see* 3810	49
R.Gamliel II (ben R.Shimon)	*see* 3828	67
R.Elazar ben Azaryah	*see* 3844	83
R.Shimon ben Gamliel II	*see* 3878	117
R.Yehuda HaNassi	*see* 3925	164
R.Gamliel III (ben R.Yehuda)	*see* 3949	188
R.Yehuda Nessia I (ben Gamliel)	*see* 3949	188
R.Gamliel IV (ben Yehuda)	*see* 3990	229
R.Yehuda Nessia II (ben Gamliel)	*see* 3990	229
R.Gamliel V (ben Yehuda)	*see* 4060	299
R.Yehuda Nessia III (ben Gamliel)	*see* 4069	308
Hillel II (ben Yehuda)	*see* 4119	358
R.Gamliel (ben Yehuda)	*see* 4189	428

- *Exact dates are not known for the Nessi'im.*
- *The year listed here is a reference to the main text where this Nassi is mentioned.*
- *Note that these Nessi'im extend over a period of more than 630 years — thus the list is not confined to this chapter, but extends through chapters 8, 9, and into 10.*
- *After Hillel, all the Nessi'im were his direct descendants, except for R.Elazar ben Azarya. He was elected when R.Gamliel II was removed from the position — and although he was reinstated a short while later, they shared the presidency for some 20 years (see 3864 / 104).*

3760 -1

Herod I lay dying, and rumor spread that he had died. Some religious scholars and students tore down the offensive golden eagle at the gates of the Beit Hamikdash (see 3750\-11), but they were caught and Herod had them burned alive. He also ordered the arrest of a member of each Jewish family, ordering his sister Salome II (see 3761\1) to have them killed on the day he died — creating a Jewish day of mourning *[Meg.Tan.11 per Dor.Har. 2.673-9]*.

3761 1

Herod I appointed his son Archelaus to rule over Yehuda *(Judea)* — subject to the consent of the Roman emperor — after having killed some of his other sons *[Tzem.Dav./ Sed.Had.]*.

When Herod I died on the 2nd Shvat, his sister, Salome II, did not notify anyone, but sent word to the prison guard that the king had ordered the release of all the recent prisoners (members of each family) (see 3760\-1). Once that had been accomplished she announced that Herod was dead *[Meg.Tan.11 per Dor.Har. 2.678-9/Tzem.Dav./Sed.Had.]*.

When Archelaus succeeded his father, many Jews were still languishing in prison, and Herod's non-Jewish officials were still in control. Archelaus forcefully stopped the Pesach sacrifice on the 14th Nissan, in a bloodbath where thousands were killed. The Jews sent a delegation to the emperor — which was joined by many Jews of Rome (see 3688\-73) — requesting that no king be approved. Archelaus went to Rome and he prevailed, although he was not approved by the emperor as a full king *[Tzem.Dav./ Sed.Had./Dor.Har.2.680-82, 688, 698-700]*.

When Archelaus was in Rome, the Roman High Commissioner of Syria sent in his legions to quell a 'possible' uprising in Yehuda *(Judea)*. This was an unfounded charge which, when conveyed to the emperor, assisted Archelaus' approval to rule. The general of these troops used his household guards to ruthlessly extort money from Jews, creating a universal outcry for his withdrawal. Although the High Commissioner had him withdrawn, this episode set an atmosphere of anarchy in Yehuda *(Judea)* (see 3770\10, 3781\21) *[Dor.Har.2.692-7]*.

3769 9

Hillel died.

Hillel, who had brought the Sanhedrin back to its original power (see 3715\-46), was succeeded by his son Shimon, to the (now elevated) position of Nassi *(President)* of the Sanhedrin (see 3729\-32). Shimon did not live long, and was succeeded in turn by his son Rbn.Gamliel I — also the first to be called "Raban". Thus the leadership of the Jews of Yehuda *(Judea)* was in the hands of a dynasty of descendants of King David *[Tal.Shab.15a/Sifri Dev. 357/ Tzem.Dav./Sed.Had.Vol.2/Dor.Har.2.670-2, 707-8]*.

Hillel's greatest disciple was Yonatan ben Uziel, who wrote an Aramaic translation (Targum) of the NEVI'IM *(Prophets, Bible)* (see *ILLUSTRATIONS TEXT A, #2; Text B, #2)* *[Tal.Meg.3a, B.B.134a, Av.Dr.Nat.14.1]*. *[Thus the Targum Yonatan on CHUMASH, it is said [Shem.Hag. 2.57b(114)], is in fact Targum Yerushalmi, and the author of what is now published as (a very sparse) Targum Yerushalmi in the CHUMASH is unknown. However, the author of what is now labelled as Targum Yonatan on the CHUMASH — is also unknown.]*

3770 10

The Jews sent a delegation to the emperor to protest against the extreme brutality of Archelaus. The emperor subsequently removed him and sent him to exile *[Tzem.Dav./Sed.Had./ Dor.Har.2.705]*.

Anarchy — which began at the beginning of Archelaus' rule (see 3761\1) — continued to spread. Arab gangs (taking revenge for Herod's brutality), small militia groups (of troops expelled from Herod's army years earlier), and some corrupt Roman commanders, all plundered and killed throughout the country *[Tzem.Dav./Sed.Had./Dor.Har.2. 696-7, 700, 713]*.

With the removal of Archelaus, the Romans annexed Yehuda *(Judea)*, and installed their own governor *(procurator)*. Antipas, the brother of Archelaus (son of Herod I) ruled in a limited way, in the Northern part of Yehuda *(see maps)* *[Sed.Had.]*.

The Tzedukim became politically active at around this time, and they established their own 'sanhedrin' *[Tal.San.52b/ Dor.Har.2.632-3]*.

3775 15

At around this time there was an unusual disturbance — with anti-Semitic overtones (see 3750\-11) — against the Jews of Bavel *(Babylonia)*, as a result of the activities of two Jewish (private) militia leaders. Much of the local (rural) Jewish population had to relocate and concentrate around the larger cities *[Dor.Har.1.121-125, 126]*.

3781 21

Agrippa I (the grandson of Herod I) — who spent much of his time in Rome — had been imprisoned for displaying a lack of loyalty to the ruling emperor. He was released with the ascent of a new emperor to the throne, and he was sent to Yehuda *(Judea)* to rule in a limited way. He became popular with the people, accepted by the TANNA'IM, and he broadened his original (territorial) mandate to rule. He became so popular that some people almost idolized him *[Tal.Sot. 41a, Ket.17a, Pes.107b, Rashbam/Mid.Rab.Vay.3.5/ Tos.Y.T.Bik. 3.4/Yuch.5.158/Tzem.Dav./Sed.Had.]*.

The position of Kohen Gadol had long been used as a source of revenue for the powers that be (see 3668\-93, 3680\-81), and some of the Roman authorities began increasing their personal profit by appointing Kohanim to this post as often as a few times a year (instead of having them serve their full lifetime as required). Many of the ex-kohanim gedolim who were corrupt formed their own strong-arm groups (even militia). This contributed further to the anarchy, lawlessness, and violence that plagued Yehuda *(Judea)* (see 3761\1, 3770\10) *[Tal.Yom.9a, Tos./ Dor.Har.2.713, 715; 3.6]*.

3789 — 29

The Sanhedrin moved from the Beit Hamikdash. With all the lawlessness, violence, and bloodshed — much of it stemming from the ex-kohanim gedolim (see 3781\21) — the Sanhedrin despairingly decided to withdraw from a center of activities it could not control. They left their respected place in the Beit Hamikdash, and moved to the Holy Mount. This automatically downgraded the spiritual and legal status of all the courts. (It was no longer possible to pass the death sentence.) *[Tal. A.Z.8b, Shab.15a, R.H.31a-b, Rashi/Tzem.Dav./Sed.Had./Dor. Har.2.719; 3.112]*.

R.Tzadok, one of the TANNA'IM, perceived an emerging national calamity and began to fast daily, until 3829 *[Tal.Git. 56a-b/Zoh.1.149]*.

3790 — 30

Jesus — according to Christian tradition (see 3671\-90) — had criticized the strong arm-groups of ex-kohanim gedolim controlling the Beit Hamikdash (see 3781\21). They captured him and delivered to him to the Romans, who later killed him on charges of treason.

3800 — 40

The emperor Caligula insisted on being worshipped, and ordered that a statue of him be placed everywhere — including in the Beit Hamikdash, and in synagogues in Egypt (see 3610\-151). The Jews of Yehuda *(Judea)* expressed their religious objection, and Petronius, the (Roman) Syrian high commissioner, convinced that this was not an expression of rebellion, sought to have the order withdrawn. Caligula was furious, but died before his cruel reply reached Yehuda *(Judea)*. Philo(n), the Jewish philosopher from Alexandria *(Egypt)*, made representations in Rome on this issue *[Yuch.5.158-9/ Sed.Had./Dor.Har.3.25, 149]*.

3804 — 44

Agrippa II (the son of Agrippa I) became a very limited ruler in 3804, at a time when the Romans controlled Eretz Yehuda *(Judea)* through their governors *(procurators)*. He had some powers transferred to him from his uncle Herod II — a regional ruler. He collaborated with the Romans (see 3825\65), and aligned himself with some of the strong-arm groups of the ex-kohanim gedolim, as they had ways and means of collecting money (see 3781\21). This they shared with (Agrippa II and) the Roman procurators — in return for political considerations *[Tal.A.Z.55a/Tzem.Dav./Sed.Had./ Dor.Har.2.633; 3.8, 14-15]*.

3810 — 50

Rbn.Gamliel I (ben Shimon, ben Hillel) died.

R.Shimon ben Gamliel I succeeded his father as the Nassi *(President)* of the Sanhedrin, and R.Yochanan ben Zakkai was the Av *(Head)* Bet Din *[Tal.Shab.15a, Sot.47a/Rashi R.H.31b/Tzem/Dav./Sed.Had.2/Dor.Har.3.52]*.

Queen Helena and King Munbaz, from the vicinity of Bavel *(Babylonia, Persia)*, converted to JUDAISM and came to see Yerushalayim. They later made contributions to alleviate food shortages there *[Tal.B.B.11a/ Mid.Rab.Br.46.10/ Yuch.5.159-60/Sed.Had./Dor.Har.1.99-101]*.

The 'sanhedrin' of the Tzedukim was active at this time (see 3770\10) *[Dor.Har.2.632-3]*. The Kuthim *(Samaritans)* attacked Jews on their way to the Beit Hamikdash for the festivals *[Dor.Har.3.58]*.

3815 — 55

Anarchy was increasing in Eretz Yehuda *(Judea)*, and various political groups emerged. Some were hoping to restore peace and order, even if it meant living under tight Roman rule, provided the rule was honest and allowed for basic human and religious freedom. Others — such

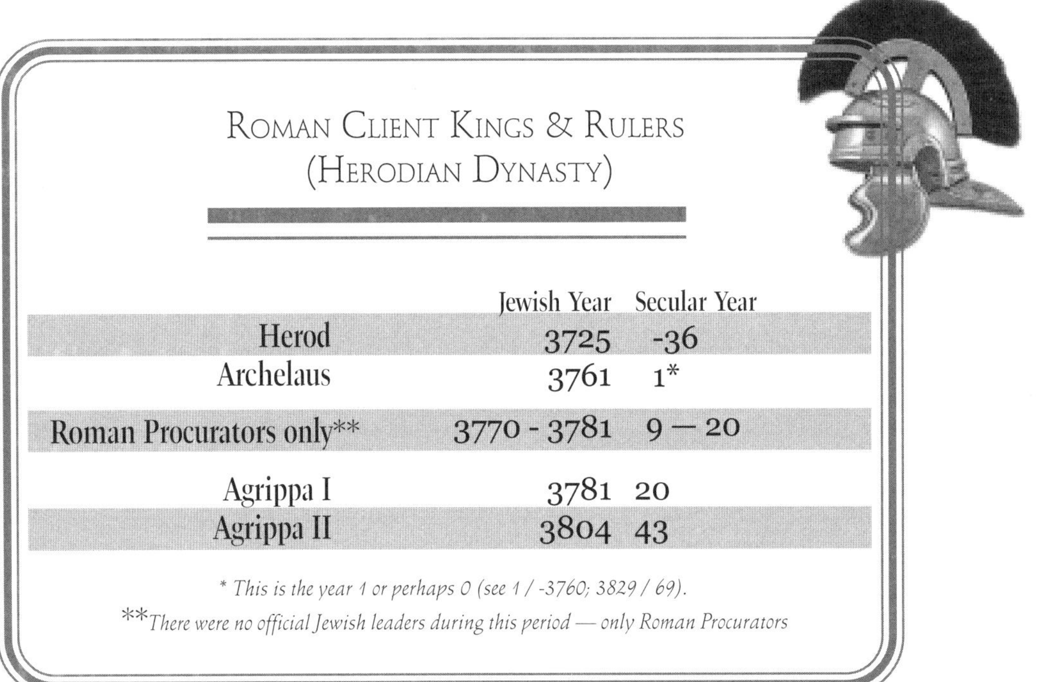

ROMAN CLIENT KINGS & RULERS (HERODIAN DYNASTY)

	Jewish Year	Secular Year
Herod	3725	-36
Archelaus	3761	1*
Roman Procurators only**	3770 - 3781	9 — 20
Agrippa I	3781	20
Agrippa II	3804	43

** This is the year 1 or perhaps 0 (see 1 / -3760; 3829 / 69).*

***There were no official Jewish leaders during this period — only Roman Procurators*

as Agrippa II, ex-kohanim gedolim, and the Tzedukim — were seeking wealth and power. Others — radical nationalists — sought to fight the Romans and expel them from Eretz Yehuda. There were many factions and splinter groups within these general categories *[Dor.Har.2.715; 3.3, 10, 17, 34-5]*.

3825 ≈ 65

A rebellion by most Jewish factions (see 3815\55) against the ruling Roman procurator *(governor)* — who was exceptionally greedy, brutal and dishonest — was sparked by his disdainful handling of an incident concerning the harassment by (local) non-Jews of a synagogue in Caesaria. Agrippa II (a collaborator, see 3804\44) disagreed with the findings of an independent Roman investigator, who had concluded that this uprising was directed only against this individual (the procurator) and not against the Roman empire. Agrippa II insisted that the procurator retain his position (which suited his own power maneuvers) *[Dor. Har.3.14-15, 19, 149]*.

Most of the Jews were so outraged that they took to the streets of Yerushalayim and forced Agrippa II to flee with the procurator. Agrippa II — and some power groups — then attempted to have the Syrian high commissioner intervene, on the grounds that this was certainly a rebellion against Rome. They eventually succeeded, after some radical kohanim rejected a sacrifice sent by a Roman official. Roman legions together with the troops of Agrippa II marched on Yerushalayim. They had to withdraw after a bloody battle, and the radical nationalists then proclaimed Yerushalayim a "free" city *[Tal.Git.56a/Sed. Had./Dor.Har.3.20-1, 25-8]*.

Factional infighting increased in Yerushalayim. Those who were hoping for a return to peaceful law and order — under the Romans — despaired when the Romans aligned themselves with Agrippa II and his corrupt and lawless power groups; whilst the defeat of Roman legions at the gates of Yerushalayim encouraged the radicals to believe that they could ultimately succeed in militarily driving out the Romans *[Tal. Av.Dr.Nat.4.5/Dor.Har.3.35]*.

Emperor Nero sent a massive army, under Vespasian and his son Titus, to restore Roman authority *[Tzem.Dav./ Sed.Had.]*. Total anarchy reigned in Yehuda *(Judea)*, and Jews were being killed by the local non-Jewish population *[Tal.Toseph.Git.3.14/Dor.Har.3.28, 141-2]*.

3826 ≈ 66

Vespasian arrived in Yehuda to reassert Roman authority.

Yosef ben Mattityahu (Josephus) was a close friend of Agrippa II, who in turn was an old acquaintance of Nero and Vespasian. He had ma neuvered himself into an important military position — in the northern part of Yehuda *(Judea)* — from which R.Shimon ben Gamliel I (unsuccessfully) sought to have him removed, because of this allegiance with Agrippa II and the Romans. He surrendered to the Romans not long after Vespasian commenced his military campaign in the north, and he subsequently travelled with them, recording the battles and the destruction of Yehuda *(Judea)*, Yerushalayim, and the Beit Hamikdash, from inside the Roman camp *[Tzem.Dav./Sed.Had./Dor.Har.1.43; 3.1, 10, 12, 15(7), 39, 179]*.

3827 ≈ 67

With the fall of the surrounding country to Vespasian's army, the infighting and power struggles in Yerushalayim turned into open and bloody civil war, with factions fighting other factions (see 3815\55), even though they may have shared similar goals. Groups of militia set fire to the vast food storage facilities — which had contained enough to last for years — and some groups also formed an internal siege — not letting anyone out. A number of groups (some say) even minted their own coins, each (separately) claiming a 'free' state, under their own leader *[Tal.Git.56a/Mid.Rab.Eych. 1.31/Tzem.Dav./Sed.Had./Dor.Har.3.33-5]*.
Many Jews from all over Yehuda *(Judea)*, who had come to the Beit Hamikdash for Pesach, were caught in the siege and could not return home *[Dor.Har.3.80]*. R.Shimon ben Gamliel I died during the siege, possibly a targeted fatality of the civil war *(see 3826\66)* [See Appendix C] *[Mrsha.Sot.49a/ Dor.Har.3.179]*.

3828 ≈ 68

R.Yochanan ben Zakkai — the last disciple of Hillel — escaped from the internal siege of Yerushalayim (see 3827\67), and from an imminent forced confrontation with the Romans. He personally negotiated an agreement with Vespasian to allow the continuance of the studies of the Sanhedrin in Yavneh — under R.Gamliel II (son of R.Shimon ben Gamliel I) as Nassi *(President)*. Vespasian returned to Rome — after the death of Nero — and Titus laid siege to Yerushalayim, causing serious hunger and disease in the overpopulated city (see 3827\67) *[Tal.Git.56a-b, Av.Dr.Nat.4.5;6.3;14.1/Mid.Rab.Eych.1.31/ Dor.Har.3.33-5, 61-3]*.

3829 ≈ 69

The 2nd Beit Hamikdash was destroyed.

All factions in Yerushalayim *(see 3827\67)* had no option but to (unite and) fight the Romans — which they did valiantly — despite their weak and starved condition *[Tal.Av.Dr.Nat. 6.3/Dor.Har.3.38]*. (A Roman historian *(Dio Cassius)* recorded that Titus was wounded during the fighting, and that some Roman soldiers deserted (to the Jewish side) because they did not believe they could conquer Yerushalayim).

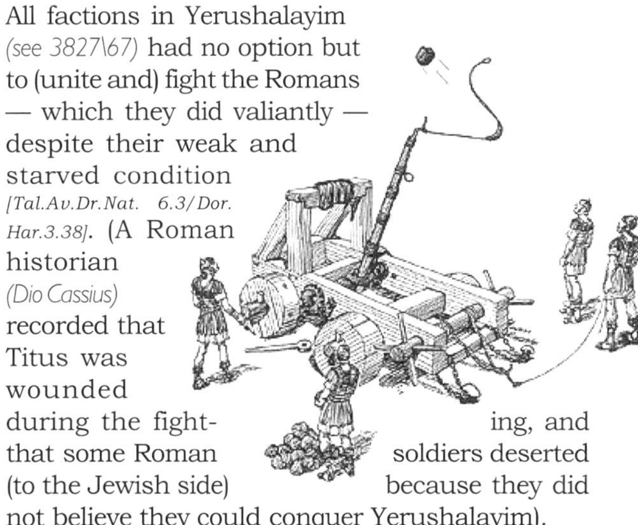

On the 17th Tammuz the walls in Yerushalayim were penetrated, and the Romans advanced with difficulty, until they reached the Beit Hamikdash and set fire in it, on the 9th Av 3829. The western wall was all that remained of the structure, and the Romans took many of the holy utensils to Rome (see 4215\455) *[Tos.A.Z.9b/Mmn.Hak.L'Yad]*.
Vast numbers of Jews (over one million recorded) died — in the battle, from hunger, and from disease *[Tal.Tan.28b/Tzem. Dav./Sed.Had./Dor.Har.3.80]*.
Some say that the second Beit Hamikdash was destroyed in 3828 *[Rashi A.Z.9b, Erch.12b]*. (The secular date usually given for the destruction is 70 (3830\70). This one year difference could be accounted for by an adjustment based on the naming of the Jewish year 1. See 1\-3760)

[3829\69 is continued in chapter 9.]

Chapter 9

The Talmudic Era — The Mishna

Section III

Chapter 9

The Talmudic Era – The Mishna

Jewish Year		Secular Year
3834	R.Yochanan ben Zakkai died.	74
3846	Sanhedrin moved from place to place, under R.Gamliel II.	86
3893	Betar fell, and "Bar Kochba's" revolt ended in tragedy.	133
3894	Judaism was banned, and R.Akiva was imprisoned.	134
3949	**R.YEHUDA HANASSI COMPLETED THE MISHNA AROUND THIS TIME.**	**189**

Section III
RIVERS OF BABYLON, CONVULSIONS IN YEHUDA (JUDEA)

Chapter 9

The Talmudic Era — The Mishna

The ninth Chapter (Tekufa) in Jewish history focuses on the struggle for Jewish survival in Eretz Yisrael under Roman conquest, and the development of the Mishna as a written body of Jewish law.

The chapter ends when the Mishna was completed. Later scholars accepted a total adherence to the Mishna, and would not consider overruling any of its statements.

[3829\69 is continued from chapter 8c.]

3829 69

Almost 100,000 Jews were taken to Rome as captives, and many of them were forced to fight wild animals in the Roman coliseums. The Romans were selective in their punishment of the various (factional) leaders of the revolution — some were brutally killed, whilst others were imprisoned — indicating that they were aware that some of the leaders had been drawn into direct conflict — against their better judgement (see 3815\55, 3827\67, Av 3829\69) *[Mid.Rab.Eych. 1.45/ Tzem.Dav./ Sed.Had./Dor.Har.3.37-8, 48, 75, 80, 138]*.

Some Jewish fortresses resisted the Romans for one or two years after the destruction of the Beit Hamikdash (see 3831\71), while roaming bands of legionnaires killed many people of all ages in those parts of Yehuda *(Judea)* already conquered. This random killing decreased after many prisoners had been gathered — including some of the factional leaders — and taken to Rome specifically for Titus' triumphant march, (approximately nine months after the destruction of the Beit Hamikdash) *[Tal.Git.55b/ Dor.Har.3.37-8, 128, 138-9]*.

The Sanhedrin continued studies (as an academy) in Yavneh (see 3828\68) under the leadership of R.Gamliel II (ben Shimon ben Gamliel I) as Nassi *(President)*. R.Yochanan ben Zakkai, the Av Bet Din (see 3810\50), came only periodically to Yavneh (for sessions) because he had moved elsewhere — some say in order not to cast his shadow over the leadership of the (young) inheritor of the dynasty of his mentor Hillel (see 3810\50, 3828\68) *[Tal.San.32b, Git.56b, Av.Dr.Nat.14.6/Toseph. Mas.2.2/ Mid.Rab.Koh.7.7.2/Sed.Had.2/Dor.Har.3.24, 61-71]*.

3830 70

R.Yehoshua (ben Chananyah) travelled to Rome (see 3841\81, 3856\96) to negotiate for the release of Jewish captives there. He had many dialogues with the emperor and his daughter (see 3856\96) *[Tal.Git.58a, Hor.10a, Shab.119a, Tan.7a, Chag.5b, Chul.59b-60a, Bech.8b/ Tzem.Dav./ Sed.Had.2/ Dor.Har.3.48-50]*.

Josephus wrote his history under the auspices of his friends in Rome, and in consultation with Titus — and Agrippa II, whom the Romans had appointed ruler in the Galil (which was considered separate to Yehuda) *(see maps)*. He presented events from (and as a justification of) his political perspective (see 3826\66); these (slanted) writings could not have served to decrease Roman anger and cruelty to the Jews whom he portrayed in a negative light *[Tal.Kid.110a/ Mmn.Hil.Kid. Hach.4.4, Ish.13.16, Shmitt.7.9/ Dor.Har.1.15(9), 19-20(12), 70(35), 193-4; 2.693; 3.38-40, 85, 129]*.

The groups of ex-kohanim gedolim (see 3804\44, 3815\55) ceased to exist, and the remnants of the Herodian Dynasty (including Agrippa II) eventually disappeared through intermarriage with the Romans *[Dor.Har.3.38-40, 51, 354]*.

3831 71

The Romans had conquered all of Yehuda (see 3829\69) (except for the fortress of Massada, which fell later), order was restored, and the Roman troops stopped their wanton killings (see 3829\69). Vespasian issued a decree — through his governor — that all properties left by Jews killed in the war were to be transferred to the emperor. The rightful heirs had great difficulties in subsequently securing their family estates and rightful inheritances from Roman officers *[Tal.Shab. 116a-b, Git.55b, Yer.Git.5.7/ Dor.Har.3.127-136, 140]*.

3834 74

R.Yochanan ben Zakkai died.

R.Yochanan ben Zakkai made adjustments to adapt Jewish life without a Beit Hamikdash, to the laws of the Torah, *[Tal. R.H.29b-31b, Suk.41a/ Dor.Har.3.122-125]*, and when he died — approximately five years after the destruction of the Beit Hamikdash — R.Yehoshua ben Chananyah (one of his five most prominent disciples) succeeded him as the Av Bet Din *[Tal.Av.2.9, B.K.74b, Nid.7b, Yer.San.1.2(6a)/ Sed.Had.1,2/ Dor.Har.3.203, 210-11, 277(24), 307-11, 337]*.

R.Eliezer ben Hyrkanos, another of the five most prominent disciples, (who married Iyma Shalum, a sister of R.Gamliel II), was author of the Midrash called Pirkei D'Rebbi Eliezer. He became the Chacham *(supreme scholar)* of the Sanhedrin-Academy, a special appointment made out of respect and in recognition of his brilliant scholarship *[Tal.Av.2.8, Bert.-end, Shab.116a, Mak.27a, Git.83a, Nid.7b, Yer.San.1.2(6a)/Mid.Rab.Sh.Hsh.1.3.1/ Pir.Dr.El.1, 2/ Tzem.Dav./Sed.Had./Dor.Har.3.210-11, 291-6]*.

When the three leaders of the Sanhedrin-Academy, R.Gamliel II (Nassi), R.Yehoshua (Av), and R.Eliezer, gathered in Yavneh (after the death of R.Yochanan ben Zakkai), they began regular sessions of the Sanhedrin in order to consolidate and clarify the laws of Torah, by ruling on the differences of opinion that had arisen (primarily since Hillel and Shamai) *[Tal. Shab.138b, Eruv.13b, Yer.Yev.1.6(9a)/Av.Dr.Nat.14.6/Toseph.Ed.1.1/Mid.Rab.Koh.7.7.2/ Tos.B.K.94b/ Dor.Har.3.203-5, 210-12, 284].*

R.Eliezer ben Yaakov I, who was known for his precise articulation, taught the accurate measurements of the Beit Hamikdash as part of the Mishna, and R.Shimon Ish HaMitzpeh taught the order of the Yom Kippur services (in the Beit Hamikdash) *[Tal.Yom.14b, Yev.49b, Yer.Yom.2.2(12a)/Dor.Har. 3.82, 181-2].*

3835 — 75

The Jews began to regain some stability, but antagonistic Christians — many of whom belonged to Jewish Christian sects (see 3893\133) and therefore mingled freely among Jews — continuously "informed" the Romans on Jewish progress. The Roman governor, Tirentius Rufus I, attempted to capture and kill R.Gamliel II (as a descendant of King David, see 3769\9). He also plowed-under the whole city of Yerushalayim, and the site of the Beit Hamikdash, on the 9th of Av *[Tal.Tan. 29a, Yer.Tan.4.5(25a)/Dor.Har.3.71-78].*

3836 — 76

As part of the Torah clarification process of Yavneh (see 3834\74) Shimon HaPakuli (a TANNA) was entrusted by R.Gamliel II to standardize the eighteen blessings of Shmona Esrei (from the various versions existing then) (see 3426\-335). R.Gamliel II also wanted a nineteenth blessing added as a prayer against the "informers" (see 3835\75, 3877\117, 3894\134), and Shmuel HaKatan (TANNA) composed it *[See Appendix C] [Tal.Ber.28b, Meg.18a/ Mmn.Hil.Tfi.2.1., Kes.Mish/Dor.Har.3.145-7, 172-3].*

3841 — 81

Titus became emperor after the reign of his father Vespasian, and he ruled in a surprisingly mild manner. R.Eliezer, R.Yehoshua and R.Gamliel II travelled to Rome to appeal for better conditions in Eretz Yisrael. However, Titus died while they were there, and he was succeeded by his cruel brother Domitian, who drafted a decree to exterminate the Jews. He killed many Romans, but a powerful political acquaintance the Jewish leaders had made in Rome, gave his life to have the decree against the Jews suspended *[Tal.Yer. San. 7.13(41a)Mid.Rab.Dev.2.24,Yal.Teh.754/Dor.Har. 3.275-8].*

When these three leaders returned from Rome, having witnessed the ruthlessness of the new emperor — particularly towards Romans suspected of being friendly to Jews — they maintained a low profile in Yavneh, and did not call any more full sessions of the Sanhedrin-Academy, but decided on all matters amongst the three of them, (after discussions in which R.Eliezer was respected as the supreme scholar, see 3834\74) *[Tal.Git.83a/Mid.Rab. Sh.Hsh.1.3.1/ Dor. Har.3.280-1, 283].*

Onkelus II — who had converted to Judaism after his uncle Titus died — was a disciple of R.Yehoshua (ben Chananyah) and R.Eliezer (ben Hyrkanos). He translated the CHUMASH *(Bible, the five Books of Torah)* into Aramaic based on their teachings *(see ILLUSTRATIONS TEXT A, #3)*. This was not Onkelus I who was a disciple of Hillel and Shamai. *[Tal.Meg.3a, Git.56b-57a, A.Z.11a, B.B.99a/Zoh. Vay.73a/ Rashi Kid.49a/Tzem.Dav./Sed. Had.2].*

3842 — 82

R.Eliezer had unilaterally ruled on matters of law, without the prior consent of the other two leaders (see 3841\81), and when he refused to withdraw these judgments — claiming that the others were insincere in their opposition — he was (completely) removed from the circle of scholars by R.Gamliel II, with the support of the others. R.Gamliel II and R.Yehoshua thus remained the sole leaders of the Sanhedrin-Academy affairs, and without the respected presence of R.Eliezer, friction emerged between them (see 3844\84) *[Tal.B.M.59b, Git.83a, Nid.7b, Yad.4.3, Yer.M.K. 3.1(10b), Korb.HaE./Dor.Har.3.293-6, 302].*

3844 — 84

R.Gamliel II had dealt harshly with R.Yehoshua in a confrontation about the setting of the month, a function usually reserved for the Av Bet Din — which was R.Yehoshua, who was also an accomplished astronomer. More than a year later (at a public lecture) he was again harsh in his treatment of R.Yehoshua. Those present were most upset and offended, and insisted that R.Gamliel be replaced as Nassi *(President)* *[Tal.R.H.2.7, 2.8, Bert., 2.9, Rashi 31b, Ber.27b-28a, Yer.Ber.4.1(32b)/Dor.Har. 3.302-6, 318, 324, 330].*

Seventy two scholars were present when

R.Elazar ben Azaryah — a young wealthy Kohen, and direct descendant of Ezra — was appointed Nassi to replace R.Gamliel II. They took this rare opportunity of a full session of the Sanhedrin-Academy (see 3841\81) to decide on many issues. That session is referred to (in the Talmud) as "*that day*". R.Elazar ben Azaryah later shared the leadership with R.Gamliel II, who was re-instated *[Tal.Ber.27b-28a, Zev.11b, Yad.3.5, 4.3/Dor.Har.3.319-24, 327, 338; 5.177]*.

3846 — 86

Sanhedrin moved from place to place, under R.Gamliel II.

The Romans increased their troops in Eretz Yisrael and continued to persecute the Jews there — particularly the scholarly leadership, which had to leave Yavneh and move to Usha in the Galil (see 3830\70). Even while there, R.Gamliel II and his court were under pressure. They moved to Teverya *(Tiberius)*, and then wandered from place to place *[Tal.Shab. 115a, Eruv.101b/ Toseph.Ter.2.13, San.2.6/Sifri Dev.33.3/ Dor.Har.3.344, 346-8]*.

3856 — 96

The ruthless emperor Domitian (see 3841\81) had died, and R.Gamliel II, R.Yehoshua, R.Elazar ben Azaryah and R.Akiva travelled to Rome in the month of Tishrei to make representations to the new emperor (the ageing Nerva), for some relief and freedom from persecution (see 3841\81, 3846\86). Some say he subsequently removed the heavy tax being paid by the Jews of Eretz Yisrael *[Tal.Mak.24a, Suk.23a, 41b/Dor. Har.3.349-50]*.

When the delegation of four elders arrived in Rome, they were asked many questions about their religion by the many Romans who were fascinated by Judaism — particularly after Domitian's virulent anti-Jewishness (see 3841\81) — and they were now free to inquire about it. R.Yehoshua was very well known for his brilliant dialogue in these matters (see 3830\70). Upon their return to Eretz Yisrael, they moved the Sanhedrin-Academy back from the Galil, to Yavneh (see 3846\86) *[Tal.A.Z.54b, R.H.31a-b, Chag.5b, Eruv.53b, D.E.5/Sifri 33.3/Dor.Har.3 349-52]*.

3858 — 98

The emperor Nerva died, and was succeeded by Trajan who harbored a deep hatred for the Jews — his father had headed a legion in the action that led to the destruction of the Beit Hamikdash. The Sanhedrin-Academy at Yavneh was abandoned once again, and the elders settled (privately) in Lod, where they called days of fast and prayer over the persecutions they were suffering *[Tal.R.H.18b, 31a-b, Yer.Tan.2.12(12b), Betz.3.5/Toseph.Pes.3.9, 10.8/ Dor.Har. 3.352-62]*.

3864 — 104

The Roman persecutions (see 3858\98) had become so extreme that R.Akiva had to travel to Bavel *(Babylonia)* to fulfil one of the functions of the Sanhedrin (setting of the new month). R.Gamliel II died in Lod, and R.Elazar ben Azaryah continued in the role of Nassi *(President)* (see 3844\84) in Lod *[Tal.M.K.27a, B.M.59b, Yev.122a, San.32b, Yad.4.3, Yer.Ber.3.1(22a)/Dor.Har.3.358-66]*.

3867 — 107

R.Elazar ben Azaryah presided over a minor regeneration of the Sanhedrin-Academy (in Lod), where there were as many as 32 scholars attending sessions. However, the Roman persecutions (see 3858\98) forced them to leave and go to the Galil once again (see 3856\96), and even there they were forced to stay in hiding, in Tzippori *(Sepphoris)* *[Toseph. Kel.B.B.2, Mik.8.6, Meg.2.2/Dor.Har.3.363, 367-71]*.

3874 — 114

The Greek population of Egypt, (part of the Roman Empire), took advantage of Trajan's hatred for the Jews (see 3858\98) — which was by now magnified because the Jews of Bavel *(Babylonia)* (see 3610\-151) had just fought in the defense of Babylonia against his invading forces. The Greeks conducted a massive massacre in Alexandria (see 3610\151) which almost wiped out the entire community of over 1,000,000 Jews (see 3454\-307) while the Romans stood by and watched *[Tal.Suk. 51b, Yer.Suk.5.1(23a)/Dor.Har.3.393-404, 407-8]*.

The Jews of Cyprus and of Cyrene *(North Africa, west of Egypt)* were well organized, and managed to fight off similar attacks by large local Greek populations, also under Roman control. The Greeks then attempted to incite the Romans by claiming that these incidents of Jewish battle were proof that the Jews were staging an international uprising. Their claims were not heeded by Trajan, who was in Babylonia, and occupied with extending the Roman Empire to its greatest size ever (see 3877\117) *[Tal.Yer.Suk.5.1(23a)/Dor.Har.3.409-11, 414]*.

3877 — 117

When Trajan died, Hadrian became emperor, and chose a relatively peaceful path for the Roman Empire. He withdrew from the furthest conquests, and even granted permission to the Jews to rebuild the Beit Hamikdash. At the request of the surviving Jews of Egypt (see 3874\114), he brought to trial those responsible for the massacre in 3874, punished them with death, and ordered that the Jewish section of Alexandria be rebuilt *[Mid.Rab.Br.64.10/Dor.Har.3.397-99, 404, 406-7, 426-32; 4.574-5]*.

Hadrian had the governor of Eretz Yisrael (his political enemy) killed, and some Jewish prisoners were subsequently released *[Tal.Tan.18b, Sma.8.(47b)/Dor.Har.3.421, 423, 431]*.

However, Hadrian had a change of heart after he was advised of the "dangers" of allowing the Jews too much independence; this advice given (some say) by "informers" (see 3836\76). Permission for rebuilding the Beit Hamikdash was withdrawn *[Mid.Rab. Br.64.10/Dor.Har.3.428(3), 432]*.

3878 — 118

R.Elazar ben Azaryah had died, and the Sanhedrin-Academy came out of hiding (see 3867\107) and was established in Usha once again (see 3846\86), under the leadership of the elderly R.Yehoshua as Av Bet Din (see 3834\74), and R.Shimon ben Gamliel II as the "son of the Nassi" — without the full responsibilities of Nassi (see 3550\-211) *[Tal. R.H.31a-b, Toseph.Eruv.5.6/Mid.Rab.Br.64.10/Dor.Har.3.425-6, 432; 4.433-9, 445-47]*.

3880 — 120

When R.Yehoshua died (see 3878\118), a skilled voice was lost in debating the early Christians (see 3830\70, 3835\75, 3856\96). The elderly R.Akiva (who had lost thousands of disciples in a plague) succeeded him as Av Bet Din in Usha (see 3878\118) *[Tal.Chag.5b, Yev.62b, Ket.62b-63a, Ned.50a, Eruv.53b, Smach.8.(47b)/Dor.Har.4.439-42, 574, 746, 763]*.

3883 — 123

Hadrian's change of heart towards the Jews in Eretz Yisrael (see 3877\117) became complete. He issued a decree against some major religious observances — Shabbat, Mila, Mikva — and revealed plans to rebuild Yerushalayim as a secular city (under another name), complete with a temple for worshipping Jupiter on the place of the Beit Hamikdash (see 3835\75). He also began deporting — to North Africa — some of the (millions of) Jews who were still living in Eretz Yisrael (see 3438\-323) *[Tal. Yev.72a, Rashi, B.B.60b, Rashi, Me'i.17a, Toseph.Ber.2.13/ Mid.Rab.Eych.4.5/Dor.Har.4.577-84]*.

Many Jews took to hiding (underground) in order to keep those now forbidden religious observances, and in those instances when the Romans came to seek them out, they resisted with armed combat. This resistance developed into a revolution, with Jewish guerrilla forces making sporadic surprise attacks on the Roman legions. The regular meetings of the Sanhedrin-Academy ceased during these difficult times *[Dor.Har. 4.577-90, 603, 717, 744]*.

3887 — 127

The Jewish revolt, against the harsh decrees of the Romans, grew from its initial stages (see 3883\123), and the Jews had built underground trenches and tunnels from which they staged successful attacks on the Roman legions. Under the leadership of *Shimon Bar Kuziba* — *[as he is named in the Talmud]*; or now commonly known as BAR KOCHBA; and also as *Shimon Bar Kochab* *[Otz.HaMid.p433.1]* — the attacks became increasingly audacious and successful, and eventually they emerged into the open battle fields. 'BAR KOCHBA' then led the well prepared forces — which included Jewish volunteers from other countries — to conquer cities from the Romans. He eventually conquered Yerushalayim, declared it a 'free city', and coins were minted for the new Jewish 'free state'. R.Akiva (see 3880\120) then indicated that 'BAR KOCHBA' appeared to be the Mashiach (*Messiah*) *[Tal.Yev.72a, Rashi, San.93b, B.K.97b, Rashi, Yer.Mas.Shen.1.1(4a), Yer.Tan. 4.5(24a)/ Mid.Rab.Eych.2.4/Dor.Har.4.580, 589-93, 600-3, 613-4, 620-1, 626-8, 632(85)]*.

3893 — 133

Betar fell and "BAR KOCHBA's" revolt ended in tragedy.

'BAR KOCHBA' (Bar Kuziba) ruled in Yerushalayim

for over two years, and the Romans had to send troop reinforcements to recapture Eretz Yisrael. They did not engage in open battle with the apparently more powerful army of 'BAR KOCHBA', but began staging sporadic attacks on outlying posts and towns *[Tal.San.93b, 97b/Rashi Yev.72a/Dor.Har.4.585, 590-4, 601, 613-4]*.

R.Yishmael and R.Shimon ben HaSgan were captured and killed, in the outlying areas. They were the first two of the ASARA HARUGEI MALCHUT *(Ten Martyrs)* *[see Appendix C]*, and upon hearing of their death, R.Akiva realized that 'BAR KOCHBA' was not the Mashiach *(Messiah)* (see 3387\127). The Romans continued their partial conquests, capturing many fortresses and towns (Hadrian himself came to supervise the conquest) until they had retaken much of Eretz Yisrael. They then captured Yerushalayim, and 'BAR KOCHBA' and his forces withdrew to Betar (a fortress near Yerushalayim). The Romans laid siege to Betar, but the battle continued for over three years amid death and starvation. 'BAR KOCHBA' was killed in the battle, together with vast numbers of Jews (580,000). Many more died of starvation, and many more were killed when Betar fell, on the 9th Av (Tisha B'Av). The Romans then attacked and destroyed many cities, killing indiscriminately. Jews were forbidden to bury their dead (see 3908\148) and many were captured and sold as slaves *[Tal. Tan.26b, Git.57a, Av.Dr.Nat.38.3 (and Smach. 8(47a) per Dor.Har. 3.177-181), Yer.Tan.4.5/ Mid.Rab.Eych.2.4/ Tos.Y.T.Chal.4.10/Mmn.Hil.Tan.5.3/Dor.Har.4. 590-4, 596, 598, 602-3, 613-4, 616- 8, 634-41, 710]*.

The Jews were expelled from Yerushalayim (see 4374\614), and the Romans also began to discriminate against the Jewish Christian sects (see 3835\75), which contributed to their decline *[Dor.Har.4.664-5]*.

3894 — 134

Judaism was banned, and R.Akiva was imprisoned.

The Romans forbade all Jewish religious practices in a decree of SHMAD, and the very elderly R.Akiva was imprisoned on the 5th Tishrei. He remained imprisoned for an extended time, and his close disciple, R.Yochanan HaSandlar (a descendant of king David) asked him questions through the cell window. A short while later, tortures and death were instituted as punishments for keeping the religion; many Jews were discovered keeping these practices in hiding. (The Romans were receiving information from Jewish informers, see also 3836\76.) R.Akiva was killed, as was R.Yishmael (see 3893\133), who composed the Mechilta *(a form of commentary on the CHUMASH (Bible))*. Other TANNA'IM were killed, some of them later became known as the ASARA HARUGEI MALCHUT *(Ten Martyrs)* *[See Appendix C]*. The massacres (see 3893\133) continued (under Tinius Rufus II) until the total destruction of Yehuda *(Judea)*. The country lay waste and all hope was lost. Jewish life in Eretz Yisrael did not recover for nearly 2,000 years *[Tal.Ber.61b, Pes.112a, Yev.108b, San.12a, 14a, A.Z.18a, Smach.8(47b), Yer.Pea.7.1(31b), Yer.Chag.2.1(9b), Yer.Sot. 5.5(25a), Yev.12.5(68b)/Tur B.Y.O.C.580/Dor.Har.3.76-78; 4.628, 635-46, 658, 660-2, 664, 670-2, 679, 710, 793; 5.283]*.

The great TANNA'IM of Yavneh (see 3867\107) had all died or been killed, and many of the younger TANNA'IM (disciples of R.Akiva) fled from Eretz Yisrael *[see Appendix C, note 2]*, and settled in Bavel *(Babylonia)*, where R.Yehuda ben Beteira was (in Netzivin) *[Tal.Ber.63b, San.14a, Sot.25a, Yer.San.8.6(42b-43a), Chag.3.1(15a-b), Yev.62b, 108b/Sif.Dev.80(Re.28)/ Dor.Har.4.635, 672-83, 691, 696(20), 710]*.

3903 — 143

Hadrian had died, and when some Jews of Eretz Yisrael emerged from their hiding to return to normal life, some Romans interpreted this as a new uprising, and the Jews were massacred once again. Some time later the TANNA'IM began to return from Bavel *(Babylonia)* (see 3894\134), and they met in small gatherings, without re-establishing the formal Sanhedrin-Academy (see 3883\123) *[Tal.Yer.Chag. 3.1 (15a)/ Mid.Rab.Sh.Hsh.2.Sam.3(15a)/ Dor.Har.4.704-10, 712-13]*.

3908 — 148

The Romans, confident that the Jews were no longer a threat, began a program of public construction, and normalization of commercial life in Eretz Yisrael. The TANNA'IM had cautiously called sessions of the Sanhedrin-Academy (in Usha) in the Galil (see 3903\143), in order to reconstruct the process of clarification of the Torah laws that had previously been commenced in Yavneh (see 3834\74); and a group of Babylonian TANNA'IM settled in Eretz Yisrael. They were headed by R.Natan, the son of the (Babylonian) REISH GALUTA *(EXILARCH)*, and (some say) the basic author of Avot D'Reb Natan *[Tal.Shab.33b/ Tos.B.K.94b/Sed.Had.2.R.Natan/Dor.Har.4.717-8, 722, 724, 727, 735, 768, 823-4, 829]*.

R.Shimon ben Yochai was sent to Rome to plead to the emperor (Antoninus Pius), and to have the bans on Jewish observances officially lifted. He had succeeded in his original mission, and permission was also granted, on the 15th Av, to bury all the dead (see 3893\133). The TANNA'IM gathered (temporarily) in Yavneh and instituted another blessing in Birkat HaMazon *(Grace After Meals)* (see 2928\-833), in commemoration *[Tal.Ber. 48b, Yer.Ber. 7.1(52a), Tan.31a, Me'i.17a-b/ Mid.Rab.Br.76.8/ Dor.Har. 4.736, 738-40, 743-4]*.

The Sanhedrin-Academy was subsequently established, with caution, in Shepharam *(in the Galil, near Usha)*. R.Natan was the Av Bet Din, R.Meir was the Chacham (*supreme scholar*, see 3834\74), and R.Shimon ben Gamliel II (who was appointed later) was the Nassi, (see 3878\118), although (some say) he was not active, or in regular attendance, for security reasons — the Romans could have interpreted his (inherited) presidency, as a measure of self-rule and rebellion. The Academy continued the process of clarification of the law, and organized the body of law into sections (called Masechtot) *[Tal.R.H.31a-b, B.M.86a, Eruv.13b, Hor.13b, Kel.30.4/ Igg.R.Sher.G./ Dor.Har. 4.744, 764-8, 770-3, 775, 718-22; 5.81, 89-90, 105]*.

3909 — 149

R.Yehuda (Bar Ila'i) had praised the Romans (in private) for their renewal of commercial life in Eretz Yisrael (see 3908\148), and R.Shimon (Bar Yochai) had countered that they had only done so out of self interest. Word of this private discussion reached the Roman authorities, who declared that R.Yehuda should be honored with leadership, R.Shimon killed, and R.Yossi (ben Chalafta) (author of *Seder Olam*), who had been present at the conversation, but made no comment, should be placed under "house arrest" in Tzippori *(Sepphoris)* *[Tal.Shab.33b]*.

This presented the Jews with an opportunity to make an officially sanctioned public appointment of leadership (see 3908\148). Thus R.Yehuda was appointed to the position of *Rosh HaMedabrim* *("chairman")* of the Sanhedrin-Academy. R.Meir — also called R.Nehorai, considered the outstanding scholar (see 3908\ 148) — had lost popularity with the people, (some say) because he retained a respectful relationship with Elisha (ben Avuya) — also called Acher — his former mentor, who had become an informer *(see 3894\134)*. R.Shimon (Bar Yochai) escaped and hid in a cave — for 13 years — with his son, R.Elazar (who wrote many PIYUTIM under the name of R.Elazar HaKalir *[Tos.Chag.13a/ Hag.Mmn. Hil.Tef.6.3/ Rosh Ber.5:21]*). *[Tal.Shab.33b, Rashi, Eruv.13a, Chul.142a, Yer.Shvi. 9.1(25a-b), Yer.M.K.3.1(10-b), Yer. Chag. 2.1 (9b)/ Mid. Rab. Br.79.6/ Tashbatz.1.33/ Dor.Har. 4.640-1, 769-73, 775-80, 791-5]*.

Berurya, the learned daughter of R.Chanina ben Tradyon *[see Appendix C]*, was the wife of R.Meir *[Tal.Pes.62b, Toseph.Kel.(B.K.)4.9, Kel.(B.M.)1.3]*.

3925 — 165

The leaders of the Sanhedrin-Academy (R.Shimon ben Gamliel II, R.Natan, R.Meir, and R.Yehuda, see 3908\148, 3909\149) had all died; the Romans — who were fighting defensive battles against the Parthians *(the rulers of Persia, which included Babylonia)* — brought their legions through Eretz Yisrael, and once again began to suppress Jewish life. The Jews appealed, the oppressions were lifted, and (some say) R.Yehuda ben R.Shimon (ben Gamliel II) met the new emperor *(Marcus Aurelius Antoninus)*, who agreed to the full and formal restoration of the Sanhedrin-Academy, with an official active Nassi (see 3908\148). R.Yehuda thus succeeded his father, and became known as R.Yehuda HaNassi — the first officially active Nassi since the decrees of Hadrian (see 3883\123). He maintained a friendship with the benevolent and intellectual emperor *[Tal.Sot. 49b/ Igg.R.Sher.Gaon/ Rashi B.M.33b/ Dor.Har. 4.809-17, 818-9]*.

R.Yehuda HaNassi — who was also called *Rebbi* — continued the clarification of Torah laws (see 3908\148), most of which had already been clarified and organized by his father and R.Natan *[see Tal.Suk.19b, Rashi]*. He consolidated the various opinions into one body of law, the Mishna, which — when edited in its specific succinct style of syntax — became established as the final word of Jewish law *[Tal.B.M.86a, Kel.30.4, Tif.Yis.Bo./ Igg.R.Sher.G./ Tos.B.K.94b/ Dor.Har. 4.817-824, 829, 858-9, 866, 870, 873, 877; 5.79, 89-90, 105]*.

Although the Jews of Eretz Yisrael were suffering continuous persecutions from the Romans, many scholars came from Bavel *(Babylonia)*, and strengthened the Jewish community and the Sanhedrin-Academy there (and even established their own synagogue(s) in Eretz Yisrael, see 4098\338) *[Tal.Git.55b, 58b-59a, Suk.20a, Ket.103b, Chul.86a, Yer.Ber.5.1(37b)/ Dor.Har. 5.282-5, 289-91, 403]*.

3949 — 189

R.Yehuda HaNassi completed the Mishna at around this time.

R.Yehuda HaNassi died around 3949 — some say he died around 3979 *[This is generally due to calculations based on the assumption that Rav "settled" — rather than "visited" — in Bavel (Babylonia), during the* *lifetime of R.Yehuda HaNassi (see 3979\219). An associated error crept into Igg.R.Sher.G., which says he settled in Bavel during the life of R.Yehuda HaNassi instead of during the life of R.Yehuda Nessia [Dor.Har.5.215].]* He had completed the final editing of the Mishna before he died *(See ILLUSTRATIONS, TEXT C, D, E, F, #1)* *[Sef.Hak.q. Tzem.Dav. 3975/ Dor.Har.4.687; 5.1-3, 32-33, 307-8]*.

He was succeeded by his son, R.Gamliel III, as the Nassi of the Sanhedrin-Academy. He died after a short while, and was in turn succeeded by his son, R.Yehuda Nessia I after a short while *[Tal.Ket.103b/ Dor.Har.5.20-1]*.

Many of the colleagues and major disciples of R.Yehuda HaNassi — some of whom were still considered TANNA'IM — continued the process of clarification of the law, in the Sanhedrin-Academy, by teaching (orally) the total body of the Mishna law and explaining the exact meanings of sections of the Mishna. Many explanations and clarifications were recorded in the form of *Beraitot* (primarily by R.Chiya, R.Oshiya, Bar Kappara), *Sifra* and *Sifri* (by Rav); and additional material was recorded in the Tosephta *[Tal.Eruv.92a, Rashi, Nid.62b, Tos., Git.76b, Rashi, A.Z.35b, Rashi, 36a Tos.(Asher), 37a, Mak.21b, Rashi, Chul.141a-b, Rashi, Yer.Shab.1.2(6a)/Igg.R.Sher.G./Rashi Eruv.19a (ben Zakkai), Betz 29a (Tanna DeBey Shmuel), B.M.48a (UBadka Levi)/Rashbam B.B.52b-end/Tos.B.K.94b/ Dor.Har.5.19-20, 34-36, 40-46, 48-9, 53, 55-57, 60, 77-79, 114, 126-136, 145-6, 153, 181, 253, 256]*.

Chapter 10

The Talmudic Era — The Gemara

Section III

Chapter 10

The Talmudic Era — The Gemara

Jewish Year		Secular Year
3979	**Rav Left Eretz Yisrael and settled in Bavel (Babylonia).**	**219**
4007	Shmuel was the Talmudic authority in Bavel.	247
4014	R.Yochanan was the leading Talmudic authority.	254
4050	R.Huna was the leading Talmudic authority.	290
4058	R.Yehuda was the leading Talmudic authority.	298
4060	R.Chisda was the leading Talmudic authority.	300
4069	Rabbah was the leading Talmudic authority.	309
4081	R.Yosef was the leading Talmudic authority.	321
4085	Abayey was the leading Talmudic authority.	325
4098	Rava was the leading Talmudic authority.	338
4119	**Hillel II (who established the calendar) became Nassi.**	**359**
4152	R.Ashi was the leading Talmudic authority.	392
4187	**R.Ashi died after the compilation of the Gemara.**	427
4235	**THE TALMUD WAS COMPLETE, WHEN RAVINA II DIED.**	**475**

Section III

RIVERS OF BABYLON,
CONVULSIONS IN YEHUDA (JUDEA)

Chapter 10

The Talmudic Era — The Gemara

The tenth Chapter (Tekufa) in Jewish history focuses on the growth of the Talmud, as the Gemara explains, interprets, and extends the words of the Mishna.

The Chapter ends when the Gemara was concluded.

3979 ≈ 219

Rav Left Eretz Yisrael and settled in Bavel.

The attacks and persecutions on the Jews of Eretz Yisrael (see 3925\165) intensified at this time, and it was dangerous for Jews to be in certain areas *[Tal.Git.16b-17a, Shab.145b-end, Yer.Dma.6.1(25a), A.Z.2.8(16a)/ Dor. Har.5.284-8]*.

Rav (Abba Aricha, *"the tall Abba"*), was an elderly disciple of R.Yehuda HaNassi who had — on previous occasions — returned to Bavel *(Babylonia, Persia)*, his country of origin *[Tal.Git.59a, Yer.Sot.9.2(41a)/ Dor.Har.5.213-5, 223, 403]*. In 3979 he returned once again, and settled in Neharde'a — the major center of the Jews in Bavel — where R.Shila was head of the Babylonian scholars (since the death of R.Yehuda HaNassi) *[Rashi Chul.137b/Igg.R.Sher.G. per Dor.Har.5 212-5/Tzem.Dav./Sed.Had./Dor.Har.4.701; 5.165, 167-8, 182-4, 403, 411]*.

3986 ≈ 226

Bavel *(Babylonia)* was part of the Persian Empire ruled by the (centuries-old) Parthian government, which was overthrown — and replaced by the Sassanids — at this time. They allowed the rulers of the local provinces *(satrapies)* to continue (see 4311\551), under the central rule of a supreme king, but the introduction of their religion caused conflict with the local Jewish population in Bavel (see 4229\469, 4234\474) *[Tal.Git.16b-17a/Dor.Har.5.64, 409, 450; 6.101]*.

3990 ≈ 230

R.Yehuda Nessia I had died, and his son R.Gamliel IV did not succeed in maintaining the Sanhedrin-Academy in the greatness anticipated of the dynastic leadership of descendants of Hillel. R.Gamliel IV did not live long, and he was succeeded by his young son, R.Yehuda Nessia II. For centuries, the Sanhedrin-Academy had asserted a leadership role among the Jews of Eretz Yisrael, as well as the Jews of Bavel *(Babylonia, Persia)*, through the direct contact it maintained with the political leader of Babylonian Jewry, the Reish Galuta *(Exilarch)*. With decline of the leadership of the Nassi, a number of scholars of the Mishna established their own metivta *(Yeshiva)* (see 3995\335) and continued their teaching and studies in different locations, which further eroded the centrality of the role of the Nassi and the Sanhedrin-Academy. Eventually the Nassi in Eretz Yisrael retained a similar status — amongst Jews — to that of the Reish Galuta in Bavel which was not essentially a role of scholarship, but of political leadership, (and the various incumbents were only mentioned in the Talmud by name, if they were also scholars in their own right). The Reish Galuta — (invariably) a descendant from the House of King David — was a (political) leader formally recognized by the Babylonian government, who even wore the golden sash *(Kamara)* of official *(Persian)* office *[Tal.San.5a, Rashi, 11b, Hor.13b-end, Rashi Yer.Meg.1.5(7b), Pn.Mosh., Chal.4.4(25b-end)/ Mmn.Hil.San.4.12/Dor.Har.5. 23-4, 28-9, 34-39, 48, 210-12, 222-3, 228, 251, 253-254, 258, 332-5, 346-7, 406]*.

When R.Shila had died (see 3979\219), Rav left Neharde'a, leaving the succession there in favor of Shmuel — his colleague's son — and he settled in Sura, where (in the absence of any major scholarship there) he established a metivta *(Yeshiva)*, began teaching the Mishna there, and eventually rejuvenated Jewish life in the whole vicinity. Shmuel (later) established a formal metivta in Neharde'a *[Igg.R.Sher.G./Dor.Har.5.35 210-12, 222-5, 403, 407]*.

Those scholars who were teaching the Mishna were called Amora'im. There were many living in various generations who had the same names (see 4112\352, 4191\431), although this chronological identification is not indicated when they are quoted or mentioned in the Talmud *[Sed.Had.2/Dor.Har.5. 210, 228, 283, 582, 588; 6.12, 89-91]*.

3995 ≈ 235

R.Yochanan established a metivta in Teverya (the old city of *Tiberius*, which was in a different location to the 'new' *Tiberius*) *[Tal.Yer.Meg.1.1(2b)/Dor.Har.5.72]*.

A few years later, after R.Oshiya — who had established a metivta in Kessarin *(Caesaria)* — had died, the metivta of his disciple R.Yochanan became the central focal point of Talmud study in Eretz Yisrael (see 4007\247, 4050\290), and eventually even for Bavel *(Babylonia, Persia)* (see 4014\254) *[Tal.Eruv.53a, B.K.117a/Tzem.Dav./Sed.Had./Dor.Har.5. 212, 253-5, 257-8, 298, 309-10, 329]*.

The metivta *(Yeshiva)* acquired a special form. The scholars and the disciples of the Metivta would gather two times in the year — in the month of Elul, and the month of Adar, which were called Yarchei Kalla — each scholar identifying with his Metivta. (Other Yeshivot existed, but they were not central focal points as were the "official" metivtot.) There was a specific protocol of titles and seating (in rows) in the official Metivta to facilitate the range of calibre. This was a continuation of the original system of the Sanhedrin — which had originated with the seventy elders accompanying Moshe — and which (after the destruction of the second Beit Hamikdash) had evolved into the Sanhedrin-Academy (see 3829\69 3990\230). In the METIVTOT of Bavel *(Babylonia, Persia)*, the REISH GALUTA *(Exilarch)* took part in some of the ceremonial proceedings (even though his position was essentially political, see 3990\ 230) *[Tal.B.K.117a, Rashi, Meg.28b, Chul.137b/Mmn. Hil.San.1.3,7, 4.1/Dor.Har.6. 156(2), 159, 192-3, 216-9, 221-3, 267-8]*.

4007 ≈ 247

Shmuel was the Talmudic authority in Bavel.

Rav — who lived to very old age — had died by this time, and no one was appointed to succeed him as the ROSH METIVTA of Sura (see 3990\230). Shmuel — the ROSH METIVTA in Neharde'a (see 3990\230) — became the leading Talmudic authority in Bavel *(Babylonia, Persia)*, while R.Yochanan was the leading authority in Eretz Yisrael (see 3995\235), where once again, there were many persecutions of the Jews *[Tal.Chul.95b/Igg.R.Sher.G./Sed.Had2/Dor.Har.5.222(24), 272, 315-7, 403, 408-11, 416, 481]*.

4014 ≈ 254

R.Yochanan was the leading Talmudic authority.

When Shmuel had died in Neharde'a (see 4007\247), no one was appointed to succeed him (see 4018\258, 4019\259, 4058\298) for a few years, and at this stage (the elderly) R.Yochanan (in Eretz Yisrael) was the senior Talmudic authority (see 3995\235, 4050\290) *[Igg.R.Sher.G./Dor.Har.5.222(24), 408, 410-11]*.

4018 ≈ 258

R.Huna had become ROSH METIVTA of Sura (see 4007\247) and the central Talmudic authority passed from Neharde'a to Sura (see 4014\254, 4019\259, 4050\290) *[Dor.Har.5.411-2, 416-7, 481]*.

4019 ≈ 259

The Jewish community in Neharde'a was destroyed (see 3979\219, 4014\254) by the invading cavalry and archers of Pappa bar Nazer, a (corrupt) military commander from Tadmor *(Palmyra, N.Syria)*, when he invaded cities in Bavel *(Babylonia, Persia)* — in support of Rome — during a war between the Persians and the Romans *[Tal.Ket.51b, Rashi/Igg.R.Sher.G. /Dor.Har.4.702-3; 5.250, 411, 413-4]*.
R.Yehuda (bar Yechezk'el) established a METIVTA (see 3995\235) in Pumpedita *(Bavel)* at around this time (see 4798\1038) *[Dor.Har.5.417]*.

4020 ≈ 260

Twelve thousand Jews were killed — in one of the Persian empire possessions — when Shabur I (king of Bavel) suppressed a revolt in which they had participated *[Tal.M.K.26a, Rashi]*.

4046 ≈ 286

The Roman emperor Diocletian divided the Roman Empire into two separate empires (east and west), and he took control of the eastern part which included Eretz Yisrael. He was in Eretz Yisrael when he declared that all wines were to be made sacramental except for Jewish wine. The Kuthim *(Samaritans)* did not choose to classify themselves as Jews, and consequently they were further removed *(see 3426\-335)* from being accepted as Jews in Halacha *[Tal.Yer.A.Z.5.4(33b-end)/Dor.Har.5.340(46), 341, 344]*.

4050 ≈ 290

R.Huna was the leading Talmudic authority.

R.Yochanan died at around this time — at the approximate age of 110 years — a few years after R.Shimon ben Lakish (Reish Lakish) his brother-in-law, who had shared some of the leadership of his METIVTA. His METIVTA had been the central place of Talmud study in Eretz Yisrael (see 3995\235). All the explanations of the Mishna that he taught were from what he had heard directly from R.Yehuda HaNassi — when he was a young orphan boy — and then from his disciples. All this became the basis of the Talmud Yerushalmi (sometimes called the Talmud of Eretz Yisrael, see 4111\351) *[Tal.Yom.82b, Kid.31b, B.K.117a, Rashi, Chul.137b/Dor.Har.5.299,302-3,306-11,321-3]*. Some of the AMORA'IM quoted in Talmud Yerushalmi were of a later period — there are instances where R.Yochanan is directly quoted in Bavli *[Tal.Ber.4b]* and quoted (on the same point) in the name of a disciple in Yerushalmi *[Tal.Yeru.Ber.30b]* — which confirms the opinions that the Yerushalmi was still developing after R.Yochanan (see 4111\351).
R.Ami succeeded R.Yochanan, yet the central focal point of Talmud study moved to Bavel *(Babylonia, Persia)*, to R.Huna (see 4018\258) — who was the recognized leader of all scholars — and later to R.Yehuda (bar Yechezk'el) (see 4058\298) *[Tal.Git.59b, Kid.70a, Yer.Chag.1.8(7a)/Dor.Har.5.332, 348, 417, 421]*.
The AMORA'IM of Bavel and Eretz Yisrael were always in close contact and consultation (see 4058\

298) *[Tal.Chul.95b/Dor.Har.5.358, 467-70, 472]*.

4058 — 298

R.Yehuda was the leading Talmudic authority.

R.Huna had died in Bavel and was buried in Eretz Yisrael. Although he was succeeded by R.Chisda as Rosh Metivta of Sura, and the "Metivta of Neharde'a" (see 4019\259) had been re-established in Mechuza by R.Nachman I; the Talmudic authority passed over to R.Yehuda (bar Yechezk'el) in Pumpedita (see 4018\258, 4019\259) *[Tal.Kid.70a, Rashi, M.K.25a, Rashi/Igg.R.Sher.G./Dor.Har.5.222, 269, 416(90), 417-9, 421, 481]*.

4060 — 300

R.Chisda was the leading Talmudic authority.

R.Yehuda (bar Yechezk'el) had died and Rabbah (bar Nachmani) (reluctantly) succeeded him as Rosh Metivta of Pumpedita — with his colleague R.Yosef stepping aside — but the central Talmudic authority in Bavel *(Babylonia, Persia)* passed over to R.Chisda in Sura (see 4058\298) *[Tal. Hor.14a, Ket.42b/Igg.R.Sher.G./Sed.Had./Dor.Har.5.222, 347-8, 421, 432-4, 481]*.

R.Yehuda Nessia II died — after R.Yehuda bar Yechezk'el in Bavel — and he was succeeded by his son R.Gamliel V as Nassi in Eretz Yisrael (see 3990\230) *[Tal.M.K.17a /Dor.Har.5.347-8]*.

The elderly R.Ami — who had yet been a disciple of R.Oshiya — was the last of the famous Roshei Metivta in Eretz Yisrael (see 4050\290). He had to relocate the Metivta from Teverya *(Tiberius)* to Kessarin *(Caesaria)* (see 3995\235) because of Roman persecutions. He was (later) consulted by scholars of Bavel on difficult questions. R.Avahu was the senior scholar in Kessarin *(Caesaria)* after R.Ami died *[Tal.Git.63b, Chul.86b/Sed.Had./Dor.Har.5.315-7, 349-52, 355-6, 373(62)]*.

4069 — 309

Rabbah was the leading Talmudic authority.

R.Chisda died and no one succeeded him as the Rosh Metivta of Sura. The central Talmudic authority passed to Rabbah in Pumpedita *[Dor.Har.5.222, 434, 481]*.

R.Gamliel V had died (previously) and was succeeded as Nassi by his son R.Yehuda Nessia III *[Tal.M.K.22b-end /Dor.Har.5.347-8, 393-4]*.

4073 — 313

The Roman emperor Constantine I, who established his capital in the Greek city of Byzantium — re-named Constantinople *(then later Istanbul)* — gave formal recognition to Christianity. He later had churches built on their *(Christian)* holy places in Eretz Yisrael.

4081 — 321

R.Yosef was the leading Talmudic authority.

Rabbah (bar Nachmani) died in seclusion — he had been slandered to the government, and was being sought. He was succeeded by his (blind) colleague R.Yosef (see 4060\300) as Rosh Metivta of Pumpedita, and as the central Talmudic authority *[Tal.B.M.86a, Hor.14a Eruv.54a, Rashi/Igg.R.Sher.G. /Dor.Har.5.306, 432-4, 437-8, 440-1, 447, 454-5]*.

4085 — 325

Abayey was the leading Talmudic authority.

The persecutions increased in Eretz Yisrael (see 4073\313) and many of the Amora'im had fled to Bavel *(Babylonia, Persia)* from where many of them had originally come *(see 3925\165)* *[Dor.Har.5. 356, 390-1, 435, 455, 467-9, 473-4]*.

R.Yosef had died in 4083 and some two years later — from among four candidates, two of whom were from Eretz Yisrael — Abayey was selected to succeed him *[Tal.Hor.14a /Igg.R.Sher.G./Dor.Har.5.432-3, 437-8, 440-1, 447, 461, 473-74]*.

The Christian council of Nicaea *(N.W. Turkey)*, called by Constantine I (see 4073\313), passed measures to distance Christianity from Judaism, and to limit the rights of Jews in the Roman empire. They considered disengaging the date of Easter from the Jewish date of Pesach *(Passover)* — which was dependent on the monthly decision of the Jewish Beit Din as to when the new moon would inaugurate the month, see 4121\361. The council also discussed transferring the Sabbath from Saturday to Sunday. Some twenty years earlier, a council in Elvira *(Spain)* had forbidden Christians from keeping the Jewish Shabbat, eating with Jews, or marrying them.

4098 — 338

Rava was the leading Talmudic authority.

Abayey had died by this time and Rava succeeded him as Rosh Metivta of Pumpedita. He moved the Metivta — and the central Talmudic authority — to Mechuza (see 4058\298) (where he had always lived) *[Igg.R.Sher.G./Dor.Har.5.367, 437-8, 441, 494-6]*. A number of Roman Jews (see 4715\955) had settled in Mechuza, and established their own synagogue (see 3925\165) *[Tal.Meg.26b, Rashi/Dor.Har.5.496]*.

4111 ≈ 351

Gallus, the (corrupt) Roman ruler in the east (see 4046\286), and his general (Ursicinus) waged a military campaign — distinct with the flavor of a religious crusade (see 4073\313, 4085\325) — against the Jewish community in Eretz Yisrael, claiming to be suppressing a rebellion (which was in fact raging elsewhere, in the Western Roman Empire). The Romans attacked and devastated cities, and also prohibited the Sanhedrin to maintain the system of establishing and aligning the Jewish calendar on a monthly basis (by means of the reportage of a visual sighting of a new moon) (see 4121\361) *[Tal.San.12a, Rashi/Yer.Meg.3.1(24a), Yev.16.3(82b)/Sed.Had./Dor.Har.5.286, 356, 366, 373-6, 378; 6.124-6]*.

Most of the AMORA'IM of Eretz Yisrael fled to Bavel *(Babylonia, Persia)*. The basics of the Talmud of Eretz Yisrael, which came to be called the Talmud Yerushalmi, thus remained in its rudimentary form, as it was being taught — and memorized — from the time of the end of the Mishna until this time (see 4050\290, 4152\392)). *[Rashi Sot.49b/Hag.M.Hil.Shab.23.4/Pn.Mosh.Yer.Br.58. "VeRoshei Chadashim"/Dor.Har.5.373, 376, 390-1, 467, 472, 526-9, 535-6; 6.103, 106-137]*.

The Talmud Yerushalmi is in Hebrew and Western Aramaic *(Galilean-Syrian)*. The Talmud Bavli — in the Eastern Aramaic language — had also taken form by this stage (see 4152\392), based on the explanations of the Mishna that the early AMORA'IM had conveyed, and the further comments of later AMORA'IM — particularly through the clarification undertaken by Abayey and Rava *(Haviyot D'Abayey VeRava)* of the laws — in Pumpedita, then the place of central Talmudic authority (see 4069\309) *[Tal.B.B.134a, Rashi, Suk.28a, Rashi/Rashi Kid.13a (Linkutinhu)/ Igg.R.Sher.G./ Dor.Har.5.473, 480-4, 489-90, 493-4, 500, 519, 551-62; 6.116-9, 123]*.

Some names of AMORA'IM appear differently in Talmud Bavli than they do in Talmud Yerushalmi. For example: R.Abba - R.Ba; R.Yossi - R.Assi; R.Yehuda - R.Yudan; R.Avun - R.Bun *[Dor.Har.5.459, 461-2. 6.114]*.

4112 ≈ 352

Rava died (see 4098\338), and although there was no central Talmudic authority for a while (see 4131\371), R.Nachman II (bar Yitzchak) succeeded him as ROSH METIVTA of Pumpedita. R.Pappa — and R.Huna Brei D.R.Yehoshua — opened a METIVTA in the vicinity of Sura, in Naresh, and many AMORA'IM were also studying in Neharde'a (where Ameimar had a central role), and in Pum Nahara (where R.Kahana had a central role). *[There were as many as six AMORA'IM at various times named R.Kahana (see 3990\230).]* *[Sed.Had.2/Dor.Har.5.367, 373, 381, 481, 496-9, 505, 515-9, 228]*.

4119 ≈ 359

Hillel II (organizer of the continuous calendar) became Nassi.

R.Yehuda Nessia III had died and was succeeded by his son Hillel II as Nassi of the Jewish remnants *(see 4111\351)* in Eretz Yisrael. He recognized that continuity of the monthly Jewish calendar-fixing system was in serious jeopardy *(see 4085\325, 4111\351)*, so he (later) established the (continuous) Jewish calendar system (see 4121\361) *[Ramban Sefer HaZechut Git.34b (Rif.18a) / Dor.Har.5.348, 393-8]*.

4121 ≈ 361

Julian (called *the Apostate* because he rejected Christianity, see 4073\313) became the new emperor of Rome. In his letters to the Jews he encouraged the rebuilding of Beit Hamikdash. During the 20-month respite of Julian's reign (see 4111\351, 4123\363), Hillel II, who was the Nassi in Eretz Yisrael, called a session of the Talmud scholars and established the continuous calendar system that no longer required the monthly moon sightings (see 4119\359). This system is still in use today. *[Mmn.Kid.Hach.5.3/Ramban Sefer HaZechut Git.34b (Rif.18a)/Dor.Har.5.24-5, 375-6, 348, 393-8]*.

4123 ≈ 363

After the death of Emperor Julian *(see 4121\361)* at battle — possibly from natural causes — the Christians attacked the Jews of Eretz Yisrael.

4131 ≈ 371

R.Pappa died, and R.Ashi became ROSH METIVTA in the vicinity of Sura (see 4112\352) at Mata Mechassiya. He developed wider recognition and achieved the emergence of a (reconstituted) central Talmudic authority *(see 4112\352, 4152\392)* *[Igg.R.Sher.G. per Dor.Har. 5.497-8/Dor.Har.5.498-9, 505, 507, 549, 593-4, 599]*.

4152 ≈ 392

R.Ashi was the leading Talmudic authority.

R.Ashi, together with his colleague *[Eruv.63a]* Ravina I — and all the senior AMORA'IM — undertook the editing of the Talmud of Bavel; gathering all the organized statements on the Mishna of the earlier AMORA'IM (see 4111\351); adding to them the clarifications of the later AMORA'IM — and comparing them with the earlier Talmud Yerushalmi of Eretz Yisrael (see 4111\351) *[Hag..M.Hil Shab..23.4]*; deciding on issues that were still unresolved; and presenting it in a comprehensible logical style. This was called the Gemara (see 4187\427) *[Tal.B.M.86a/Rif Eruv.-end(on Tal. Eruv.35b)/ Dor.Har.5.526, 535-6, 539, 549-50, 551-62, 573, 589, 591; 6.102-13, 116-9, 123, 127]*.

Two sections (Sedarim) of the Mishna were not organized with the Gemara statements of AMORA'IM (*Seder Zera'im, Seder Taharot*) — most of their concepts are explained elsewhere *[Rashi Suk.14a (Mishum Hachi)]*.

4155 ≈ 395

The Jews left Corinth *(Greece)* after the invasion of the Visigoths *(a people of the Germanic group called Barbarians, see 4215\455)* who came from the vicinity of present-day Sweden.

4174 ≈ 414

The Jews were expelled from Alexandria by the Christian authorities.

4178 ≈ 418

Many Jews of Minorca *(a Mediterranean island near Majorca)* were killed, and the rest — 540 — were subjected to FORCED BAPTISM.

4181 ≈ 421

Ravina I died *(see 4152\392)* *[Sed.Had./ Dor.Har.6.10, 85]*.

4187 ≈ 427

R.Ashi died after the compilation of the Gemara.

R.Ashi died after almost sixty years of leadership in Mata Mechassiya *(near Sura)*, during which time he presided over the complete compilation of the Gemara — the Talmud Bavli — into a final form (see 4152\392).

Many of the AMORA'IM in his METIVTA — the central Talmudic authority — also lived long lives, and those that were present at his deliberations were still called AMORA'IM, though some of them lived on for many years (see 4235\475).

Mareimar succeeded R.Ashi as the ROSH METIVTA — now in nearby Sura (although some scholars and students remained in Mata Mechassiya, see 4131\371) — and the AMORA'IM continued to add minor editorial material to the Gemara (see 4236\476, 4320\560) *[Igg.R.Sher.G./Dor.Har. 5.309, 498, 597-9, 600-2; 6.10, 19-20, 21-2, 64-5]*.

4189 ≈ 429

R.Gamliel VI had died, and the Roman emperor *(Theodosius II)* prohibited further raising of funds for the office of Nassi — the office effectively ceased to exist.

4191 ≈ 431

Mareimar died and was succeeded — as ROSH METIVTA of Sura — by R.Iddi (bar Avin, who was the second AMORA with exactly this name *[Sed.Had.4192/Dor.Har.6.89-91]* (*see 3990\230*)) *[Igg.R.Sher.G./ Dor.Har.5.598, 601; 6.7, 89-91]*.

4211 ≈ 451

R.Iddi (bar Avin) died and was succeeded by R.Nachman III (bar Huna) as ROSH METIVTA of Sura *[Igg.R.Sher.G./Dor.Har.5.598, 601; 6.7, 89-91]*.

4214 ≈ 454

R.Nachman III (bar Huna) had died, and the elderly Mar (Tivyumi) bar Rav Ashi succeeded him as ROSH METIVTA of Sura (at Mata Mechassiya) (see 4187\427) *[Tal.B.B.12b /Igg.R.Sher.G./ Dor.Har.5.598; 6.7, 93]*.

4215 ≈ 455

The king *(Yesdegerd II)* prohibited the Jews of Bavel *(Persia)* from keeping the Shabbat — among other decrees. He was later killed by a snake *[Igg.R.Sher.G. /Dor.Har.5.598; 6.89, 93]*.

The Vandals *(a people of the Germanic group called Barbarians (see 4155\395) who came from the vicinity of present-day Norway)* sacked Rome, looted, and (some say) took utensils of the Beit Hamikdash (see 3829\69, 5629\1869) to Africa, which they also conquered. This westward move of the Barbarians (see 4155\395) — which some say was caused by the advance of Attila the Hun and his hordes from the east — contributed to the fall of the Western Roman Empire, some twenty years later.

4227 ≈ 466

Mar (Tivyumi) bar Rav Ashi died on the 11th Tishrei *(Motza'ei Yom Kippur)*, and he was succeeded by Rabbah Tospha'a *[Igg.R.Sher.G./Dor.Har.5.598]*.

4229 ≈ 469

Three Jewish notables, R.Ameimar (bar Mar Yenuka), Huna (bar Mar Zutra) — the REISH GALUTA *(Exilarch)* — and R.Mesharshiya (bar Pekod), were all arrested in Bavel in Tevet, by orders of the king (Firuz "*Reshi'a*" — "the wicked" — who was the son of Yesdegerd, see 4215\455). R.Mesharshiya and Huna were killed on the 18th Tevet, and R.Ameimar was killed in Adar *[Tal.Chul.62b/Igg.R.Sher.G. /Dor.Har. 6.8, 73, 99-100]*.

4234 ≈ 474

Rabbah Tospha'a had died by this time, and he was succeeded as the ROSH METIVTA of Sura by Ravina II (R.Avina, nephew of Ravina I) *[Tal.Ket.100b/Igg.R.Sher.G./ Dor. Har.6.9, 13-14, 100-1]*.

All the synagogues were closed in the city of Babylon *(later called Baghdad, in Bavel-Babylonia, Persia)*, and many of the Jews — mostly children — were handed over to the priests (see 3986\226, 4229\469) *[Igg.R.Sher.G./Dor.Har.6.8, 22, 100-3]*. Some say these persecutions led to Jewish emigrations from Bavel to other places — to Arabia, Egypt, North Africa and (southern) Europe — (see 4285\525, 4397\637).

4235 ≈ 475

The Talmud was complete when Ravina II died.

Ravina II (R.Avina), the last of the AMORA'IM who had been part of R.Ashi's deliberations (see 4187\427), died on 13th Kislev very soon after Rabbah Tospha'a *[Tal.B.M.86a /Igg.R.Sher.G. per Dor.Har.6.7-9/ Sef.Hak.q.Sed.Had.4134 /Dor.Har.5.598, 602, 6.7-9, 15-7, 19, 22-3, 98]*.

The Talmud was complete at this stage *(see ILLUSTRATIONS, TEXT E, F)* (see 4187\427) and no further additions were made, except for the minimal editing undertaken by the (Rabbanan) SAVURAI (see 4236\476) *[Igg.R.Sher.G./Dor.Har.6.17, 19, 21-23]*.

The Talmud was henceforth not to be disputed, but logical deductions could be made from it — to cover new situations as they arise *[Mmn.Hakd.L'Yad]*.

Chapter 11

The Talmudic Academies of Bavel

Section III

Chapter 11

The Talmudic Academies of Bavel

Chapter 11a — The Rabbanan Savurai

Jewish Year		Secular Year
4311	Mar Zutra proclaimed Jewish self-rule in Babylonia.	551

Chapter 11b — The Ge'onim, and Arabic Dominion

Jewish Year		Secular Year
4349	The Metivta of Pumpedita was reconstituted.	589
4369	The Metivta of Sura was reconstituted.	609
4374	The Persians conquered Eretz Yisrael.	614
4374	**JEWS WERE ALLOWED TO RETURN TO YERUSHALAYIM.**	**614**
4389	The Byzantine (E.Roman) Empire reconquered Eretz Yisrael.	629
4396	R.Yitzchak was the last GAON of Neharde'a (Firuz-Shabur).	636
4397	**The Arabs conquered Eretz Yisrael.**	**637**
4405	One of the "TAKKANOT HAGE'ONIM" was enacted at this time.	645
4515	R.Acha(i) Gaon left Bavel (Iraq) for Eretz Yisrael.	755
4519	R.Yehudai became GAON of Sura.	759
4519	The Halachot Gedolot (BaHaG) was written at this time.	759
4548	Another of "TAKKANOT HAGE'ONIM" was enacted at this time.	788
4618	**R.Amram (who wrote the Siddur) became GAON of Sura.**	**858**
4688	Rbnu.Saadya was appointed GAON of Sura.	928
4715	"Four Captives" were ransomed at around this time.	955
4728	R.Sherira became GAON of Pumpedita.	968
4757	R.Hai became (the last) GAON of Pumpedita.	997
4798	**R.HAI GAON DIED, AND THE ACADEMIES OF BAVEL DECLINED.**	**1038**

Section III

RIVERS OF BABYLON

CONVULSIONS IN YEHUDA (JUDEA)

Chapter 11

The Talmudic Academies of Bavel

The eleventh Chapter in Jewish history covers the period of time where the scholars of Bavel *(Babylonia, Persia)* were the focal point of the Jewish people.

This era is viewed in two parts:

1) the Rabbanan SAVURAI, *whose status merged almost seamlessly with the last of the* AMORA'IM *in the Gemara;*

2) the GE'ONIM *who maintained the structure and activity of the* AMORA'IM *and Rabbanan* SAVURAI *— yet considered themselves remote disciples of those past, and thus focused mainly on verbatim review of the Talmud. It is however, a concealed period remembered primarily for the* TAKKANOT *(regulations) enacted by the* GE'ONIM (see chart).

This chapter concludes when this influential role of Bavel suffered a sharp decline.

Chapter 11a

The Rabbanan SAVURAI

4236 — 476

R.Yosef was the ROSH METIVTA of Pumpedita at this time. He and his colleagues were called the (Rabbanan) SAVURAI (the generation of Talmud scholars immediately following the Amora'im). They added very minor editorial (and Halacha) clarifications to the Gemara (see 4187\427, 4320\560) where necessary. (Some say that the word "Vehilcheta" precedes the opinion of the SAVURAI *[Rishonim]* and others say the word "Vehaidna" serves the same purpose *[Kasher, Sod HaIbbur, Tor.Shl. 13.p161a]*. Some say that the Hagaddah of Pesach was finalized at this time *[Hagaddah Shleima p 26—28]*.

This first generation of (Rabbanan) SAVURAI included R.Rechumai, R.Tachana, a Mar Zutra, and two by the name of R.Achai (one of whom is mentioned in the Talmud *[Zev.102b, see Tos. — **where the words "She'assa She'iltot" appear to have been added later**/ Dor.Har.6.56—9]* as were others {see 4300\540}) *[Igg.R.Sher.G./ Dor.Har.6.3, 6, 13, 21, 24—6, 28, 56—9]*.

Some say that it was this first generation of (Rabbanan) SAVURAI who actually recorded the Talmud in writing *[Dor.Har.6.25—6]*.

4246 — 486

The persecutions of the Jews of Bavel (see 4229\469, 4234\474) had lost their intensity when Firuz died. A new form of persecution arose under his successor, who endorsed a religious cult that all Babylonians were required to follow *[Dor.Har.6.8, 61—3]*.

4280 — 520

R.Yosef had died by this time, and R.Simuna succeeded him as ROSH METIVTA of Pumpedita. R.Eyna became ROSH METIVTA of Sura for a while (there having been no successor since the death of Ravina II and the persecutions of Firuz) (see 4300\540) *[Igg.R.Sher.G./ Dor.Har.6.24—7, 30—3, 34, 61, 158]*.

Huna (bar Kahana) — the REISH GALUTA *(Exilarch)* — and many of his family, had died shortly after he had a political disagreement with his father-in-law R.Chinena *(Exilarch)* — one of the leading Talmud scholars. Huna had punished the older scholar in a cruel demeaning way. Huna was survived by a posthumous son, who was (later) named Mar Zutra (I) (see 4298\538) *[Sed.Ol.Zut.q. Dor.Har.6.38—46/ Dor.Har.6.38—46]*.

4285 — 525

Yussuf — convert to Judaism — was king of the Hymarites, a nation in South Arabia *(Yemen)* which included many Jews (see 4234\474) and many more who had converted to JUDAISM. He was killed in battle when his country was conquered by the Ethiopians.

4295 — 535

Justinian I, emperor of the Byzantine *(E.Roman)* Empire, ordered the closing of all synagogues — among other repressive decrees — and although this was not fully carried out, there were forced conversions to Christianity.

At this stage (according to some) there was a decree against reciting the SHMA, consequently — as a 'camouflage' — it was inserted in the KEDUSHA *(prayer)* of MUSSAF *(prayer)*.

4298 — 538

Through the representations of the elderly R.Chinena (see 4280\520), his 15 year old grandson Mar Zutra (I) replaced the (temporary) REISH GALUTA *[Dor.Har.6.44]*.

4300 — 540

R.Simuna had died by this time, and he was succeeded as ROSH METIVTA of Pumpedita by R.Reva'i — who was from Rov — who is (yet) mentioned in the Talmud *[San.43a, Rbnu.Chananel]*.

R.Eyna (see 4280\520) had also died, but there was no successor to his position as ROSH METIVTA of Sura because of local persecutions *(see 4280\520, 4311\551)* *[Sef.Hak.q.Dor.Har.6.28/Igg.R.Sher.G./ Sed.Had./ Dor.Har.6.28—30, 34, 38—46, 106, 158]*.

4311 — 551

Mar Zutra proclaimed Jewish self-rule.

In a local persecution *(see 4300\540)*, R.Yitzchak, one of the great scholars of Bavel, was killed. The REISH GALUTA *(Mar Zutra (I), see 4298\538)* rebelled against the local rulers *(see 3986\226)*, and established a certain level of Jewish independence in his area *(see 4318\558)* *[Sef.Hak.q.Dor.Har.6.28/Sed.Ol.Zut.q.Dor.Har.6.38—46/ Igg.R.Sher.G./ Sed.Had./ Dor.Har.6.28—30, 34, 38—46]*.

4318 ≈ 558

The Babylonian *(Persian)* forces overpowered the forces of Mar Zutra (I), after seven years of Jewish self government. Mar Zutra (I) was hanged — together with his elderly grandfather R.Chinena — in the city of Mechuza *(a suburb of the capital, Ctesiphon)*, and the Jews of Bavel suffered increasing persecutions (see 4320\560). A son was born to Mar Zutra (I) at the time he was killed, and he was named Mar Zutra (II) *[Sed.Ol.Zut.q.Dor.Har.6.38—46/ Dor.Har.6.38—46]*.

4320 ≈ 560

R.Reva'i (see 4300\540) had died at a very advanced age, and because of local persecutions (see 4246\486, 4318\558) the METIVTA of Pumpedita was later transferred to Firuz-Shabur *(in the vicinity of Neharde'a)* (see 4349\589).
The Talmud scholars of this specific period — the last of the (Rabbanan) SAVURAI, wich included R.Giza and R.Sama (some say R.Huna and R.Dimi Surgo) — made very minor editorial adjustments to the final version of the Gemara (such as placing subheadings from the Mishna, where the Gemara begins a new subject) (see 4187\427, 4236\476). No new additions — or deletions — were made in their time, nor editorial adjustments, and it was accepted that no such changes were to be made after them. Some minor variations were later erroneously made by copier scribes, particularly in the time of the GE'ONIM (see 4349\589), whose explanations on the Talmud were also in Aramaic and were thus sometimes (somewhat confusingly) recorded in the margins of the text by their disciples (see 4519\759). *[Sed.Tan.VeAm.q. Dor.Har. 6.3, 21, 30, 35, 48—9/Igg.R.Sher.G./ Mmn.Hil.Mal.VeLov.15.2/Sh.Mkbtzt. B.M.13b(48b), 15b(55b)/ Dor.Har.6.28—35, 36—8, 44—6, 55, 138—46, 166, 169, 198, 200, 227.]*
Some say the Rabbanan SAVURAI also compiled the smaller secondary sections, MASECHTOT KETANOT, of the Talmud — *Sofrim, Smachot, Kalla,* and so on, currently printed at the end of *Seder Nezikin* in standard versions of the Talmud — from the sayings of TANNA'IM and AMORA'IM *[Dor.Har.6.38]*.

Chapter 11b
The GE'ONIM & Arabic Dominion

4336 ≈ 576

500 Jews of Clermont-Ferrand *(France)* were subjected to FORCED BAPTISM, and the remainder fled (see 4342\582).

4342 ≈ 582

The Frankish king (Chilperic I) forced many Jews to become Christians (see 4336\576), but most of them remained secretly Jewish.

4349 ≈ 589

The METIVTA of Pumpedita was reconstituted by R.Chanan.

The persecution of Jews in Bavel (see 4318\558) had lessened, and R.Chanan (from Ishkiya) returned to Pumpedita (see 4320\560), and he reconstituted the METIVTA there, although the METIVTA at Firuz-Shabur remained (more) active, under R.Maari Surgo (the son of R.Dimi, see 4320\560). This ushered in the era of the GE'ONIM.
The "GAON" was the head of a Yeshiva in Bavel (ROSH METIVTA) — an official position and title (see 3995\235) that was usually conferred to an elderly and suitable candidate *[Igg.R.Sher.G./ Dor.Har.6.35—6, 45—6, 54, 164, 166—7, 218]*. Some say that greatly respected Talmud scholars in any country in that period were given the title GAON *[Mmn.Hakd.L'Yad]*. During the four centuries of the GE'ONIM, Bavel was considered the center of Jewish life. The GE'ONIM received many questions on Halacha matters from many countries, which

were discussed amongst the scholars of the METIVTA. The responses — released under the name of the presiding GAON — were often very brief and did not reflect the internal discussions. They were written in the same language as the Talmud *(Aramaic)*, and in a similar style. The METIVTA itself also retained the same style that it had developed at the time of the AMORA'IM (see 3995\235) *[Igg.R.Sher.G./ Dor.Har.6.154, 191, 215, 223, 245, 266—8]*.

At around this time, Mar Zutra (II) (see 4318\558) left Bavel and settled in Eretz Yisrael, where he was accepted as a leader of the Talmud scholars — and some say he was given the title of "head of the Sanhedrin" (see 4189\429), which passed on to his descendants *[Sed.Ol.Zut.q.Dor.Har.6.39/ Dor.Har.6.47—8, 50]*.

4368 ≈ 608

R.Chanan (from Ishkiya) died, R.Maari Surgo (see 4349\589) was called to be the GAON of Pumpedita, and he was succeeded as GAON of Firuz-Shabur by R.Chanina (Min Bei Gihara) *(Chanina I of GE'ONIM)* *[Igg.R.Sher.G./ Dor.Har.6.167, 172—3, 190]*.

4369 ≈ 609

The METIVTA of Sura was reconstituted.

The METIVTA of Sura was reconstituted (see 4300\540), and R.Mar (bar R.Huna) became the GAON *[Igg.R.Sher.G./ Dor.Har.6.172]*.

4372 ≈ 612

When the Christian Visigoths (see 4155\395) had gained complete control of the country, the Jews of Spain were ordered to convert or leave. The order was apparently not strictly enforced, although many left. However it was re-issued a number of times in later years (see 4454\694), when some were forced to convert, and some were expelled from certain locations.

4374 ≈ 614

Jews were allowed to return to Yerushalayim.

The Persians captured Eretz Yisrael — including Yerushalayim — from the Byzantine *(E.Roman)* Empire (see 4389\629), and the Jews were allowed to settle in Yerushalayim after almost 500 years (see 3893\133, 4389\629).

4380 ≈ 620

At around this time R.Chana Gaon succeeded R.Maari Surgo as GAON of Pumpedita, and R.Chanina *(Chanina II of GE'ONIM)* succeeded R.Mar (bar R.Huna) as GAON of Sura *[Igg.R.Sher.G./ Dor.Har. 6.172—3]*.

4389 ≈ 629

The Byzantine Empire reconquered Eretz Yisrael.

When the Byzantine Empire *(Romans)* reconquered Eretz Yisrael (see 4374\614), many Jews were killed, many fled, and the rest were expelled from Yerushalayim again (see 4374\614 and 4397\637). The Byzantine emperor (Heraclius) later decreed (unsuccessfully) that all Jews in the empire should be subjected to FORCED BAPTISM.

4392 ≈ 632

A number of the many battles Muhammad fought in northern Arabia were against Jewish tribes — who did not accept his new religion — and he massacred and expelled many Jews from there. Under the claim of fulfilling his wish, many were later expelled after he died in 4392\632 — having become the strongest leader in Arabia — and Jews have never been allowed to live in parts of Arabia since then (thus effectively becoming the longest-lasting expulsion.)

4396 ≈ 636

R.Yitzchak was the last GAON of Neharde'a (Firuz-Shabur).

R.Yitzchak Gaon *(Yitzchak I of GE'ONIM)* succeeded R.Chanina (I, Min Bei Gihara) as GAON of Firuz-Shabur (see 4368\608). He was the last GAON of the METIVTA of Firuz-Shabur *(Neharde'a)* (see 4420\660) *[Igg.R.Sher.G./ Dor.Har.6.164—8, 171, 173]*.

4397 ≈ 637

The Arabs conquered Eretz Yisrael.

The Muslim Arabs conquered many countries at this time, including Bavel *(Babylonia)* from the Persian empire, Eretz Yisrael from the Byzantine *(E.Roman)* Empire, Syria, Egypt, North Africa and (later) Spain. Communication became easier between the Jewish communities of these countries (see 4234\474) and the Metivtot of Bavel *(Iraq at this stage)*.

4400 ≈ 640

At around this time, R.Rava *(Rava I of GE'ONIM)* succeeded R.Chana as GAON of Pumpedita (see 4380\620), and R.Huna *(Huna I of GE'ONIM)* succeeded R.Chanina (II) as GAON of Sura (see 4380\620) *[Igg.R.Sher.G./ Dor.Har.6.173—5, 177]*.

4405 ≈ 645

One of the "TAKKANOT HAGE'ONIM" was enacted at this time.

R.Rava (I), GAON of Pumpedita (see 4400\640), enacted a TAKKANA *(regulation, see Chart)* together with R.Huna (I), GAON of Sura (see 4400\640), that a woman should be given an immediate divorce, if she refuses to live with her husband. (This enactment was not unanimously accepted as part of HALACHA beyond those times, except as it relates to financial rights.) *[Igg.R.Sher.G./ Rif Ket.27a (on Tal.Ket.63b), Shilt.Gib. / Mmn.Hil.Ish.14.14, Mag.Mish./ Tur E.H.77, B.Y./ Dor.Har.6.173—5, 177, 215/ see also Mmn.Hil. Mal.VeLov.2.2]*.

4410 ≈ 650

R.Bustenai (Gaon) succeeded R.Rava (I) as GAON of Pumpedita (see 4400\640), and R.Sheshna (Mesharshiya bar Tachlifa) succeeded R.Huna (I) of Sura (see 4400\640) *[Igg.R.Sher.G./ Dor.Har.6.175—7]*.

4420 ≈ 660

At around this time R.Sheshna (see 4410\650) died, and for a number of years the REISH GALUTA *(Exilarch)* was involved in political manipulation (see 4449\689) in the appointment of successors as GAON of Sura *[Igg.R.Sher.G./ Dor.Har.6.152, 159, 176—7, 192]*.

Muhammad's cousin *(Calif Ali)* was his son-in-law — and eventually a successor, although controversy over this lead to the splitting of the Islamic nation, with his followers becoming the Shi'ite sect *[from the phrase shi-at Ali — the party of Ali]*. He came to Iraq *(Bavel)* at around this time, and R.Yitzchak (I) Gaon (see 4396\636) of Firuz-Shabur went out to meet him with a large contingent of the estimated 90,000 Jews of Neharde'a and its environs, and was accepted favorably *[Igg.R.Sher.G./ Dor.Har.6.166—8, 178]*. Bustenai — of whom many stories are told — was the first REISH GALUTA *(Exilarch)* under the new Arab Islamic rule of Bavel. A controversy later developed about the status of some of his children, who were said to be of an (unconverted) wife (of the recently conquered Persian royal family) given to him by the caliph *[Yuch.3.138/ Sed.Had.4420/ Dor.Har. 6.169—171(3)]*.

4421 ≈ 661

The new Muslim Arab caliph of Yerushalayim built a large wooden mosque on the site of the Beit Hamikdash. He also confiscated Jewish property in Eretz Yisrael, which he redistributed to Arab settlers.

4449 ≈ 689

Mar R.Chanina(i) *(Chanina III of GE'ONIM)* became GAON of Sura, after many years of political manipulations by the REISH GALUTA *(Exilarch)* (see 4420\660). Mar R.Huna Mari *(Huna II of GE'ONIM)* was GAON of Pumpedita, having succeeded R.Bustenai (see 4410\650) *[Igg.R.Sher.G./ Dor.Har.6.176—7, 192, 233]*.

4454 ≈ 694

The Jews of Spain were accused of plotting to overthrow the Christian Visigoth government, which had been continuously enacting laws to convert or expel them (see 4372\612). Many fled (some say to Morocco), but many were forcibly converted (see 4471\711).

4457 ≈ 697

Mar R.Nahilai succeeded Mar R.Chanina(i) (III) as GAON of Sura (see 4449\689) *[Igg.R.Sher.G./ Dor.Har.6.233]*.

4471 ≈ 711

When the Moors (Muslims) invaded Spain the Jews welcomed them (see 4454\694). Many Jews who had converted and lived publicly as Christians — while secretly remaining practicing Jews — returned to Judaism completely. The Jews became indigenous allies to the invaders and helped them conquer and then to rule. Subsequently Jewish life in Spain began to flourish.

4475 ≈ 715

Mar R.Yaakov HaKohen *(Yaakov I of GE'ONIM)* succeeded Mar R.Nahilai as GAON of Sura (see

4457\697) [Igg.R.Sher.G./ Dor.Har.6.233].

4479 — 719

Mar R.Chiya had succeeded Mar R.Huna (II) Mari as GAON of Pumpedita (see 4449\689), and Mar R.Rava *(Rava II of GE'ONIM)* succeeded him. Around this time (4479), Mar R.Natrunai *(Natrunai I of GE'ONIM)* succeeded Mar R.Rava (II) *[Igg.R.Sher.G./ Dor.Har.6.192, 233].*
The son-in-law of Mar R.Natrunai (I) (Mar R.Yaneka) was a member of the (royal) family of the REISH GALUTA *(Exilarch)*. He wielded his influence (see 4449\689) and exercised harsh authority over the scholars of Pumpedita, which caused many to leave (to Sura) *[Igg.R.Sher.G./ Dor.Har.6.192].*

4482 — 722

Many Jews were forced to accept Christianity in the Byzantine *(E.Roman)* Empire, and many left Constantinople and other parts of the empire.

4493 — 733

Mar R.Shmuel *(Shmuel I of GE'ONIM)* — the grandson of R.Rava (I), (see 4410\650) — succeeded Mar R.Yaakov (I) as GAON of Sura (see 4475\715) *[Igg.R.Sher.G./ Dor.Har. 6.233].*

4499 — 739

R.Yehuda *(Yehuda I of GE'ONIM)* had succeeded Mar R.Natrunai (I) as GAON of Pumpedita (see 4479\719), and in 4499, R.Yosef *(Yosef I of GE'ONIM)* succeeded him *[Igg.R.Sher.G./ Dor.Har.6.233].*

4500 — 740

The Khazars *(a people said to originate from the vicinity of Turkey)* lived at this time, in a region between the Caspian and the Black seas. Their king and many of his people converted to JUDAISM (see 4715\955) *[Kuzari 1.1, 1.47].*

4508 — 748

Many died in an earthquake in Eretz Yisrael.
R.Shmuel *(Shmuel II of GE'ONIM)* succeeded R.Yosef (I) as GAON of Pumpedita (see 4499\739) *[Igg.R. Sher. G./ Dor.Har.6.233].*

4511 — 751

R.Mari Kohen *(Mari I of GE'ONIM)* succeeded Mar R.Shmuel (I) as GAON of Sura (see 4493\733) *[Igg.R.Sher.G./ Dor.Har.6.233].*

4515 — 755

R.Acha(i) GAON left Bavel (Iraq) for Eretz Yisrael.

R.Natroy succeeded R.Shmuel (II) as GAON of Pumpedita (see 4508\748) *[Igg.R.Sher.G./ Dor.Har.6.212, 233].* R.Acha(i) Gaon — who had written a work called *She'iltot d'R.Acha(i) (Talmudic Halacha/Agada, in the order of the CHUMASH (Bible), and in the style of the Talmud)* — was passed over in the appointment of R.Natroy (due to the involvement of the REISH GALUTA *(Exilarch)*, Shlomo bar Chisdai, see 4519\759). He left Bavel and settled in Eretz Yisrael *[Igg.R. Sher.G./ Sef.Hak.q.Dor. Har.6.270 /Yuch.3.139/ Dor.Har.6.192—3, 212, 270].*

4519 — 759

R.Yehudai became GAON of Sura.

R.Avraham *(Avraham I of GE'ONIM)* succeeded R.Natroy as GAON of Pumpedita (see 4515\755) *[Igg.R.Sher.G./ Dor.Har.6.212, 233].*
Mar R.Acha *(Acha I of GE'ONIM)* succeeded R.Mari (I) Kohen for half a year (see 4617\857) as GAON of Sura (see 4511\751), and he was succeeded by R.Yehudai Gaon *(Yehuda II of GE'ONIM)*, who was brought to Sura by the REISH GALUTA *(Exilarch)* Shlomo bar Chisdai (himself a Talmud scholar) *(see 4515\755) [Tsh.Hag.Zich.LeRi.183.q.Dor.Har.6.213 /Igg.R.Sher.G./ Dor.Har.6.213—4, 233].* R.Yehudai Gaon — who was blind — was known for his lucid clarifications on the Talmud (some of which crept into the text, because his disciples had written them in the margins from where they were later mistakenly appended, see 4320\560) *[Tos.B.K.53b, Rashal/Yuch.3.139/Sh.Mkbtzt. B.M.13b(48b), 15b(55b)/ Dor.Har.6.139, 196—201].*

The Halachot Gedolot (BaHaG) was written at this time.

R.Yehudai had already written many (of his own) Halachic decisions (see 4349\589), and R.Shimon Kaira, who lived at this time, collected many of them. He also collected those from the *She'iltot of R.Acha(i)* (see 4515\755), and of other GE'ONIM, and wrote the Halachot Gedolot *(in the order of the Talmud)*, which is known as the BaHaG. It is probably the first work to have a HAKDAMA *(Introduction) [Tsh.Hag.Zich.LeRi.376.q. Dor.Har.6.211/B.HaMa.Shab.25b (Rif12a)/ Sef.Hak./Sed.Had. /Shem. Hag.2.26/ Dor.Har.6.191, 200—8, 211].*

4521 ≈ 761

R.Davidai — the brother of R.Yehudai (II) Gaon (see 4519\759) — succeeded R.Avraham (I) as GAON of Pumpedita (see 4519\759) *[Igg.R. Sher.G./ Dor.Har.6.212, 233]*.

4523 ≈ 763

Mar R.Achunai Kahana succeeded R.Yehudai (II) Gaon, as GAON of Sura (see 4519\759) *[Igg.R.Sher.G./ Dor.Har.6.230—1, 233]*.

Anan ben David founded a sect (of Jews) — some say because he was passed over when his brother was appointed REISH GALUTA *(Exilarch)*. This sect later became known as (or merged with) the Kra'im *(Karaites)* (see 3628\-133) *[Igg.R.Sher.G./ Yuch.2.130; 3.139/Tzem.Dav.4515 /Sed.Had.4515]*.

4524 ≈ 764

R.Chanina *(Chanina IV of GE'ONIM)* succeeded R.Davidai as GAON of Pumpedita (see 4521\761) *[Igg.R.Sher.G./ Dor.Har.6.233]*.

4528 ≈ 768

Mar R.Chanina Kahana *(Chanina V of GE'ONIM)* succeeded Mar R.Achunai as GAON of Sura (see 4523\761) *[Igg.R.Sher.G./ Dor.Har.6.230—1, 233]*.

4531 ≈ 771

R.Malka *(Malka I of GE'ONIM)* succeeded R.Chanina (IV) as GAON of Pumpedita (see 4524\764) *[Igg.R.Sher. G./ Dor.Har.6.233]*.

At this time there was a controversial challenge (see 4577\817) to the leadership of the REISH GALUTA *(Exilarch)* (Zakkai bar Achunai), and when the challenger (Natrunai) was removed by the intervention of the METIVTOT, he left Bavel *(Iraq)* for the west *[Igg.R.Sher.G./ Dor.Har.6.231—2]*.

4533 ≈ 773

Mar R.Rava *(Rava III of GE'ONIM)*, the son of R.Davidai (see 4524\764), succeeded R.Malka (I) as GAON of Pumpedita (see 4531\771) *[Igg.R.Sher.G./ Dor.Har.6.233]*.

4536 ≈ 776

Mar R.Mari HaLevi *(Mari II of GE'ONIM)* succeeded Mar R.Chanina (V) Kahana as GAON of Sura (see 4528\768) *[Igg.R.Sher.G./ Dor.Har.6.230—1, 233]*.

4540 ≈ 780

Mar R.Bibi HaLevi succeeded Mar R.Mari (II) HaLevi as GAON of Sura (see 4536\776) *[Igg.R.Sher.G./ Dor.Har. 6.234]*.

4542 ≈ 782

R.Shanui succeeded Mar R.Rava (III) as GAON of Pumpedita (see 4533\773) *[Igg.R.Sher.G./ Dor.Har. 6.233]*.

4543 ≈ 783

R.Chanina Kahana *(Chanina VI of GE'ONIM)* — the son of R.Avraham (see 4521\761) — succeeded R.Shanui as GAON of Pumpedita (see 4542\782) *[Igg.R.Sher.G./ Dor.Har.6.234, 235]*.

4546 ≈ 786

R.Chanina (VI) Kahana was removed from office by the REISH GALUTA *(Exilarch)* and Mar R.Huna Mar HaLevi *(Huna III of GE'ONIM)* succeeded him as GAON of Pumpedita (see 4543\783) *[Igg.R.Sher.G./ Dor.Har.6.234, 270]*.

4548 ≈ 788

Another of "TAKKANOT HaGe'onim" was enacted at this time.

Mar R.Huna Mar HaLevi, GAON of Pumpedita (see 4546\786), together with Mar R.Bibi HaLevi, GAON of Sura (and R.Menasheh, who was to succeed Mar R.Huna, see 4549\789), enacted a TAKKANA *(regulation, see Chart)* enabling a widow to collect her ketuba and dowry (and enabling creditors to collect debts), not only from real estate, but from any belongings of the husband *[Igg.R.Sher.G./ Mmn.Hil.Ish.16.7, Mag.Mish./ Dor.Har.6.232, 234]*.

4549 ≈ 789

R.Menasheh (see 4548\788) succeeded Mar R.Huna Mar (III) HaLevi as GAON of Pumpedita *[Igg.R.Sher.G./ Dor.Har.6.234]*.

4550 ≈ 790

Mar R.Hilai *(Hilai I of GE'ONIM)* succeeded Mar R.Bibi

HaLevi as GAON of Sura (see 4540\780) *[Igg.R.Sher.G./ Dor.Har.6.281]*.

4556 — 796

Mar R.Yeshayah HaLevi succeeded R.Menasheh as GAON of Pumpedita (see 4549\789) *[Igg.R.Sher.G./ Dor.Har.6.281]*.

4558 — 798

R.Yaakov HaKohen *(Yaakov II of GE'ONIM)* succeeded R.Hilai (I) as GAON of Sura (see 4550\790), and Mar R.Yosef *(Yosef II of GE'ONIM)* succeeded Mar R.Yeshayah HaLevi as GAON of Pumpedita (see 4556\796) *[Igg.R.Sher.G./ Dor.Har.6.281]*.

4560 — 800

The caliph in Baghdad placed Yerushalayim under the protection of Charlemagne, the Frankish king, and newly proclaimed emperor of the reorganized (see 4215\455) Western Roman Empire. Charlemagne — who strengthened the power of the Church in his dominions — is said (by some) to have settled some Talmud scholars in Germany and France.

4565 — 805

Mar R.Kahana — the son of R.Chanina VI (see 4543\783) — succeeded Mar R.Yosef (II) as GAON of Pumpedita (see 4558\798) *[Igg.R.Sher.G./ Dor.Har.6.281]*.

4571 — 811

Mar R.Avimai *(Ivumai, Avimai I of GE'ONIM)* succeeded Mar R.Kahana (his nephew, see 4565\805) as GAON of Pumpedita (see 4565\805) *[Igg.R.Sher. G./ Dor.Har.6.235, 281]*.

4573 — 813

R.Avumai *(Avumai II of GE'ONIM)* succeeded R.Yaakov (II) (his nephew) as GAON of Sura (see 4558\798) *[Igg.R.Sher.G./ Dor.Har.6.241—2, 281]*.

4575 — 815

Mar R.Yosef *(Yosef III of GE'ONIM)* succeeded Mar R.Avimai (I) as GAON of Pumpedita (see 4571\811) *[Igg.R.Sher.G./ Dor.Har.6.281]*.

4577 — 817

Mar R.Avraham *(Avraham II of GE'ONIM)* succeeded Mar R.Yosef (III) as GAON of Pumpedita (see 4575\815) *[Igg.R.Sher.G./ Dor.Har.6.281]*.
There was a challenge to the leadership of the REISH GALUTA *(Exilarch)* (see 4531\771), and the challenger appointed another GAON for Pumpedita (R.Yosef IV). The issue of REISH GALUTA was resolved, and R.Yosef (IV) stepped aside (see 4588\828) when it became evident that the people were perturbed by the presence of two GE'ONIM *[Igg.R.Sher.G./ Dor.Har.6.239]*.

4581 — 821

Mar R.Tzadok succeeded R.Avumai (II) as GAON of Sura (see 4573\813) *[Igg.R.Sher.G./ Dor.Har.6.281]*.

4583 — 823

R.Hilai *(Hilai II of GE'ONIM)* succeeded Mar R.Tzadok as GAON of Sura (see 4581\821) *[Igg.R.Sher.G./Dor. Har. 6.281]*.

4587 — 827

Mar R.Kiyumi *(Kiyumi I of GE'ONIM)* — who some say was a brother of R.Tzadok (see 4583\823) — succeeded R.Hilai (II) as GAON of Sura (see 4583\823) *[Igg.R.Sher.G./ Dor.Har.6.281]*.

4588 — 828

R.Yosef *(Yosef IV of GE'ONIM)* (see 4577\817) succeeded Mar R.Avraham (II) as GAON of Pumpedita (see 4577\817) *[Igg.R.Sher.G./ Dor.Har.6.281]*.

4590 — 830

R.Moshe (or R.Mesharshiya) (the son of R.Yaakov (II), see 4573\813) succeeded Mar R.Kiyumi (I) as GAON of Sura (see 4587\827) *[Igg.R.Sher.G./ Sef.Hak. q.Dor.Har.6.242/ Dor.Har.6.241—2]*.

4593 — 833

Mar R.Yitzchak *(Yitzchak II of GE'ONIM)* succeeded R.Yosef (IV) as GAON of Pumpedita (see 4588\828) *[Igg.R.Sher.G./ Dor.Har.6.240, 271, 281]*.

4598 — 838

Mar R.Yosef *(Yosef V of GE'ONIM)* — who had been

passed over in the appointment of Mar R.Yitzchak (II) as GAON of Pumpedita (see 4593\833) — succeeded R.Yitzchak *[Igg.R.Sher.G./ Dor.Har.6.240, 271, 281]*.

4601 — 841

R.Paltui succeeded Mar R.Yosef (V) as GAON of Pumpedita (see 4598\838) *[Igg.R.Sher.G./ Dor.Har.6.281]*. R.Moshe (Mesharshiya) died (see 4590\830), and he was not replaced as GAON of Sura for two years *[Igg.R.Sher.G./ Dor.Har.6.281]*.

4603 — 843

R.Kohen Tzedek (Kohen Tzedek I of GE'ONIM) — the son of R.Avumai II — became GAON of Sura, after the position was vacant for two years (see 4601\841) *[Igg.R.Sher.G./ Dor.Har.6.259, 281]*. The REISH GALUTA *(Exilarch)* Ukva attempted to redirect some of the funds raised for the METIVTA of Sura to his own advantage (see 4420\660), and R.Kohen Tzedek was instrumental in stopping this. Ukva was eventually expelled from his position, and from the central Jewish areas of Bavel *(Iraq) (from which some infer that other serious matters were also involved)*. He later managed to have himself reinstated (by the caliph) (see 4613\853), but was expelled once again due to public outcry *[Yuch.2.133/ Dor.Har.6.257, 249—262]*.

4608 — 848

R.Sar Shalom succeeded R.Kohen Tzedek as GAON of Sura (see 4603\843) *[Dor.Har.6.241—6, 259, 281]*.

4610 — 850

The Jews of Bavel *(Iraq)* were required by their Muslim Arab rulers to wear a yellow patch. Some say the decree was originally issued in 4478\718 and was re-issued in this year.

4613 — 853

R.Natrunai (Natrunai II of GE'ONIM) — the son of R.Hilai (II) (see 4587\827) — succeeded R.Sar Shalom as GAON of Sura (see 4608\848) *[Dor.Har.6.241—6, 259, 281—2]*. Some say that during the controversy with the REISH GALUTA Ukva (see 4603\843) R.Amram was appointed (by Ukva) to be GAON of Sura — during the tenure of R.Natrunai II — but he did not exercise any of the rights or powers of that position *[Igg.R.Sher.G./ Dor.Har.6.259(34)]*.

4617 — 857

R.Acha (Acha II of GE'ONIM) succeeded R.Paltui as GAON of Pumpedita (see 4601\841) for half a year (see 4519\759), and he was succeeded by R.Menachem (the son of R.Yosef IV, see 4593\833). Not all the scholars of the METIVTA accepted the appointment of R.Menachem, and some followed R.Mattityahu (see 4619\859). This was the only documented case — in four centuries of GE'ONIM — where there was active internal dissent among the scholars *[see Dor.Har.6.240, 269—75]* regarding the leadership of the METIVTOT of Bavel *(Babylonia, Persia-Iraq)* *[Igg.R. Sher.G./ Dor.Har.6.240, 271—2, 282]*.

4618 — 858

R.Amram (who wrote the Siddur) became GAON of Sura.

R.Amram Gaon succeeded R.Natrunai (II) as GAON of Sura (see 4613\853). R.Amram had the system (*seder*) of prayers committed to writing, and it was sent to the Jews of Spain (see 4471\711). This was the earliest (known) book of written prayers — which is now commonly called a SIDDUR *(Prayer Book)* *[Tzem.Dav. 4600/ Shem.Hag. 2.34a/ Dor.Har.6.241—6, 259, 282]*.

4619 — 859

R.Mattityahu (see 4617\857) — who some say was the brother of R.Yosef (V) (see 4598\838) — succeeded R.Menachem as GAON of Pumpedita (see 4617\857) *[Igg.R.Sher.G./ Dor.Har.6.240, 242—3, 282]*.

4628 — 868

R.Abba — a grandson of R.Shmuel (II) (see 4515\755) — succeeded R.Mattityahu as GAON of Pumpedita (see 4619\859) *[Igg.R.Sher.G./Dor.Har. 6.249, 282]*.

4631 — 871

R.Tzemach *(Tzemach I of GE'ONIM)* — the son of R.Paltui (see 4617\857) — succeeded R.Abba as GAON of Pumpedita (see 4628\868) *[Igg.R.Sher.G./ Dor.Har.6.282]*. R.Tzemach was asked to rule on the validity of the (singular) Halachic opinions con-

veyed by the traveller Eldad HaDani, who claimed to be from the lost tribe of Dan (see 3205\556) *[Mord.Chul.2a / Sed.Had./Shem.Hag.2.110]*.
The Byzantine emperor (Basil I) decreed that the Jews of southern Italy were to be forcibly converted to Christianity. R.Shephatia ben Amittai — from the town of Oria in that region, a scholar well versed in KABBALA who was the author of PIYUTIM — travelled to Constantinople, and managed (some say) to have the decree lifted for the Jews of his town (and surroundings). His son R.Amittai succeeded him as a leader in the community, and he also wrote many PIYUTIM, some of which may be ascribed to his grandfather of the same name. They were one of many families reputed to have been in this part of Italy since they were brought there by Titus after the destruction of the Second Beit HaMikdash (see 3829\69 *[in Chap.9]*).
R.Silano of Venosa *(Southern Italy)* wrote PIYUTIM.

4636 — 876

R.Nachshon, the son of R.Tzadok (see 4583\823, 4587\827), succeeded R.Amram Gaon as GAON of Sura (see 4618\858) *[Igg.R.Sher.G./ Dor.Har.6.282]*.

4640 — 880

R.Hai *(Hai I of GE'ONIM)* succeeded R.Tzemach (I) as GAON of Pumpedita (see 4631\871) *[Igg.R.Sher.G. / Sef.Hak.q.Dor.Har.6.241/ Dor.Har.6.240—1, 282]*.

4644 — 884

R.Tzemach *(Tzemach II of GE'ONIM)* succeeded his (maternal) half-brother R.Nachshon as GAON of Sura (see 4636\876) *[Igg.R.Sher.G./ Dor.Har.6.282]*.

4648 — 888

Mar R.Kiyumi *(Kiyumi II of GE'ONIM)*, the son of R.Acha (II) (see 4617\857), succeeded R.Hai (I) as GAON of Pumpedita (see 4640\880) *[Igg.R. Sher.G./ Dor.Har.6.248, 282]*.

4652 — 892

R.Malka *(Malka II of GE'ONIM)* succeeded R.Tzemach (II) as GAON of Sura (see 4644\884) for only a few weeks, and he was succeeded by Mar R.Hai *(Hai II of GE'ONIM)*, the son of R.Nachshon (see 4644\884). Many of the (other) elderly scholars of the METIVTA of Sura died within a three-month period (see 4671\911) *[Igg.R.Sher.G./ Dor.Har.6. 246—7, 263, 282]*.

4658 — 898

Mar R.Hilai *(Hilai III of GE'ONIM)*, the son of R.Natrunai (II) (see 4618\858), succeeded Mar R.Hai (II) as GAON of Sura (see 4652\892) *[Igg.R.Sher.G./ Dor.Har. 6.248, 282]*.

4665 — 905

Mar R.Shalom succeeded Mar R.Hilai (III) as GAON of Sura (see 4658\898) *[Igg.R.Sher.G./ Dor.Har.6. 282]*.

4666 — 906

R.Yehuda *(Yehuda III of GE'ONIM)* succeeded Mar R.Kiyumi (II) as GAON of Pumpedita (see 4648\888) *[Igg.R.Sher.G./ Dor.Har.6.248, 282]*.

4671 — 911

R.Yaakov *(Yaakov III of GE'ONIM)* succeeded Mar R.Shalom as GAON of Sura (see 4665\905).
At this stage the number of scholars in the METIVTA of Sura had decreased significantly, many of them having joined the METIVTA of Pumpedita (see 4652\892) *[Igg.R.Sher.G./ Yuch.2. 133/Dor.Har.6.247, 263, 283]*.

4677 — 917

R.Mevasser, the son of Mar R.Kiyumi (II) (see 4648\888) was appointed by the scholars of the METIVTA of Pumpedita to succeeded R.Yehuda (III) (see 4666\906) as GAON. However, David (ben Zakkai) the REISH GALUTA *(Exilarch)* sought to appoint Mar R.Kohen Tzedek *(Kohen Tzedek II of GE'ONIM)* (see 4686\926). The disagreement continued for five years after which R.Mevasser was recognized as GAON by David (the REISH GALUTA) — although some scholars remained with R.Kohen Tzedek (II) Kahana *[Igg.R.Sher.G./ Dor.Har.6.249, 251—2, 260, 271—2, 282]*.

4683 — 922

Aharon ben Meir, the ROSH METIVTA in Eretz Yisrael, announced there that Rosh HaShana of this year should be on a Tuesday — while the

[continued on page 174]

TAKKANOT HaGE'ONIM

The greatest impact of the otherwise obscured era (TEKUFA) of the GE'ONIM are the TAKKANOT *(regulations)* they were known to have enacted. Although the impact of these TAKKANOT was universal *[Rashba 729/B.Y.C.M.2]* and the term "TAKKANOT HaGE'ONIM" appears quite often in HALACHA writings, nevertheless there exists no defining description or systematic list of them. The following is a relatively comprehensive list, gleaned from the various sources as they emerged in practical HALACHA writings.

In the years 4405\645 and 4548\788 two TAKKANOT are listed. Besides these known TAKKANOT (known when — and by whom of the GE'ONIM — they were enacted) the following were enacted:

A. The *script* the Kohen says at a PIDYON HABEN. This included a blessing for the Kohen which did not become minhag ASHKENAZ — although the rest is universal *[Rosh Kid.41, Karb.Net.; Bech.8.8/Pit.Tesh.Y.D.305.4]*.

B. To be standing when saying the prayer of Vehu Rachum (on Monday and Thursday) *[B.Y. O.C. 134. q. Mahari Abuhab]*.

C. To read the relevant portions in the Torah — for the MAFTIR on YOM TOV — describing the sacrifices for that day (some say they instituted all MAFTIR readings except for the special four, which preceded them) *[B.Y.488 q Rosh, Mord., Ran; Mag.Av.O.C.488.3/Agur Shab.397]*.

D. To say the phrases of Zachreinu and Mi Kamocha in SHMONA ESREI of the YAMIM NORA'IM *(High Holy Days)* *[Avudraham/Rosh/TBY.O.C.582]*.

E. To say the Aneinu *(prayer in SHMONA ESREI)* only at MINCHA of a fast day (not at MAARIV or SHACHARIS) *[Tos.Shab.24a]*.

F. To ensure completion of the Mila *(circumcision)* by hand *[Meiri Magen Avot 14]*.

G. Meat that was not salted — as required by HALACHA *(in order to draw out the blood)* — during the first three days after SHECHITA, may no longer be cooked *(in liquid)*, although it may be broiled. *[Tur Y.D.69/Pit.Tesh.Y.D.81.7.1]*. *(SEPHARDIM do not even broil it; whereas ASHKENAZIM have accepted a provision that if it is washed-down within these three days, then the three-day cycle is interrupted. [Rivash 86/Bin.Zev.328].)*

H. To disallow special consideration for CHALUTA *(a "snap-cook" process, which is considered — in a number of instances — to be a circumvention of the technical-halachic concept of cooking)* because the exact procedure is unknown to us *[Tur Y.D.73]*.

I. To discontinue the practice of taking oath in THE HOLY NAME *[Ra'avad Hil.Shev.11.13]*.

J. That a person cannot disallow another (by NEDER *(oath)*) from his share — as a member of the public — of a public property. *[B.Y.Y.D.224 q. Ra'avad and peers]*.

K. A provision that even though the laws of PENALTY PAYMENTS (Knass) do not apply in the absence of the Beit Hamikdash, the BEIT DIN should place the offender under a NIDDUI *(form of excommunication)* until he pays an equivalent amount — in order to maintain the dignity of the offended *[Tur E.H.177, Perisha 45; C.M.1.5]*.

L. A special blessing for the consummation of a woman's first marriage *[BaHag/Rosh Ket.1.15/B.Y.E.H.120.14]*.

M. The rights for litigants to make — in BEIT DIN — a sweeping CHEREM *(excommunication)* to apply to anyone who makes false statements in the case being heard *[Mmn.Yad.Hil.ShluchVeshut.3.11]*.

N. The requirement — due to the increase of dishonesty — that DAYANIM *(judges)* delve carefully and deeply into character and reputation to ensure they are hearing true statements *[Mord.B.M.222(p.6a) q. Rab.Tam/B.Y.C.M.75.1(p.115b)]*.

O. The procedure that in the event someone admits (in BEIT DIN) that he owes, but currently has nothing to pay with, he takes an oath to that effect — including in the statement that he will pay immediately as the funds come to him. The BEIT DIN itself also makes a sweeping CHEREM *(excommunication)* to apply to anyone who knows of possessions belonging to this person which he may be hiding *[Mmn.Yad.Hil.Mal.Velov.14.12/T.B.Y.C.M.99]*.

P. The layout/form/style of writing a GET *[B.Y.125(p.14b]*.

Q. That the BEIT DIN may accept testimony in the absence of a litigant, if the presence of the litigant will generate future agitation and dispute between the parties involved. They may also conceal the identity of those testifying. (Some say that this TAKKANA only applies to a case involving interpersonal disputes unrelated to direct financial matters.) *[Ramo C.M.28.15]*.

R. The empowerment for a lender to write a document of assignment (HARSHA'A) for a loan (to protect the lender from a fleeing borrower) *[Mmn.Yad.Hil.Shluch Veshut.3.7/TBY.C.M.123.1]*.

S. The (above) document of assignment may be attached to a part of the assigner's (theoretical) share in Eretz Yisrael (some say only if there exists no communal property on location in which he has a more tangible share, such as a SHUL *(synagogue)*) *[Mmn.Yad.Hil.Shluch Veshut.3.7/Ramban Git.8b/TBY.CM.123]*.

KITNIYOS & Rice on PESACH

In a number of HALACHA writings the restriction on eating KITNIYOS *(beans, peas and rice etc.)* is attributed to the GE'ONIM *[Maharsham Sec.2.50]*. However a number of questions arise that cast significant doubt around this attribution.

1. SEPHARDI scholars did not incorporate this restriction in their halacha decisions — whereas ASHKENAZIM did — yet the SEPHARDI communities were more directly connected to the GE'ONIM in Bavel *(Iraq)* (see 4715\955; Takkana A. & G. above).

2. The earliest mention of this restriction are in writings — all from the same period of time — of the S'mak, the Hagahot Maymunit and the Mordechai. The latter two were disciples of Maharam MeRottenburg (see 5058\1298, 5059\1298) and the former was a peer of his (perhaps he was older) (see 5040\1280).

3. The S'mak was a disciple (and son-in-law) of R.Yechiel of Paris (see 5040\1280) — one of the BA'ALEI TOSAPHOT — who is documented as not having adhered to this restriction *[Mord.Pes.588(p.31d)]*. (Although the Mordechai there *[Pes.588]* refers to R.Yechiel as his brother-in-law, it would be assumed that he was essentially a generation removed *(see #2)*.)

4. What is striking about all of them is that they were all in the late 1200's (at the end of the TOSAPHOT era) — which was almost 250 years after the last of the GE'ONIM. In the interim we have the halachic writings of the Rif and the Rambam (who mention the GE'ONIM on numerous occasions), neither of whom mention this restriction.

It therefore appears safe to assume that the restriction on KITNIYOS emerged sometime during the period of those "brilliant scholars" (small "g" ge'onim) we now refer to as TOSAPHOT — most likely at the very end, after (or concurrent with) R.Yechiel of Paris — and was respectfully attributed to them, as ge'onim.

After having cautiously come to this conclusion, further research has discovered precisely this attribution — in a comment aside — by the Chassam Sofer "...... we can say that this was not the intention of the restriction imposed by these early ge'onim, the Hagahot Maymuni, the S'mak and the Mordechai." [Sec.1 O.C.122]

[continued from page 171]

calculations of the GE'ONIM in Bavel *(Iraq)* established it for Thursday. This created a serious division, and Rbnu.Saadya Gaon (of Egypt) took a prominent stand, in lucid and articulate communications, supporting the GE'ONIM of Bavel — who eventually prevailed — after a few years of serious disruption in the calendars of the many local communities which had split into opposing factions *[See Otz.Hag.2.128—35]*.

4683 — 923

R.Yom Tov Kahana succeeded R.Yaakov (III) as GAON of Sura (see 4671\911), although he had not been one of the full time scholars of the METIVTA (see 4671\911) *[Igg.R.Sher.G./ Dor.Har.6.263, 283]*.

4685 — 925

Some Jews were killed and many were enslaved when the city of Oria *(southern Italy)* (see 4631\871) was attacked by Arabs.

4686 — 926

Mar R.Kohen Tzedek Kahana (II) (see 4677\917) was accepted as the successor to R.Mevasser as GAON of Pumpedita *[Igg.R.Sher.G./ Dor.Har.6.249, 251—2, 282]*.

4687 — 927

R.Yom Tov Kahana died (see 4683\923), and the remaining scholars of the METIVTA of Sura considered disbanding, and moving to Pumpedita. The REISH GALUTA *(Exilarch)* (David ben Zakkai) appointed Mar R.Natan to become GAON, but he died before he took office, and a suitable candidate was not immediately found (see 4688\928) *[Igg.R. Sher.G./ Dor.Har.6.247, 263—4, 283]*.

4688 — 928

Rbnu.Saadya was appointed GAON of Sura.

The REISH GALUTA *(Exilarch)* David ben Zakkai appointed the (relatively) very young Rbnu.Saadya Gaon (see 4683\922) as GAON of Sura (see 4687\927), with the hope — shared by the scholars of Pumpedita — of breathing new life into the METIVTA *[Igg.R.Sher.G./Yuch.2.134/Dor.Har.6.159, 264—5, 283]*.

4690 — 930

Rbnu.Saadya — GAON of Sura, author of *Emunot VeDeyot (philosophy)*, and of PIYUTIM questioned some official documents of judgement favoring David ben Zakkai, the REISH GALUTA *(Exilarch)* and he refused to sign them. A severe (political) dispute broke out, during which time David appointed R.Yosef — who was not an outstanding scholar — as GAON of Sura. Rbnu.Saadya appointed the brother of David as REISH GALUTA, and the strife spilled out into a wider circle, involving the need for the approval of the Caliph for the REISH GALUTA (see 3990\230) (and the accompanying monetary representations customary at that stage).

The Caliph endorsed David — who was of greater stature — and Rbnu.Saadya withdrew from public life until the dispute — in which many people had taken sides — had receded. (R.Yosef was (nominal) GAON of Sura in his absence) *[Igg.R.Sher.G./ Yuch.2.134—5, 3.140/ Dor.Har.6.159, 258, 261, 274—9]*.

Rbnu.Saadya wrote many works, and was actively engaged in refuting the claims of the Kra'im (see 4523\763) who were very influential in Eretz Yisrael at this time.

4692 — 932

In parts of Italy Jews were forced to convert. In Bari *(Italy)* they were massacred. Some say that Chisdai ibn Shaprut — a very influential Jewish statesman (see 4715\955) — accomplished the withdrawal of an expulsion order.

4695 — 935

R.Tzemach *(Tzemach III of GE'ONIM)* succeeded Mar R.Kohen Tzedek (II) as GAON of Pumpedita (see 4686\926) *[Igg.R.Sher.G./ Dor.Har.6.265, 283]*.

4699 — 939

R.Chanina *(Chanina VII of GE'ONIM)*, the son of R.Yehuda III (see 4677\917), succeeded R.Tzemach (III) as GAON of Pumpedita (see 4695\935), more than a year after he had died *[Igg.R.Sher.G./ Dor.Har.6.249, 283]*.

4704 — 944

R.Aharon succeeded R.Chanina (VII) as GAON of Pumpedita (see 4699\939) *[Igg.R.Sher.G./ Dor.Har.6.265—6, 283]*.

4705 — 945

A new fanatic dynasty took control of Bavel *(Iraq)*, and the Jews suffered persecutions during its century of reign (see 4757\997).

4715 955

"Four Captives" were ransomed at around this time.

Four great Talmudic scholars were said to have left Bari *(S. Italy)* (see 4692\932) on a journey across the Mediterranean Ocean — to collect money for charity — when they were captured by a Spanish warship.
One of them, R.Chushiel, was sold in North Africa, and went to Kairou'an *(Tunisia)*.
R.Moshe — who had travelled with his wife and young son — was sold (with his son, R.Chanoch, one of the scholars) in Spain, and thus arrived in Cordova, where he was appointed head of the local yeshiva by Chisdai ibn Shaprut (see 4692\932). (R.Moshe's wife had taken her own life at sea because of the pirates' intentions for her.)
R.Shemaryahu was sold in Alexandria *(Egypt)* from where he went to Cairo.
These four scholars, each in his respective location, raised the level of scholarship and transformed the local style in a remarkable way. The Talmud scholars of Italy — from where they originated — were quite independent from the GE'ONIM of Bavel *(Iraq)* (see 4098\338). Their style of scholarship was based on their own logical deductions from the Talmud — as distinct from the Babylonian style of strict adherence to (and emphasis on) directly transferred tradition. They tended to rely on the scholars (and the tradition — NUSSACH) of Eretz Yisrael, which was mostly under the same (Roman) government as Italy (as was most of Europe — ASHKENAZ), a distinction that quite probably reflects the origin of SEPHARDI and ASHKENAZI traditions *[Sef.Hak. q.Dor.Har. 6.283—4/ Sef.Hay.619/ Rosh R.H.(Chap.4) 35a(p.40a)/ Yuch.5.182/ Sed.Had.4790/ Dor.Har.6.234, 283—90, 293—4, 295—7, 298—300, 301—2]*.
[Recent archival findings pose questions for this account of how the scholars arrived at these locations. However, the answer may lie in the fact that there seems to have been another R.Shemaryahu ben Elchanan (slightly later) (see Dor.Har.6.299(47), 299—300) and possibly another R.Chushiel.]
R.Menachem (ben Yaakov) ben Saruk, the Spanish author of a dictionary of HEBREW words — that he called *Machberet* — was the secretary to Chisdai ibn Shaprut, who (some say) sent a letter to Joseph, the Jewish king of the Khazars (see 4500\740).
R.Donash ben Lavrat of Baghdad — a disciple of Rbnu.Saadya Gaon — was a grammarian who disagreed with many things in R.Menachem's dictionary. He also wrote poems and PIYUTIM.

4720 960

R.Nechemyah — son of Mar R.Kohen Tzedek (II) (see 4695\935), who had sought to be GAON of Pumpedita earlier — succeeded R.Aharon (see 4704\944) as GAON , although not all the scholars — including R.Sherira — accepted his leadership (because it lacked scholarly stature) *[Igg.R.Sher.G./ Dor.Har.6.265—6, 279, 283]*.

4728 968

R.Sherira became GAON of Pumpedita.

R.Sherira Gaon, the son of R.Chanina (VII) (see 4704\944) — a descendant of King David — succeeded R.Nechemyah as GAON of Pumpedita (see 4720\960) *[Igg.R.Sher.G./ Dor.Har.6.47, 279—80]*.

4757 997

R.Hai became (the last) GAON of Pumpedita.

R.Sherira Gaon wrote a detailed letter (IGGERET) in answer to some questions posed to him about the historical background of the Talmud tradition. This letter has served as a basis for the clear chronology of the METIVTOT of Bavel *(Babylonia, Persia-Iraq)* *[Igg.R.Sher.G./ Dor.Har.4.682(18); 6.28, 162—3, 166—7, 180]*.
R.Sherira lived to almost 100 years of age. Some say that he stepped aside, and his son R.Hai Gaon *(Hai III of GE'ONIM)* succeeded him as GAON of Pumpedita (see 4728\968).
R.Sherira was slandered to the caliph *(see 4705\945)*, who arrested him and his son R.Hai (III), confiscated their property, then released R.Hai and had R.Sherira hanged *[Igg.R. Sher.G./ Yuch.3.141; 5.181/ Sef.Hak.q. Dor.Har.6.279—80/ Dor.Har.6.252, 279—80]*.

4764 1004

Arab Muslim rulers of Eretz Yisrael forced some Jews to convert. Synagogues were burned down, and the Jews of Egypt were required to wear a distinctive sign on their clothing.

4767 1007

Many Jews were killed, and many were forced to convert to Christianity, in riots throughout France. Most of the converts returned to Judaism a few years later, after the riots had ceased.

4772 ≈ 1012

When a priest converted to Judaism in Mayence *(Mainz, Germany)*, the Jews were forced to convert or leave. The expulsion order was withdrawn within the year.

At around this time there was one R.Amnon in Mayence *(Mainz, Germany)*, of whom it is told that he asked for three days to consider whether to convert to avoid the punishment of death; and then — regretting having even asked for time — he pleaded for his (mis-spoken) tongue to be cut out. However, other limbs were hacked off for his refusal to convert. He asked to be brought to the synagogue on Rosh HaShana in his deathbed, where he composed the prayer *Unetaneh Tokef* as he was dying.

R.Shimon HaGadol (ben Yitzchak), also of Mayence — author of many PIYUTIM that are standard in the prayers of the YAMIM NORA'IM *(High Holy Days)* — lived at this time, and he served on the BEIT DIN of the city together with Rbnu.Gershom Me'or HaGola.

R.Shlomo (ben Yehuda) HaBavli, also author of PIYUTIM, had died approximately 25 years earlier.

R.Yekutiel (ben Moshe) — of the famous Klonymos family in Speyer *(Bavaria)* at this time — also wrote PIYUTIM now prominent in the MACHZOR *(prayer book for the High Holy Days)*.

Another PAYTAN *(author of PIYUTIM)* — R.Eliyahu (ben Shemayahu) of Bari *(S. Italy)* — lived at this time.

4773 ≈ 1013

Many Jews were killed when the Berbers *(of Northern Africa)* conquered Cordova *(Spain)* and divided Spain into many provinces *(see maps page 326)*. R.Shmuel HaNagid fled to Granada where he became very influential (see 4815\1055).

4785 ≈ *1024*

R.Chanoch — who had been one of the "Four Captives" (see 4715\955) — died a few days after he fell in the synagogue on Simchat Torah, in Tishrei 4785\ *1024* (some say it occurred in 4775\ *1014*) *[Sef.Hak.q. Yuch.3.143/ Dor.Har.6.301—2]*.

4795 ≈ 1035

6,000 Jews were massacred (in what some say was an invasion) in Fez *(Morocco)* at around this time.

4798 ≈ 1038

R.Hai GAON died.

The elderly R.Hai Gaon, son of R.Sherira Gaon, the last — and most influential — of the GE'ONIM, died in Pumpedita on the 20th Nissan. He had maintained communications with an ever-increasing range of (scattered) Jewish communities throughout the whole world, but after his death the influential role of the METIVTOT of Bavel *(Iraq)* rapidly declined (see 4705\945, 4715\955, 4800\1040) *[Yuch.3.141/ Dor.Har.6.156, 304—5]*.

R.Hai (III) was succeeded by R.Chizkiyah — the grandson of David ben Zakkai (see 4690\930) — who was killed two years later (see 4705\945, 4800\1040).

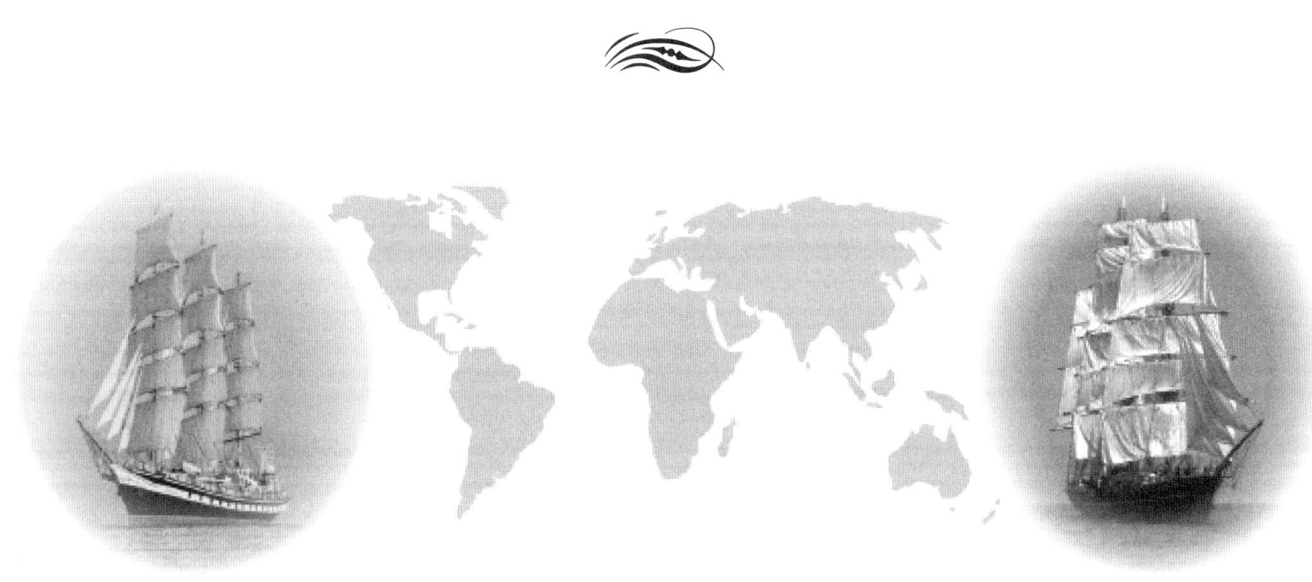

UNIVERSAL DISPERSION

Section IV

Chapter 12

The Rishonim — Early Scholars

Section IV

Chapter 12

The Rishonim — Early Scholars

Chapter 12a — Early Rishonim, Tosaphot, and the Crusade Massacres.

Jewish Year		Secular Year
4800	Rbnu.Gershom Me'or HaGola died.	1040
4848	The Rif arrived in Spain (from Morocco).	1088
4856	CRUSADERS (1ST) DESTROYED JEWISH COMMUNITIES.	**1096**
4859	Yerushalayim was captured by the Crusaders.	**1099**
4863	The Rif Died.	1103
4865	RASHI DIED, AND THE ERA OF THE TOSAPHOT BEGAN.	**1105**
4895	THE RAMBAM (MAIMONIDES) WAS BORN.	**1135**
4904	THE FIRST (RECORDED) BLOOD LIBEL TOOK PLACE.	**1144**
4907	Crusaders (2nd) attacked Jewish communities.	**1147**
4907	Rabbenu Tam was captured by the Crusaders.	1147
4908	The Rambam's and the Radak's families left Cordova.	1148
4925	The Rambam visited Eretz Yisrael.	1165
4931	Rabbenu Tam died.	1171
4935	The Rashbam died.	1175
4944	The young son of the Ri was killed.	1184
4948	Jews were allowed to return to Yerushalayim.	**1187**
4949	R.Yaakov D'Orleans was killed in London.	1189
4950	Jews were massacred in England, in the 3rd Crusade.	**1190**
4951	The Radak wrote his commentary.	1191
4954	The Ramban (Nachmanides) was born.	1194
4959	The Ra'avad died.	1198
4965	The Rambam died.	*1204*
4996	Rampaging mobs massacred Jews in France.	1236
5002	A massive burning of the Talmud took place in Paris.	**1242**
5004	Yerushalayim was sacked by Egyptians and Turks.	1244
5012	The Inquisition began to use torture.	1252
5027	The Ramban (left Spain and) settled in Eretz Yisrael.	1267
5030	The Ramban died.	**1270**
5046	The Maharam MeRothenburg was imprisoned.	**1286**
5050	New works advanced the study of KABBALA.	**1290**
5050	THE ERA OF THE TOSAPHOT CONCLUDED AT AROUND THIS TIME.	**1290**

Chapter 12b — Later Rishonim, Persecutions, and Expulsions.

Jewish Year		Secular Year
5050	**All Jews were expelled from England.**	**1290**
5053	The Maharam MeRothenburg died in prison.	1293
5058	**The Rindfleisch massacres began.**	**1298**
5058	The 'Mordechai' and Hagahot Maimoniyot were killed.	1298
5065	The Rashba placed a limited ban on philosophy.	1305
5065	The Rosh (and his son, the Tur) arrived in Spain.	1305
5066	All Jews were expelled from France.	1306
5070	The Rashba died.	1310
5080	Jews were massacred by the Pastoureaux Crusaders.	1320
5088	The Rosh died.	1327
5096	Jews of Germany were massacred by the Armledder bands.	1336
5098	The Ralbag wrote his commentary on the Bible.	1338
5109	**THE BLACK DEATH MASSACRES SWEPT ACROSS EUROPE.**	**1349**
5127	The Ran, Rivash, and other scholars in Spain, were imprisoned.	1367
5151	**Jews of Spain were massacred — many became Marranos.**	**1391**
5151	The Rivash and Rashbatz left Spain.	1391
5155	**The Final expulsion of Jews from France.**	**1394**
5173	R.Yosef Albo was in a forced debate with Christians.	1413
5181	**Jews in Austria were massacred in the Wiener Gezera.**	**1421**
5235	**THE INVENTION OF PRINTING WAS USED FOR JEWISH BOOKS.**	**1475**
5241	**The Inquisition was established in Spain.**	**1481**
5248	R.Ovadya Bertinura settled in Yerushalayim.	1488
5251	Columbus consulted R.Avraham Zacuto for his travels.	1491
5252	**ALL JEWS WERE EXPELLED FROM SPAIN AND SICILY.**	**1492**

Major Rishonim

Rbnu.Gershom Me'or Hagola	b. 960?	d.1040?
Rbnu.Chananel	b. 985?	d.1057?
R.Shmuel HaNagid	b. 993	d.1056?
Rif (Alfasi)	b.1013	d.1103
Rashi	b.1040	d.1105
Rashbam	b.1080?	d.1174?
R.Avraham ibn Ezra	b.1089?	d.1164
Rabbenu Tam	b.1100?	d.1171
Ri (R.Yitzchak)	b.1120?	d.1200?
Ra'avad	b.1120?	d.1198
Ba'al HaIttur	b.1120?	d.1193?
Ba'al Hama'or	b.1125?	d.1186
Rambam (Maimonides)	b.1135	d.1204
R.Yehuda HaChasid	b.1150?	d.1217
Roke'ach (R.Elazar)	b.1160?	d.1237?
Radak (Kimchi)	b.1160?	d.1235?
Rbnu.Yona (Gerondi)	b.1180?	d.1263
Ramban (Nachmanides)	b.1194?	d.1270?
Maharam MeRothenburg	b.1215?	d.1293
Rashba	b.1235?	d.1310?
Mordechai (Pirush)	b.1240?	d.1298
Hagahot Maimoniyot	b.1240?	d.1298
Me'iri (R.Menachem)	b.1249?	d.1315?
Rosh (R.Asher)	b.1250?	d.1327
Rbnu.Bachya II	b.1265?	d.1340?
Tur (R.Yaakov ben Asher)	b.1275?	d.1349?
Ralbag (Gersonides)	b.1288	d.1344
Ran (R.Nissim)	b.1290?	d.1380?
Rivash	b.1326	d.1408?
Maharil	b.1360?	d.1427
Rashbatz	b.1361?	d.1444

Section IV
UNIVERSAL DISPERSION

Chapter 12

The Rishonim — Early Scholars

The twelfth Chapter (Tekufa, era) in Jewish history begins with the emergence of great scholars in the regions of North Africa, Spain, Provence (S.E. France), Germany and France. This developed into a distinct new era of Torah scholarship.

This chapter covers the beginning of the codification of the laws of the Talmud (led by the Rif and the Rambam), and the great commentaries to the Talmud (led by Rashi and Tosaphot).

The chapter concludes when the Jews were expelled from Spain, after having been expelled from England, France and Austria, and having been decimated by persecutions and local (area) expulsions in Germany, Bohemia, Moravia, Switzerland and Italy — virtually the whole of Central and Western Europe.

Chapter 12a

Early Rishonim, Tosaphot, & the Crusade Massacres

4800 — 1040

Rbnu.Gershom Me'or HaGola died.

Rbnu.Gershom ben Yehuda Me'or HaGolah — a disciple of R.Yehuda ben Meir HaKohen (Rbnu.Leontin) — died in Mayence *(Mainz, Germany)* where he headed the first famous YESHIVA in Europe. (Some say he died as many as thirty years later). He was a prolific scribe who copied accurate versions of many works, and composed some PIYUTIM. He is most remembered for his CH'RAMIM (bans) and TAKKANOT (enactments), particularly the one for monogamy.
R.Chizkiyah (Gaon) (see 4798\1038) was slandered to the king, arrested and tortured, and then killed.

4810 — 1050

Rbnu.Nissim Gaon died in 1050, and Rbnu.Chananel (ben Rbnu.Chushiel) — who wrote a Talmud commentary — died shortly thereafter (although some say he died ten years earlier). They both lived in Kairou'an *(Tunisia)* and were disciples of Rbnu.Chushiel and followers (through correspondence) of R.Hai Gaon.

4815 — 1055

R.Shmuel HaNagid died.

R.Shmuel HaNagid — a disciple of R.Chanoch, and author of *Mavoh LaTalmud* *(Introduction to the Talmud)* — was an influential statesman in the province of Granada *(Spain)*, and a prosperous, generous, Talmud scholar. He died in 4815\1055, and his son R.Yosef HaNagid — who was a son-in-law of R.Nissim Gaon — succeeded him (see 4827\1066).
R.Shlomo ibn Gvirol — to whom the PIYUT Adon Olam is attributed — was a grammarian and poet who lived (in Spain) at this time, and he wrote Tikkun Middot HaNefesh *(Mussar)* (see 4928\1167).
R.Meir ben Yizchak, a scholar often quoted by Rashi — he was also called *R.Meir Sheliach Tzibbur*, presumably because he wrote many PIYUTIM, including the famous *Akdamos* PIYUT of Shavuot — lived in Germany at this time.
R.Moshe HaDarshan of Narbonne *(Provence, S.E.France)* also lived at this time (see 4866\1105).

4827 — 1066

R.Yosef ben Shmuel HaNagid of Granada *(Spain)* (see 4815\1055), was killed at the gates of the city on Shabbat the 9th **Tevet** 4827\1066, and 4,000 Jews were killed in the ensuing massacre. The influential Jewish community of Granada ceased to exist for a while.
R.Yosef Tuv Elem I — author of many famous PIYUTIM, who is quoted in Rashi *[Chul.114b]* and in Tosaphot *[A.Z.74b, Pes.116a]*— lived at around this time.

4848 — 1088

The Rif arrived in Spain.

The Rif, R.Yitzchak ben Yaakov Alfasi HaKohen (see 4863\1103), was (some say) a disciple of Rbnu.Chananel and Rbnu.Nissim Gaon. Some say he was called Alfasi because he lived in Fez *(Morocco)* (Al Fazi, Rif — R.Isaac Fazi) *[see Hakd.SMaG]*. He fled Morocco in his later years, in 1088, because he was denounced, and was appointed rabbi in Alusina *(Lucene, Spain)* (which was a completely Jewish town) shortly after his arrival there.

4856 — 1096

Crusaders (1st) destroyed Jewish communities.

The Pope *(Urban II)* declared a crusade to capture Yerushalayim, because of the way the Moslems were treating Christian pilgrims in Eretz Yisrael. The masses who gathered in Europe for the crusade, attacked many Jewish communities before they left. Some Jewish communities gave immense sums of silver and valuables, which in the end only sufficed to delay the attacks.
The Jews of Speyer *(Bavaria)* were massacred in this first Crusade, on Shabbat the 8th **Iyar**, and the Jews of Virmyze *(Worms, Germany)* on the 23rd. The Jews of Cologne *(Germany)* were saved, on the 25th **Iyar** *(see Tammuz)*, when the Crusaders could not enter the city because the bishop had ordered

the gates closed. A number of local bishops made attempts to divert a local massacre, and some needed to hide for their own safety.
Those Jews of Virmyze *(Worms)* who took refuge in a castle *(see Iyar)*, were massacred (during the prayer of Hallel for Rosh Chodesh) on the 1st **Sivan**.
R.Klonymos of Rome — who succeeded R.Yaakov ben Yakar (see 4865\1105) in Worms — was killed. One Jew (Simcha ben Yitzchak HaKohen) stabbed the bishop's nephew while being subjected to FORCED BAPTISM, and was killed for this.
On the 2nd **Sivan**, Crusaders massacred the Jews of Neuss *(Prussia)*, 1,000 Jews of Mayence *(Mainz, Germany)* were massacred on the 3rd, and the Jews of Bachrach *(Germany)* were massacred Erev Shavu'ot (5th **Sivan**).
On the 1st day of Shavu'ot, a number of Jews in Cologne *(see Iyar)* chose to be killed, rather than be subjected to FORCED BAPTISM — as was the case in many instances during the Crusade — and on the 5th **Tammuz** the Jews of Xanten *(Germany)* took their own lives, rather than be massacred or subjected to FORCED BAPTISM — as did many other Jews in other cities.
The Jews of Mehr *(Germany)* were massacred on the 6th **Tammuz** and Jews of Cologne were attacked on the 7th, although they escaped total destruction *(see Iyar, Sivan)*.
The Crusaders also attacked Jews in the cities of Troyes and Metz *(France)*, Regensburg *(Germany)*, Prague *(Bohemia)*, Pressburg *(Hungary)*, and in other towns and cities in these countries before the Hungarians put an end to their excesses.
The dead numbered in the tens of thousands (according to some), and many were subjected to FORCED BAPTISM, although most of them continued as secretly practicing Jews. Those who were baptized were allowed to openly return to JUDAISM one year later by Henry IV.
Many German Jews moved east — to Poland-Lithuania — taking their language, which later became YIDDISH.

4859 — 1099

Yerushalayim was captured by the Crusaders.

When the Crusaders reached Yerushalayim, they laid a siege to it on the 15th **Sivan**, and conquered it on the 23rd **Tammuz**. They forced all Jews into a synagogue, which they set on fire, killing almost all; very few escaped from the city. The Christian 'Kingdom of Jerusalem' was established in which Jews were not allowed to live (see 4948*1187* and 4389\629, 4925\1165).

Living in the Year 1100

Rif (Alfasi)	*b.*1013,	*d.*1103.
Rashi	*b.*1040,	*d.*1105.
Rashbam	*b.*1080?,	*d.*1174?.
R.Avraham ibn Ezra	*b.*1089?,	*d.*1164.
Rabbenu Tam	*b.*1100?,	*d.*1171.

4863 — 1103

The Rif died.

The Rif, R.Yitzchak Alfasi (see 4848\1088), died at the age of 90 in Alusina *(Lucene, Spain)* on the 11th **Iyar**. Some say he died in **Nissan** 1123. His major Halacha work 'Halachot' follows the order (and is in the form of a summary) of the Talmud and is similar in style to the works of the GE'ONIM *(see ILLUSTRATIONS, TEXT G, H)*. The Ri Migash — R.Yosef HaLevi ibn Migash, his young disciple — succeeded the Rif in his position in Alusina.

4865 — 1105

Rashi died, and the era of the Tosaphot began.

Rashi — R.Shlomo (Yarchi) ben Yitzchak, (R.Shlomo Yitzchaki) — died on the 29th **Tammuz** in Troyes *(France)*, where he was born. Rashi's commentaries on Bible and Talmud *(see ILLUSTRATIONS TEXT A, #4; TEXT B #3; TextE #3)* were — in their simple clarity — a unique departure from the style which had prevailed until this time (see 4863\1103). Rashi — a descendant of R.Yochanan HaSandlar, who also wrote PIYUTIM (see 4815\1055) — was the disciple of R.Yaakov ben Yakar (who was a disciple of Rbnu.Gershom Me'or HaGola), and of R.Yitzchak ben Asher I HaLevi, among others *[Rashi Bet.24b-end/ Shem.Hag.35a-b]*.
Rashi's disciple R.Simcha — author of the Machzor Vitry — died in the same year.
Rashi was succeeded by the Rashbam — R.Shmuel ben Meir, his grandson and disciple — who also wrote a (lengthier) commentary on Talmud and the CHUMASH (Bible) *((see ILLUSTRATIONS TEXT A, #5)*.
The Rivan — R.Yehuda ben Natan, a son-in-law of Rashi — has part of his commentary printed in the place of Rashi — around a section of the Talmud (Makot) — at the point where Rashi had died. He is mentioned in Tosaphot *[Tan.27b, Zev.96a, Bech.50b, etc.]*.
At this time R.Yehuda HaLevi ben Shmuel — a disciple of the Rif and the Ri Migash who was renowned for his poetry — wrote (some say edited) the Kuzari (see 4928\1167) *(philosophy based*

on a dialogue with the king of the Khazars (see 4500\740)].
The Riva — R.Yitzchak ben Asher II, a disciple of Rashi — was one of the earliest scholars mentioned in Tosaphot *[Nid.39b, etc.]*.
Tosaphot were considered 'additional' explanations to Rashi's commentary on the Talmud (see 5050\1290), and followed a new style of scholarship, involving logical deductions from the Talmud *[See Dor.Har.6.295]*.

4866 — 1105

The Ba'al HeAruch, R.Natan ben Yechi'el — who (some say) was a disciple of Rbnu.Chananel and R.Moshe HaDarshan — died in Rome in 4866\1105. It was there that he wrote the Sefer HeAruch *(a Talmudic Aramaic-Hebrew dictionary)*, which some say he completed one year before he died.

4885 — 1125

All Jews were expelled from Ghent *(Belgium)*, and from the rest of the province of Flanders.

4886 — 1126

R.Baruch ben Yitzchak I — a disciple of the Rif — died in **Elul** 1126. His disciple (and nephew) was R.Avraham ben David (ibn Daud), Ra'avad I, author of Sefer HaKabbala *(narrative-history)*, who was (later) killed for refusing to convert to Christianity.

4895 — 1135

The Rambam (Maimonides) was born.

The Rambam — R.Moshe ben Maimon, a descendant of King David — was born on 14th **Nissan**, and was a child when he saw — and was blessed by — the Ri Migash (see 4863\1103). The Rambam then considered him as his teacher *[Shem.Hag.1.49a/Mmn.Hil. Sh.Up.5.6]*.

Living in the Year 1140

Name	Born	Died
Rashbam	b.1080?,	d.1174?.
R.Avraham ibn Ezra	b.1089?,	d.1164.
Rabbenu Tam	b.1100?,	d.1171.
Ri (R.Yitzchak)	b.1120?,	d.1200?.
Ra'avad	b.1120?,	d.1198.
Ba'al HaIttur	b.1120?,	d.1193?.
Ba'al Hama'or	b.1125?,	d.1186.
Rambam (Maimonides)	b.1135,	d.1204.

4901 — 1141

The Ri Migash (see 4895\1135) died on the 30th **Nissan**.

4904 — 1144

The first recorded blood libel took place.

On the second day of Pesach 1144, the Jews of Norwich *(England)* were accused of using Christian blood for Pesach *(Passover)* ritual purposes. This was the first recorded anti-Jewish BLOOD LIBEL (see **Av** 5050\1290).

4906 — 1146

R.Peter ben Yosef — a disciple of Rabbenu Tam (see 4950\1190) — was killed (according to some) in Austria.

4907 — 1147

Crusaders (2nd) attacked Jewish communities.

When the remnants of the first Crusaders lost some territory in the Middle East to the Turks, the Pope *(Eugene III)* proclaimed a second Crusade to restore Christian power in the area. These Crusaders also massacred Jews (see 4856\1096) before leaving for the Middle East, where they failed.
The Jews of Wurtzburg *(Germany)* were massacred on the 24th **Adar**, and the Jews of Cologne *(Germany)* were attacked on the 23rd **Nissan**, although many Jews fled to the safety of the mountains or castles. The Jews of Bachrach *(Germany)* were attacked on the 5th **Sivan** (Erev Shavu'ot).

Rabbenu Tam was captured by the Crusaders.

Rabbenu Tam, R.Yaakov ben Meir (see 4931\1171), was a grandson of Rashi and a son of R.Meir (who is mentioned in Tosaphot *[Kid.59a, Shab.56a, etc.]*). Rabbenu Tam — one of the leading BA'ALEI TOSAPHOT *(authors of Tosaphot)* (see 4865\1105, 5050\1290) — was captured by the Crusaders in Ramerupt *(France)*, on the second day of Shavu'ot. They ransacked his home and tore his Sefer Torah scroll into pieces. He escaped the next day — with serious injuries — after being left in a field; some say he escaped with the help of a friendly knight.

4908 — 1148

The Rambam's family, and the Radak's father, left Cordova.

The Jews of Cordova *(Spain)* were attacked by ANTI-JEWISH RIOTERS, and many synagogues were destroyed on the 24th **Tammuz** 1148. When a fanatical Islamic sect took power in Cordova, the Jews were forced to convert (which some did, retaining their Jewish religion secretly) and many fled the country, including R.Maimon ben Yosef, father of the Rambam, and his family (see 4925\1165); R.Yosef Kimchi, father of the Radak (see 4951\1191), who settled in Narbonne *(Provence, S.E.France)*; and R.Yehuda ibn Tibbon (see 4928\1167) who settled in Lunel *(Provence)*.

4910 — 1150

R.Zerachyah (ben Yitzchak) HaLevi — called the RaZah and the Ba'al HaMa'or — was writing his work HaMa'or *(comments on the "Halachot" of the Rif)* *(see ILLUSTRATIONS, TEXT G)* in 1150 in Lunel *(Provence, S.E.France)*. *(The Rambam appears to take extreme exception to one of his Halacha rulings [Mmn.Hil.Mam. 4.1/ HaMa'or HaKatan on Rif Pes.7a(Tal.Pes.28a), Ra'avad/TBY.O.C.443])*.

4919 — 1158

R.Avraham ibn Ezra (see 4924\1164) wrote a letter about Shabbat, in London on the 14th of **Tevet**.

Living in the Year 1160

Rashbam	b.1080?, d.1174?.
R.Avraham ibn Ezra	b.1089?, d.1164.
Rabbenu Tam	b.1100?, d.1171.
Ri (R.Yitzchak)	b.1120?, d.1200?.
Ra'avad	b.1120?, d.1198.
Ba'al HaIttur	b.1120?, d.1193?.
Ba'al Hama'or	b.1125?, d.1186.
Rambam (Maimonides)	b.1135, d.1204.
R.Yehuda HaChasid	b.1150?, d.1217.
Roke'ach (R.Elazar)	b.1160?, d.1237?.
Radak (Kimchi)	b.1160?, d.1235?.

4921 — 1161

Rbnu.Bachya I ben Yosef (ibn Paquda) (Rabbenu Bachaye) wrote Chovat HaLevavot *(Mussar)* in Arabic (see 4928\1167), around 1161 (in Spain). Some say it was written earlier.

R.Eliezer ben Natan, the Ravan — a disciple of the Riva — wrote Even HaEzer *(Halacha, Customs)* and corresponded with Rabbenu Tam and the Rashbam. He is mentioned in Tosaphot *[Shev.26b, Shab.69b, etc./Shem.Hag.1.10b]*.

R.Eliezer of Metz *(France)* (R'EM, R.Eliezer MiMetz) was a disciple of Rabbenu Tam and the Ri. He wrote the Sefer Yere'im *(Halacha, Ethics)*, and is mentioned in Tosaphot *[Shab.36a, 64a, Chul.26b, etc.]*.

4924 — 1164

R.Avraham ben Meir ibn Ezra — who wrote a commentary on the Bible *(see ILLUSTRATIONS TEXT A, #6)* — died on Rosh Chodesh **Adar** 1164, after his wife and children had all died (on separate occasions). There are other opinions as to when he died *[Sed. Had.5934]*. He had discussions with Rabbenu Tam, on his many wanderings (see 4919\1158), and is mentioned in Tosaphot *[R.H.13a, Tan.20b, Kid.37b.]*. He was a close contemporary of R.Yehuda HaLevi — many say they were related — and he is still known in the world of mathematics.

4925 — 1165

The Rambam visited Eretz Yisrael.

After fleeing Cordova (see 4908\1148) where he was born, the Rambam spent some time travelling, before settling in Fez *(Morocco)* for some five years. Due to forced Islamic conversions by radicals (see 4958\1198), he left Fez with his family and sailed to Eretz Yisrael. His ship was threatened by a storm, but reached Acco *(Acre)* on the 3rd **Sivan**. Six months later, he visited Yerushalayim (see 4859\1099). He subsequently left Eretz Yisrael for Egypt, and settled in Fostat (old Cairo), where he reversed the overriding influence of the Kra'im (see 4523\763) that then prevailed *[Mmn.Hil.Mel.5.7, Radvaz]*.

4928 — *1167*

R.David ben Levi — of whom little else is known — was killed in Virmyze *(Worms, Germany)* on the 21st **Cheshvan**, 4928*1167*.

R.Yehuda ibn Tibbon (see 4908\1148) translated a number of works from Arabic into HEBREW. These included: Emunot VeDeyot (see 4690\930), the Kuzari (see 4865\1105), Tikkun Middot HaNefesh (see 4815\1055), and Chovat HaLevavot (see 4921\1161).

There was a BLOOD LIBEL in Gloucester *(England)* in 1168 *(see 4904\1144)*.

4931 — 1171

Rabbenu Tam died.

Fifty-one Jews were burned at the stake (because of a BLOOD LIBEL) in Blois *(France)* on the 20th **Sivan**, and — according to some — Rabbenu Tam (see 4907\1147) declared it a fast day, before his death (only two weeks later) on the 4th **Tammuz**.

Rabbenu Tam was a brother of the Rashbam (see 4865\1105) — and his disciple — and of the Rivam (who had died at a young age, leaving seven orphans, and some PIYUTIM still said today). Rabbenu Tam wrote the Sefer HaYashar *(Pirush Sugiyot and SH'ELOT UTESHUVOT)*, and his BEIT DIN was considered the leading Talmudic authority in his generation *[Tos.Git.36b/ Sed.Had.4930/ Shem.Hag.]*. Rabbenu Tam had eighty disciples sitting before him when he lectured (see 4935\1175) *[Yam.Sh.Sh.Hakd.]*.

4932 — 1172

The Ra'avad (III) was imprisoned (in Provence, *S.E. France*) for a short while on a false charge.

4933 — 1173

Binyamin ben Yona of Tudela *(Spain)* travelled extensively, and recorded what he saw in Masa'ot Binyamin (or Sefer HaMasa'ot), a valuable record of Jewish communities at this time.

R.Petachyah of Regensburg also travelled extensively at this time, and a description of his travels was documented in a book called Sivuv.

4935 — 1175

The Rashbam died.

The Rashbam was very old when he died in 4935\1174 (see 4931\1171).

The Ri — or 'Ri HaZaken', R.Yitzchak ben Shmuel of Dampierre *(France)* — was one of the leading BA'ALEI TOSAPHOT (see 4865\1105, 5050\1290). He was a grandson of R.Simcha (see 4865\1105), a great-grandson of Rashi, and a disciple of his uncle, Rabbenu Tam (see 4931\1171). He lectured to sixty disciples (see 4931\1171), each one of them thoroughly conversant in a different section (Mesechta) of the Talmud, which allowed them instant clarification of any issue.

4939 — 1179

The Ba'al HaIttur, R.Yitzchak ben Abba Mari of Marseilles, completed forty years of work on his encyclopedic Halacha work, Sefer HaIttur, in which he often mentions the Sefer Yere'im (see 4921\1161).

4941 — 1181

Jews were seized in Paris while attending services on Shabbat 25th **Adar**, and were held for ransom. There was a BLOOD LIBEL in Bury St.Edmunds *(England)* in 1181.

4942 — 1182

There was a BLOOD LIBEL in Saragossa *(Spain)*. All Jews were expelled from part of France (see 4958\1198).

4944 — 1184

The young son of the Ri was killed.

R.Elchanan — the son and disciple of the Ri (see 4935\1175) — was killed in Dampierre *(France)* in 1184 during the life of his father *[Otz.Hag.2.155]*. He composed PIYUTIM and is mentioned in Tosaphot *[Zev.45b, Shev.25a, B.M.111b, etc.]*.

4946 — 1186

Aaron of Lincoln *(England)* — the richest man in England, who was said to be worth over 15,000 pounds when died — had (in addition) such vast sums owed to him that the king *(Henry II)* immediately seized his estate, and royal officials set up the "exchequer of Aaron" *(Scaccarium Aaronis)* to deal with it. After sixteen years they only succeeded in recovering approximately half of the debts owed him. Some of his debtors included kings, counts, the archbishop *(of Canterbury)*, and many other nobles. This laid the ground for a system of debt registries for Jewish loans in various cities of England, which enabled the king to oversee Jewish lending and facilitate easier raising of JEW-TAXES.

4948 — 1187

Jews were allowed to return to Yerushalayim.

Jews were allowed to return to Yerushalayim when Saladin — Sultan of Egypt, whose personal physician was the Rambam (see 4925\1165) — recaptured it from the Christians (see 4859\1099).

R.Shimshon ben Avraham of Shantz *(Sens, France)* later emigrated to Eretz Yisrael *(see 4962\1202, 4971\1211)*. He was one of the leading BA'ALEI TOSA-

PHOT (see 5050\1290), is referred to in Tosaphot as 'Rashba', and is also called Ish Yerushalayim. He was the author of Tosaphot Shantz and the Pirush Rash, a commentary on some Mishna *(see ILLUSTRATIONS, TEXT D, #2)*. His older brother, R.Yitzchak, is referred to in Tosaphot as the 'Ritzba', as 'Ri HaBachur' (to distinguish him from 'Ri HaZaken' (see 4939\1179)), and sometimes as the 'Riva' *[Otz.Hag.5.211a]*, (although Riva usually refers to R.Yitzchak ben Asher II (see 4865\1105)) *[Shem.Hag. 35a-b]*. Both brothers were disciples of Rabbenu Tam and the Ri (see 4931\1171, 4935\1175).

Living in the Year 1190

Ri (R.Yitzchak)	b.1120?,	d.1200?.
Ra'avad	b.1120?,	d.1198.
Ba'al HaIttur	b.1120?,	d.1193?.
Ba'al Hama'or	b.1125?,	d.1186.
Rambam (Maimonides)	b.1135,	d.1204.
R.Yehuda HaChasid	b.1150?,	d.1217.
Roke'ach (R.Elazar)	b.1160?,	d.1237?.
Radak (Kimchi)	b.1160?,	d.1235?.
Rbnu.Yona (Gerondi)	b.1180?,	d.1263.

4949 — 1189

R.Yaakov D'Orleans was killed in London.

R.Yaakov of Orleans — a disciple of Rabbenu Tam who hinself is mentioned in Tosaphot *[Ket.47a, Zev.55b, Nid.8a, etc.]* (and sometimes as "Rabbenu Tam") — was killed with many other Jews in the ANTI-JEWISH RIOTS which took place in **Elul**, in London, at the coronation of Richard I (the Lion-Hearted). King Richard later went on a Crusade to try and recapture Yerushalayim (see 4948*1187*).

4950 — 1190

Jews massacred in England in the 3rd Crusade.

A crusading enthusiasm swept England *(see 4949\1189, 4952\1192, 4956\1196)*. The Jews of Norwich were massacred on 28th **Shvat** *(see 4904\1144)*, and the Jews of Stamfordfair were massacred on 27 **Adar**. The Jews of York refused to be subjected to FORCED BAPTISM, and R.Eliyahu — a disciple of Rabbenu Tam *(see 4906\1146)* — was killed there, (another disciple of Rabbenu Tam was killed in York in 1191 *(see 4951\1191)*; while on the 7th **Nissan** many brought about their own mass deaths *(and since then the Jewish custom is not to stay overnight in York.)*. On the 9th of **Nissan**, fifty-seven Jews were killed in Bury St.Edmunds *(England)*.

One hundred Jews were burned to death in France, by order of the king.

R.Shmuel ben Eli HaLevi was head of the vibrant YESHIVA in Baghdad which had been reconstituted — by his father who was a descendant of Shmuel HaNavi (the Prophet) — from the old academies in Sura and Pumpedita. He was not completely successful in his attempt, in 1190, to have the position of REISH GALUTA (Exilarch) abolished so that the funds could be diverted to the YESHIVA. He had a Halacha disagreement with the Rambam, and had a very learned daughter who gave Torah lectures (in a special arrangement, so that the (male) students could not see her).

4951 — 1191

The Radak wrote his commentary.

R.David ben Yosef Kimchi of Narbonne *(Provence, S.E.France)*, the Radak, (who was very young when his father died, see 4908\1148), wrote his commentary on the T'NACH (Bible) at around this time (see 4992\1232)*(see ILLUSTRATIONS, TEXT B, #4)*.

A disciple of Rabbenu Tam, R.Yom Tov — author of Omnam Kein *(PIYUT which is said on Yom Kippur evening)* — was killed in York *(England)* (see 4950\1190).

4952 — 1192

R.Yaakov of Corbeil — a disciple of Rabbenu Tam who is mentioned in Tosaphot *[Shab.27a, Bet.6b, Ket.12b, etc.]* — was killed (some say in Corbeil) in 1192 (see 4950\1190, 4051\1191).

4953 — 1193

There was a BLOOD LIBEL in Winchester *(England)* (see 4950\1190).

4954 — 1194

The Ramban was born.

R.Moshe ben Nachman, the Ramban (see 5030\1270), was born in Gerona *(Spain)* on the 12th **Elul**.

4956 — 1196

Fifteen Jews (including an advisor to the duke) were massacred in Vienna by participants in the 3rd Crusade (see 4950\1190).

R.Yitzchak ben Asher III (see 4948\ *1187*) — who was named after his grandfather the 'Riva' (see 4865\1105) — was killed in Speyer *(Germany)*.

4957 1197

On the 6th **Adar** 1197, R.Shmuel ben Natrunai — a son-in-law and disciple of the 'Ravan' (see 4921\1161) — was tortured and then killed, with many other Jews in Neuss *(France)*.
Another son-in-law of the Ravan — R.Yoel ben Yitzchak HaLevi, a disciple of R.Ephrayim of Regensberg (who in turn was a disciple of Rabbenu Tam) who also wrote PIYUTIM — lived in Bonn for many years before he became rabbi in Cologne (see 4977\1217).

4958 *1197*

R.Elazar ben Yehuda Roke'ach — of Virmyze *(Worms, Germany)* (see 4998\1237), author of the Roke'ach — was wounded (some say by Crusaders) who killed his wife and children on the 22nd **Kislev**.

4958 1198

Jews were allowed to return to the areas of expulsion in France in 1198 (see 4942\1182).
Jews of North Africa — even those who had openly converted to Islam, whilst secretly remaining Jews (see 4925\1165) — were required to wear SPECIAL DRESS (see 4610\850).

4959 *1198*

The Ra'avad died.

The Ra'avad — (Ra'avad III), R.Avraham ben David of Posquieres *(Provence, S.E.France)* (see 4932\1172) a son-in-law of Ra'avad II, (**R.Av**raham ben Yitzchak **Av Beit din**) — died on the 26th **Kislev**. He was born in Narbonne *(Provence, S.E.France)*, established a YESHIVA in Posquieres, and wrote Hasagot *(critical comments, sometimes acerbic)* on the Rambam *(see ILLUSTRATIONS, TEXT I, #2)*, on the Rif and on HaMa'or (see 4910\1150).

4962 1202

A letter was sent to the Torah scholars of Lunel *(Provence, S.E.France)* — by (the young) R.Meir ben Todros Abulafia HaLevi, the 'Ramah' of Toledo *(Spain)* (see 5004\1244) — raising doubts about the philosophical views of the Rambam. He requested, unsuccessfully, that study of the Rambam's philosophical works be prohibited below a certain age (see 4992\1232). He also raised these doubts with the scholars in northern France, and R.Shimshon (Ba'al Tosaphot Shantz, see 4948\ *1187*) replied with respect and admiration for the Rambam, whose works he had apparently just seen.

4963 1203

R.Yaakov HaChasid (HaLevi) of Marvege *(France)* recorded an entry in his SH'ELOT UTESHUVOT Min HaShamayim (Responsa from Heaven) on the 29th **Elul** 4963 (1203).
R.Baruch ben Yitzchak II — a disciple of the Ri — wrote the Sefer HaTeruma, and is mentioned in Tosaphot *[A.Z.9b, 76a, Yom.46b]*. He later settled in Eretz Yisrael.
R.Avraham ben Natan HaYarchi — who had left Lunel *(Provence, S.E.France)* (hence the name HaYarchi, for 'lunar'), and had travelled through Germany and Provence — settled in Spain where he wrote his Sefer HaManhig.

4965 *1204*

The Rambam died.

The Rambam, R.Moshe ben Maimon (Maimonides), died on 20th of **Tevet**. R.Avraham, his 19-year-old son (and disciple) succeeded him. The Rambam's Halacha code, Yad HaChazaka - Mishneh Torah *(see ILLUSTRATIONS, TEXT I, #1)* — an encyclopedic compilation (in HEBREW) of all Talmudic law in a brilliant and original systematic arrangement (which was a departure from previous works, see 4863\1103, 4865\1105) — was rapidly accepted as the final word in Jewish law in the SEPHARDIC communities (see 4996\1236) *[Tsh.Mhrm.Alashkar.96.p.260-end/etc.]*. In a letter, five years before his death, he had praised and encouraged R.Shmuel ben Yehuda ibn Tibbon — the son of a translator, see 4928\1167 — for his work on translating his Moreh Nevuchim *(Guide for the Perplexed, philosophy)* from Arabic into HEBREW. Among other works, the Rambam also wrote a commentary on Mishna (see 5070\1310) *(see ILLUSTRATIONS, TEXT D, #3)*.

4966 1206

A number of Jews were killed in Halle *(Germany)* and the rest were expelled.

4969 — 1209

Two hundred Jews were killed in a massacre in Beziers *(Provence, S.E.France)*, on the 19th **Av**.

4971 — 1210

Jews were imprisoned (for ransom) in England, by order of the king, on the 13th **Cheshvan**.

4971 — 1211

A group of 300 Talmud scholars (from France and England) emigrated to Eretz Yisrael, subsequent to the emigration of R.Shimshon (Ba'al Tosaphot Shantz, see 4948*1187*, 4962\\1202) *[See Encpd.Jud.14.778]*.

4977 — *1216*

The Pope *(Innocent III)* issued an order in **Tevet** for Jews to wear a BADGE, in order to distinguish them from the rest of the population *(see 4610\850, 4958\1198)*. (This order was followed in various ways, and in different countries, for five centuries.) Many Jews in England paid money in order to be exempted from wearing the BADGE (see **Av** 5050\\1290), and Jews in Spain threatened to leave the Christian controlled part of the country.

4977 — 1217

R.Yehuda HaChasid of Regensburg *(Germany)* — a disciple of the Ri, and author of Sefer HaChasidim *(Mussar, Halacha, KABBALA-Customs)*, and the assumed author of the Anim Zemirot PIYUT — died on the 13th **Adar**. He learned his KABBALA concepts from his father — R.Shmuel HaChasid (ben Klonymos), about whom it is said that he composed the Shir HaYichud *[Maharal, R.Yaakov Emden]* — who had received them from his ancestors (see 4998\\1237). He was a leader of a group of extremely devout scholars, called CHASSIDEI ASHKENAZ. He is mentioned in Tosaphot *[B.M.5b]*.
R.Eliezer ben Yoel HaLevi, — the 'Raviyah', a disciple of (his grandfather) the 'Ravan', R.Yehuda HaChasid, and R.Eliezer of Metz — lived in Germany, succeeded his father as rabbi in Cologne (see 4957\\1197), and was the author of Avi HaEzri and Avi Assaf *(both Halacha)*. He is mentioned in Tosaphot *[Tan.13a, Pes.100b, Chul.47b]*.

Although the Mongol ruler Genghis Khan was the greatest conqueror of all times — *(his empire being three times the geographical size of Alexander's)*, and despite his having conquered areas of Jewish populations *(Persia, Bukhara, etc.)* — nevertheless there is no documentation of any effect on Jewish life (see 5020\\1260, 5051\\1291).

Living in the Year 1220

Roke'ach (R.Elazar)	b.1160?,	d.1237?.
Radak (Kimchi)	b.1160?,	d.1235?.
Rbnu.Yona (Gerondi)	b.1180?,	d.1263.
Ramban (Nachmanides)	b.1194?,	d.1270?.
Maharam MeRothenburg	b.1215?,	d.1293.

4981 — 1221

Many Jews were killed in Erfurt *(Germany)* in a massacre on the 25th **Sivan**, and some threw themselves into the flames of the burning synagogue.
The Jews of Sicily and Pisa *(Italy)* were ordered to wear a blue BADGE, and to grow beards (see 4977*1216*).

4985 — 1225

All Jews were expelled from Cremona and Pavia *(N. Italy)* — within fifty years they were resettling there.

4988 — *1227*

R.Ezra (HaNavi) of Gerona *(Spain)* — a disciple of R.Yitzchak Sagi Nahor (the blind son of the 'Ra'avad', who was extremely well versed in the KABBALA he had learned from his father) — was a teacher of the Ramban, and is mentioned in Tosaphot *[Shev.25a, B.B.28a, Git.88a]*. He died on the 9th **Tevet**.
R.Shmuel HaSardi of Spain was a contemporary and disciple of the Ramban, and he wrote Sefer HaTerumot.

4990 — 1230

Jews of Wiener-Neustadt *(Austria)* were attacked for eleven days by ANTI-JEWISH RIOTERS.
Many Jews were killed, and many were forced to convert to Christianity in Astorga *(Spain)*.

4992 — 1232

The Jews were massacred in Marrakesh *(Morocco)*.

R.Shlomo (ben Avraham, Min HaHar) — of Montpelier *(Provence, S.E.France)*, who was respected by his contemporaries, the Ramban and the 'Ramah' — was concerned over the tendency towards the study of philosophy; he attempted to prohibit such studies (see 4962\1202), including the Rambam's works. This raised a controversy involving others (see 5024\1263), in which the Ramban, a recognized leader, appeared to be a mediator, and the (elderly) Radak supported the Rambam's works. Nevertheless, the controversy passed into non-Jewish hands, and there was a burning of the Rambam's works (see 5002\1242).

4995 — 1235

Seven Jews were tortured and burned at the stake, in Bischofsheim *(Germany)*, on the 10th **Shvat**.

4996 — *1235*

Thirty-four Jews were killed in Fulda *(Germany)* in a BLOOD LIBEL, on the 18th **Tevet** (see 5007\1247).

4996 — 1236

R.Moshe ben Yaakov of Coucy *(France)* travelled through Provence and Spain, encouraging Jews in keeping Mitzvot — particularly Tefillin — and preventing intermarriage in Spain. He wrote the Sefer Mitzvot Gadol (S'MaG) — which made use of the Rambam's work — and it received broad acceptance in the ASHKENAZI communities (see 4965*1204*). He is mentioned in Tosaphot *[Me.16a, A.Z.13a, Ber.14b, etc.]*. His brother in law was R.Shimshon, mentioned in Tosaphot as HaSar MiCoucy (the Count — or sir — of Coucy) *[Me.9b, Ber.9a, 14a, etc.]*.

Rampaging mobs massacred Jews in France.

Over 2,500 Jews were killed in France by rampaging mobs (some say crusaders). The Jews of Narbonne *(Provence, S.E. France)* were saved, and in commemoration they instituted a local Purim (which is the first recorded) on the 21st **Adar**.

4998 — *1237*

R.Avraham Maymuni HaNagid — the only son of the Rambam (see 4965*1204*) — died on the 18th **Kislev** 4998\1237. He was succeeded by his son R.David HaNagid (see 5045\1285), who wrote DeRashot R.David (or Midrash David).
R.Elazar ben Yehuda Roke'ach (see 4958\1197) was a disciple of R.Yehuda HaChasid, and he wrote the Sefer Roke'ach *(Halacha, Customs, Mussar)* in which some of his teaching are attributed to direct transmission (through R.Yehuda HaChasid) all the way back to R.Shimon HaPakuli (see 3836\76, 4977\1217) *[Shem.Hag.1.11a]*.

Living in the Year 1240

Rbnu.Yona (Gerondi)	b.1180?,	d.1263.
Ramban (Nachmanides)	b.1194?,	d.1270?.
Maharam MeRothenburg	b.1215?,	d.1293.
Rashba	b.1235?,	d.1310?.
Mordechai (Pirush)	b.1240?,	d.1298.
Hagahot Maimoniyot	b.1240?,	d.1298.

5000 — 1240

The Pope *(Gregory IX)* ordered the confiscation of all copies of the Talmud and other Jewish books, on the 16th **Tammuz** 1239; and consequently on the 7th **Adar-2** 1240, all copies of the Talmud were confiscated in France. R.Yechi'el of Paris — who is mentioned in Tosaphot *[Yom.18b]*, and was a disciple of R.Yehuda of Paris (who was a descendant of Rashi) — was forced to DEBATE (see 5014\1254) the *meshumad (apostate)* who had libeled the Talmud. R.Moshe of Coucy (see 4996\1236) also attended the DEBATE, which began on the 4th **Tammuz** 1240. Despite the eloquence of the defenders, the Talmud was burned two years later, see 5002\1242.
All Jews were expelled from the province of Brittany *(France)* by the local duke, in **Tammuz** 1240.

5001 — 1241

Most of the Jews of Frankfort am Main were massacred, and the Jewish quarter was destroyed on the 14th **Sivan**.
Many Jews were killed in Bohemia when the Tartars invaded the country.
The Jews in (Christian) Spain were forced to attend CONVERSION SERMONS by an order of the king *(James I of Aragon)* issued in 1241 (see 5023\1263).

5002 — 1242

A massive burning of the Talmud in Paris.

Twenty-four wagon loads of handwritten copies of the Talmud, as well as other Jewish books — all hand-written and hand-made before the invention of printing (see 5235\1475) — were burned, in **Tammuz**, as a result of events two years earlier, see 5000\1240. This Erev Shabbat Parshat Chukat was observed as a fast day for generations, to commemorate the monumental loss from which Torah scholarship in France never really recovered (see 5066\1306). Some say that this burning took place at the same location in Paris as had another burning nine years earlier (see 4992\1232).

5003 — 1243

Jews were burned to death in Belitz *(near Berlin, Germany)* in the first recorded libel of RITUAL DESECRATION. (The charge — called 'DESECRATION OF THE HOST' — was that Jews purposely desecrated one of the Christian sacraments.)
Eleven Jews were killed in a BLOOD LIBEL in Kitzingen *(Germany)*.

5004 — 1244

Egyptians and Turks sacked Yerushalayim.

Most Jews fled from Yerushalayim, but some were killed by the hordes who sacked the city and massacred the inhabitants, leaving almost no Jews there (see 4948*1187*, 5027\1267).
On the 26th **Adar**, the Pope *(Innocent IV)* ordered further burnings of the Talmud (see 5002\1242).
The 'Ramah' of Toledo *(Spain)* (see 4962\1202) — a close contemporary of the Ramban, who was well versed in KABBALA and was author of Yad Ramah *(Chidushim)* — died on the 18th **Nissan**.
R.Yeshayahu HaZaken of Trani *(Italy)*, who wrote Tosaphot Rid (R.Yeshayahu D'Trani), was the leading Torah scholar in Italy. He had great respect for his contemporary, R.Yitzchak (ben Moshe) of Vienna — who was a disciple of the 'Raviyah', R.Yehuda HaChasid, and R.Yehuda of Paris. R.Yitzchak of Vienna wrote the Sefer Or Zaru'a, which was later abbreviated by his son, R.Chaim (Eliezer).

5007 — 1247

Many Jews were killed, and others were FORCIBLY CONVERTED to Islam, in Meknes *(Morocco)*, with the rise of a new radical government.
Emperor Frederick II had planned to kill all the Jews (in his Holy Roman Empire) if the BLOOD LIBEL in Fulda (see 4995\1235) were true. Upon much investigation, he concluded that BLOOD LIBELS were false. The Pope *(Innocent IV)* who had ordered the burning of the Talmud (see 5004\1244), stated in 1247 that BLOOD LIBELS were false.
However, that same year many Jews in Valreas *(France)* were tortured — some mutilated, others killed, and all the rest imprisoned (with Jewish properties confiscated) — in a BLOOD LIBEL.

5008 — 1248

In France, Christians were forbidden to have contact with Jews.

5010 — 1250

The Jews of Tunisia *(Northern Africa)* were required by their Muslim rulers to wear a SPECIAL BADGE *(see 4610\850, 4977\1216)*.
A new government which oppressed the Jews, began to rule in Egypt (and spread to surrounding countries in Northern Africa). Conditions of Jewish life in that region declined significantly.

5012 — 1252

The Inquisition began to use torture.

The Inquisition was a series of (localized, church) courts empowered — by the central authority, the presiding Pope — to investigate and judge Christian heretics, who could be punished and/or killed. Initially established in 1184 by the Pope, to "do away with" the growing heresy in southern France, it was reenforced in the 1230's. In 1252, the Pope *(Innocent IV)* (see 5007\1247, 5013\1253) allowed the use of torture during these investigations of heresy. The Inquisition was later expanded to other areas of Europe (see 5038\1278, 5241\1481, 5301*1540*), and later to Central and Southern America (see 5330\1570).
Jews were subsequently open to such charges of 'heresy' — just for being Jewish — (see 5038\1278) and torture was a tool for extracting "confessions".

5013 — 1253

The Pope *(Innocent IV*, see 5013\1253) ordered the expulsion of all Jews from Vienne *(France)* in **Av**.

5014 ≈ 1254

A Jewish participant in a religious DEBATE *(see 5000\1240, 5023\1263)* in Cluny *(France)* was killed by a Christian knight.

5015 ≈ 1255

Many (prominent) Jews were killed in England, in the BLOOD LIBEL of Lincoln, on the 24th **Elul** 1255 — the same year that R.Eliyahu Menachem ben Moshe was removed from his position of Chief Rabbi in London, because he refused to force his fellow Jews to pay a heavy tax.

5017 ≈ 1257

All Jews of Rome were required to wear a JEW'S BADGE in 1257 (see 4977*1216*, 5019\1259).

5019 ≈ 1259

The Jews of Mayence *(Mainz, Germany)* were required to wear a JEW'S BADGE *(see 5017\1257)*.

Living in the Year 1260

Rbnu.Yona (Gerondi)	b.1180?,	d.1263.
Ramban (Nachmanides)	b.1194?,	d.1270?.
Maharam MeRothenburg	b.1215?,	d.1293.
Rashba	b.1235?,	d.1310?.
Mordechai (Pirush)	b.1240?,	d.1298.
Hagahot Maimoniyot	b.1240?,	d.1298.
Me'iri (R.Menachem)	b.1249?,	d.1315?.
Rosh (R.Asher)	b.1250?,	d.1327.

5020 ≈ 1260

R.Yechi'el of Paris left France to settle in Eretz Yisrael *(see 5000\1240, 5002\1242, and 4971\1211)*, which was under threat of invasion by the Mongols (who had conquered Syria, and massacred Jews see 4977\1217, 5051\1291).
R.Tzidkiyah ben Avraham HaRofeh — a cousin and disciple of the 'Rivevan', R.Yehuda ben Binyamin — wrote the Shibbolei HaLeket *(Customs, Halacha)* in Italy.

5023 ≈ 1263

The Ramban was forced by the king *(James I)* of Aragon *(Spain)* (see 5001\1241) to DEBATE *(see 5014\1254)* a *meshumad* *(apostate)* on the 12th **Av** 1263, and although he did so quite successfully, nevertheless he had to leave Aragon because of the ensuing controversy. The king ordered that all references to (early) Christianity be censored and removed from the Talmud — the most elaborate of the very few (independent) works that contain documentation of that era.

5024 ≈ *1263*

Rbnu.Yona — (HaChasid) (ben Avraham) Gerondi *(Gerona, Spain)*, who was a disciple and supporter of R.Shlomo Montpelier (see 4992\1232) — died in **Cheshvan** 5024\1263. He was a cousin and *mechutan* of the Ramban, and the author of Sha'arei Teshuva *(Mussar)* and Chidushim.

5024 ≈ 1264

Jews of Arnstadt *(Germany)* were attacked and massacred by ANTI-JEWISH RIOTERS on 11th **Av**.

5025 ≈ 1265

Twenty Jews were killed in Koblenz *(Germany)*.

5026 ≈ 1266

R.Avraham, a *ger tzedek* from Augsburg *(Germany)*, was killed on the 22nd **Kislev** 5026\1265.
Twelve Jews were killed in Cologne *(Germany)* in **Tammuz**.
All Jews were ordered to wear SPECIAL HATS in parts of Poland *(see 5027\1267, 5039\1278)*.

5027 ≈ 1267

All Jews of Poland (see 5026\1266), Austria, and Silesia *(a region between Germany and Poland)*, were required to wear a SPECIAL HAT (see 4977*1216*), by an order issued in **Shvat**.

The Ramban settled in Eretz Yisrael.

The Ramban arrived in Eretz Yisrael (see 5023\1263 and 5020\1260), and when he visited Yerushalayim in **Elul**, he established a house for prayer for Rosh HaShana. He renewed the Jewish settlement in Yerushalayim, since the city had been sacked (see 5004\1244).

5028 — 1268

All Jews of Spain were exempted from wearing a JEW'S BADGE (see 5027\1267, 4977*1216*), but were required to wear a round cape in its stead.

5029 — 1269

All Jews of France were ordered to wear a YELLOW BADGE in **Tammuz**. They were also expelled from Carpentras *(Provence, S.E.France)* — but returned a few years later when that area (around Avignon) was ceded by the king to the Pope.

5030 — 1270

The Ramban died.

The Ramban, R.Moshe ben Nachman (Nachmanides) (see 4988\1227, 5027\1267) — who wrote a commentary on the Bible *(see ILLUSTRATIONS TEXT A, #7)*, *chidushim*, and many other works — died on the 11th **Nissan**.
The 'Me'iri' — R.Menachem ben Shlomo Me'iri of Provence *(S.E.France)*, author of Beit HaBechira, *(basic commentary on the Mishna-Talmud)* — corresponded with (and had great respect for) the Rashba (see 5065\1305, 5070\1310), who was a disciple of the Ramban, and rabbi in Barcelona *(Spain)*.

5031 — 1271

All Jews of Brabant *(province in the Netherlands and Belgium)* were to be expelled by an order left in the will of the duke. However, his widow received a declaration from Thomas Aquinas — a famous Christian scholar significantly influenced by the Rambam's philosophy — in which he indicated that heavy taxes should be extracted instead, and that the Jews should wear a SPECIAL BADGE *(see 5029\1269)*.

5035 — 1275

All Jews were expelled from Worcester *(England)* (see 5039\1278).

5037 — 1277

The Jews were attacked in an ANTI-JEWISH RIOT in Pamplona *(Spain)*, and their houses were destroyed.

5038 — 1278

R.Yitzchak Males, rabbi of Toulouse *(France)*, was burned at the stake on the 9th **Shvat**, by the Inquisition (see 5012\1252), which was well established by this time in the central and western parts of Europe.
On the 14th **Av**, an order was issued by the Pope *(Nicholas III)* that Jews must attend CONVERSION SERMONS by Christian priests (see 5001\1241). The order was enforced in England shortly thereafter (see 5039\1278, **Av** 5050\1290), and then sporadically at various times in various countries (see 4977*1216*).

5039 — *1278*

Over a number of years, the Jews of England were subjected to very restrictive laws — in business, in the parts of the country they could live — and they were continuously forced to pay very high taxes *(see 5015\1255, 5035\1275, 5038\1278)*. On the 10th **Cheshvan** 5039*1278*, many were imprisoned and killed on charges of circulating counterfeit money. Subsequently, on the 18th **Nissan** 1279, a number of Jews were killed in London in a BLOOD LIBEL.
The Jews of Poland were required to wear a RED BADGE *(see 5026\1266)*.

5039 — 1279

By order of the Church Council of Buda (Budapest) Jews were forbidden to lease land and required to wear the JEWS BADGE.

Living in the Year 1280

Maharam MeRothenburg	b.1215?,	d.1293.
Rashba	b.1235?,	d.1310?.
Mordechai (Pirush)	b.1240?,	d.1298.
Hagahot Maimoniyot	b.1240?,	d.1298.
Me'iri (R.Menachem)	b.1249?,	d.1315?.
Rosh (R.Asher)	b.1250?,	d.1327.
Rbnu.Bachya II	b.1265?,	d.1340?.
Tur (R.Yaakov ben Asher)	b.1275?,	d.1349?.

5040 — 1280

The S'MaK — R.Yitzchak of Corbeil (also called R.Yitzchak Ba'al HaChotem) — was author of Sefer Mitzvot Katan (S'MaK, or Amudei HaGola),

and son-in-law and disciple of R.Yechi'el of Paris. He died in 1280 (some say in 1270).
R.Avraham (ben Shmuel) Abulafia — a controversial personality from Spain *[Tsh.Rashba.548/ Shem.Hag.2.19a/Otz.Hag.2.33]* — travelled to Rome to convert the Pope *(Nicholas III)* to JUDAISM. Although a stake had been prepared to burn him at — upon arrival — he did not turn back — not until he heard that the Pope had died.

5041 1281

Jews were killed in a BLOOD LIBEL in Mayence *(Mainz, Germany)*, and the synagogue was burned down (see 5043\1283).

5043 1283

There was another BLOOD LIBEL in Mayence (see 5041\1281), and one in Bachrach *(Germany)*, and many Jews were killed in the ensuing massacres.

5045 1285

180 Jews were killed in a BLOOD LIBEL in Munich (see 5043\1283).
R.David ben Avraham HaNagid — the grandson of the Rambam (see 4998\1237) — was removed from his position in Cairo (by the Sultan), and he left for Eretz Yisrael, where he defended the works of the Rambam (see 4992\1232, 5065\1305). Five years later he was asked to return (see 5050\1290).
A very prominent *sefer* was published anonymously at around this time and scholars have not succeeded in establishing the identity of the author, although many consider the author to have been a disciple of the Rashba. *Sefer HaChinuch* — first published in Venice in 1523 — is a comprehensive description of the 613 commandments, arranged according to their appearance in the Chumash *(Bible)* and in accordance to the listing of the Rambam.

5046 1286

The Maharam MeRothenburg was imprisoned.

Maharam MeRothenburg — R.Meir ben Baruch, a disciple of R.Yitzchak of Vienna and of R.Yechi'el of Paris — was the leading Halacha authority in Germany. He wrote thousands of SH'ELOT UTESHUVOT, as well as Tosaphot on Yoma, now printed as the standard Tosaphot (see 5050\1290).
The Maharam MeRothenburg intended to leave the country — because of the continuous dangers and difficulties Jews were experiencing (see 5043\1283) — but he was denounced by a *meshumad* *(apostate)*, and then imprisoned on the 4th **Tammuz** in the fortress at Ensisheim. A huge ransom was imposed for his release, but he refused (on Halacha grounds) to allow it to be paid (so that a precedent not be set). He continued his teaching for seven years (see 5053\1293) — in the fortress — where his disciple R.Shimon ben Tzadok visited him regularly and recorded his Halacha rulings in a work called Tashbetz *(as distinct from "Tashbatz"; see 5168\1407)*.
On the same day that the Maharam MeRothenburg was interned, forty Jews were killed in a BLOOD LIBEL in Oberwesel *(Germany)* (see 5045\1285); and this was followed by a massacre in Bachrach *(Germany)* in 1287 (see 5043\1283).

5048 1288

Thirteen Jews were burned at the stake by the Inquisition in Troyes *(France)*, in a BLOOD LIBEL on 20th **Iyar**, and others were killed in a BLOOD LIBEL in Neuchatel *(Switzerland)*.

5050 1289

All Jews were expelled from Anjou and Le Mans *(in France)*.

5050 1290

New works advanced the study of KABBALA.

KABBALA (Torah mysticism) was handed down orally (and discreetly) through the generations *(see Adar 4977\1217, 4988\1227)* (hence the name KABBALA — received teachings).
R.Menachem (ben Binyamin) of Recanti *(Italy)* wrote a KABBALA commentary on the CHUMASH (Bible), and Piskei HaRecanti *(Halacha)*.
R.Moshe de Leon *(Spain)* found (and copied) a KABBALA manuscript, that has been accepted by Talmud scholars as the Zohar, composed by R.Shimon bar Yochai, the TANNA *[see 5051\1291]*.

≈ R.Yosef ben Avraham Gikatilya (of Spain) wrote Sha'arei Ora *(Kabbala)*.

The Tosaphot era concluded at around this time.

≈ R.Peretz ben Yitzchak — of Corbeil *(France)*, a disciple of R.Yechi'el of Paris — composed one of the last Tosaphot writings, called Tosaphot Rbnu.Peretz, (part of) which is now printed as the standard Tosaphot on a section of the Talmud (Avoda Zara).

≈ R.Eliezer of Touques *(France)* also wrote one of the last Tosaphot, called Tosaphot Tuch (Touques), which is an abbreviated version of Tosaphot Shantz (see 4948*1187*) — edited to include other Tosaphot.

≈ Although Tosaphot Tuch now comprises the major part of the Tosaphot printed around the Talmud *(see Illustrations, Text E#4)*, many other independent Tosaphot were written *[Tos.Shev.35a, B.M.111a, M.K.20b, Yom.2b, Mrsha 'A"N N"L'/See 5004\1244, 5046\1286]*.

≈ The authors, the Ba'alei Tosaphot, included more than 100 scholars of France and Germany and extended over a period of almost 200 years (see 4865\1105). It is therefore not certain which Tosaphot writings were included in the standard version now available (see 5046\1286) *[Tos.A.Z.9b-end/ Sh.Mkbtzt.Ket.31b-end/ Yam.Sh.Sh.Yev.4.34/ Yad.Mlchi.Klly.HaTos.2.14/ Shem.Hag.2.54a-b]*.

≈ Many earlier (and other) scholars are quoted in Tosaphot. These include:

- R.Yehudai Gaon *[Pes.30a, B.K.53b, etc.]*,
- Halachot Gedolot (BaHaG) *[Pes.30a, etc.]*,
- She'iltot D'R.Acha(i) *[Pes.30a, etc.]*,
- R.Saadya Gaon *[Git.2a, etc]*,
- R.Tzemach Gaon *[M.K.20b, etc.]*,
- Shimusha Rabba *[Min.29b, 34b, Ber.60b]*,
- R.Hai Gaon *[A.Z.58b, etc.]*,
- Rbnu.Gershom Me'or HaGola *[Betz.24b, etc]*,
- the Rif *[Eruv.104a, etc]*,
- (R.Natan Ba'al) HaAruch *[Shab.27b, etc]*,
- Machzor Vitry *[Ber.14a, etc.]*,
- Rambam *[Min.42b, Ber.44a/ see Yam.Sh.Sh.Hakd]*,
- Ra'avad *[Tem.12b, etc.]*.

In 1290, R.David HaNagid was reinstated in Cairo (see 5045\1285).

Chapter 12b

Later Rishonim, Persecutions, and Expulsions

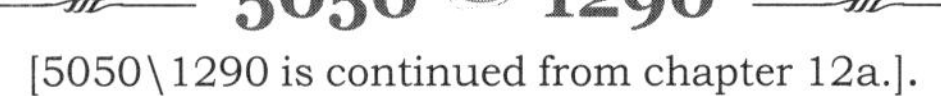

5050 ≈ 1290

[5050\1290 is continued from chapter 12a.].

All Jews were expelled from England.

England was the first European country to have a blood libel (see 4904\1144), was amongst the first to require Jews to wear a special badge (see 4977*1216*), and was the first to force Jews to attend conversion sermons (see 5038\1278). On Tisha B'Av in 1290, England became the first European country to completely expel all Jews from its borders (see 5416\1656). Sixteen thousand Jews left, and most settled in Germany and some provinces of France.
The Jews of Naples, Bari (see 4692\932) and other towns in southern Italy were massacred and subjected to forced baptism (see 5071\1311), in a blood libel in 1290, and many left.

5051 ≈ 1291

Rbnu.Bachya ben Asher — a disciple of the Rashba (in Spain) — wrote Midrash Rbnu.Bachya (Bachaye), a commentary on Chumash (Bible) which includes Kabbala from the Zohar (see 5050\1290).
A Jewish physician — who had risen to the highest power, under the Mongol ruler of Persia *(Arghun Khan)* — was assassinated by enemies on the 3rd **Nissan**, and many Jews were massacred.

5052 ≈ 1291

The Sultan of Egypt conquered Acco *(Acre)*, killed many Jews, and imprisoned others — including R.Yitzchak (ben Shmuel) *De'Min Acco* (of Acco), a disciple of the Ramban (see 5027\1267) who was well versed in Kabbala. When released he went to Spain, and he wrote a commentary on the Ramban's Chumash (Bible) commentary, and an authentication of the Zohar (see 5050\1290).

5053 ≈ 1293

The Maharam MeRothenburg died in prison.

The Maharam MeRothenburg died in the fortress of Ensisheim (see 5046\1286) on the 19th **Iyar**, but his body was not released for burial for fourteen years (see 5067\1307).

R.Aharon HaLevi, the 'Ra'ah', a descendant of the Razah and disciple of the Ramban, wrote Chidushim and also Bedek HaBayit *(a critique on the Rashba's Torat HaBayit)* (see 5070\1310). They were both rabbis in Barcelona — and the Rashba wrote Mishmeret HaBayit (anonymously, at first) in response

A number of Jews were forced to convert to Islam in Iraq.

5054 — 1294

A number of Jews were killed in Berne *(Switzerland)* in a BLOOD LIBEL, and the rest were expelled. They were allowed to return after paying an enormous amount of money, and also agreeing that all debts owed to them be annulled. (The annulment of debts owed to Jews was not uncommon in Europe.)

5058 — 1298

The Rindfleisch massacres began.

A knight by the name of Rindfleisch led a mob of people on a journey of Jewish massacre. It began in Rottingen *(Germany)* on the 7th **Iyar**, and spread out to some 150 Jewish communities within a few months, causing many thousands of deaths (as many as 100,000) in the course of a few years. The BLOOD LIBEL charges of previous years *(see 5043\1283, 5046\1286, 5048\1288, 5054\1294)* were still prominent in the minds of those who participated in these slaughters.

Jews were massacred in Wiener-Neustadt *(Austria)* on the 12th **Tammuz**, in Ifhauben *(Austria)* on the 13th, and 250 Jews were killed in Rothenburg A.T. *(Germany)* on the 14th. The Jews of Morgentheim *(Austria)* were massacred on the 18th **Tammuz**, the Jews of Wurtzburg *(Germany)* on the 13th **Av**, and Jews of Bischofsheim A.T. *(Germany)* on the 14th.

The 'Mordechai' was killed in the Rindfleisch massacres.

R.Mordechai (ben Hillel) (Ashkenazi) — a disciple of Maharam MeRothenburg, and author of the 'Mordechai' *(Halacha)*, was killed with his wife and five children on the 22nd **Av**, together with 728 other Jews of Nuremberg *(Germany)*. The Mordechai and his peer Hagahot Maimoniyot were the first to document the prohibition of *kitniyos* (beans) on Pesach — as accepted by ASHKENAZIM (*see CHART TAKKANOT HAGE'ONIM*).

R.Avraham ben Baruch — who, some say, was the brother of Maharam MeRothenburg — was killed with his wife and children in Mayence *(Mainz, Germany)* [Otz.Hag.2.101].

Ten Jews were killed in Korneuburg *(Austria)* in a RITUAL DESECRATION libel *(see 5003\1243)*.

5059 — 1298

The Hagahot Maimoniyot killed in the Rindfleisch massacres.

R.Meir (ben Yekutiel) HaKohen — the author of Hagahot Maimoniyot (notes on the Rambam's Yad HaChazaka) *(see ILLUSTRATIONS TEXT I; #3)* — was a disciple of the Maharam MeRothenburg and R.Peretz of Corbeil. He was killed with his family in the Rindfleisch massacres. The Hagahot Maimoniyot documented the restriction on the use of *kitniyos* (beans) on Pesach (*see CHART TAKKANOT HAGE'ONIM*).

200 Jews of Heilbronn *(Germany)* were killed on the 12th **Cheshvan**.

Living in the Year 1300

Rashba	b.1235?,	d.1310?.
Me'iri (R.Menachem)	b.1249?,	d.1315?.
Rosh (R.Asher)	b.1250?,	d.1327.
Rbnu.Bachya II	b.1265?,	d.1340?.
Tur (R.Yaakov ben Asher)	b.1275?,	d.1349?.
Ralbag (Gersonides)	b.1288,	d.1344.
Ran (R.Nissim)	b.1290?,	d.1380?.

5062 — 1301

The Jews of Renchen *(Germany)* were massacred in 1301, in a continuation of the Rindfleisch massacres (see 5058\1298).

5062 — 1302

In **Nissan** the Jews of Barcelona were ordered to kneel when passing Christian priests.

5063 — 1303

The Jews of Gotha *(Germany)* were attacked in

the Rindfleisch massacres (see 5062\1301), and the Jews of Weissensee *(Germany)* were massacred on the 7th **Nissan**.
Many Jews in Egypt were forced to convert to Islam (see 5010\1250), and all Jews were henceforth required to wear YELLOW turbans.
The Rosh (see 5088*1327*) — a disciple of Maharam MeRothenburg, and a leading Halacha authority in Germany — was consulted on many questions arising from the Rindfleisch massacres, (particularly on property where no inheritors survived). Concerned that he might be imprisoned for ransom — as was his teacher, the Maharam (see 5046\1286) — he left Germany with his family, as the Maharam had attempted to do (see 5065\1305).
R.Yitzchak (ben Meir) of Dura *(Duren, Germany)* — a disciple of Maharam MeRothenburg — wrote Sha'arei Dura (She'arim BeIssur VeHeter, *Dietary Halacha)*, which was widely accepted in ASHKENAZI communities.

5065 — 1305

The Rashba placed a limited ban on the study of philosophy.

R.Abba Mari of Montpelier *(Provence, S.E.France)* — who was concerned over the tendency of the young, in Provence, to study philosophy — appealed to the Rashba (see 5030\1270, 5070\1310) — who was the leader of Spanish Jews and had a great influence over all Jewish communities through his SH'ELOT UTESHUVOT *(responsa)* — to prohibit the study of philosophy under 25 years of age (see 4962\1202, 4992\1232). The Rashba did prohibit such study — although he endorsed the Rambam's integrity and greatness — but allowed the study of medicine (which was considered a form of philosophy in those days — as were all "sciences" — before the movement to focus on the empirical study of facts and data, see 5500\1740).

The Rosh arrived in Spain.

The Rosh — who arrived in Barcelona in 1305 (see 5063\1303), where he was warmly received by the Rashba — agreed to the ban. He became rabbi in Toledo *(Spain)* shortly thereafter — some say with the assistance of the Rashba — bringing (some say) the French/German (Tosaphot) style of Talmud analysis to Spain (see 5050\1290, 5088*1327*). He was surprised to find that the Jewish courts in Spain were actually using the death sentence (under the imprimatur of the government) (see 3789\29) *[Tsh.HaRosh.17.8/ Mmn.Hil.Chov.UMaz.8.10, 11/ See Sed.Had.5421].*

5066 — 1306

All Jews were expelled from France.

The Jews of France were arrested, their property was confiscated, and they were expelled in 1306, on the day after Tisha B'**Av**.
Although they were allowed to return nine years later (see 5075\1315), Talmud scholarship in France deteriorated further (see 5002\1242).
Among the refugees leaving France were:
♦Rbnu.Yerucham (see 5095*1334*);
♦R.Aharon the father of R.Menachem ibn Zerach (see 5088\1328);
♦R.Shimshon ben Yitzchak of Chinon, author of the Sefer Keritut *(principles of the Talmud)*;
♦R.Aharon ben Yaakov HaKohen of Lunel, author of Orchot Chayim *(Halacha)*;
♦R.Eshtori HaParchi — a disciple of the Rosh and
♦R.Eliezer ben Yosef of Chinon (see 5082*1321*) — who travelled to Spain, Egypt, and then Eretz Yisrael. He later wrote Kaftor VaPherach *(a scholarly book on the geography of Eretz Yisrael in Halacha)*, which identifies many historical sites.

5067 — 1307

The body of the Maharam MeRothenburg was released for burial on the 4th **Adar** 1307 (see 5053\1293), through the efforts of R.Alexander ben Shlomo (Susskind) Wimpen, who was subsequently buried near him.

5069 — 1309

110 Jews were killed by a mob in Born (Limburg, province of the Netherlands), and many were killed (after refusing to be subjected to FORCED BAPTISM) in neighboring Louvain (Belgium).

5070 — 1310

The Rashba died.

The Rashba — R.Shlomo ben Avraham ibn Aderet (see 5030\1270, 5065\1305), a disciple of the Ramban and Rbnu.Yona (Gerondi) — wrote Chidushim, thousands of SH'ELOT UTESHUVOT, Torat HaBayit and Avodat HaKodesh *(both Halacha)*, as well as Mishmeret HaBayit (see 5053\1293). He was instrumental in

having the Pirush HaMishna of the Rambam translated into HEBREW (see 4965\ *1204*).
After the Rashba died in Barcelona, the Rosh became the leading Halacha authority, and students came to him (in Toledo) from as far away as Bohemia and Russia *[Tsh.HaRosh.51.2-end]*.

5071 — 1311

Forced converts in southern Italy (see Av, 5050\1290) were severely punished for (secretly) returning to JUDAISM.

5072 — 1312

Many Jews were killed at around this time, in a RITUAL DESECRATION libel *(see 5003\1243)* and a BLOOD LIBEL, in Fuerstenfeld and Judenberg *(Styria, province of Austria)*.

5075 — 1315

Jews were allowed to return to France (see 5066\1306) by the new king, Louis X the Quarreller, son and successor of Phillip the Fair who had expelled them.

5079 — 1319

The Ritva — R.Yom Tov ben Avraham (ibn Ashvili), a disciple of the Rashba and the 'Ra'ah' — wrote an exhaustive commentary on the Talmud (in Spain), which includes an overview of previous writings. He wrote many other works, among them are some attributed to others, and some attributed to him are by others.
The Inquisitor ordered the Talmud burned in Toulouse and Perpignan *(France)* in 1319, and several Jews were burned at the stake in Tudela *(Spain)*.

Living in the Year 1320

Name	Born	Died
Rosh (R.Asher)	b.1250?,	d.1327.
Rbnu.Bachya II	b.1265?,	d.1340?.
Tur (R.Yaakov ben Asher)	b.1275?,	d.1349?.
Ralbag (Gersonides)	b.1288,	d.1344.
Ran (R.Nissim)	b.1290?,	d.1380?.

5080 — 1320

Jews were massacred by the Pastoureaux Crusaders.

Forty thousand teenage shepherds *(pastoureaux)* marched through France, from north to south, on a crusade to fight the Muslims in Spain. They attacked the Jews of 120 towns on their way, forcing conversions — which the Inquisition later insisted were valid, although they were forced — looting, and killing (including 500 Jews seeking refuge in Verdun).
All Jews were expelled from Milan *(Italy)* (see 4985\1225).
An order for the expulsion of the Jews of Rome came from Avignon *(Provence, S.E. France)* where the popes were residing at this time (see 5029\1269) — and the Jews were expelled before the news of a withdrawal of the order reached Rome (see 5082\1322).

5082 — *1321*

One hundred and sixty Jews were burned to death on the second day of Rosh HaShana 5082\ *1321*, in Chinon, Tours and Vitry (Le Brule) *(all in France)* (see 5082\1322) — on a charge of poisoning the water wells (in conjunction with the local lepers).
Among those killed were R.Eliezer ben Yosef (see 5066\1306) — a brother in law of R.Peretz of Corbeil (see 5050\1290) — and his two brothers.

5082 — 1322

All Jews were expelled from parts of France *(see 4942\1182, 5066\1306, and 5082\1321)*.
The Talmud was burned in Rome (see 5085\1320).

5086 — 1326

Twenty-seven Jews were killed in a RITUAL DESECRATION libel *(see 5003\1243)* in Constance *(Germany)*.

5088 — *1327*

The Rosh died.

R.Asher ben Yechi'el, the Rosh (see 5063\1303, 5065\1305, 5070\1310) — who had eight sons — died in **Cheshvan** 5088\ *1327*. He wrote a Halacha-Commentary — which, like the Rif, follows the order of the Talmud, in contrast to the Rambam's system *[Tsh. HaRosh.31.9]* (see 4863\1103, 4965\ *1204*, 5065\1305). He also wrote SH'ELOT UTESHUVOT, and Tosaphot HaRosh (see 5065\1305).

R.Yehuda — one of his (younger) sons, (who had married his niece the daughter of the Tur) — succeeded his father.

5088 ≋ 1328

Six thousand Jews of the province of Navarre *(Spain)* were killed in ANTI-JEWISH RIOTS. In the town of Estella, R.Menachem ben Aharon ibn Zerach — author of Tzeida LaDerech — survived (some say he was rescued by a knight) after his parents and four brothers were killed (see 5066\1306). He went to Toledo to study, and became a disciple of R.Yehuda, son of the Rosh. The Tur (see 5100\1340) — R.Yaakov ben Asher, son of the Rosh — encouraged Jews to leave Germany (as he had done with his father, see 5063\1303), because it was a dangerous place for them to live *[Otz.Hag.5.75]*.

5092 ≋ 1332

Three hundred Jews were killed in a BLOOD LIBEL in Uberlingen *(Germany)* when a mob set the synagogue on fire.

5095 ≋ *1334*

Rbnu.Yerucham (see 5066\1306) — a disciple of the Rosh and R.Avraham ben Ismael (who was a disciple of the Rashba) — wrote Meisharim and Adam VeChava *(Halacha)* (in which there appear to be errors in the copying).
The Jews of Poland received renewed promises of certain rights in **Cheshvan** 5095*1334*.

5096 ≋ 1336

Jews of Germany were massacred by the Armledder bands.

Bands of peasants — who wore leather arm bands (armledder) — roamed through Germany and Alsace *(region between France and Germany)* for three years, killing Jews and ravaging 120 communities.
Fifteen hundred Jews were killed in Ribeuville, and all the Jews of Deggendorf *(Germany)* were killed because of a RITUAL DESECRATION libel there *(see 5003\1243)*.
R.Shem Tov ben Avraham ibn Gaon — a disciple of the Rashba who emigrated to Eretz Yisrael — wrote Migdal Oz a (somewhat controversial) commentary on the Rambam's Yad HaChazaka *(see Illustrations, Text I, #4)* *[Yam.Sh.Sh.Hakd./Shach Chosh.Mish. Hil.Ed.36.S.K.6-end]*.

5097 ≋ 1337

Many Jews were killed in massacres in Bohemia.

5098 ≋ 1338

The Ralbag wrote his commentary on the Bible.

The Ralbag — R.Levi ben Gershom (Gersonides) of France, a descendant of the Ramban — wrote a commentary on the T'NACH *(Bible)* *(see ILLUSTRATIONS, TEXT B, #5)*, and also Milchamot HaShem *(philosophy)* for which he was criticized *[see Mhrl.MiPrg. Hakd.Gevrt.HaSh.]*, although his stature as a Talmud scholar was undiminished. He wrote works on mathematics, and invented the Jacob Staff (an instrument used in astronomy). A crater on the moon has been named 'Rabbi Levi' after him.
Jews were burned at the stake in Pulkau *(Austria)* in a RITUAL DESECRATION libel in 1338 *(see 5003\1243)*, and the massacre spread to twenty-seven towns.

5100 ≋ 1340

R.Yaakov ben Asher (see 5088\1328) wrote the

Living in the Year 1340

Name	Born	Died
Rbnu.Bachya II	b.1265?,	d.1340?.
Tur (R.Yaakov ben Asher)	b.1275?,	d.1349?.
Ralbag (Gersonides)	b.1288,	d.1344.
Ran (R.Nissim)	b.1290?,	d.1380?.
Rivash	b.1326,	d.1408?.

Tur (the Arba'a Turim) — an encyclopedic compilation of Halacha, quoting most of the preceding Halacha works — in the systematic arrangement of daily life (see 5088*1327*), which was a departure from the previous systems of the Rif and the Rambam (see 4863\1103, 4965*1204)*. This system later became the basis for the SHULCHAN ARUCH (see 5323\1563).
The Tur also wrote a commentary on the CHUMASH (Bible), some of which is printed (as Ba'al HaTurim) *(see ILLUSTRATIONS, TEXT A, #8)*. He died on the 12th **Tammuz** 1340 (some say in 1348), in Toledo *(Spain)* *[Otz.Hag.5.75]*.

5102 ≋ 1342

R.David (ben Yosef) Abudraham — a disciple of the Tur — wrote Abudraham *(prayer guide and commentary)*.
R.Shimon — the eighth son of the Rosh — died in a plague on the 12th **Elul**.

5104 1344

The Ralbag (Gersonides) (see 5098\1338), died on the 6th **Iyar**.
R.Vidal di Tolose *(Spain)* — also called AnVidal *(abbreviation for Adon Vidal)* — wrote the Maggid Mishneh commentary on the Yad HaChazaka of the Rambam *(see Illustrations, Text I, #5)*. He was a colleague of the Ran — R.Nissim ben Reuven (see 5127\1367) — who wrote a commentary on the Rif and on (parts of) the Talmud *(see Illustrations, Text H, #2)*.

5109 1349

The Black Death massacres swept across Europe.

An epidemic of plague — mostly *bubonic* but also *pneumonic* and *septicemic*, all with a very high death rate *(30%-100%)*, and apparently bought from China by Italian trading ships in spring of 1348 — was spread across Central and Western Europe *(carried by the very people who were fleeing it)* killing as many as half of the total population *(75 million)* in three years. *(See chart below. Some estimates are 25 million or one third of the population)*.
On the 23rd **Kislev** 5109*1348* it was announced in Lausanne *(Switzerland)* that Jews (one named Agimet, who apparently was ignorant of the Bible *[Middle High German chronicle of Von Königshofen (1346-1420) 1698 ed.]*.) had confessed (after torture) to poisoning the water wells. Word of this spread throughout Europe. The Jews were savagely attacked and massacred. by sometimes hysterical mobs — normal social order had disintegrated because of the mass deaths and the panic of the living — who were encouraged by the rumors of Jewish confessions to the crime. In some towns all Jews were expelled, and in others they were massacred before the plague had even arrived (cancellation of debts to Jewish money-lenders was motivation in some instances.)
The killings continued despite statements from the Pope *(Clement VI)* that the Jews were innocent,

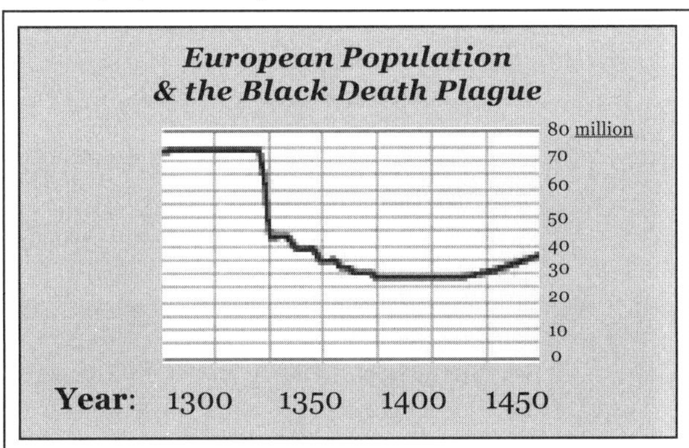

and despite the fact that the Jews were also dying *(see Tammuz)* in the Black Death plague. More than three quarters of the Jews of Saragossa *(Spain)* died, and the Jewish cemetery in Vienna (where there were no massacres) was extended because of the large number dying of the disease.
The Jews of Berne *(Switzerland)* were burned to death as soon as information on the confessions came from Lausanne, and they were accused of sending the poison on to Basel *(see Shvat)*. The Jews of Colmar *(Alsace, a region between France and Germany)* were imprisoned on the 8th **Shvat** for well poisoning, and burned to death seven months later.
Six hundred Jews of Basel *(Switzerland)* were burned to death on the 19th **Shvat** in a specially constructed house on the Rhine, and 140 children were subjected to FORCED BAPTISM. The Jews of Speyer *(Bavaria)* perished on the 2nd **Adar-1**, when they set their houses afire, rather than face destruction by mob violence. The Jews of Freiburg *(Germany)* were killed in these on the 10th **Adar-1**, and the Jews of Uberlingen *(Switzerland)* were massacred on the 22nd. 2,000 Jews were burned to death (on a scaffold in the cemetery) in Strasbourg *(Alsace)* on the 25th. All Jews were expelled from Burgsdorf *(Switzerland)* on the 27th, and Jews of Zurich were burned (and some expelled) on 2nd **Adar-2** *(see 4th Nissan)*. The Jews of Virmyze *(Worms, Germany)* set fire to their own homes and perished, on the 10th **Adar-2**.
Some Jews of Zurich were burned to death *(see 2nd Adar-2)*, and the rest were expelled on the 4th **Nissan**. The Jews of Muehlhausen *(Germany)* and 3,000 Jews in Erfurt *(Germany)* were killed on Erev Pesach. Some say that R.Alexander Zisslin — a disciple of R.Yitzchak of Dura, and author of the Aguda *(Halacha)* — was killed in Erfurt. Sixty Jews were killed in Breslau *(Silesia, a region between Germany and Poland)* on the 10th **Sivan**, in the RIOTS that followed a disastrous fire.
R.Yehuda — the son of the Rosh (see 5088*1327*) — died of the Black Death plague (as did some of his family) on the 17th **Tammuz** 1349. The Jews of Frankfort were massacred on Erev Tisha B'Av (8th **Av**), and 300 Jews were killed in Tarrega *(Spain)* on the 10th **Av**. Some Jews of Mayence *(Mainz, Germany)* were killed fighting a RIOTING mob; many others — 6,000 — set fire to their homes and died in the flames on the 7th **Elul**. The Jews of Cologne did the same two days later.

5110 *1349*

The Jews of Krems *(Austria)* were massacred in the Black Death RIOTS on the 16th **Tishrei** 5110*1349*; the Jews in Augsburg *(Germany)* on the 17th **Kislev**;

560 Jews of Nuremberg *(Germany)* were killed and burned on the 23rd; and Jews were massacred in Hanover *(Germany)* and in Brussels on the 24th.
R.Peretz (ben Yitzchak) HaKohen left Provence because of the Black Death massacres, and settled in Barcelona where he became a rabbi at the same time as the Ran (see 5127\1367).

5110 — 1350

All Jews of Cheb *(Eger, Bohemia)* were massacred.

Over 300 Jewish communities were completely destroyed by the Black Death massacres and expulsions, particularly in Germany. Jewish communities of Provence *(S.E.France)* also suffered severe destruction, while France, Belgium, the Netherlands and Spain were less severely affected. Many Jews moved east to Poland-Lithuania (see 4856\1096), which were the only countries (besides Austria) where the Jews did not suffer an irreversible setback, economically and in Torah scholarship (see 5195\1435).

5115 — 1355

1,200 Jews were killed in a Christian and Moslem mob attack on the Jewish section of Toledo *(Spain)*, on the 25th.

5118 — 1358

Hundreds of Jews were killed in Catalonia *(a province of Spain)* on the day after Tisha B'Av.

Living in the Year 1360

Ran (R.Nissim)	b.1290?,	d.1380?.
Rivash	b.1326,	d.1408?.
Maharil	b.1360?,	d.1427.

5120 — 1360

Many Jews of Breslau *(Silesia, a region between Germany and Poland)* were killed in ANTI-JEWISH RIOTS following a fire, and the rest were expelled.
All Jews were expelled from Hungary, but were allowed to return a short while later.
Shmuel ben Meir HaLevi Abulafia, a wealthy and generous Jew in Castille *(Spain)*, was arrested and tortured to death; his enormous wealth was confiscated.

5123 — 1363

R.Mattityahu ben Yosef Treves — a descendant of Rashi who studied in Spain and returned to Paris to open a YESHIVA — was appointed Chief Rabbi by the king of France.

5127 — 1367

The Ran, Rivash, and other scholars, were imprisoned.

The Jews of Barcelona were accused of a RITUAL DESECRATION *(see 5003\1243)*, three Jews were killed, and all the Jews were held prisoner in the synagogue for three days.
The Ran (see 5104\1344), was imprisoned — on what may have been a related charge — together with R.Chisdai Crescas I (ben Yehuda) and his young grandson — R.Chisdai Crescas II (ben Avraham ibn/ben Yehuda) — as well as his young disciple the Rivash (see 5151\1391), and others *[Tsh.Rivash 373, 376]*. They were released after a short period.

5130 — 1370

Many Jews were killed as a result of a civil war in Castille *(Province of Spain)*; R.Menachem ben Zerach lost all his belongings (see 5088\1328), and moved (back) to Toledo *(Spain)*, where 8,000 Jews had been killed.
Hundreds of Jews were burned alive in Brussels, in a RITUAL DESECRATION libel *(see 5003\1243)*, and the remainder were expelled in 1370.

5137 — 1377

Some Jews of Huesca *(Spain)* were tortured and burned to death in a RITUAL DESECRATION libel *(see 5003\1243)*.

5141 — 1380

Jews of Paris were killed by ANTI-JEWISH RIOTERS in **Kislev**.
R.Yisrael of Krems *(Austria)* wrote Hagahot Ashri on the Talmud commentary of the Rosh.

5148 — 1388

After the devastation of German Jewry (see 5109\1349), R.Meir ben Baruch HaLevi (Ma-

Living in the Year 1380

Ran (R.Nissim)	b.1290?, d.1380?.
Rivash	b.1326, d.1408?.
Maharil	b.1360?, d.1427.
Rashbatz	b.1361?, d.1444.

haram Levi) of Vienna introduced SEMICHA for rabbis, to ensure minimum qualifications for those officiating in marriages and divorces (etc.). He empowered R.Yeshayahu ben Abba Mari of France to be Chief Rabbi there, and to confer the SEMICHA on suitable rabbis. This led to a dispute with R.Yochanan Treves who had succeeded his father (see 5123\1363). R.Yochanan consulted the Rivash and R.Chisdai Crescas II (in Spain), but the matter ended when all Jews were expelled from France (see 5155*1394*) *[Tsh.Rivash.369-372]*.

5149 — 1389

3,000 Jews were killed in Prague on the day after Pesach, their houses were burned, and the cemetery was desecrated.
R.Yitzchak Abohab I wrote Menorat HaMa'or *(Mussar)* *[Otz.Hag.5.222]*.

5151 — 1391

Jews of Spain were massacred — many became Marranos.

4,000 Jews of Seville (more than half) were killed on the 1st **Tammuz**, in a massacre that spread throughout Spain and Portugal, killing a total of 50,000 Jews. Women and children were sold as slaves to Muslims, and many synagogues were forcibly converted into churches. Many Jews — (mostly the wealthy), who saved their lives by openly converting to Christianity, while remaining secretly Jewish — were called ANUSSIM ('the forced ones') Marranos, or Conversos. They numbered about 200,000 in Aragon and Castille *(provinces of Spain)*.
4,000 Jews were killed in Ja'en and Toledo on the 17th **Tammuz**, and the Jewish community of Valencia was destroyed on the 7th **Av**. Jews were massacred in Barcelona and in the whole of Catalonia *(province of Spain)* on the 22nd **Av**; in Palma (Majorca) on the 1st **Elul**; and in Gerona on the 9th. The Jews of Perpignan (France, near the Spanish border) were also attacked.

The Rivash and Rashbatz left Spain.

The Rivash — R.Yitzchak ben Sheshet Perfet (see 5127\1367), a disciple of the Ran and R.Peretz HaKohen (see 5110\1349) — fled the massacres of Spain (some say he lost two sons in Majorca on his way to North Africa, *see 1st Elul*). He went to Algiers where he was appointed rabbi of the community.
Some say R.Vidal Ephrayim Gerondi, also a disciple of the Ran, was killed in the massacres. His disciple, the Rashbatz, also fled to Algiers, and R.Ephrayim ben Yisrael AlNakava fled to North Africa after his father was killed.
Although his son was killed, R.Chisdai Crescas II stayed in Spain and tried to rebuild the Jewish communities, which no longer included the wealthy and influential Jews. He wrote Or HaShem *(philosophy)* and Bitul Ikarey HaNotzrim *(responses to Christianity)*.
R.Yitzchak (R.Profiat) ben Moshe HaLevi Duran (HaEphodi) — a disciple of R.Chisdai Crescas II who was affected before he left Spain, *[Sed.Had.5154]* — also wrote works in answer to Christianity, Kelimat HaGoyim and Al Tehi KeAvotecha *(satire)*.

5152 — 1392

A Jew was burned alive in Damascus and other Jews were tortured after being accused of setting fire to a mosque.

5153 — 1393

The Nimukei Yosef, R.Yosef Chaviva, wrote a commentary on the Halacha of the Rif in Spain *(see ILLUSTRATIONS, TEXT G, #3)*.
R.Shalom (ben Yitzchak) of Vienna, a disciple of R.Yisrael of Krems, was a prominent rabbi in Wiener-Neustadt *(Austria)*.
Almost all the Jews fled Baghdad when the Tartars conquered the city (see 5160\1400).
All Jews of Venice were required to wear a YELLOW BADGE (see 4977*1216*).

5155 — *1394*

The Final expulsion of Jews from France.

The Jews of Paris were attacked on Yom Kippur 5155*1394*, and seven Jews were imprisoned on the charge that they had captured a *meshumad* *(apostate)* to force him to return to JUDAISM.

Shortly thereafter, all Jews were expelled from all of France (see 5082\1322) except for Narbonne, Montpelier and other parts of Provence *(S.E.France)* (see 5261\1501).

5157 — 1397

All Jews were expelled from Basel *(Switzerland)*.

5159 — 1399

Eighty Jews were killed in Prague, because a *meshumad* *(apostate)* accused them of denigrating Christianity (see 5160\1400).
R.Yom Tov Lipman (ben Shlomo) Millhausen of Prague — author of the sought-after Sefer HaNitzachon (a brilliant book *(collection of responses to Christianity)* which was discreetly passed around) — was imprisoned with other Jews. He managed to escape, and Sefer HaNitzachon was eventually published (in Latin, by a priest who added counter refutations). The Pope forbade the Jews to have the book, and it was the subject of many later Christian refutations (known as ANTI-LIPMANNIANA).

Living in the Year 1400	
Rivash	b.1326, d.1408?.
Maharil	b.1360?, d.1427.
Rashbatz	b.1361?, d.1444.

5160 — 1400

The Jews were massacred in Syria when the Tartars conquered the country (see 5153\1393).
Seventy-seven Jews were killed in ANTI-JEWISH RIOTS in Prague in **Elul** (see 5160\1399).

5161 — 1401

Thirty Jews were burned at the stake in a BLOOD LIBEL in Schaffhausen *(Switzerland)* on the 14th **Tammuz** (see 5157\1397).

5164 — 1404

Many Jews were killed in Salzburg *(Austria)* in a RITUAL DESECRATION libel *(see 5003\1243)*, and the rest were expelled — they returned a few years later.

5166 — 1406

The Jews of Corfu *(island of Greece)* were required to wear a SPECIAL BADGE.

5168 — *1407*

The Jews of Cracow *(Poland)* were attacked by riotous mobs (in a BLOOD LIBEL) on the 25th **Cheshvan** 5168*1407*. One Jew was publicly tortured, then burned at the stake — on a charge of counterfeiting — and a number of Jews were FORCIBLY CONVERTED.
The Rashbatz, R.Shimon ben Tzemach Duran, was appointed rabbi in Algiers after the death of the Rivash (see 5151\1391). He refused (on principal) to accept any confirmation of the appointment by the government (in contrast to his predecessor), although he maintained that a rabbi should be paid by the community (he was a physician), in order to allow total devotion to the work. He wrote many SH'ELOT UTESHUVOT (collected in Tashbatz *[as distinct from "Tashbetz", see 5046\1286]*), and Magen Avot *(philosophical-ideological, with commentary on Pirkei Avot, and responses to Christianity, see 5151\1391)*.

5172 — 1412

A *meshumad* *(apostate)* — who had become bishop of Burgos *(Spain)* and an advisor to the king of Castille *(province of Spain)* — instigated anti-Jewish laws which seriously affected the economic position of the Jews, who had already lost many of the wealthy and influential among them (see 5151\1391). They were also required to wear a RED BADGE and distinctive clothing — besides having to let their hair and beards grow long (see 4977*1216*, 5029\1269).

5173 — 1413

R.Yosef Albo was in a forced DEBATE with Christians.
R.Yosef Albo — a disciple of R.Chisdai Crescas II, and author of Sefer HaIkkarim *(principles of religion)* — was a leader of those Jews who were forced to DEBATE a *meshumad* *(apostate)* — a follower of the bishop in Burgos, see 5172\1412) — in Tortosa *(Spain)*, under very intimidating circumstances. The twenty-one month DEBATE — which was presided over by *[one of a few who claimed to be]* the Pope *(Benedict XII)* — resulted in Jews being forced to convert, and in an order that all anti-Christian statements (as defined by

the *meshumad*) *(apostate)* be removed from the Talmud (see 5023\1263).

5178 1418

All Jews were expelled from Koblenz *(Germany)* and Cochem *(Germany)*.
Jewish women in Salzburg *(Austria)* were ordered to wear bells on their dresses (see 4977*1216*).

Living in the Year 1420

Maharil	b.1360?, d.1427.
Rashbatz	b.1361?, d.1444.

5181 1421

Jews in Austria were massacred in the Wiener Gezera.

The Jews of Austria were imprisoned, and their possessions confiscated on the 10th **Sivan** 1420, after a RITUAL DESECRATION libel *(see 5003\1243)* in Enns *(Austria)* in which the accused were tortured. Many children were subjected to FORCED BAPTISM, and many Jews took their own lives rather than accept Christianity. Later, on the 9th **Nissan** 1421, 212 Jews were burned at the stake, and R.Aharon (Blumlein) of Neustadt was also killed. He was a disciple of R.Shalom of Vienna — whose son, R.Yona, was killed — and author of Hilchot Nida. His disciple and nephew, R.Yisrael Isserlein (see 5220\1460), fled after his mother was killed.
Fifty-eight Jews of Styria *(Austria)* were burned on the 10th **Sivan**, and the rest of the Jews in (most of) Austria were expelled, after many had been killed in the war of the Hussites — a new Christian sect, whom the Jews were accused of supporting — against the Catholics.
The Jews of Chomutov *(Komotov, Bohemia)* were massacred by the Hussites, and the Jews of Cheb *(Eger, then Bohemia)* (see 5110\1350, 5190\1430) and Iglau *(Jihlava, Bohemia)* (see 5186\1426) were expelled for (allegedly) supporting the Hussites.

5184 1424

All Jews were expelled from Cologne *(Germany)*.

5186 1426

All Jews were expelled — again — from Iglau *(Jihlava, Bohemia)* (see 5181\1421, 5195\1435).

5187 1427

All Jews were expelled from Berne *(Switzerland)* on the 13th **Iyar** (see 5054\1294, 5157\1397).
The Maharil — R.Yaakov (ben Moshe) HaLevi Moellin of Mayence *(Mainz, Germany)*, a disciple of R.Shalom of Vienna (see 5181\1421) — was a leading rabbi in Germany. He died on the 21st of **Elul** and his opinions are recorded in Minhagey Maharil *(customs and ritual)* and SH'ELOT UTESHUVOT.

5188 1428

All Jews were expelled from Fribourg *(Switzerland)* (see 5187\1427).
On the 18th of **Shvat**, the Jews of Sicily were ordered to attend CONVERSION SERMONS.

5190 1430

Fifteen Jews were burned to death in a BLOOD LIBEL in Constance, Lindau, and Ravensburg *(Germany)*, and the rest were expelled. All Jews were also expelled from Miessen and Thuringa *(Germany)* and — again — from Cheb *(Eger, Bohemia)* (see 5181\1421, 5195\1435).

5194 1434

Jewish men were required to wear YELLOW BADGES and women were required to wear YELLOW pointed veils, in Augsburg *(Germany)* (see 4977*1216*).

5195 1435

200 Jews were FORCIBLY CONVERTED in Majorca in 1435 (after a BLOOD LIBEL in 1432), and the rest fled to North Africa.
The Jewish community in Speyer *(Germany)* had been rebuilt after the Black Death massacres (see 5109\1349), and since then the Jews were expelled twice (in 1405 — returning in 1421, and in 1430 — returning in 1434). On 6th **Iyar** 1435 the Jews were expelled once again, and were not allowed to return until thirty years later. This was similar to the pattern of settlement in many communities after the devastation of the Black Death massacres *(see 5120\1360, 5130\1370, 5155\1394, 5181\1421, 5184\1424, 5211\1450, 5233\1473, 5251\1491)*.

5196 1436

All Jews were expelled from Zurich *(see 5188\1428)*.

5202 — 1442

All Jews were expelled from Upper Bavaria *(province of Germany)* (see 5211\1450, 5311\1551).

Living in the Year 1440

Rashbatz	b.1361?,	d.1444.
R.Yitzchak Abarbanel	b.1437,	d.1508.
Yuchasin	b.1440?,	d.1515.

5204 — 1444

The Rashbatz (see 5168\1407) died in 1444, and was succeeded by his son, R.Shlomo ben Shimon Duran as rabbi in Algiers.

5206 — 1446

All Jews were expelled from Berlin and the whole province of Brandenburg *(Germany) (see 5202\1442)*, but they were permitted to return in 1447 *(see 5195\1435)*.

5209 — 1449

Many Jews were killed in an attack in Lisbon *(Portugal)*, and many houses were destroyed.

5211 — *1450*

On the 29th of **Tishrei** 5211*1450*, all Jews were expelled from forty cities in Lower Bavaria (see 5202\1442, 5206\1446, 5238\1478) after paying a huge ransom (see 5195\1435).

5211 — 1451

R.Yaakov (ben Yehuda) Weil — the Mahariv, a disciple of the Maharil (see 5187\1427) — was a leading rabbi in Germany. He wrote Shechitot UBedikot *(Halacha pertaining to meat)* which was printed with SH'ELOT UTESHUVOT Mahariv, and has been reprinted over seventy times.
Jews were forbidden to have social contact with non-Jews by order of the Pope *(Nicholas V)* on 24th **Adar** (see 5007\1247).
All Jews were ordered to wear a JEW'S BADGE (see 4977*1216*) in Hanover *(Germany)*.

5212 — *1451*

On the 25th **Tishrei** 5212\1451, all Jews in Arnhem (Holland) were ordered to wear a JEW'S BADGE.

5213 — 1453

Forty-one Jews were burned at the stake in Breslau *(Silesia, a region between Germany and Poland)* on the 28th **Tammuz** — and the rest of the Jews were expelled (see Iyar 5195\1435, 5120\1360, 5509\1749) — in a RITUAL DESECRATION libel *(see 5003\1243)*, to which some had confessed after being tortured. The libel was instigated by a travelling Italian priest who made an identical charge in Schweidnitz *(Silesia)*, in which seventeen Jews were burned at the stake — including, some say, R.David who taught R.Yisrael Brunna (see 5214\1454) — on the 8th **Elul** 1453. The rest of the Jews were expelled from there and from some of the surrounding towns.
Jews were invited to settle in the Turkish *(Ottoman)* empire (see **Av** 5252\1492) after the Turks had conquered Constantinople *(later called Istanbul)*.

5214 — 1454

Many Jews were killed in ANTI-JEWISH RIOTS in Cracow *(Poland)* after the Italian priest (see 5213\1453) visited in 1454, and all Jews were expelled from Brno and other cities of Moravia *(province)* on the 28th **Av** 1454, after he visited there. R.Yisrael (ben Chaim) — of Brunna *(Brno)* (see 5234\1474), a disciple of the Maharay (see 5220\1460) and the Mahariv (see 5211\1451) — moved to Regensburg *(Germany)*, (some say before the expulsion).

5216 — 1456

R.Yisrael Brunna (see 5214\1454) was arrested in Regensburg over the refusal of the Jewish community to pay an exorbitant tax.

5217 — 1457

All Jews were expelled from Hildesheim *(Germany)*.

5218 — 1458

All Jews were expelled from Erfurt *(Germany)*.

5219 — 1459

Sixty Jews were killed in ANTI-JEWISH RIOTS in Carpentras *(Provence, S.E.France)*.

5220 1460

All Jews were expelled from Mayence *(Mainz, Germany)* (see 5195\1435, 5233\1473), and the rabbi, R.Moshe (Maharam Mintz I) — a disciple of the Mahariv (see 5211\1451) — eventually settled in Posen *(Poznan, Poland)*.

R.Yisrael (ben Petachyah) Isserlein (Maharay) (see 5181\1421) — a leading rabbi who wrote Terumat HaDeshen — died in Austria.

Living in the Year 1460

R.Yitzchak Abarbanel	b.1437,	d.1508.
Yuchasin	b.1440?,	d.1515.
R.Ovadya Bertinura	b.1445?,	d.1524?.
Eyn Yaakov (R.Yaakov ibn Chaviv)	b.1445?,	d.1516?.
R.Yaakov Pollak	b.1460?,	d.1530?.

5223 1463

R.Yitzchak (ben Yaakov) Kanpanton was over one hundred years old when he died in Spain.

5224 1464

The Jews were attacked in Seville *(Spain)* in ANTI-JEWISH RIOTS on the 27th **Nissan**.

Thirty Jews were killed in ANTI-JEWISH RIOTS in Cracow *(Poland)* on 4th **Iyar** (see 5214\1454).

5225 1465

Jews were massacred in a revolt in Fez *(Morocco)*.

5226 1466

Some Jews were killed in Arnstadt *(Germany)*, and the rest were expelled.

The Jews of Rome were forced to run HUMILIATING RACES before jeering crowds in the Christian Carnival *(festive period preceding Lent)*. These humiliating 'performances' became an annual event for two centuries (see 5427\1667).

5227 1467

Eighteen Jews were burned to death in a BLOOD LIBEL in Nuremberg *(Germany)*.

R.Shlomo ben Shimon Duran died, and his sons — R.Shimon Duran and R.Tzemach Duran — succeeded him as rabbis in Algiers. Together they wrote Yachin UBo'az *(Sh'elot UTeshuvot)*.

5229 1468

The Jews of Landau *(Germany)* were forced to wear YELLOW BADGES in **Cheshvan** (see 4977*1216*).

5230 1470

R.Eliyahu and his two brothers (see 5290\1530) were killed in a BLOOD LIBEL in Endingen *(Germany)*, and all Jews were subsequently expelled from the whole province of Baden.

5232 1472

All Jews were expelled from Schaffhausen *(Switzerland)* (see 5196\1436), and the Jews of Muehlhausen *(Germany)* were required to wear a YELLOW BADGE (see 4977*1216*) and were forbidden to enter non-Jewish houses.

5233 1473

Jews were allowed to return to Mayence *(Mainz, Germany)* (see 5220\1460, 5195\1435).

Jews were massacred in Cordova on Purim (see 5224\1464, 5234\1474).

5234 1474

360 Jews were killed in a massacre in Sicily.

Jews were massacred in Segovia *(Spain)* on the 29th **Iyar**.

R.Yisrael Brunna (see 5214\1454) was arrested in Regensburg *(Germany)* in a BLOOD LIBEL, instigated by a *meshumad* *(apostate)* who later confessed.

5235 1475

The invention of printing was used for Jewish books.

Less than thirty-five years after the invention (in Germany) of movable type for printing, Rashi's commentary on CHUMASH (Bible) was printed in Reggio di Calabria *(Italy)* on the 10th

Adar. It was the first Jewish book to be (dated and) printed. The Tur (see 5100\1340) was printed on 28th **Tammuz**, in Piove Di Sacco *(Italy)*.
Many Jews of Trent *(N. Italy)* were tortured and killed in a BLOOD LIBEL in 1475, some were subjected to FORCED BAPTISM, and the rest were expelled.

5237 — 1477

All Jews were expelled from Tuebingen *(Germany)* and from Nancy and the whole duchy of Lorraine *(France)*.

5238 — 1478

Ten Jews were killed in a RITUAL DESECRATION libel *(see 5003\1243)* in Passau *(Bavaria, Germany)*, and the rest were expelled (see 5211*1450*). All Jews were expelled from Bamberg *(Germany)*.
There was a BLOOD LIBEL in Mantua *(N. Italy)*.

5239 — 1479

All Jews were expelled from Shlettstadt *(Selestat, Germany)* (see 5238\1478).

5240 — 1480

R.Yosef (ben Shlomo) Kolon, the Maharik, died in Italy.
Three Jews were burned at the stake in a BLOOD LIBEL in Venice *(Italy)*.

5241 — 1481

The Inquisition was established in Spain.

The Spanish Inquisition — established with the intention of exposing secret Jews, ANUSSIM (Marranos) — began to function in 1481. It devoted its efforts to anti-Jewish activity to a greater extent than any previous (localized) Inquisition (see 5012\1252).
The first public sentencing and burning (AUTO DA FE) by the Spanish Inquisition was held at Seville on the 7th **Adar**. On the 4th **Sivan** the Pope *(Sixtus IV)* instructed all his local bishops to send back to Spain all those Jews who had fled the Inquisition there.

Living in the Year 1480

R.Yitzchak Abarbanel	b.1437, d.1508.
Yuchasin	b.1440?, d.1515.
R.Ovadya Bertinura	b.1445?, d.1524?.
Eyn Yaakov (R.Yaakov ibn Chaviv)	b.1445?, d.1516?.
R.Yaakov Pollak	b.1460?, d.1530?.
Radvaz	b.1463?, d.1573?.
R.Yosef Yoselman	b.1478?, d.1555?.

5243 — 1483

Tomas de Torquemada was appointed head of the Spanish Inquisition in **Cheshvan** 5244*1483*, and the persecutions grew worse (see 5241\1481). All Jews were expelled from Andalusia *(province of Spain which included Seville and Cordova)*, making it easier for the Inquisition to isolate the ANUSSIM (Marranos) who remained (see 5241\1481).
All Jews were expelled from Warsaw *(Poland)*, and also from Mayence *(Mainz, Germany)* (see 5233\1473, 5239\1479).
R.Yitzchak Abarbanel (see 5269*1508*) — Don Yitzchak Abravanel, a scholarly member of a wealthy aristocratic family who were descendants of King David — had succeeded his father as treasurer to the king of Portugal. He fled to Spain in 1483 — when he was suspected of being in a conspiracy against a new king — and he subsequently became important in the court of the Spanish king (see 5252\1492). Some say that his grandfather had originally been a royal treasurer in Spain, but left for Portugal to revert to open JUDAISM, after having been FORCIBLY CONVERTED (see 5151\1391).

5245 — 1485

The Jews were attacked in ANTI-JEWISH RIOTS in many towns of Provence *(S.E.France)* in 1484, and again in 1485; many were killed.
The Spanish Inquisition burned twenty-two ANUSSIM (Marranos) in Perpignan (France near the Spanish border, see 5151\1391).
All Jews were expelled from Perugia *(Italy)* in 1485 (see 5235\1475), and then from Gubbio and Vicenza *(Italy)* in 1486.

5247 — 1487

R.Yaakov (ben Yehuda) Landau — a German Talmud scholar residing in Naples *(Italy)* — wrote Sefer HaAgur *(Halacha)* (printed in Naples 1487 *(see 5235\1475)*). This was probably the first book to be printed during the life of the author, and the first work to be published with Haskamot (approbations), a practice which later included warnings of copyright to extend over a number of years.

5248 — 1488

R.Ovadya Bertinura settled in Yerushalayim.

R.Ovadya Bertinura — a disciple of the Maharik — arrived in Yerushalayim on the 13th **Nissan**, after two years of travel from Italy, via Egypt. He became the leading rabbi in Yerushalayim (which suffered from extreme poverty). He subsequently finished his popular commentary to the Mishna *(see Illustrations, Text C, #2)*.
R.Yosef Karo (see 5335\1575) was born.
Sixteen Jews were burned at the stake in Toledo *(Spain)* on 22nd **Av**. Forty Anussim (Marranos) were burned in Toledo *(Spain)* during this year (see 5250\1490), and over 100 bodies were exhumed and also burned. By this time, the Spanish Inquisition had burned over 700 Anussim (see 5241\1481).

5249 — 1489

The Jews were attacked in parts of Provence *(S. E. France)*, some were forcibly converted, and the rest were ordered to leave. The expulsion was enforced only later (see 5261\1501).
All Jews were expelled from Lucca *(Italy)* (see 5245\1485).

5250 — 1490

422 Anussim were burned in Toledo (see 5248\1488).
All Jews were expelled from Geneva (see 5232\1472), and (for the third or fourth time) from Heilbronn *(Germany)*.

5251 — 1491

All Jews were expelled from Thurgau *(Switzerland)*, leaving almost no Jews in Switzerland (see 5250\1490).
Jews were expelled from Ravenna *(Italy)* and the synagogue was burned (see 5249\1489).

5252 — *1491*

A Jew was burned at the stake in Avila *(Spain)* on a blood libel in the month of **Kislev** 5252*1491*, and another was stoned to death by an angry mob. In the same month, all Jews of Granada were given permission to depart peacefully, before the Castillian (Christian) forces took control from the Moors (Muslims), and completed Christian control over all of Spain *(see map page 326)*.

Columbus consulted R.Avraham Zacuto for his travels.

Christopher Columbus — who, some say, may have been of Jewish origin — consulted (and was encouraged by) R.Avraham Zacuto (see 5264\1504) — a disciple of the Maharyah (see 5252\1492). He was famous for his knowledge of astrology, achievements in astronomy, and for his refinement of the astrolabe (an instrument for navigation). Columbus used R.Avraham's improved tables of astronomical movement, which once saved the lives of the whole expedition. (A menacing native tribe was pacified by Columbus, when he threatened to take away the light of the moon — which he knew was going to be eclipsed.)

5252 — 1492

All Jews were expelled from Spain and Sicily.

It is estimated that 100,000 to 300,000 Jews were expelled from Spain, and many became Marranos (Anussim). This added to the large number of Anussim (Marranos) already existing (see 5151\1391), even though 13,000 of them had already been exposed by the Inquisition (see 5241\1481).
R.Yitzchak Abarbanel (see 5243\1483) attempted to use his (wealth and) influence to have the Spanish expulsion order withdrawn.
Most of the Jews — who had all left Spain by the 9th **Av** — settled in Turkey (where they were welcomed, see 5213\1453), North Africa, and Italy (see 5253\1493, 5249\1489).
Many (some say 150,000) went to Portugal, where R.Yitzchak Abohab II — the Maharyah (see 5253\1493), the leading Talmud scholar in Castille *(province of Spain)* — convinced the king of Portugal to allow a number of Jews to settle. The Jews were forced to pay a tax for temporary residence in Portugal, and 700 young Jews were forcibly expelled — sent to populate an island off the coast of central Africa.
All Jews were also expelled from Sicily and Sardinia, which were under Spanish rule, and

an estimated 37,000 to 100,000 Jews left. Among the refugees leaving Spain were: the Maharyah (see 5253\1493), and his disciples;

- R.Yaakov ibn Chaviv (see 5276\1516);
- R.Yaakov Bei Rav (see 5298\1538) who was not yet 18;
- R.Avraham Zacuto (see 5257*1496*);
- R.Yitzchak Abarbanel (see 5253\1493);
- Maharam Alashkar (see 5270\1510);
- R.Ephrayim Karo with his family (including his 4 year old son, R.Yosef) (see 5282\1522);
- R.Yosef Saragossi and his disciple, the Radvaz (see 5277\1517), who was not yet 13, (some say the Radvaz left Spain earlier);
- R.Meir (ib)n Gabbai, who was almost 13, and was later known as the author of Avodat HaKodesh and other KABBALA works.

5253 — *1492*

Twenty seven Jews were burned in Mecklenburg *(province of Germany)* in a RITUAL DESECRATION libel *(see 5003\1243)*, and the rest were expelled, on 3rd **Cheshvan** 5253*1492*. All Jews had also been expelled from Olesnica *(Silesia, a region between Germany and Poland)*.

Chapter 13

The Kovim

The Great Scholars of the Shulchan Aruch & Torah Consolidation

Section IV

Chapter 13

The Kov'im*

The Great Scholars of the Shulchan Aruch & Torah Consolidation

Jewish Year		Secular Year
5253	R.Yitzchak Abarbanel arrived in Naples, from Spain.	1493
5257	**All Jews were expelled from Portugal.**	**1496**
5276	The Eyn Yaakov was printed.	1516
5276	The Turks (Ottoman Empire) conquered Eretz Yisrael.	1516
5285	R.Yosef Yoselman saved many Jews during the Peasants War.	1525
5314	A mass burning of Jewish books took place in Rome.	1553
5323	**The Shulchan Aruch was completed by R.Yosef Karo.**	**1563**
5330	**SHULCHAN ARUCH PUBLISHED WITH SUPPLEMENTS OF RAMO.**	1570
5332	**The Ari'zal died in Tzfat (Safed).**	**1572**
5333	The Maharal came to Prague.	1573
5334	The Maharshal died.	1573
5335	R.Yosef Karo died in Tzfat.	1575
5359	The Maharal returned to Prague again.	1599
5374	The Maharsha became Rabbi in Lublin.	1614
5377	The Tosaphot Yom Tov commentary was concluded.	1616
5382	The Shaloh arrived in Eretz Yisrael.	1621
5389	R.Yom Tov Lipman Heller was imprisoned in Prague.	1629
5400	R.Yoel Sirkes, the Bach, died.	1640
5406	**The Shach and Taz (on Shulchan Aruch) were printed.**	**1646**
5408	**JEWS WERE MASSACRED BY CHMIELNITZKI'S FORCES.**	1648

**See Appendix D*

Section IV

UNIVERSAL DISPERSION

Chapter 13

The Kovim *

The Great Scholars of the Shulchan Aruch & Torah Consolidation

The thirteenth chapter in Jewish history begins with the Jewish expulsion from Spain, and ends with the massacre of the Jews of Poland, during the Cossack uprising under Chmielnitzki.

This chapter is notable for the ultimate development and consolidation of Halacha — with the broad acceptance of the Shulchan Aruch, and other aspects of Torah study, and for the calibre of the Torah scholars living at that time.

So great was the effect of this era, that it represents a chapter (Tekufa) all on its own. (See Appendix D.)

* *See Appendix D*

Major Kovim

RYitzchak Abarbanel	b1437	d1508
Yuchasin	b1440?	d1515
ROvadya Bertinura	b1445?	d1524?
Eyn Yaakov (RYaakov ibn Chaviv)	b1445?	d1516?
RYaakov Pollak	b1460?	d1530?
Radvaz	b1463?	d1573?
Beit Yosef (RYosef Karo)	b1488	d1575
Maharshal	b1510?	d1573
Maharal of Prague	b1512?	d1609
Shitta Mekubetzet (RBetzAshkenazi)	b1520?	d1594?
Ramak (Cordovero)	b1522?	d1570
Ramo (RMoshe Isserles)	b1525?	d1573?
RMordechai Yaffe (Levush)	b1530	d1612
Ari'zal (RYitzchak Luria)	b1534	d1572
Sma (RYehoshua Falk)	b1540?	d1614
RChaim Vital	b1542?	d1620
Lechem Mishneh (RAvraham di Boton)	b1545?	d1588
Kli Yakar (RShlomo Ephrayim)	b1550?	d1619
Maharsha (RShmuel Edels)	b1555	d1631
Bach (RYoel Sirkes)	b1560?	d1640
Shaloh (RYeshayahu Horowitz)	b1560?	d1630
Tosaphot Yom Tov (Lipman Heller)	b1579	d1654
Taz (RDavid ben Shmuel)	b1586	d1667
Chelkat Mechokek (RMoshe Lima)	b1605?	d1658
Shach (RShabbetai Kohen)	b1621	d1663?

Chapter 13a

The Kovim,

The Great Scholars of the Shulchan Aruch & Torah Consolidation

5253 — 1493

R.Yitzchak Abarbanel arrived in Naples from Spain.

The overcrowded ships arriving with Jewish refugees from Spain had been allowed to land in Genoa *(N. Italy)* for three days only. At the beginning of 1493, this permission was also withdrawn. R.Yitzchak Abohab II (see 5252\1492) — a disciple of R.Yitzchak Kanpanton — died in Portugal in 1493; and R.Yitzchak Abarbanel — who had studied under him — arrived in Naples *(Italy)* (see 5254\1494).

All Jews — including refugees from Spain — were expelled from Perpignan *(France, near the Spanish border, see 5255\1485)* on Yom Kippur 5254\ *1493*.

As many as 20,000 Spanish Jews died in Morocco of attacks, disease and famine, and some returned to Spain and converted.

5254 — 1494

Sixteen Jews were killed in Tyrnau *(Trnava, Slovakia; Nagyszombat, Hungary)* in a BLOOD LIBEL (see 5297\1537).

All Jews were expelled from Campo S. Pietro and Brescia *(Italy)* (see 5251\1491), and from Arles *(Provence, S.E.France)* (see 5261\1501).

R.Yitzchak Abarbanel's home in Naples *(Italy)* (see 5253\1493) was looted by invading French troops, and he moved to the island of Corfu for a while, before returning when the French left *(see 5269\1508)*.

5255 — 1495

All Jews were expelled from Lithuania, and allowed to return eight years later (see 5263\1503).

Most of the Jews of Cosenza *(S.Italy)* were subjected to FORCED BAPTISM.

5256 — 1496

After having been allowed to return to parts of Austria (see 5181\1421), all Jews were again expelled (see **Iyar** 5195\1435) from Carinthia and Styria *(provinces of Austria)* in the month of **Adar**.

5257 — 1496

All Jews were expelled from Portugal.

An expulsion order was issued — in the month of **Tevet** 5257\ *1496* — giving all the Jews living in Portugal (see 5252\1492) one year to convert or to leave the country. Many Jews resisted the force — including torture — that was used to convince and convert them (see 5257\1497).

Among the refugees leaving Portugal was R.Avraham Zacuto (see 5252\1492, 5264\1504), who was consulted on astronomy and navigation *(see 5252\1491)* by the explorer Vasco da Gama before a trip to India (where, some say, he captured a travelling Jew, subjecting him to FORCED BAPTISM).

R.Yitzchak Karo — uncle of R.Yosef Karo who had settled in Portugal before the Spanish expulsion — left for Constantinople *(Istanbul, Turkey)*.

5257 — 1497

From the first day of Pesach, many Jewish children — aged 4 through 14 — were captured and subjected to FORCED BAPTISM in Portugal (see 5257\ *1496*). This led to some of the parents converting in order to remain in the country with their children. The government of Portugal also connivingly brought 20,000 Jews to Lisbon, and assembled them in a palace where they were then denied food and water and subjected to FORCED BAPTISM. These became the ANUSSIM (Marranos) of Portugal.

5258 — 1498

All Jews — including refugees from Spain — were expelled from Navarre (province of Spain on the French border) (see 5253\1493), and from the island of Rhodes.

All Jews were expelled from Nuremberg *(Bavaria,*

Living in the Year 1500

R.Yitzchak Abarbanel	b.1437,	d.1508.
Yuchasin	b.1440?,	d.1515.
R.Ovadya Bertinura	b.1445?,	d.1524?.
Eyn Yaakov (R.Yaakov ibn Chaviv)	b.1445?,	d.1516?.
R.Yaakov Pollak	b.1460?,	d.1530?.
Radvaz	b.1463?,	d.1573?.
R.Yosef Yoselman	b.1478?,	d.1555?.
Beit Yosef (R.Yosef Karo)	b.1488,	d.1575.

Germany) in **Tammuz** (see 5211*1450*, 5311\\1551), although some settled in the surrounding villages.
All Jews were again expelled (see 5164\\1404) from Salzburg *(Austria)*.

5259 ≈ 1499

Seventy-five ANUSSIM (Marranos) were burned at the stake in Avila *(Spain)*, and the bones of twenty-six Jews were exhumed and burned.

5260 ≈ 1500

R.(Asher) Lemlein predicted that the Mashiach *(Messiah)* was about to come, and he propelled a movement of Teshuva *(repentance)*, which spread to many communities in Europe. R.Zeligman Gans — grandfather of the author of Tzemach David — demolished his special matza-baking oven, because next year he would be in Eretz Yisrael *[Tzem.Dav. 5260]*. There was disappointment, when R.Lemlein died but no documented negative movements *[See Encpd.Jud.11.11]*.

5261 ≈ 1501

All Jews were expelled from Provence *(S.E.France)* (see 5155*1394*) except for that part which belonged to the Pope's court *(see 5029\\1269, 5080\\1320, 5329\\1569)*.

5262 ≈ 1502

A number of Jews (refugees from Spain) were burned at the stake in Dubrovnik *(Yugoslavia)*.

5263 ≈ 1503

R.Yaakov Pollak, — a leading rabbi who established a YESHIVA in Cracow *(Poland)*, after leaving Prague — introduced his sharp (and somewhat controversial) style of Talmud scholarship *(Chilukim)* into Poland-Lithuania *[Mrsha.B.M. 85a-"DeLishtakach"/ Tzem.Dav.5290/ Chav.Yair.152]*.

Jews were permitted to return to Lithuania, (see 5255\\1495).

5264 ≈ 1504

R.Avraham Zacuto (see 5257*1496*) had settled in Tunisia (see 5270\\1510) after the expulsion from Portugal (he was twice taken prisoner on his journey). He concluded his Sefer Yuchasin *(history)* in 1504, and later travelled to Turkey, Damascus, and some say Eretz Yisrael.
All Jews were expelled from Pilsen *(Bohemia)* in a RITUAL DESECRATION libel *(see 5003\\1243)*.

5265 ≈ 1505

All Jews were expelled from Orange *(S.E.France)* (see 5261\\1501).

5266 ≈ 1506

Two thousand ANUSSIM (Marranos) were killed in Lisbon (see 5257\\1497).
An angry crowd in a BLOOD LIBEL in Venice stoned a Jew to death.

5269 ≈ *1508*

R.Yitzchak Abarbanel (see 5243\\1483) died (some say in **Tishrei** 5269*1508*) in Venice *(N. Italy)* where he had settled in 1503 (see 5254\\1494), and he was buried nearby in Padua. He wrote a commentary to the Bible, and Rosh Emanah *(philosophy)*, as well as other works.

5270 ≈ *1509*

R.Chaim ben Yitzchak Katz (of whom little else is known) was killed in Prague, in a LIBEL on the 28th **Tishrei** 5270*1509*.

5270 ≈ 1510

All Jews were expelled from Colmar *(Alsace, a region between France and Germany)* in **Shvat**, and from Coltbus *(Germany)*.
Some of the wealthy Jews were allowed to remain in Naples *(S. Italy)* where the rest were expelled.
Jewish books were confiscated in Frankfort am Mai at the instigation of a *meshumad (apostate)*, but were returned — less than two months later — in **Sivan**.
Thirty-eight Jews were burned at the stake in Berlin, in **Av** in a RITUAL DESECRATION libel *(see*

5003\1243), and the rest were expelled from the whole province of Brandenburg (see 5206\1446, and 5303\1543).

R.Moshe (ben Yitzchak) — the Maharam Alashkar, who had settled in Tunisia after the expulsion from Spain (see 5252\1492) — left there in 1510, when Spanish forces landed in parts of North Africa and imprisoned a number of Jews. He settled in Greece for a while, and then moved to Cairo, where he remained for an extended time writing many SH'ELOT UTESHUVOT. He went to Eretz Yisrael shortly before he died.

5275 — 1515

All Jews were expelled from Laibach *(Austria, now Ljubjana, Slovenia)* in **Tevet** 1515 (see 5256\1496); and from Genoa *(N. Italy)* (see 5253\1493), where they were allowed to return a short while later (see 5310\1550).

5276 — 1516

The Eyn Yaakov was printed.

After leaving Spain, R.Yaakov (ben Shlomo) ibn Chaviv (see 5252\1492) settled in Salonika *(Greece)* (some say he went to Portugal first). He wrote — and began printing— the Eyn Yaakov *(collection of the Agada quotes from the Talmud, with his compiled commentary)*, but it was completed (after his death) by his son R.Levi, who later settled in Yerushalayim (see 5298\1538).

The (Ottoman Turks) conquered Eretz Yisrael.

Eretz Yisrael was conquered by the Turks becoming part of a rapidly expanding empire *(see map page 329)*.

All Jews were expelled from Lowicz *(Poland)*.

In the month of **Iyar** the Jews of Venice were ordered to move out of the city to a restricted area where there had previously been a foundry ('getto' in Italian). It is assumed that this is the origin of the term 'ghetto', although there were many earlier cases of Jews being forced into separate — if not so remote — living areas (and apparently the term 'get' was used much earlier in Rome, to signify a separated section of a town.)

It was in Venice — a year later, in **Kislev** 5278\1517 — that the popular CHUMASH Mikra'ot Gedolot *(with commentaries) (see ILLUSTRATIONS, TEXT A)* was printed for the first time.

5277 — 1517

The Radvaz, R.David (ben Shlomo) ibn (Avi) Zimra, had settled in Egypt, having been in Tzfat *(Safed)* and (some say) in Fez *(Morocco)* after leaving Spain (see 5252\1492). When the Turks conquered Egypt in 1517, and the system of Jewish communal structure changed, the Radvaz became the leader of Egyptian Jews (see 5313\1553). He formally ended the Minyan Shtarot (see 3449\-313) which was still being used there, and he was consulted on Halacha questions from many countries *[Radvaz Hil.Mel.5.7]*.

Much Jewish property was destroyed when the Turks conquered Tlemcen *(Pomaria, Algeria)* and the Jews were subsequently required to wear a YELLOW PATCH on their headgear.

5278 — 1518

The Jews of Hevron were attacked; many were killed and many fled.

5279 — 1519

All Jews were expelled from the region of Wuertemberg *(Germany)* and from Regensburg *(Bavaria, Germany)* (see 5211*1450*, 5311\1551).

5282 — *1521*

The Jews of Yerushalayim were blamed for a severe water shortage in **Kislev** 5282*1521*, and were required to pay heavy fines.

5282 — 1522

R.Ephrayim Karo — the father of the young R.Yosef Karo (see 5252\1492) — had settled in Constantinople *(Istanbul, Turkey)*, after the expulsion from Spain — some say they were in Portugal until the expulsion from there. After his father died R.Yosef became the disciple of his uncle R.Yitzchak Karo (see 5257*1496*). He began writing the Beit Yosef *(a thorough study of the development of*

Living in the Year 1520

R.Ovadya Bertinura	b.1445?,	d.1524?.
R.Yaakov Pollak	b.1460?,	d.1530?.
Radvaz	b.1463?,	d.1573?.
R.Yosef Yoselman	b.1478?,	d.1555?.
Beit Yosef (R.Yosef Karo)	b.1488,	d.1575.
Maharshal	b.1510?,	d.1573.
Maharal of Prague	b.1512?,	d.1609.
Shitta Mekubetzet (R.Betz.Ashkenazi)	b.1520?,	d.1594?.

Halacha, written as a commentary on the Tur) in 1522 after he had moved to Adrianople *(Turkey)*. From there he moved to Nikopol *(Bulgaria)*.
Between 2,000 and 3,000 Jews had been captured and brought as slaves to the island of Rhodes (see 5258\1498). In 1522, these Jewish slaves helped the Turks conquer Rhodes, which subsequently became a vibrant Jewish center.

5283 — 1523

Most of the Jews left Cranganore (S.W. India) when the Portuguese conquered the territory. Many settled in Cochin (S.W. India), where they were granted certain protections by the local rajah (prince).

5284 — 1524

All the Jews of Cairo were to be massacred unless they paid an exorbitant tax. However on the day the money was to be paid, the (local) ruler was killed in a (counter) rebellion, and to commemorate the event the Jews instituted Purim Mitzrayim on the 28th **Adar**.

5285 — 1525

R.Eliyahu Mizrachi — leading rabbi in Turkey and author of a famous work on Rashi's CHUMASH (Bible) commentary — died in Constantinople *(Istanbul, Turkey)*.
All Jews of Carpentras — *(Provence, S.E. France)*, part of the papal territory (see 5080\1320, 5261\1501) — were ordered to wear YELLOW HATS by the Pope *(Clement VII)* in **Sivan** 1525 (see 4977*1216*).

R.Yosef Yoselman saved many Jews during the Peasants War.

R.Yosef Yoselman the SHTADLAN (see 5290\1530) saved the Jews of Alsace *(a region between France and Germany)* during the bloody Peasants War (revolt) through brave negotiations.

5287 — *1526*

All Jews were expelled from Hungary in **Kislev** 5287*1526* (see 5120\1360) as the Turks *(Ottoman Empire)* invaded the country. Many crossed to the Balkan countries *(which include Greece, Bulgaria, SE Romania, Slovenia, Croatia, Serbia and Montenegro, Bosnia and Hercegovina, Albania, and Macedonia)* which were under Turkish rule *(see map page 329)* — although some continued to live in small towns (see 5289\1529), and some returned to the larger towns a few years later (see 5120\1360).

5288 — 1528

Although the Spanish government required settlers in Mexico to prove that they had been Christian for four generations, many ANUSSIM (Marranos) managed to emigrate (see 5310\1550) — some were burned at the stake in 1528.

5289 — 1529

Thirty Jews were burned to death in Pezinok *(Poesing, Slovakia; Bazin, Hungary)* in a BLOOD LIBEL in **Sivan** 1529, and the rest were expelled from there (see 5287\1526) and from a number of other towns.

5290 — 1530

R.Yosef Yoselman of Rosheim *(E. France, near Germany)* (see 5285\1525, 5303\1543) — a scholar and a great SHTADLAN *(advocate and negotiator for Jewish causes)* whose great uncles had been killed in a BLOOD LIBEL, see 5230\1470 — was forced to DEBATE a *meshumad (apostate)* on the Rosh Chodesh **Av** 1530. The *meshumad* was subsequently expelled from Augsburg *(Germany)*.
R.Yosef Yoselman also succeeded in convincing the emperor that Jews were not spying for the Turks *(Ottomans)*. He was outstanding as a SHTADLAN, by virtue of the broad sphere of influence he managed to maintain, and in the number of times he interceded for Jewish causes.
All Jews of Germany were required to wear a YELLOW BADGE in 1530 (see 4977*1216*).

5293 — 1532

Shlomo Molcho was an ANUSS (Marrano) from Portugal who returned to (open) Jewish practice — by the influence of David Re'uveni (as did many) — when David came to Portugal to involve the king in a war against the growing Turkish *(Ottoman)* empire (see 5276\1516, 5277\1517, 5287\1526 *(map page 329)*). David's plan — which he skillfully succeeded in making credible — was that the Jews would take Eretz Yisrael, and that this would be the advent of Mashiach (the Messiah). Shlomo left Portugal — with David, who was forced to leave — and after much journey, he took up David's mission, apparently indicating that he himself was Mashiach. They both travelled to Regensburg *(Germany)* (see 5279\1519), where the emperor had them arrested and imprisoned. Shlomo was burned at the stake in **Kislev** 5293\1532 for refusing to convert to Christianity. David Re'uveni — whose country of origin was unclear, but believed to be

Africa or Arabia — died in prison a few years later (some say he was burned at the stake).

5293 1533

All Jews were expelled from Constance *(Germany)*.

5294 1534

Many Jews were massacred in Tlemcen *(Pomaria, Algeria)* when the Spanish conquered the town (see 5270\1510, 5277\1517), and 1,500 were enslaved (see 5295\1535).

5295 1535

Many Jews were killed in Tunis and many were captured and sold as slaves when invaders (see 5270\1510, 5294\1534) ransacked the city.

5296 1536

R.Yosef Karo (see 5282\1522), moved to Eretz Yisrael after his three children (and first wife) had died — some say he spent three years in Salonika *(Greece)* and they died there. He settled in Tzfat *(Safed)*, where he considered himself a disciple of R.Yaakov Bei Rav (see 5298\1538) — whom he may have studied under, during a previous stay in Egypt.

5297 1537

When the brothers who established the first Jewish printing press in Poland (Cracow) converted to Christianity, the Jews there boycotted their books until the king issued an order in **Nissan** 1537 which broke the boycott *[see Ency.Jud. 5.1037, 7.1189]*.
Jews were killed in Tyrnau *(Trnava, Slovakia; Nagyszombat, Hungary)* in a BLOOD LIBEL (see 5299\1539).

5298 1538

R.Yaakov Bei Rav was a very young) rabbi in Fez *(Morocco)* after he left Spain (see 5252\1492). He travelled (on business matters) to Egypt and Syria, before settling in Tzfat *(Safed)*, where he was accepted as a leader by such scholars as R.Yosef Karo (see 5296\1536). R.Yaakov attempted — by use of the Rambam's Halacha — to re-introduce the original SEMICHA (ordination) which would enable for rulings and judgements on all matters, including capital punishments. Although he was supported by the scholars of Tzfat, he was vigorously opposed by R.Levi ibn Chaviv (see 5276\1516) and other rabbis.

5299 1539

All Jews were expelled from Tyrnau *(Trnava, Slovakia; Nagyszombat, Hungary)* in **Adar** 1539, after a BLOOD LIBEL two years earlier (see 5297\1537, and 5254\1494).

5301 *1540*

The well acclaimed *[Resh.Choch.Sh.HaTesh.7]* anonymous work *Orchot Tzadikim* *(Mussar)* — written in YIDDISH — appeared in this year.
The Portuguese Inquisition — which began to function (see 5012\1252, 5241\1481) with the intention of seeking out ANUSSIM (Marranos) (see 5257\1497) — had some burned to death in Lisbon on the 19th **Tishrei** 5301*1540*. Eventually 1,200 ANUSSIM were burned to death by this Inquisition (see 5266\1506).

Living in the Year 1540

Radvaz	b.1463?,	d.1573?.
R.Yosef Yoselman	b.1478?,	d.1555?.
Beit Yosef (R.Yosef Karo)	b.1488,	d.1575.
Maharshal	b.1510?,	d.1573.
Maharal of Prague	b.1512?,	d.1609.
Shitta Mekubetzet (R.Betz.Ashkenazi)	b.1520?,	d.1594?.
Ramak (Cordovero)	b.1522?,	d.1570.
Ramo (R.Moshe Isserles)	b.1525?,	d.1573.
R.Mordechai Yaffe (Levush)	b.1530,	d.1612.
Ari'zal (R.Yitzchak Luria)	b.1534,	d.1572.
Sma (R.Yehoshua Falk)	b.1540?,	d.1614.

5301 1541

There was a massacre of Jews in Bohemia, after an order was issued expelling them from the country (see 5317\1557).
All the Jews who had resettled in Naples *(S.Italy)* were expelled again (see 5270\1510).

5302 1542

R.Yosef Karo finished his Beit Yosef commentary on the Tur (see 5282\1522) on the 11th **Elul,** and it brought him great respect amongst leading Talmud scholars of the time.
R.Ovadya Seforno of Italy wrote a commentary

on the CHUMASH (Bible) *(see ILLUSTRATIONS, TEXT A, #9)*.
The Jews of Kalisch *(Poland)* were attacked in ANTI-JEWISH RIOTS.

5303 1543

All Jews were expelled from Muehlhausen *(Saxony, province of Germany)* (see 5232\1472) and from other towns of the province, as a result of the influence of Martin Luther (a German Christian reformer) who had turned against the Jews — some say in disappointment that the Jews did not accept his form of (less "paganistic") Christianity.
R.Yosef Yoselman (see 5290\1530) had attempted to intercede there, without success, although — through his representations — Jews were allowed to return to live in Brandenburg *(province of Germany)* (see 5270\1510, 5333\1573). Some say that he (R.Yosef) is the Jew with whom John Calvin (a French Christian reformer) engaged in a DEBATE (recorded in Calvin's writings) see 5290\1530.

5305 1545

200 Jews were killed, and 5,000 houses destroyed in a fire in Salonika *(Greece)* on the 4th of **Av**.

5307 1547

Many Jews were killed in Treviso *(N. Italy)* in ANTI-JEWISH RIOTS, and the rest left town.

5310 1550

All Jews were expelled from Genoa *(N. Italy)* (see 5275\1515).
Some say that at this point there were more ANUSSIM (Marranos) in Mexico City than there were Christians (see 5288\1528).

5311 1551

The Jews of Bratslav *(Podolia, Poland)* were attacked by the Tartars who invaded the town.
The Jews in Austria were required to wear a YELLOW BADGE, (see 4977*1216*).
The last Jews of Bavaria were expelled (see 5211*1450*, 5238\1478, 5258\1498, 5279\1519).

5313 1553

The (elderly) Radvaz (see 5277\1517) settled in Eretz Yisrael, in Yerushalayim at first, and then in Tzfat *(Safed)*, where he lived for some twenty years. He wrote many SH'ELOT UTESHUVOT, and a commentary on sections of the Rambam's Yad HaChazaka *(see ILLUSTRATIONS, TEXT I, #6)*.
He was succeeded in Egypt by his disciple R.Betzalel Ashkenazi, author of the Shitta MeKubetzet *(collection — from unpublished manuscripts — of the commentaries and Tosaphot of early scholars on the Talmud)*. Later, R.Betzalel also went to Eretz Yisrael, where some say he had been born.
The Ari'zal — R.Yitzchak Luria Ashkenazi (see 5330\1570), who was born in Yerushalayim — was brought to Cairo by his mother (after his father died), to her wealthy brother, who later became his father-in-law. He was a disciple of the Radvaz, and also of R.Betzalel — although R.Betzalel and the Ari'zal later wrote the Shitta MeKubetzet on (the Talmud tractate) Zevachim together *[Shem.Hag.1.37a]*.

5314 1553

A mass burning of Jewish books in Rome.

A *ger tzedek* *(convert to Judaism)* who had previously been a monk was burned alive in **Elul** 5313\1553 in Rome.
The Pope *(Julius III)* ordered the burning of the Talmud — and the cessation of its printing — because of alleged anti-Christian content (see 5002\1242, 5023\1263). On the first day of Rosh HaShana 5314*1553* the Inquisition staged a massive burning of the Talmud and other Jewish books in Rome, and Jewish books were subsequently burned in many cities in Italy (see 5319\1559, and 5361\1601). In Venice, over 1,000 copies of the Talmud and 500 copies of the Rif were burned on the 13th **Cheshvan** 5314*1553*.

Dona Gracia (Mendes) Nassi — a distinguished Jewish stateswoman who used her vast wealth and aristocratic contacts to conduct a network for aiding her fellow ANUSSIM (Marranos) to leave Portugal — left Ferrara (Italy, see 5343\1583) and settled in Constantinople *(Istanbul, Turkey)*. She was born into a family of ANUSSIM in Portugal (see 5257\1497), had left Portugal after her husband's (untimely) death, and had later openly declared herself Jewish. In Constantinople, she extended her financial support to further Jewish study, and Jewish causes.

5315 1555

The Jews of Rome (and other cities) were ordered by the Pope *(Paul IV,* see 5316\1556) to live in ghettos and lock the doors of the ghetto at night. Men were to wear YELLOW HATS, and women YELLOW

KERCHIEFS — and they were subjected to severe economic restrictions (see 5558\1798).

5316 — 1556

Twenty-six Portuguese ANUSSIM (Marranos) who had openly returned to JUDAISM were burned to death in Ancona *(Italy)* on the 3rd of **Iyar**, by order of the Pope (*Paul IV*, see 5315\1555).
Three Jews were killed in Sochatchev *(Poland)* in a RITUAL DESECRATION libel *(see 5003\1243)*.

5317 — 1557

The Jews of Bohemia — who had returned since the last expulsion (see 5301\1541) were expelled from the major cities (although they were allowed to return a short while later); a few Jews were allowed to remain in Prague.
Among those leaving Prague was R.Mordechai Yaffe (see 5352\1592). He was a disciple of the Ramo and the Maharshal, and author of the Levushim, which is known as Levush *(Halacha)*. He lived in Italy for approximately ten years, before becoming rabbi in Hurodno *(Grodno, Lithuania)*, Lublin *(Poland)*, and then Kremeniec *(Poland)*. He participated in the VA'AD ARBA ARATZOT *(see 5340\1580)*.

5318 — 1558

7,500 Jews — many of them exiles from Portugal and Spain — died in a cholera epidemic in Marrakesh *(Morocco)* (see 5253\1493).

5319 — 1559

10,000 Jewish books were burned in Cremona *(N. Italy)* under the instructions of the Inquisition (see 5314*1553*). However, the Zohar was printed there in the same year, by a recently established press — of non-Jewish ownership — which also published (in the following year) a CHUMASH (Bible) with a YIDDISH translation by someone Jewish.

5323 — 1563

The SHULCHAN ARUCH was completed by R.Yosef Karo.

R.Yosef Karo — who was already greatly respected by most Talmud scholars (see 5302\1542) — finished writing the SHULCHAN ARUCH *(code of law)* *(see ILLUSTRATIONS, TEXTS J K L & M,, #1)* — which was an abbreviated extension of his commentary, the Beit Yosef, see 5282\1522) — on the 17th **Adar**.
He corresponded with the Ramo, who later supplemented R.Yosef's SEPHARDI oriented SHULCHAN ARUCH with the ASHKENAZI rulings and customs. This helped consolidate the eventual role of the SHULCHAN ARUCH as the ultimate word in Halacha.
All Jews were expelled from Neutitschein *(Novy Jicin, Moravia)* in **Elul.**

Living in the Year 1560

Name	Born	Died
Radvaz	b.1463?,	d.1573?.
Beit Yosef (R.Yosef Karo)	b.1488,	d.1575.
Maharshal	b.1510?,	d.1573.
Maharal of Prague	b.1512?,	d.1609.
Shitta Mekubetzet (R.Betz.Ashkenazi)	b.1520?,	d.1594?.
Ramak (Cordovero)	b.1522?,	d.1570.
Ramo (R.Moshe Isserles)	b.1525?,	d.1573.
R.Mordechai Yaffe (Levush)	b.1530,	d.1612.
Ari'zal (R.Yitzchak Luria)	b.1534,	d.1572.
Sma (R.Yehoshua Falk)	b.1540?,	d.1614.
R.Chaim Vital	b.1542?,	d.1620.
Lechem Mishneh (R.Avraham di Boton)	b.1545?,	d.1588.
Kli Yakar (R.Shlomo Ephrayim)	b.1550?,	d.1619.
Maharsha (R.Shmuel Edels)	b.1555,	d.1631.
Bach (R.Yoel Sirkes)	b.1560?,	d.1640.
Shaloh (R.Yeshayahu Horowitz)	b.1560?,	d.1630.

5324 — *1563*

Ivan the Terrible captured the city of Polotzk *(Lithuania)* and thirty Jews were drowned in the Dvina *(Daugava)* River on the 25th **Kislev** (first day Chanuka) for refusing to be subjected to FORCED BAPTISM.

5325 — 1565

The Maharam Padua — R.Meir (ben Yitzchak) Katzenellenbogen, a disciple of R.Yaakov Pollak and of R.Yehuda of Mintz (Mahari Mintz, whose granddaughter he married) — died on the 10th **Shvat**.

5326 — 1566

Jewish men were required to wear YELLOW HATS in Lithuania, and the women were required to wear YELLOW KERCHIEFS.

5327 — 1567

Jews were expelled from the rest of the province of Genoa *(N. Italy)* (see 5310\1550), although they returned after a short while.

5329 ≈ 1568

R.Yisrael (ben Yeshayahu) HaLevi Horowitz — a great-uncle of the Shaloh, and of R.Pinchas (see 5345\1585) — was burned to death together with his son-in-law, R.Moshe ben Yoel in Prague on 27th **Kislev**.

5329 ≈ 1569

In **Adar**, all Jews were expelled from the Papal States *(most of central Italy, including Bologna and Recanti)* by the Pope *(Pius V)*. The expulsion excluded Rome and Ancona, but included Carpentras *(Provence, S.E.France)* (see 5261\1501).

5330 ≈ 1570

The Shulchan Aruch was published with the supplements of the Ramo.

The Ramo — R.Moshe Isserles (ben Yisrael - Isserel), a disciple (and son-in-law) of R.Shalom Shachna (who was a disciple of R.Yaakov Pollak, see 5263\1503) — wrote Darkei Moshe *(supplement to the Beit Yosef on the Tur)*, and then Hagahot *(supplementary comments to the Shulchan Aruch (see 5323\1563))*. These supplements *(see Illustrations, Texts J K L & M, #2)* — which included Ashkenazi Halacha decisions and customs, and was also known as the Mappa ('tablecloth' to the *shulchan*) — helped consolidate the eventual role of the Shulchan Aruch as the ultimate word in Halacha (see 5374\1614). The Ramo (see 5333\1573) wrote many other works — including Torat HaChattat *(Halacha)*, Torat Ha'Olah *(Kabbala)*, as well as Sh'elot UTeshuvot.

With the establishment of an investigatory tribunal in Peru in **Shvat**, the Inquisition officially 'arrived' in South America (see 5310\1550).

The Ari'zal (see 5313\1553, 5332\1572) — who had spent many years in secluded study near Cairo — settled in Tzfat *(Safed)*. He arrived (in Tzfat) just before the Ramak (R.Moshe Cordovero) — from whom he was eager to learn — died there on the 23rd **Tammuz**.

The Ramak — author of Pardes Rimmonim *(Kabbala)* and of a commentary on the Zohar, among other works — was a disciple of R.Yosef Karo, and of his own brother-in-law, R.Shlomo HaLevi Alkabetz (author of the piyut Lecha Dodi).

R.Menachem Azaryah of Fano *(Italy)* — the Rama MiFano, who was the author of many works of Kabbala (as well Alfasi Zuta *(summary of the Rif)*) — helped the Ramak (financially) in publishing his works.

5331 ≈ 1571

Anti-Jewish riots began in Berlin, because of accusations that a court Jew — whose name has been recorded as Lippold — had (wrongly) exploited his power as a royal administrator (see 5333\1573).

5332 ≈ 1572

The Ari'zal died in Tzfat (Safed).

The great Kabbala scholar, the Ari'zal (see 5330\1570, 5334*1573*), R.Yitzchak Luria — who had attracted as many as thirty disciples in the short period of some two years (or less) that he lived in Tzfat — died during an epidemic on the 5th **Av**, at the very young age of 38. He had earned his living (it appears) as a merchant, and his daughter married the son of R.Yosef Karo.

His teachings — which he transmitted orally — gave a new dimension to the study of Kabbala.

R.Chaim Vital — his major disciple — who was approximately 29 — had previously been a disciple of the Ramak, and was a disciple of R.Moshe Alshich. He recorded the Ari'zal's Kabbala in notes, and the other disciples agreed to the superior authenticity of these notes (some say the Ari'zal had instructed only him to take notes). He lived almost fifty years longer and wrote many works, including Etz Chaim and Pri Etz Chaim (Kabbala).

5333 ≈ 1573

The Maharal came to Prague.

R.Yehuda Liva (Loew, Leib) (ben Betzalel) — a descendant of King David, known as the Maharal (of Prague) — left Nikolsburg *(Mikulov, Moravia)* — where he had been rabbi of the province of Moravia for twenty years — and he settled in Prague — for eleven years (see 5317\1557, 5352\1592) — where he opened a yeshiva which was called the 'Klaus'.

Lippold (see 5331\1571) was executed in Berlin in **Shvat** when he refused to convert, and (consequently) all Jews were expelled from Berlin and the whole province of Brandenburg (see 5303\1543, 5430\1670).

The Ramo, see 5330\1570, died on 18th **Iyar** (Lag B'Omer) *[Taz.OC.420]* at a very young age — opinions varying from an age of 33 *[Shem.Hag.1.46b]* to 47.

5334 — 1573

The Maharshal died.

The Maharshal — R.Shlomo Luria (a descendant of Rashi, and related to the Ramo and the Ari'zal) — died in Lublin *(Poland)* on the 12th **Kislev**. He wrote (among other works) Yam Shel Shlomo *(on the Talmud)* and Chochmat Shlomo *(now printed at the end of standard editions of the Talmud) (see Illustrations, Text N, #1)*.

5335 — 1575

R.Avraham di Boton — a disciple of R.Shmuel de Medina (Maharashdam) in Salonika *(Greece)* — was writing Lechem Mishneh *(commentary on the Rambam's Yad HaChazaka) (see Illustrations, Text I, #8)* when he saw the Kesef Mishneh of R.Yosef Karo (which was a similar work) *(see Illustrations, Text I, #7)* on the 5th **Adar** *[Lech.Mish.Hil.Tef.11.15]*.
R.Eliyahu de Vidas — a disciple of the Ramak (see 5330\1570) — completed writing Reishis Chochma *(Mussar)* in Tzfat *(Safed)* on the 18th **Adar-2.**

R.Yosef Karo died in Tzfat.

R.Yosef Karo died in Tzfat *(Safed)* on the 13th **Nissan**, shortly after the sixth edition of the Shulchan Aruch (see 5323\1563) and his Kesef Mishneh, were printed.
R.Moshe Alshich — his disciple, also a rabbi in Tzfat — wrote Torat Moshe Alshich *(comments and homily on the Bible)*.
R.Shmuel Uceda (Uzida) — a disciple of the Ari'zal — wrote Midrash Shmuel *(commentary on Pirkei Avot)*.
R.Gedalyah ibn Yachya left Italy to settle in Alexandria *(Egypt)*. He was author of the chronicle Shalshelet HaKabbala, which attracted much criticism from scholars *[Shem.Hag.1.(2a-b, 3-4), 1.85-end, etc./Dor.Har.5.267/ Otz.Hag.3.75]*.

5337 — 1577

Twenty Jews were killed in anti-Jewish riots in Posen *(Poznan, Poland)*.
All Jews of Rome and Ancona (see 5329\1569) were ordered to attend conversion sermons in churches (see 5038\1278), by order of the Pope (*Gregory XIII*, who calculated the Gregorian calendar).

5340 — 1580

The Va'ad Arba Aratzot *(Council of Four Lands, provinces of an extended Poland, see at end of paragraph)* — an autonomous Jewish body, which served as the leadership of all Jews of Poland for some 200 years (see 5524\1764) — administered the social (welfare), monetary (taxes), and legal (Halacha) matters of Polish Jews. Many of the great rabbis participated in the Va'ad *(see 5317\1557, 5374\1614, 5400\1640, 5414\1654)*. Meetings usually took place in an appointed city at the time of a fair, and its Beit din would (also) sit in judgement. The Council used its powers to implement the decisions it had made.
*[**The Four Lands**: Great Poland (Poznan), Little Poland (Crakow and Lublin), Red Rus' (Lemberg [now Lvov in Ukraine]), and Volhynia (Ostrog and Kremieniec), see maps].*

Living in the Year 1580

Maharal of Prague	b.1512?,	d.1609.
Shitta Mekubetzet (R.Betz.Ashkenazi)	b.1520?,	d.1594?.
R.Mordechai Yaffe (Levush)	b.1530,	d.1612.
Sma (R.Yehoshua Falk)	b.1540?,	d.1614.
R.Chaim Vital	b.1542?,	d.1620.
Lechem Mishneh (R.Avraham di Boton)	b.1545?,	d.1588.
Kli Yakar (R.Shlomo Ephrayim)	b.1550?,	d.1619.
Maharsha (R.Shmuel Edels)	b.1555,	d.1631.
Bach (R.Yoel Sirkes)	b.1560?,	d.1640.
Shaloh (R.Yeshayahu Horowitz)	b.1560?,	d.1630.
Tosaphot Yom Tov (Lipman Heller)	b.1579,	d.1654.

5343 — 1583

Yosef Saralvo — one of the Portuguese Anussim (Marranos, see 5257\1497) who returned to Judaism — was arrested in Ferrara, a town *(in N. Italy)* that had served as a refuge for oppressed Jews. He was burned at the stake in Rome on the 27th **Shvat**, with other Jews (some say two others) of similar background. He claimed to have returned 800 Anussim to Judaism.

5344 — 1584

R.Yissachar Ber (ben Naftali) HaKohen — known as Berman Ashkenazi, who (some say) was a disciple of the Ramo — finished writing Matanot Kehuna *(commentary on Midrash Rabba)* in Poland.
At this time, R.Shmuel (ben Yitzchak) Yaffe (Ashkenazi) — rabbi of the Ashkenazi community in Constantinople *(Istanbul, Turkey)* — was writing Yefei To'ar *(commentary on Midrash Rabba)*.

5345 — 1585

R.Pinchas HaLevi Horowitz (see 5329*1568*) — a Talmud scholar from Prague, who married Miriam Beilla, the sister of the Ramo (who was famous for her scholarship and piety) in Cracow *(Poland)* — became the head of the VA'AD ARBA ARATZOT *(see 5340\1580)*.

5349 ≈ 1589

All Jews who had returned to Cochem *(Germany)* (see 5178\1418) were again expelled, and at around this time the Jews were also expelled from a number of provinces of Germany.

5350 ≈ 1590

Sevety-six Jews died in a fire in Posen *(Poznan, Poland)* on the 9th **Sivan**, and eighty Torah scrolls were burned. The Jewish section there was abandoned for two years (see 5380\1620).
All Jews were expelled from Petrokov *(Piotrkow, Poland)* after a BLOOD LIBEL.

5352 ≈ 1592

The Maharal of Prague — who had left Prague for four years (see 5333\1573), before returning in 1588 — left Prague again four years later, to become rabbi in Posen *(Poznan, Poland)* (see 5350\1590).
R.Mordechai Yaffe, the Levush, was then appointed rabbi in Prague *(see 5317\1557, 5359\1599)*.
R.Elazar Azkiri (Azikri) wrote the Sefer Charedim *(Mussar)* in Tzfat *(Safed)*.
The Jews of Vilna were attacked, and their houses and shops were plundered (see 5395\1635).

5354 ≈ *1593*

Many Jews were massacred in Bucharest on the 28th **Cheshvan** 5354*1593*, when the local residents revolted against the Turkish *(Ottoman)* rule.
In 1594 Rodrigo de Castro — a physician from Lisbon, who was one of the Portuguese ANUSSIM (Marranos) — settled in Hamburg *(Germany)* where he became a physician to royalty. He became openly Jewish, at the persuasion of a fellow physician, Shmuel Cohen, who had also been one of the Portuguese ANUSSIM (Marranos).

5355 ≈ 1595

The Jews of Patras *(Greece)* were murdered and plundered by sailors from Naples and Sicily.

5357 ≈ 1597

All Jews were expelled from the Italian province of Milan (although there were no longer any Jews living in the actual city of Milan, see 5080\1320).

Living in the Year 1600

Name	Born	Died
Maharal of Prague	b.1512?,	d.1609.
R.Mordechai Yaffe (Levush)	b.1530,	d.1612.
Sma (R.Yehoshua Falk)	b.1540?,	d.1614.
R.Chaim Vital	b.1542?,	d.1620.
Kli Yakar (R.Shlomo Ephrayim)	b.1550?,	d.1619.
Maharsha (R.Shmuel Edels)	b.1555,	d.1631.
Bach (R.Yoel Sirkes)	b.1560?,	d.1640.
Shaloh (R.Yeshayahu Horowitz)	b.1560?,	d.1630.
Tosaphot Yom Tov (Lipman Heller)	b.1579,	d.1654.
Taz (R.David ben Shmuel)	b.1586,	d.1667.

5359 ≈ 1599

The Maharal returned to Prague again.

The Maharal returned to Prague again (see 5352\1592), and R.Mordechai Yaffe, the Levush, took his position in Posen *(Poznan, Poland)*. The Maharal wrote many works, including Gur Aryeh *(commentary on Rashi's commentary on the Chumash (Bible))*, but he is most famous for the *Golem of Prague*.
R.Yeshayahu Menachem — who was rabbi in Cracow *(Poland)*, and a leading participant in the VA'AD ARBA ARATZOT *(see 5340\1580)* — was the originator of the HETER ISKA (a document to circumvent paying direct interest on loans). He died on the 25th **Av**.

5361 ≈ 1601

Mordechai (ben Shmuel) Meisel — a wealthy philanthropist — died in Prague, and — although he left huge sums of money for charity under the Maharal of Prague — the emperor seized all his properties, and the inheritors (he had no children) were tortured to have them declare any other properties.
The Church authorities in Rome confiscated and burned Jewish Holy books in the month of **Shvat** (see 5314*1553*).

5362 ≈ 1602

Seven Jews were hanged in Mantua *(N. Italy)*.

5365 ≈ 1605

The Jews of Bisenz *(Bzenec, Moravia)* were mas-

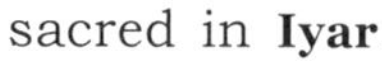

sacred in **Iyar**.
A Jew was killed in a RITUAL DESECRATION libel *(see 5003\1243)* in Bochnia *(Poland)*.

5369 — 1609

The Maharal of Prague (see 5333\1573, 5359\1599), died on the 18th **Elul** at the age of at least 83.
R.Shlomo Ephrayim Lunshitz (see 5379\1619) was (already) a rabbi in Prague since five years earlier (see 5375\1615).

5373 — 1613

The Tzemach David — R.David Gans, a disciple of the Ramo and author of Tzemach David *(history-chronology)* — died in Prague in **Elul.** Ten days later, R.Yitzchak Chayes — author of Appey Ravrevei *(Halacha in verse)* — also died in there.

5374 — 1614

The Maharsha became rabbi in Lublin.

The Maharsha — R.Shmuel HaLevi Edels, who wrote a commentary on Talmud, Rashi and Tosaphot (which is now printed in standard editions of the Talmud) *(see Illustrations, Text N, #2)* — became rabbi in Lublin *(Poland)*, where he stayed for eleven years (see 5392*1631*). He had previously been rabbi in Chelm *(Poland)* for nine years, after the death of his mother-in-law (Edel), who had supported him and his disciples for twenty years.
R.Yehoshua Falk HaKohen (Katz) — known as the Sma for his commentary on the SHULCHAN ARUCH *(commentaries and extension)* called Sefer Me'irat Enayim (Sma, printed in standard editions on the Choshen Mishpat section *(see ILLUSTRATIONS, TEXT M, #4)*) — died on the 19th of **Nissan**.
The importance he placed on every word of the SHULCHAN ARUCH further consolidated its acceptance as the ultimate word in Halacha (see 5406\1646).
The Sma — who participated in the VA'AD ARBA ARATZOT *(see 5340\1580)*, and was a disciple of the Ramo and the Maharshal — also wrote the Derisha and Perisha *(commentaries on the Tur)*.
His wife Beilla — who was known for her scholarship and great piety — contributed to two Halacha decisions *[See Hakd.LeDerisha/Mag.Av.O.C.263.12, Caf.HaChym.43, etc.]*.
The Jews of Virmyze *(Worms, Germany)* repelled an attack on the Jewish quarter on Erev Tisha B'Av. The Jews of Frankfort am Main were attacked in the month of **Elul,** and forced to leave the city for awhile.

5375 — 1615

The Shaloh (see 5382\1621) — who had been the rabbi in Frankfort (see **Elul** 5374\1615) for eight years, after having previously been rabbi in a number of towns — became a rabbi in Prague (see 5369\1609, 5379\1619).

5376 — 1616

R.Meir (ben Gedalyah) of Lublin, Maharam Lublin — who had been ROSH YESHIVA in Lublin *(Poland)* at a very young age; then rabbi and ROSH YESHIVA in Lvov *(Lemberg, Poland)*; and later in Cracow *(Poland)*, before returning to Lublin — died in **Iyar**.
He wrote Me'ir Eynei Chachamim, *(a commentary on Talmud, Rashi and Tosaphot)* (now printed at the end of standard editions of the Talmud, as the 'Maharam') *(see ILLUSTRATIONS, TEXT N, #3)*.

5377 — 1616

The Tosaphot Yom Tov commentary was concluded.

R.Yom Tov Lipman Heller (see 5400\1640) had become a DAYAN at the age of 18 in Prague, where he was a disciple of the Maharal of Prague and R.Shlomo Ephrayim (see 5369\1609). He finished his writing of Tosaphot Yom Tov *(commentary on the Mishna) (see Illustrations, TEXT C, #3)* on the 22nd **Cheshvan** 5377\1616 at the age of 38. He later left Prague to become rabbi in Vienna, before eventually returning (see 5389\1629).

5379 — 1619

A Jew was killed in Sochatchev *(Poland)* in a BLOOD LIBEL.
R.Shlomo Ephrayim of Lunshitz — a disciple of the Maharshal, and author of Kli Yakar *(commentary on Chumash (Bible) (see Illustrations, Text A, #10))* and Ollelot Ephrayim *(homiletic Mussar)* — died on the 7th of **Adar** in Prague, where he was rabbi (see 5369\1609) at the same time as the Shaloh (see 5375\1615).
The Bach (see 5400\1640) became rabbi in Cracow *(Poland)*, after having previously been rabbi in six or seven other towns.

5380 — 1620

The Jews of Posen *(Poznan, Poland)* were expelled from a temporary area of settlement outside of the city (in which they had settled after their second fire in 1613, see 5350\1590).

Living in the Year 1620

R.Chaim Vital	b.1542?,	d.1620.
Maharsha (R.Shmuel Edels)	b.1555,	d.1631.
Bach (R.Yoel Sirkes)	b.1560?,	d.1640.
Shaloh (R.Yeshayahu Horowitz)	b.1560?,	d.1630.
Tosaphot Yom Tov (Lipman Heller)	b.1579,	d.1654.
Taz (R.David ben Shmuel)	b.1586,	d.1667.
Chelkat Mechokek (R.Moshe Lima)	b.1605?,	d.1658.

5382 — *1621*

The Shaloh arrived in Eretz Yisrael.

The Shaloh (HaKadosh) — R.Yeshayahu (ben Avraham) HaLevi Horowitz — left Prague (see 5375\1615) when his wife died, and arrived in Yerushalayim in **Kislev** 5382*1621*, where he wrote Shnei Luchot HaBrit (SHaLoH) *(Kabbala-Mussar)*.

5382 — 1622

The (third edition of) Tzena URena (an uncomplicated YIDDISH Midrashic work, intended for the otherwise uneducated women) by R.Yaakov Ashkenazi, was published.

5385 — 1625

Fifteen scholars, including the Shaloh (see 5382\1621), were arrested in Yerushalayim on Shabbat the 11th **Elul,** and released after a ransom was (later) paid. The Shaloh subsequently settled in Tzfat *(Safed)*, and later in Teverya *(Tiberius)*, where he died.
When the Portuguese recaptured Bahia *(Brazil)* from the Dutch, they allowed all the Dutch to leave (including the Jews), but five Portuguese ANUSSIM (Marranos) — who had become openly Jewish under Dutch rule — were captured and killed (see 5407\1647).

5389 — 1629

R.Yom Tov Lipman Heller was imprisoned.

The Tosaphot Yom Tov, R.Yom Tov Lipman Heller (see 5377\1616), was imprisoned on the 5th **Tammuz** for a short while. He had been slandered — by some people who had considered the tax assessments for the THIRTY YEAR WAR *(see 5409\1648, between the Catholics and the Protestants)* to be unfair — because he was one of the assessors. He was released on the revised (and more lenient) conditions; that he was forbidden to be rabbi in Prague; and that those parts of his books that had been slandered, were to be censored — after having originally been entirely banned.

5390 — 1630

Moshe Shmuler was killed in Przemysl *(Poland)* in a RITUAL DESECRATION libel *(see 5003\1243)*.
Invading German troops expelled all Jews of Mantua *(N. Italy)* after confiscating their possessions.
Eighteen Jewish children were subjected to FORCED BAPTISM in Reggio Emilia *(Italy)*.
All Jews of Venice and of Prague were forced to attend Christian CONVERSION SERMONS (see 5337\1577).
After the Dutch had conquered the area from the Portuguese, Jews were permitted to live in Recife *(N.W.Brazil)*, and many ANUSSIM (Marranos) became openly Jewish (see 5385\1625, 5407\1647, 5414\1654). At this time Recife was the only town in colonial Latin America to allow open Jewish life and Jews prospered there. A whole military company made up of Jewish soldiers was exempted from guard duty on Shabbat, and at one point the Jews became a majority (see 5310\1550).

5391 — *1630*

R.Meir Schiff, the Maharam Schiff, finished his Chidushim on Talmud Bava Kama, in **Cheshvan** 5391*1630*.

5392 — *1631*

The Maharsha (see 5374\1614) died on the 5th **Kislev** 5392*1631*, in Ostraha *(Ostrog, Volhynia, region in W.Poland)* where he had been rabbi in his last seven years.

5395 — 1635

The Jews of Vilna were attacked and their houses were ransacked (see 5352\1592, 5448*1687*).

5396 — 1636

R.Eliyahu ben Moshe Loanz — who was called R.Eliyahu Ba'al Shem of Virmyze *(Worms, Germany)* — died on the 21st **Tammuz**. He was a grandson of R.Yosef Yoselman the SHTADLAN, and the author of Michlal Yofi *(commentary on Kohelet (Ecclesiastes)*.
There were at least two other personalities called R.Eliyahu Ba'al Shem — they lived at around the same time *[Otz.Hag.2.183, 184/Great Maggid, N.Y.1974.p.31]*.
The Jews of Lublin *(Poland)* were attacked — and some were killed — after a BLOOD LIBEL trial.

Living in the Year 1640

Bach (R.Yoel Sirkes)	b.1560?,	d.1640.
Tosaphot Yom Tov (Lipman Heller)	b.1579,	d.1654.
Taz (R.David ben Shmuel)	b.1586,	d.1667.
Chelkat Mechokek (R.Moshe Lima)	b.1605?,	d.1658.
Shach (R.Shabbetai Kohen)	b.1621,	d.1663?.
Beit Shmuel (R.Shmuel)	b.1630?,	d.1700?.
Magen Avraham (R.Avr.Abele Gombiner)	b.1637?,	d.1683.

The Jews of Brisk *(Brest-Litovsk, Lithuania)* were attacked in an ANTI-JEWISH RIOT.

5399 ≈ 1639

Twenty Jews were arrested and tortured in a BLOOD LIBEL in Lunshitz *(Leczyca, Poland)*. Two were later publicly killed in front of the synagogue, and their bodies mutilated.

5400 ≈ 1640

R.Yoel Sirkes, the Bach, died.

The Bach, R.Yoel Sirkes, wrote a commentary on the Tur (**Ba**yit **Ch**adash - BaCH) and Hagahot *(notations)* on the Talmud *(see ILLUSTRATIONS, TEXT E)*. He died in Cracow *(see 5379\1619)* on the 20th **Adar**. He was succeeded (a few years later) by the Tosaphot Yom Tov (see 5377\1616), who — after he was forced to leave Prague (see 5389\1629) — had moved from place to place and participated in the VA'AD ARBA ARATZOT *(see 5340\1580)*, (and was victim of further hatred).

R.Yehoshua (ben Yosef) Falk — author of Meginei Shlomo *(defending Rashi on the questions posed by the Tosaphot)* and of SH'ELOT UTESHUVOT Pnei Yehoshua I — was a disciple of the Maharam Lublin and the Sma. He became ROSH YESHIVA in Cracow *(Poland)* in 1640 — upon the death of R.Natan Shapiro (author of Megaleh Amukot) — after having previously been rabbi in a number of communities. His greatest disciple, the Shach *(see 5406\1646, 5415\1655)*, moved to Cracow with him. R.Moshe Lima (see 5415\1655) — another disciple of the Meginei Shlomo — was author of Chelkat Mechokek *(commentaries and extension)* on the Even HaEzer section of the SHULCHAN ARUCH, (now in standard editions *(see Illustrations, Text L, #4)*). He was rabbi in Slonim *(then Poland)* and later became rabbi in Vilna.

5402 ≈ 1642

R.Yitzchak Abohab III da Fonseca was born in Portugal to a family of ANUSSIM (Marranos) who escaped (with him as a child), and they raised him as an open Jew in Amsterdam. In 1641 he left his position as a rabbi in Amsterdam, and arrived in Recife *(Brazil)* in 1642, to become the first rabbi in the Western Hemisphere (see 5390\1630).

5404 ≈ 1644

A Spanish nobleman — Lopa de Vera Y Alarcon) who decided to convert to JUDAISM (after studying the Bible) — was arrested and tried by the Inquisition. In prison he circumcised himself and changed his name to Yehuda HaMa'amin (the believer). He refused to renounce JUDAISM, despite torture, and his burning at the stake in **Tammuz** left a deep impression on the ANUSSIM (Marranos) of Spain (see 5407\1647).

5405 ≈ 1645

The Jews of Mogilev *(Poland, Russia)* were attacked by RIOTERS (including the mayor) during Tashlich on Rosh HaShana.

5406 ≈ 1646

The Shach and Taz (on SHULCHAN ARUCH) were printed.

R.David (ben Shmuel) HaLevi, the Taz (see 5414\1654), was a disciple of the Bach, whose scholarly daughter, Rivka, he married. He had previously been rabbi in Posen *(Poznan, Poland)* for twenty years, before he became rabbi in Ostraha *(Ostrog, Volhynia, region in W.Poland)*. There — in the course of some five years — he wrote, and then published (in 1646), Turei Zahav (TaZ) *(commentaries and extension)* on the Yoreh De'a section of the SHULCHAN ARUCH. He later wrote on other sections, as well as writing other works.

R.Shabbetai (ben Meir) HaKohen, the Shach (see 5400\1640), wrote and published Siftei Kohen (ShaCh) *(commentaries and extension)* on Yoreh De'a, although he was not yet twenty-five years old; he later wrote on the section of Choshen Mishpat. Both the Taz and the Shach are printed in standard editions of the SHULCHAN ARUCH *(see ILLUSTRATIONS, TEXTS J K L & M)*, and the importance they placed on every word of the SHULCHAN ARUCH further consolidated its acceptance as the ultimate word in Halacha (see 5374\1614).

5407 ≈ 1647

R.Yitzchak de Castro (Tartas) was burned alive in Lisbon for teaching JUDAISM to ANUSSIM (Marranos) in Portuguese Brazil (see 5385\1625). His cries of Shma Yisrael at his death, left a deep impression on the ANUSSIM (Marranos) of Portugal (see 5404\1644).

5408 — 1648

Jews were massacred by Chmielnitzki's forces.

The Cossacks, under the leadership of Bogdan Chmielnitzki, sought to establish an independent Ukraine — by rebelling against (the aristocratic) Polish rule — and they received military assistance from the Tartar rulers of Crimea *(region in S.W. Russia)* in battles that lasted twenty years *(see map page 331)*. In the first years the peasants rioted uncontrollably, wreaking chaos and havoc, and — whether warriors or not — attacked the Jews, who were usually the middle-men between them and the absentee landlord princes whose properties they leased and managed. The rabble tortured many, FORCIBLY CONVERTED some, massacred tens of thousands, and mutilated their remains.
300 Jewish communities were destroyed, and between 100,000 and 300,00 Jews were killed in the massacres, which became known as Gezerot Tach VeTat — for the years 5 thousand 408 and 409, which many had expected *(based on prediction of the Zohar)* would be the year (in 408) when the Mashiach *(Messiah)* would come *[Zoh.1.139b/Or HaChama (Ramak) Sh.(2).10]*.
Poland-Lithuania — which had been a relatively prosperous haven for the Jews for many years (see 5110\1350) — became a scene of massive Jewish devastation. On the 20th **Sivan** 6,000 Jews of Nemirov *(Poland)* were killed, and this day was later declared a fast (see 4931\1171, 5410\1650), to mark the beginning of the massacres. 1,000 Jews were tortured, then killed on the 4th **Tammuz** in Tulchin *(Poland)*; 10,000 were killed in Polannoe *(Polonnoye, Volhynia, region in W.Poland)* on the 3rd **Av**, including R.Shimshon of Ostropole (a maggid and writer of KABBALA) and 3,000 Jews were killed in Staro-Konstantinov *(Poland)* on Tisha B'Av (including those who had taken refuge in the city).

5409 — *1648*

R.Naftali — the son of Yitzchak HaKohen Katz (of Lublin), son-in-law of the MahaRal of Prague) — was killed on the 5th **Tishrei** 5409*1648* by Chmielnitzki's forces.
4,000 Jews of Dubno *(Poland)* were killed on the 15th **Tishrei**, when the Poles did not allow them to seek refuge in a fortress.
12,000 Jews in Narol *(Poland)* were drowned, or killed in the synagogue — which was then set on fire — on the 17th of **Cheshvan**. Some 40,000 Jews who had fled from other parts of the country — seeking refuge in the vicinity of Narol — were all massacred.
The Jews of Medzibuzh *(Miedzyborz, Poland)* were saved from Chmielnitzki's troops by someone called Mordechai and his wife Esther. They instituted the 12th of **Tevet** as MORDECHAI PURIM, in commemoration.
The parents of R.Avraham Abele Gombiner, the Magen Avraham (see 5433\1673), were killed in the massacres, and the Taz (see 5406\1646) left Ostraha *(Ostrog, Volhynia, region in W.Poland)* and took refuge in a fortress (see 5414\1654).
Many Jews moved to other countries such as Rumania, Hungary, and the provinces of Moldavia and Transylvania. Germany was then also in a state of ruin at the conclusion of the THIRTY YEAR WAR (see 5389\1629, 5415\1655). (Estimates are that the population of Germany fell from 17 million to 8 million over these thirty years of war, famine and plague.)
The Jews of Prague were presented with a banner in recognition of their defense of the city against Swedish invaders.

Chapter 14

The Acharonim — Later Scholars

Section IV

Major Acharonim

Beit Shmuel (R.Shmuel)	b.1630?, d.1700?
Magen Avraham (R.Avr.Abele Gombiner)	b.1637?, d.1683.
Siftei Chachamim (R.Shabbetai Bass)	b.1641, d.1718.
Mishneh LeMelech (R.Yehuda Rosannes)	b.1657?, d.1727.
Pnei Yehoshua (R.Yaakov Yehoshua Falk)	b.1680, d.1756.
R.Yaakov Culi (Me'am Lo'ez)	b.1689?, d.1732.
R.Yonatan Eybeshutz	b.1690?, d.1764.
Sha'agat Aryeh (R.Aryeh Leib Gunzberg)	b.1695?, d.1785.
Or HaChayim (R.Chaim (ib)n Attar)	b.1696, d.1743.
R.Yaakov Emden	b.1697?, d.1776.
Korban HaEida (R.David Frankel)	b.1707, d.1762.
Pnei Moshe (R.Moshe Margolis)	b.1710?, d.1781.
Noda BiYehuda (R.Yechezk'el Landau)	b.1713, d.1793.
Vilna Gaon	b.1720, d.1797.
Chida (Azulai)	b.1724, d.1806.
Pri Megadim (R.Yosef Te'omim)	b.1727?, d.1792.
R.Shneur Zalman (Rav of Lyady)	b.1745, d.1813.
Ketzot HaChoshen (R.Aryeh Leib Heller)	b.1745?, d.1813.
Chayei Adam (R.Avraham Danziger)	b.1748, d.1820.
Yismach Moshe (R.Moshe Teitelbaum)	b.1759, d.1841.
Chavat Da'at (R.Yakv.of Lissa/Netivot)	b.1759?, d.1832.
R.Ephrayim Zalman Margolis	b.1760, d.1828.
R.Akiva Eger	b.1761, d.1837.
Chassam Sofer	b.1762, d.1839.
Tiferet Yisrael (R.Yisrael Lipshutz)	b.1782, d.1860.
Tzemach Tzedek (of Lubavitch)	b.1789, d.1866.
Divrei Chaim (of Tzanz)	b.1793, d.1876.
Chidushei HaRim (of Gur)	b.1799, d.1866.
Minchat Chinuch (R.Yosef Babad)	b.1800?, d.1874.
Kitzur Shulchan Aruch (R.Shl.Ganzfried)	b.1804, d.1886.
Malbim (R.Meir Leib[ush])	b.1808?, d.1879.
Pitchei Teshuva (R.Avraham Tzvi Hirsch)	b.1813, d.1868.
Aruch HaShulchan (R.Yechi'el Epstein)	b.1829, d.1908.
Sdei Chemed (R.Chaim Chizkiyah Medini)	b.1832?, d.1904.
Ben Ish Chai (R.Yosef Chaim Al-Chakkam)	b.1833?, d.1909.
Chafetz Chaim (R.Yisrael Meir Kagan)	b.1838, d.1933.
Darkei Teshuva (R.Tzvi Hirsch Shapira)	b.1845?, d.1913.
'Sfass Emess' (of Gur)	b.1847, d.1905.
R.Chaim Brisker	b.1853, d.1918.
Rogatchover Gaon (R.Yosef Rozin)	b.1858, d.1936.
Torah Temima (R.Baruch Epstein)	b.1860, d.1942.
Kaf HaChayim — R.Yaakov Chaim (Sofer)	b. 1870, d.1939.
Chazon Ish — R.Avraham Yeshaya Karelitz	b. 1878 d. 1953.
R.Meir Shapiro — Daf Yomi	b. 1887 d. 1934.

Section IV
UNIVERSAL DISPERSION

Chapter 14

The Acharonim — Later Scholars

The fourteenth chapter in Jewish history begins after the devastating massacres of the Cossack uprisings, and ends with the total devastation of European Jewry by the Nazi Holocaust.

This period of time includes the Acharonim and the development of the movement of Chasidim as a dynamic force among observant Jews, which provided leadership against the many eroding factors of the industrial and social revolutions.

During this time the Jewish people were rocked by the disruptive influence of the false Messiahs. The social emancipation of the Jews led to the Haskala and the Reform movements, and the persistent persecutions in Eastern Europe led to massive emigrations (to the U.S. of America), and to the emergence of Zionism as a strong nationalistic force.

Chapter 14

The Acharonim — Later Scholars.

Chapter 14a, Early Acharonim and East European Massacres

Jewish Year		Secular Year
5414	The first Jews settled in New Amsterdam (New York).	1654
5415	Many Jews killed in Russian and Swedish invasions of Poland.	1655
5416	Jews were permitted to live in England.	1656
5416	Baruch Spinoza was excommunicated.	1656
5433	**The Magen Avraham (on Shulchan Aruch) was completed.**	**1673**
5437	**SHABBETAI TZVI DIED AS A MUSLIM.**	**1676**
5449	**The Beit Shmuel (on the Shulchan Aruch) was printed.**	**1689**
5458	**THE BA'AL SHEM TOV WAS BORN.**	**1698**
5463	The Pnei Yehoshua's family were killed in an explosion.	1702
5472	The Siftei Chachamim was arrested.	1712
5484	R.Yaakov Culi (Me'am Lo'ez) arrived in Constantinople.	1724
5487	The Mishneh LeMelech died.	1727
5494	**Jews were massacred by the Haidamack bands.**	**1734**

Chapter 14b, Acharonim and Early Chassidim.

Jewish Year		Secular Year
5501	The Or HaChayim arrived in Eretz Yisrael.	1741
5507	R.Moshe Chaim Luzzatto (Ramchal) died in Acco (Acre).	1747
5510	R.Yonatan Eybeshutz became Rabbi in Hamburg.	1750
5515	The Noda BiYehuda became Rabbi in Prague.	1754
5518	**The Frankists instigated mass burnings of the Talmud.**	**1757**
5519	Frankists supported blood libel charges in public DEBATE.	1759
5520	**The Ba'al Shem Tov died.**	**1760**
5524	The VA'AD ARBA ARATZOT was discontinued.	1764
5528	**Despite resistance the Haidamacks massacre thousands.**	**1768**
5532	**The Maggid of Mezeritsch died.**	**1772**
5542	R.N. Adler and Chassam Sofer visited the Noda BiYehuda.	1782
5546	R.Elimelech of Lizensk died.	1786
5551	**The Pale of Settlement was established in Russia.**	**1791**
5553	Jews suffered in Reign of Terror of French Revolution.	1793
5558	The Vilna Gaon died.	1797

Jewish Year		Secular Year
5559	The Ba'al HaTanya was released from first imprisonment.	1798
5559	Napoleon led an army expedition through Eretz Yisrael.	1799
5566	The Chida (R.Chaim Yosef David Azulai) died.	1806
5566	The Chassam Sofer became Rabbi in Pressburg.	1806
5570	R.Levi Yitzchak of Berditchev died.	1809
5571	R.Nachman of Bratslav died.	1810
5574	R.Akiva Eger became Rabbi in Posen.	1814
5575	Kozhnitzer Maggid and Yehudi of Pershisskha, both died.	1814
5575	Chozeh of Lublin, and R.Mendel of Rymanov, both died.	1815
5579	Anti Jewish (Hep Hep!) riots spread throughout Germany.	1819
5587	**Russia began conscripting Jewish children to the army.**	**1827**
5600	Adm.R.Yisrael of Ruzhin was released from imprisonment.	1840

Chapter 14c, Later Acharonim and Changing Society.

5603	The Tzemach Tzedek of Lubavitch was repeatedly arrested in Russia.	1843
5606	Sir Moshe Montefiore visited Russia to help local Jews.	1846
5609	R.Yisrael Salanter left Vilna.	1848
5611	R.Shimshon Rapha'el Hirsch became Rabbi in Frankfort am Main.	1851
5619	R.Menachem Mendel of Kotzk died.	1859
5624	The Malbim was imprisoned, and then expelled from Rumania.	1864
5626	Chidushei HaRim, Tiferet Shlomo, and Tzemach Tzedek, died.	1866
5633	The Chafetz Chaim was published.	1873
5634	The Minchat Chinuch died.	1874
5638	Petach Tikva agricultural settlement was established.	1878
5641	**MANY JEWS BEGAN LEAVING RUSSIA AFTER A WAVE OF POGROMS.**	**1881**
5646	R.Shlomo Ganzfried (author of Kitzur Shulchan Aruch) died.	1886
5652	R.Chaim (Brisker) became Rabbi in Brisk.	1892
5665	The Sfass Emess died.	1905
5665	**Many Jews were killed in (official) Russian pogroms.**	**1905**
5671	Chazon Ish was published.	1911
5674	**Over 500,000 Jewish soldiers fought in World War I.**	**1914**
5678	**Over 60,000 Jews were killed during Russian Revolution.**	**1918**
5684	**Daf HaYomi study cycle commenced.**	**1923**
5687	The Lubavitcher Rebbe was released from Soviet prison.	1927
5699	Jews were attacked in the Kristallnacht pogroms in Germany.	1938

Chapter 14a

Early Acharonim and East European Massacres

5409 — 1649

Ninety-six Marranos were burned to death in Mexico (see 5288\1528, 5310\1550).

5410 — 1650

Many Jews were killed in Jassy *(Moldavia)* by the Cossacks (see 5413*1652*).
The VA'AD ARBA ARATZOT proclaimed the 20th **Sivan** as a fast day in commemoration of the Chmielnitzki massacres (see 20th **Sivan** 5408\1648), and VA'AD MEDINAT LITA *(Council of Lithuania, similar to VA'AD ARBA ARATZOT (see 5340\1580))* instituted three years of memorial mourning, (forbidding such things as music at weddings).
A Jew was killed in a BLOOD LIBEL in Kadan *(Bohemia)*, and the rest of the Jews were expelled.

5411 — 1651

Many Jews were killed in Bar *(Ukraine)* by the Cossacks and the Tartars (see 5408\1648).

5413 — *1652*

David ben Chaim — of whom little else is known — was burned to death in Podhayetz *(Podgaitsy, Poland)*, on the 17th **Kislev** 5413*1652*.
Manuel Fernandes de Villareal, a Portuguese diplomat, was discovered to be secretly Jewish. He was executed — by the Inquisition, during Chanuka — in Lisbon, and (subsequently) some of his relatives became openly Jewish in Livorno *(Leghorn, Italy)*.
Many Jews were killed in Jassy *(Moldavia)* by invading Cossacks (see 5410\1650).

5414 — 1654

After the Chmielnitzki massacres, the Taz (see 5409*1648*) had travelled around for a few years (he spent a few days in the house of the Shach), and he became a rabbi of Lemberg *(Lvov, Poland)* in 1654 (see 5424\1664). He participated in the VA'AD ARBA ARATZOT *(see 5340\1580)*.
R.Yom Tov Lipman Heller — the Tosaphot Yom Tov (see 5400\1640) — died in **Elul,** and was succeeded (as rabbi in Cracow, *Poland*) by the Rebbe R.Heschel, R.Yehoshua Heschel, who had previously been ROSH YESHIVA and rabbi in Lublin *(Poland)*.

The first Jews settled in New Amsterdam (New York).

Recife *(Brazil)* was reconquered by the Portuguese (see 5390\1630, 5407\1647), and the Jews fled — most of them (including the rabbi, see 5402\1642) — to Holland. Twenty-three of them settled in New Amsterdam — the first Jews in what later became New York — where they were not readily accepted by the governor *(Peter Stuyvesant)*.

5415 — 1655

Avraham Nunez Bernal, a leader of Spanish ANUSSIM (Marranos), was burned at the stake in Cordova *(Spain)*, in **Nissan**; his open proclamation of allegiance to JUDAISM aroused many ANUSSIM. His nephew was also burned within a few months.

Many Jews were killed in Russian and Swedish invasions of Poland.

Many Jews (some say as many as 25,000) were killed when Vilna was attacked by invading Russian forces on the 23rd **Tammuz** (see 5416*1655*, 5420*1659*) — an extension of the carving of Poland initiated by Chmielnitzki *(see map page 331)*.
The Shach — (see 5406\1646, 5416*1655*) who was part of the Vilna BEIT DIN of R.Moshe Lima (the Chelkat Mechokek, see 5400\1640) — fled from the city (see 5416*1655*), as did:

- R.Moshe Rivkes — the author of Be'er HaGola *(bibliography on the SHULCHAN ARUCH)*, which was published in Amsterdam, where he was allowed to settle for a while. He was not sent on to Germany with other refugees because of the influence R.Shaul Levi Morteira and R.Yitzchak Abohab III (see 5416\1656) had exercised on his behalf.
- R.Ephrayim HaKohen — a disciple of R.Moshe Lima, and author of Sha'ar Ephrayim *(SH'ELOT UTESHUVOT)* — also left Vilna (see 5420\1660) as did his son-in-law.
- R.Yaakov Sak (see 5420\1660) — who had been left for dead in the fighting — also managed to escape.
- R.Hillel — author of Beit Hillel *(on SHULCHAN ARUCH)* (who some say was a nephew of R.Yehoshua

Heschel, see 5414\1654 — was also a member of the BEIT DIN of R.Moshe Lima.
Cracow *(Poland)* was captured by the Swedes, and many Jews fled — including some who had previously sought refuge there from Chmielnitzki's forces, and from the Thirty Year War in Germany (see 5409*1648*).
Those remaining suffered under the two year Swedish occupation, and under (Stefan Czarnetzki) the leader of Polish resistance against the invaders *(see 5417\1656, 5419\1659)*.
150 Jews of Chmielnick *(Poland)* were accused of helping the Swedes, and were killed by the Polish resistance forces.
The parents of the Siftei Chachamim, R.Shabbetai (Meshorer) Bass (see 5449\1689), were both killed by the Polish in Kalisch *(Poland)*, (see 5419\1659).

5416 — 1655

The Jews of Mogilev *(then part of Poland)* — who had been living under the occupying Russian forces (see 5414\1654) — were massacred early in **Tishrei** 5416*1655*, when Polish forces approached the town to counter attack.
On the 14th **Tishrei**, thousands of Jews were killed in Lublin *(Poland)*, where the Shach had fled to (see 5415\1655). He fled once again, this time to Moravia, where he became a rabbi in Holeschau *(Holesov)* until his death (at the young age of 41-42).
R.Aharon Shmuel Kaidanover (Maharshak, author of Birkat HaZevach) also fled, after his two young daughters were killed at Lublin. He later became rabbi in Nikolsburg *(Mikulov, Moravia)*.
Most of the Jews of Tzoozmir *(Sandomierz, Poland)* and Tarnobrzeg *(Poland)* were killed, and the rest were expelled.

5416 — 1656

Jews were permitted to live in England.

Menasheh ben Yisrael — a scholar from Amsterdam whose father had escaped from Portugal, after being captured as a Marrano — made repeated written and personal representations to the government of England (recently re-organized under the protectorate of Oliver Cromwell) until permission was granted for Jews to live there (see 5050\1290).
Menasheh — who had personal contact with Rembrandt — had established a Jewish printing press, and wrote a number of works, including a code of Jewish law for returning ANUSSIM (Marranos).
350 Jewish families were killed in Krotoszyn *(Poland)* by the Polish resistance, in the war against Sweden (see 5415\1655, 5416*1655*).
200 families were killed in Apta *(Opatow, Poland)*, 100 families in Brest Kuyavsk *(Brzesc Kujawski, Poland)*, 50 families in Cheshanov *(Poland)*, 40 families in Brzeziny *(Poland)*, and 150 Jews were killed in Checiny *(Poland)*.

Baruch Spinoza was excommunicated.

R.Shaul Levi Morteira *(see 5415\1655, 5458\1697)*, R.Yitzchak Abohab III *(see 5402\1642, 5414\1654, 5415\1655)* and other rabbis of Amsterdam placed the young (24 year old) Baruch Spinoza in CHEREM *(excommunication)*, when he did not retract on his views (which included questioning the authenticity of the Bible).

5417 — 1656

3,000 Jews were killed when the Polish recaptured Lunshitz *(Leczyca, Poland)* from the Swedes (see 5416\1656), and (some say) 600 Torah scrolls were burned.

5418 — 1658

Three Jews were killed in Cracow *(Poland)* on Erev Shavu'ot (see 5415\1655).

5419 — 1659

Hundreds of Jews were killed in Kalisch *(Poland)* (see 5415\1655, 5468\1708) at the end of the war with Sweden.
Eight Jews were killed in Przemysl *(Poland)* in **Nissan**.

Living in the Year 1660

Taz (R.David ben Shmuel)	b.1586,	d.1667.
Shach (R.Shabbetai Kohen)	b.1621,	d.1663?.
Beit Shmuel (R.Shmuel)	b.1630?,	d.1700?.
Magen Avraham (R.Avr.Abele Gombiner)	b.1637?,	d.1683.
Siftei Chachamim (R.Shabbetai Bass)	b.1641,	d.1718.
Mishneh LeMelech (R.Yehuda Rosannes)	b.1657?,	d.1727.
Chacham Tzvi (R.Tzvi Ashkenazi)	b.1660,	d.1718.
Seder HaDorot (R.Yechi'el Heilprin)	b.1660?,	d.1747?.

5420 1659

R.Yisrael ben Shalom and R.Tuvyah Bachrach were killed in Ruzhany *(Poland)* on Rosh HaShana 5420*1659*, in a BLOOD LIBEL.
300 Jews were killed in Bichov *(Poland-Lithuania)* when the Russians captured the town in **Tevet** (see 5415\1655, 5416*1655*).

5420 1660

When the Shach was in Kalisch *(Poland)* (see 5419\1659), he met R.Avraham Abele, the Magen Avraham (see 5433\1673).
R.Ephrayim HaKohen (see 5415\1655) became rabbi in Budapest, where he was accompanied by his son-in-law R.Yaakov Sak (see 5415\1655), and his newborn grandson, who grew up to become the Chacham Tzvi (see 5446\1686).

5421 1661

R.Menachem Mendel Krochmal — a disciple of the Bach, author of Tzemach Tzedek I *(SH'ELOT UTESHUVOT)* — died on the 2nd **Shvat** in Nikolsburg *(Mikulov, Moravia)*, where he was rabbi of the province (see 5333\1573).
Many Jews of Persia had been forced to convert to Islam over the previous twenty years — although they remained secretly Jewish — but in 1661, they were allowed to return to practising JUDAISM openly.

5422 1662

The Jews fled Cochin (S.W. India) — when the Portuguese rulers (see 5283\1523) attacked them and plundered their property, blaming them after the Dutch had attempted to conquer the territory — but they returned a year later, when the Dutch were successful in conquering the area (see 5385\1625).

5424 1663

Mattityahu Kalahora, a physician, was dismembered and burned in Cracow *(Poland)* on the 14th **Kislev** 5424*1663* (see 5516*1755*), after being accused of cursing Christianity.

5424 1664

Many Jews were massacred in Bratslav *(Podolia, Poland)* in a Cossack invasion.
Many Jews were killed — including R.Mordechai and R.Shlomo (sons of the Taz) — in ANTI-JEWISH RIOTS in Lvov *(Lemberg, Poland)* during **Iyar**. The Taz died three years later.
Isaac Newton (who probably never met anyone Jewish *(see 5416\1656)*, yet had apparently spent much time studying Jewish matters) introduced a new style in scientific study — especially with his painstaking investigation of the effects of gravitational force — that depended on the meticulous observation of facts *(chochmas ha'teva)*, as opposed to previous "sciences" which tended to be theories *(chochmas umos ha'olam)* upheld by anecdotal evidence. Many beneficial discoveries and inventions (see 5500\1740) have followed.

5425 1665

Shabbetai Tzvi publicly proclaimed himself as "the Mashiach" *(Messiah)* while in Eretz Yisrael in **Sivan**. He did so with the strong support of a follower — Natan of Gaza, who was well versed in KABBALA, and claimed to be a prophet.
Notwithstanding that he had previously been banished by various rabbis from towns in which he had lived (Izmir-Smyrna, Salonika, Constantinople-Istanbul) — for unusual and unacceptable behavior, and transgressions of Halacha (for which he made a blessing "...he who permits the forbidden...") — nevertheless, word of his proclamation as the "Mashiach" spread all over with exceptional speed. The word was sometimes preceded by apparently unassociated rumors that the ten lost tribes were marching towards Eretz Yisrael.
Many stories — about "miracles" he had supposedly performed — were circulated; and "proofs" — from Torah and KABBALA — were discovered to validate his claim; resulting in a broad acceptance. Many Jews, including rabbis, from virtually every country in the world were electrified with anticipation and enthusiasm. *(The countries included Algeria, Bohemia, Egypt, England, Eretz Yisrael, Germany, Greece, Holland, Iraq, Kurdistan, Moravia, Morocco, Persia, Poland-Lithuania, Russia, Slovakia, Tripoli, Turkey, Yemen).*
Many rabbis, however, raised their voices — opinions ranging from doubt to outright opposition. He had also been banished from Yerushalayim, a fact that did not apparently receive much publicity.
He travelled to his home town, Izmir *(Smyrna, Turkey)*, and whipped up much excitement, through his charismatic speeches and a feverish prayer style — which (some say) included ecstatic (and hysterical) congregational chanting of the Shem

HaMephorash *(the complete and Holy name)* — as well as female participation in the Torah reading ceremonies. The exciting atmosphere he generated gained him many supporters, who rallied in masses against those who would question — or disbelieve in the fulfillment of one of the principal beliefs of Judaism — the coming of the Mashiach. (To his followers it was apparently obvious that any skepticism about Shabbetai Tzvi was equivalent to a complete denial in the belief of the redemption; and in an emotive atmosphere, even sages become vulnerable to such an accusation.)
However, it appears that at least some rabbis who met him at times of subdued behavior found him to be a dignified scholar with a touch of nobility, and consequently considered his case seriously. It was reported that the Taz (see 5424\1664) sent his son and his stepson from Poland to investigate. They were suitably impressed, and Shabbetai Tzvi sent a silk garment to honor the Taz.
Nevertheless, those who saw him in a state of euphoria, were witness to his strange — although extremely charismatic — behavior, and his flaunting of Halacha (which he claimed — with distorted references and contentions based on Kabbala — was no longer neccessary). It is plausible that some rabbis — not being witness to his neutralization of Halacha — may also have been swept along by the charisma and excitement.
He was arrested by the Turkish authorities when he travelled to Constantinople *(Istanbul, Turkey)*, but was treated more leniently (see 5426\1666) than someone who was leading a revolt. (Eretz Yisrael — over which, as "Mashiach", he was to be king — was part of the Turkish-Ottoman Empire, see 5276\1516.)

5426 — 1666

In **Nissan**, a Jew from Tunis disrupted proceedings at his FORCED BAPTISM in Rome by committing suicide.
Shabbetai Tzvi (see 5425\1665) managed to use his detainment — in the Turkish fortress of Gallipoli — as if it were a royal court; receiving followers and delegations from all over. This posture in captivity, increased his stature and following.
In **Elul,** however, he was brought before the Sultan in Adrianople *(Turkey)*, and given the choice of death or conversion to Islam. He chose Islam, and some of his followers also converted (see 5443\1683).
Most of the Jewish world were stunned in disbelief — and confused for generations.
However, many followers persisted with interpretations of his actions, developing a new mystical style (pseudo KABBALA) that continued along the lines of Shabbetai Tzvi's own divergence from KABBALA (see 5437*1676*).

5427 — 1667

The Jews of Podgaitsy *(Podhayetz, Poland)* were massacred when the Tartars invaded the town.
The Jews 'performed' their annual HUMILIATING RACES at the Carnival in Rome for the last time (see 5226\1466).

5428 — 1668

A number of Jews were expelled from parts of Morocco.

5430 — 1670

R.Raphael Levi was burned to death at the beginning of 1670 on a BLOOD LIBEL charge in Metz *(France)*.
All Jews were expelled from Austria (see 5256\1496) — including Jews who had settled there after the Chmielnitzki massacres in Poland — and the last Jews left Vienna on Tisha B'Av. They were allowed to return twenty-three years later.
Fifty (wealthy) families were permitted to settle in the province of Brandenburg, and some of them subsequently settled in Berlin (see 5333\1573).
Among those leaving Vienna was the rabbi, R.Gershon Ashkenazi (Olif) who then became rabbi in Metz *(N.E. France)*. He was a disciple of the Bach, of the Meginei Shlomo, and of his father-in-law, R.Menachem Mendel Krochmal (see 5421\1661), and he was author of Avodat HaGershuni *(SH'ELOT UTESHUVOT)* among other works.

5433 — 1673

The Magen Avraham (on SHULCHAN ARUCH) was completed.

R.Avraham Abele HaLevi Gombiner, rabbi in Kalisch *(Poland)*, had completed writing (his major work) Magen Avraham *(commentaries and extension)* on the Orach Chayim section of the SHULCHAN ARUCH (now printed in standard editions, *(see ILLUSTRATIONS, TEXT J, #4)*.) Although he had gathered HASKAMOT (approbations), he did not manage to have his work — which he had originally named Ner Yisrael — printed during his

lifetime. His son later printed it as Magen Avraham N"Y (**N**er **Y**israel).
R.Reuven Katz of Prague — author of the Yalkut Re'uveni *(collected sayings on the CHUMASH (Bible))* — died.
R.Chaim Benveniste — author of Knesset HaGedola *(supplements to the SHULCHAN ARUCH)* — died on the 19th **Elul** in Izmir *(Smyrna, Turkey)* where he was rabbi.

5436 ≈ 1676

R.Aharon Shmuel Kaidanover — rabbi of Nikolsburg *(Mikulov, Moravia)* (see 5416*1655*) — died on the 19th of **Tammuz** during a session at a gathering of rabbis in Chmielnick *(Poland)*.

5437 ≈ *1676*

Shabbetai Tzvi died as a Muslim.

Shabbetai Tzvi — the self proclaimed Messiah who had converted to Islam (see 5426\\1666) — died on Yom Kippur 5437*1676* in Dulcigno *(Albania)*, where he had been exiled by the Turkish authorities because of his unacceptable behavior (see 5425\\1665). Some individuals claimed to be his successor — and many of his followers continued the movement he began, as mostly secret sects, called Shabbateans — for many generations, particularly in Turkey, Italy and Poland-Lithuania *(see 5443\\1683, 5478\\1718, 5490\\1730, 5518\\1757, and 5461\\1700, 5490\\1730)*.

5437 ≈ 1677

Four Jews were killed in Cracow *(Poland)*, and 1,000 died of a plague (see 5440\\1680) in Kazmierz (part of Cracow).

5438 ≈ 1678

All Jews were expelled from Yemen after many synagogues had previously been demolished. They were allowed to return a year later, after the general population suffered from the loss. Many communities were not re-established.

5440 ≈ 1680

More than 3,000 Jews — in Prague — died of a plague (see 5437\\1677).

Living in the Year 1680

Beit Shmuel (R.Shmuel)	b.1630?,	d.1700?.
Magen Avraham (R.Avr.Abele Gombiner)	b.1637?,	d.1683.
Siftei Chachamim (R.Shabbetai Bass)	b.1641,	d.1718.
Mishneh LeMelech (R.Yehuda Rosannes)	b.1657?,	d.1727.
Chacham Tzvi (R.Tzvi Ashkenazi)	b.1660,	d.1718.
Seder HaDorot (R.Yechi'el Heilprin)	b.1660?,	d.1747?.
Pnei Yehoshua (R.Yaakov Yehoshua Falk)	b.1680,	d.1756.

5442 ≈ 1682

Many Jews were killed in Cracow *(Poland)* in **Adar**, in ANTI-JEWISH RIOTS (see 5437\\1677).

5443 ≈ 1683

All the Jews of Uhersky *(Ungarish Brod(a), Moravia)* were killed, including R.Natan Nata Hanover — who had chronicled the Chmielnitzki massacres in his book Yeven Metzula — who was killed in the attack, during his prayers, some say by Hungarian rebels (see 5464\\1704).
300 followers of Shabbetai Tzvi converted to Islam in Salonika *(Greece)* — in emulation of their leader (see 5426\\1666), who was now dead for seven years — and most of them (secretly) maintained their Shabbatean beliefs (as a group).

5446 ≈ 1686

Many Jews were killed during the Austrian siege of Budapest — including the wife and baby daughter of the Chacham Tzvi (see 5420\\1660, 5470\\1710), who had returned to Budapest after studying in Salonika *(Greece)* where he became a CHACHAM (SEPHARDI rabbi). He had also been in Belgrade *(Yugoslavia)* and had adopted the name Ashkenazi.
When the Austrian forces subsequently invaded and captured the city, they plundered the Jewish section and burned the Torah scrolls.

5448 ≈ *1687*

Although the Jews of Posen *(Poznan, Poland)* fought a successful three-day battle (in **Kislev** 5448*1687*) to defend the Jewish section of the city from ANTI-JEWISH RIOTERS, they suffered heavy losses.
The Jews of Vilna were attacked (and their property damaged) in ANTI-JEWISH RIOTS (see 5395\\1635, 5415\\1655).

5449 — 1689

The Beit Shmuel (on the SHULCHAN ARUCH) was printed.

R.Shmuel ben Uri Shraga Faivish — a disciple of R.Yehoshua Heschel (see 5414\1654) — was rabbi in Shidlov *(Szydlowiec, Poland)*, where he wrote Beit Shmuel *(commentaries and extension)* on the Even HaEzer section of the SHULCHAN ARUCH, (now printed in standard editions, *(see Illustrations, Text L, #5)*.) It was printed two years before he became rabbi in the prestigious community of Fiyorda *(Fuerth, Germany)*.

The Beit Shmuel was the first book printed in the new printing press of the Siftei Chachamim, R.Shabbetai (Meshorer) Bass (see 5415\1655, 5472\1712), author of Siftei Chachamim *(commentary on Rashi) (see ILLUSTRATIONS, TEXT A, #11)* and Siftei Yesheinim *(bibliography)*.

R.Ya'ir Chaim Bacharach — author of Chavat Ya'ir *(SH'ELOT UTESHUVOT)* — fled to Metz *(N.E. France)* when the French army occupied Virmyze *(Worms, Germany)* in 1689. He was the son of R.Moshe Shimshon — the previous rabbi of Virmyze — who was the son of Chava, the learned daughter of R.Yitzchak HaKohen Katz (see 5409*1648*). R.Ya'ir Chaim returned to Virmyze ten years later to become rabbi (three years before he died). He intended the name of his SH'ELOT UTESHUVOT, "Chaves Yo'ir", to be in memory of his grandmother (Chava), who herself had written comments on Torah.

R.Menachem Mendel Auerbach — a disciple of the Bach and author of Ateret Zekeinim *(on the SHULCHAN ARUCH, printed in standard versions)* — died on the 20th **Tammuz** in Krotoszyn *(Poland)*, where he was rabbi.

R.Yosef Shmuel of Cracow *(Poland)* — who wrote Hagahot HaShas *(annotations on the Talmud)* and edited Mesorat HaShas *(bibliography on the Talmud)* — became rabbi of Frankfort *(Germany)* four years before he died.

Three hundred Jewish houses and eleven synagogues were destroyed in a fire in Prague (see 5440\1680).

5450 — 1690

R.Aharon (ben Moshe) Te'omim — author of Matteh Aharon *(commentary on the Hagada)* — had just become the rabbi of Cracow *(Poland)*, having previously been rabbi in Virmyze *(Worms, Germany)*. He was arrested by soldiers on Shabbat late afternoon — for no apparent reason, while in Chmielnik *(Poland)* for a meeting of the VA'AD ARBA ARATZOT, *(see 5340\1580)*, — and he died of the cruel beatings while being taken away on the 2nd **Av.**

5451 — 1691

Glikl (Glueckel) of Hameln *(Germany)* began writing her memoirs — which give a rich description of Jewish life in Germany — when her (first) husband died in 1691, leaving her with 12 children.

5452 — 1692

R.Chizkiyah ben David da Silva printed his work, Pri Chadash *(on the SHULCHAN ARUCH)* — in Amsterdam, when he was there on a mission from Eretz Yisrael — only a few years before he died at a very young age.

5456 — 1696

The Jewish section of Brody *(Russia)* was destroyed by fire.

5458 — *1697*

R.Moshe Zacuto — the RaMaZ (or ReMeZ), who had been a disciple of R.Shaul Levi Morteira in Amsterdam (see 5416\1656) before he went to Poland-Lithuania to study — was an outstanding scholar of KABBALA, in which he was a disciple of (the elderly) R.Binyamin HaLevi, a follower of the Ari'zal. He wrote many works, and died — on the second day of Sukkot 5458*1697* — in Mantua *(Italy)*, where he had been rabbi for some twenty-four years (after being rabbi in Venice for approximately twenty-eight years).

5458 — 1698

The Ba'al Shem Tov was born.

R.Yisrael ben Eliezer, the Ba'al Shem Tov (see 5494\1734), was born on the 18th **Elul.** Both his parents died when he was a young child.

5461 — *1700*

R.Yehuda Chasid (Segal) — an extremely pious scholar — travelled around Europe, encouraging Jews to repentance because the Mashiach

(Messiah) was about to come. He emigrated to Eretz Yisrael with a large group of followers, but only a fraction of them reached their destination, and R.Yehuda died a few days after arriving in Yerushalayim, in **Cheshvan** 5461*1700*. Further problems developed, as some of the group were suspected Shabbateans (see 5437*1676*), (and as a consequence the leader's reputation was also questioned (posthumously) by some, see 5490\\1730).

Living in the Year 1700

Beit Shmuel (R.Shmuel)	b.1630?,	d.1700?.
Siftei Chachamim (R.Shabbetai Bass)	b.1641,	d.1718.
Mishneh LeMelech (R.Yehuda Rosannes)	b.1657?,	d.1727.
Chacham Tzvi (R.Tzvi Ashkenazi)	b.1660,	d.1718.
Seder HaDorot (R.Yechi'el Heilprin)	b.1660?,	d.1747?.
Pnei Yehoshua (R.Yaakov Yehoshua Falk)	b.1680,	d.1756.
R.Yaakov Culi (Me'am Lo'ez)	b.1689?,	d.1732.
R.Yonatan Eybeshutz	b.1690?,	d.1764.
Sha'agat Aryeh (R.Aryeh Leib Gunzberg)	b.1695?,	d.1785.
Or HaChayim (R.Chaim (ib)n Attar)	b.1696,	d.1743.
R.Yaakov Emden	b.1697?,	d.1776.
Ba'al Shem Tov	b.1698,	d.1760.
Maggid of Mezeritsch (R.Dov Ber)	b.1698?,	d.1772.

5463 — 1702

The Pnei Yehoshua's family were killed in an explosion.

R.Yaakov Yehoshua Falk (see 5478\\1718) — author of Pnei Yehoshua *(CHIDUSHIM on Talmud)* and a grandson of R.Yehoshua Falk *(the* Meginei Shlomo *and* Pnei Yehoshua I*)* — was living in Lvov *(Lemberg, Poland)*. He was teaching his disciples on the 3rd **Kislev** (5463*1702*) — as he describes in the hakdama to his work — when a gunpowder storehouse exploded. Thirty-six Jews were killed, including his wife, daughter and mother in law, but he survived even though he had been buried in the rubble.

5464 — 1703

The Jews of Belaya Tzerkov *(then Poland)* were attacked in — was what later marked as the beginning of — the Haidamack massacres (see 5496\\1736).

5464 — 1704

Many Jews were killed, at this time — and many more were displaced (see 5443\\1683, 5474\\1714) — during the (unsuccessful) Hungarian revolution.

The Jews of Krotoszyn *(Poland)* (see 5416\\1656) were attacked, and their property looted, in ANTI-JEWISH RIOTS.

5466 — 1706

Forty-five Jews were killed in a fire, in Kalisch *(Poland)* (see 5468\\1708).

The Jews of Lissa *(Leszno, Poland)* were attacked and plundered by the invading Russian soldiers *(of Peter the Great)*, and the whole Jewish section of the town was burned (see 5469\\1709).

5468 — 1708

Four hundred and fifty Jews died in a plague in Kalisch *(Poland)* (see 5419\\1659, 5466\\1706).

A fire destroyed the Jewish section of Vitebsk *(then Poland)*.

5469 — 1709

The Jews of Lissa *(Leszno, Poland)* (see 5466\\1706) were accused of spreading a plague, and were expelled. They were allowed to return when the plague was over.

5470 — 1710

Jews were expelled from Groningen *(N. Netherlands)*.

R.Tzvi Ashkenazi — the Chacham Tzvi, who had spent eighteen years as a ROSH YESHIVA in Altona *(part of Hamburg, Germany)* — succeeded the father of his second wife (see 5446\\1686) R.Meshulam Zalman, as rabbi there. However, he returned to his studies, after a short while, because of a Halacha dispute with another rabbi, and in 1710 he became the rabbi (see 5478\\1718) of the relatively new ASHKENAZI community — in the predominantly Sephardi community (see 5402\\1642, 5416\\1656) — of Amsterdam.

Adel (Ethel) — the daughter of Moshe Kikinish of Lvov *(Lemberg, Poland)*, a wealthy descendant of Yona HaNavi) — was killed on the 26th **Elul,** when she confessed to a BLOOD LIBEL to save the lives of other Jews.

5471 — 1711

R.Yechi'el Heilprin — author of Seder HaDorot *(history; chronological, biographical)* — became rabbi in Minsk

(then Poland) until he died some thirty-six years later.
A fire broke out in the house of R.Naftali Katz, the rabbi of Frankfort, which destroyed the whole Jewish section. R.Naftali — a great scholar (especially in KABBALA) — was maliciously maligned: some accused him of preventing the flames to be extinguished, so that he could test his KAMEYOT *(amulets)* for fire extinguishing. Although he was cleared of any charges, he was compelled to leave Frankfort.

5472 — 1712

The Siftei Chachamim was arrested.

R.Shabbetai (Meshorer) Bass — the author of Siftei Chachamim (see 5449\1689) — was arrested on the charge that his printing press in Dyhernfurth *(Silesia, a region between Germany and Poland)* was printing books that were spreading hatred against Christians. He was later released.
R.Eliyahu Shapiro of Prague (see 5514\1754) — a disciple of the Magen Avraham, and a brother in law of the Chok Yaakov (see 5494*1733*) — was author of Eliyahu Rabba and Zuta *(Halacha, on the Levushim)*. He died on the 8th **Nissan**.

5474 — *1713*

R.Yoel Ba'al Shem (ben Yitzchak Halpern) — a grandson of R.Yoel (also a Ba'al Shem), and author of Toldot Adam *(KABBALA)* — died on the 4th **Tishrei** 5474*1713*.

5474 — 1714

R.Meir Eisenstadt — known as the Maharam Esh (or Ash) (an abbreviation of Eisenstadt) — became rabbi in Eisenstadt, which had just recovered from the Hungarian Revolution (see 5464\1704). He wrote Panim Me'irot *(Chidushim and SH'ELOT UTESHUVOT)*.

5475 — 1715

Eight hundred and ninety-two Jews died in a plague in Boskowitz *(Moravia)*.

5476 — 1716

The Jews of Posen *(Poznan, Poland)* were attacked — a few years after an epidemic *(of Ergot disease)* had decimated the community — and many Jews subsequently left the town *(see 5496\1736)*.

5478 — 1718

The Chacham Tzvi had left Amsterdam after residing there for four years (see 5470\1710). His leaving was due to his placing a prominent Shabbatean (see 5437*1676*) in CHEREM *(excommunication)*, and the subsequent controversy and differences with the older Portuguese (SEPHARDI) congregation. He had travelled to England, Germany, and Poland, before becoming rabbi in Lvov *(Lemberg, Poland)* shortly before he died there, on Rosh Chodesh **Iyar** 1718.
He was succeeded by the Pnei Yehoshua (see 5490\1730) — who had (previously) left Lvov, after losing his family (see 5463*1702*) — and had since then been the rabbi in a number of towns.

5479 — 1719

The whole Jewish section of Nikolsburg *(Mikulov, Moravia)* was completely destroyed by fire.
Shimshon Wertheimer — an extremely wealthy SHTADLAN from Vienna, who was a scholar, and financially supported other scholars, besides his many activities on behalf of Jews throughout Europe — organized the raising of funds to rebuild the community.

5480 — 1720

The Jews of Budapest *(Hungary)* were attacked

Living in the Year 1720

Mishneh LeMelech (R.Yehuda Rosannes)	*b.*1657?,	*d.*1727.
Seder HaDorot (R.Yechi'el Heilprin)	*b.*1660?,	*d.*1747?.
Pnei Yehoshua (R.Yaakov Yehoshua Falk)	*b.*1680,	*d.*1756.
R.Yaakov Culi (Me'am Lo'ez)	*b.*1689?,	*d.*1732.
R.Yonatan Eybeshutz	*b.*1690?,	*d.*1764.
Sha'agat Aryeh (R.Aryeh Leib Gunzberg)	*b.*1695?,	*d.*1785.
Or HaChayim (R.Chaim (ib)n Attar)	*b.*1696,	*d.*1743.
R.Yaakov Emden	*b.*1697?,	*d.*1776.
Ba'al Shem Tov	*b.*1698,	*d.*1760.
Maggid of Mezeritsch (R.Dov Ber)	*b.*1698?,	*d.*1772.
Ramchal (Luzzatto)	*b.*1707,	*d.*1747.
Korban HaEida (R.David Frankel)	*b.*1707,	*d.*1762.
Pnei Moshe (R.Moshe Margolis)	*b.*1710?,	*d.*1781.
Noda BiYehuda (R.Yechezk'el Landau)	*b.*1713,	*d.*1793.
R.Elimelech of Lizensk	*b.*1717?,	*d.*1786.
R.Zushya of Annopol	*b.*1718?,	*d.*1800.
Vilna Gaon	*b.*1720,	*d.*1797.

and their homes plundered (see 5474\1714).

5481 ≈ 1720

Arabs broke into the Ashkenazi synagogue in Yerushalayim — which had been built in honor of R.Yehuda Chasid (see 5461\ *1700*) — and they burned the Torah scrolls, on 8th **Cheshvan** 5481\ *1720*. The Ashkenazi Jews had to flee (they could not return), and the synagogue remained in disrepair for many years (see 5597\1837), thus attracting the name Churvat R.Yehuda Chasid.

5483 ≈ 1723

R.Yeshayahu (ben Avraham) HaLevi — grandson of the Taz and author of the first Ba'er Heitev (1) *(summary of commentaries on the Orach Chayim section of Shulchan Aruch) (see Illustrations, Text J, #5)*— was burned to death (see 5424\1664) with his wife and daughter, in a fire in Mogilev *(then Poland)*. They were on their way to Eretz Yisrael.

R.Yehuda ben Shimon of Tiktin *(Tykocin, N.E.Poland)* also wrote Ba'er Heitev (2) *(a (full) commentary on the Shulchan Aruch)*. Although it covers all four sections of the Shulchan Aruch, it is only his Ba'er Heitev on the Orach Chayim and Even HaEzer sections that are now printed in standard editions *(see Illustrations, Text J, #5, L, #6)*.

R.Zecharyah Mendel of Belz *(Poland)* also wrote a Ba'er Heitev (3) *(summary of commentaries)*, which is printed (in standard editions of the Shulchan Aruch) on the sections of Yoreh De'a and Choshen Mishpat *(see Illustrations, Text K, #5, M, #6)*.

R.Moshe (ben Shimon) Frankfurter also wrote a Ba'er Heitev (4) *(summary of commentaries)*, on the Choshen Mishpat section of Shulchan Aruch.

5484 ≈ 1724

R.Yaakov Culi (Me'am Lo'ez) arrived in Constantinople.

R.Yaakov Culi came to Constantinople — to print the works of his grandfather (R.Moshe ibn Chaviv) — and there he became a disciple of R.Yehuda Rosannes. Later — after R.Yehuda died (see 5487\1727) — he edited his work (Mishneh LeMelech, see 5487\1727), and wrote Me'am Lo'ez *(extensive basic commentary, homily)* on Bereshit and Shmot (Chumash, Bible). This he wrote in Ladino, a Judeo-Spanish language similar in concept to (Germanic) Yiddish. After he died (at an early age), further volumes of the Me'am Lo'ez were written by others, who continued his work (partly from manuscript he had left). This popular work played an important role in the Torah re-orientation of Sephardim, after the confusion left by Shabbetai Tzvi *(see 5426\1666, 5437\1676, 5494\1734)*.

5486 ≈ 1726

The Jews were attacked in Jassy *(Moldavia)* after a blood libel, and the synagogues were desecrated.

5487 ≈ 1727

The Mishneh LeMelech died.

R.Yehuda Rosannes of Constantinople *(Istanbul, Turkey)* — author of the Mishneh LeMelech *(commentary on the Rambam's Yad HaChazaka) (see Illustrations, Text I, #9)* (see 5484\1724) — died on the 22nd **Nissan**, Acharon Shel Pesach *(the last day of Pesach)*.

5488 ≈ 1728

Two brothers — after being charged that they had attempted to convince a *meshumad (apostate)* to return to Judaism, and that they had 'profaned Christian symbols' — R.Chaim, a rabbi, and R.Yehoshua Reitzes, a Rosh Yeshiva, were tortured and then burned in Lvov *(Lemberg, Poland)* on Erev Shavu'ot. (Some say R.Yehoshua took his own life in prison, and his body was then mutilated and burned.)

5490 ≈ 1730

The Pnei Yehoshua (see 5478\1718, 5494\ *1733*) had left Lvov *(Lemberg, Poland)* — because of a controversy over his public cherem *(excommunication)* of the Shabbateans *(see 5437\1676, 5478\1718)* — and he had not settled until he became rabbi in Berlin in 1730 (see 5430\1670).

R.Moshe Chaim Luzzatto (see 5507\1747) — known as the Ramchal, a brilliant young scholar of Italy — was suspected of being influenced by the Shabbateans, because of his personal mystical style and his Kabbala writings (which he subsequently undertook to cease). He later left Italy and settled in Amsterdam for a while (see 5507\1747).

The Kabbala, and its transference through the

generations (see 5050\1290), is not as strictly defined as the Talmud and Halacha, and does not have the same clear structure. It can be possible for '*analysts*' to assume that the origins of some works were Shabbatean, when they may have been from other (discreet) sources. It is also possible — within the unstructured nature of transference of the KABBALA tradition — that some (sometimes even scholars) may (mistakenly) accept the authenticity of KABBALA works — most likely without the guidance of an elder mentor — which were in fact influenced by Shabbetai Tzvi's divergence from KABBALA (see 5426\1666).

5494 — *1733*

R.Yaakov Reisher — author of Shvut Yaakov, Minchat Yaakov, and Chok Yaakov *(Halacha)*, and rabbi of Metz *(N.E. France)* — died on the **10th Tevet** 5494*1733*. A year later he was succeeded by the Pnei Yehoshua (see 5490\ 1730), who was remarried (see 5463\ *1702*) to a scholarly woman.

R.Alexander Sender (ben Ephrayim Zalman) Schorr published Simla Chadasha *(Halacha of Shechita)* with his own commentary called Tevu'ot Shor four years before he died.

5494 — 1734

Jews were massacred by the Haidamack bands.

Twenty-seven Jews were massacred in Korsun *(Poland)* by the roaming Haidamack bands (see 5463\1703, 5496\1736).

For a number of years, the Ba'al Shem Tov had kept company with the itinerant TZADIKIM NISTARIM (see 5546\1786), a grouping who were covertly active — after the Chmielnitzki massacres, and the confusion left by Shabbetai Tzvi, see 5408*1648*, 5426\1666, 5437\ *1676*) — to alleviate the massive economic and spiritual plight of the Jews in and around Poland-Lithuania. He became a leader in their clandestine society, and began teaching his concepts of CHASIDUT publicly in 1734 at the age of thirty-six.

5496 — 1736

The Haidamacks — roving bands of armed peasants and their assorted colleagues — attacked travellers, and the smaller towns (see 5464\ *1703*, 5494\1734, 5528\1768) in Polish Ukraine. In 1736 they massacred thirty-five Jews in Pavoloch and fourteen Jews in Pogrebishche.

Many Jews were imprisoned and tortured in a BLOOD LIBEL in Posen *(Poznan, Poland)*, and the community deteriorated further (see 5476\ 1716, 5516*1755*).

5497 — 1737

A number of Jews were tortured and killed in a BLOOD LIBEL in Yaroslav *(Poland)*.

5498 — 1738

Joseph Oppenheimer — financial advisor to the Duke (Karl Alexander) of Wurtemberg, who had previously settled Jews in places that were forbidden to them — was slandered by the envious for his successful management. He decided to escape danger and leave the country, and made a last-night visit to the Duke who was supporting him. Unfortunately the Duke died on that very night, Oppenheim was arrested by enemies — and although he was not a Halacha-observant Jew, and two of his siblings had "embraced" Christianity — he resisted attempts to force him to conversion, and was hanged saying SHEMA YISRAEL on the 14th **Shvat**.

Baruch Leibov and the Russian naval officer Alexander Vosnitsyn — whom he introduced to JUDAISM — were both tortured and burned at the stake in S.Petersbrg (Russia).

Living in the Year 1740

Seder HaDorot (R.Yechi'el Heilprin)	b.1660?,	d.1747?.
Pnei Yehoshua (R.Yaakov Yehoshua Falk)	b.1680,	d.1756.
R.Yonatan Eybeshutz	b.1690?,	d.1764.
Sha'agat Aryeh (R.Aryeh Leib Gunzberg)	b.1695?,	d.1785.
Or HaChayim (R.Chaim (ib)n Attar)	b.1696,	d.1743.
R.Yaakov Emden	b.1697?,	d.1776.
Ba'al Shem Tov	b.1698,	d.1760.
Maggid of Mezeritsch (R.Dov Ber)	b.1698?,	d.1772.
Ramchal (Luzzatto)	b.1707,	d.1747.
Korban HaEida (R.David Frankel)	b.1707,	d.1762.
Pnei Moshe (R.Moshe Margolis)	b.1710?,	d.1781.
Noda BiYehuda (R.Yechezk'el Landau)	b.1713,	d.1793.
R.Elimelech of Lizensk	b.1717?,	d.1786.
R.Zushya of Annopol	b.1718?,	d.1800.
Vilna Gaon	b.1720,	d.1797.
Chida (Azulai)	b.1724,	d.1806.
Pri Megadim (R.Yosef Te'omim)	b.1727?,	d.1792.
R.Levi Yitzchak of Berditchev	b.1740,	d.1810.

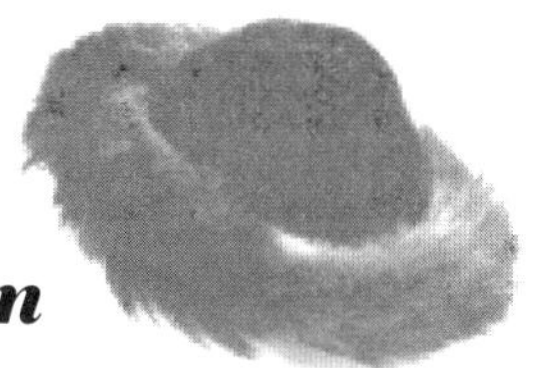

Chapter 14b,
Acharonim and Early Chassidim

5500 — 1740

The year 5500 carried a centuries-old prediction from the Zohar (see 5050\1290) — that the GATES OF WISDOM would be opened in the "*sixth hundred year of the sixth (thousand)*" (5500) *[Zoh.1.117a]* — which coincides with the increased development of the new sciences and technologies of the Industrial Revolution, ushering in a new era in the history of mankind.

5501 — 1741

The Or HaChayim arrived in Eretz Yisrael.

Due to persecutions and famine, R.Chaim (ib)n Attar — author of Or HaChayim *(commentary on CHUMASH (Bible)) (see ILLUSTRATIONS, TEXT A, #12)* and other works — left Morocco, where he was born. He travelled to Italy (via Algiers), where he sought to publish his works. His popular reception there inspired him to seek (financial) support for his proposed YESHIVA in Yerushalayim (some disciples had followed him). After more than a year in Italy, he sailed (with 30 people) to Eretz Yisrael, arriving in 1741. He stayed in Acco *(Acre)* for a year because of a plague (see 5507\1747) in Yerushalayim, where he finally arrived, only to live one year before he died (at 47).

R.Yonatan Eybeshutz (see 5510\1750) — an orphan who was raised by the Maharam Esh (see 5474\1714) — was author of Creti UPeleti and Urim VeTumim *(Pilpul (fine and sharp distinctions) on Halacha)*. He was appointed rabbi in Metz *(N.E. France)* in 1741, when the Pnei Yehoshua left (see 5494*1733*, 5514\1754). Before R.Yonatan had a chance to leave, the French army attacked Prague (see 5505\1745), but they permitted him to leave for Metz *(in France)*. However, the (defending) Austrian government confiscated his belongings for this "treason".

5502 — 1742

All Jews were expelled from — most of what was then — Russia (see 5532\1772).

5503 — 1743

R.David Frankel (Mirels) — author of Korban HaEida *(commentary on Talmud Yerushalmi, now printed in standard editions) (see Illustrations, Text F, #4)*— was appointed rabbi of Berlin.

5505 — 1745

A number of Jews were massacred in Roudnice *(Bohemia)*, and — in a decree issued by Maria Theresa (empress of Austria) (see 5506\1746, 5534\1774) in 1744 — all Jews were expelled from Prague (see 5501\1741). They were allowed to return three years later.

R.Shneur Zalman (see 5530\1770) — the son of R.Baruch, who was a direct descendant of the Maharal of Prague — was born on the 18th **Elul** (see 5369\1609, 5458\1698). His mother, Rivka, was a scholarly woman who had daily SHI'URIM *(study-sessions)*.

5506 — 1746

All Jews were expelled (by Maria Theresa, see 5505\1745) from Buda *(Budapest, Hungary)*.

5507 — 1747

R.Moshe Chaim Luzzatto (Ramchal) died in Acco (Acre).

R.Moshe Chaim Luzzatto (see 5490\1730) — author of Mesilat Yesharim *(Mussar)* and other works, who had left Amsterdam and settled in Eretz Yisrael — died, in a plague (see 5501\1741) in Acco *(Acre)* on the 26th **Iyar**, some four years after he had arrived there. Many Jews in nearby Tzfat *(Safed)* also died of a plague (see 5520*1759*).

Five Jews were killed in a BLOOD LIBEL in Izyaslav *(Poland)*.

R.Avraham Gershon of Kitev *(Kuty, Poland)* — a Torah scholar respected by R.Yonatan Eybeshutz and the Noda BiYehuda — left Europe to settle in Eretz Yisrael at the request of his brother-in-law, the Ba'al Shem Tov, of whom he was a follower.

5509 1749

The Jews of Breslau *(Silesia, a region between Germany and Poland)* — who had recently returned (see 5213\1453) — were killed in the RIOTS that followed the explosion of a gunpowder storehouse.

5510 1750

R.Yonatan Eybeshutz became rabbi in Hamburg.

R.Yonatan Eybeshutz (see 5501\1741) became rabbi in the combined communities of Hamburg Altona and Wandsbek. R.Yaakov Emden — the son of the Chacham Tzvi (see 5470\1710) — was living there, after having been rabbi in Emden *(Germany)* for a few years. When R.Yonatan arrived, there was an 'epidemic' — in which many women died at childbirth — and the community turned to the new rabbi, who was also renowned for his expertise in PRACTICAL KABBALA. R.Yonatan wrote KAMEYOT *(amulets)*, some of which were later opened by R.Yaakov Emden and interpreted by him to be of Shabbatean content (see 5490\ 1730).
Although R.Yonatan had been a participant in a CHEREM *(excommunication)* of the Shabbateans (see 5437*1676*) — in Prague (in 1725), and he had restated his position regarding them — nevertheless a prolonged and widespread *(see 5514\1753, 5514\1754)* controversy ensued (which also extended outside of the Jewish communities). R.Yaakov Emden (see 5536\1776) maintained his accusations — from Amsterdam, when he had to leave Hamburg — and R.Yonatan presented explanations for his KAMEYOT.

5513 1753

Eleven Jews were (skinned alive and) killed — and thirteen were forced to convert to Christianity — in a BLOOD LIBEL in Zhitomir *(then Poland)*.

5514 *1753*

R.Yonatan Eybeshutz was cleared of suspicion (see 5510\1750) by the scholars of the VA'AD ARBA ARATZOT in Yaroslav, on the 3rd **Cheshvan** 5514*1753*.

5514 1754

The Noda BiYehuda became rabbi in Prague.

Two years after his proclamation of mediation — allowing both sides in the Emden-Eybeshutz controversy a dignified retreat (see 5510\ 1750), R.Yechezk'el Landau — author of Noda BiYehuda *(SH'ELOT UTESHUVOT)* and other works — became rabbi of Prague (see 5505\1745) and all of Bohemia. He was not kind in his (later) statements about the Chasidim.
The Pnei Yehoshua (see 5501\1741) had left Metz *(N.E. France)*, and then been rabbi in Frankfort am Main for ten years. He left there after becoming involved in the Emden-Eybeshutz controversy (see 5510\1750) in favor of R.Yaakov Emden (see 5490\1730). He was living in Virmyze *(Worms, Germany)* when the Chida (see 5566\1806) — while on his travels as an emissary for Eretz Yisrael — visited him, (somewhat over a year) before the Pnei Yehoshua died.
Most of the Jewish section of Prague was destroyed by a fire in which many writings of R.Eliyahu Shapiro (Eliyahu Rabba, see 5472\1712) were burned.

5515 1755

Hertzl Levi was killed in Colmar *(Alsace, a region between France and Germany)*, after a (LIBEL) trial.

5516 *1755*

R.Aryeh Leib ben Yosef Kalahora the Darshan *(preacher)* was killed (see 5424*1663*) on the 18th **Kislev** 5516*1755*, only a few weeks after Yaakov ben Pinchas (a community trustee) and Wolf Winkler were killed, in a BLOOD LIBEL in Posen *(Poznan, Poland)* (see 5496\1736).

5517 *1756*

R.Yitzchak (Chizkiyah) Lampronti — author of the monumental Talmudic encyclopedia Pachad Yitzchak — died in the month of **Cheshvan** 5517*1756* (at age 78) in Ferrara *(Italy)*, where he served a rabbi, ROSH YESHIVA, and doctor. His burial place is unknown, because the Inquisition (see 5012\1252) had forbidden Jews to erect tombstones.

5518 *1757*

The Frankists instigated mass burnings of the Talmud.

Jacob Frank had returned to Poland after he had spent many years in Turkey with members of Shabbatean sects (see 5437*1676*). There he apparently acquired SEPHARDI style — for which, some say, he was nick-named 'frenk' — and he subsequently adopted the name 'Frank'. He became a leader (see 5519\ 1759) among the mostly secret Shabbatean followers in Europe, and began to encourage them to express their beliefs openly.

A CHEREM *(excommunication)* was proclaimed in Brody *(then Russia)*, against the now identifiable Shabbatean followers of Frank (who were later called Frankists). The CHEREM included a ban against the study of KABBALA under the age of 40 (see 5065\1305).

The Frankists had begun developing close relations with the Bishop of Kaminetz-Podolski *(then Poland)*, who subsequently organized a DEBATE, in his city, between the Shabbatean-Frankists and leaders of traditional Jews. At the DEBATE the Frankists degraded the Talmud, and as a result the bishop declared that all copies were to be confiscated and burned (see 5314*1553*). A mass burning took place in Kaminetz-Podolski in **Cheshvan-Kislev** 5518\ *1757*, where the bishop died at the time of the burnings — a miracle attributed to the Ba'al Shem Tov. Jewish books were also burned in other towns in Poland, including Lvov *(Lemberg)*, Zholkva *(Zolkiew)* and Brody.

5519 ≈ 1759

Frankists supported BLOOD LIBEL charges, in public DEBATE.

Jacob Frank (see 5518*1757*) had drawn his Shabbatean followers closer to Christianity. After the DEBATE of *1757* he was involved with Christians in organizing another DEBATE with (traditional) Jews, in which he and his followers were to prove (among other things) that Jews did in fact use non-Jewish blood for ritual purposes. It was also understood, that after the DEBATE, he and his followers would participate in a MASS CONVERSION to Christianity (although they secretly intended to retain their Shabbatean beliefs, see 5443\1683).

R.Chaim HaKohen Rappaport — the distinguished rabbi of Lvov *(Lemberg, Poland)*, and a secret follower of the Ba'al Shem Tov — was the leading spokesman for the (traditional) Jews (some say the Ba'al Shem Tov himself was not among those present) in the highly charged (but inconclusive) DEBATE that took place in 1759 in Lvov.

There were no resultant burnings of the Talmud (see 5518*1757*), but Jacob Frank led many of his followers (some say thousands) to baptism in Lvov after the DEBATE, and he himself was baptized again later. However, many of his followers did not convert, yet remained devoted to him without following his (stated) *'path through the religions, to a world higher than any religious order'*.

Frank was arrested a short while later, because of Christian suspicions about his ('heretic' personal Messianic) ambitions and intentions, and because of the scandalous nature of some of the (pseudo-religious) orgies that the Shabbateans indulged in. He remained imprisoned in the fortress at Chestochova *(Czestochowa, Poland)* for thirteen years (see 5532\1772).

5520 ≈ 1759

200 Jews died in an earthquake in Tzfat *(Safed)* in **Cheshvan** 5520*1759*, and most of the survivors began leaving the town (see 5507\1747, 5597\1837).

5520 ≈ 1760

The Ba'al Shem Tov died.

The Ba'al Shem Tov — (Besht) (see 5494\ 1734),

Living in the Year 1760

R.Yonatan Eybeshutz	b.1690?,	d.1764.
Sha'agat Aryeh (R.Aryeh Leib Gunzberg)	b.1695?,	d.1785.
R.Yaakov Emden	b.1697?,	d.1776.
Ba'al Shem Tov	b.1698,	d.1760.
Maggid of Mezeritsch (R.Dov Ber)	b.1698?,	d.1772.
Korban HaEida (R.David Frankel)	b.1707,	d.1762.
Pnei Moshe (R.Moshe Margolis)	b.1710?,	d.1781.
Noda BiYehuda (R.Yechezk'el Landau)	b.1713,	d.1793.
R.Elimelech of Lizensk	b.1717?,	d.1786.
R.Zushya of Annopol	b.1718?,	d.1800.
Vilna Gaon	b.1720,	d.1797.
Chida (Azulai)	b.1724,	d.1806.
Pri Megadim (R.Yosef Te'omim)	b.1727?,	d.1792.
R.Levi Yitzchak of Berditchev	b.1740,	d.1810.
R.Shneur Zalman (Rav of Lyady)	b.1745,	d.1813.
Ketzot HaChoshen (R.Aryeh Leib Heller)	b.1745?,	d.1813.
Chozeh of Lublin	b.1745?,	d.1815.
Chayei Adam (R.Avraham Danziger)	b.1748,	d.1820.
R.Chaim Volozhiner	b.1749,	d.1821.
Yismach Moshe (R.Moshe Teitelbaum)	b.1759,	d.1841.
Chavat Da'at (R.Yakov of Lissa/Netivot)	b.1759?,	d.1832.
R.Ephrayim Zalman Margolis	b.1760,	d.1828.

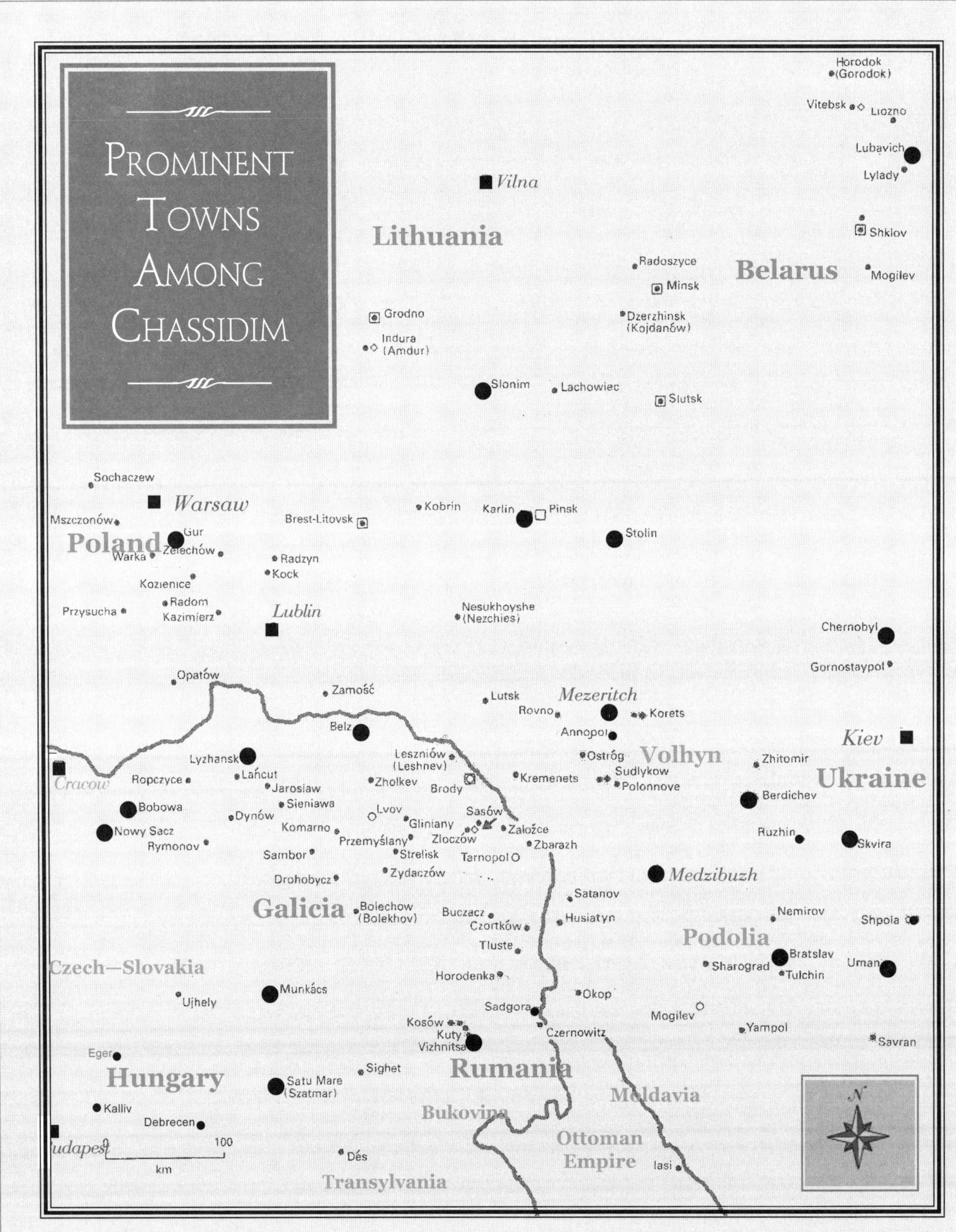

Prominent Towns Among Chassidim
Horodok (Gorodok)
Vitebsk
Liozno
Lubavich
Lylady
Vilna
Lithuania
Shklov
Radoszyce
Belarus
Mogilev
Minsk
Grodno
Dzerzhinsk (Kojdanów)
Indura (Amdur)
Slonim
Lachowiec
Slutsk
Sochaczew
Warsaw
Kobrin
Karlin
Pinsk
Mszczonów
Brest-Litovsk
Gur
Stolin
Poland
Warka
Żelechów
Radzyn
Kock
Kozienice
Radom
Przysucha
Kazimierz
Lublin
Nesukhoyshe (Nezchies)
Chernobyl
Gornostaypol
Opatów
Zamość
Lutsk
Mezeritch
Rovno
Korets
Belz
Annopol
Kiev
Leszniów (Leshnev)
Ostróg
Volhyn
Zhitomir
Lyzhansk
Łańcut
Kremenets
Sudlykow
Ukraine
Cracow
Ropczyce
Zholkev
Brody
Polonnove
Jaroslaw
Berdichev
Bobowa
Sieniawa
Dynów
Lvov
Sasów
Nowy Sacz
Gliniany
Załoźce
Ruzhin
Skvira
Komarno
Rymonov
Przemyślany
Zloczów
Zbarazh
Sambor
Strelisk
Tarnopol
Zydaczów
Medzibuzh
Drohobycz
Satanov
Galicia
Bolechow (Bolekhov)
Buczacz
Husiatyn
Nemirov
Czortków
Shpola
Podolia
Tluste
Bratslav
Czech—Slovakia
Sharograd
Tulchin
Uman
Horodenka
Munkács
Okop
Ujhely
Sadgora
Mogilev
Kosów
Yampol
Kuty
Czernowitz
Vizhnitsa
Savran
Eger
Sighet
Hungary
Rumania
Satu Mare (Szatmar)
Moldavia
Kalliv
Bukovina
Debrecen
Ottoman Empire
Budapest
100
km
Dés
Iasi
Transylvania
N

Major Admurim & Chassidic Leaders

Listed in order of date of birth.
(*) Date of birth unknown.
Estimated on life of 60 years.

Ba'al Shem Tov	b. 1698	d. 1760.
Maggid of Mezeritsch (R.Dov Ber)	b. 1698?	d. 1772.
R.Avraham Gershon of Kitev (*)	b. 1701?	d. 1761.
R.Nachman of Horodenka (*)	b. 1705?	d. 1765.
R.Elimelech of Lizensk	b. 1717?	d. 1786.
R.Zushya of Annopol	b. 1718?	d. 1800.
R.Yechi'el Michel of Zlotchov	b. 1721?	d. 1786?
R.Yaakov Yosef of Polannoe (*)	b. 1724?	d. 1784?
The Shpoler Zeideh	b. 1725	d. 1812.
R.Shmelke of Nikolsburg	b. 1726?	d. 1778?
R.Pinchas of Koretz	b. 1728	d. 1790.
R.Menachem Mendel of Vitebsk	b. 1730?	d. 1788.
R.Nachum of Chernobyl	b. 1730	d. 1797.
R.Pinchas Horowitz	b. 1730	d. 1805.
R.Yisrael (Maggid) of Kozhnitz	b. 1733?	d. 1814.
R.Aharon of Karlin	b. 1736	d. 1772.
R.Shlomo of Karlin	b. 1738	d. 1792.
R.Levi Yitzchak of Berditchev	b. 1740	d. 1810.
R.Avraham of Kalisk	b. 1741	d. 1809.
Adm.R.Yitzchak Aisik of Kalliv	b. 1744?	d. 1821.
R.Shneur Zalman (Rav of Lyady)	b. 1745	d. 1813.
Chozeh of Lublin	b. 1745?	d. 1815.
R.Baruch of Medzibuzh	b. 1753?	d. 1811.
Adm.R.Avrham YhoshuaHeschel of Apta	b. 1755	d. 1825
Adm.R.Mnachem Mendel of Rymanov (*)	b. 1755?	d. 1815
Yismach Moshe (R.Moshe Teitelbaum)	b. 1759	d. 1841
Adm.R.Meir of Apta	b. 1760	d. 1827
Adm.R.Naftali Tzvi of Ropshytz	b. 1760	d. 1827
Adm.R.Klonymos Kalman of Cracow (*)	b. 1763?	d. 1823
Adm.R.Asher of Stolin	b. 1765	d. 1826
The Yehudi of Pershisskha	b. 1766	d. 1814
Adm.R.Simcha Bunim of Pershisskha	b. 1767	d. 1827
Adm.R.Mordechai of Chernobyl	b. 1770	d. 1837
R.Nachman of Bratslav	b. 1772	d. 1811
Adm.R.Dov Ber of Lubavitch	b. 1774	d. 1827
Adm.R.Shalom of Belz	b. 1779	d. 1855
Adm.R.Meir(el) Premishlaner	b. 1780?	d. 1850
Bnei Yissachar (of Dynov)	b. 1783?	d. 1841
Adm.R.Elazar Nissan Teitelbaum	b. 1786?	d. 1856
R.Mendel of Kotzk	b. 1787	d. 1859
Tzemach Tzedek (of Lubavitch)	b. 1789	d. 1866
Divrei Chaim (of Tzanz)	b. 1793	d. 1876
R.Yisrael of Ruzhin	b. 1797	d. 1850
Chidushei HaRim (of Gur)	b. 1799	d. 1866
Adm.R.Shlomo of Radomsk	b. 1803	d. 1866
Adm.R.Aisik of Komarno	b. 1806	d. 1874
Adm.R.Yekutiel Yehuda of Sighet	b. 1808	d. 1883
Divrei Yechezk'el (of Shinev)	b. 1811?	d. 1899
Adm.R.Yitzchak of Skvira	b. 1812	d. 1885

continued ....

.....continued

Adm.R.Tzadok HaKohen of Lublin	b. 1823	d. 1900
Adm.R.Yehoshua of Belz	b. 1825	d. 1894
Adm.R.Dovid Moshe of Czhortkov	b. 1828	d. 1904
AdAdm.R.Menachem Mendel of Vizhnitz	b. 1830	d. 1884
Adm.R.Shmuel of Lubavitch	b. 1834	d. 1882
Adm.R.Chananyah Yom Tov Lipa of Sighet	b. 1836	d. 1904
Adm.R.Avraham of Sochatchev	b. 1839	d. 1910
Darkei Teshuva (of Munkatch)	b. 1845?	d.1913
'Sfass Emess' (of Gur)	b. 1847	d. 1905
Adm.R.Shlomo of Bobov	b. 1848	d. 1906
Adm.R.Yeshaya Kerestirer	b. 1852	d. 1925
Adm.R.Yissachar Dov Rokeach I of Belz	b. 1854	d. 1926
Adm.R.Yisrael Hager of Vizhnitz	b. 1860	d. 1935
Adm.R.Sholom DovBer of Lubavitch	b. 1860	d. 1920
Adm.R.Avraham Mordechai of Gur	b. 1866	d. 1948
Adm.R.Chaim Elazar of Munkatch	b. 1871?	d. 1937
Adm.R.Ben Zion of Bobov	b. 1874	d. 1941
Adm.R.Aharon of Belz	b. 1880	d. 1957
Adm.R.Chaim Tzvi Teitelbaum of Sighet	b. 1880?	d. 1926
Adm.R.Yosef Yitzchak of Lubavitch	b. 1880	d. 1950
Adm.R.Chaim Meir Hager of Vizhnitz	b. 1881	d. 1972
Adm.R.Yoel(ish) of Satmar	b. 1888	d. 1979
Adm.R.Yisrael of Gur	b. 1894	d. 1977
Adm.R.Yaakov Yosef of Sqver	b. 1895?	d. 1968
Adm.R.Simcha Bunim of Gur	b. 1896	d. 1992
Adm.R.Menachem Mendel Schneersohn	b. 1902	d. 1994
Adm.R.Yekutiel Yehuda of Klausenberg	b. 1905	d. 1994
Adm.R.Shlomo of Bobov	b. 1908	d. 2000
Adm.R.Moshe of Sighet, Satmerer Rov	b. 1915	
Adm.R.Pinchos Menachem Alter of Gur	b. 1926	d. 1996
Adm.R.Naftali Halberstam of Bobov	b. 1931	
Adm.R.Yaakov Aryeh of Gur	b. 1933	

the founder of the movement of Chasidim — died on (Wednesday, the first day of) Shavu'ot. He had attracted thousands of followers (called CHASIDIM) — some of them secret, see 5494\1734, 5519\1759, 5543\ 1783 — to his 'new' (joyous) expression of JUDAISM (based in KABBALA), in which the 'quality' of spiritual dedication *(in the heart)* was considered as important as the 'quantity' of intellectual (Torah) information *(in the mind)*, and in which the ability to feel close *(love)* to the Creator became as important as the need to stand distant *(fear, respect)*. He also stressed the need to love all fellow Jews (AHAVAT YISRAEL), regardless of status and background.

A veritable literature of stories, tales, and legends has evolved about his miraculous healing of both bodies and souls, and about rescues and other wondrous accomplishments.

This personal charismatic centrality in the role of TZADIK, or REBBE, contributed to serious suspicions that this new movement was yet another group of Shabbetai Tzvi'niks (Shabbateans) (see 5437*1676*, 5518*1757*) (and the VA'AD ARBA ARATZOT threatened to make a CHEREM).

Another contributing factor to the suspicions about Chasidim was the 'new' emotional and expressionful style of Chasidim — in prayer and mitzvot, and in life in general — a style accompanied by the (spiritual) desire to be unobtrusive (and often secretive) in the fulfillment of good deeds. The latter style and conduct relegated much of the refinement of the movement beyond the eye of casual observation.

Chasidim became known (by many) as THE SECT (HaCat), particularly in the circles of the scholars, whose suspicions were amplified because of the Ba'al Shem Tov's PEOPLE ORIENTATION — even the unlearned could participate in the dedication of the heart, and were in fact encouraged (with the warm personal attention of AHAVAT YISRAEL) to do so — which stood in stark contrast to their own SUBJECT ORIENTATION (with an elitist emphasis on accumulated knowledge and intellectual skills). These suspicions (see 5532\1772), and their often harsh social consequences, increased the need and thus the incidence of secret followers of the new movement — a fact which probably, in turn, further increased the suspicion...

The Ba'al Shem Tov — who lived in Medzibuzh *(Miedzyborz, then Poland)* — had begun a mass re-orientation among the Jews of Poland and Eastern Europe, who had not recovered (economically or spiritually, see 5494\1734) from the decimation of the Chmielnitzki massacres (see 5408\1648), and from the confusion left in the wake of Shabbetai Tzvi (see 5426\1666, 5484\1724, 5518*1757*).

R.Dov Ber (see 5533*1772*), the Maggid of Mezeritsch *(Poland)* succeeded the Ba'al Shem Tov as the leader of the movement, although some of the other major disciples (see 5507\1747, 5524\1764) — which included R.Pinchas of Koretz *(Poland)*, R.Yechi'el Michel of Zlotchov *(Poland)*, and R.Yaakov Yosef of Polannoe *(Polonnoye, Volhynia, region in W.Poland)* (author of Toldot Yaakov Yosef, see 5541\1781) — had many followers (CHASIDIM) of their own.

All Jews were expelled from Courland *(region in S.W. Latvia)*.

5522 — 1761

Many Jews were killed in Mogilev-Podolski *(then Poland)*, and a number of Jews of Wojslawice *(Poland)* were killed in a BLOOD LIBEL supported by the Frankists (see 5519\1759).

5522 — 1762

The Jews of Emden *(Germany)* were attacked in ANTI-JEWISH RIOTS in **Sivan**.

5523 — 1763

Four Jews were killed in Kalisch *(Poland)* in a BLOOD LIBEL.

5524 — 1764

The VA'AD ARBA ARATZOT was discontinued.

The VA'AD ARBA ARATZOT *(see 5340\1580)* was dissolved by the government of Poland — which sought to end the Jewish autonomy — and devised another method of collecting Jewish taxes.

R.Yonatan Eybeshutz (see 5501\1741) died on the 21st **Elul,** and R.Yitzchak Horowitz was appointed rabbi in Hamburg (with the approval of R.Yaakov Emden). R.Yitzchak, known as 'Reb Itzikel MeHamburg', eventually managed to restore dignity to both sides in the Emden-Eybeshutz controversy (see 5510\1750).

R.Nachman of Horodenka *(Poland)* settled in Eretz Yisrael (see 5507\1747) together with some other disciples of the Ba'al Shem Tov.

5527 — 1767

Twenty Jews were killed when a fire destroyed the whole Jewish section of Lissa *(Leszno, Poland)*.

R.Malachi (ben Yaakov) HaKohen published Yad Malachi *(principles and methods of Talmud and Halacha study)*.

5528 — 1768

Despite Jewish resistance, the Haidamacks massacred thousands.

The Haidamacks (see 5496\1736) brutally killed many Jews in the Polish-Ukrainian towns of Fastov, Lysyanka, Zhabotin, Kanyev, Tetiyev, Korsun (see 5494\1734), and Balta (where some had come to seek refuge). Many fled to the fortified city of Uman *(then Poland)*, where on the 5th **Tammuz**, many Jews fought the attackers until they were overwhelmed. Thousands of Jews in Uman were massacred in the synagogues, which were subsequently burned together with the Torah scrolls which had been desecrated.

5529 — 1769

R.Netanel Weil of Prague — descendant of the Mahariv, and author of Korban Netanel *(commentary on the Rosh)* — died in Karlsruhe *(Germany)* where he was succeeded by his son as rabbi.

5530 — 1770

R.Yechi'el Hillel Altshuler completed and printed his father's commentaries on the T'NACH (Bible), Metzudat David and Metzudat Tzion *(see Illustrations, Text B, #6, #7)*.

R.Shneur Zalman (see 5532\1772, 5559\ *1798*) — a disciple of the Maggid of Mezeritsch, who, in 1767, had been appointed Maggid in his hometown of Liozhna *(then Poland-Lithuania)* — began writing an edition of the SHULCHAN ARUCH.

This undertaking — assigned to him by the Maggid of Mezeritsch, who treated him as one of his favored disciples (even though he was probably the youngest) — was based on the original, but included all important opinions on Halacha since the SHULCHAN ARUCH of R.Yosef Karo and the Ramo (see 5330\1570). It is written in one synthesized (descriptive) text, and is commonly called 'SHULCHAN ARUCH HaRav'.
800 Jews died in a plague in Zholkva *(Zolkiew, Poland)*.

5532 — 1772

At a public DEBATE — held in Shklov *(then Poland-Lithuania)*, on *"The Movement of Chasidim"* (see 5520\1760), and organized by their opponents (called *Mitnagdim*) — the Chasidim were represented by two disciples of the Maggid of Mezeritsch, R.Shneur Zalman (see 5530\1770), the Ba'al HaTanya VeShulchan Aruch, and R.Avraham of Kalisk, (who, some say, was a former disciple of the Vilna Gaon).
Although the Chasidim demonstrated that they were great scholars — and that they were not diverging from Halacha (as had the Shabbateans, to whom they had been compared, see 5520\ 1760) — the questioners concentrated on the issue of some excesses of R.Avraham's disciples (which included public levity in the disparaging of intellectual elitism, see 5520\1760).
The meeting did not deliver a peaceful resolution. A CHEREM *(excommunication)* against the Chasidim (see 5541\1781) — which included the signature of the Vilna Gaon — was proclaimed in **Nissan** by the BEIT DIN in Vilna. Letters (of the CHEREM) were circulated to many communities, which resulted in harsh persecutions of Chasidim. (The Chasidim were the subject of many CH'RAMIM *(excommunications)* in many locations, over an extended time, and they occasionally countered in kind.)
R.Shneur Zalman and R.Menachem Mendel of Vitebsk *(Poland-Lithuania)* — disciples of the Maggid of Mezeritsch who had many followers in the regions of Lithuania *(then Poland)* — later (unsuccessfully) attempted to meet the Vilna Gaon, to explain the direction of the new movement (he left town until they departed).
In 1772, Austria, Prussia *(Germany)*, and Russia all divided (partitioned) large sections of Polish territory and incorporated these sections into their own empires. The Austrian (Hapsburg, Holy Roman) Empire thus contained the largest Jewish population in Europe (see 5534\1774). The Russians freed Jacob Frank (see 5519\1759) from his prison, which was in the territory they had annexed.

5533 — *1772*

The Maggid of Mezeritsch died.

The Mezeritscher Maggid — R.Dov Ber, (the Rebbe R.Ber), the disciple and successor of the Ba'al Shem Tov (see 5520\1760), who, some say, was previously a disciple of the Pnei Yehoshua — died on the 19th **Kislev** 5533*1772*.
His major disciples included (see 5537\1777)
- his son R.Avraham,
- R.Aharon of Karlin *(then Poland-Lithuania)* — who had died half a year earlier (at age 35),
- R.Elimelech (see 5546\1786) of Lizensk *(Lezajsk, Poland)* and his brother,
- R.Zushya of Annopol *(Poland)*,
- R.Yisrael (the Maggid) of Kozhnitz *(Kosienice, Poland)* (see 5575*1814*),
- R.Levi Yitzchak (see 5570*1809*) of Berditchev *(Poland)*,
- R.Menachem Mendel of Horodok (see 5537\1777) and Vitebsk *(then Poland-Lithuania)*,
- R.Pinchas Horowitz of Frankfort (see 5542\1782) and his (older) brother,
- R.Shmuel Shmelke of Nikolsburg *(Mikulov, Moravia)*,
- R.Shlomo of Karlin (see 5552\1792),
- R.Nachum (see 5558*1797*) of Chernobyl *(then Poland)*, and
- R.Shneur Zalman (see 5559*1798*) of Liozhna and Lyady *(then Poland-Lithuania)*.

Most were leaders in their own towns and regions, where they developed their own followings.

5533 — 1773

R.Meir (ben Yosef) Te'omim died in Lvov *(Lemberg, then Austrian Poland)*, and his son — R.Yosef, author of the Pri Megadim *(on SHULCHAN ARUCH)* — came from Berlin to succeed him, until he left for Frankfort *an der Oder* some eight years later.
Some followers of Jacob Frank (see 5532\1772) converted (to Christianity) in Prossnitz *(Prostejov, Czech.)*.

5534 — 1774

All Jews were expelled from Hodonin *(Moravia)* by Maria Theresa — the Austro-Hungarian Empress (see 5505\1745), who was generally considered to be generous, kind and respectful of the rights of others (she had initiated laws (in 1771) to bring relief to the serfs) — six years before she died, after ruling for forty years. Her son — Joseph II, who succeeded her — was said to be more liberal (see 5542\1782), probably because his commitment to the Catholic Church was considerably less.

5536 — 1776

R.Yaakov Emden (see 5510\1750) (Yavetz - **Ya**akov **b**en **Tz**vi) — author of She'ilat Yavetz *(Sh'elot UTeshuvot)*, Siddur Yavetz *(with commentary)*, among other works — died on Rosh Chodesh **Iyar**.

Many Jewish people — who favored, and were loyal to the American Revolution — fled from New York during the British occupation of that city.

5537 — 1777

R.Menachem Mendel of Vitebsk *(Poland-Lithuania)* led a group of more than 300 Chasidim (including R.Avraham of Kalisk, see 5532\ 1772) to settle in Eretz Yisrael.

R.Shalom Shar'abi of Sana *(Yemen)* died. He was a rabbi and Rosh Yeshiva in Yerushalayim who was renowned for his knowledge and experience in Kabbala.

5538 — 1778

All Jews were expelled from Kitzingen *(Germany)*.

Living in the Year 1780

Sha'agat Aryeh (R.Aryeh Leib Gunzberg)	b.1695?,	d.1785.
Pnei Moshe (R.Moshe Margolis)	b.1710?,	d.1781.
Noda BiYehuda (R.Yechezk'el Landau)	b.1713,	d.1793.
R.Elimelech of Lizensk	b.1717?,	d.1786.
R.Zushya of Annopol	b.1718?,	d.1800.
Vilna Gaon	b.1720,	d.1797.
Chida (Azulai)	b.1724,	d.1806.
Pri Megadim (R.Yosef Te'omim)	b.1727?,	d.1792.
R.Levi Yitzchak of Berditchev	b.1740,	d.1810.
R.Shneur Zalman (Rav of Lyady)	b.1745,	d.1813.
Ketzot HaChoshen (R.Aryeh Leib Heller)	b.1745?,	d.1813.
Chozeh of Lublin	b.1745?,	d.1815.
Chayei Adam (R.Avraham Danziger)	b.1748,	d.1820.
R.Chaim Volozhiner	b.1749,	d.1821.
Yismach Moshe (R.Moshe Teitelbaum)	b.1759,	d.1841.
Chavat Da'at (R.Yakv.of Lissa/Netivot)	b.1759?,	d.1832.
R.Ephrayim Zalman Margolis	b.1760,	d.1828.
R.Akiva Eger	b.1761,	d.1837.
Chassam Sofer	b.1762,	d.1839.
R.Nachman of Bratslav	b.1772,	d.1811.

5540 — 1780

R.Elchanan (ben Shmuel) Ashkenazi — author of Sidrei Tahara *(on Yoreh De'a section of Shulchan Aruch)*, and rabbi in Shottland, part of Danzig *(Gdansk, Poland)* — died there in **Elul.**

5541 — 1781

R.Moshe (ben Shimon) Margolis — author of Pnei Moshe *(commentary on Talmud Yerushalmi, now printed in standard editions) (see Illustrations, Text F, #3)* — died in Brody *(then Austria)*, while traveling in search of the means to continue printing his work.

The Kalliver Rebbe — Adm.R.Yitzchak Aisik (Taub), a disciple of R.Shmelke of Nikolsburg and R.Elimelech of Lizensk — became rabbi in Kalliv *(Kallo, Hungary)*, where he lived for forty years.

A new cherem *(excommunication)* — which again included the signature of the Vilna Gaon — was proclaimed in Vilna against the Chasidim (see 5532\1772). As a result, the book Toldot Yaakov Yosef (see 5520\1760) was publicly burned. (It was the first book published by Chasidim, and a contemporary — Sephardi, hence probably objective — observer, the Chida, praised it). The cherem resulted in further persecutions of Chasidim, and some of the leaders had to leave their towns. ♦ R.Yechi'el Michel of Zlotchov left Brody *(then part of Austria)*, ♦ R.Shlomo left Karlin *(then Russia)*, and ♦ R.Levi Yitzchak of Berditchev left his position as rabbi in Pinsk *(Russia)*.

5542 — 1782

R.Natan Adler and 'Chassam Sofer' visited the Noda BiYehuda.

R.Natan (HaKohen) Adler left Frankfort, where he was a Rosh Yeshiva — to become rabbi in Boskowitz *(Moravia)* — after a controversy with the 'official' congregation, including R.Pinchas Horowitz (see 5543\1783), the rabbi there. The controversy surrounded the issue of his separate (private) congregation, in which he followed the Nussach *(liturgy)* of the Ari'zal — which R.Pinchas followed clandestinely — and other (practical) Kabbala oriented ritual. When he passed through Prague — with the 'Chassam Sofer' (see 5566\1806), who was one of his group of disciples (which also included R.Yitzchak (Ai)Sekel Wormser, later known as the Ba'al Shem of Michelstadt) — he was well

received by the Noda BiYehuda.
R.Natan returned to Frankfort a few years later, but the CHEREM *(excommunication)* against him was not removed until **Elul** 5560\1800, just weeks before he died.
Some restrictions on Jews were abolished in (expanded) Austria (see 5532\1772, 5534\1774). However, they were directed to open German-language schools for their children — or to send them to general schools — and they were forbidden to use HEBREW or YIDDISH in business and in communal records (see 5547\1787).
These measures — that increased the assimilation (see 5547\1787) of Austrian Jews, as some say they were designed to do, (see 5580\1820) — were opposed by the Noda BiYehuda, rabbi of Prague (see 5514\1754) (which was then part of the Austrio-Hungarian Empire).

5543 — 1783

Moshe Mendelssohn — Moses of Dessau (previously a disciple of the Korban HaEida, R.David Frankel) — became a rationalist philosopher of the ENLIGHTENMENT. He believed in Jewish integration into the surrounding society — opposing, for example, the use of YIDDISH *(see 5542\1782)*; insisting on the use of the GERMAN language; and supporting an increased emphasis on secular studies as a necessary preparation for Jews being recognized as equal (SOCIAL EMANCIPATION, see 5547\1787).
This ideology became the foundation of the Haskala movement (the JEWISH-ENLIGHTENMENT).
Mendelssohn — who had previously been criticized by R.Yaakov Emden for some advice he had given a Jewish community — published a GERMAN translation and commentary (Bi'ur) on the Bible in 1783. It was severely criticized by the Noda BiYehuda and R.Pinchas Horowitz — the rabbi of Frankfort — author of Sefer Hafla'a *(Halacha-Pilpul)*, and a disciple (some say secret) of the Maggid of Mezeritsch (see 5533*1772*). (The Bi'ur was later tacitly approved by the scholars of Vilna.)
Although it appears that Mendelssohn's personal lifestyle conformed to Halacha — and he certainly frowned on converting to Christianity to gain the social acceptance he promoted — four of his six children did convert. At least one of the remaining Jewish grandchildren (Abraham) converted his whole family (in 1816), including his seven year old son Felix — later regarded by many as one of the most prolific and gifted composers (although dying at age 38) — who chose to retain the name Mendelssohn and not use the German-sounding name the family had adopted (see 5547\1787).
The Haskala rapidly spread its ideology, particularly by opening schools for Jewish children — such a school already being in existence in Berlin since 1778.

5545 — 1785

The 'Sha'agas Aryeh', R.Aryeh Leib (ben Asher) Gunzberg — author of Sha'agat Aryeh *(SH'ELOT UTESHUVOT)* and other works — died in Metz *(N.E. France)*, where he was rabbi for approximately twenty years.

5546 — 1786

R.Elimelech of Lizensk died.

R.Elimelech of Lizensk *(Lezajsk, Poland)* — author of No'am Elimelech, who had previously been one of the 'itinerant Tzadikim' (see 5494\1734) — was the most influential disciple of the Maggid of Mezeritsch in Galicia *(region of S.E.Poland, annexed by Austria)*. His many disciples continued to gain followers (CHASIDIM) in the region after he died on the 21st **Adar**.

5547 — 1787

The Constitution of the (newly independent) United States of America granted Jews full equality together with other citizens (SOCIAL EMANCIPATION). This concept spread, with time, to other countries *(see 5542\1782, 5549\1789, 5550\1790, 5570\1810, 5629\1869)*, affording the opportunity for all to (integrate, and then) assimilate, into the society around them (see 5570\1810). Inasmuch as society was also changing (see 5500\1740) — and many people (non-Jews) were relaxing the intensity of (and even leaving) their religious beliefs and practices (becoming non-religious) — a new alternative emerged for Jews to assimilate with non-Jews, without having to accept (and convert to) their religion.
All Jews of Austria were forced *(see 5542\1782)* to choose German-sounding names, from a prepared list.

5548 — 1788

R.Aryeh Leib HaKohen Heller — respected author of Ketzot HaChoshen and Avnei Millu'im *(commentaries on the Choshen Mishpat and Even HaEzer sections of SHULCHAN ARUCH)* (see *ILLUSTRATIONS, TEXT M, #9*), as well as other works — became rabbi in Stry *(Stryj, then Poland)*.

5549 — 1789

Jews had slowly returned to France *(see 5155\1394)*, particularly to Alsace *(region between France and Germany)*. The Declaration of the Rights of Man — in 1789, at the beginning of the ten year French Revolution — implied that Jews were to be equal to all citizens *(see 5547\1787)*. Equality (SOCIAL EMANCIPATION) was fully granted two years later (see 5553\1793).

5550 — 1790

A Jew was killed in Grodno *(Hurodno, Lithuania)* in a BLOOD LIBEL.
The Jews of Warsaw were attacked by ANTI-JEWISH RIOTERS in **Sivan**.
The Jews of Florence *(Italy)* were attacked by mobs who were angry that the Jews had been granted some CIVIL RIGHTS (see 5547\1787).

5551 — 1791

The Pale of Settlement was established in Russia.

Russia *(under Catherine the Great)* restricted the residence of the Jews — in its newly annexed territories (see 5532\1772) — to an area later known as the Pale of Settlement *(see 5613\1853, 5677\1917)*. This area *(see map page 319)* covered regions of former Poland — where dense Jewish population already existed — as well as the steppes of southern Russia, which they sought to populate *(see 5564\1804)*. She later relieved the Karaites of the JEWS TAX although decrees still refered to them as "Jews" (see 5587\1827).

5552 — 1792

R.Shlomo of Karlin — successor of R.Aharon (see 5533*1772*) — was killed during prayers on the 22nd **Tammuz**, in the Polish rebellion *(see 5554\1794)*. He was succeeded by his disciple, R.Asher (son of R.Aharon), who settled in Stolin *(Russia, near Karlin)*.

5553 — *1792*

50 Jews of Ofran *(Ifran, Morocco)* chose to be burned alive on the 17th **Tishrei** rather than convert to Islam. The rest of the Jews left the city.

5553 — 1793

Jews suffered in Reign of Terror of French Revolution.

During the 'Reign of Terror' — a one-year period of the ten year French Revolution, in which many thousands of people were guillotined — a number of Jews were among the 200,000 people imprisoned. Although equality had been granted to Jews in France (see 5549\ 1789), many synagogues were closed; all Jewish books in Strasbourg were confiscated to be burned; and the YESHIVA in Metz *(N.E. France)* was closed (see 5501\1741, 5545\1785).

5554 — 1794

When the Poles — under the leadership of Kosciuszko, a Polish commander who had fought against the British in the American Revolution — rebelled against the occupying Russian and (German) Prussian forces (see 5532\1772), many Jews were killed (see 5552\1792, 5555\1795). Yosef Shmuel Zbitkower, a wealthy government contractor, paid large sums of money (through his excellent political connections) to rescue Jews from the fighting.

5555 — 1795

Jews were killed by RIOTERS in Vilna following the Polish rebellion (see 5554\1794), and many Jews were killed in Warsaw in a similar incident.

5558 — *1797*

The Vilna Gaon died.

The Vilna Gaon, the "Gra" (for **G**aon **R**.**E**liyahu) — who had become a living legend of scholarship in Talmud (and KABBALA) — died on the 19th **Tishrei** 5558*1797* *(Chol HaMo'ed Sukkot)*. Many of his teachings and annotations were published by his disciples after his death from the notes they had recorded *(see Illustrations, TextE, #7, J K L, #6)*.
R.Nachum of Chernobyl *(Ukraine, then Russia)* died on the 11th **Cheshvan** 5558*1797*, and he was succeeded as ADMUR (REBBE, 'TZADIK') by his twenty-eight-year-old son, R.Mordechai (R.Mottel) (see 5577\1837).

5558 — 1798

When Napoleon invaded Italy, conditions for the Jews (see 5315\1555) generally improved in the occupied areas, although the Jews of Ancona *(Italy)* were attacked by RIOTERS, as were the Jews of Rome (before the French occupation), and (later) the Jews of Siena *(Italy)*. After Napoleon's army withdrew (in success), the Jews of Pesaro *(Italy)* were attacked, many were killed, and the two synagogues were plundered. The Jews of Senigallia *(Italy)* were (later) also attacked.

5559 ≈ *1798*

The Ba'al HaTanya was released from his first imprisonment.

After the death of the Vilna Gaon — who had reaffirmed his opposition to Chasidim one year before his death see 5558*1797* — the *Mitnagdim (opponents of Chasidim)* in Lithuania denounced (to the Russian government) the Rav (of Lyady, the Ba'al HaTanya VeShulchan Aruch), whose Tanya *(major, intellectually presented, treatise on the teachings of the Ba'al Shem Tov)* had recently been published. He was arrested, together with twenty-two other Chasidim — who were directly released — including Adm.R.Asher of Stolin (see 5552\\1792) and Adm.R.Mordechai of Lechevitch, both from Russia. The Rav was cleared of the charges (including treason, for sending money to the Turkish *(Ottoman)* dominated Eretz Yisrael), and was released from prison (after fifty-three days) on the 19th **Kislev** 5559*1798* (see 5533*1772*). He subsequently continued to expound his particular intellectually oriented (Chabad) style of CHASIDUT.

5559 ≈ 1799

Napoleon led an army expedition through Eretz Yisrael.

Napoleon had led a successful army expedition to Egypt, and from there he moved northeastward, through Eretz Yisrael (see 5571\\ *1810*) until he reached Acco *(Acre)* in the north, where he was halted, and he subsequently retreated to Egypt in the south. It was reported (in Europe) that Napoleon had issued a proclamation in Eretz Yisrael, promising that the Jews would be returned to their country.

5561 ≈ *1800*

The Rav (of Lyady) (see 5559*1798*) was requested to report to the Russian capital — exactly two years after his first arrest — on renewed charges, attributable to further denunciations by *Mitnagdim.*

Living in the Year 1800

Name	Born	Died
R.Zushya of Annopol	b.1718?,	d.1800.
Chida (Azulai)	b.1724,	d.1806.
R.Levi Yitzchak of Berditchev	b.1740,	d.1810.
R.Shneur Zalman (Rav of Lyady)	b.1745,	d.1813.
Ketzot HaChoshen (R.Aryeh Leib Heller)	b.1745?,	d.1813.
Chozeh of Lublin	b.1745?,	d.1815.
Chayei Adam (R.Avraham Danziger)	b.1748,	d.1820.
R.Chaim Volozhiner	b.1749,	d.1821.
Yismach Moshe (R.Moshe Teitelbaum)	b.1759,	d.1841.
Chavat Da'at (R.Yakv.of Lissa/Netivot)	b.1759?,	d.1832.
R.Ephrayim Zalman Margolis	b.1760,	d.1828.
R.Akiva Eger	b.1761,	d.1837.
Chassam Sofer	b.1762,	d.1839.
R.Nachman of Bratslav	b.1772,	d.1811.
Tiferet Yisrael (R.Yisrael Lipshutz)	b.1782,	d.1860.
Bnei Yissachar (R.Tzvi Elmlch.of Dynov)	b.1783?,	d.1841.
R.Mendel of Kotzk	b.1787,	d.1859.
Tzemach Tzedek (of Lubavitch)	b.1789,	d.1866.
Divrei Chaim (of Tzanz)	b.1793,	d.1876.
R.Yisrael of Ruzhin	b.1797,	d.1850.
Chidushei HaRim (of Gur)	b.1799,	d.1866.
Minchat Chinuch (R.Yosef Babad)	b.1800?,	d.1874.

He was released from this second imprisonment, but was required to remain in the capital (outside of the Pale of Settlement) until a further investigation was concluded. Subsequently — in what was the second document signed by the young Czar Alexander I (after the assassination of his father, Czar Paul I, on 28th **Adar** 5561\\1801) — he was granted total freedom, after which he decided to settle in Lyady *(then Russia)*.

5561 ≈ 1801

128 Jews were killed in ANTI-JEWISH RIOTS in Bucharest, after a BLOOD LIBEL.

5564 ≈ 1804

The Jews of Russia were prohibited from living in the villages — by an edict which, among other things, also prohibited them from selling alcohol to the peasants — this order amounting to a major expulsion, because of the vast numbers living in the numerous SHTETLACH *(villages)*. However, this was not fully enforced, partly because of problems with resettlement (some of which was to be in the steppes, see 5551\\1791).

Expulsions from the SHTETLACH *(villages)* were resumed later (see 5582\1822, 5642\1882).

5565 — *1804*

The Maggid of Dubno — R.Yaakov Krantz, who was famous for his MESHALIM *(parables and metaphors)* — died on the 17th **Tevet** 5565\ *1804*.

5565 — 1805

Naftali Busnach — an extremely wealthy (generous and pious) Jewish statesman (who unofficially controlled the Algerian government) — was assassinated in Algiers by dissatisfied Turkish soldiers (of the Ottoman Empire.) The Jewish community was attacked, and 200 to 500 Jews were killed in the massacre. Naftali was succeeded as head of the Jewish community by his relative and business partner, David Bakri (see 5571\1811).

5566 — 1806

The Chida (R.Chaim Yosef David Azulai) died.

The Chida — R.**Ch**aim **Y**osef **D**avid **A**zulai, author of Machazik Bracha, Birkei Yosef *(Halacha)* and Shem HaGedolim *(biographic-bibliography)* — died on the 11th **Adar** in Livorno *(Leghorn, Italy)*, where he had lived for the last eight years of his life (after he had left Eretz Yisrael, where he was born).

The 'Chassam Sofer' became rabbi in Pressburg.

The 'Chassam Sofer' — R.Moshe Sofer, a disciple of R.Natan Adler and R.Pinchas Horowitz (see 5542\1782) (and later, with his second marriage, a son-in-law of R.Akiva Eger) — became the rabbi of Pressburg *(later Bratislava, Slovakia)*, which was then the most important community in Hungary. He established a famous YESHIVA there, became the leading rabbi in the effort to stop the movement of reforms (see 5570\1810), and he wrote many SH'ELOT UTESHUVOT.

5567 — 1807

Napoleon convened an assembly of Jews — many of whom were rabbis — wanting them to approve certain 'religious' regulations, which a previous assembly of laymen had approved. This assembly — which was called the 'French Sanhedrin' — met in the month of **Adar**, and approved a number of the 'regulations', which were designed to blur the religious distinction between Jews and non-Jews in a freer (socially emancipated) society.

Many Jews were killed during the British bombardment of Copenhagen in the month of **Av**.

The Machatzit HaShekel *(commentary on Orach Chayim section of SHULCHAN ARUCH, now printed in standard editions) (see ILLUSTRATIONS, TEXT J, #7)* was published, and (some say) the author — R.Shmuel (ben Natan) HaLevi Kelin (of Kolin, *(Bohemia)*) — died in the same year.

5568 — 1808

The Yismach Moshe — Adm.R.Moshe Teitelbaum of Uhel, a disciple of the Chozeh of Lublin, and author of Yismach Moshe *(commentary on Bible)* and Heshiv Moshe *(SH'ELOT UTESHUVOT)* — became rabbi (and REBBE, ADMUR) in Uhel *(Ujhely — Satoraljaujhely — N.E. Hungary)*.

5569 — 1809

The Chavat Da'at — R.Yaakov (Lorberbaum of) Lissa, a disciple of his relative the Pri Megadim (who raised him, because his father died before he was born) — became rabbi in Lissa *(Leszno, then Prussian Poland)* (see 5582\1822). His work Chavat Da'at *(on the Yoreh De'a section of SHULCHAN ARUCH)* had previously been published anonymously (gaining him a great reputation). He later wrote Netivot HaMishpat *(commentary on the Choshen Mishpat section of SHULCHAN ARUCH) (see ILLUSTRATIONS, TEXT M, #10)*, among other works.

R.Menachem Mendel of Shklov — a disciple of the Vilna Gaon, who had been instrumental in publishing his works (see 5558\ *1797*) — arrived in Tzfat *(Safed)* to settle together with a group of (some say 70) people. R.Yisrael of Shklov, another disciple of the Vilna Gaon, also emigrated to Eretz Yisrael, where he wrote Pe'at HaShulchan *(Halacha of Eretz Yisrael)*.

5570 — *1809*

R.Levi Yitzchak of Berditchev died.

R.Levi Yitzchak of Berditchev (see 5533\ *1772*, 5541\1781) — author of Kedushat Levi and a disciple of the Maggid of Mezeritsch with a strong personal following — died on the 25th **Tishrei** 5570\ *1809*. (Some say he had studied with the Pri Megadim earlier in his life.) He was famous for his ability to only see the good in his fellow Jews, (and to intercede on their behalf).

R.Avraham of Kalisk (see 5537\1777) — another disciple of the Maggid — died on the 4th **Shvat**.

5570 1810

R.Avraham Danziger — a disciple of the Noda BiYehuda, who was an (honorary) DAYAN in Vilna — published his work Chayei Adam *(a clear and simple (layman's) presentation of the laws in the Orach Chayim section of the SHULCHAN ARUCH)*. He later wrote other similar works.
After Napoleon gained control of much of (western) Germany, and equal rights (see 5549\1789) were granted to the Jews (SOCIAL EMANCIPATION), the movement of REFORM in JUDAISM was founded. Initially, laymen instituted changes in the prayer services — to reflect the general society, in which Jews could now freely mix. Later, suitably secular-oriented scholars were attracted to function as leaders of these transformed congregations (see 5578*1817*). Many congregations split when reforms were introduced (see 5614\1854).
The first introduction of an organ into synagogue services — probably the most controversial of the REFORM changes — was made by Israel Jacobson in 1810. He had previously (in 1801) founded (and supported) a school, in Seesen *(W.Germany)*, that *emphasized* modern and vocational subjects, and then he conducted an inaugural service in part of the school — which by then also had some non-Jewish children. He arrived — to conduct the service of hymns sung in GERMAN, and accompanied by the organ — dressed in the robes of a Protestant *(Christian)* clergyman. (Most of Jacobson's own ten children were eventually baptized.)

5571 *1810*

R.Nachman of Bratslav died.

R.Nachman of Bratslav *(then Russia)* — a great-grandson of the Ba'al Shem Tov, grandson of R.Nachman of Horodenka, and author of Likutei MoHoran — died on the 18th **Tishrei** (during Sukkot) 5571*1810*. He had visited Eretz Yisrael in 1798 (and spent Rosh HaShana in the newly rebuilt village of Haifa), but left when Napoleon invaded the country (see 5559\1799), and later he became involved in controversies with his peers over some of his teachings. His followers (CHASIDIM) are unique in that they have never appointed a successor.

5571 1811

David Bakri (see 5565\1805) was beheaded by the government of Algeria (see 5575\1815). He was replaced — as head of the Jewish community — by David Duran (of a rival family, see 5575\1815), who was also killed in the same year. Joseph Bakri (father of David) became head of the community.

5572 *1811*

R.Aryeh Leib — 'Der Shpoler Zeideh', who was considered a disciple of the Ba'al Shem Tov — had a strong following among the common people (see 5520\1760) because of his extreme warmth and emotional piety. He died on the 6th **Tishrei** 5572*1811* (at the age of 85).
R.Baruch of Medzibuzh *(Miedzyborz, then Russia)* — a grandson of the Ba'al Shem Tov who had thousands of followers, and considered himself the rightful heir of (all) Chasidic leadership — died on the 18th **Kislev**.

5572 1812

The Jews were attacked, and several synagogues were burned, by Greek revolutionaries (see 5581\1821), in Galati *(Rumania)*.

5573 *1812*

Napoleon's conquest of Eastern Europe was seen by many Jews as fulfillment of the prophecies of wars before the arrival of Mashiach *(Messiah)*, particularly in light of statements he reportedly had made in Eretz Yisrael (see 5559\1799). R.Mendel of Rymanov felt that the conquests would be beneficial for the Jews, but others — including the Maggid of Kozhnitz, and Adm.R.Naftali of Ropshytz, a disciple of R.Mendel — felt that this would have negative effects on the Jews of Poland and Russia.
The Rav of Lyady (see 5561*1800*), R.Shneur Zalman, had strong convictions that a victory for Napoleon would be detrimental for the Jews, and he even rendered assistance to the Russian war effort. When Napoleon's army advanced towards Lyady *(Russia)*, he (hastily) left the town, and spent five months journeying (even after Napoleon's defeat). He died — on the 24th **Tevet** 5573*1812*, while in a small village — and was succeeded by his son, Adm.R.Dov Ber, who settled in Lubavitch *(Russia)*.

5574 1814

R.Akiva Eger became rabbi in Posen.

R.Akiva Eger — author of SH'ELOT UTESHUVOT, Chidushim, and many other works — became rabbi in Posen *(Poznan, then Prussian Poland)*, despite strong opposition from the MASKILIM (see 5581\1821).

5575 1814

The Kozhnitzer Maggid, and the Yehudi of Pershisskha, died.

R.Yisrael — the Maggid of Kozhnitz *(Kosienice, Austrian Galicia)*, a disciple of the Maggid of Mezeritsch, R.Shmelke of Nikolsburg and R.Elimelech of Lizensk — was among those who brought the teaching of the Ba'al Shem Tov to Poland. He was author of a number of works on Talmud, Halacha, and KABBALA. He died on the 14th **Tishrei** (Erev Sukkot) 5575\ *1814* (when he was, some say, over 80 years old).

Adm.R.Yaakov Yitzchak of Pershisskha *(Prsyzucha, Austrian Galicia)* — a leading disciple of the Chozeh of Lublin — was called HaYehudi HaKadosh *(the Holy Jew)*, because (some say that) the other disciples of the Chozeh did not want to call him by name — inasmuch as his first names were identical with those of the Chozeh — so they gave him an appropriate pseudonym.

Although he died ten months before the Chozeh — on the 19th **Tishrei** (during Chol HaMo'ed Sukkot) before he was 49 — he had already established his own following, to a variation of the (current Polish-Galician) style of Chasidim. He placed a different emphasis on the role of the REBBE (ADMUR, 'TZADIK') — as being more of a spiritual guide and inspiration for honest introspective devotion in prayer and the study of Torah, rather than being a 'miracle worker' — and he demanded higher standards — in Torah study, and in prayer — from his followers (CHASIDIM). This difference of style caused friction between him and other disciples of the Chozeh, and eventually with the Chozeh himself. He was succeeded (primarily) by his leading disciple Adm.R.Simcha Bunim of Pershisskha.

5575 1815

The Chozeh of Lublin, and R.Mendel of Rymanov, died.

Adm.R.(Menachem) Mendel of Rymanov *(Austrian Galicia)* — a disciple of R.Elimelech of Lizensk — died on the 19th **Iyar**.

The Chozeh of Lublin — R.Yaakov Yitzchak Horowitz, a follower (CHASID) of the Maggid of Mezeritsch, and a disciple of R.Elimelech of Lizensk — died on Tisha B'Av. He was the leading REBBE (ADMUR, 'TZADIK') in Poland and Galicia *(region of S.E.Poland, annexed by Austria)*, and many of his disciples were the leading ADMURIM in these regions. He was called the Chozeh *(seer)* by his followers (after his death, according to some) because of his reputation for predicting personalities and events.

R.Yitzchak Albuker, the rabbi of Algiers, was killed with seven other Jewish leaders, when internal Jewish (family) rivalries (see 5571\1811) spilled out into the wider community.

5578 1817

The first congregation initially founded on a REFORM basis in Germany (see 5570\1810) was opened in Hamburg, in the month of **Tishrei** 5578\ *1817* (despite the vehement opposition of R.Mordechai Benet); and a prayer book — with significant ideological changes — was printed there a year later.

5579 1819

Anti-Jewish (Hep! Hep!) riots spread throughout Germany.

An ANTI-JEWISH RIOT broke out in Wurtzburg *(Germany)* with the attacking mobs using the cry of "Hep! Hep!", and similar RIOTS quickly spread to many towns. (The MASKILIM and the REFORMERS refrained from reporting — in their periodicals — details on these destructive incidents, lest they

Living in the Year 1820

Chayei Adam (R.Avraham Danziger)	b.1748,	d.1820.
R.Chaim Volozhiner	b.1749,	d.1821.
Yismach Moshe (R.Moshe Teitelbaum)	b.1759,	d.1841.
Chavat Da'at (R.Yakv.of Lissa/Netivot)	b.1759?,	d.1832.
R.Ephrayim Zalman Margolis	b.1760,	d.1828.
R.Akiva Eger	b.1761,	d.1837.
Chassam Sofer	b.1762,	d.1839.
Tiferet Yisrael (R.Yisrael Lipshutz)	b.1782,	d.1860.
Bnei Yissachar (R.Tzvi Elmlch.of Dynov)	b.1783?,	d.1841.
R.Mendel of Kotzk	b.1787,	d.1859.
Tzemach Tzedek (of Lubavitch)	b.1789,	d.1866.
Divrei Chaim (of Tzanz)	b.1793,	d.1876.
R.Yisrael of Ruzhin	b.1797,	d.1850.
Chidushei HaRim (of Gur)	b.1799,	d.1866.
Minchat Chinuch (R.Yosef Babad)	b.1800?,	d.1874.
Kitzur Shulchan Aruch (R.Shl.Ganzfried)	b.1804,	d.1886.
R.Shimshon Raphael Hirsch	b.1808,	d.1888.
Malbim (R.Meir Leib[ush])	b.1808?,	d.1879.
R.Yisrael Salanter	b.1810,	d.1883.
Divrei Yechezk'el (of Shinev)	b.1811?,	d.1899.
Pitchei Teshuva (R.Avraham Tzvi Hirsch)	b.1813,	d.1868.

have a negative influence on the attitude of Jews to their non-Jewish neighbors.)

5580 ≈ 1820

R.Shlomo Kluger — a disciple of the Maggid of Dubno — became rabbi in Brody *(then part of Austria)*, where he stayed for 50 years until his death.
A law was issued in Austria (in 1820) that required all rabbis to study philosophy, preach in the local language, and also required Jewish children to attend Christian schools (see 5542\1782). These laws were instituted after the lobbying by one of the MASKILIM (see 5605*1844*) — who had also proposed that beards and traditional Jewish dress be outlawed, and many traditional Jewish writings (including the Talmud) be banned and censored.

5581 ≈ 1821

R.Chaim Volozhiner — a disciple of the Vilna Gaon, and (some say) of the Sha'agat Aryeh, and author of Nefesh HaChayim *(MUSSAR)* — died in **Sivan**. He was the founder of the famous YESHIVA of Volozhin *(Lithuania)* which set a precedent and created a model now almost universally followed — in that the YESHIVA provided its own facilities as well as all the needs (food and board) of its students — and whose graduates were viewed as the elite.
R.Shlomo Zalman Lifshitz — author of Chemdat Shlomo *(SH'ELOT UTESHUVOT)* — became rabbi of Warsaw. R.Akiva Eger had once visited him there at the same time as the Chavat Da'at was visiting, with the Chidushei HaRim also present. R.Shlomo had previously declined to return (as rabbi) to his hometown of Posen *(Poznan, Prussian Poland)*, because he wanted to protect his children from the influence of the Haskala which was prevalent there (see 5574\1814, and 5496\1736).
Hundreds of Jews were killed in Jassy *(Moldavia, Rumania)* (see 5587\1827) — by Greek volunteers in a revolt against the Turkish *(Ottoman)* Empire (see 5582\1822 and 5572\1812) — and (some say) as many as 5,000 Jews were killed in Greece itself during the revolt.
The Jews were attacked in ANTI-JEWISH RIOTS in Odessa *(Russia)*.

5582 ≈ 1822

The Chavat Da'at left his position as rabbi in Lissa *(Leszno, then Prussian Poland)*, because of his rift with a large part of the community, due to his strong stand against the reformers (see 5570\1810). He declined to become rabbi in any community until eight years later, when he became rabbi in Stry *(Stryj, Austrian Poland)*.
The expulsion of Jews from Russian SHTETLACH *(villages)* (see 5564\1804, 5585\ 1825), was resumed.
60 Jews were killed in Bucharest on Purim by Turkish soldiers suppressing the Greek revolution (see 5581\1821).
The Jewish section of Schaffa *(Safov, Moravia)* was destroyed by a fire, on the 24th **Sivan**.

5583 ≈ 1823

Adm.R.Klonymos Kalman of Cracow died on the 1st **Tammuz**. He was a disciple of R.Elimelech of Lizensk, and of the Chozeh of Lublin, author of Ma'or VaShemesh *(commentary (CHASIDUT) on CHUMASH (Bible))*, and had attracted many followers (CHASIDIM) in Cracow and the region of S.W.Galicia *(then Austria)*.

5584 ≈ 1824

A group of Jews seceded from the congregation in Charleston *(S.Carolina, U.S.A.)*, when the reforms they wanted to introduce (see 5570\1810) were not accepted. They established the first REFORM group (later congregation) in the U.S.A.

5585 ≈ 1825

All Jews were expelled from the SHTETLACH *(villages)* around Mogilev and Vitebsk *(Russia)*, and removed to the cities (see 5582\1822).
When the order for expulsion (from the villages) was received, the Apta Rav — Adm.R.Avraham Yehoshua Heschel of Opatow *(Austrian Galicia)*, a disciple of R.Elimelech of Lizensk — had declared a fast day.
He died on the 5th of **Nissan**, in Medzibuzh *(Miedzyborz, then Russia)* — where he had lived for his last years, during which time he was regarded as the 'elder statesman' of Polish-Galician Chasidim, being the last of R.Elimelech's leading disciples — and he is remembered by the (sole) epitaph (some say) he requested: "Oheiv Yisrael".
Adm.R.Dov Ber of Lubavitch visited R.Akiva Eger when passing through Posen (see 5574\1814).

5587 ≈ 1827

Adm.R.Naftali Tzvi of Ropshytz *(Ropczyce, Austrian Galicia)* — a disciple of R.Elimelech of Lizensk, and (later) of the Chozeh of Lublin, the Maggid of Kozhnitz, and of Adm.R.Mendel of Rymanov (see 5575\1815) — died on the 11th **Iyar**.

Adm.R.Meir of Apta *(Opatow, Austrian Galicia)* — a leading disciple of the Chozeh of Lublin — died on the 25th **Tammuz**.

Many Jews were killed by a fire in the Jewish section of Jassy *(Moldavia)* (see 5581\1821).

Moshe Montefiore (later Sir Moses) — who was the brother-in-law (and stockbroker) of Nathan Mayer Rothschild (son of the original Rothschild *(for his "red shield")* Mayer Anschel *(see 5596\1836)*) — had retired from business at age forty. He then visited Eretz Yisrael for the first time, and recommitted himself to Jewish religious (Halacha) observance (later he would take a shochet *(ritual meat slaughterer)* with him on all his travels). He commanded respect in many circles — being a tall man, who lived for over 100 years — and was a great SHTADLAN *(advocate and negotiator for Jewish causes) (see 5600\1840, 5606\1846, 5618\1858, 5624\1864, 5627\1867)*. He supported Jewish scholars, and the Jews of Eretz Yisrael — which he visited 7 times — and was a major force in confining the spread of REFORM in England.

Isaac (Adolphe) Cremieux — an assimilated Jew who rose to high positions in the French government, and was an active advocate and negotiator for Jewish causes — was instrumental in the abolition of the humiliating OATH MORE JUDAICO, which Jews in Europe had often been required to take (in various forms) for many centuries.

Adm.R.Simcha Bunim of Pershisskha *(Prsyzucha, Austrian Galicia)* — who (some say) had previously studied under R.Mordechai Benet — was a disciple of the Chozeh of Lublin, and the Yehudi of Pershisskha whom he succeeded. He continued to develop the Pershisskha style (see 5575*1814*), and his followers included many outstanding scholars. He died on the 12th **Elul,** and was succeeded (primarily) by Adm.R.Mendel of Kotzk *(Austrian Galicia)*.

Russia began conscripting Jewish children into the army.

Czar Nicholas I (of Russia) issued a decree (during **Elul**), that Jewish males between the ages of 12 and 25 were to be drafted into military service. (In the same year Karaites (see 5551\ 1791, 5596\1836) from Crimea were exempted from the military draft.) Local communal leaders were held personally responsible for delivering the inflated quotas of conscripts, and because there were virtually no volunteers for this military service, CHAPPERS *(snatchers, kidnappers)* grabbed children as young as 8-9 (mostly from the poor).

Children of under 18 years old — who were 'trained' in the *cantonments (barracks that had been established for children of the military)*, hence the name CANTONISTS — came under strong pressure (including torture) to convert to Christianity. When they turned 18, they were required to serve 25 years in the army. It is estimated that 30-100,000 CANTONISTS were 'drafted' under this decree — in force until 1856 (see 5613\1853) — and there were many stories of bravery, but (some say) that at least half eventually succumbed to this FORCED BAPTISM (see 5588*1827*).

5588 — *1827*

Adm.R.Dov Ber of Lubavitch *(Russia)* — author of many works (of CHASIDUT), who was denounced to the (Russian) government, and detained for questioning — was totally exonerated on the 10th **Kislev** 5587*1826*. Exactly one year less a day later — on the 9th **Kislev** (his birthday), in 5588*1827* — he died. He was succeeded (eighteen months later) by his son-in-law, the Tzemach Tzedek, Adm.R.Menachem Mendel, a grandson of the Rav (of Lyady) — who had raised him from the age of two (when his mother died) — and he was his close disciple. Thus, at the age of 38, he was a direct recipient of the transmission of teachings *(an important ingredient in studies relating to KABBALA (see 5050\1290, also 5520\1760, and 5490\1730)* from (the inner circle of) the Maggid of Mezeritsch (see 5530\1770), which was unique at this stage (see **Nissan** 5585\1825).

He organized a clandestine group of his followers (CHASIDIM) at once, to combat the CANTONIST conscription law (see 5587\1827). They assisted communities to negotiate lower quotas; they paid (illegal) ransoms for conscripted children; and they sent (special) people to comfort the children at assembly points, and to encourage them to be loyal to JUDAISM. (Some of the organizers were later imprisoned for these efforts.)

He also organized visiting rabbis for the new agricultural colonies (see 5564\1804), and later bought land and negotiated government assistance to help resettle Jews on the land (see 5585\1825).

5588 — 1828

R.Ephrayim Zalman Margolis died. He was author of Beit Ephrayim *(SH'ELOT UTESHUVOT)*, Yad Ephrayim *(on SHULCHAN ARUCH)*, and Matteh Ephrayim *(Halacha)*, among other works, who had supported himself with a business in Brody *(then Austria)*. He had edited the work of his brother, R.Chaim Mordechai, called the Darkei Teshuva *(on Orach Chayim section of SHULCHAN ARUCH, collection of additional (updated) Halacha notes,(see 5616\1856).)*

5590 — *1829*

All Jews had been ordered to leave (expelled from) Kiev *(then Russia)*, and later from the Russian port cities of Nikolayev and Sevastopol, in **Cheshvan** 5590*1829*, although none of these expulsion orders were immediately enforced.

5590 — 1830

The Divrei Chaim — Adm.R.Chaim Halberstam, a disciple of Adm.R.Naftali Tzvi of Ropshytz and Adm.R.Tzvi Hirsch of Zydachov *(Austrian Galicia)*, and son-in-law of R.Baruch Frankel (author of Baruch Ta'am) — was appointed rabbi of Tzanz *(Nowy Sacz, Austrian Galicia)*, where he became REBBE (ADMUR, 'TZADIK'), and attracted many followers (CHASIDIM).
Adherents to the REFORM movement gained control of the Jewish communal administration in Fiyorda *(Fuerth, Germany)*, and had closed the YESHIVA of R.Avraham Binyamin (Wolf) Hamburg, expelling over 100 students (with the help of local police) (see 5641\1881).

5591 — 1831

Many Jews were killed in Oshmyany *(Lithuania)* when Russian soldiers initiated a fire after a Polish rebellion.
R.Moshe Mintz (Muenz, Maharam Mintz II) — the highly respected rabbi of O-Buda *(Old Buda, Hungary)* — died in **Elul.**

5596 — 1836

The Karaites succeeded (some say in 1835) in having the Jews expelled from the town of Troki *(Lithuania)* (see 5587\1827, 5613\1853).
R.Tzvi Hirsch Kalischer — a disciple of the Chavat Da'at and R.Akiva Eger — had met (some say) with Mayer Anschel Rothschild — an extremely wealthy and Halacha-observant Jew — proposing the bringing of Mashiach *(Messiah)* by buying (parts of) Eretz Yisrael (at least Yerushalayim) from the Turkish Sultan.

5597 — 1837

R.Yisrael Lipshutz — author of Tiferet Yisrael *(commentary on Mishna) (see ILLUSTRATIONS, TEXT C, #4)* — became rabbi in Danzig *(Gdansk, Prussian Poland)*, where he lived for the rest of his life.
Adm.R.Mordechai of Chernobyl *(then Russia) (see 5558\1797)* — The Chernobler Maggid — died on the 20th **Iyar**. He was succeeded as ADMUR (REBBE, 'TZADIK') by his eight sons — each in his own location — including Adm.R.Yitzchak of Skvira *(then Russia)*.
4,000 Jews died in an earthquake in Tzfat *(Safed)* (see 5520*1759*) on the 24th **Tevet**, and 700-1,000 died in Teverya *(Tiberius)* from the same earthquake. Many of the survivors eventually moved — including Chabad (Lubavitch) Chasidim, who subsequently joined the Chabad settlement in Hevron (established ten years earlier, by Adm.R.Dov Ber) — and they rejuvenated the community there.
The Churvat R.Yehuda Chasid synagogue (see 5481*1720*) was re-opened in Yerushalayim at the end of **Tevet**, after it had been reconstructed.

5598 — 1838

R.David Luria — rabbi of Bichov *(Russia)*, and author of Chidushei HaRadal *(on Midrash Rabba)*, an active leader against the (local) MASKILIM and the reformers — was released from prison, when the evidence supporting his denunciation was found to be forged.
Russian authorities — charging that two Jewish people were killed by fellow Jews (for informing and illegal exploitation) — arrested and tortured hundreds of Jews for being involved. Many died from their sentence of hard labor.

5599 — 1839

The Chassam Sofer died, and he was succeeded as rabbi in Pressburg *(Hungary)* by his oldest son, R.Avraham Shmuel Binyamin (Zev), the Ktav Sofer (see 5629\1869).
Many Jews of Meshed *(Persia)* were killed in an ANTI-JEWISH ATTACK, and the remainder were forced to convert to Islam, although they remained secretly Jewish (see 5421\1661). Most eventually migrated to other places, where they could be Jewish openly.

Chapter 14c
Later Acharonim & Changing Society

5600 ≈ 1840

Adm.R.Yisrael of Ruzhin was released from imprisonment.

Adm.R.Yisrael of Ruzhin *(Russia)* — a great-grandson of the Maggid of Mezeritsch, and a grandson of R.Nachum of Chernobyl — was released from prison, where he had been for almost two years. He had been denounced — on a charge of having (revolutionary) ambitions to be ruler of the Jews (his regal lifestyle was cited as evidence), and for implication in the informers affair (see 5598\1838) — and although he was released, he was kept under continuous surveillance. He subsequently left Russia, and settled in Sadgora *(Austrian Bukovina)*, where he continued his regal lifestyle, which caused a controversy with other Chasidim in the region.

Many Jews were arrested in a notorious BLOOD LIBEL in Damascus (known as the Damascus Affair), including over sixty children (in order to extract a confession from their mothers). Two Jews died of torture, a number confessed, and one converted (to Islam). It became an international affair — involving the governments of Turkey, Egypt, France, and Austria — and on the island of Rhodes, the rabbi and leading Jewish people were also arrested (by the Turks). The release of all the Jews was negotiated by a delegation of international Jewish notables, including Sir Moshe Montefiore *(see 5587\1827).*

This act of (successful) Jewish international cooperation spurred the eventual formation of the ALLIANCE ISRAELITE UNIVERSELLE (see 5620\1860).

Living in the Year 1840

Name	Born	Died
Yismach Moshe (R.Moshe Teitelbaum)	b.1759,	d.1841.
Tiferet Yisrael (R.Yisrael Lipshutz)	b.1782,	d.1860.
Bnei Yissachar (R.Tzvi Elmlch.of Dynov)	b.1783?,	d.1841.
R.Mendel of Kotzk	b.1787,	d.1859.
Tzemach Tzedek (of Lubavitch)	b.1789,	d.1866.
Divrei Chaim (of Tzanz)	b.1793,	d.1876.
R.Yisrael of Ruzhin	b.1797,	d.1850.
Chidushei HaRim (of Gur)	b.1799,	d.1866.
Minchat Chinuch (R.Yosef Babad)	b.1800?,	d.1874.
Kitzur Shulchan Aruch (R.Shl.Ganzfried)	b.1804,	d.1886.
R.Shimshon Raphael Hirsch	b.1808,	d.1888.
Malbim (R.Meir Leib[ush])	b.1808?,	d.1879.
R.Yisrael Salanter	b.1810,	d.1883.
Divrei Yechezk'el (of Shinev)	b.1811?,	d.1899.
Pitchei Teshuva (R.Avraham Tzvi Hirsch)	b.1813,	d.1868.
Aruch HaShulchan (R.Yechi'el Epstein)	b.1829,	d.1908.
Sdei Chemed (R.Chaim Chizkyah Mdini)	b.1832?,	d.1904.
Ben Ish Chai (R.Yosef Chaim Al-Chakkam)	b.1833?,	d.1909.
Chafetz Chaim (R.Yisrael Meir Kagan)	b.1838,	d.1933.

5601 ≈ *1840*

R.Avraham David of Butshatsh *(Buczacz, Austrian E.Galicia)* — a disciple of R.Levi Yitzchak of Berditchev, author of Da'at Kedoshim *(Halacha)* among other works — died on Erev Rosh Chodesh **Cheshvan** 5601*1840.*

5601 ≈ 1841

The Bnei Yissachar, Adm.R.Tzvi Elimelech of Dynov — a disciple of the Maggid of Kozhnitz, the Chozeh of Lublin, and R.Menachem Mendel of Rymanov, and author of Bnei Yissachar, among many other works — was rabbi and REBBE (ADMUR, 'TZADIK') in many towns, including Dynov *(Austrian Galicia)* and Munkatch *(Munkacevo, Austrian Hungary, near Galicia)*. He died on the 18th **Tevet** 5601\1841.

The Yismach Moshe, Adm.R.Moshe Teitelbaum (see 5568\1808), died on the 28th **Tammuz** in Uhel *(Ujhely — Satoraljaujhely — N.E. Hungary)*. He was succeeded as REBBE (ADMUR, 'TZADIK') by his only son, Adm.R.Elazar Nisan — who was the rabbi of Drahavitsch *(Drogobych, then Austrian E.Galicia)* — and by his grandson (and disciple), Adm.R.Yekutiel Yehuda of Sighet *(Marmaros-Sziget, N.W.Rumania)* (see 5618\1858), who became rabbi of Uhel until he was forced to leave by the *Mitnagdim (opponents to Chasidim)*.

Some manuscripts of R. Chaim Palaji were destroyed in a fire in Izmir *(Turkey)*— nevertheless, 26 of his works survived. *(He would make a festive meal and ate a new fruit, for the blessing of "She'he'cheyanu.", each time he published a new book.)*

5603 ≈ 1843

The Tzemach Tzedek of Lubavitch was repeatedly arrested in Russia.

The Russian government convened a commission — which included the Tzemach Tzedek (representing Chasidim) and R.Yitzchak (son of R.Chaim) of Volozhin (*Mitnagdim*), a businessman, and a secular oriented scholar (MASKILIM) — to discuss many Jewish issues. In the forefront was the issue of secular education for Jewish children, which Max Lilienthal (a German Jewish MASKIL, and educator) had been lobbying for in government circles (see 5580\1820), and had been heavily promoting among the Jews (see 5543\1783).
The Tzemach Tzedek was detained for his outspoken views twenty two times during the course of the conference. Although the immediate outcome (see 5605*1844*) of the commission was unclear, the government did repeal the (1836) ban on publication and importation of certain Jewish books — essentially KABBALA and CHASIDUT, which the MASKILIM viewed as particularly irksome — and also suspended the expulsion of Jews from the SHTETLACH *(villages)* (see 5582\1822, 5642\1882).

5605 ≈ *1844*

The Russian government *(of Czar Nicholas, see 5587\1827)* ordered the establishment of state schools for Jewish children (conceived by Lilienthal, see 5603\1843) — and a secret clause in the decree indicated that the purpose was to attract Jews to Christianity. The government also ordered the establishment of RABBINICAL SEMINARIES in the style of the MASKILIM, with secular education (see 5639\ 1879); the abolition of the older style Jewish community structure; and the introduction of GOVERNMENT APPOINTED RABBIS (graduates of the government RABBINICAL SEMINARIES).
Although many of these decrees were difficult to enforce — and these APPOINTED RABBIS rarely had serious influence in the Jewish communities, but primarily served as 'clerks' for recording births, marriages, etc. — the Jewish communal structure lost much of its power, including the power to control the establishment of new institutions in the community. This presented the MASKILIM with the opportunity to openly disseminate their views on Jewish life in the vast number of East European communities of Russia and Poland, as they had already done in the freer countries of Western Europe. They also encouraged parents to send their children to the government schools — which leaders of both Chasidim and *Mitnagdim* were discouraging — claiming that all such children would receive exemption from the conscription laws *(see 5587\1827)*.
Lilienthal (see 5603\1843) — who became very unpopular, even among the MASKILIM (for political reasons) — left Russia amid a controversy over (alleged) misappropriation of funds and settled in the U.S.A.. There he was active in the REFORM movement — together with (his friend) Isaac Mayer Wise, who spread the REFORM ideology throughout the U.S.A. (see 5641\1881) in his frequent travels, particularly to the scattered communities.

5606 ≈ 1846

Sir Moshe Montefiore (see 5587\1827) visited Russia in an attempt to intercede for the Jews, and to negotiate a relaxation of the harsh and discriminatory decrees *(see 5582\1822, 5587\1827, 5605\1844, 5613\1853)*. He met with the Chidushei HaRim (in Warsaw), R.Yitzchak Volozhiner, and R.David Luria, among other Jewish leaders and government officials.

5609 ≈ *1848*

R.Yisrael Salanter left Vilna.

Many Jews died in an epidemic of cholera in Vilna, and R.Yisrael Salanter (Lipkin) — who was the original propounder of a new movement (in Lithuania) to study and practice MUSSAR *(ethical and introspective behavior and demeanor)* — was very active in helping the sick. When doctors claimed that — in order to maintain a healthy resistance to the disease — Jews should not fast on Yom Kippur (5609*1848*), R.Yisrael set a public example, by eating in the synagogue. In the same year, he was asked to head the new government sponsored RABBINICAL SEMINARY in Vilna (see 5605*1844*), which — although encouraged to do so by R.Yitzchak Volozhiner — he refused. He was consequently compelled to leave Vilna, and he settled in Kovno *(Lithuania)*, where he stayed for nine years (see 5617\1857).

5610 ≈ 1850

Adm.R.Meir(el) Premishlaner — a popular REBBE (ADMUR, 'TZADIK') of Chasidim, who had developed a wide reputation as a miracle worker — died on the 29th **Iyar**.

5611 — 1851

R.Shimshon Rapha'el Hirsch became rabbi in Frankfort am Main.

R.Shimshon Rapha'el Hirsch — who had previously been rabbi in a number of towns — became rabbi in Frankfort am Main, where he established his ideology on a congregational (KEHILLA) basis. He had already written some of his major works, setting out his ideology — which was based on traditional JUDAISM, but reflected the new cultural environment of the nineteenth century — without changing the structure of Jewish law, as the REFORM movement (in Germany) had done a few years earlier (when they formally rejected sections of the Halacha, including dietary prohibitions). He had attracted the friendship of such people as Abraham Geiger (a leading REFORM scholar) and Heinrich Graetz (a REFORM scholar and historian, who had even spent some time studying under R.Shimshon Rapha'el), although both their relationships with him eventually cooled.

Other congregations in Germany joined his new KEHILLA concept, and he founded Jewish schools which offered the traditional Jewish education, yet also included secular studies.

R.Shimshon Rapha'el Hirsch was instrumental in consolidating and enhancing the position of the Halacha-observant (ORTHODOX) Jews of Germany (see 5629\1869), at a time when — besides the influences of the REFORM movement and the Haskala — outright assimilation had jeopardized their continued existence, to the extent that practical Halacha observance in many cities (including Frankfort) was almost eliminated.

5613 — 1853

The Czar *(Nicholas I)* increased the quota of Jewish conscripts (and CANTONISTS, see 5587\1827) during the Crimean War with England, France, and Turkey, which started with a dispute over control of the Christian holy places in Yerushalayim.

The Russian government also issued decrees RESTRICTING the Jewish STYLE OF DRESS, and classifying Jews into various discriminatory economic classes. The Kra'im *(Karaites)* — some 2,500 in Russia, and 7,500 in Crimea —were later (1863) totally exempted from Russian ANTI-JEWISH laws (see 5596\1836, **Nissan** 5702\1942).

The decree of the CANTONISTS was repealed — some three years later, after the death of Czar Nicholas I — and among other things, the right was granted for some (upper economic-class) Jews to live outside the Pale of Settlement.

5614 — 1854

A group of people broke away from the synagogue in Mainz *(Germany)* when an organ was installed (see 5570\1810), and they formed their own (ORTHODOX) congregation. Meir (Marcus) Lehman — who wrote many historical novels — became their rabbi.

5615 — 1855

Adm.R.Shalom of Belz *(Austrian Galicia)* — a disciple of the Chozeh of Lublin and the Apta Rav — died on the 27th **Elul.** He was succeeded as REBBE (ADMUR, 'TZADIK') by his son, Adm.R.Yehoshua.

5616 — 1856

R.Avraham Tzvi Hirsch Eisenstadt — author of Pitchei Teshuva *(on the Shulchan Aruch — except the Orach Chayim section — (see ILLUSTRATIONS, TEXT K, #7, L, #8))*, collection of additional updated Halacha notes (see 5588\1828) — left Grodno *(Russian Lithuania)* to become rabbi in Uttina *(Uttian, Russian Lithuania)*.

5617 — 1857

R.Yosef Shaul Nathanson, author of Sho'el UMeshiv *(Sh'elot UTeshuvot)*, became rabbi of Lvov *(Lemberg, then Austria)*. He permitted the use of machines to bake Matza — which created a widespread Halacha controversy — and he was active in combatting the introduction of the new education of the MASKILIM (see 5543\1783).

R.Yisrael Salanter *(see 5609\1848, 5643\1883)* — who went to Germany for medical reasons, and remained there for a few years — attracted Jewish university students to his lectures — SHI'URIM on Bible, Talmud, and MUSSAR *(ethics)* — which he gave in GERMAN, dressed in German fashion. He later settled in the town of Memel *(border of Lithuania and Germany)*.

A Jew was attacked by a mob in Tunisia and later killed for (allegedly) insulting Islam.

5618 — 1858

Adm.R.Yekutiel Yehuda Teitelbaum (see 5601\1841), author of Yetev Lev, became rabbi of Sighet *(Marmaros-Sziget, N.W.Rumania)*, and was also REBBE (ADMUR, 'TZADIK'), succeeding his father (see

5601\1841), who had died two years earlier.
R.Meir Leib(ush) ben Yechi'el Michel — the Malbim, famous for his commentary on the Bible — became rabbi in Bucharest, where he faced strong opposition from the REFORMERS (see 5624\1864).
A 6-year-old Jewish boy — Edgardo Mortara — was forcibly taken from his parents in Bologna *(Italy)* by the church authorities. After being subjected to FORCED BAPTISM, the child was raised as a Christian — despite an international outcry, which included the intervention of Francis Joseph I (the Austrian emperor who had very friendly relations with the Jews) and the representations of England's Sir Moshe Montefiore. The boy later became a church dignitary and theologian.

5619 — 1859

R.Menachem Mendel of Kotzk died.

Adm.R.Menachem Mendel of Kotzk *(Poland)* — a disciple of the Chozeh of Lublin, the Yehudi of Pershisskha, and of Adm.R.Simcha Bunim of Pershisskha (whom he succeeded) — died on the 22nd **Shvat**, after having spent almost twenty years in seclusion in his room. He was succeeded (primarily) by the Chidushei HaRim, Adm.R.Yitzchak Meir (who lived in Warsaw, but subsequently moved to Gur). The Chidushei HaRim maintained the high demands of R.Mendel — in the depth of Torah study — but reduced the intense pressure his predecessor had exerted (and instilled in his CHASIDIM) in the search of absolute truth.
Many Jews were killed in an attack by RIOTERS in Galati *(Rumania)* (see 5627\1867), and the Jews were also attacked in (the nearby) Odessa *(Russia)* (see 5631\1871).

5620 — 1860

The Jews of Tetuan *(Morocco)* were massacred, and throughout Morocco many Jews fled when the Spanish attacked. Some took refuge in Gibraltar, whilst some subsequently settled in Eretz Yisrael (see 5625*1864*).
The ALLIANCE ISRAELITE UNIVERSELLE was established *(see 5600\1840)* as an organization through which Jews living in (countries of) more fortunate circumstances could help those in poorer conditions. The organization undertook diplomatic activities, emigration assistance, and also educational endeavors. The education included French language and culture — which became a major factor in the organization's decline in some places, because of its challenge to traditional Jewish education and culture (see 5543\1783), and in other places because of the rise of local nationalism.

5621 — 1861

R.Moshe Schick — the Maharam Schick, a disciple of the Chassam Sofer and author of SH'ELOT UTESHUVOT Maharam Schick — became rabbi in Chust *(Hungary)*. He developed the community — in the eighteen years until he died — into the most important in northern Hungary. Although he was vehemently opposed to the REFORMERS (see 5629\1869), he maintained — in what was progressive for his time and place — that it was permissible (where necessary) for a rabbi to preach in the local language, instead of YIDDISH (or HEBREW.)
R.Yisrael Zev Horowitz — a disciple of the Chassam Sofer, and a direct descendant of R.Pinchas Horowitz (see 5345\1585) — was a rabbi in Uhel *(Ujhely — Satoraljaujhely — N.E. Hungary)* (see 5601\1841), before he settled in Eretz Yisrael. He died in Teverya *(Tiberius)* on the 18th **Sivan**.

5623 — *1862*

An order expelling Jews from Tennessee *(U.S.A.)* was approved, by General Grant in **Kislev** 5623*1862* — less than two weeks before President Lincoln's Emancipation Proclamation — during the American Civil War. He was instructed — three weeks later, by the President — to revoke the order.

Living in the Year 1860

Tiferet Yisrael (R.Yisrael Lipshutz)	b.1782,	d.1860.
Tzemach Tzedek (of Lubavitch)	b.1789,	d.1866.
Divrei Chaim (of Tzanz)	b.1793,	d.1876.
Chidushei HaRim (of Gur)	b.1799,	d.1866.
Minchat Chinuch (R.Yosef Babad)	b.1800?,	d.1874.
Kitzur Shulchan Aruch (R.Shl.Ganzfried)	b.1804,	d.1886.
R.Shimshon Raphael Hirsch	b.1808,	d.1888.
Malbim (R.Meir Leib[ush])	b.1808?,	d.1879.
R.Yisrael Salanter	b.1810,	d.1883.
Divrei Yechezk'el (of Shinev)	b.1811?,	d.1899.
Pitchei Teshuva (R.Avraham Tzvi Hirsch)	b.1813,	d.1868.
Aruch HaShulchan (R.Yechi'el Epstein)	b.1829,	d.1908.
Sdei Chemed (R.Chaim Chizkyah Mdini)	b.1832?,	d.1904.
Ben Ish Chai (R.Yosef Chaim Al-Chakkam)	b.1833?,	d.1909.
Chafetz Chaim (R.Yisrael Meir Kagan)	b.1838,	d.1933.
Darkei Teshuva (R.Tzvi Hirsch Shapira)	b.1845?,	d.1913.
'Sfass Emess' (of Gur)	b.1847,	d.1905.
R.Chaim Brisker	b.1853,	d.1918.
Rogatchover Gaon (R.Yosef Rozin)	b.1858,	d.1936.
Torah Temima (R.Baruch Epstein)	b.1860,	d.1942.

5624 1864

The Malbim was imprisoned, and then expelled from Rumania.

The Malbim (see 5618\1858) was arrested, after being denounced by assimilationist REFORM Jews of Bucharest. He was released — after personal representations on his behalf by Sir Moshe Montefiore — on the condition that he leave Rumania. He was subsequently rabbi in a number of towns — where he continued to be persecuted by the REFORMERS and MASKILIM — and he did not find favor with the Chasidim.

5625 *1864*

Jews of many cities in North Africa (see 5620\1860), including Tunis and Tripoli, were massacred on Yom Kippur 5625*1864* by insurgent tribes.

5626 1866

Chidushei HaRim, Tiferet Shlomo, and Tzemach Tzedek, died within one month.

The Chidushei HaRim — Adm.R.Yitzchak Meir of Gur *(Poland)*, a disciple of the Maggid of Kozhnitz and Adm.R.Simcha Bunim of Pershisskha, and author of Chidushei HaRim *(on Talmud and SHULCHAN ARUCH)* — died on the 23rd **Adar**. He was succeeded four years later — all his (thirteen) sons had died in his lifetime — by his young grandson (and disciple), the Sfass Emess.
Adm.R.Shlomo HaKohen of Radomsk *(Poland)* — a disciple of Adm.R.Meir of Apta, and author of Tiferet Shlomo *(CHASIDUT on CHUMASH (Bible))* — died Erev Rosh Chodesh **Nissan**.
The Tzemach Tzedek (see 5603\1843) — Adm.R.Menachem Mendel of Lubavitch — author of Tzemach Tzedek II *(Sh'ELOT UTESHUVOT, and Halacha notes)* among other works — died on the 13th **Nissan**. He was succeeded, in Lubavitch, by his youngest son, Adm.R.Shmuel, although — except for the oldest — his (four other sons became REBBE (ADMUR, 'TZADIK') in their own towns.

5627 1867

All Jews were expelled from many SHTETLACH *(villages)* in Rumania (see 5619\1859) — some drowned in the Danube in their flight — and the remainder were harassed with discriminatory laws, which Sir Moshe Montefiore (in a personal visit) attempted to have repealed.

5629 1869

One year after Hungary had granted the Jews equal rights (SOCIAL EMANCIPATION), most of the ORTHODOX (Halacha-observant) Jews split from the central (government recognized) communal structure, because — at a communal congress — the REFORMERS (Neologs) rejected demands that the communal regulations be subject to the authority of the SHULCHAN ARUCH. The Ktav Sofer (see 5599\1839) was an active organizer of the ORTHODOX — who subsequently established their own separate communal structure, with the support of the Maharam Schick (see 5621\1861) — and this structure was later recognized by the government.
R.Shimshon Rapha'el Hirsch (see 5611\1851) followed the example of Hungarian ORTHODOXY, and (subsequently) established German ORTHODOXY on a separate basis.
R.Azriel Hildesheimer — rabbi in Eisenstadt *(Austrian Hungary)* — had disagreed with the establishment of the separate Orthodox communal structure, which created friction between him and many rabbis in Hungary. He left in 1869 to become rabbi in Berlin, where he followed the style of R.Shimshon Rapha'el Hirsch.
R.Yosef Chaim (ben Eliyahu) Al-Chakkam of Baghdad visited Eretz Yisrael. He was a Halacha authority whose PIYUTIM have been incorporated in the Iraqi liturgy, and author of the very popular Ben Ish Chai *(homily with Halacha and KABBALA)*, among many other (unpublished) works.
R.Raphael Meir Penijel returned to Eretz Yisrael and described in his book *(Lev HaMarpeh)* how he had befriended the Pope, who had shown him some of the holy utensils of the Beit HaMikdash taken by the Romans (see 4215\455).

5631 1871

The Jews were attacked in ANTI-JEWISH RIOTS in Odessa *(Russia)* (see 5619\1859) during Pesach.

5632 1872

R.Shmuel Strashun of Vilna — a disciple of the Chayei Adam and author of Hagahot HaRaShash *(notes on Talmud)* — died.

5633 1873

The Chafetz Chaim was published.

R.Yisrael Meir HaKohen (Kagan) (see 5672\ 1912) (anonymously) published his work Chafetz Chaim

(Halacha of slander/gossip etc.). He later became known as the Chafetz Chaim, and wrote the widely accepted Mishna Berura *(commentary and updated Halacha notes on the Orach Chayim section of SHULCHAN ARUCH, published as a separate work, rather than "SHULCHAN ARUCH with commentary")*.

5634 ≈ 1874

Adm.R.Yitzchak Yehuda Yechi'el of Komarno *(Austrian Galicia)* — R.Aisik(el) Komarno, a nephew of Adm.R.Tzvi Hirsch of Zydachov (who was a disciple of the Chozeh of Lublin) — was a prolific writer. He died on the 10th **Iyar**.

The Minchat Chinuch died.

R.Yosef Babad — author Minchat Chinuch *(commentary on Sefer HaChinuch)*, and rabbi of Tarnopol *(then Austria)* — died, some say on the 25th **Elul.**

R.Yechi'el Michel Epstein — author of Aruch HaShulchan *(Halacha update based on SHULCHAN ARUCH)* — became rabbi in Novardok *(Novogrodek, Russia)*, where he remained until he died. His son (and disciple) was R.Baruch, author (some say controversial) of the popular Torah Temima *(collection of Talmud statements on the CHUMASH (Bible) — respected for its accuracy in exactness of Biblical notations (Mesorah) [see Mmn.Hil.Tfillin.8.4 re:ben Asher])*.

5636 ≈ 1876

The Divrei Chaim — Adm.R.Chaim (Halberstam) of Tzanz (see 5590\1830), who died on the 25th **Nissan** — was succeeded as a REBBE (ADMUR, 'TZADIK') by his six sons. Prominent among them was Adm.R.Yechezk'el Shraga of Shinev *(Sieniawa, Austrian Galicia)*, known as the Divrei Yechezk'el, who later visited Eretz Yisrael, (and, some say, later considered settling in the United States). The Divrei Chaim was also succeeded by his grandson, Adm.R.Shlomo of Bobov *(Bobowa, Austrian Galicia)*.

5638 ≈ 1878

Petach Tikva agricultural settlement was established.

The agricultural village of Petach Tikva was established in Eretz Yisrael, by a group of (Halacha-observant) Jews from Yerushalayim and (recent immigrants) from Hungary. This was the first such settlement to be established in Eretz Yisrael (in almost 2,000 years), and they faced the problems of malaria and Arab attacks — problems which the many subsequent settlements (primarily secular Zionist) also faced. This was also probably the first time that some Jews from Yerushalayim sought to take original action to establish their own economic independence, rather than subsisting on the Chaluka *(stipends of charity funds collected overseas)*, as had been the custom for centuries.

5639 ≈ 1879

R.Shimon Sofer (son of the 'Chassam Sofer') was rabbi in Cracow *(Austrian Galicia)*, and together with Adm.R.Yehoshua of Belz *(Austrian Galicia)*, he founded an organization (MACHAZIKEI HADAT) to counter the activities of the MASKILIM, who were well organized. The MASKILIM already held three seats in the Austrian Parliament (see 5580\1820), and were planning to open a RABBINICAL SEMINARY (see 5605*1844*). MACHAZIKEI HADAT had four candidates for the next parliamentary election, and R.Shimon was (the only one) elected.

5640 ≈ 1880

R.Yaakov AbiChatzira of Morocco — author of many works, renowned for his expertise in practical KABBALA, and possessor of a wide reputation for miraculous deeds — died in Egypt, on his way to Eretz Yisrael, on the 20th **Tevet**.

5641 ≈ 1881

Many Jews began leaving Russia after a wave of POGROMS.

The Jews were blamed when Czar Alexander II

Living in the Year 1880

Kitzur Shulchan Aruch (R.Shl.Ganzfried)	b.1804,	d.1886.
R.Shimshon Raphael Hirsch	b.1808,	d.1888.
R.Yisrael Salanter	b.1810,	d.1883.
Divrei Yechezk'el (of Shinev)	b.1811?,	d.1899.
Aruch HaShulchan (R.Yechi'el Epstein)	b.1829,	d.1908.
Sdei Chemed (R.Chaim Chizkyah Mdini)	b.1832?,	d.1904.
Ben Ish Chai (R.Yosef Chaim Al-Chakkam)	b.1833?,	d.1909.
Chafetz Chaim (R.Yisrael Meir Kagan)	b.1838,	d.1933.
Darkei Teshuva (R.Tzvi Hirsch Shapira)	b.1845?,	d.1913.
'Sfass Emess' (of Gur)	b.1847,	d.1905.
R.Chaim Brisker	b.1853,	d.1918.
Rogatchover Gaon (R.Yosef Rozin)	b.1858,	d.1936.
Torah Temima (R.Baruch Epstein)	b.1860,	d.1942.
Kaf HaChayim - R.Yaakov Chaim (Sofer)	b.1870,	d. 1939.
Chazon Ish - R.Avraham Yeshaya Karelitz	b.1878,	d. 1953.

See also chart "Noteworthy Contemporaries" page 311

— despite having made many (mild) changes in Russia — was assassinated by revolutionaries on 12th **Adar-2**. POGROMS *(ANTI-JEWISH RIOTS)* broke out in southern Russia (see 5642\ 1882), and swept across the whole country (often with the open encouragement of local officials). The POGROMS continued (sporadically) over the next three years, resulting in many injuries, enormous damage to Jewish property (including synagogues), and the desecration of Torah scrolls.
MASKILIM were disillusioned by the attitude of non-Jewish intellectuals, who often demonstrated open support for the RIOTERS.
Assimilationists (mostly socialists) were disillusioned at the expressions of rejection from all strata of the Russian society (into which they believed they had successfully assimilated).
Many Jews directed their thoughts to Eretz Yisrael. Small groups were formed — generally called Chovevei Tzion *(Lovers of Zion)* — to discuss emigration *(Aliya)*. They were supported and joined by some rabbis (see 5653\1893, 5655\1895, 5656\1896). Others saw Jewish nationalism as an alternative ideology — giving momentum to a developing secular nationalistic concept of 'the Return to Zion' (see 5655\1895) — as distinct from those seeking only to emigrate, settle, and work the land, with no political goals.
For many, living in Russia became untenable — 2 million left in the next 32 years. Most emigrated to the economically appealing U.S.A., where approximately 280,000 Jews were living at this stage *(see 5660\1900, 5685\1925)*, and (some say) 200 synagogues already existed at this stage — only twelve of which were not REFORM *(see 5605\1844)*.
Many of those arriving in the U.S.A. discontinued religious observances — work on Saturday was mandatory (see 5698\1938) — and focused on Jewishness as a culture and ethnic identity.
Some of the idealistic Chovevei Tzion groups emigrated to Eretz Yisrael — where over 20,000 Jews at this stage *(see 5675\1915)* were living under harsh economic conditions. These groups were small (the famous Bilu group were only 53 immigrants — and number of them returned or left for the U.S.A.).
The YESHIVA (of Chabad) in Starodub *(Russia)* was closed by the government after a denunciation by one of the local MASKILIM (see 5590\1830).

5642 ≈ 1882

The Jews were attacked in Algiers and other cities of Algeria, in ANTI-JEWISH RIOTS that arose (sporadically) over the course of a few years (see 5657\1897). Many Jews were killed, some synagogues were sacked, and Torah scrolls were desecrated.
An inquiry by the Russian government into "the POGROMS of 1881" concluded that Jews were to blame, because of their 'economic exploitation' of others. Consequently, the government passed a series of laws (called the May Laws) in which — among other discriminatory provisions — all Jews were expelled from the SHTETLACH *(villages and rural settlements)* and were only allowed to live in the towns (see 5603\1843, 5651\1891). Although there is no evidence the expulsion was fully accomplished, it was immortalized by the YIDDISH writer Sholom Aleichem — in a story to become famous as *Fiddler on the Roof* (which portrayed Jews as required to leave legendary "Anatevka".) (Shalom Rabinovitz *(YIDDISH writers used pseudonyms then, usually because they were spurned by the intelligentsia and MASKILIM who idealized HEBREW)* created (and immortalized) — in humorous satires — many characters and terms that became part of classic YIDDISH. *(Among them: Shver tzu Zayn a Yid; Tsezeyt un Tsershpreyt; Boiberick; Yehupetz.)*)
A number of Jews were accused in a BLOOD LIBEL in Tisza-Eszlar *(Hungary)*, and — although they were later acquitted — the accusation led to many ANTI-JEWISH RIOTS throughout the country.

5643 ≈ *1882*

Adm.R.Shmuel of Lubavitch, had travelled to Western Europe a number of times, attempting to influence large bankers to withhold much-needed loans to the Russian government, until there was a change in their "Jewish policy" (see 5641\1881, 5642\1882). He died on 13th **Tishrei** 5643*1882*, and was succeeded — ten years later — by his second son (twenty-two years old, at this stage) Adm.R.Shalom Dov Ber.

5643 ≈ 1883

R.Yisrael Salanter had lived in Paris for two years (see 5617\1857) before returning to Germany, where he died on the 25th **Shvat**.
The Yetev Lev, Adm.R.Yekutiel Yehuda Teitelbaum (see 5618\1858), died on the 6th **Elul,** and he was succeeded by his son Adm.R.Chananyah Yom Tov Lipa, as rabbi and REBBE (ADMUR, 'TZADIK') in Sighet *(Marmaros-Sziget, N.W.Rumania)*.
R.Shmuel Ehrenfeld died. He was a grandson of the Chassam Sofer, author of Chatan Sofer *(Halacha)*, and rabbi in Mattesdorf *(Mattesburg-Nagymarton, Austria)*.

5645 ≈ *1884*

Adm.R.Menachem Mendel of Vizhnitz — a grandson of Adm.R.Menachem Mendel of Kossov *(then Austria)*, and a son-in-law of Adm.R.Yisrael of Ruzhin — was the rabbi and Rebbe (Admur, 'Tzadik') of Vizhnitz *(Vizhnitza, then Austria)*, and author of Tzemach Tzadik *(Chasidut)*. He died on Erev Rosh Chodesh **Cheshvan** 5645\ *1884*, and was succeeded by his son Adm.R.Baruch.

Adm.R.Avraham (ben Yitzchak Mattityahu) — a disciple of Adm.R.Moshe of Kobrin (who was a disciple of R.Mordechai of Lechevitch) — was author of Yesod HaAvodah *(chasidut)* and other works, and Rebbe (Admur, 'Tzadik') in Slonim *(then Russia)*. He died on the 11th **Cheshvan**.

5645 ≈ 1885

At a Pittsburgh conference, the Reform movement in U.S.A. *(see 5641\ 1881)* adopted a *platform of principles* which denied current validity to Halacha *(Jewish Law) (see 5611\1851)*. Reaction to this position eventually caused many more traditional — but not fully Halacha-observant — scholars (and laymen) to develop what was later called Conservative (movement.)

5646 ≈ 1886

R.Shlomo Ganzfried (author of Kitzur Shulchan Aruch) died.

R.Shlomo Ganzfried — author of the Kitzur Shulchan Aruch *(Halacha)* and Kesset HaSofer *(Halacha for scribes)* among other works — was rabbi in Ungvar *(Uzhgorod, Hungary)*. The Kitzur *(abridged)* Shulchan Aruch was already so popular during his lifetime that it had been published in fourteen editions, and had sold almost 250,000 copies by the time he died in **Tammuz** 1886.

R.Chaim Yeshayahu Halbesberg had already written Misgeret Hashulchan *(a commentary on the Kitzur Shulchan Aruch)*, which was later printed in an edition of the Kitzur Shulchan Aruch that also included a number of his editorial refinements.

5648 ≈ 1888

R.Meir Simcha HaKohen — author of Or Same'ach *(commentary on the Rambam's Yad HaChazaka)* — became a rabbi in Dvinsk *(Duenaburg, Daugavpils, Latvia)*, where he remained for almost forty years, until his death.

There were already some 130 Orthodox synagogues in New York at this stage (see 5641\ 1881). Many congregational rabbis — as well as self proclaimed (immigrant) rabbis — were acting independently as Halacha authorities, particularly in the financially rewarding area of kashrut supervision. One of the largest congregations — in association with other congregations — brought R.Yaakov Yosef from Vilna to the U.S.A. to become their rabbi, and also the Chief Rabbi of New York. Although R.Yaakov Yosef had some initial success in consolidating a structure of central religious authority, there were powerful (and ruthless) self-interest groups who resisted. By 1902 — when he died at 59, in poverty, ill health, and an almost forgotten man — there were already 250 synagogues (with increased petty rivalries, stemming primarily from the different geographic origins of the people). The Jewish 'community' of New York settled into irreversible anarchy *[def: absence of any cohesive form of unity and/or authority]*.

5649 ≈ 1889

R.Yosef Rozin — the Rogatchover Gaon, a great Talmud scholar of a calibre unknown for many generations — wrote a number of works (all) entitled Tzaphnat Pane'ach, which are often only cryptic notes (without the aid of commentary). He became the rabbi of the Chasidic community in Dvinsk *(Duenaburg, Daugavpils, Latvia)* (see 5648\1888).

5650 ≈ 1890

R.Nathan (Marcus) Adler, chief Rabbi of the British Empire — when it was said "the sun never sets on the empire" *(because of Australia)* — died on the 29th **Tevet**. When he had applied for a position in London (R.Shimshon Raphael Hirsh also applied) he was recommended by the queen *(Victoria)*. She once was in Hanover *(Germany)* and about to give birth two months prematurely when he (as the local rabbi) had advised her (through R.Moshe Monetfiore) that she should hurry to a British ship, sail three miles out to sea, and solve the problem of her child's eligibility *(later Edward VII)* to the throne (as a local German citizen.)

A committee was established in Eretz Yisrael to make Hebrew a language of daily use.

5651 ≈ 1891

All Jews were expelled from Moscow (see 5642\1882) and 30,000 were forced to (sell their properties and) leave. Some wealthy merchants — and some Cantonists who had completed their full military service, see 5587\1827 — were permitted to stay.

5652 — 1892

R.Chaim (Brisker) became rabbi in Brisk.

R.Chaim Solovetchik — who had been a MAGGID SHIUR *(lecturer)* of a select group (some say he was the ROSH YESHIVA, see 5653\1893) in the Volozhin YESHIVA — left there when the YESHIVA was closed (see 5653\1893). He became rabbi in Brisk *(Brest-Litovsk, Lithuania)* where he succeeded his father — R.Yosef Ber Solovetchik — who had also previously been in Volozhin as a ROSH YESHIVA. R.Chaim (Brisker) developed a YESHIVA (Etz Chaim) in Brisk, and is known for introducing an analytical style of Talmud study.

5653 — 1893

R.Naftali Tzvi Yehuda Berlin, the Netziv — author of Meishiv Davar *(SH'ELOT UTESHUVOT)* and Ha'amek Davar *(commentary on CHUMASH)* — was a son-in-law of R.Yitzchak Volozhiner, whom he had succeeded as ROSH YESHIVA in Volozhin. When the Russian government had demanded that secular studies be taught at the YESHIVA, and that the number of students be reduced, the Netziv failed to fully accomplish either demand — although (some say) lectures in Russian were introduced. The YESHIVA was closed, and he left Volozhin, hoping to settle in Eretz Yisrael — an ideal he supported (see 5641\1881). However he died in Warsaw in 1893, eighteen months after the YESHIVA was closed.

5655 — 1895

A Jewish captain in the French army (Alfred Dreyfus) was falsely convicted of spying in 1895, which aroused much anti-Jewish expression throughout the country. A newspaper reporter from Vienna, Theodore Herzl (of an assimilated Hungarian Jewish family), was profoundly moved by this wave of anti-Jewish sentiment, which sparked a Jewish identity crisis in him. He consequently developed the idea of creating a Jewish state (with its own political self-rule), and became obsessed with the idea — meeting with wealthy Jews, statesmen and politicians to promote it. He persevered, despite the ridicule he received (some say he saw himself as a visionary redeemer akin to Shabbetai Tzvi.) Within two years he convened a congress of all the various groups that were promoting a return to Eretz Yisrael (see 5641\1881), thus establishing the Zionist movement — which developed into a powerful political (if controversial) force under his leadership.
Many rabbis and virtually all ADMURIM (Chasidic 'TZADIKIM') strongly opposed the Zionist movement — because of its secular orientation — which (ironically) was blended with a subtle messianic overtone. There were also rabbis who were strong proponents of RELIGIOUS ZIONISM — which led to the later establishment of Mizrachi *(from '**M**erka**Z** **R**u**CH**an**I**')* in Vilna (in 1902) — as a religious faction within the Zionist movement.

5656 — 1896

R.Yitzchak Elchanan Spektor, rabbi of Kovno *(Lithuania)* was very involved in Russian communal affairs, and supported the wave of enthusiasm for settling in Eretz Yisrael (see 5641\1881). He died in **Adar**.
Solomon Schechter (a CONSERVATIVE-PROGRESSIVE scholar *(see 5645\1885)* — who was later responsible for the formal organization of the CONSERVATIVE movement in the U.S.A.) — extracted a large collection of (approximately 100,000) ancient Jewish manuscripts from Cairo, and took them back to Cambridge University in England. This GENIZA was in the attic of the very old Ezra synagogue — built in 882\4642, in Fostat *(Old Cairo, Egypt)* — in which it is said that the Rambam had taught. The existence of the books and documents — more of which were subsequently taken by other large libraries — had been known for a long time, but they had remained untouched because of local fears and (others say, superstitious) beliefs.

5657 — 1897

Jews were attacked by ANTI-JEWISH RIOTERS in Mostaganem *(Algeria)* (see 5642\1882).

5658 — *1897*

A general Jewish socialist workers-union *(Bund)*, was founded at a secret meeting in Vilna. The Bund later became involved in Russian revolutionary activity — in alliance with Communists — and was at the forefront of a movement which promoted YIDDISH as the basis of a secular (often overtly non-religious) culture (see 5680\1920).
Jews were attacked in a POGROM in Bucharest, in **Kislev** 5658*1897*.

5659 — 1899

R.Chaim Chizkiyah Medini, author of Sdei Chemed *(Halacha encyclopedia)*, had been rabbi in Crimea *(S.W. province in Russia)* for over thirty years, after living in Constantinople *(Istanbul, Turkey)* for fourteen years. In

1899 he returned to Yerushalayim, where he had been born — declined to become SEPHARDI Chief Rabbi *(Rishon LeTziyon)* — and became rabbi in Hevron.
Leopold Hilsner was sentenced to death in Bohemia, in a BLOOD LIBEL which aroused strong anti-Jewish expressions in the press. His sentence was later reduced to life imprisonment.

5660 — 1900

Reb Tzadok HaKohen of Lublin — author of Pri Tzadik *(Chasidut)*, among other profound works *(he also wrote scholarly essays on astronomy, geometry, and algebra)* — died on the 9th **Elul**. He was a disciple of R.Mordechai Yosef Izbitzer (author of Mey Shilo'ah *(Chasidut)*) and of R.Leibele Eger (both were disciples of R.Mendele Kotzker), whom he succeeded in 1888 (some say he was a peer of R.Leibele).
At this stage there were 50,000 Jews in Eretz Yisrael *(see 5641\1881, 5675\1915)*, and 1 million Jews in the U.S.A. *(see 5641\1881, 5675\1915, and 5648\1888)*.

5663 — 1903

49 Jews were killed, 500 were injured, and many houses were destroyed (2,000 Jewish families were said to be left homeless) in Kishinev *(Moldova — Romanian: Chisinau — then Russia)*, in a POGROM (see 5668\ *1907*) which began with a BLOOD LIBEL — in **Nissan**, around Pesach-time *(also Easter)* as usual — and was further incited by hateful newspaper attacks. Russian officials openly supported the perpetrators of the POGROM as a means of diverting public attention from the country's fermenting revolution (see 5641\1881, 5665\1905).
Eight Jews were killed in Homel *(Gomel, Russia)* in a POGROM in **Elul.** Thirty-six of the Jews who fought in self defense were charged with committing a POGROM against Russian citizens.

Living in the Year 1900

Name	Born	Died
Aruch HaShulchan (R.Yechi'el Epstein)	b.1829,	d.1908.
Sdei Chemed (R.Chaim Chizkyah Mdini)	b.1832?,	d.1904.
Ben Ish Chai (R.Yosef Chaim Al-Chakkam)	b.1833?,	d.1909.
Chafetz Chaim (R.Yisrael Meir Kagan)	b.1838,	d.1933.
Darkei Teshuva (R.Tzvi Hirsch Shapira)	b.1845?,	d.1913.
'Sfass Emess' (of Gur)	b.1847,	d.1905.
R.Chaim Brisker	b.1853,	d.1918.
Rogatchover Gaon (R.Yosef Rozin)	b.1858,	d.1936.
Torah Temima (R.Baruch Epstein)	b.1860,	d.1942.
Kaf HaChayim - R.Yaakov Chaim (Sofer)	b.1870,	d. 1939.
Chazon Ish - R.Avraham Yeshaya Karelitz	b.1878,	d. 1953.
R.Meir Shapiro - Daf Yomi	b.1887,	d. 1934.
R.Shlomo Yosef Zevin - Talmud Encyclopedia	b.1890,	d. 1978.
Baba Sali *[Praying Father]* R.Yisroel Abuchatzeira	b.1890,	d. 1984.

See also chart "Noteworthy Contemporaries" page 311

5664 — *1903*

Marcus Jastrow — a Polish CONSERVATIVE-PROGRESSIVE scholar (see 5645\1885), and author of an Aramaic-English dictionary (popular for decades among English speaking Talmud students) — died in **Tishrei** 5664\ *1903*, in the U.S.A.

5664 — 1904

Adm.R.Chananyah Yom Tov Lipa Teitelbaum (see 5643\1883) died in **Shvat**, and was succeeded by his sons, Adm.R.Chaim Tzvi — author of Atzei Chayim, who was rabbi and REBBE (ADMUR, 'TZADIK') in Sighet *(Marmaros- Sziget, N.W.Rumania)* — and Adm.R.Yoel(ish) — who later (see 5688\1928) became rabbi and ADMUR — in Satmar *(Szatmarnemeti, Satu Mare province, N.W.Rumania)*.
R.Yaakov Chaim (Soffer) of Baghdad, author of Caf HaChayim *(on SHULCHAN ARUCH)*, settled in Eretz Yisrael.

5665 — 1905

The 'Sfass Emess' died.

The Sfass Emess — Adm.R.Yehuda Leib Alter of Gur, author of Sfat Emet *(CHASIDUT, and separate Chidushim)* — had maintained regular contact with his followers (CHASIDIM) fighting at the front (who even sent him letters containing Torah discussion) in the Russian war with Japan. He died on the 5th **Shvat**, and was succeeded by his son, Adm.R.Avraham Mordechai.

Many Jews were killed in (official) Russian POGROMS

Russia — having just lost a war with Japan — was stirring with revolutionary agitation. The last Czar *(Nicholas II)* was forced to establish a parliament, and it suited government officials and Czarist supporters to divert the attention of the masses through ANTI-JEWISH incitement (see 5663\1903).
As a result almost 700 (sanctioned) POGROMS were carried out against the Jews — and more than 800 Jews were killed — over the course of less than two years (see 5666\1906).
25 Jews were killed in Zhitomir in **Nissan** (including 10 who were killed on their way from another town to help fight). 120 Jews were killed in Yekaterinoslav *(Dnepropetrovsk)* in **Tishrei** 5666\ *1905*, 40 were killed in Simferopol *(Crimea, S.W. Russia)*, 50 in Rechitsa *(Russia)*, and 300 Jews were killed in Odessa.

5666 — 1906

70 Jews were killed — and 70 were seriously injured — in a POGROM (see 5665\1905) in Bialystok *(then Russia)* in **Sivan**. 30 Jews were killed in Shedlitz *(Siedlice, Russia)* in **Elul.**
R.Yosef Engel — who wrote many works on Halacha and KABBALA — became rabbi in Cracow.

5668 — *1907*

30 Jews were killed — and 250 women and children were abducted — in tribal riots in Casablanca *(Morocco)*.
19 Jews were killed in a POGROM (see 5665\1905) in Kishinev *(Russia)* in **Cheshvan** (see 5663\1903).

5669 — 1909

R.Shmuel Salant — Chief Rabbi of the ASHKENAZIM in Yerushalayim, where he had lived for almost 70 of his 93 years — died in **Av**, and was succeeded by R.Chaim Berlin. Since his arrival in Yerushalayim in 1841, he saw the Jewish community grow from 500 people to 30,000 *(see 5660\1900, 5675\1915)*.
The city of Tel Aviv was founded as a suburb of Yaffo *(Jaffa)* (see 3342\-419).

5670 — 1910

Adm.R.Avraham of Sochatchev *(Poland)* — son-in-law of R.Mendel of Kotzk, and author of Eglei Tal and Avnei Nezer *(Halacha, SH'ELOT UTESHUVOT)* — died on the 11th **Adar-1**.

5671 — 1911

Chazon Ish was published.

R.Avraham Yeshayahu Karelitz — the Chazon Ish (see 5714\1953) — anonymously published the first volume of Chazon Ish *(on SHULCHAN ARUCH)*.
On extremely weak evidence Menachem Mendel Beilis was accused of murder — in a BLOOD LIBEL in Kiev *(then Russia)* — and was imprisoned for two years. This raised an international outcry — he was later given a trial (in 1913), and subsequently freed.

5672 — 1912

An organization (political in nature) was formed — to maintain and strengthen Jews in the adherence to Halacha (see 5638\1878 — because of the eroding influences of the REFORMERS, assimilationists, socialists and YIDISHISTS (see 5658*1897*). The organization — Agudat Yisrael, which was founded in the month of **Sivan** at a conference in Kattowitz *(Silesia, a region between Poland and Germany)* — included the ORTHODOX communities of Germany and Hungary, as well as the Halacha-observant Jews of Poland, Russia, and Lithuania. The conference was opened by the Chafetz Chaim (a revered Torah leader), and was supported by (see 5674\1914) such notables as R.Chaim Brisker and the ADMUR (REBBE 'TZADIK') of Gur (see 5674\1913).

5674 — *1913*

Adm.R.Tzvi Hirsch Shapira — a great grandson of the Bnei Yissachar and a disciple of the Divrei Chaim (Tzanzer) who was rabbi and REBBE (ADMUR, 'TZADIK') in Munkatch *(Munkacevo, Austrian Hungary, near Galicia)* — was author of Darkei Teshuva *(commentary and update on the Yoreh De'a section of SHULCHAN ARUCH)* and Be'er LaChay Ro'i *(commentary on Tikkunei Zohar)*. He was opposed to Hungarian Halacha-observant Jews joining the Agudat Yisrael (see 5672\1912) (not to be influenced by the modernity of the German contingent). He died on the 16th **Tishrei** (2nd day of Sukkot) and was succeeded by his son Adm.R.Chaim Elazar, who was vehemently opposed to the recent settlement of Eretz Yisrael, and was involved in many controversies (including some with other Chasidic Rebbes (ADMURIM)).

5674 — 1914

R.Yitzchak HaLevi Rabinowitz (of Lithuania) — rabbi of Hamburg, and author of Dorot HaRishonim *(exhaustively erudite — if cumbersome and emotive — defence of classical-traditional Jewish history)* — had been one of the motivators for the formation of Agudat Yisrael (see 5672\1912), and he died on the 20th **Iyar**.

Over 500,000 Jewish soldiers fought in World War I.

Germany declared war on Russia on Tisha B'Av, which marked the opening of the Eastern European front of World War I *(The Great War — "to end all wars")*, during which some 400,000 Russian Jews and over 100,000 German Jews were drafted.
Some 12,000 Jewish German soldiers were killed during the four year war, and many more Russian Jews were killed in the upheavals that rocked that country over the next seven years *(see 5677\1917, 5678\1918, 5680\1920)*.
50,000 Jews served as soldiers in the English armies, suffering heavy casualties (10,000).

When the Russians suffered defeat and losses, they sought to blame the Jews, as the front battle-lines passed through densely Jewish populated areas. Many were accused of treason and espionage, and tens of thousands were sent to the Russian interior. All Jews were expelled from towns near the front line, and printing in HEBREW characters — which included YIDDISH — was prohibited. This effectively silenced the YIDDISH newspapers — the major source of information for most Jews there — blacking-out vital precautionary information on military clashes near populated areas.
Germany and Austria conquered territory with a total Jewish population of over 2,250,000.
33 Jews were killed as the invading German army set fire to the Jewish section of Kalisch *(Poland)*.

5675 — 1915

Of the 85,000 Jews living in Eretz Yisrael at this stage *(see 5660\1900, 5685\1925)* — under the rule of *(Ottoman)* Turks, who were on the German side of the war — thousands died of starvation during the war, and many left.
There were approximately 3,250,000 Jews in the U.S.A. *(see 5660\1900, 5685\ 1925)* — who raised very substantial sums of money to assist the Jews in Russia, the occupied areas of the war, and in Eretz Yisrael.
Leo Frank had been charged with murder, based on flimsy evidence . He was lynched *(killed)* by an ANTI-SEMITIC MOB in Georgia *(U.S.A.)*, in **Elul.**

5677 — 1917

Widespread strikes and street demonstrations in Russia crippled the authority of the Czar *(Nicholas II)* who was forced to resign. For a few months the country was ruled by a (WHITE) provisional government, which abolished most of the discriminatory restrictions against the Jews, including the abolishment of the Pale of Settlement (see 5551\1791). This government failed to gain full control, and the (RED) communist Bolsheviks seized power, plunging Russia into a civil war — which lasted until 1921 — in which the Jews suffered many attacks *(see 5678\1918, 5679\1918, 5679\1919, 5680\1920)*.

5678 — *1917*

When Sarah Schenirer started a small school called Bais Yaakov, to teach girls traditional Jewish studies — in Cracow *(Poland)* — it grew rapidly, and became the beginning of a new direction in the traditional education of women and girls.
The British — who were also in the Middle Eastern front of World War I — had just announced (in the 'Balfour Declaration') that they supported the Zionist concept of a national country (see 5655\1895) for the Jews in Eretz Yisrael.
In what has become known as history's last great mounted charge (an already outdated military tactic), the Australian 4th Light Horse Brigade — in a stunning achievement — re-captured the town and the water wells of Beersheeba on 15th **Cheshvan**.
The British captured Tel Aviv and Yaffo *(Jaffa)* from the Turkish *(Ottoman)* Empire (see 5276\ 1516) at the beginning of **Kislev**, and the Jews — who had been expelled by the Turks — returned. The British then captured Yerushalayim.
50,000 Jews were left homeless (according to some) when a fire destroyed much of Salonika *(Greece)*. This, along with subsequent government restrictions and other hardships, caused many of them to leave the country.

5678 — 1918

Over 60,000 Jews were killed during the Russian Revolution.

The Ukrainians (under Simon Petlyura, see 7th **Tammuz** 5701\1941) established their independence from Russia which was in the throes of a civil war, and the Jews were massacred in POGROMS (see 5408\1648) for over two years, by troops from both sides (WHITE and RED), nationalists, and peasant bands.
Over 525 communities were attacked, 60,000 Jews were killed, and many times that number were wounded *(see 5679\1919, 5680\1920)*.
90 Jews were killed in **Nissan** in NovgorodSeversk *(Ukraine)*, in an ANTI-JEWISH ATTACK by the RED Russian army — while retreating from the Germans.
R.Chaim Brisker (see 5652\1892) died on the 21st of **Av**.

5679 — *1918*

70 Jews were killed in Lvov *(Lemberg, Poland)* in a POGROM in **Kislev** 5679*1918*, by Polish soldiers fighting the Ukrainians (see 5678\1918) for control of the region *(eastern Galicia)*.

5679 — 1919

1,700 Jews were killed in **Adar** — in a four hour POGROM by the Ukrainian Nationalists (see 5678\1918) — in Proskurov *(Ukraine)*, and 80

Jews were killed in Zhitomir *(Ukraine)*.
35 Jews were EXECUTED — in the month of **Nissan**, by the Polish — in Pinsk *(then Poland)*, on dubious allegations, and two Jews were killed in a POGROM in Kalisch *(Poland)*.
700 Jews of Cherkassy *(Ukraine)* were killed by Cossacks in POGROMS in **Iyar**, and 250 were later killed by the WHITE Russian Army in **Av**.
400 Jews were killed by peasant bands in a POGROM in Trostyanets *(Ukraine)* in **Iyar** *(see 5678\ 1918)*; 317 were killed (in another POGROM) in Zhitomir *(Ukraine)*; 170 in Tulchin *(Ukraine)*; and 80 Jews were killed by Polish troops in Vilna *(then Poland)*.
40 Jews were massacred in Bugoslav *(Ukraine)* by the WHITE Russian Army on the 30th **Av**.
36 Jews of Kiev *(Ukraine)* were executed by Petlyura's Ukrainian army in **Elul,** and 1,500 Jews were killed by the WHITE Russian army, in a POGROM in Fastov *(Ukraine)*.

5680 1919

Adm.R.David (ben Yitzchak) of Skvira (see 5597\1837) died on the 15th **Kislev** 5680\ *1919*, in Kiev *(Ukraine-Russia)* — where he had moved with his whole family, because of the POGROMS and unrest in the other parts of the Ukraine — and many of his family died in the same year.

5680 1920

Arab nationalists attacked many of the new Jewish settlements in northern Eretz Yisrael in **Adar** (see 5638\1878), and a number of defenders were killed — eight of them at Tel Chai — including Yosef Trumpeldor, a decorated (Jewish) Russian officer who had come to assist in the defense. 5 Jews were killed in **Nissan** during Pesach, in an Arab attack in Yerushalayim.
Although there were a high proportion of Jews in the early leadership of communist Russia (see 5658\ *1897*) — almost half of the RED Army officers were Jewish — there was an ideological commitment among many of these leaders to eradicate the distinctiveness of Jews, exceeding their major assault on all religion. A special government 'Jewish section' had been established (the YEVESEKTZIA) — which used the assistance of the police and the dreaded internal security forces — to close down synagogues and all places of Jewish learning. Religious observance was singled out for particularly cruel and venomous suppression, and rabbis, Shochtim *(ritual slaughterers)*, and teachers risked their lives to fulfill their communal religious obligations *(see 5684\1924, 5687\1927, 5693\1933,* ***Av*** *5704\1944)*.
Halacha-observant Jews were also totally destabilized economically — because of the new economic laws, and economic order of Communism.
Adm.R.Shalom Dov Ber of Lubavitch *(see 5643\ 1882)* had to leave the shtetl of Lubavitch *(Russia)* — late in 1915, as a result of World War I, and the revolution — and he settled in Rostov *(Russia)*. He had established a YESHIVA in Hevron in 1911, based on the particular Chassidic style of the YESHIVA he had established (in 5657\ 1897) in Lubavitch. He died on the 2nd **Nissan**, and was succeeded by his only son, Adm.R.Yosef Yitzchak, who immediately continued and expanded his activities, assisting Jews of Russia who were desperate in religious and economic needs — millions of Russians had died of starvation by the time the civil war ended, with the Bolshevik Communists victorious. (The population of Petrograd *(S.Petersburg, Leningrad)* had fallen from 2.5 million in 1917 to 0.6 in 1920.)
The British took formal control of Eretz Yisrael in **Iyar** (see 5678\1917), under the authority of the internationally endorsed Palestine Mandate.
A newly established council (Rabbanut) of Yerushalayim invited R.Avraham Yitzchak Kook — returning to Eretz Yisrael after six-years of the war — to be Av BEIT DIN and (the first) ASHKENAZI Chief Rabbi of Eretz Yisrael. This council was opposed by R.Yosef Chaim Sonnenfeld — a disciple of the Ktav Sofer — and by R.Yitzchak Yerucham Diskin, because secular Zionists were involved in its formation. They subsequently established their own council, which became known as Eda HaCharedit.
4,000 Jews were killed by armed bands in a POGROM in Tetiyev *(Ukraine)*.
R.David AbiChatzira was killed by a canon shot in Morocco.

5681 1921

47 Jews were killed in Arab RIOTS in Yaffo *(Jaffa)* in **Nissan** *(see Adar 5680\1920)*; 4 Jews were killed while defending Petach Tikva from an Arab attack.
R.Shraga Faivel Mendelovitz — who had settled in the U.S.A. in 1913 — became ROSH YESHIVA in New York where he was active in attempts to reassert the traditional study of Torah in the U.S.A.

5682 1922

Mordechai Kaplan — born in Vilna and emigrated to the U.S.A. with his family (at age eight) in 1889 — was a Halacha-observant rabbi when he was a founder of a major ORTHODOX organization. He later became a leading and highly influential CONSERVAtive lecturer and scholar (see 5645\1885), and also founder of Reconstructionism. It is claimed that he introduced the bat-mitzva ceremony, which he performed for his daughter in the congregation he had established. The ceremony — postponed for six months, because there was no congregation which would allow it — was eventually held on Wednesday the 15th **Adar** (*Shushan Purim*). *(Some claim [Bat Mitzvah, Dat Israel U'Medinat Israel, New York, 1951, pp.136- 139] that he had heard of a Bat Mitzvah celebration taking place (somewhere) in Eastern Europe (in 1902) and was duplicating it in the U.S.A. Others cite similar earlier celebrations in France (no time or place given). Much has been written in contemporary She'elot Uteshuvot (responsa) about this growing custom (in an era when women have been granted 'equality'.) [Kol.Mev.2.48/Ser.Esh.2.39.p460/Igg.Mosh. O.C.1.104; 2.97; 4.36/Yab.Om.6.29. q.Ben Ish Chai/Tzi.El. Vol.18.33]).*

5684 ≈ 1923

Daf HaYomi study cycle commenced.

R.Meir Shapira — a leading rabbi in Poland known as the Lubliner Rav, and member (for a while) of the Polish parliament — instituted the practice of studying one two-sided page of Talmud per day, in a system called Daf HaYomi *(the daily page)*, which began on Rosh HaShana 5684\ *1923. The cycle lasts approximately seven years. (2,750 pages ÷ 365 days = 7.46 years; however the Jewish lunar year is shorter.)*

5684 ≈ 1924

Adm.R.Yosef Yitzchak of Lubavitch had organized a mass underground network of Jewish religious institutions in Russia (see 5680\ 1920), and when any melamed *(teacher)*, Shochet *(ritual slaughterer)* or rabbi was arrested for this work, the Lubavitcher Rebbe's followers (Chassidim) were prepared to replace them — at great personal risk. He was forced to leave Rostov *(Russia)* — by internal security forces, instigated by the Yevesektzia *(see 5680\1920)* — and he moved to Leningrad *(Petrograd, S.Petersburg)*, where he continued his secret work (see 5687\1927).

Living in the Year 1920

Chafetz Chaim (R.Yisrael Meir Kagan)	b.1838,	d.1933.
Rogatchover Gaon (R.Yosef Rozin)	b.1858,	d.1936.
Torah Temima (R.Baruch Epstein)	b.1860,	d.1942.
Kaf HaChayim - R.Yaakov Chaim (Sofer)	b.1870,	d.1939.
Chazon Ish - R.Avraham Yeshaya Karelitz	b.1878,	d. 1953.
R.Meir Shapiro - Daf Yomi	b.1887,	d. 1934.
R.Shlomo Yosef Zevin - Talmud Encyclopedia	b.1890,	d. 1978.
Baba Sali [Praying Father] R.Yisroel Abuchatzeira	b.1890,	d. 1984.

See also chart "Noteworthy Contemporaries" page 311

5685 ≈ 1925

There were approximately 120,000 Jews in Eretz Yisrael at this stage *(see 5675\1915, 5689\ 1929)*, and 4,500,000 Jews in the U.S.A. *(see 5675\1915)* — the largest Jewish community in the world, and the largest single ethnic group in the U.S.A. (although much greater numbers of non-Jewish immigrants arrived from Italy alone, over the same years.)

R.Menachem Kasher — a disciple of Adm. R.Avraham of Sochatchev and author of Torah Sheleima *(encyclopedic collection of Talmud and Midrash on the passages of the Chumash (Bible))*, among other *(encyclopedic)* works — settled in Yerushalayim, where he was Rosh Yeshiva in the yeshiva established by the Imrey Emess, Adm.R.Avraham Mordechai of Gur.

The (original) yeshiva of Slobodka *(Russia)* was transferred to Eretz Yisrael, in Hevron.

R.Isser Zalman Meltzer became a Rosh Yeshiva in Yerushalayim where he settled. He was a disciple of R.Chaim Brisker and the Chafetz Chaim; author of Even HaEzel *(on Yad HaChazaka of the Rambam);* and Rosh Yeshiva in Slutzk *(Russia).*

5687 ≈ 1927

Soviets released Lubavitcher Rebbe from prison.

Adm.R.Yosef Yitzchak of Lubavitch was arrested on the 15th **Sivan** by the communist regime — for his "underground" organization of religious activity (see 5684\ 1924) — he was abused, tortured (see 5710\ 1950), and sentenced to death without a trial, which raised an international outcry.

He was given notice of release on the 12th **Tammuz** (his 47th birthday), and expelled from Soviet Russia. He settled in Riga *(Latvia)*, but even from a distance he did not cease his "underground" organizing — although restricted to providing long-distance guidance and funds.

5688 ≈ 1928

Adm.R.Yoel Teitelbaum (see 5664\1904) was appointed rabbi (amid opposition) in Satmar *(Szatmamemeti, Satu Mare province, N.W.Rumania)*. A conflict ensued, and his supporters prevailed after six years.

5689 ≈ 1929

There were 150,000 Jews in Eretz Yisrael at

this stage *(see 5685\1925, 5699\1939)*.
Many were killed in a clergy-incited Arab POGROM *(see 5681\1921)* — 60 in Hevron, where the community was destroyed (see 5696\1936) and survivors moved to Yerushalayim *(see 5680\1920, 5685\1925)*.
After seven years of paralysis, Franz Rosenzweig — a German Jew who had become interested in JUDAISM, after almost converting to Christianity — died (at the age of 43). After a fifteen-year search for a meaningful Jewish expression, he arrived at a full observance of Halacha. His works of those years had a major impact on (German-Jewish) secular-oriented scholars.
Adm.R.Yosef Yitzchak of Lubavitch visited Eretz Yisrael and the U.S.A. — to encourage religious observance *(see 5641\1881)* and to collect funds. He arrived on **Elul** 12th — just weeks before the great Wall Street stock-market crash of 25th **Tishrei** *(October 29th, 1929)*. He spent ten months in the U.S.A. — visited eight major cities, and had audience with the President *(Hoover)* — before he returned to Europe and later settled in Warsaw.

Living in the Year 1930

Chafetz Chaim (R.Yisrael Meir Kagan)	b.1838,	d.1933.
Rogatchover Gaon (R.Yosef Rozin)	b.1858,	d.1936.
Torah Temima (R.Baruch Epstein)	b.1860,	d.1942.
Kaf HaChayim - R.Yaakov Chaim (Sofer)	b.1870,	d.1939.
Chazon Ish - R.Avraham Yeshaya Karelitz	b.1878,	d. 1953.
R.Meir Shapiro - Daf Yomi	b.1887,	d. 1934.
R.Shlomo Yosef Zevin - Talmud Encyclopedia	b.1890,	d. 1978.
Baba Sali *[Praying Father]* R.Yisroel Abuchatzeira	b.1890,	d. 1984

See also chart "Noteworthy Contemporaries" page 311

5693 — 1933

R.Yechezk'el Abramsky, author of Chazon Yechezk'el *(commentary on Tosephta)*, had been released after two of years of hard labor (see 5680\1920) in Soviet Russia. He was permitted to leave and he settled in London, where he became a very influential rabbi.
The Nazis — a virulently ANTI-JEWISH, extreme right-wing political party, led by Adolph Hitler — came to power in Germany on the 3rd **Shvat**. The 500,000 Jews of Germany (see 5699\1939) began to suffer immediate hardships (economic sanctions, arrests, torture, and in some cases murder).
The Chafetz Chaim died on the 24th **Elul.**

5694 — 1934

25 Jews were killed, and many were wounded in attacks by the (French-incited) Muslim population of Constantine *(Algeria)*. The attacks ceased when the Jews organized a resistance.

5695 — 1935

R.Avraham Yitzchak Kook (see 5680\1920) — author of many works, who was considered a philosopher and a mystic — died on 3rd **Elul**. He had narrowed the sphere of his influence as ASHKENAZI Chief Rabbi of Yerushalayim (and Eretz Yisrael) by some of his politically unpopular opinions.
On December 25, 5696\1935, the head of the Liberal (REFORM) Rabbis Association in the city of Offenbach *(Germany)* ordained a woman *(Regina Jonas)* to serve as a rabbi.

5696 — 1936

18 Jews were killed in Arab RIOTS in Tel Aviv in **Nissan** (see 5689\1929) — strikes, terror and unrest continued for three years — called "the Arab Revolt" (against Jewish immigration *(see 5699\1939)*).
A total of almost 500 Jews were killed, despite well organized HAGANA *(Jewish-defense)* units. The Jewish community of recently resettled Hevron (see 5689\1929) ceased to exist again.
Nevertheless, some 60,000 Jews entered Eretz Yisrael (legally and illegally) during those three years (164,000 had arrived in the previous 3 years).
Three Jews were killed and 60 wounded in a POGROM in Przytyk *(Poland)*.
Two Jews were killed in a bomb attack in Timisoara *(Temesvar, then Rumania)*.

5698 — 1938

The Jews were attacked in many cities of Poland during this year.
The five day (forty-hour) working week was introduced in the U.S.A. — other countries followed later. This allowed for increased levels of Shabbat observance in the industrialized Western countries (see 5641\1881).
On the 7th **Tammuz,** delegates of 32 countries met in Evian *(France, near Swiss border, on Lake Geneva)* — at the request of the U.S. President *(Franklin D. Roosevelt)* — to facilitate Jewish emigration from Germany and Aus-

tria, and solve the growing refugee problem. All delegates expressed sympathy for the refugees, yet all countries (except for the Dominican Republic) offered excuses for not accepting refugees. Later (in 1939 and 1940) a bill to admit 20,000 Jewish refugee children was defeated in the U.S. Senate.
All Jews of foreign origin were expelled from Italy in **Elul** *(by the extreme right wing government of Mussolini, who had been in power since 1922)*.

5699 — 1938

Jews were attacked in the Kristallnacht POGROMS in Germany.

The Nazi government of Germany incited a massive series of countrywide POGROMS, which swept through Germany and Austria on the night of the 16th **Cheshvan**. 36 Jews were killed — and many hundreds took their own lives — 30,000 were arrested and sent to CONCENTRATION *(prison)* CAMPS. 300 synagogues — and over 1,000 private Jewish properties — were completely destroyed. Hundreds of Torah scrolls were desecrated and destroyed — over 60 in the cities of Bamberg and Darmstadt alone — and many Jewish cemeteries were ruined.
The POGROM was called Kristallnacht because of all the broken glass.

5699 — 1939

In **Shvat** Hitler indicated that there would be a war, and that all the Jews of Europe would be exterminated.
There were over 400,000 Jews in Eretz Yisrael *(see 5689\1929, 5696\1936, 5709\1949)* — when the British Government announced their new policies for Eretz Yisrael *(called "the White Paper")*, which restricted Jewish immigration *(see 5696\1936)* to 10,000 a year, and also restricted the ability of Jews to buy land there.
A German ship arrived in Cuba with 1,000 Jews fleeing Europe, but they were not permitted to disembark, and no country would agree to accept them. They eventually returned to Europe — only 287 were SURVIVORS of World War II.
300,000 German Jews had left the country — since the Nazi rise to power *(see 5693\1933)* — when the German troops started World War II by invading Poland on the 17th **Elul**. 55,000 had gone to Eretz Yisrael; 70,000 to England and France; and 65,000 to the U.S.A.
Over 100,000 Jews had left Austria since the Nazi-German annexation in **Adar-2** 5698\1938, and 66,000 had remained. 10,000 had gone to Eretz Yisrael, 30,000 to England, and 28,000 to the U.S.A.

[5699\1939 continued in Chapter 15a.]. 

Chapter 15

The Melaktim & the Current Era

Section IV

Chapter 15,
The Melaktim & the Current Era.

Chapter 15a — The Holocaust.

Jewish Year		Secular Year
5699	**GERMANY STARTED WORLD WAR II, AND MASS KILLING OF JEWS.**	**1939**
5701	Nazi-Germany unexpectedly invaded Russia.	1941
5701	**200,000 Jews were killed at Babi Yar and Ponary.**	**1941**
5702	**400,000 Jews of Warsaw were sent to DEATH CAMPS.**	**1942**
5703	Nazi-Germany experienced massive losses in the battle of Stalingrad.	1943
5703	**THE REMAINING JEWS IN WARSAW STAGED A MASSIVE UPRISING.**	**1943**
5703	Jewish uprisings at Treblinka, Sobibor, and Bialystock.	1943
5703	The Danish people quietly rescued 93% of their Jews to safety.	1943
5704	**300,000 Hungarian Jews were killed in 3 months.**	**1944**
5705	Uprising in Auschwitz DEATH CAMP just before freedom.	1944
5705	**Nazi-Germany was conquered, and World War II ended.**	**1945**
5705	**6,000,000 JEWS WERE KILLED BY THE NAZIS DURING THE WAR.**	**1945**

Chapter 15b — The Independent State of Israel.

Jewish Year		Secular Year
5707	Publication of the Talmud Encyclopedia was commenced.	1947
5708	The United Nations divided Eretz Yisrael.	1947
5708	Arabs attacked in Eretz Yisrael, to gain territory.	1947
5708	**THE STATE OF ISRAEL WAS ESTABLISHED IN ERETZ YISRAEL.**	**1948**
5708	**Eretz Yisrael was invaded by many Arab countries.**	**1948**
5709	**The "War of Independence" (in Eretz Yisrael) ended.**	**1949**
5710	All Jews left the ancient Jewish community of Iraq.	1950
5710	Almost all Jews of Yemen emigrated to Eretz Yisrael.	1950
5717	Jewish forces invaded Egypt and conquered the Sinai Desert.	1956
5727	**YERUSHALAYIM RE-UNITED UNDER JEWISH RULE, IN SIX-DAY-WAR.**	**1967**
5734	2,500 Jewish soldiers were killed in the Yom-Kippur-War.	1973
5742	Massive enemy arsenals were discovered in Lebanon.	1982
5753	**A secret agreement signed in Oslo.**	**1993**
5754	**The Last Lubavitcher Rebbe died.**	**1994**

Chapter 15c — The Post-Holocaust Era.

Jewish Year		Secular Year
5756	**Yitzchak Rabin was assassinated.**	1995
5760	Court rules that Revisionist Historians are Nazi sympathizers	2000
5761	TERRORISM AGAINST AMERICA EXPLODES INTO A WORLD WAR (III)	2001
5763	Jewish astronaut with Torah scroll in fiery return from space.	2003

Section IV
UNIVERSAL DISPERSION

Chapter 15

The Melaktim & the Current Era

The fifteenth Chapter (Tekufa) in Jewish history
covers the history of our time.

The title "The Current Era" is dominated by (1) the Holocaust, and (2) the establishment of an autonomous Jewish state in the Holy Land of Eretz Yisrael. In the frame of this work, it should also be called THE MELAKTIM — *"The Collectors"* — for the many authors and works of comprehensive (and often encyclopedic) Torah material — collections of law and custom — often one subject spanning a number of volumes (and much of this in the English laguage.) However it is too early to establish (and list) those who will leave a permanent mark on history.

It also appears however, that — with almost engineered precision of timing — another new dimension is unfolding — THE POST-HOLOCAUST.

We witness signs of depletion, strains of weariness and fatigue, that begin to replace what was — for fifty years — a deep sub-conscious "national hysteria" of rebuilding. Rebuilding institutions, great learning houses, and dynasties, existing in pre-war Europe; re-populating the statistics of a nation been butchered; building a nation powerful enough to rank in the international listings of research, medicine, military prowess, economics and invention — without mentioning the personal achievements of many HOLOCAUST SURVIVORS.

Almost engraved in the calendar is the year 5755\1995,
as a turning point on many fronts.

- *political leaders in Eretz Yisrael were negotiating compromises within themselves;*
- *post-Zionism introduced into Jewish schools curricula faulting and even accusing those who established a Jewish refuge — homeland and then state — in "Arab" land;*
- *a timidity for demands that Arab schools cease the teachings of hate against Jews — the holiness of murder and the heroism of suicide martydom;*
- *some began to view the Israel Defense Forces as an institution to avoid;*
- *Observant Jews were also finding disillusioned children in their homes and schools;*
- *the panorama of Jewish landscape was levelled of leaders;*
- *Holocaust-denial gained respectability;*
- *and not the least, our natural gravitation towards convenience over committment..*

See page 294

Chapter 15a — The Holocaust

[5699\1939 is continued from chapter 14c.].

5699 1939

Germany started World War II, and mass killings of Jews.

The following chronology is not comprehensive — it is but a list of incidents — incidents that serve to illustrate, and incidents that can be placed in a chronological context.

The Germans started World War II by invading Poland on the 17th **Elul.** They massacred Jews in their conquests. In Chestochova *(Czestochowa)* *(see Tammuz 5703\1943)* they killed several hundred Jews on the 19th **Elul.** On the 25th **Elul** they set afire a synagogue in Bendin *(Bedzin)* — the fire spread to the whole Jewish section — and no Jews were permitted to escape alive. Several hundred perished in the fire (as was the case in similar incidents elsewhere).

The beginning of the war marked the beginning of the campaign to kill all the Jews in Europe *(see Shvat 5699\1939)*. An estimated 6,000,000 were killed during the 6 years of World War II — many died of disease and starvation — and the Jews were treated in the most hideous ways, many of which defy adequate description.

Russia annexed the eastern part of Poland — in accord with a secret agreement with Germany *(see 27th Sivan 5701\1941)* — and many Jews in those parts of Poland fled eastward into Russia. The Soviet Russians prohibited most (organized) Jewish activity *(see 5680\1920)*, and many Jews were transported further east — deeper into Russia — to work camps. This resulted in a larger percentage of HOLOCAUST SURVIVORS among Polish Jews who were on the Russian side of Poland (than of those who were trapped under Nazi-German rule.) Among them was R.Dov Ber Wiedenfeld of Tschebin *(Trzebinia, Galicia)*, author of Dovev Meisharim *(SH'ELOT UTESHUVOT)*, who settled in Yerushalayim after the War.

5700 1939

500 Jews were killed in Premyshl *(Przemysl, Poland)* after the Germans captured the town on Rosh HaShanah, the 1st of **Tishrei**.

Ostrov Mazovyetzka *(Poland)* became a border town — between the German and Russian armies *(see Elul 5699\1939)* — and the 560 Jews (out of 7,000) who did not escape to the Russian side were killed by the Nazi-German troops on the 29th **Tishrei**.

On the 13th **Cheshvan** the Nazis began to use Polish Jews for slave labor.

They placed the Jews of Petrokov *(Piotrkow, Poland)* into a ghetto on the 15th **Cheshvan**. This was the beginning of a campaign in which they eventually relocated most of Polish Jewry into crowded ghettos — mainly in Warsaw, Cracow, and Lublin — and as many as 30% died of disease and starvation under the consequent intolerable conditions.

5700 1940

After spending the first months of the war in Nazi-occupied Warsaw, Adm.R.Yosef Yitzchak of Lubavitch traveled via a dangerous route — through Berlin to Latvia *(see 5687\1927)* — and then directly to the U.S.A.. He was met at the port by thousands of Jews on the 9th **Adar-2**, and within days of his arrival, he had established a YESHIVA; embarked on a massive educational re-orientation program for young and old, which included publications in English and YIDDISH, SHI'URIM *(study sessions)* — and founded schools in towns outside of New York.

Although 1,750,000 Jews in the U.S.A. *(see 5675\1915, 5685\1925)* spoke YIDDISH at home *[U.S. census, 1940]* there was a prevailing notion that *'things are different in America'* — with regard to the religious observances kept in their countries of origin *(see 5641\1881)* — and it was this attitude that he consciously (and conscientiously) set out to combat.

He was joined fifteen months later by his son-in-law Adm.R.Menachem Mendel Schneersohn (who was in conquered Paris, before he escaped).

The Nazis transported Jews (packed standing densely into freight trains) — from one place to another, from SHTETLACH *(villages)* and towns — mostly to ghettos CONCENTRATION CAMPS *(for slave labor)* and DEATH CAMPS *(where they instituted systematic killing of the Jews)*. The largest DEATH CAMP was opened on the 8th **Sivan**, at Auschwitz *(Oswiecim, Poland)*. This camp eventually covered an area of forty square kilometers, and could hold 140,000 prisoners. 2,500,000 Jews were killed there — and half a million died of starvation and disease — during its five-year existence.

By the 16th **Sivan** the Germans had also conquered Denmark, Norway, Holland, Belgium and France.

5701 — 1940

Several thousand Jews had arrived 'illegally' in Eretz Yisrael from Rumania, and the British determined a policy to deport them *(see 5699\1939)*. 1,700 of them were placed on the steamer 'Patria', which sank on the 24th **Cheshvan** (through miscalculated Jewish political sabotage), while still in the port of Haifa. 250 Jews died.

In Constanta *(S.E. Rumania)*, government representatives looked on as armed bands of Macedonian refugees confiscated Jewish businesses on the 13th **Kislev** 5701*1940*. Those who resisted, disappeared — yet the city continued to serve as an escape port for Jews fleeing Europe.

1,800 Jews of Chelm *(Poland)* were taken on a DEATH MARCH — on the 19th **Kislev** — and 1,400 were shot on the way.

The Imrey Emess, Adm.R.Avraham Mordechai of Gur — who (some estimate) had 250,000 followers (CHASIDIM), and was the recognized leader of Polish Halacha-observant Jewry — escaped from Warsaw, and arrived in Eretz Yisrael *(see 5685\1925)*, (where he had property, bought on previous visits).

5701 — 1941

Many Jews (120) were killed in POGROMS in Bucharest in **Tevet**.

Many Jews (120 - 180) were killed in a massacre in Baghdad *(Iraq)* in **Sivan**, on the first day of Shavu'ot.

The Nazi-Germans had already conquered Yugoslavia and Greece at this stage.

On the 9th **Sivan**, Jewish property was confiscated by the Republic of Croatia — which, together with Rumania, Hungary and Bulgaria, had joined Nazi-Germany — and Jews were ordered to wear a YELLOW BADGE.

Nazi-Germany unexpectedly invaded Russia.

When, on the 27th **Sivan**, the Nazi-Germans suddenly attacked Russia — whom they had previously neutralized by signing a peace agreement *(see Elul 5699\1939)* — they committed a decision that almost defied all logical explanation. According to military analysts *(then and later)*, the German-Nazis could have held their conquests in Europe — for decades, if not more — had they not propelled Russia out of 'neutrality' and into joining the war on the side of the Allies *(England (and nations in its 'Empire') — later the U.S.A. — as well as the remnants and refugee armies of Poland and France)*.

(It also had the affect of emboldening Japan to act — as Russia (their long-time foe) became a reduced threat. When Japan later attacked the United States many young Jews were among those called into active service.)

Although this attack on Russia changed the eventual direction of the war *(see Shvat 5703\1943)*, and shortened the duration of Nazi rule to five years (not decades, as feared) — saving at least some SURVIVORS of European Jewry, and the survival of English Jewry — nevertheless, tragically, in the interim this attack led to the direct decimation of the already oppressed Jewish population (under the Soviet regime) in the eastern part of Poland, virtually all of Lithuania, Latvia and western Russia.

The Nazi- German troops were welcomed with flowers by many non-Jewish Lithuanians as they entered Vilna.

35,000 Jews of Vilna were massacred and buried at Ponary.

The Nazis immediately rounded up and began killing 35,000 Jews in the Ponary forest near Vilna, and 100,000 were eventually killed there.

1,000 Jewish men of Augustow *(Poland)* were killed by the Nazis on the 27th **Sivan**.

When the Nazis conquered Lithuania within one week, the great YESHIVOT of Lithuania were closed. Some students were among the thousands who escaped eastward (through Russia) to Shanghai *(China)*, having received visas from the Japanese diplomat Chiune Sugihara who continued hand-writing visas —although instructed to cease and leave — even as his moving train was leaving the station.

The Amshinover Rebbe, Adm.R. Shimon Shalom, was an active proponent for the exodus of thousands of bachurim in Mir, Kletzk, Radin, Novardok, and other YESHIVOT to Japan and Shanghai at the outbreak of World War II — when there were estimates of some 4,000 students in over 80 Novardoker YESHIVOT throughout Poland, (distinct in the MUSSAR style of R.Yosef Yoizel Horowitz, Der Alter of Novardok, discple of R.Yisroel Salanter and Der Alter of Kelm). "Reb. Shimon Shalom" was an active communal leader upon arriving in the east, and is reported to have explained to Japanese officials that the German (allies of Japan) hated the Jews "because of our Oriental origins."

Rabbi Eliezer Silver — a disciple of the Rogatchover Gaon and R.Chaim Ozer Grodzinski (see 5648\1888, 5649\1889) — as president of the Agudath Harabonim of America (where he arrived in 1907) spearheaded the effort of their Vaad Hatzalah in rescuing as many European Torah scholars as possible. He helped save an estimated 10,000 Jewish lives by raising millions of dollars, which he channelled through passport counterfeiters, smugglers, and Nazi officers.

Some of the great Lithuanian Talmud scholars were killed by the Nazis, including:

- ❖ R.Elchanan Wasserman (ROSH YESHIVA of Baranowice),
- ❖ R.Avraham Yitzchak Bloch and
- ❖ R.Azriel Rabinovitz (ROSHEI YESHIVA, in Telz).

A number of the great Lithuanian Talmud scholars died a natural death during this very short period, including:

- ❖ R.Shimon Shkop (ROSH YESHIVA in Grodno) who had died a year earlier,
- ❖ R.Boruch Ber Leibovitz (the Kaminetzer ROSH YESHIVA), and
- ❖ R.Chaim Ozer Grodzinski — rabbi in Vilna, and author of Achi'ezer (*SH'ELOT UTESHUVOT*) — had both died in this same year.

A number of the great Lithuanian Talmud scholars escaped the war (although some lost their families):

- ❖ R.Aharon Kotler (ROSH YESHIVA in Kletzk *(Lithuania))* escaped (via Japan) to the U.S.A., and he established a new YESHIVA — with great success — in Lakewood *(New Jersey)*.
- ❖ R.Yosef Kahaneman (rabbi and ROSH YESHIVA in Ponevitch *(Panevezys, Lithuania)*) was overseas when the war broke out, and he settled in Eretz Yisrael, where he (later) established the Ponevitcher YESHIVA in Bnei Brak.
- ❖ R.Eliezer Yehuda Finkel (ROSH YESHIVA of Mir) escaped from war-torn Europe to Yerushalayim, where he established a YESHIVA called Mir. A separate branch of the Mir YESHIVA which operated in Shanghai during the war years was later transferred to New York (two years after the war).
- ❖ R.Eliyah Meir Bloch was raising funds in the U.S.A. (with R.Mordechai Katz) when the war broke out, and they founded the YESHIVA of Telz in Cleveland *(U.S.A.)* less than half a year after the original YESHIVA was closed in Lithuania.

The Jews of Kovno *(Kaunus, Lithuania)* were massacred by the Lithuanian Nazi-sympathizers on the 1st **Tammuz** *(see Av 5701\1941)*; 800 Jews were killed by invading Rumanian troops in Novoselitsa *(Bessarabia, Russia)* on the 2nd **Tammuz**, and the Germans killed over 6,000 Jews of Kovno in the ten days following the 3rd **Tammuz**. 12,000 Jews were killed in Jassy *(Rumania)* by German and Rumanian soldiers in a two-day massacre that started on the 3rd **Tammuz**; 1,000 Jews were burned in a synagogue in Bialystok *(Poland)* on the 3rd **Tammuz**; and 3,300 were killed there *(see Av 5703\1943)* in the following two weeks.

5,000 Jews were killed outside Brisk *(Brest-Litovsk, Poland-Lithuania)* on the 4th **Tammuz**.

Many Ukrainians had welcomed the Nazi-German invasion, and on the 7th **Tammuz** the Germans instigated POGROMS in Lvov *(Lemberg, Poland)* and in Borislav *(Poland)*, by reminding the local population of the assassination of Petlyura — their previous independence leader *(see 5678\1918)* — who was killed by a Jew (in 1926). More than 2,000 Jews were killed in these POGROMS, and 3,500 Jews were killed by Ukrainians in Zlotchov *(Poland)* on the 8th **Tammuz**.

400 Jews were killed by the German-Nazis in Drogobych *(Drahavitsch, Ukraine) (see Elul 5702\1942)* on the 8th **Tammuz**; 3,000 were killed in a fortress outside of Lutzk *(Poland)* on the 9th **Tammuz** *(see Elul 5702\1942)*; and 5,000 Jews were killed in Tarnopol *(Poland) (see Iyar 5702\1942)* in the following week.

German and Rumanian troops captured Chernovitz *(Rumania)* from the Russians on the 10th **Tammuz**, and they massacred over 2,000 Jews. 200 Jews were killed in Chortkov *(Czortkow, Poland)* on the same day, and German and Rumanian troops shot 2,000 Jews in Hotin *(Bessarabia, Russia)* on the 12th **Tammuz**. 1,200 Jews were killed by the Nazis on the outskirts of Slonim *(then Poland)* on the 22nd **Tammuz** *(see Elul 5701\1941)*. 3,000 Jews of the port town of Libava *(Liepaja, Latvia) (see Kislev 5702\1941)* were killed at the lighthouse on the 29th **Tammuz**, and 700 Jews were killed outside of Oshmyany *(Lithuania)* on the 1st **Av**.

Many REBBES (ADMURIM, 'TZADIKIM') were killed by the Nazis *(see Elul 5702\1942)*, and some escaped *(see Adar-2 5700\1940, 5701\1940, Tishrei 5704\1943, Kislev 5705\1944)*. Adm.R.Ben Tziyon (ben Shlomo) of Bobov *(see 5636\1876)* was killed on the 4th **Av**,

and his son Adm.R.Shlomo escaped, and succeeded him — after the war — in the U.S.A.
The Nazis killed 900 Jews of Vilkovishk *(Vilkaviski, Lithuania)* on the 4th **Av**; 400 on the 8th **Av** (Erev Tisha B'Av); 500 in Kishinev *(Bessarabia, Russia)* on the 11th **Av**; and 3,000 in Ostraha *(Ostrog, Poland) (see Elul 5701\1941)*. They killed 1,000 Jews of Kovno *(Kaunus, Lithuania)* on the 14th **Av** *(see Tammuz 5701\1941)*; 1,500 Jews of Zambrov *(Poland)* were killed on the 26th **Av** (1,000 were killed there two weeks later), and 350 Jews were killed in the outskirts of Koretz *(Poland) (see Sivan 5702\1942)* on the 27th **Av**.
1,400 Jews were killed near Tiktin *(Tykocin, Poland-Lithuania)* on the 2nd **Elul**; 7,000 Jews were killed in Marijampole *(Lithuania)*; 2,500 in Ostraha *(Ostrog, Poland) (see Av 5701\1941, Cheshvan 5702\1941)* on the 9th **Elul**; 1,700 in Radomyshl *(Poland)* on the 14th; and 9,000 Jews on the outskirts of Slonim *(then Poland)* on the 22nd **Elul** *(see Tammuz 5701\1941)*. A few who had escaped from the large pits into which they were thrown came back to the ghetto hospital, but were seized by the Nazis, returned to the pits, and shot.
There were 30,000 Jews in Zhitomir *(Ukraine)* before the war, and on the 27th **Elul** the Nazis killed them all — except for those who had fled.

5702 ≋ 1941

28,000 Jews of the vicinity of Vinitza *(Ukraine)* were killed there on Rosh HaShanah, most by Ukrainian militia — many of whom performed their destruction on horseback.
The methods used by the Nazis for killing Jews had not met their desired standards of efficiency *(see Sivan 5702\1942)*. Accordingly — at this stage — they began using poisonous gas in the Auschwitz DEATH CAMP *(see Sivan 5700\1940)*. They also extended the camp (by including Birkenau), in order to increase the intake capacity.

34,000 Jews of Kiev massacred and buried at Babi Yar.

On the 8th and 9th **Tishrei** (Erev Yom Kippur), the Nazis machine-gunned 34,000 Jews on the outskirts of Kiev *(Ukraine)* into the ravine of Babi Yar, where they were buried — many of them while still alive, *(see Elul 5701\1941)* — and a woman gave birth during the slaughter.
The total number of Jews eventually killed and buried there was 100,000.
When the Nazis ordered the Jews of Tuchin *(Poland)* to assemble on the 12th **Tishrei**, the heads of the Judenrat decided that everyone should revolt. Many were killed when the Nazis broke into the ghetto, but 2,000 escaped to the forests. 300 returned when the Nazis promised to allow volunteer returnees to live in the ghetto — but they were taken to the cemetery and shot. Many others were delivered back to the Nazis by local Ukrainians.
All 30,000 Jews of the ghetto in Berditchev *(Ukraine)* had been killed by the 14th **Tishrei** (Erev Sukkot), and 500 Jews were killed outside of Peremyshlany *(Ukraine)* on that day. 10,000 Jews were killed in the Jewish cemetery in Stanislav *(Poland) (see Shvat 5703\1943)* on Hoshana Rabba (21st **Tishrei**), and on that day the head of the Judenrat in Chortkov *(Czortkow, Poland) (see Elul 5702\1942)*, Shmuel Kruh, was killed, for his strong stand against cooperating with the Nazis *(see 4th Cheshvan 5703\1942)*.
Rumanian Legionnaires *(see Sivan 5701\1941)* entered Odessa *(Russia)* on the 25th **Tishrei**, and killed 8,000 Jews. They killed another 40,000 within the next ten days.
2,500 Jews were killed outside Kossov *(Poland)* on the 25th and 26th **Tishrei**, and all the Jews (1,700) of Kaidanov *(Russia)* were killed on the 30th **Tishrei**.
3,000 Jews were killed in Ostraha *(Ostrog, Poland) (see Elul 5701\1941)* on the 4th **Cheshvan**; 4,000 were killed in Kletzk *(Lithuania) (see Av 5702\1942)* on the 5th **Cheshvan**; 5,000 were killed in Nesvizh *(Lithuania) (see Av 5702\1942)* on the 9th **Cheshvan**; and 2,500 Jews were killed in Nadvorna *(Poland)* on the 16th — the day that 18,000 Jews of Rovno *(Poland) (see Tammuz 5702\1942)* were machine-gunned by the Nazis in a forest. 12,000 Jews from the ghetto of Minsk *(Russia)* were also killed in a similar manner on the 17th, and another 5,000 two weeks later *(see Adar 5702\1942)*. Their houses were used by the Germans to settle Jews who had been deported from Germany and Austria.
The Nazis killed 1,500 Jews in Mir *(Russia)* on the 19th **Cheshvan**; 800 Jews were killed in Zaleshchiki *(Poland)* on the 24th **Cheshvan**; and 700 Jews from the ghetto of Lubavitch *(Russia)* were killed.
On the 10th **Kislev**, 10,500 Jews of Riga *(Latvia)* were shot to death in a nearby forest; another 16,000 — including the historian Simon Dubnow — were killed during the ensuing week; and 1,500 Jews were killed in the forest near Borislav *(Poland) (see Tammuz 5701\1941, Adar-I 5703\1943)*. 400 Jews of Novardok *(Novogrodek, Russia) (see Av 5702\1942)* were killed on the 17th **Kislev** *(the day Japan attacked the United States at Pearl Harbor)*; 3,500 were killed in Libava *(Liepaja, Latvia) (see Tammuz 5701\1941)* on the first and second days of

Chanukah (25th and 26th **Kislev**); and 900 Jews were killed outside of Zobalotov *(Ukraine)* on the 2nd **Tevet** (the last day of Chanukah).
While on burial duty at the Chelmno death camp, someone found his wife and children amongst the corpses just gassed.

5702 — 1942

More than 15,000 Jews were killed in Drobitzky Yar outside of Charkov *(Russia)* in **Tevet** and **Shvat**; 1,400 Jews of Novi Sad *(Yugoslavia)* were shot and dumped into the icy waters of the Danube on the 5th **Shvat**; and 3,000 Jews were killed in Brailov *(Russia)* by the Nazi-Germans on the 25th **Shvat**.
The 'Struma' — a ship with 769 Jewish refugees on board, which the British had rejected from Eretz Yisrael *(see 5699\1939)* — was sunk by the Nazi-Germans in (or near) the Black Sea on the 7th **Adar** *(see Cheshvan 5701\1940)*.
The Nazis killed several thousand Jews — including all the children in the orphanage — in Minsk *(Russia)* on the 13th **Adar** *(see Cheshvan 5702\1941, Av 5702\1942)*. The Jews in the Minsk ghetto underground were well organized, and they eventually helped 10,000 Jews escape to the forests, despite the ruthless reprisals imposed, if discovered.
Many Jews — some say over 25,000 — formed partisan groups *(armed guerrillas)* in the forests, and they attacked the Nazis sporadically *(see Nissan 5703\1943, Cheshvan 5705\1944)*.
1,500 Jews were killed on Purim (14th **Adar**) in Dolhinov *(Poland) (see Sivan 5702\1942)*; 800 Jews were killed in Radoshkovichi *(Poland)* on the 22nd **Adar;** and 1,000 were killed in Ilya *(Poland)* on the 28th **Adar**.
2,000 Jews were killed outside Rogatyn *(Poland)* on the 2nd **Nissan;** 1,500 Jews were killed near Horodenka *(Gorodenka, Poland)* on the 17th (the 3rd day of Pesach); and 900 were killed in Kitev *(Kuty, Poland)* on the 23rd **Nissan** when the Germans set fire to Jewish houses.
On the 29th **Nissan** the Nazis proclaimed the Crimean peninsula *(S.W. Russia)* — a region in which some 60,000 Jews had lived before the war — to be 'Judenrein' ('free' of any Jews), because in a previous decision (18th **Tevet** 1939) they had declared the Kra'im (Kara'ites) not to be Jews (see 5613\1853) – a notion supported by Talmudists they consulted , who sought to spare them – but the Kra'im vacillated between indifference to the Jewish cause and in some cases actual collaboration with the Germans.
1,000 Jews were shot in a forest near Tarnopol *(Poland) (see Tammuz 5701\1941)* on the 8th **Iyar**; over 2,800 Jews of Dunayevtsy *(Ukraine)* were killed by the Nazi-Germans on the 15th **Iyar**; all the Jews of Dokshytz *(then Poland)* were taken outside the town and killed on the 18th **Iyar** (Lag B'Omer); and 2,000 Jews from Radin *(Lithuania)* were killed on the 23rd **Iyar**.
2,200 Jews were killed in Koretz *(Poland) (see Av 5701\1941)* on the 5th **Sivan** (Erev Shavu'ot); over 2,500 Jews were killed in Dolhinov *(Poland) (see Adar 5702\1942)* on the 6th **Sivan** (Shavu'ot); 1,500 Jews were killed in Radziwillow *(Poland)* on the 13th; 4,000 were killed in Kobrin *(Poland) (see Cheshvan 5703\1942)* on the 17th; and 3,000 Jews were killed by the Nazis in Braslav *(Poland)* in three days commencing the 18th **Sivan** *(see Adar-2 5703\1943)*.
The chief Nazi exterminator of Jews *(Reinhard Heydrich)* was killed in **Sivan** by Czechoslovak partisans. The Nazis used this as a pretext to accelerate the massive program of extermination of Jews. They substituted the previous method of gassing Jews — in closed motor-vans with their exhaust fumes fed into them — for the more efficient system of gassing rooms *(see Tishrei 5702\1941)*. The mass-burial disposal of bodies was substituted with cremating furnaces. Trains brought 6,000 to 10,000 Polish Jews a day to the DEATH CAMPS, mainly Treblinka, and also Maidanek, Belzec, Sobibor, Chelmno, and Auschwitz. The latter began its highly efficient extermination of Jews — at an achieved rate of 10,000 a day — on the 5th **Tammuz** *(see Tishrei 5702\1941)*.
On the 2nd **Tammuz** the Nazis shot at Jews escaping from the ghetto in Druya *(Lithuania)*, and they set the ghetto on fire, killing all 1,500 Jews.
2,500 Jews were killed outside Glubokoye *(Poland) (see Av 5703\1943)* on the 4th **Tammuz**, and the Nazis killed 5,000 Jews of Rovno *(Poland)* on the 28th **Tammuz** *(see Cheshvan 5702\1941)*.
The first transport of Dutch Jews arrived at Auschwitz on the 3rd **Av**, and the head of the Nazi-Party SS (from Schutzstaffel: Protective Squadron — independent of the Army — of which the Gestapo [from Geheime Staats-Polizei] were a branch) Heinrich Himmler himself supervised their gassing.

1,000 Jews were killed in the ghetto of Kletzk *(Lithuania) (see Cheshvan 5702\1941)* when the Nazis set it afire on the 7th **Av**; and on the 8th **Av** (Erev Tisha B'Av), the Jews remaining in the ghetto of Nesvizh *(Lithuania) (see Cheshvan 5702\1941)* tried to resist the Nazi-Germans, but most were

killed, and only a few escaped to the forests.
The mass deportation of Jews from the Warsaw ghetto *(see Kislev 5700\1939, Sivan 5702\1942)* to the DEATH CAMPS began on Erev Tisha B'**Av**, at a daily rate of 5,000 or more *(see Elul 5702\1942)*. The Nazis lured the starving people to the assembly points — with food and promises for resettlement — although most Jews had grave doubts. Adam Czierniakov, the head of the Judenrat *(Nazi approved Jewish self government of the ghetto)*, committed suicide rather than co-operate in the deportations. Most of the Jews were deported to the Treblinka DEATH CAMP — 100 kilometers away — where they were killed.
More than 200 Jews were killed in Ivye *(Poland-Lithuania)* on the 9th **Av** (Tisha B'Av); 10,000 Jews of Minsk *(Russia)* were massacred on the 14th **Av** *(see Adar 5702\1942, Shvat 5703\1943)*; over 5,000 Jews of Novardok *(Novogrodek, Russia) (see Kislev 5702\1941)* were killed on the 24th **Av**; and 40,000 Jews from Lvov *(Lemberg, Poland)* were killed in two weeks, commencing the 27th **Av** *(see Tammuz 5701\1941, Sivan 5703\1943)*.
700 Jews were killed in Gorlice *(Poland)* on the 1st **Elul**; on the 4th **Elul** 600 Jews were killed — when thousands were deported — in Drogobych *(Drahavitsch, Poland) (see Tammuz 5701\1941)*; during five days, commencing on the 6th **Elul**, 7,000 Jews were killed on a hill outside Lutzk *(Poland) (see Tammuz 5701\1941)*; and 1,000 were killed in Minsk-Mazowiecki *(Poland)* on the 8th **Elul.** The children, sick, and elderly — 500 Jews — were killed in Chortkov *(Czortkow, Poland) (see Tammuz 5701\1941)* on the 15th **Elul,** when thousands of others were transported to the DEATH CAMPS; 4,000 Jews were killed in the prison courtyard of Ludmir *(Vladimir Volynski, Poland)* beginning the 19th **Elul**; and — outside of the town — another 14,000 were killed within two weeks. 1,000 Jews were killed in Dzialoszyce *(Poland)* — and thousands more were deported — on the 21st **Elul,** the same day that over 600 Jews were killed in Lachva *(Poland-Lithuania)* when they resisted the Nazi invasion of the ghetto — and many escaped to the forests.
The Nazis killed all of the 11,000 Jews of Stolin *(Russia)* (in a nearby forest) — including Adm.-R.Moshe of Karlin-Stolin *(see 5552\1792)* — on the 29th **Elul**, Erev Rosh HaShanah.
90,000 Jews were deported from the Warsaw ghetto *(see Av 5702\1942)* on Erev Rosh HaShanah, the 29th **Elul**, completing a total of 300,000 deportations and killings in 53 days *(see Nissan 5703\1943)*.
Hillel Zeitlin, a writer and thinker — who had returned to Jewish religious observance — wore his Tallit at the deportation assembly point; his exhortations of the young to fight created an immediate skirmish. He was killed on that Erev Rosh HaShanah in Treblinka; Shaindel — the daughter of Adm.R.Yosef Yitzchak of Lubavitch *(see Adar-2 5700\1940)* — was killed there on the 2nd day of Rosh HaShanah 5703*1942*.

5703 — *1942*

3,000 Jews of Baranowice *(Poland-Lithuania)* were killed by the Nazi-Germans on the day after Yom Kippur (11th **Tishrei**) 5703\1942.
The Jews of Kobrin *(Poland) (see Sivan 5702\1942)* attacked their Nazi killers on the 3rd **Cheshvan** *(see Adar-2 5703\1943)*; the Jews of Bereza Kartuska *(Poland)* set their ghetto on fire on the 4th **Cheshvan** — when the Nazi's came to remove them — and members of the Judenrat *(see Av 5702\1942)* took their own lives. The Nazis killed many of the Jews in the burning ghetto, and 1,800 Jews were killed outside of the town.
The Nazi-Germans shot 300 Jewish children — of the orphanage in Cracow *(Poland)*, together with the patients and inmates of the Jewish hospital and the old age home *(see 15th Elul 5702\1942)* — when they were selecting 6,000 Jews to be sent to Belzec DEATH CAMP, on the 17th **Cheshvan** 5703\1942.
The last 16,000 Jews in Pinsk *(Russia)* were killed by the Nazis on the 18th **Cheshvan** 5703\1942, and the last 3,000 Jews of Baranowice *(see Tishrei)* were killed on the 9th **Tevet**.

5703 — 1943

250 Jewish children and old people were shot by the Nazis *(see Cheshvan 5703\1942)* in the ghetto of Chestochova *(Czestochowa, Poland)* on the 27th **Tevet** *(see Elul 5699\1939)*, the day after some Jewish resistance fighters fought a battle there; hundreds of Jews were shot in Radomsk *(Poland)* on the 28th **Tevet**, when they resisted the deportation of thousands of Jews to the Treblinka DEATH CAMP. 10,000 Jews were killed in Stanislav *(Poland) (see Tishrei 5702\1941)*.

Nazi-Germany experienced massive losses in the battle of Stalingrad.

The turning point of World War II came *(see 5701\1941)* when the Germans lost the battle for Stalingrad *(Volgograd, Russia)* — surrendering to the Russians on the 25th **Shvat** — a deciding factor being a new airplane (La-5) designed by a Jewish engineer. *(Another engineer — Mikhail Gurevich*

— designed the MiG airplanes named after him.)

- Over 250,000 German soldiers were killed, and
- almost 100,000 were captured,
- including 24 generals.

1,500 Jews of Minsk *(Russia)* were killed by the Nazi-Germans on the 26th **Shvat** *(see Av 5702\1942)*; 2,500 Jews of Butshatsh *(Buczacz, Poland)* were killed outside the town on the 26th **Shvat** and 27th; 600 women, children and elderly Jews were killed *(see Tevet)* in the city slaughterhouse of Borislav *(Poland)* on the 11th **Adar-1** *(see Kislev 5702\1941)*; 2,000 of the last Jews in the Cracow ghetto *(see Kislev 5700\1939)* were killed on the 6th **Adar-2** — and 8,000 were sent to the DEATH CAMPS; and 900 Jews were killed in the cemetery of Sambor *(Poland)* on the 7th **Adar-2**.

On the 8th **Adar-2** the Nazis began transporting the 44,000 Jews of Salonika *(Greece)* to the DEATH CAMPS. Some Jews of Braslav *(Poland) (see Sivan 5702\1942)* resisted deportation *(see Cheshvan 5703\1942)* to the DEATH CAMPS on the 12th **Adar-2** — until they ran out of ammunition. 127 Jews were killed in Chestochova *(Czestochowa, Poland)* on the 13th **Adar-2** *(see Elul 5699\1939)*, and 750 Jews were killed outside of Skalat *(Poland) (see Iyar 5703\1943)* on the 2nd **Nissan**.

The remaining Jews in Warsaw staged a massive uprising.

Word of the fate of deported Jews was smuggled back to the Warsaw ghetto *(see Av 5702\1942)* — some say an underground fighter had been sent to establish why the same train carriages (supposedly taking Jews for resettlement) were returning within a very short time (each carriages has an identification number). The Treblinka DEATH CAMP was only 100 kilometers away. Accordingly there had already been some resistance to the Nazis.

R.Menachem Zemba— a great Torah scholar, respected by the Rogatchover Ga'on (who was noted for his reluctance to endorse other scholars) — together with other rabbis had declared Erev Rosh Chodesh **Nissan** as a day of fast and repentance, in light of the impending doom.

On the 14th **Nissan** (Erev Pesach) the remaining 35,000 Jews in the Warsaw ghetto — from an original 450,000) — staged an organized uprising, and they drove back the Nazis with a rain of bullets, when they arrived to carry out the final removal of all Jews. This resistance lasted for almost a month.

On the same Erev Pesach, a train full of deportees was derailed in Belgium by the Jewish underground *(partisans, see Adar 5702\1942)* and non-Jewish rail workers. Hundreds of Jews were saved from being taken to the DEATH CAMPS.

R.Menachem Zemba had reportedly declined offers of escape from the Warsaw ghetto, and was killed there in **Nissan**, during the uprising which he is said to have supported. Mordechai Anilevitch, the 24 year old commander of the Warsaw ghetto uprising, was killed during the fighting on the 3rd **Iyar**, and the Warsaw ghetto uprising came to an end on the 10th. Although the ghetto was burned to the ground, some stray SURVIVORS hid in the rubble and fired sporadically at Nazis for another two months.

660 Jews were killed in Skalat *(Poland) (see Nissan 5703\1943)* on the 4th **Iyar**; 1,000 were killed in the cemetery in Stry *(Poland)* on the 17th; 3,000 were killed in the cemetery in Tluste *(Tolstoye, Poland)* on the 22nd **Iyar**; and another 1,000 on the 3rd **Sivan**.

Most of the remaining Jews in the ghetto of Lvov, *(see Av 5702\1942)* were killed in a six day massacre that began on the 18th **Sivan**. 4,000 Jews of Disna *(Lithuania)* were killed outside the town, and 2,000 escaped to the forests — where they joined partisan groups — although most of them were eventually captured by the Nazis.

On the 2nd **Tammuz** the Vilna ghetto underground had freed their leader — Yitzchak Wittenberg — from Nazi captivity, an act which almost triggered a previously-planned uprising. The Nazis immediately proclaimed that — unless he gave himself in — they would demolish the whole ghetto and its total population; Wittenberg decided that such dramatic loss of life was inexpedient, and surrendered himself. Two months later the Vilna ghetto underground resisted (for a few weeks) the massive deportation of Jews to the DEATH CAMPS.

5,000 Jews were killed in Kamenka-Bugskaya *(Poland)* on the 7th **Tammuz**, and 500 were killed at the Jewish cemetery in Chestochova *(Czestochowa, Poland)* on the (fast of the) 17th **Tammuz**.

The prisoners of Treblinka DEATH CAMP revolted and escaped.

The prisoners of Treblinka staged a revolt on the 1st **Av** — which was triggered off a crucial hour earlier than planned, because of a mishap. Nevertheless hundreds of prisoners escaped, although most were caught within a few weeks, and there were only 50 SURVIVORS at the end of the war. *(Estimated total killed in Treblinka: 750,000.)* The Jews of Bendin *(Bedzin, Poland)* attempted to resist their deportation to the DEATH CAMPS on the 3rd **Av**.

An organized uprising began in the Bialystok ghetto.

An organized uprising broke out in the ghetto of Bialystok *(Poland)* on the 15th **Av** which was suppressed after a few days, and the Nazis deported all the remaining 40,000 Jews *(see Tammuz 5701\1941)* to the DEATH CAMPS. When the Jews of Glubokoye *(Poland)* *(see Tammuz 5702\1942)* attempted to resist deportation to the DEATH CAMPS — on the 19th **Av** — the whole ghetto was set afire by the Nazis, and over 1,000 Jews perished.

The Danish people quietly rescued 93% of their Jews to safety.

With the help of Danish captains and fishermen — in the three weeks before Rosh HaShanah — over 7,000 Jews escaped across the straits from Denmark to neutral Sweden. When the Nazi-Germans came to round up the Jews — on the night after Rosh HaShanah — less than 500 Jews remained, most of whom were also fortunate and became SURVIVORS of the war.

5704 — 1943

Jews escaped in the Sobibor DEATH CAMP uprising.

When the transports of new victims to the Sobibor DEATH CAMP had ceased, the remaining 300 forced laborers realized that they were no longer needed and would certainly be killed. They staged an uprising on the 15th **Tishrei**, and 170 escaped alive, although all but 30 were captured again, and killed. *(Estimated total killed in Sobibor: 250,000.)*

The Nazi-Germans subsequently shut down the Janowska Road CONCENTRATION CAMP *(near Lvov, Ukraine)* on the 22nd **Cheshvan**, for fear of an uprising there. They removed all traces of this particularly brutal DEATH CAMP where Jews were tortured for the entertainment of Nazi officers. (A laundry cleaner later testified that she had regularly to clean the very bloodied clothes of a German officer.)

Adm.R.Aharon (ben Yissachar Dov) of Belz *(see 5615\1855)* had managed to move from ghetto to ghetto during the course of the war until he escaped to Eretz Yisrael via Hungary.

5704 — 1944

300,000 Hungarian Jews were killed in 3 months.

The Germans invaded Hungary (their previous ally *(see Sivan 5701\1941)*) on the 25th **Adar**, and deportations of Hungarian Jews to Auschwitz started shortly thereafter. The Nazis convinced these Jews — with the assistance of Jewish collaborators *(see Kislev 5705\1944)* — that because Germany was losing battles in the war (the 933 day siege of Leningrad had just been broken on the 2nd **Shvat**) they were no longer killing Jews but merely resettling them. This tactic made for smooth and accelerated deportations to the DEATH CAMPS — mainly Auschwitz — and 300,000 Hungarian Jews were killed within three months.

When deportations to Auschwitz began, Carl Lutz — Swiss Vice-Consul to Hungary — increased his staff from 15 to 150 and started to issue tens of thousands of "protective letters", even though he only had eight thousand official certificates. In order to hide this, he always repeated the numbers 1 to 8,000, and then grouped each 1,000 together into one Swiss collective passport placing them under formal Swiss protection. He helped 62,000 Jews survive the war — including thousands of Jewish children emigrating to Eretz Yisrael — and when the Budapest Jews were herded into a ghetto, he placed some 30,000 people into protected houses.

Many Jews escaped from the Koldychevo CONCENTRATION CAMP on the 27th **Adar**, and 10 Nazi guards were shot.

The Nazis forced all the Jews of the ancient community of Canea *(Crete)* into a boat which was towed out to sea and sunk, on the 9th **Sivan**.

Almost one year after the Italians had removed Hitler's friend Mussolini from power, the Allied forces that had landed in Italy pushed back German armies, and entered Rome — the first capital city to be LIBERATED from the Nazis — on the 13th **Sivan**. Jews of Rome — SURVIVORS of the deportations — emerged from their hiding places. Two days later, on the 15th **Sivan**, 150,000 service-men of the Allied forces landed on the beaches of Normandy *(France)* — using over 5,000 ships and 11,000 airplanes to secure a beach-head — taking nearly 10,000 casualties, with over 4,000 killed.

The retreating Nazi-Germans began evacuating some of the DEATH CAMPS and CONCENTRATION CAMPS by marching the inmates to other locations in what became known as DEATH MARCHES, as many of the captives died on the way. They also began eliminating — killing — many of their Jewish slave laborers, 3,000 of them at Ponary *(see Sivan 5701\1941)* on the 12th **Tammuz**.

On the 15th **Av** the Nazis discovered the Amsterdam family hideout of Anne Frank — a 15 year old girl of a family of Jewish-German refugees — whose diary of suffering *(discovered and published after the war)* was later received internationally with acclaim. She later died in the Bergen-Belsen CONCENTRATION CAMP during a typhus epidemic.

R.Levi Yitzchak Schneersohn — a direct descendant of the Tzemach Tzedek *(of Lubavitch)* had been sent to Russian exile four years earlier — after having previously spent a year in prison — for fulfilling his duties as a rabbi (see 5680\1920). He died on the 20th **Av** in his exile in Alma Ata *(Asian Russia)*. The many comments and notes *(particularly on the Zohar)* — that he had written in exile, on the sides of his book, with ink prepared by his wife from local roots and herbs — were later published by his son and disciple Adm.R.Menachem Mendel of Lubavitch.

R.Michal Dov Weismandel — a son-in-law of the Rav of Nitra, and a Jewish (Czech.) resistance leader working to rescue Jews — had tried (from his hiding place in a cave) to warn the Hungarian Jews of their impending doom. He was found and captured by the Nazis, shortly after he sent a letter (including maps) to the outside world, demanding that the Allied forces *(U.S.A., England, etc.)* bomb the Auschwitz DEATH CAMP in order to disable it. He escaped this capture by jumping off the moving transport train — as did many of the few war SURVIVORS — as it headed for Auschwitz. He survived, and later settled in the U.S.A.

5705 — 1944

Jewish uprising in the Auschwitz DEATH CAMP.

Jews were forced to assist in cremating the bodies — of those killed by gassing — at the Birkenau part of Auschwitz DEATH CAMP *(see Tishrei 5702\1941)*, and on the 20th **Tishrei** they staged an uprising, killing some of the Nazis. Some escaped, but none were ultimately SURVIVORS.

Chanah Senesh was a 23 year old Hungarian girl who had already settled in Eretz Yisrael. She had returned to the war-zone — by parachuting into Nazi territory with 31 others — to assist partisans *(see Adar 5702\1942)* and rescue Jews. She was caught, and was executed in Budapest on the 20th **Cheshvan**.

Two train-transports totaling 1,686 Jews were released by the Nazi-Germans in order that the occupants be enabled to leave Europe. One train of 318 was released on the 29th **Av** 1944, and another carrying 1,368 — from the Bergen Belsen CONCENTRATION CAMP — on the 20th **Kislev** 5705*1944*. Their release was secured by Rudolf Kasztner — head of the Zionist rescue operations in Hungary — whom the Germans had granted the privilege to travel around Europe, including Germany. After the war he was seriously implicated — in a prolonged trial — of collaborating with the Nazis, by knowingly allowing, and even assisting, in the deportation of hundreds of thousands of Hungarian Jews to the DEATH CAMPS *(see Adar 5704\1944)*, in return for the release of this relatively small number of Jews.

Adm.R.Yoel of Satmar was among those released from Bergen Belsen; he went to Eretz Yisrael for a few years, and later settled in New York, in 1947.

5705 — 1945

Raoul Wallenberg — a diplomat representing neutral Sweden, who used his position to save and rescue tens of thousands of Hungarian Jews from the Nazi killings — disappeared on the 3rd **Shvat**, when he was taken by the advancing Russian army.

The Auschwitz DEATH CAMP was captured and liberated.

The Russian army reached the Auschwitz DEATH CAMP on the 12th **Shvat** and LIBERATED the 2,819 Jewish SURVIVORS *(see Sivan 5700\1940, Tishrei 5702\1941)*.

- Estimated total Jews killed in the Auschwitz DEATH CAMP: 2.5 million.

On the 17th **Nissan**, the Nazis killed 'Maria of Paris', a Russian nun who saved the lives of many French Jews from Nazi extermination.

After the Russians had LIBERATED the Lublin and Auschwitz DEATH CAMPS *(see Sivan 5704\1944, Shvat 5705\1945)*:

- The U.S. army captured and LIBERATED the Buchenwald DEATH CAMP on the 29th **Nissan**, finding 20,000 Jewish SURVIVORS.
- The British captured and LIBERATED the Bergen Belsen CONCENTRATION CAMP on the 2nd **Iyar,** with 40,000 SURVIVORS.
- Dachau was captured by the U.S. on the 16th **Iyar**, and
- Mathausen was LIBERATED on the day of Nazi-Germany's surrender, the 24th **Iyar.**

(Some of the liberators reported that the crematoria were still warm — the defeated Nazis had been killing until the last moment.)

On the 28th **Nissan** the advancing U.S. Army *(104th Infantry Division)* entered the Mittelbau-Dora Concentration Camp at Nordhausen *(Germany)* and discovered 3,000 corpses and 750 sick and emaciated prisoners (who had been left behind when the SS took most of the inmates on death marches.) *(Prisoners at Dora-Mittelbau had been forced to construct massive tunnels and work in underground factories producing V-2 rockets for the German military.)* A young girl (18 or 19) — Lili Meier — was one of the sick left behind. *(She had been deported from Bilke (Carpatho-Ruthenia, then Hungary) to Auschwitz with her family on the 2nd Sivan 5604\1944, and when the Russian forces were approaching, was evacuated from Auschwitz and ended in the Dora camp, more than 400 miles away.)* She was looking around in an evacuated and deserted SS barracks when she found a picture-album (with more than 200 pictures) of the "processing" of a trainload of arrivals at Auschwitz-Birkenau. She immediately recognized the rabbi of her town (R.Naftali Tzvi Weiss); then some friends, relatives, and family, and she took possession of the album. This collection — it has since been recognized — was the only time the Nazis photographed the entire "processing" (except for the actual gassing and cremation.) Its purpose (and how it came to Dora, so far away) is unknown. *[The collection was copied by the Jewish Museum in Prague, and eventually donated (minus some pictures she gave away to people who recognized family in them) to Yad Vashem — the Holocaust museum in Yerushalayim. The 3 pictures on page 284 are from that collection.]*

Nazi-Germany was conquered, and World War II ended in Europe.

Nazi-Germany was militarily defeated, and was compelled to surrender unconditionally, which they did on 24th **Iyar.** Adolph Hitler was reported to have committed suicide on the 17th **Iyar**.

The Theresienstadt GHETTO-CAMP — which had served as a massive staging area for the deportation of some 140,000 Jews to the DEATH CAMPS — was liberated three days after the surrender, on the 27th **Iyar**. Among the SURVIVORS there was Leo Baeck — previously a prominent liberal (REFORM) rabbi in Berlin, and president of the Nazi-created "Reich Representation of German Jews" from 1933 until his deportation to Theresienstadt in early 1943. He had refused the opportunity to leave Germany, even when the imminent danger was clear. He settled in London after the war.

On the 27th and the 30th **Av** the United States Air Force delivered "Atom Bombs" on the Japanese cities Hiroshima and Nagasaki — causing destruction of a completely new magnitude. The Pacific war ended and the world entered the nuclear age. Many Jewish scientists were at the forefront of the new technologies, Albert Einstein being the most prominent (because of his notable and celebrated theories of relativity.)

Many SURVIVORS died after the camps were LIBERATED — from weakness, disease, and the inability to properly digest food after years of starvation.

Jews from all over Europe — SURVIVORS of the wartime massacre of 6,000,000 Jews, the Holocaust — were placed by the victorious Allied forces into special camps for DISPLACED PERSONS. Most of them began looking for relatives and friends among the SURVIVORS, and a country to make their new home. Besides the vivid memories of horror that they carried in their minds, and the loss of loved ones that left an emptiness in the heart, most of them carried serial numbers on their arms — tattooed there by the Nazi-Germans — who had reduced the significance of a Jew to a number; the ultimate aim of which was to reach the number zero.

Many of the Nazi murderers were not captured, or managed to escape (see 5707\1946).

Adm.R.Yekutiel Yehuda of Klausenberg *(Cluj, Rumania)* — a great grandson of the Divrei Chaim (Tzanzer) and a son-in-law of Adm.R.Chaim Tzvi of Sighet — was among the SURVIVORS of the war. He lost his wife and eleven children — as did many other SURVIVORS — and he later remarried. He settled in New York at first, and later in Eretz Yisrael, where he established a community in Netanya called Kiryat Tzanz.

R.Mordechai Gifter — who was born in Portsmouth *(Virginia, U.S.A.)* — was (probably) the first American-born Talmud scholar to become a ROSH YESHIVA (in Telz YESHIVA, in Cleveland *(see Sivan 5701\1941)*).

R.Eliezer Yehuda Waldenberg, a rabbi in Yerushalayim, published the first volume of Tzitz Eliezer *(SH'ELOT UTESHUVOT, dealing with many issues involving technological and scientific advances)*.

Chapter 15b
The Independent State of Israel,

5706 ≈ 1945

The Jewish resistance movement in Eretz Yisrael — operating underground against restrictive British rule (see 5699\1939) — freed 208 Jews on the 3rd **Cheshvan** 5706*1945* by attacking a British camp for internment of ILLEGAL IMMIGRANTS. Although they continued their attempts to 'smuggle' in more Jews from the European DISPLACED PERSONS camps, the British intercepted most of the ILLEGAL IMMIGRANT boats before they arrived in Eretz Yisrael, and interned the occupants in special camps on Cyprus.

5706 ≈ 1946

The U.S. Army published an edition of the Talmud in Germany — called The Survivors' Talmud — for the refugees in the DISPLACED PERSONS camps.

From the dedication published in the Survivors' Talmud

... This special edition of the Talmud, published in the very land where, but a short time ago, everything Jewish and of Jewish inspiration was anathema, will remain a symbol of the indestructibility of the Torah ... (see 5706\1946)

The British maintained their restrictions on Jewish immigration into Eretz Yisrael — consequently the Jewish underground resistance movement (see 5706*1945*) continued to attack British military installations. They blew up many bridges on the borders, and consequently many Jews — political leaders — were arrested on the 30th **Sivan**.
42 Jewish SURVIVORS of the Holocaust were killed in a POGROM in Kielce *(Poland)* on the 5th **Tammuz**.
On the 23rd **Tammuz**, a group of Jewish (underground) fighters blew up the British headquarters in Yerushalayim — the British did not believe a message of warning — and 80 people were killed.

5707 ≈ 1946

Some of the leaders of Nazi-Germany had been captured after the war, and many others had escaped (see 5722\1962). The captured were brought to trial in an international court at Nuremberg *(Germany)*, and many were sentenced to death. They were hanged on the 21st **Tishrei** for their crimes against Jews and humanity during World War II.
The Pope *(Pius XII)* – in a letter dated November 20, 1946 – approved the decision instructing the Catholic church in France not to return Jewish children to their families who placed in the church's care to save them from Nazi murder. This added to the controversy surrounding this Pope and his war-time record. The letter was sent to Angelo Roncalli *(later Pope John XXIII)*, who had a reputation — when in Istanbul — for favoring Jews. He disobeyed the Vatican instructions.

5707 ≈ 1947

Publication of the Talmud Encyclopedia was commenced.

The first volume of the Talmud Encyclopedia was published in Eretz Yisrael, under the editorship of R.Shlomo Yosef Zevin. He was also one of the editors of Otzar HaPoskim *(comprehensive encyclopedic Halacha update, on* Even HaEzer *section of* SHULCHAN ARUCH*)* — the first volume was also published in 1947 — together with R.Yitzchak Hertzog (ASHKENAZI Chief Rabbi of Eretz Yisrael) and R.Isser Zalman Meltzer (see 5685\1925).
Two ships arrived in Eretz Yisrael with ILLEGAL IMMIGRANTS (see 5706*1945*) on the 18th **Tevet**, and they were taken by the British for internment on Cyprus (see 5706*1945*). On the 1st **Av** the British seized the ship *Exodus 1947* — causing three deaths among the 4,000 Jewish immigrants on board — and forced it to return to Germany.

5708 ≈ 1947

The United Nations divided Eretz Yisrael.

The problem of the Jewish war SURVIVORS in Europe

— who had nowhere to go (see Iyar 5705\ *1945*) — was the focus of international attention. On the 16th **Kislev** 5708\1947 the United Nations *(an organization including most countries in the world)* voted to withdraw the mandate given to the British (see 5680\1920) over Palestine (Eretz Yisrael), and agreed to a plan partitioning the country. Some of the land was to be for Jews, and some for Arabs. Yerushalayim (according to the plan) was to be an international city on its own.

Arabs attacked the Jews of Eretz Yisrael, to gain territory.

On the 17th **Kislev,** the day after the United Nations had voted to give a partitioned area of Eretz Yisrael into Jewish control, Arabs living there — backed and supported by of other Arab countries — began attacking Jews. The Arabs did not approve of the U.N. partition arrangement, and sought to forcibly occupy as much territory as possible — while the British governors of Palestine (Eretz Yisrael) were, at best, neutral onlookers to the attacks (see Adar 5708\1948).

On the 19th **Kislev** 75 Jews were killed in Arab ANTI-JEWISH RIOTS in Aden *(Yemen)*, which was also under British rule. The Jews of Aleppo *(Syria)* were attacked, all synagogues were destroyed, and 6,000 Jews fled the country.

On the 16th **Tevet** a ship — crammed with Jewish immigrants, SURVIVORS of the Holocaust — arrived in Eretz Yisrael, only to be driven away by the British (see Av 5707\1947).

5708 — 1948

Many Jews were killed by a bomb exploding in the center of Yerushalayim on the 12th **Adar** — and although there were many bombings and attacks by Arabs against Jews in Eretz Yisrael during this time — a British hand was also suspected in this bombing.

The roads to Yerushalayim were cut off by Arab forces, and the Jewish population of the city came under siege — which was broken on the 6th **Nissan**.

The British rule over Eretz Yisrael officially ended on the 5th of **Iyar**, and their troops had almost all left. 30,000 Jews of Eretz Yisrael were already enlisted into an army, but there was a severe shortage of arms and ammunition. Although a few hundred Jews had already been killed in fighting with Arabs, the major cities and roads were under Jewish control — except that the road to Yerushalayim was cut off again, returning the city to life under siege. The Palestinian Arabs had been beaten back and defeated, and many had fled their homes in fear.

The State of Israel was established in Eretz Yisrael.

The Jewish political leaders in Eretz Yisrael — headed by David Ben Gurion *(David Green from Plonsk (Poland) — a secular Zionist)* — established an autonomous and independent Jewish state — the State of Israel — which commenced to govern when the British left.

The provisional government of the new state immediately acted to assure free Jewish immigration to Eretz Yisrael (see 5708\1947), and the right for Jews to freely purchase land there *(see 5699\1939)*.

Some Halacha-observant Jews saw the formation of Jewish self-government in Eretz Yisrael as the beginning of the Ge'ula *(messianic redemption)*. Others accepted it graciously, as a form of ge'ula — in establishing a homeland for the many homeless Jews — yet disappointed that the ultimate Ge'ula — with the long awaited advent of the Mashiach *(Messiah)* — seemed to have slipped out of grasp. (Many were troubled that Jewish government was in the hands of secular — and often anti religious — Jews). Other Halacha-observant Jews were against the establishment of an autonomous Jewish state (see 5674\1913, 5739\1979), and claimed that this could not be done without the prophetic advent of the Mashiach.

Eretz Yisrael was invaded by surrounding Arab countries.

On the day after the State of Israel was declared, the armies of all Arab countries surrounding Eretz Yisrael — Egypt, Jordan, Syria, Lebanon, and Iraq — invaded the country. Saudi Arabia joined the war a few days later, and Yemen also declared war. The intention of the Arab countries was to crush the new State of Israel, and destroy the Jewish population of Eretz Yisrael — in their words: "to drive the Jews into the sea". The fighting began with the bombing of Tel Aviv on the 6th **Iyar**. The invading armies were fully equipped with tanks, planes, and heavy artillery, which the Jewish forces did not have — often having to rely on makeshift weapons. Nevertheless Jewish fighters managed to hold most areas — except for the Jewish quarter in the Old City of Yerushalayim where the 'Churvat R.Yehuda Chasid' synagogue *(see 5597\1837)* was destroyed. This section fell to the Arabs on the 19th **Iyar** — even though the construction of a rough new road had once again lifted the siege off Yerushalayim itself.

An American colonel, David (Mickey) Marcus — who was among the many Jews who came to Eretz Yisrael to join the fight — was killed accidentally outside his headquarters on the 3rd **Sivan**.

A ship (the *Altalena*) bringing a privately organized shipment of much needed arms to Eretz Yisrael — as well as some 900 immigrant-fighters — was blown up on arrival *(see Cheshvan, 5701\1940)*. 20 Jews were killed in the "affair". A statement by David Ben Gurion — in the Provisional State Council on 17th **Sivan,** blessing the "holy canon" that fired the shot — increased the indication that it was a calculated Jewish action — by the dominant political *(left-wing)* party and their military arm. The action, some say, was taken to thwart what was claimed to be a plot by the rival *(right-wing)* party (who had until this time maintained their own revolutionary militia under the British) to use these arms for a power-grab — although they had reportedly agreed to be absorbed in the larger military as a unified national force. (Yitzchak Rabin was reportedly the commander to give the actual order to fire.)

Adm.R.Avraham Mordechai Alter of Gur, the 'Imrey Emess' (see 5701*1940*) died on Shavu'ot during the siege of Yerushalayim and he was buried in the courtyard of the YESHIVA he had established there (see 5685\1925). He was succeeded by his son, Adm.R.Yisrael — later called the 'Bais Yisroel'.

20 Jews were killed in Cairo when a bomb was thrown into the Jewish quarters on the 13th **Sivan**, and over 100 Jews were killed in sporadic RIOTS.

The last of the British armed forces left Eretz Yisrael on the 23rd **Sivan**.

Yerushalayim was bombed from the air on the 4th **Tammuz**, and newly purchased Jewish planes — on their way to Eretz Yisrael — bombed Cairo in retaliation on the 7th **Tammuz**. Yerushalayim was also under the continuous bombardment of heavy Arab guns, and the water supply was cut off when the Arabs blew up a pumping station.

The fighting continued throughout the country, and a few hundred thousand Arabs fled from their homes during the battles and after Jewish victories (see Iyar 5708\1948). Most did not immediately return, because the Arab governments vowed to throw the Jews of Eretz Yisrael into the sea, and return the whole land to the Arabs. (There were also many instances where the Arab forces required their brethren to leave their homes temporarily, so that they could conduct the battle more effectively.)

R.Shlomo Zalman Broin of Budapest had settled in New York, where he published the first volume of his She'arim HaMetzuyanim BeHalacha *(Halacha update on Kitzur Shulchan Aruch)*.

Jewish SURVIVORS of the Holocaust were attacked by anti-Jewish mobs in Plungyan *(Plunge, Lithuania)* in a BLOOD LIBEL on Erev Rosh HaShanah.

5709 — 1949

The British released the (remaining) 25,000 Jewish ILLEGAL IMMIGRANTS — from a total of over 50,000 — being held on Cyprus, on the 18th **Tevet** (see 5706*1945*).

By this time there were 1,000,000 Jews in Eretz Yisrael, almost 300,000 more than a year earlier *(see 5699\1939, 5719\1958)*.

The 'War of Independence' (in Eretz Yisrael) ended.

The State of Israel signed separate armistice agreements with all its neighboring Arab countries (see Iyar 5708\1948), and the war was ended. Almost 8,000 square miles of Eretz Yisrael was under Jewish control — compared to the 6,200 that the United Nations had originally planned (see Kislev 5708\1947) — however Yerushalayim remained divided (see 19th Iyar 5708\1948), with the Western Wall (see Av 3829\69) remaining under Arab control.

4,000 Jewish soldiers had died in the war, and 2,000 Jewish civilians perished. Arabs continued sporadic and isolated attacks on Jews for many years (see Cheshvan 5717\1956).

5710 — 1950

On the 10th **Shvat** Adm.R.Yosef Yitzchak Schneersohn of Lubavitch died in New York (see 5700\1940). He had established a network of organizations — from the confinement of a wheelchair, a result of his tortures (see 5687\ 1927) — for the furtherance of Jewish religious observance and Torah studies in the U.S.A., Canada, Eretz Yisrael — where he founded a settlement for his followers (CHASIDIM) — England, France, Morocco, and Australia. He was succeeded by his son-in-law Adm.R.Menachem Mendel Schneersohn (see Av 5704\1944) — revered for his very exceptional Torah scholarship. He increased and expanded his father in law's work (see 5754\1994) in a very significant way.

The Jews left the ancient Jewish community of Iraq.

The government of Iraq — which had treated the Jews harshly in the preceding few years (see Sivan 5701\1941, Iyar 5708\1948) — allowed Jews living there to leave on condition that they took none of their possessions along. During the fifteen months beginning **Sivan** 1950, 110,000 Jews — almost all of the Jews living there — left Iraq for Eretz Yisrael, leaving behind possessions worth $200 million. This was the effective end of a Jewish community dating back to before the destruction of the first Beit Hamikdash (see 3319\-442, Av 3338\-423).

The Jews of Yemen emigrated to Eretz Yisrael.

16,000 Jews of Yemen had emigrated to Eretz Yisrael from 1919 to 1948, and a remaining 45,000 were brought to Eretz Yisrael in a massive airlift which lasted less than a year, and ended in **Elul.** This effectively ended most of the ancient Jewish community of Yemen (see Iyar 5708\1948).

There were some secular Zionists who — in attempting to assist (these and other immigrants from "primitive" cultures) to adapt to modern society — actively discouraged traditional Jewish religious practice. Later (see 5755\1995), a commission of inquiry was established to investigate accusations that many children of these large Eastern immigrant families were kidnapped and sold for adoption. (Many parents claimed they had bought a healthy child to hospital, were told to leave the child for some treatment *(medical treatment was completely foreign to them)*, and upon return they were told that the child had died.)

5711 — 1951

The Knesset *(Parliament)* of the State of Israel declared the 27th **Nissan** as Yom HaSho'a *(Holocaust Remembrance Day)*, in memory of the six million Jews killed during World War II.

5712 — 1952

26 Jews — including secular YIDDISH writers (see 5658*1897)* — were killed by the Russian authorities on the 21st **Av**, as part of their program to eradicate Jewish religion and culture (see 5680\1920).

On the 20th **Elul,** the government of West Germany agreed to pay money for the losses caused to Jews by the Nazis. The prominent negotiator for these "reparation" funds was the SHTADLAN Nachum Goldmann — founder of the World Jewish Congress — who created a storm of controversy (whether to take money for the blood.) The State of Israel received a total of $845 million over the next fourteen years, and countless individuals benefited directly with payments for lost possessions.

5714 — 1953

R.Avraham Yeshayahu Karelitz, the Chazon Ish (see 5671\1911) — who had settled in Eretz Yisrael in 1933 — died on the 15th **Cheshvan**. He had gained worldwide recognition for his Torah scholarship without serving in any position as rabbi or ROSH YESHIVA.

R.Isser Zalman Meltzer (see 5685\1925, 5707\1947) died three weeks later on the 10th **Kislev**.

5717 — 1956

Jewish forces invaded Egypt and conquered the Sinai Desert.

An increasing number of Jews were being killed — aproximately 1,300 since 1949 — by Arab infiltrators into Eretz Yisrael, many of them from Egypt.

Egypt — which was receiving large quantities of quality Russian arms and ammunition — nationalized the *(international)* Suez Canal, and promptly disallowed ships to pass to and from Israel. In response, Israeli forces invaded the Sinai peninsula on the 24th **Cheshvan**, and conquered most of it in a lightning strike that lasted only eight days.

The Egyptian army was totally routed — fleeing in a completely disorganized manner — leaving large quantities of almost unused arms, and thousands of soldiers dead or taken prisoner. 171 Jewish soldiers were killed in the campaign. Jewish forces were withdrawn shortly afterwards — due to (political) pressure from the U.S.A. and Russia — and they were replaced by troops of the United Nations, who were to serve as a buffer.

Many Jews left Hungary in **Cheshvan** during the unsuccessful revolt against the Soviet-Russian backed communist government.

5718 — 1958

When it was declared that the State of Israel would begin registering as a Jew anyone stating that they were Jewish — without the need for certification acceptable by Halacha — a serious and prolonged controversy arose. The controversy is known as Mihu Yehudi *(who is (considered) a Jew)*.

5719 — 1958

A new water reservoir was opened in **Kislev** to ensure Yerushalayim with an adequate water supply *(see 5282\1521, Tammuz 5708\1948)*.
There were 1,800,000 Jews in Eretz Yisrael at this time, an increase of over one million in eleven years *(see 5709\1949, 5729\1969)*.

5719 — 1959

R.Moshe Feinstein — who settled in the U.S.A. in 1937 — published the first volume of Iggrot Moshe *(Sh'elot UTeshuvot)*. He had escaped the Stalinist regime of Russia in 1936, settling in New York as a rosh yeshiva.
In **Elul** the head of Soviet Russia *(Nikita Khrushchev)* visited the U.S.A., and on a train trip in California a resourceful reporter — Gershon Jacobson, a Jewish (Halacha observant) Russian immigrant — reported that he had an impromptu interview with him *("Let him in — he is the only journalist here who speaks Russian...")* When asked about his country's treatment of Jews he denied that they were being persecuted, and claimed that they were free but didn't want to leave Russia. Jacobson (later a prominent journalist and Yiddish news publisher) also reported on an interview with the President of Egypt *(Nasser), (just after the Six-Day-War, see 5727\1967)* who cited the Nazi desire to annihilate the Jews as proof that they (Jews) were bad and dangerous.

5720 — 1960

In an earthquake in Agadir *(Morocco)* on the 2nd **Adar**, hundreds of Jews died — some say 800 — including students at the yeshiva (of Lubavitch).
More than half of the 250,000 Jews of Morocco had already settled in Eretz Yisrael, and within a few years almost all of the rest had left, many going to France. Of the 130,000 Jews of Algeria, only 7,700 settled in Eretz Yisrael, most of the rest emigrating to France.

5721 — 1961

On the 26th **Nissan** a Russian pilot was the first person to leave earth and fly into space. Among other things, he later said that he flew into the heavens, he looked and looked, and saw no Creator *(see 5729\1969, 5763\2003)*.

5722 — 1962

Adolph Eichmann — the Nazi overseer of the German *(World War II)* plan to exterminate the Jews — was captured (see 5707\1946) in Argentina. He was publicly tried in a court in Eretz Yisrael, and privately hanged in 1962.

5723 — 1962

R.Aharon Kotler (see Sivan 5701\1941) — a son-in-law of R.Isser Zalman Meltzer *(see 5685\1925, 5707\1947)* and a leader of Torah scholars in the U.S.A. and in Eretz Yisrael — died on the 2nd **Kislev**.

5724 — 1964

The Palestinian Arab refugees had been (permanently) placed in refugee camps — by their Arab bretheren in the countries into which they had fled (see Sivan 5708\1948) — while the Jewish refugees from Arab countries *(see 5710\1950, 5720\1960)* were absorbed into normal life in Eretz Yisrael.
Delegations from these Arab countries met in Egypt, and established the Palestinian Liberation Organization (P.L.O.), which was to have an army (of Palestinian Arabs) to carry out attacks against Jews in Eretz Yisrael (see 5717\1956).
A terrorist group called Al Fatah was independently established along the same lines as the P.L.O., but the fighters were more extreme.

5725 — 1965

Martin Buber was a famous philosopher, who — although himself not a practicing religious Jew — had popularized the Chassidim and their tales and ideology amongst intellectual Western Jews. He died on the 13th **Sivan**.

5727 — 1967

Yerushalayim was re-united under Jewish rule in the Six-Day-War.

Terrorist attacks against Jews in Eretz Yisrael reached unbearable proportions (see 5724\1964), and Arab armies were preparing for a battle to

finally destroy the Jewish state *(see Sivan 5708\1948)*. Egypt dismissed the buffering United Nations force in Sinai *(see Cheshvan 5717\ 1956)*; began deploying its forces against the borders of Israel; and once again *(see 5717\1956)* closed the Suez canal to all ships to and from Eretz Yisrael.
In the morning of 26th **Iyar**, Israeli planes attacked Egypt and Syria — in a miraculous action that lasted only three hours — and destroyed 452 Arab planes *(391 of them still on the ground)*, while losing only 19.
For six days the Jewish soldiers made spectacular advances, and completely shattered the Arab armies of Egypt, Syria and Jordan — both of whom joined the action, convinced that this would be the victory they had always spoken of.
The Old City of Yerushalayim was captured from Jordan *(see 5709\1949)*, and Jews could visit the Western Wall for the first time in many years (although no one suggested the removal of the Arab mosque from the holiest Jewish place). Yerushalayim was under complete Jewish control — for the first time since "Bar Kochba" (Bar Kuziba) *(see 3887\127)*. Many of the Jewish holy places *(synagogues etc.)* were found to have been desecrated and vandalized by the Jordanian Arabs.

2,700 square miles of Eretz Yisrael — including Kever Rachel and Ma'arat HaMachpela and 23,500 square miles of Sinai desert — came under Jewish control *(see 5709\1949)*. The government of Israel (some say too hastily) indicated that — except for Yerushalayim — captured territories could be returned in exchange for peace.
777 Jewish soldiers were killed in the war. Immense quantities of arms and ammunition were captured.
Jews all over the world had been aroused in an unprecedented manner — when the threat of war became reality — and many Jews came to Eretz Yisrael to join the battle and many came to help.
In the aftermath of the miraculous victory, many Jews were reawakened to religious observance — particularly the young — and this reawakening eventually developed into the long-lasting Ba'al Teshuva Movement, which involved many thousands of Jews returning to Jewish ritual and Halacha observance.
R.Adin Steinsaltz — a brilliant scholar (and Ba'al Teshuva) living in Eretz Yisrael — published the first volume of the Talmud, with many embellishments designed to make it more accessible to the untrained.
A project to enter all the available SH'ELOT UTESHUVOT into a computer — for quick and comprehensive reference — was commenced in Eretz Yisrael. Later — with the advance of personal computers and their ability to read (rapidly) dense recordings of data — this information was available to everyone at home.

5729 — 1968

In a broadcast from space on the 4th **Tevet** the astronauts (on the American spacecraft Apollo 8) — inspired by the view of Earth from space, which they shared in the broadcast — read from the opening passages of the Bible *("In the beginning....") (see 5721\1961, 5763\2003)*.

5729 — 1969

9 Jews were publicly executed in Damascus on the 8th **Shvat**.
R.Aryeh Levin, often called *'The Tzadik of Yerushalayim"* — for his kind heart and good deeds to the sick, poor and others in need — died on 9th **Nissan**.
The Arab countries surrounding Eretz Yisrael — who had been re-equipped *(see 5727\1967)* with arms and ammunition by Russia — still refused to recognize the existence of a Jewish state in Eretz Yisrael, and P.L.O. infiltrators *(see 5724\1964)* had staged many damaging attacks and bombings. On the 4th **Iyar**, Egypt began a war of attrition against Israel, with daily artillery shelling across the Suez Canal.
There were 2,400,000 Jews living in Eretz Yisrael at this time *(see 5719\1958, 5752\1992)*.

5730 — 1970

Libya ordered the confiscation of Jewish property on the 17th **Tammuz**.
At this stage the P.L.O. *(see Iyar 5729\1969)* had developed a new technique of terrorism — hijacking international aircraft, and holding the passengers as hostages — until their (often unrealistic) demands were met.

5731 — 1971

Ten Jews were arrested in Russia on Tisha B'Av — and sent to jail — because they were commemorating this tragic day by visiting Babi

Yar *(see Tishrei 5702\1941)*. This was part of a series of such arrests, which did not succeed in curbing the increasing courage with which the Jews of Russia *(see 5712\1952)* began to speak up, particularly in their petitions and requests to leave for Eretz Yisrael. 1,000 Jews were permitted to leave Russia in 1970, and 14,500 were permitted to leave in 1971 *(see 5735\1975)*.

5732 ≈ 1972

Arab terrorists captured Israeli athletes at the Munich Olympic Games on 26th Elul. Eleven Jews were killed in the international incident.

5734 ≈ 1973

2,500 Jewish soldiers were killed in the Yom-Kippur-War.

Egyptian and Syrian troops had been gathering at the frontiers of Eretz Yisrael for a number of days, but the government of the State of Israel was confident that this did not signal an imminent war. In the early afternoon of Yom Kippur, Egypt and Syria attacked. The Arab armies were initially successful in advancing on both fronts, due to surprise and numbers — less than 500 Jewish soldiers were on duty (Yom Kippur) defending 100 miles along the Suez Canal — they were attacked by 70,000 Egyptian soldiers. Nevertheless within days, the Israeli defense forces staged a successful counter attack, crossed the Suez Canal into North Africa, and (in Syria) advanced to within firing range of Damascus. Russia — which was continuously airlifting new supplies of arms to the Arabs during the fighting — used the United Nations to intervene and stop the fighting, in which the Arabs had lost very large numbers of soldiers (18,500) and massive amounts of arms (2,100 tanks). The war was over after twenty days of fighting, in which 2,522 Jewish soldiers were killed.
After the defeat in the Yom Kippur War, the Arab countries threatened not to sell their crude-oil to countries who supported the Jewish state — which proved an effective weapon, considering they were the world's largest oil suppliers — and the State of Israel became politically isolated particularly in the United Nations. It became increasingly difficult to purchase armaments.

5734 ≈ 1974

A group of mostly young religious nationalists — calling themselves Gush Emunim — established a settlement in the newly captured Syrian territory, in **Iyar**, in an attempt to pre-empt the Israeli government from withdrawing from that territory. They saw this as their first action towards their goal — of establishing settlements in all parts of Biblical Eretz Yisrael, captured since 1967, that the government of Israel had consistently maintained could be "returned" to the Arabs.

5735 ≈ 1975

100,000 Jews from Russia had arrived in Eretz Yisrael since 1967 *(see 5731\1971, 5752\1992)*.
The birthrate among Halacha-observant Jewish families was very high, and there were great Torah centers emerging in the U.S.A. — particularly in and around New York City — and in Eretz Yisrael, only thirty years after the total destruction of the European Torah centers.

5736 ≈ 1976

100 Jews — who had been passengers on a plane hijacked by Arab terrorists (see 5730\1970) — were held as hostages in the Entebbe airport near Kampala *(Uganda, Africa)*. They were miraculously rescued — from deep in the African continent — in a spectacular raid by the Jewish army of Israel.
Arab infiltrators continued their constant attacks on Jews in Eretz Yisrael, and all over the world *(see Iyar 5727\1967)*.

5737 ≈ 1977

Adm.R.Yisrael of Gur, the "Beis Yisroel", who had lost his family in the Holocaust of World War II — as did a many of his followers (Chasidim) who were a surviving minority of the pre-war predominant Polish Chasidim — died on the 2nd **Adar**, and was succeeded by his brother, Adm.R.Simcha Bunim, later called the "Lev Simcha".

5739 ≈ 1979

The president of Egypt, Anwar Sadat, had visited Yerushalayim in **Kislev** 5778\1977 — on the invitation of the newly elected prime minister of Israel, Menachem Begin — and after long negotiations, a peace treaty was signed on the 27th **Adar** 1979, supported by the U.S.A. Under the terms of the agreement all Jewish forces and settlements were withdrawn from Sinai (see 5734\1973). Menachem Begin then visited Cairo.
Adm.R.Yoel of Satmar — who was vehement in his opposition to the State of Israel (on religious grounds, see Iyar 5708\1948) — died on the 26th **Av**, and

was succeeded by his nephew, Adm.R.Moshe (ben Chaim Tzvi) of Sighet *(see 5664\1904)*.

5740 — 1980

R.Yoseph Breuer — grandson of R.Shimshon Rapha'el Hirsch (see 5611\1851) — died at the age of 98 on the 3rd **Iyar**. He had started a KEHILLA in a small apartment in New York upon his arrival after Kristallnacht (see 5798\1938) and built it into a grand community (providing a full spectrum of member's needs) which adhered with dedication to the MINHAGIM *(customs)* of the centuries of the glorious communities of ASHKENAZ *(Germany)*. He was succeeded by (his chosen assistant of 30 years) R.Shimon Schwab.

Arab terrorists killed 7 Jewish students and wounded 16 others — in Hevron on 16 **Iyar** — and the Arab mayor was deported for incitement. *(Subsequently the UN demanded the deportation be cancelled.)*

Many more Jews were allowed to leave Russia *(see 5735\1975 — 17,000 in 1977, 29,000 in 1978, 51,500 in 1979)*, however, less than half settled in Eretz Yisrael.

By this time many Jews had left Eretz Yisrael primarily for economic reasons — and as many as 500,000 had moved to the U.S.A. *(see 5689\1929, 5729\1969, and 5641\1881)*.

5741 — 1981

Iraq — which had always sent troops in the wars against Israel *(see Iyar 5708\1948)* — was dangerously close to gaining a nuclear arms capacity. A nuclear reactor near Baghdad, was bombed and destroyed — by the Jewish pilots of the Israel airforce — on 5th **Sivan**. *(The UN condemned the bombing.)*

3 Jews were killed — on 13th **Tammuz** — and 17 wounded by heavy Arab (artillery) shelling of the northern Galil *(Galilee)*.

5742 — 1982

Jewish settlements in northern Sinai were dismantled in **Adar** and the settlers — many of them resisting — were removed by force.

A Jewish Israeli diplomat of Israel was assassinated by terrorists in Paris on 10th **Nissan**.

Massive enemy arsenals were discovered in Lebanon.

Arabs in Lebanon were bombarding Jewish settlements near the border with destructive rockets and killing with other forms of terrorist attack. The killing extended into an international campaign of terror against Jews the world over. On the 17th **Sivan** Israeli defense forces invaded Lebanon to remove the P.L.O. *(see 5730\1970)* that had firmly entrenched itself there. The invading Jewish forces discovered enormous arsenals of threatening weapons that were far greater than anticipated. Although the P.L.O. had stationed their fighters amongst women and children — thus allowing them to illustrate to the compliant international media that Jews were killing helpless civilians — they were nevertheless overcome in the battle and forced to withdraw from their entrenchment in the capital Beirut. These strongholds were primarily in the festering refugee camps now thirty-four years old (see Sivan 5708\1948, 5724\1964). The P.L.O. fighters departed to other countries (primarily Tunisia). Israeli forces (later) withdrew southward, not fully withdrawing from Lebanon for another three years (see 5745\1985).

Adm.R.Eliezer Zusia Portugal of Skulen — a dedicated religious leader in Romania under Communist rule (see 5680\1920), who later built a network of institutions for poor non-religious Jews in Israeli towns — died on the 29th **Av** in the United States.

5743 — 1983

On Rosh Chodesh **Nissan**, REFORM rabbis decided that children of a Jewish father be considered "legally" Jewish (*patrilineal descent*) — even if the mother is non-Jewish *(which they defined as someone not converting to Judaism)* — if the children participate in Jewish rituals.

5744 — 1983

Most of the senior Talmudists left the Jewish Theological Seminary (JTS) when the official CONSERVATIVE seminary voted to train women as rabbis.

On the 18th **Kislev** 4,600 terrorist prisoners were exchanged for the release of 6 Jewish soldiers (see 5745\1985).

5744 — 1984

R.Yisrael AbiChatzira — who was a grandson of R.Yaakov (of Morocco), and had a wide reputation for miraculous deeds — died in Eretz Yisrael (see 5640\1880) on the 4th **Shvat**.

The Jewish population of Yerushalayim had grown to 320,000 (445,000 including non-Jews) the largest population of any city in Eretz Yisrael — except that Tel Aviv together with its surrounding city-suburbs had a total metropolitan area population of 800,000.

5745 ≈ 1985

The Israeli army completed its withdrawal from Lebanon in **Sivan**, three years after the invasion *(see 5742\1982)*. 654 Jewish soldiers had been killed, many not in actual battle but by terrorist attacks.
1,150 terrorist prisoners were exchanged for the release of 3 Jewish soldiers on 20th Iyar (see 5744\ *1983*).

5746 ≈ 1985

7 Israeli tourists were killed by an Egyptian soldier when they were touring in the Sinai desert on the 20th **Tishrei**.
On 23rd **Tishrei** Palestinian terrorists hijacked an Italian cruise ship *(the Achille Lauro)* and murdered Leon Klinghoffer, a Jewish American passenger.

5746 ≈ 1986

On the 2nd **Adar-2**, Anatoly Sharansky — a prominent Soviet Jewish dissident *(refusenik)* — was freed from prison and finally allowed to emigrate to Eretz Yisrael, where he became a prominent leader.
Elie Wiesel — a prominent Jewish personality, and an outstanding articulator of the horror of the Holocaust from whence he emerged — was awarded the Nobel Peace Prize.
The Pope *(John Paul II)* visited the Great Synagogue in Rome on the 4th **Nissan** (the first such visit ever.)
22 worshippers were killed in a terrorist attack against the prominent Neve Shalom synagogue in Istanbul *(Turkey)* on 2nd **Elul**.

5747 ≈ 1987

On the 26th **Tevet**, the President of Russia *(Mikhail Gorbachev)* formally announced the ongoing relaxation of many tight government controls over the basic freedoms of the people in all the countries it controlled under the USSR *(Union of Soviet Socialist Republics)*.
This moderation allowed for more Jewish activity — banned for seventy years *(see 5712\1952)* — and many Jews subsequently came to Russia from Israel and the United States to teach about JUDAISM — they even established schools and YESHIVOT. Over the next decades, tens of thousands (some say over 100,000) of adult Jewish men from Russia underwent *bris mila* *(circumcision)* — whether there, in Eretz Yisrael, the U.S.A., or elsewhere.
Relaxation of central control in Russia — which allowed Jews greater freedom to apply for visas to leave — also allowed local nationalistic passions to emerge in such regions as the Ukraine and Moldavia. Local pride in these regions bore a strong tone of ANTI-JEWISH sentiment and even hatred — which aroused the fears of many Jews — so that combined with the economic problem of dwindling food production and supplies, the number of Jews leaving the country increased dramatically *(see 5740\1980, 5752\1992)*.
Austrian president Kurt Waldheim — previously the head of the UN — was barred from entry into the U.S. as information had come to light that he had been an officer of the Nazi military and had participated in atrocities.
Six Jewish soldiers were killed at a camp near Kiryat Shmona by a terrorist who crossed the heavily guarded border from Lebanon on a hang-glider.

5748 ≈ 1987

Arabs in Eretz Yisrael began a violent uprising in what was called the (first) Intifada, which lasted for some five years.

5748 ≈ 1988

R.Gavriel Zinner began publication of his comprehensive work Nitey Gavriel *(an up-to-date collection of laws and customs)* that is one of the major works of this era of Melaktim.

5749 ≈ 1989

14 passengers were killed and 30 wounded on 3rd **Tammuz** when a bus — commandeered by an Arab terrorist — crashed into a ravine on the slopes of the Yerushalayim-Tel Aviv highway.

5750 ≈ 1990

Iraq invaded (and annexed) neighboring Kuwait on 18th **Av**, promptly proclaiming that any military action — by international forces — against Iraq will be met with attacks on Israel.

5751 — 1990

On 17th **Cheshvan** R.Meir Kahane was assassinated by an Arab in New York City, where years earlier he had founded a group of vigilantes — the Jewish Defense League. He had subsequently moved to Eretz Yisrael where the political party he formed was banned. It was considered ultra-extreme for his fundamentalist application — to the contemporary situation — of Biblical statements of war and expulsion.

5751 — 1991

One person was killed and much damage was caused when Iraq fired a total of 39 missiles (with conventional explosive war-heads) into Israel, as international forces led by the U.S.A. swept into Kuwait to drive the Iraqis out.

From the 27th **Nissan**, Adm.R.Menachem Mendel Schneersohn of Lubavitch *(see 5710\1950)* significantly increased his predictions of the imminent coming of the Mashiach *(Messiah)*. Many of his followers claimed that he was already here, and — privately at first — gave him petitions proclaiming their allegiance to him as Mashiach.

In a dramatic airlift *(see 5710\1950)* beginning on the 11th **Sivan**, 15,000 Jews were flown out of Ethiopia — after 20,000 had arrived in previous years, 7,000 of them in a similar operation in 5744\1984 — and although they believed themselves to be of biblical Hebrew descent there was considerable Rabbinic discussion about their ultimate acceptance as full Jews.

On the 9th **Elul** an ANTI-JEWISH POGROM broke out in the Crown Heights section of Brooklyn — after a non-Jewish black child was killed in a car accident — and Yankel Rosenbaum, a Jewish student visiting from Melbourne *(Australia)* was killed. For three days the police (apparently under orders not to further incite the attackers) stood by as ANTI-JEWISH RIOTERS attacked Jews and their property. Although virtually no Jews retaliated with violence, the news-media described the event as "Jews and blacks fighting each other".

On the 18th **Elul** the absolute rule of the Communist party *(see 5677\1917)* in Russia was ended *(see 5747\1987, 5752\1992)*, fundamentally changing the formal structure of government there.

Jews from the former Soviet Union were officially offered the right to settle in Germany — to help rebuild Jewish communities, eliminated by the country's Nazi regime.

5752 — 1991

The United States government was successful in arranging (some say co-ercing) for Israel to meet with other Arab countries on the 22nd **Cheshvan,** to discuss peace (see 5739\1979). It was anticipated that this process would be a long one; and was based on the assumption that the Jewish State would deliver territories west of the Jordan River (that had been surrendered to Israel, see 5727\1967) to some form of Arab rule. These territories had many Jewish settlements by this time, and many more were planned (see 5734\1974).

5752 — 1992

29 people were killed and 242 injured when a car bomb exploded in the Israeli Embassy in Buenos Aires,*(Argentina)* on 12th **Adar-2**.

The USSR *(Union of Soviet Socialist Republics)* was disbanded as the formal government of Russia, and was replaced by a Commonwealth of Independent States *(CIS)* which included the newly independent (Communist free) states of Russia, Byelorussia and the Ukraine. This did not have any immediate effect on the uncertain situation of Jews in these countries (see 5747\1987), nor did the structure of commonwealth survive the gravitation to localized national independence.

Adm.R.Simcha Bunim (see 5737\1977) died on the 7th **Tammuz**. He was succeeded by his half-brother Adm.R.Pinchas Menachem, another son of the Imrey Emess of Gur *(see Sivan 5708\1948)*.

Some 350,000 Jews had left "Russia" *(what was formerly the Soviet USSR)* and settled in Eretz Yisrael in the previous three years *(see 5740\1980, 5747\1987)*.

There were 4,250,000 Jews living in Eretz Yisrael at this time *(see 5729\1969)*.

5753 — 1993

A secret agreement signed in Oslo.

A secret agreement (*Declaration of Principles* of future peace) — signed in Oslo *(Norway)* on the 3rd **Elul**, between Israel and the PLO — caused serious controversy when it was publicly announced ten days after the event. Diplomats in the non-Jewish world were also startled that discussions would be held with the murderous PLO — with whom every Jewish leader had vowed not to negotiate with. In the next 5 years more Jews were killed by Palestinian terrorists than in the previous 15 years.

5754 1993

Ashkenazi Chief Rabbi of Israel — R.Yisrael Meir Lau — visited with the Pope *(John Paul II)* in Rome on 6th **Tishrei**.

5754 1994

Baruch Goldstein (a medical doctor) entered the Cave of Machpelah in Hevron on the 14th **Adar** (Purim) during Muslim (Friday) prayers and killed 29 (prostrated) Arab worshippers with his automatic assault weapon. He was instantly hacked to death. Some say he intended to preempt a *(1929 style)* clergy-incited Arab POGROM on Jews *[see Dr. C. Simons, 2003]*.
On the 18th **Adar**, in New York, an Arab opened automatic gunfire on a van of Jewish students seriously injuring some and killing 16 year old Ari Halberstam. The city named the ramp (to the Brooklyn Bridge — where the shooting took place) in his memory, and his mother was the driving force in the building of a multi-million dollar children's museum named in his memory.

The Last Lubavitcher Rebbe died.

Adm.R.Menachem Mendel, the Lubavitcher Rebbe, died on 3rd **Tammuz** after a prolonged illness. He left a legacy unequalled in perhaps centuries of Jewish history. Hundreds of volumes of his teachings have been published, and virtually no place on the planet has eluded a visit by his emissaries (SHLUCHIM), who spread the teachings of Jewish religious observance and Torah study. In the ten years after his passing some two thousand additional SHLUCHIM settled in to new locations on the globe, and hundreds of new buildings of Torah study and observance have been erected. No other individual — during his lifetime — had a greater impact on Jewish life.
He had no children, and no successor has been appointed — his followers (chassidim) unable to conceive of someone filling his place — and many of them await his return, in varying degrees of the notion. There are some who fervently await his resurrection as the Mashiach (see Nissan 5751\1991).
86 people were killed and some 300 wounded on the 10th **Av** when a bomb blast completely destroyed the seven-story Jewish community building in Buenos Aries *(Argentina)*, see 5752\1992.
After many years, a declaration officially ending the state of war between Israel and Jordan was signed on 16th **Av** (see 5739\1979.)

5755 *1994*

22 people were murdered on the 14th **Cheshvan** when an Arab suicide bomber blew himself to pieces on a crowded bus in Tel Aviv.

R.Shlomo Carlebach died.

R.Shlomo Carlebach died on the 15th **Cheshvan**. He was famous for his hundreds of musical compositions (many of them anonymous) which introduced a new style of (westernized) Jewish music — and his spirited singing, which left thousands of Jews — particularly many young and assimilated — warm to the spirit of Jewish life (although he was considered controversial in his manner of contact with followers). A legacy of Jewish prayer-style (replete with songs) has resulted in many "Carlebach Minyanim" springing up in numerous locations.

Chapter 15c – The Post-Holocaust Era.

5755 ~ 1995

A commission of inquiry was established in Eretz Yisrael on the 7th **Shvat**, to investigate allegations of disappearance of (mostly) Yemenite immigrant children between 1948 and 1954 (see 5710\1950), after reports submitted by two previous committees did not satisfy the families and the Yemenite community in Israel — the accusations persisted that many infants were spirited away from their parents to be "sold" for adoption. Eventually this commission (also) found no organized activity of this nature had taken place. This did not satisfy many, nor answer the numerous anecdotal indications (especially of parents being told their healthy infant had died, and being ignored when requesting to visit a grave).

R.Shlomo Zalman Auerbach — one of the foremost POSKIM *(halacha decision makers)* and ROSHEI YESHIVA — died on 20th **Adar**, and so many people attended the levaya *(funeral)* (300,000, some say 500,000) that many secular Jews, who had never heard his name (not having consulted this independent and politically-low-profile POSEK) — wondered why they hadn't.

5756 ~ 1995

Yitzchak Rabin was Assassinated.

Yitzchak Rabin — Prime Minister of the State of Israel — was assassinated on the 12th **Cheshvan** and a young extremist was indicted for the murder — ostensibly his vengeful response to the implementation of the Oslo Accords (see 5753\1993). As usual, many questions remained unanswered.

5756 ~ 1996

25 were killed and some 90 wounded when Arab suicide bombers (from Hamas — an extremely radical fundamentalist-Islamic group) attacked a Yerushalayim bus on 5th **Adar**; another 20 were killed when a Hamas suicide bomber blew up a bus in Yerushalayim on the 11th **Adar**; and 14 were killed and 130 wounded on 13th **Adar** *(Taanit Esther)* when a Palestinian suicide bomber blew himself up in a Purim-holiday shopping crowd at a Tel Aviv mall.

Adm.R.Pinchas Menachem Alter — the Gerer Rebbe (*Pnei Menachem),* last of the sons of the Imrey Emess (see 5708\1948) — died on 16th **Adar**, and was succeeded by his nephew Adm.R.Yisrael Aryeh Alter (son of Adm.-R.Simcha Bunim (see 5752\1992).)

5757 ~ 1997

On 29th **Tevet** — shortly after the Swiss parliament had prohibited the destruction of documents relating to "dormant accounts" *(bank accounts belonging to Jews exterminated during the HOLOCAUST, which the Swiss banks had refused to disclose for more than fifty years)* — a security guard at a bank found some documents in the shredding room that were from the HOLOCAUST era. Realizing the potential significance of these financial records, he took some to authorities. He was fired from his job, received death threats, and forced to leave his country, finding refuge in the United States where Congress passed a special bill granting permanent residence for him and his family. *(After extensive legal action by claimants, a payment settlement of U.S. $1.25 billion was eventually reached.).*

Seven school girls were murdered by a Jordanian soldier at Naharayim on the 6th **Adar-1** — the Jordanian king (later) sent $1 million for compensation to families

Suicide bombers killed 24 people in three separate attacks — one in Tel Aviv and two in Yerushalayim — on the 14th **Adar-1** (*Purim Katan*). On the 25th **Tammuz** two consecutive suicide bombings in the Mahane Yehuda market in Yerushalayim killed 16 people and wounded 178.

5759 ~ 1999

The Reform Movement's rabbinical body (numbering some 1,500 members) meeting in Pittsburgh in **Sivan**, encouraged (in a *Statement of Principles*) performance of mitzvot and returning to traditional practices (see *Pittsburgh Platform* 5645\1885, issued by less than 20 members.)

5760 2000

The Pope *(John Paul II)* visited Eretz Yisrael in **Adar-2** (see 5746\1986, 5754*1993).*

Court rules that Revisionist Historians are Nazi sympathizers.

In a book *["Denying the Holocaust: The Growing Assault on Truth and Memory" (Free Press, 1993)]*, an internationally distinguished American scholar *(Deborah Lipstadt)* acccused an "Holocaust denier" *(David Irving)* of committing serious historical misrepresentation. He, in response, sued her and her British publisher for libel (in England — where she would be the one on trial, and need to prove her statements to be true). After having to spend $3 million in defense and bringing countless witnesses, the judge ruled against Irving on the 6th **Nissan**, stating that he was essentially a Nazi sympathizer and apologist.

After suffering constant attacks, kidnappings, and harassment, Israeli troops (2,000) withdrew unilaterally from Southern Lebanon during **Iyar,** after twenty-two years of protecting the northern border of Eretz Yisrael (from that side.) Many were concerned that this would send a message to the Arab world that the Jewish people had lost their resolve and would retreat under pressure.

Adm.R.Shlomo of Bobov died on the 1st **Av** *(Rosh Chodesh).* He had come to the U.S.A. as a HOLOCAUST SURVIVOR, yet managed to re-build the greatness of the dynasty of Bobov — and even (by virtue of his constant encouragement and nurturing of other SURVIVORS) appeared to have inherited the central role of the whole Galcian Chassidic domain. He was succeeded by his son AdmR.Naftali Tzvi.

On the 22nd **Tammuz** the Palestinian leader *(Yasser Arafat)* refused to accept a peace offer (see Elul, this year) *(made at the presidential retreat of Camp David in the USA)* from the prime minister of the State of Israel *(Ehud Barak)* which would have given Palestinian Arabs more than 95% of the territory captured in 1967 (in self defense) from Egypt and Jordan, and granted them the right to create their own (Palestinian) state.

On the 7th **Av** Joseph Lieberman *(of Connecticut)* — a prominent U.S. Senator and a publicly acknowledged ORTHODOX Jew — was nominated as the candidate for Vice-President on the ticket of a major political party (Democratic).

On 28th **Elul** a visit to the HAR HABAYIT *(Temple Mount)* by the (right-wing) opposition party leader *(Ariel Sharon)* sparked a clash with Arabs who had slowly been allowed to regard this as their territory. This was used as the launching pretext (despite evidence of preparation all summer) for a four year series of clashes which became known as Intafada-2 *(see 5761\2000, 5761\2001, 5765\2004)*.

5761 2000

On the 2nd **Tishrei** *(Rosh HaShanah)*, after having been under incessant fire, the tomb of Yosef HaTzadik *(biblical Joseph)* — one of the tombs whose location is known with the utmost degree of certainty *["Tombs of the Righteous in the Land of Israel", p. 365; Dr. Zvi Ilan, archeologist]* — was destroyed, a few hours after the Jewish forces securing the site had withdrawn under an agreement Prime Minister Ehud Barak had made with the Palestinian authorities (that the site would be guarded from vandalism, and would be accessible to all).

On the 30th **Tishrei** a Jewish minister of the State of Israel *(Rehavam Ze'evi)* was assassinated by Palestinian terrorists.

There were more than 200 attacks internationally on Jewish targets — including more than 60 on synagogues — during the month of **Tishrei**.

On 5th **Tevet** Arab terrorists seeking targets for murder, chanced upon the son of R.Meir Kahane (see 5751\1990) — he was murdered together with his wife.

231,680 Jews of the former Soviet Union immigrated to the U.S.A. between 1991 and 2000, 105,598 of them settled in the New York area (see 5752\1992).

5761 2001

R.Mordechai Gifter *(see 5705\1945)* died on 24th **Tevet**.

R.Avigdor Miller — a prominent, devout and outspoken Rav and author in New York — died on 29th **Nissan**.

On 20th **Av** a terrorist blew himself up in a pizza store (crowded with children) in the center of Yerushalayim. 130 were wounded and 15 were killed; among them 15 year-old Malka Chana Roth, who had always devoted time extending aid to severely disabled children (including her sister). Her (Australian immigrant) parents

tablished a foundation for such children in her memory *(Keren Malka)*.
R.Avraham Yaakov Pam — a revered ROSH YESHIVAH with an exceptionally humble personal integrity and approach — died on 28th **Av**.

Terrorism against America explodes into a World War (III).

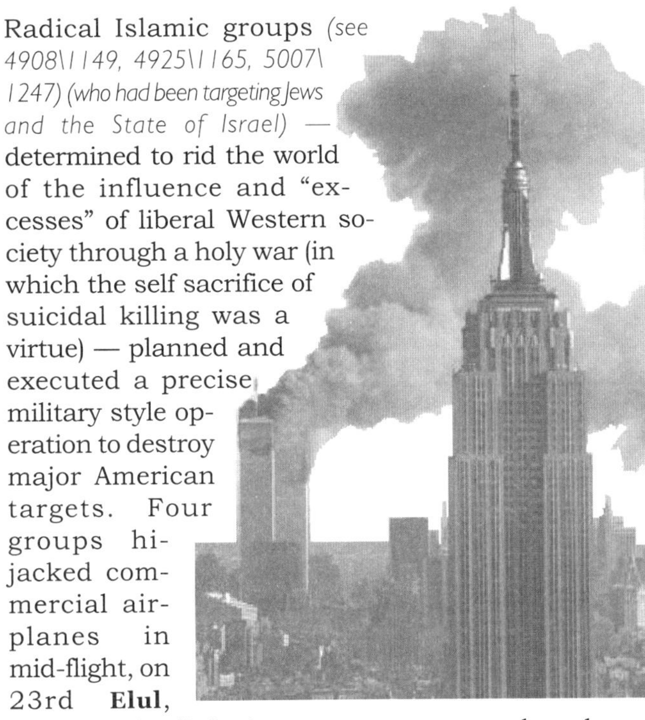

Radical Islamic groups *(see 4908\1149, 4925\1165, 5007\1247) (who had been targeting Jews and the State of Israel)* — determined to rid the world of the influence and "excesses" of liberal Western society through a holy war (in which the self sacrifice of suicidal killing was a virtue) — planned and executed a precise military style operation to destroy major American targets. Four groups hijacked commercial airplanes in mid-flight, on 23rd **Elul**, and — with all the innocent passengers aboard — flew them crashing into prominent buildings. Two crashed into — and brought down — the tallest buildings in the world, the "Twin Towers" of the World Trade Center in New York, and another crashed into the Pentagon, the hub of the USA military. The fourth airplane crashed in southern Pennsylvania as it was apparently heading towards the US Capitol or the White House in Washington DC. The passengers on that last flight, having received information by cell-phones of the other three hijackings, and realizing that they were doomed, rebelled against the hijackers and either directly or indirectly caused the plane to crash without reaching its intended target.
A total of 2,792 people were killed (including 343 fire-fighters, 75 police, 261 passengers) and 2,337 were injured. The vast majority of casualties were in New York, where despite a high Jewish population relatively few were casualties.
This signaled the official start of an international war — even though there had been previous attacks against the USA (one was a bombing of the same World Trade Center building) — because the elected government at the time recognized the motives behind the attacks. This war — against a swelling movement aiming to bring the world to a primitive social structure, without personal wealth and liberties, international finance, communications, a world where Islam reigns supreme, and where, at the appropriate times of the day, the billions of inhabitants of the Earth would bow to Mecca — appears to bear the title World War III *(some say World War IV — considering the Cold War between the Free World (USA and Allies) and the Communists as an actual war)*, although it is very different from the two previous conventional wars that were fought worlwide — but by nation against nation. This war could take decades, and could emerge in unanticipated ways and places — to be decided by "stateless" radicals who glorify murder and suicide for the cause of their religion. They recognize that many in the Western world lack the resolve to confront the issue (ironically, mostly the same people whose morals and values the Islamic fundamentalists despise the most) and consider it another sign of the decadent decline of Western society which they seek to overthrow.
The subsequent USA led invasion and freeing of the people of Afghanistan and Iraq from despotic regimes allied to terrorism were the first and the clearest actions of the war — although many in Western countries did not see these actions as subsections of the international war against fundamentalist Islam.

5762 — 2001

R.Elazar Menachem Mann Shach (see 5748\1988) — who had been imprisoned during the Russian civil war (see 5677\1917) — died in the town of Bnei Brak where he was the leading ROSH YESHIVAH — on the 16th Cheshvan (some say at age 103), and only a few hours later approximately 600,000 people were reportedly attended his funeral.

5762 — 2002

On the 18th **Tevet** a ship laden with 50 tons of weapons from the (radical Islamic republic) Iran, bound for Palestinian Arabs, was intercepted on the ocean by the navy of Israel.
One person was killed on the 14th **Shvat** and more than 100 people were injured when a woman became the first female to commit suicide with a bomb in Yerushalayim.
28 people were killed and 134 injured when a suicide bomber blew himself up at a Pesach (Passover) SEDER (14th-15th **Nissan**) in a Netanya resort hotel.

The Jewish population in Eretz Yisrael was 5.3 million in **Iyar**, and in **Tammuz** a record number (400) of North American immigrants arrived together to settle.
The total number of attacks in the 2nd Intafada (from Elul 5760\2000) until **Tammuz** 14th was 13,421. 561 were killed and 4,208 persons were injured.

5763 2003

Jewish astronaut with Torah scroll in fiery return from space.

The first Israeli astronaut *(Ilan Ramon)* (who had been a pilot in the air raid which destroyed the Iraqi nuclear reactor, see 5741\1981) — displayed to the world on the 28th **Shvat,** *(during a live tele-conference from a US space-craft, before its tragic disentigration on re-entry into the earth's atmosphere)* an exceptionally small Torah scroll that he was given to take into space (it had originally been given by a rabbi to a thirteen year old bar mitzvah boy in Bergen Belsen *(Nazi CONCENTRATION CAMP)* who was now a scientist.) He also took a silver kiddush cup for use on Shabbat (and later, together with the remains of his diary found strewn on the Texas landscape, was a page on which he had written a Shabbat prayer so that he could recite it properly while in space.

5764 2003

The Neve Shalom Synagogue (see 5746\1986) in Istanbul *(Turkey)* and another nearby synagogue were attacked by car bombs on 20th **Cheshvan** during Shabbat prayer services. 21 Jewish people (and 3 non-Jews) were killed and 60 were wounded.

5764 2004

R.David Ribiat wrote (in 5759\1999) an encyclopedic work *The 39 Melochos (halacha)* which, although intended for lay persons, was at this stage consulted often by scholars for its comprehensive bibliography. Similarly, the Hebrew work *Shemirat Shabbat KeHilchata (halacha)* of R.Yehoshua Neuwith in (5725\1965) on the laws of Shabbat was published in English. Most of the classical Torah works were at this stage published in English translation, and the leader in this field was Artscroll Publications, who actually translated their English commentary-guide on Talmud into Hebrew, thus affecting a major shift in the manner of Talmud study, especially in the proliferation of study of the *Daf HaYomi* (see 5683\1923).

Total Casualties in Eretz Yisrael

Since the establishment of the State of Israel in 1948, 22,700 people were killed in traffic accidents on the country's roads; in the same time-span 21,600 lost their lives in wars and security-related incidents.
A fence was erected (a massive wall, in places) along the border of Jewish and Arab habitation, and the casualties from terrorism were down by 44% in this year compared to the previous year, although the project is not yet complete. Casualties of Palestian-Arabs from internal skirmishes were on the rise and close to equal Jewish casualties by them.

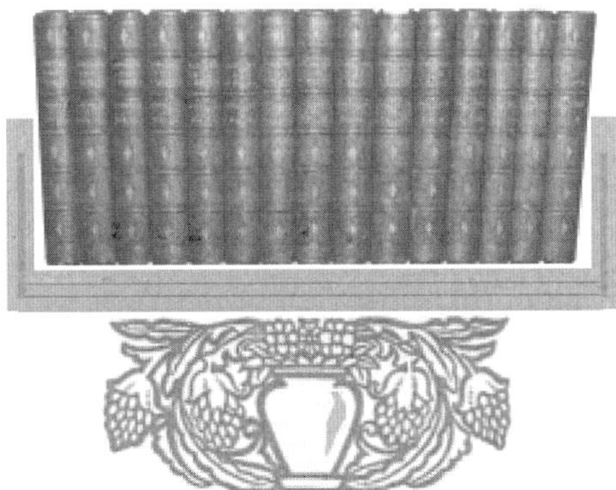

Noteworthy Contemporaries

Personalities are mentioned in this
Chronological Index of Jewish History
in three possible ways:
(i) In the major timelines, charts and headlines;
(ii) in the text of the year of an event;
(iii) in a chart or in a listing of "Living in the Year ....".

Most — if not all — of the names
in this listing here
do not appear elsewhere.
Conversely, names of prominent persons
not appearing here
are listed elsewhere —
barring human error in oversight,
for which apologies are herewith
sincerely extended.
The listing of
Current Noteworthy Personalities
are those still developing historical significance.

Noteworthy Contemporaries

Tzaddikim & Baalei Mussar, Roshei Yeshivah & Rabbonim, Talmudists & Scholars.

1. Chronological Listing

R.Yoshua Leib Diskin	*b.* 1818?	*d.* 1898
"The Alter of Kelm" — R.Simcha Zissel Ziv	*b.* 1824	*d.* 1898
Adm.R.Yosef Meir Weiss of Spinka	*b.* 1838	*d.* 1909
Adm.R.Gershon Henich of Radzin - Ba'al HaTechelet	*b.* 1839	*d.* 1891
Adm.R.Mordechai of Rachamstrivka	*b.* 1839?	*d.* 1921
R.Eliezer Gordon	*b.* 1841	*d.* 1910
R.Nosson Tzvi Finkel — Alter of Slabodka	*b.* 1849	*d.* 1927
R.Yaacov Cohen Gadisha	*b.* 1851	*d.* 1909
Adm.R.Yerachmil Yisrol Yitzchak Danziger-Alexander	*b.* 1853	*d.* 1910
Adm.R.Moshe Grunwald of Chust - Arugas Habosem	*b.* 1853	*d.* 1911
Adm.R.Avrohom Sholom Halberstam of Stropkov	*b.* 1854	*d.* 1940
Adm.R.(Elimelech) Menachem Mendel of Strikov	*b.* 1855?	*d.* 1936
R.Yehuda Fatiyah	*b.* 1859	*d.* 1942
R.Yosef Leib Bloch	*b.* 1860	*d.* 1929
R.Baruch Ber Leibowitz	*b.* 1862	*d.* 1940
Adm.R.Menachem Nachum of Boyan	*b.* 1868	*d.* 1936
R.Yosef Tzvi Dushinsky	*b.* 1868	*d.* 1948
R.Baruch Ber Lebowitz	*b.* 1870	*d.* 1941
R.Isser Zalman Meltzer	*b.* 1870	*d.* 1954
R.Naftoli Trop	*b.* 1871	*d.* 1930
R.Eliyahu Lopian	*b.* 1872	*d.* 1970
Adm.R.Menachem Mendel Halberstam of Stropkov	*b.* 1873	*d.* 1954
R.Alter Israel Perlow of NovoMinsk	*b.* 1874	*d.* 1933
R.Yeruchem Levovitz	*b.* 1875	*d.* 1936
Adm.R.Pinchos Dovid Horowitz - Bostoner Rebbe	*b.* 1876	*d.* 1941
R.Menachem Mendel Alter of Pabyanitz	*b.* 1877	*d.* 1943
Adm.R.Shulem Moshkovitz — Shotzer Rov	*b.* 1877	*d.* 1958
Adm.R.Pinchas Twerski of Ostila	*b.* 1880	*d.* 1943
Adm.R.Itzikel Gevirtzman of Antwerp-Pshevorsk	*b.* 1880	*d.* 1975
R.Zalman Sorotzkin	*b.* 1881	*d.* 1966
R."Itche Massmid" Gorovitz	*b.* 1881?	*d.* 1942
Adm.R.Shimon Sholom Kalish of Amshinov	*b.* 1883	*d.* 1954
R.Ezra Atiyah	*b.* 1885	*d.* 1970
Adm.R.Alter Yechezkel Horowitz of Dzikov	*b.* 1885?	*d.* 1943
Adm.R.Shaul Yedidya Taub - Modzitzer Rebbe	*b.* 1886	*d.* 1947

R.Yehuda Leib Ashlag — Ba'al HaSulam	b. 1886	d. 1954
R.Yosef Shlomo Kahaneman	b. 1886	d. 1969
R.Velvel (Solevetchik) of Brisk	b. 1887	d. 1959
Adm.R.Avrohom Yehoshua Heschel of Kopischnitz	b. 1888	d. 1967
Adm.R.Yisrael of Bluzhev	b. 1889	d. 1989
R.Avraham Chaim No'eh	b. 1890	d. 1954
R.Yechezkel Sarna	b. 1890	d. 1969
Adm.R.Mordechai Shlomo of Boyan	b. 1891	d. 1971
Adm.R.Shmuel Ehrenfeld of Mattersdorf	b. 1891	d. 1980
R.Yaakov Kaminetsky	b. 1891	d. 1986
Michtav M'Eliyahu — R.Eliyahu Eliezer Dessler	b. 1892	d. 1954
Adm.R.Aharon Roth — "Toldos Aharon"	b. 1894	d. 1947
Tchebiner Rav — R.Dov Ber(ish) Weidenfeld	b. 1894?	d. 1965
R.Yaakov Landau	b. 1895?	d. 1986
R.Reuven Grozovsky	b. 1896	d. 1956
Adm.R.Nachum Mordechai Perlow of NovoMinsk	b. 1897?	d. 1976
Adm.R.Yehuda Moshe Tiberg of Alexander	b. 1898	d. 1973
The Steipler Gaon — R.Yaakov Yisroel Kanievsky	b. 1899	d. 1985
Ribnitzer Rebbe - Adm.R.Chaim Zanvil Abramowitz	b. 1899?	d. 1995
R.Yaakov Shaul Katzin	b. 1900	d. 1994
R.Yaakov Halevi Ruderman	b. 1901	d. 1987
R.Chaim Shmuelevitz	b. 1902	d. 1978
Minchas Yitzchak — R.Yitzchak Yaakov Weiss	b. 1902	d. 1989
Adm.R.Yosef Greenwald of Pupa	b. 1902?	d. 1984
Adm.R.Yitzchok Friedman — Bohusher Rebbe	b. 1903	d. 1992
R.Yosef Dov Soloveichik II — "The Rav"	b. 1903	d. 1993
Adm.R.Levi Yitzchok Grunwald of Tzelem	b. 1903??	d. 1984
R.Nissan Nemenov	b. 1904	d. 1984
Adm.R.Yidel Horowitz of Dzikov	b. 1905	d. 1989
R.Yitzchok Hutner	b. 1906	d. 1980
Adm.R.Yaakov Leizer - "R.Yankele" of Antwerp-Pshevorsk	b. 1906	d. 1998
R.Mordechai Pinchos Teitz	b. 1908	d. 1995
R.Gedaliah Shorr	b. 1910	d. 1979
R.Nosson Meir Wachtfogel	b. 1910	d. 1998
Sassover Rebbe — Adm.R.Simcha Rubin	b. 1910	d. 2003
R.Beinush Finkel	b. 1911	d. 1990
R.Moshe Bick	b. 1911	d. 1997
R.Moshe Neuschloss	b. 1911	d. 1997
R.Shulem Schwadron — Yerushalaymer Maggid	b. 1911	d. 1998
Adm.R.Shalom Noach Brazovsky of Slonim	b. 1911	d. 2000
R.Moshe Stern — Debreciner Rov	b. 1911??	d. 1997
R.Pinchas Hirschprung	b. 1912??	d. 1998
R.Baruch Shimon Schneersohn	b. 1913	d. 2001
Toldos Aharon Rebbe — R.Avrohom Yitzchak Kahan	b. 1914	d. 1996
R.Chaim Kreiswirth	b. 1920	d. 2001
Adm.R.Moshe Mordechai Heschel of Kopyczynitz	b. 1927	d. 1975
R.Betzalel Rakow	b. 1927	d. 2003
R.Meir Zvi Ehrentreu	b. 1929?	d. 2000
R.Aryeh Kaplan	b. 1935	d. 1983

2. Alphabetical Listing

Adm.R. Aharon Roth — "Toldos Aharon"	b. 1894	d. 1947
R. Alter Israel Perlow of NovoMinsk	b. 1874	d. 1933
Adm.R. Alter Yechezkel Horowitz of Dzikov	b. 1885?	d. 1943
R. Aryeh Kaplan	b. 1935	d. 1983
R. Avraham Chaim No'eh	b. 1890	d. 1954
Adm.R. Avrohom Sholom Halberstam of Stropkov	b. 1854	d. 1940
Adm.R. Avrohom Yehoshua Heschel of Kopischnitz	b. 1888	d. 1967
Toldos Aharon Rebbe — R. Avrohom Yitzchak Kahan	b. 1914	d. 1996
R. Baruch Ber Leibowitz	b. 1862	d. 1940
R. Baruch Shimon Schneersohn	b. 1913	d. 2001
R. Beinush Finkel	b. 1911	d. 1990
R. Betzalel Rakow	b. 1927	d. 2003
R. Chaim Kreiswirth	b. 1920	d. 2001
R. Chaim Shmuelevitz	b. 1902	d. 1978
Ribnitzer Rebbe - Adm.R. Chaim Zanvil Abramowitz	b. 1899?	d. 1995
Tchebiner Rav — R. Dov Ber(ish) Weidenfeld	b. 1894?	d. 1965
R. Eliezer Gordon	b. 1841	d. 1910
Adm.R. Elimelech Menachem Mendel of Strikov	b. 1855?	d. 1936
Michtav M'Eliyahu — R. Eliyahu Eliezer Dessler	b. 1892	d. 1954
R. Eliyahu Lopian	b. 1872	d. 1970
R. Ezra Atiyah	b. 1885	d. 1970
R. Gedaliah Shorr	b. 1910	d. 1979
Adm.R. Gershon Henich of Radzin - Ba'al HaTechelet	b. 1839	d. 1891
Adm.R. Itzikel Gevirtzman of Antwerp-Pshevorsk	b. 1880	d. 1975
Adm.R. Levi Yitzchok Grunwald of Tzelem	b. 1903??	d. 1984
R. Meir Zvi Ehrentreu	b. 1929?	d. 2000
R. Menachem Mendel Alter of Pabyanitz	b. 1877	d. 1943
Adm.R. Menachem Mendel Halberstam of Stropkov	b. 1873	d. 1954
Adm.R. Menachem Nachum of Boyan	b. 1868	d. 1936
Adm.R. Mordechai of Rachamstrivka	b. 1839?	d. 1921
R. Mordechai Pinchos Teitz	b. 1908	d. 1995
Adm.R. Mordechai Shlomo of Boyan	b. 1891	d. 1971
R. Moshe Bick	b. 1911	d. 1997
Adm.R. Moshe Grunwald of Chust - Arugas Habosem	b. 1853	d. 1911
Adm.R. Moshe Mordechai Heschel of Kopyczynitz	b. 1927	d. 1975
R. Moshe Neuschloss	b. 1911	d. 1997
R. Moshe Stern — Debreciner Rov	b. 1911??	d. 1997
Adm.R. Nachum Mordechai Perlow of NovoMinsk	b. 1897?	d. 1976
R. Naftoli Trop	b. 1871	d. 1930
R. Nissan Nemenov	b. 1904	d. 1984
R. Nosson Meir Wachtfogel	b. 1910	d. 1998
R. Nosson Tzvi Finkel — Alter of Slabodka	b. 1849	d. 1927

	R. Pinchas Hirschprung	*b.* 1912??	*d.* 1998
	Adm.R. Pinchas Twerski of Ostila	*b.* 1880	*d.* 1943
	Adm.R. Pinchos Dovid Horowitz - Bostoner Rebbe	*b.* 1876	*d.* 1941
	R. Reuven Grozovsky	*b.* 1896	*d.* 1956
	Adm.R. Shalom Noach Brazovsky of Slonim	*b.* 1911	*d.* 2000
	Adm.R. Shaul Yedidya Taub - Modzitzer Rebbe	*b.* 1886	*d.* 1947
	Adm.R. Shmuel Ehrenfeld of Mattersdorf	*b.* 1891	*d.* 1980
	Adm.R. Shulem Moshkovitz — Shotzer Rov	*b.* 1877	*d.* 1958
	R. Shulem Schwadron — Yerushalaymer Maggid	*b.* 1911	*d.* 1998
Sassover Rebbe —	Adm.R. Simcha Rubin	*b.* 1910	*d.* 2003
"The Alter of Kelm" —	R. Simcha Zissel Ziv	*b.* 1824	*d.* 1898
	R. Velvel (Solevetchik) of Brisk	*b.* 1887	*d.* 1959
	R. Yaacov Cohen Gadisha	*b.* 1851	*d.* 1909
	R. Yaakov Halevi Ruderman	*b.* 1901	*d.* 1987
	R. Yaakov Kaminetsky	*b.* 1891	*d.* 1986
	R. Yaakov Landau	*b.* 1895?	*d.* 1986
	Adm.R. Yaakov Leizer"R Yankele" of Antwerp	*b.* 1906	*d.* 1998
	R. Yaakov Shaul Katzin	*b.* 1900	*d.* 1994
The Steipler Gaon —	R. Yaakov Yisroel Kanievsky	*b.* 1899	*d.* 1985
	R. Yechezkel Sarna	*b.* 1890	*d.* 1969
	R. Yehuda Fatiyah	*b.* 1859	*d.* 1942
	R. Yehuda Leib Ashlag — Ba'al ḤaSulam	*b.* 1886	*d.* 1954
	Adm.R. Yehuda Moshe Tiberg of Alexander	*b.* 1898	*d.* 1973
	Adm.R. Yerachmil Yisrol Yitzchak Danziger-Alexander	*b.* 1853	*d.* 1910
	R. Yeruchem Levovitz	*b.* 1875	*d.* 1936
	Adm.R. Yidel Horowitz of Dzikov	*b.* 1905	*d.* 1989
	Adm.R. Yisrael of Bluzhev	*b.* 1889	*d.* 1989
	R.Yitzchak "Itche Massmid" Gorovitz	*b.* 1881?	*d.* 1942
Minchas Yitzchak —	R. Yitzchak Yaakov Weiss	*b.* 1902	*d.* 1989
	Adm.R. Yitzchok Friedman — Bohusher Rebbe	*b.* 1903	*d.* 1992
	R. Yitzchok Hutner	*b.* 1906	*d.* 1980
	R. Yosef Dov Soloveichik II — "The Rav"	*b.* 1903	*d.* 1993
	Adm.R. Yosef Greenwald of Pupa	*b.* 1902??	*d.* 1984
	R. Yosef Leib Bloch	*b.* 1860	*d.* 1929
	Adm.R. Yosef Meir Weiss of Spinka	*b.* 1838	*d.* 1909
	R. Yosef Shlomo Kahaneman	*b.* 1886	*d.* 1969
	R. Yosef Tzvi Dushinsky	*b.* 1868	*d.* 1948
	R. Yoshua Leib Diskin	*b.* 1818?	*d.* 1898
	R. Zalman Sorotzkin	*b.* 1881	*d.* 1966

Current Noteworthy Personalities
5765\2004

Adm.R.Meshulam of Tohsh-Montreal
R.Ovadiah Yosef
R.Yechezkel Roth
R.Menashe Klein
Adm.R.Yisroel Avrohom Portugal Skulener Rebbe
Adm.R.Moshe Yehoshua of Vizhnitz, Bnei Brak
R.Yosef Shalom Elyashiv
Adm.R.Mordechai of Vizhnitz, Monsey
R.Yoel Kahan
Adm.R.Levi Yitzchok Horowitz of Boston-Har Nof
R.Mordechai Eliyahu
R.Aharon Leib Shteinman
Adm.R.Yaacov Perlow, Novominsker Rebbe
Adm.R.David Twersky of Sqver
R.Shmuel Kaminetzky
R.Moshe Yehuda Landau
R.Avrohom P. Blumenkranz
R.Moshe Wolfson, Emunas Yisrael
Adm.R.Yissachar Dov Rokeach II of Belz
R.Mattisyahu Solomon
R.Yisrael Belsky
R.Gavriel Zinner - Nitey Gavriel

Prime Ministers of Israel

David Ben-Gurion	1948 – 1953 & 1955 – 1963
Moshe Sharett	1954 – 1955
Levi Eshkol	1963 – 1969
Golda Meir	1969 – 1974
Yitzhak Rabin	1974 – 1977 & 1992 – 1995
Menachem Begin	1977 – 1983
Yitzhak Shamir	1983 – 1984 & 1986 – 1992
Shimon Peres	1984 – 1986 & 1995 – 1996
Benjamin Netanyahu	1996 – 1999
Ehud Barak	1999 – 2001
Ariel Sharon	2001 –

Official Emblem of the State of Israel

Presidents of Israel

Chaim Weizmann	1949 – 1952
Itzhak Ben-Zvi	1952 – 1963
Zalman Shazar	1963 – 1973
Ephraim Katzir	1973 – 1978
Yitzhak Navon	1978 – 1983
Chaim Herzog	1983 – 1993
Ezer Weizman	1993 – 2000
Moshe Katsav	2000 –

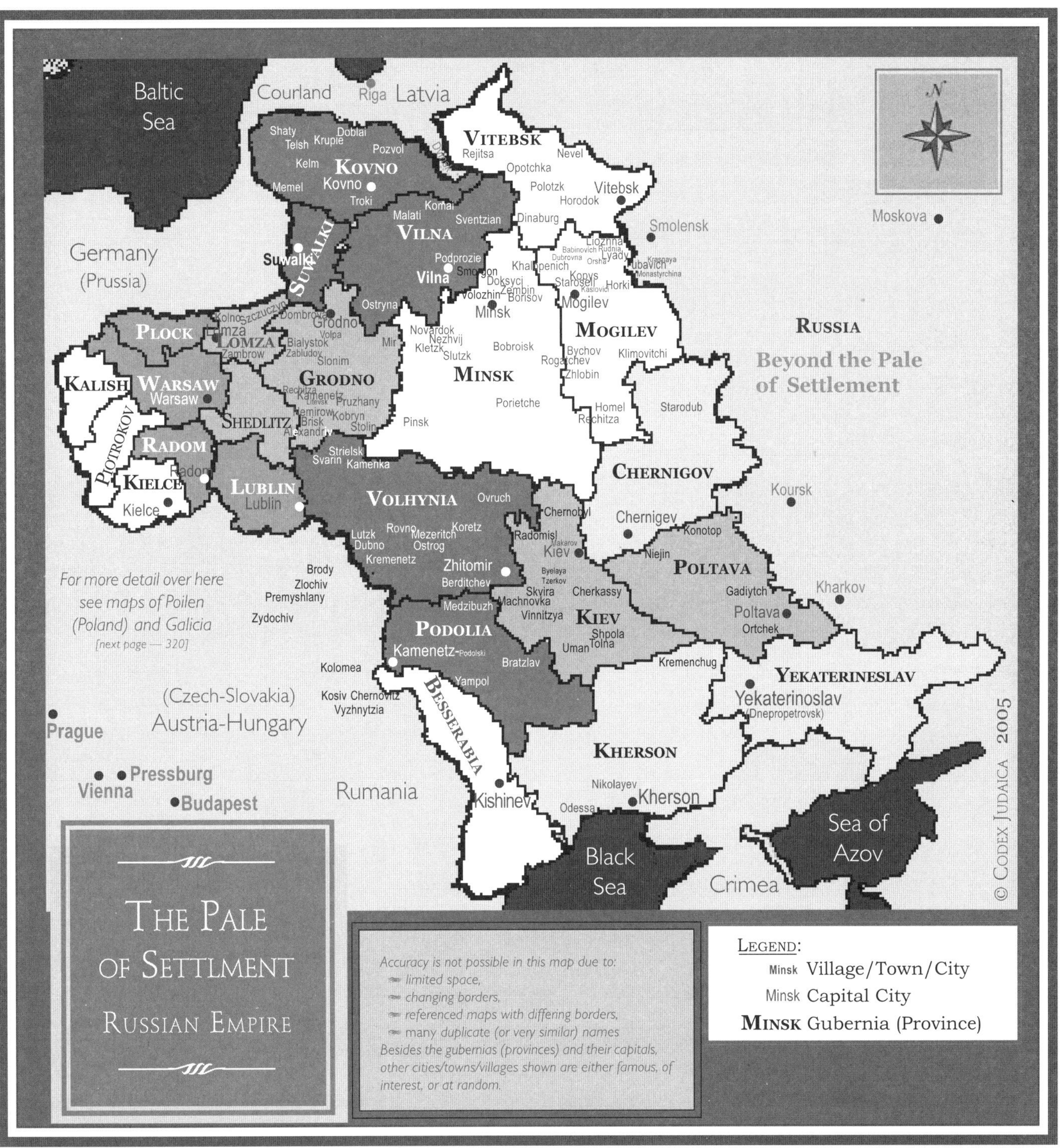

Baltic Sea
Courland
Riga
Latvia
Shaty
Telsh
Krupie
Doblai
Pozvol
Kelm
Kovno
Kovno
Memel
Troki
Vitebsk
Rejitsa
Nevel
Opotchka
Polotzk
Vitebsk
Horodok
Dinaburg
Smolensk
Moskova
Malati
Komai
Sventzian
Vilna
Suwalki
Suwalki
Podprozie
Smorgon
Vilna
Germany
(Prussia)
Khalopenich
Lyady
Lubavich
Dokšyci
Zembin
Borisov
Starosel
Horki
Volozhin
Minsk
Mogilev
Ostryna
Grodno
Kolno
Szczuczyn
Dombrova
Plock
Lomza
Lomza
Bialystok
Zabludov
Zambrow
Volpa
Slonim
Mir
Novardok
Nezhvij
Kletzk
Slutzk
Bobroisk
Minsk
Mogilev
Bychov
Rogachev
Zhlobin
Klimovitchi
Russia
Beyond the Pale of Settlement
Kalish
Warsaw
Warsaw
Grodno
Rechitza
Kamenetz
Pruzhany
Kobryn
Brisk
Stolin
Shedlitz
Alexandria
Poritche
Pinsk
Homel
Rechitza
Starodub
Piotrokov
Radom
Radom
Kielce
Kielce
Lublin
Lublin
Strielsk
Svarin
Kamenka
Volhynia
Ovruch
Chernigov
Koursk
Chernobyl
Chernigev
Konotop
Radomisl
Kiev
Niejin
Lutzk
Rovno
Mezeritch
Koretz
Dubno
Ostrog
Kremenetz
Zhitomir
Berditchev
Poltava
For more detail over here see maps of Poilen (Poland) and Galicia
[next page — 320]
Brody
Zlochiv
Premyshlany
Zydochiv
Skvira
Cherkassy
Machnovka
Vinnitzya
Medzibuzh
Kiev
Gadiytch
Kharkov
Poltava
Ortchek
Podolia
Kamenetz-Podolski
Shpola
Tolna
Uman
Bratzlav
Kremenchug
Kolomea
Yampol
Yekatérineslav
Yekaterinoslav
(Dnepropetrovsk)
(Czech-Slovakia)
Austria-Hungary
Kosiv Chernovitz
Vyzhnytzia
Besserabia
Prague
Kherson
Pressburg
Vienna
Budapest
Rumania
Kishinev
Nikolayev
Kherson
Odessa
Sea of Azov
Black Sea
Crimea
© Codex Judaica 2005
The Pale of Settlment
Russian Empire
Accuracy is not possible in this map due to:
limited space,
changing borders,
referenced maps with differing borders,
many duplicate (or very similar) names
Besides the gubernias (provinces) and their capitals, other cities/towns/villages shown are either famous, of interest, or at random.
Legend:
Minsk Village/Town/City
Minsk Capital City
Minsk Gubernia (Province)

Baltic Sea
Slupsk
Gdansk
Koszalin
Elblag
Suwalki
Swinoujscie
Olsztyn
Chojnice
Szczecin
Grudziadz
Stargard Szczecinski
Walcz
Pila
Bydgoszcz
Thrun
Ostroleka
Lomza
Bialystok
Ciechanow
Gorzów
Kostrzyn
Wloclawek
Plock
Poznan
Kouin
Warszawa
Siedlce
Biala Podlaska
Zielona Góra
Leszno
Kalisz
Skierniewice
Lódz
Sieradz
Piotrkow Trybunalski
Tomaszow Mazowiecki
Pulawy
Radom
Lublin
Chelm
Lubin
Legnica
Wroclaw
Jelenia Góra
Piotrkow
Ostrowiec Swietokrzyski
Walbrzych
Opole
Czestochowa
Kielce
Zamosc
Tarnobrzeg
Stalowa Wola
Klodzko
Bytom
Katowice
Krakow
Rzeszow
Oswiecim
Tarnow
Przemysl
Bielsko- Biala
Bielsko
Nowy Sacz
Krosno
POILEN
(POLAND)
© CODEX JUDAICA 2005
Tarnobrzeg
Bilgoraj
Nisko
Tomaszow
Sokal
Horokhiv
Volhynia
Rivne
Dubno
Mielec
Kolbuszowa
Dabrowa
Rava Ruska
Radekhiv
Liubachiv
Tarnów
Ropczyce
Lancut
Przeworsk
Jaroslaw
Brzesko
Rzeszow
Zhovkva
Kamianka
Brody
Kremianets
Yavoriv
Jaslo
Peremyshl
Horodok
Lviv
Zolochiv
Nowy Sacz
Gorlice
Brzozow
Krosno
Mostyska
Peremyshlany
Zboriv
Zbarazh
Rudky
Sianik
Dobromyl
Bibrk
Sambir
Ternopil
Skalat
Lisko
Rohatyn
Berezhany
Drohobych
Zhydachiv
Bardejov
Svydnyk
Pidhaitsi
Terebovla
Turka
Stryi
Kopychyntsi
Kalush
Presov
Dolyna
Stanyslaviv
Buchach
Chortkiv
CZECHOSLOVAKIA
Tovmach
Borshchiv
Horodenka
Zalishchyky
Uzhhorod
Nadvirna
Kolomyia
Sniatyn
Zastavna
Kholyn
Vashkivtsi
Chernivtsi
Transcarpathia
Kosiv
Vyzhnytsia
Khust
Bukovyna
Rakhiv
Trachiv
Sighetu-Marmatiei
GALICIA
© CODEX JUDAICA 2005

Courtesy of the University of Texas Libraries,
The University of Texas at Austin

From the Perry-Castañeda LibraryMap Collection,
from the Atlas To Freeman's Historical Geography,
Edited by J.B. Bury, Longmans Green and Co. 3rd Edition 1903

Ancient Persia & Babylonia

IMPERIUM PERSICUM ANTIQUUM

Map 1

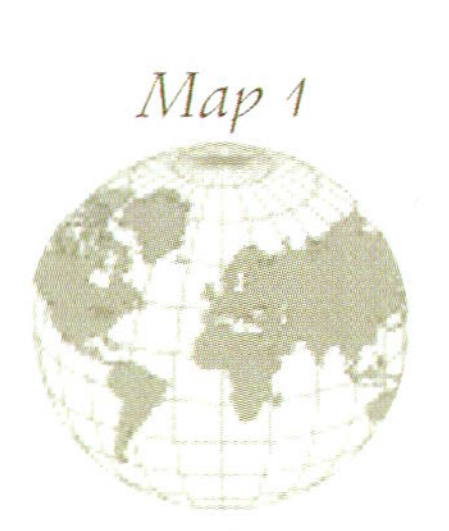

The East Roman Empire

Note:

Costantinople (later Istanbul previously Byzantium, see 4073\313) at the mouth of the Black Sea. Also Nicaea (see 4084\325) just across the Bosphorus Straits from Constantinople.

EASTERN HALF OF THE ROMAN EMPIRE

N.B. The Succi Pass does not cross the Balkan Mountains but crosses a spur from the Balkan Mountains which runs towards the south-west.

In this map Tyana should be more to the west, on the north-western side of the Taurus mountains, and about sixty miles north of Tarsus.

Map 2

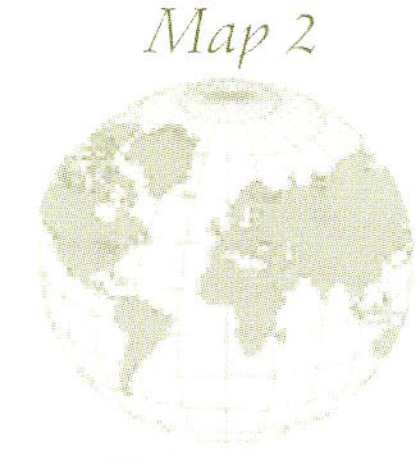

Frankish Territory 481 to 814

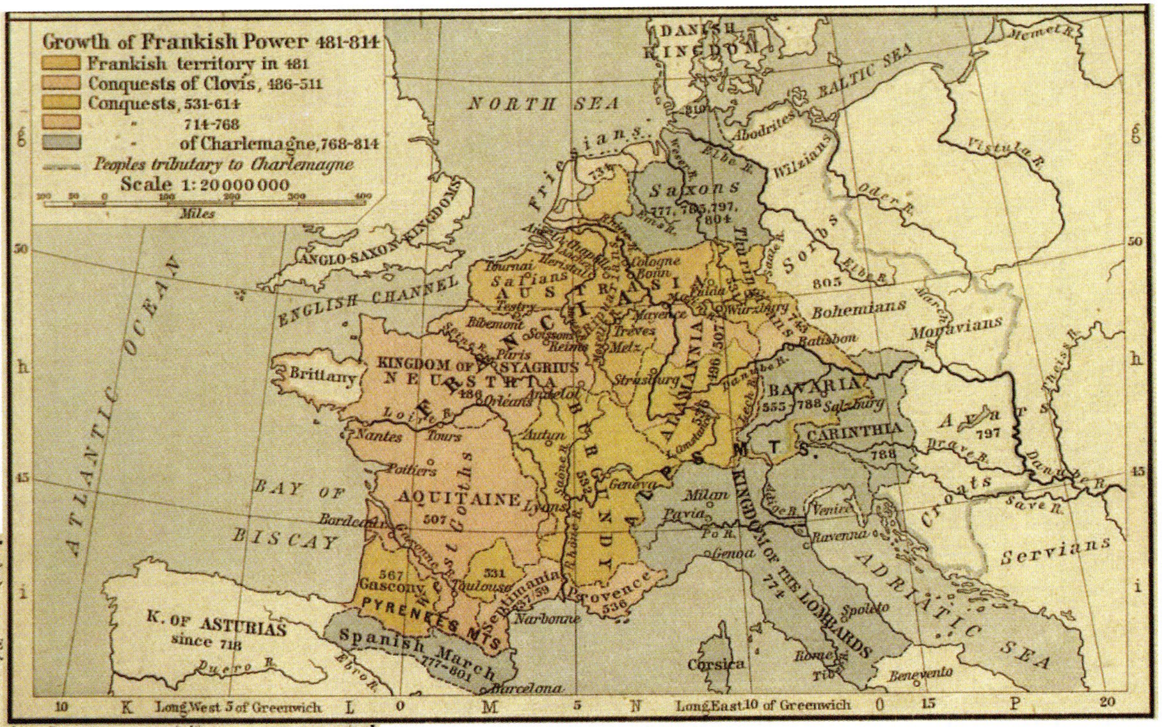

Growth of Frankish Power 481-814
Frankish territory in 481
Conquests of Clovis, 486-511
Conquests, 531-614
714-768
of Charlemagne, 768-814
Peoples tributary to Charlemagne
Scale 1:20000000
NORTH SEA
ATLANTIC OCEAN
BAY OF BISCAY
ENGLISH CHANNEL
ADRIATIC SEA
BALTIC SEA
K. OF ASTURIAS since 718
AQUITAINE
KINGDOM OF THE LOMBARDS 774
BAVARIA
CARINTHIA
Saxons
Bohemians
Moravians
Servians
Spanish March 777-801

& Germanic Kingdoms 526

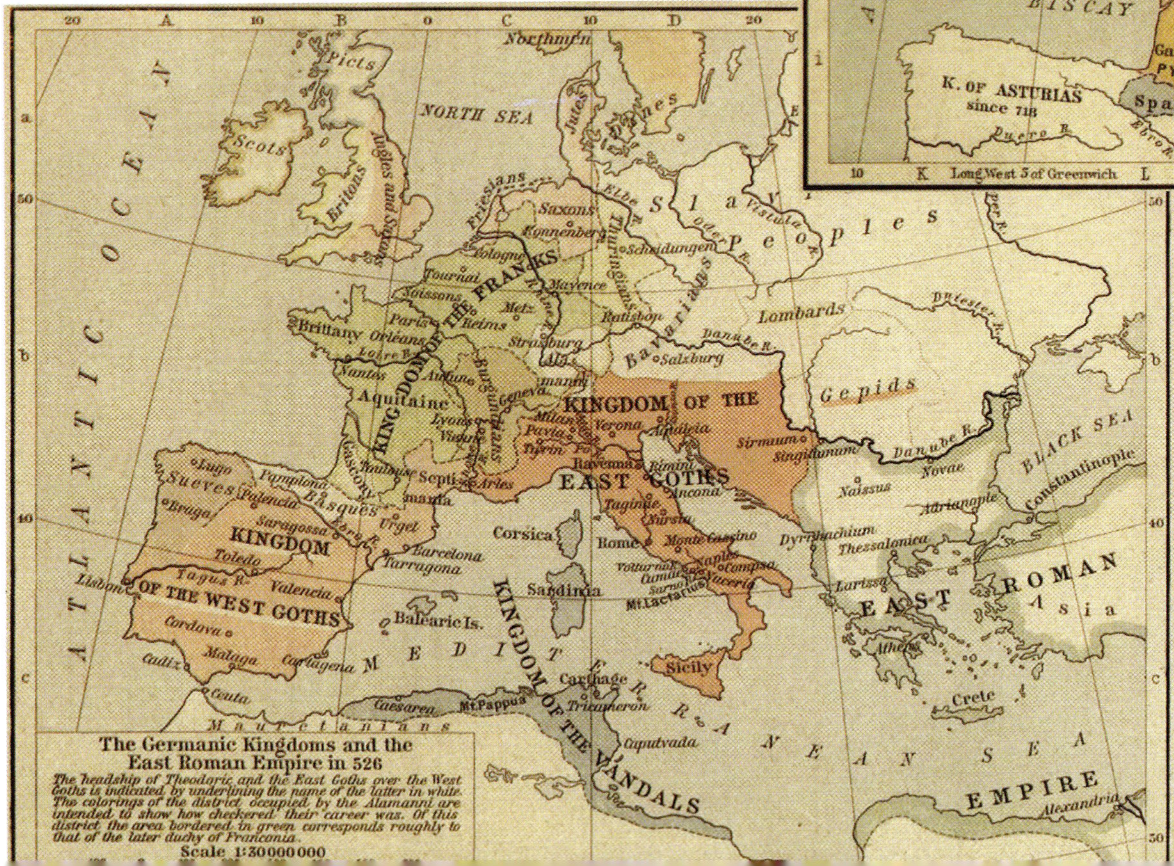

The Germanic Kingdoms and the East Roman Empire in 526
The headship of Theodoric and the East Goths over the West Goths is indicated by underlining the name of the latter in white. The colorings of the district occupied by the Alamanni are intended to show how checkered their career was. Of this district the area bordered in green corresponds roughly to that of the later duchy of Franconia.
Scale 1:30000000
ATLANTIC OCEAN
NORTH SEA
KINGDOM OF THE EAST GOTHS
KINGDOM OF THE WEST GOTHS
KINGDOM OF THE FRANKS
KINGDOM OF THE VANDALS
EAST ROMAN EMPIRE
MEDITERRANEAN SEA
BLACK SEA
Slav Peoples
Lombards
Gepids

Map 3

Islamic Conquests in the First 100 Years

The Califate in 750

Conquests of the Arabs (Saracens) up to the death of Mohammed, 632
" " " under the first three Califs, 632–656
" " " Ommiad Califs, 661–750
Boundary of the Califate
" " East Roman (Byzantine) Empire
The dates are those of conquest
Scale 1:30 000 000

Note:

The conquests include Bavel, which was the center of Jewish learning (see 4397\637)

Changing face of Spain

910

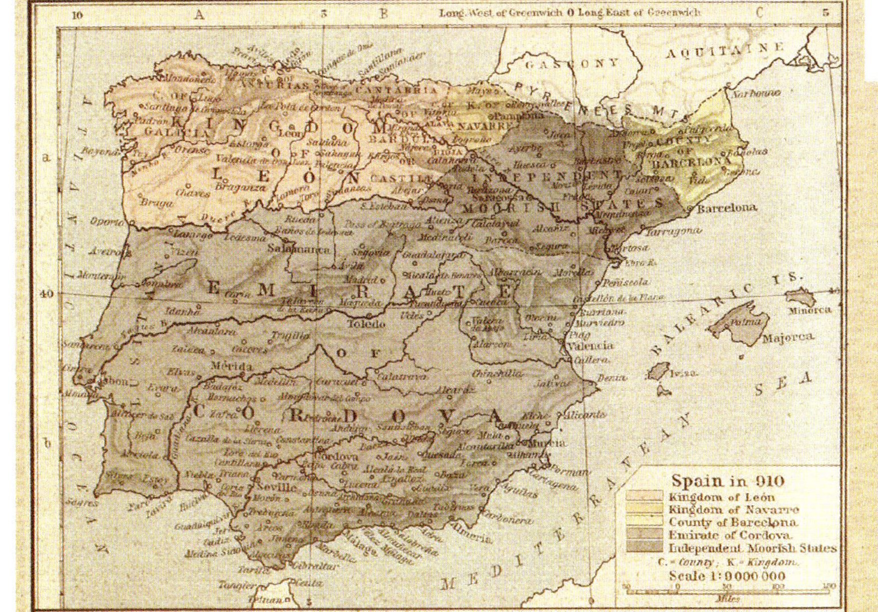

1037

Spain in 1037
Kingdoms of León and Castile
Kingdom of Navarre
Kingdom of Aragon and neighbouring principalities
County of Barcelona
Moorish States
Scale 1:9000000

1150

1492

Map 5

Kingdom of the Almohads (radical Islamic) extending into Spain (see 4908\1148)

Europe 1135

Map 6

Europe 1360

Note:

- Provence (south-east France), see Index.
- Change of rule in Spain, see other maps
- Size of Lithuania, Poland and Hungary

Population of Europe
1300 to 1600 — showing affects of the Black Death Plague

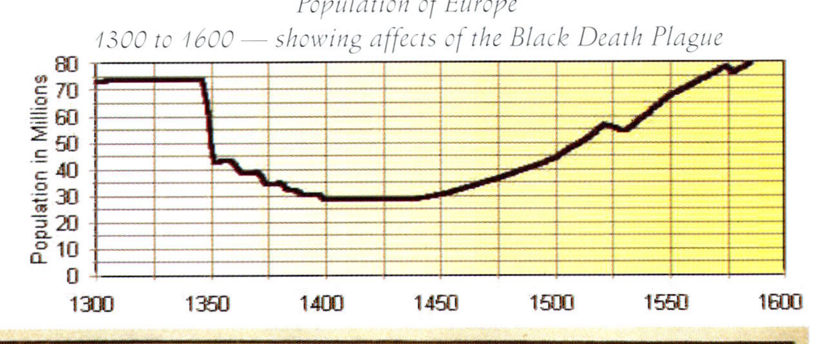

CODEX JUDAICA - *Chronological Index of Jewish History*

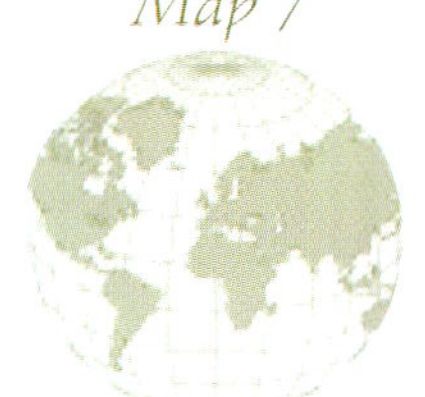

Map 7

Ottoman Empire 1481 to 1683

Map 8

Note: *The extent of Poland-Lithuania — including Ukraine — at a time of Jewish growth.*

The Ottoman Empire and the town of Galipoli (south-west of Constaninople) where Shabbetai Tzvi was interned (see 5426\1666).

Europe in 1550

Map 9

Cossack State — Ukraine 1648

See 5408\1648

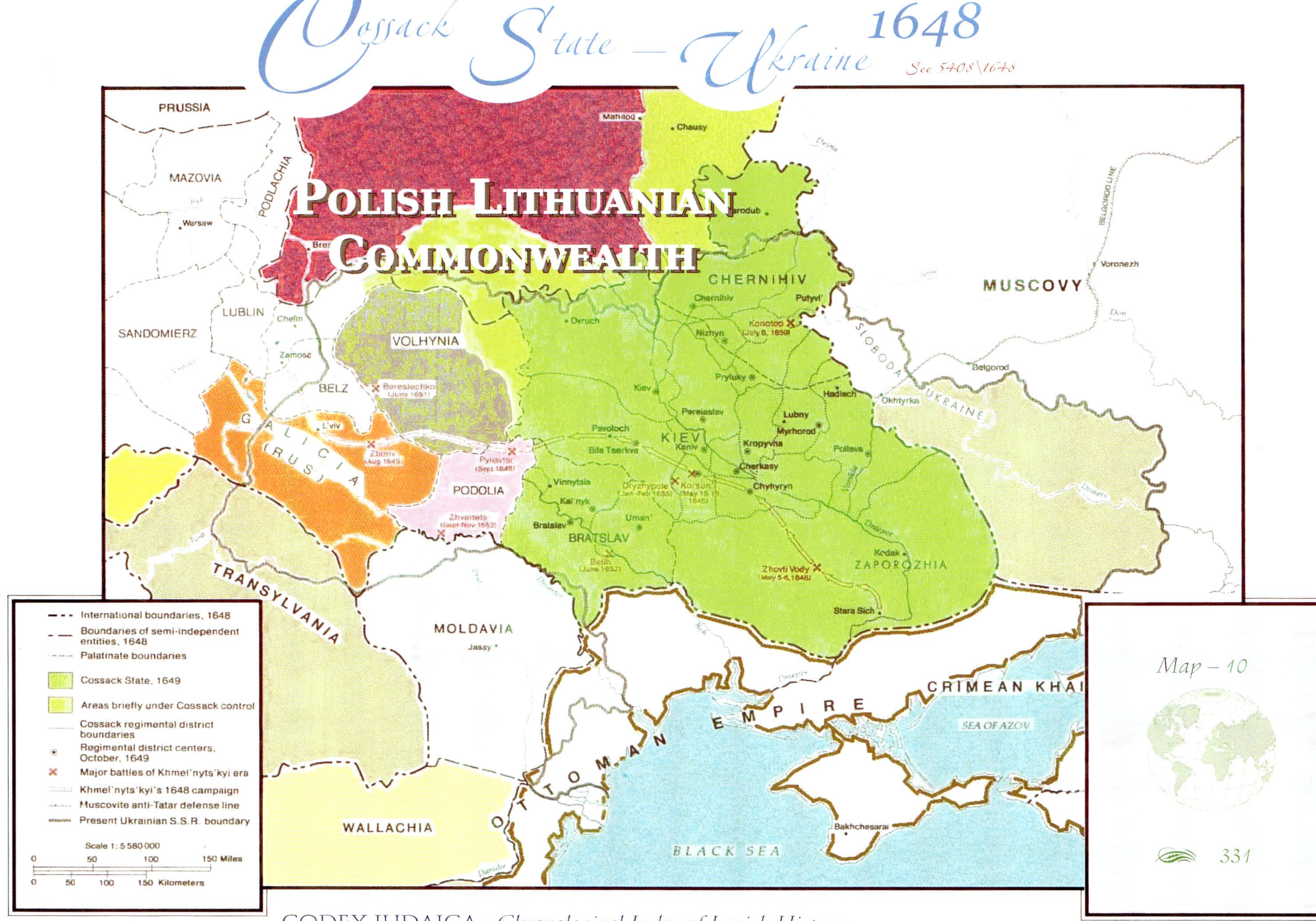

Europe 1740

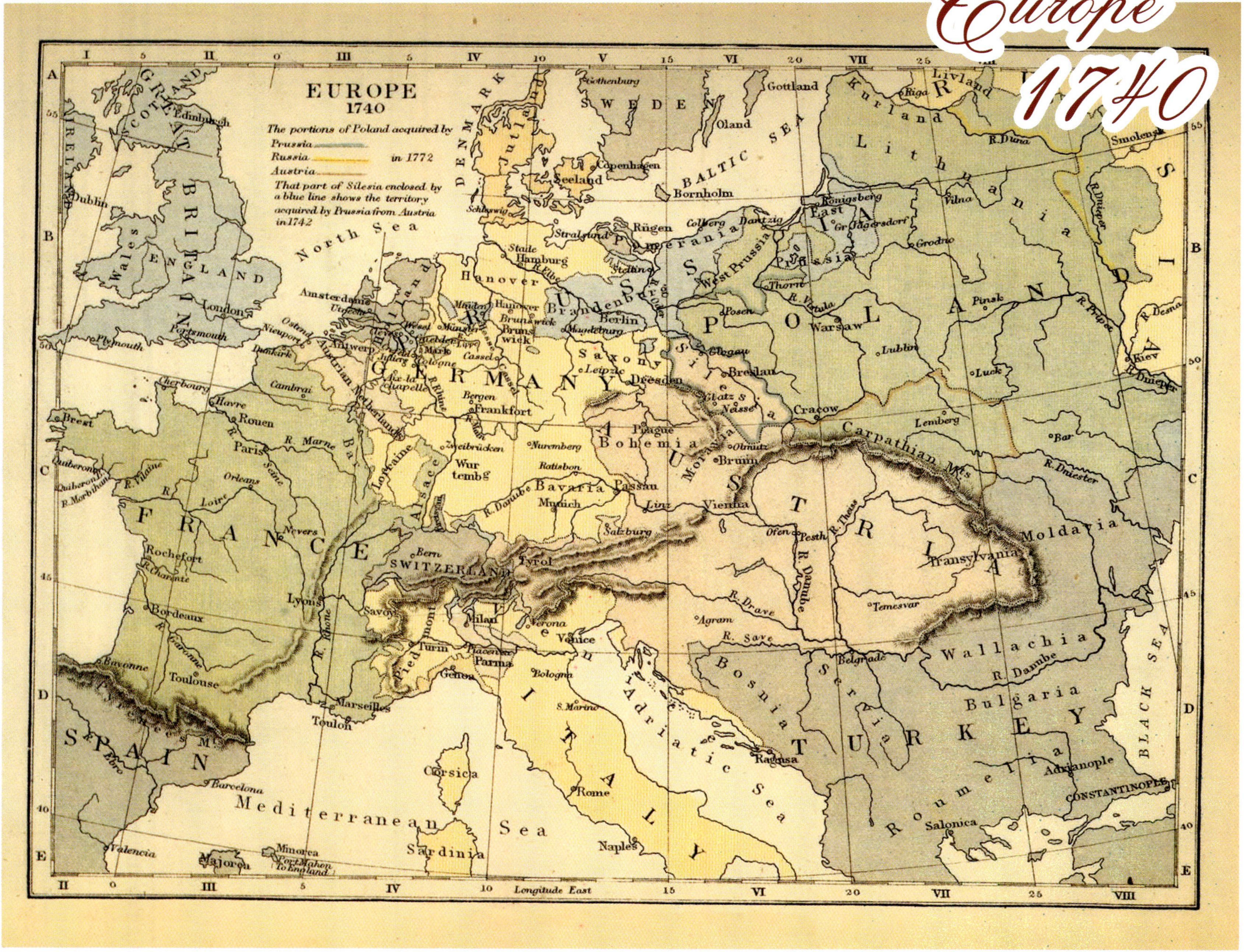

EUROPE
1740

The portions of Poland acquired by
Prussia
Russia *in 1772*
Austria

That part of Silesia enclosed by a blue line shows the territory acquired by Prussia from Austria in 1742

Longitude East

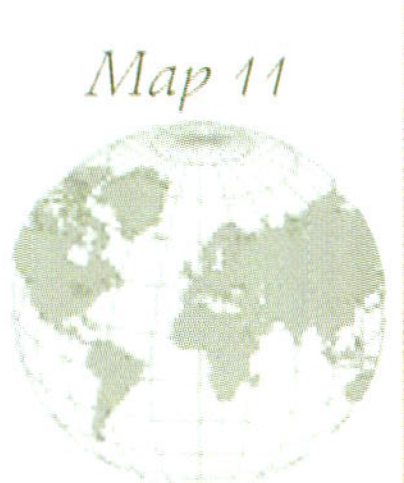

Europe 1815

Map 12

Europe 1913

before World War I

Note:

The extent of Russia that included parts of Poland.
The Austro-Hungarian Empire which also included parts of Poland, Galicia and the Ukraine.

German Empire, Austria Hungary, Italy — The Triple Alliance
France, Russia — The Dual Alliance

Scale 1:20000000.

Map 13

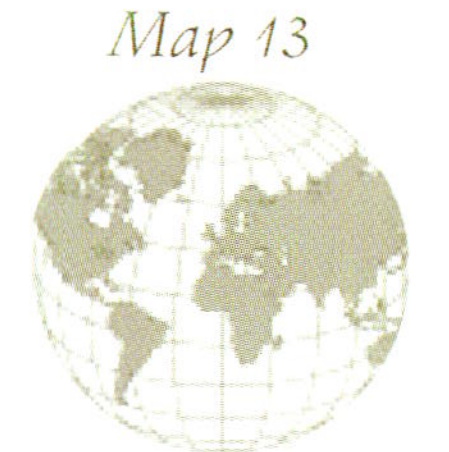

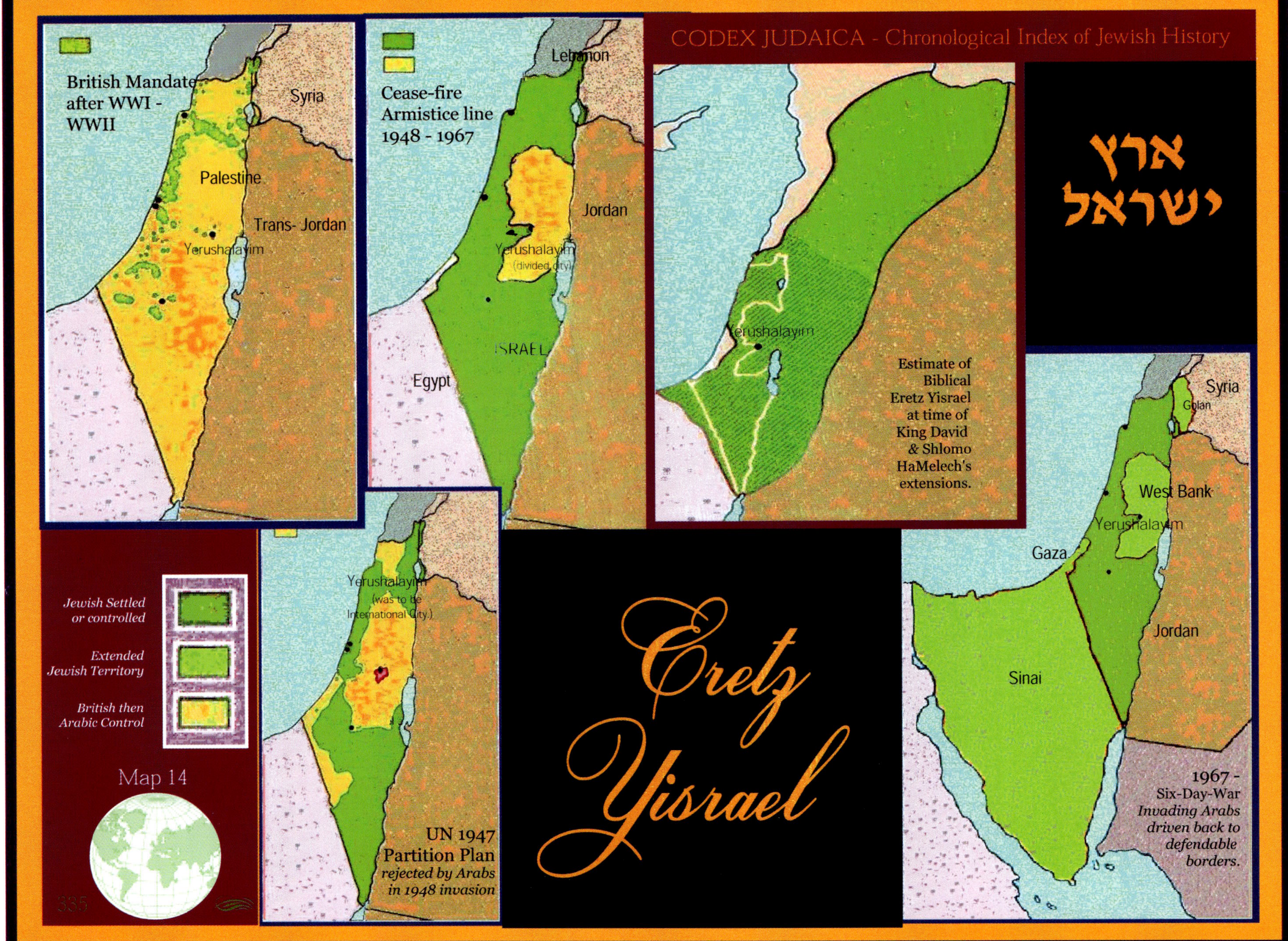

CODEX JUDAICA - Chronological Index of Jewish History
ארץ ישראל
Eretz Yisrael
British Mandate after WWI - WWII
Syria
Palestine
Trans- Jordan
Yerushalayim
Cease-fire Armistice line 1948 - 1967
Lebanon
Jordan
Yerushalayim (divided city)
ISRAEL
Egypt
Yerushalayim
Estimate of Biblical Eretz Yisrael at time of King David & Shlomo HaMelech's extensions.
Syria
Golan
West Bank
Yerushalayim
Gaza
Jordan
Sinai
1967 - Six-Day-War Invading Arabs driven back to defendable borders.
Jewish Settled or controlled
Extended Jewish Territory
British then Arabic Control
Map 14
Yerushalayim (was to be International City.)
UN 1947 Partition Plan rejected by Arabs in 1948 invasion

TORAH TOWNS OF GREATER LITHUANIA
"DER LITTEH"
Finland
HELSINKI
Gulf of Finland
Sweden
STOCKHOLM
TALLINN
Estonia
Latvia
RIGA
Russia
Dvinsk
Baltic Sea
Slobodka
Vitebsk
Ponevitch
Telz
Lubavich
Kelem
Lithuania
Shklov
Kovno
VILNA
Mohilev
Smorgon
Dnypro
Radun
MINSK
Russia
Novardok
Volozhin
KALININGRAD
Slonim
Mir
Baranovich
Kajdanow
Kletsk
Slutsk
Zhlobin
Bialystok
Dneiper
Grodno
Gdansk
Belarus
Poland
Kamentez-Litovsk
Pinsk
WARSAW
Brisk
Pozen
Oder
Lodz
KIEV
Lublin
Rovno
Germany
(Wroclaw)
Breslau
Ukraine
Vistula
Katowice
Oswiecim
(Auschwitz)
Cracow
Lemberg
(Lvov)
Kamenetz-Podolski
Czech Republic
PRAGUE
Brno
Slovakia
Moldavia
KISHINEV
(Bratislava)
PRESSBURG
Danube
Yassi
VIENNA
BUDAPEST
Romania
Austria
Hungary
(Cluj)
Klausenburg
N

APPENDICES

Appendix A
The Chronological Placement of Chanuka.

In this book, Chanuka is chronologically placed in the (Jewish) year 3621.

Some say *[Meir.Eyn.36, 53/q.Tzem.Dav.3590]* that the revolt of the Chashmona'im was (not in 3621 but) in 3590.

This, however, is inconsistent with the dates given in the Talmud. *[A.Z.9a, see Tzem.David 3621]*.

Some attempt to resolve the inconsistency by saying that the revolt and subsequent miracle of Chanuka were isolated victories, and that the Syrian (Greek) domination and religious persecution did not cease, but continued for over 20 years, until the establishment of the Kingdom of the Chashmona'im (at a later date), which would coincide with the time frame of the Talmud — 3622 *[A.Z.9a]*. Accordingly (they say) none of the brothers were kings (or rulers) (except for Shimon, the last one, who ruled in a limited way), because the Syrian (Greeks) were still in power *['Chanukah' Artscroll Mesorah Series, N.Y. 1981, p.34, 81-86]*.

This attempt at reconciliation, however, is inconsistent with:

1) the Talmud *[Shab.21b]*, which refers to the *Kingdom* of the Chashmona'im at the time of the miracle of Chanuka, and makes the specific point of [1]inserting the word "Kingdom" (Malchut) into the text (of Megillat Ta'anit) that it is quoting;

2) the Ramban *[Br.49.10 (Quoted in 'Chanukah', Artscroll (p.87, 88), and apparently misread)]*, who *clearly* refers to all of the brothers as *rulers* — who suffered the consequences of their rule (because they were Kohanim, not from the tribe of Yehuda, and therefore not supposed to rule);

3) Rashi who refers to them all in regal terms, as *rulers [Dan.11.20]*;

4) the prayer of "Al-HaNissim" composed very shortly after the miracle by Yochanan Kohen Gadol (see 3622\-139, 3623\-138, and Appendix B). This prayer (which has a *specific number of words*) indicates that only *after* they had successfully defeated their enemy (*V'achar Kach*) did they take to the dedication of the Beit Hamikdash and light the lights of the Menora *[KolBo Chan.44 p.44b, Gimat.122. p.926/Roke'ach 225 p.127/Mmn.Hakd.Pir.Mi.chap.6]*.

Much of the weight of evidence, produced by the latter work *['Chanukah', Artscroll]*, rests on the account of the events in the anonymous books of Chashmona'im (Maccabees). These books are part of the Apocrypha, a series of books, some of which are assumed to have been written in Hebrew originally, but are now only available in (Hebrew) translations from the Greek (and Latin).

It seems that the books were available, in some form, in the 1500's, because they are supposedly quoted in Tosaphot Yom Tov *[Meg.3.6]*, (although he refers to Sefer Maccabi, and may be referring to something else[2]), and in Tzemach David *[3590]*; and both authors were living in a similar time span (1550-1650 CE). The fact that the Tosaphot Yom Tov and the Tzemach David have quoted from them is used as a proof of their acceptability to traditional Talmud scholars[3].

In fact, however, it is remarkable that they (Chashmona'im) are so *rarely* referred to by Talmudists, *particularly* by the Tzemach David, who was writing history. It is equally important to note, that one of those few occasions in which he does quote Chashmona'im, is with regard to the chronological placing of Chanuka, yet *he overrules that opinion.*

The Halachot Gedolot (BaHaG) (see 4519\759) mentions a *Megillat* Chashmona'im that was written by the authors of Megillat Ta'anit. *[Hil.Sof. p.282b]*. It is unlikely[2] that this is the same book of Chashmona'im (Maccabees) referred to here, because Chashmona'im differs with Megillat Ta'anit on such a fundamental issue as to how the revolt of the Chashmona'im began. Megillat Ta'anit *[chap. 6]* ascribes it to a *personal* persecution about to be perpetrated on the family of the Chashmona'im, whilst Chashmona'im *[Maccabees I 2.17-29]* describes a public event of an altar with an idol.

The book Me'or Einayim (whose author also lived in the 1500's) also bases his chronological placement of Chanuka on the book of Chashmona'im. However, the negative attitude of Talmudists (particularly R.Yosef Karo), to Me'or Einayim is clearly stated by the Chida *[Machazik Bracha O.C.307.p.133a]*, and the Maharal of Prague categorically rejects his historical calculations. *[Ba'er HaGola Chap.6 p.127-141, Yerush.1971]*.]

This chronology is based on Biblical, Talmudic, and post Talmudic sources, and all evidence in such sources clearly places the date of the revolt of the Chashmona'im at the year 3621.

---

[1]) *Megillat Ta'anit itself distinguishes between "Beit" Chashmona'i [2.17,27, 9.3,2 7], "Bnei" Chashmona'i [3.17], and "Malchut" Chashmona'i [12.13], and one must therefore assume significance to the Talmud's insertion of the word "Malchut" (Kingdom).*

[2]) *The following accounts of Chanuka are referred to, or are actually extant:*
Megillat Antiochus [Siddur Otzar HaTefillot] reportedly written originally in Aramaic , and supposedly pre-dating Chashmona'im [see footnote there].,
Megillat Chashmona'im, referred to by the Halachot Gedolot (see further in this appendix). (Some say that this is the Megillat Antiochus.)
Midrash Ma'asei Chanuka [Manuscript, Munich],
d) Chashmona'im [Macc.2.25] refer to five other works, describing the story of Chanuka.
It is therefore quite possible, that there were also other works available (besides these).

[3]) *"Chanukah", Artscroll [p.34] also mentions (as proof to their assumption of the (Talmudic) acceptability of Chashmona'im), that Eliyahu Rabbah [O.C.671.1 - should be 670.1] also quotes them. In fact his quote is virtually verbatim as that of the Tosaphot Yom Tov, and he also calls it Sefer Maccabi.*
If Eliyahu Rabbah in fact saw the Sefer Maccabi that he quotes, then it is definitely not(2) the Sefer Chashmona'im (Maccabees), because both he and the Tosaphot Yom Tov are quoting identical words to describe an event, and those words are not found in Chashmona'im, in the description of the same event. [Macc.I 4.38-58, II 10.2-11].
If he is quoting from the Tosaphot Yom Tov, which he often did [Shem.Hag.1.Yud.92 p.52]], then the Eliyahu Rabbah cannot be used as an additional endorsement of the Talmudic acceptability of Chashmona'im.

Appendix B
The Identity Of Yochanan Kohen Gadol.

The Talmud mentions Yochanan Kohen Gadol many times, without clearly identifying who he was, and at what time he lived.

In fact there is a difference of opinion in the Talmud *[Ber.29a]* as to his identity as indicated in the following.

1) The Rambam (Maimonides), in his introduction to his explanations of the Talmud *[Pirush HaMishna, Zer.]*, devotes a chapter *[chap.6]* to clarification of identities in the Talmud. In this chapter (where he would have paid attention to be precise and accurate) he clearly states that Yochanan Kohen Gadol was the son of Mattityahu ('the famous, mentioned in the prayers', presumably the "Al-HaNissim" prayer). The Rambam also mentions Yochanan ben Mattityahu *[in chapters 4 and 7]*, as being a leading scholar of that time.

The Roke'ach, in discussing Chanuka *[225.p.127]*, states that Chanuka transpired through Yochanan Kohen Gadol. He later points out[1] that Yochanan Kohen Gadol composed the "Al-HaNissim" prayer.

The Levush *[Hil.Chan.670]*, says that the Chashmona'im, which means Yochanan Kohen Gadol, recaptured and entered the Beit Hamikdash.

It seems obvious that both the Roke'ach and the Levush concur with the opinion of the Rambam that Yochanan Kohen Gadol was the son of Mattityahu; and because he became Kohen Gadol, rather than a political leader like the other brothers, he was perhaps not as commonly identified (as they were) with military or political accomplishments.

This can be reinforced by the indication in the Talmud *[R.H.18b]* that after the victory of the Chashmona'im, it was customary to use a standardized introduction on legal documents. The statement read "In the year ____ since Yochanan Kohen Gadol...".

However, the Rambam *[Hil.Mas.9.1]* says "...Yochanan Kohen Gadol, who was after Shimon HaTzadik...", and the Bertinura *[Mas.Shen.5.15]* follows this statement. The Kesef Mishna (R.Yosef Karo) however, immediately explains that the Rambam wrote this in order to distinguish[2] between the first Yochanan Kohen Gadol, and the second Yochanan Kohen Gadol, who became a Tzeduki.

It is (incidentally) impossible to suggest that Yochanan Kohen Gadol was *directly* after Shimon HaTzadik, because of the events related in the Talmud *[Min.109b]*, regarding the jealousy of succession after Shimon HaTzadik's death (see 3488\-273). (This would probably explain why the Kesef Mishneh found it necessary to comment on the historical point, when it doesn't affect the Halacha aspect at all.)

2) There are those who say that Yochanan Kohen Gadol was the father of Mattityahu. *[Yuch.1.16, 62/Sed.Had. Sed.Tan.VeAm. Yoch.K.G./possibly the Bertinura Mas.Shen.5.15]*.

The Yuchasin quotes the Rambam *[chap. 6]*, and claims that it is a mistake, and should read Yochanan the 'father' of Mattityahu, not the 'son'. (He interprets the words 'the famous, mentioned in the prayers' as referring to Yochanan (when in fact it seems obvious that it is referring to Mattityahu)).

Would the Yuchasin claim that chap.4 and 7 in the Rambam are also mistakes?

(Toldot Am Olam *[2.412]* questions the Yuchasin, but also relies on saying that the Rambam *[chap.4]* is an inaccuracy *[Tol.Am.Ol.2.410]*, and really is referring to the son of the son (grandson) of Mattityahu (in a circumspect way). He does not quote nor address chap.6, yet it is precisely in this chapter the Rambam would not use circumspect references to a grandson as a son while attempting to clarify and be specific about identities.)

Furthermore, what would be the explanation of the (aforementioned) Talmud *[R.H.18b]*, which indicates that Yochanan Kohen Gadol was being used as a dating 'beacon' *after* the revolt of the Chashmona'im?

It is also clear that [3]Rashi *[Sot.33a]* maintains that Yochanan Kohen Gadol was after the revolt of the Chashmona'im.

3) Others say that Yochanan Kohen Gadol was Yochanan Hyrkanos (see 3642\-119) the son of Shimon, who was in turn the son of Mattityahu. *[Dor.Har.2.444/Tol.Am Ol.2.227, 410]*.

Most agree that this Yochanan (II) was the Kohen Gadol who the Talmud says became a Tzeduki. *[Yuch.1.14, 62/Tzem. David 3646/Sed.Had./Dor.Har.2.442, 444/Tol.Am Ol.2.254]*.

There is a difference of opinion in the Talmud *[Ber.29a]* as to whether Yochanan Kohen Gadol was the one who became a Tzeduki. All seem to agree that Yannai (was or) became a Tzeduki. Was Yochanan the same person as Yannai, or was he not? Abayee says he was. Rava says he was not. The Talmud appears to conclude with the opinion of Rava (as would be customary)[4].

None of the above possibilities readily accounts for a Yochanan Kohen Gadol to have served (a full) 80 years, as related in the Talmud *[Ber.29a, Yom.9a]*. This remains unclear. [5],[6],[7].

For the purposes of a Talmudic chronology, it is preferable to accept the clear statements of the Rambam, Roke'ach and Levush; that Yochanan Kohen Gadol was the son of Mattityahu the Chashmona'i.

It is plausible that there would be a blurring of identities *[Tal.Ber.29a]* between Yochanan Kohen Gadol (the son of Mattityahu), and his nephew, '*Yochanan Hyrkanos Yannai*', if they succeeded each other - which they probably did.

---

[1] *The Roke'ach claims a very long line of information transferral direct to him from Shimon HaPakuli, see 3836\76. [Shem.Hag.1. Alef.219 p.21-22].*

[2] *It is probable that the Rambam used* ***this method*** *of identification - even though Yochanan Kohen Gadol was much later than Shimon HaTzadik - because he was paraphrasing the Talmud [Yom.9a], which lists them together, because they were both famous and of long tenure.*

[3] *It appears, however, that Rashi accepts that there was only one Yannai, which raises questions resolved by Tosaphot, who indicate there were two. [Rashi Sot.22b, Ber.48a, Kid.66a, Shab.16b/ Tos.Yom.18a, Yev.61a].*

[4] *It is also apparent from the Kesef Mishna [Hil.Mas.9.1] that the conclusion of the Talmud is that they were two different people, and it was established that it was (technically) possible that Yochanan could have become a Tzeduki, but in fact he did not.*

[5] *The Tiferet Yisrael [Tal.Av.2.4(33)] says that Yochanan Kohen Gadol lived for 80 years. The Talmud, however, clearly states that he served as Kohen gadol for 80 years. [Tal.Ber.29a, Yom.9a].*
The Steinsaltz Talmud points to a possible solution [Yom.9a, Ber.29a], saying that Yochanan Kohen Gadol refers to a "group" of people, or to a period. This is more plausible in Yoma than in Berachot, and would be accepted if stated by a Rishon (Early Scholar). Rashi [Ber.29a], however, accepts the meaning as simply stated.

[6] *The Maharsha [Pes.57a] suggests (yet) another possible identity for Yochanan Kohen Gadol.*

[7] *The Me'iri [Peticha (introduction) L'Avot] appears to contradict himself. Once he says Yochanan Kohen Gadol was the son of Mattityahu [p.28 Yerush.1964], and later he says that he was the father of Mattityahu. [p.34 Sed.Hat.,Dmai].*

Appendix C
The Ten Martyrs Killed By The Romans

Ten great Tanna'im were brutally killed by the Romans, and their memory has become legend in Jewish history, particularly through a prayer that is said on the holiest day of the Jewish calendar, Yom Kippur, during the Mussaf service. It is generally accepted *[Sed.Had.3880]* that these Ten Martyrs *(Asara Harugei Malchut)* include the following Tanna'im:

1. R.Shimon ben Gamliel I[1]
2. R.Chanina Sgan HaKohanim
3. R.Yishmael (Kohen Gadol)
4. R.Akiva[2] (ben Yosef)
5. R.Yehuda ben Bava[3]
6. R.Chanina ben Tradyon[4]
7. R.Chutzpit HaMeturgeman
8. R.Yesheivav HaSofer
9. R.Elazar ben Shamu'a

There is a considerable difference of opinion as to who was the tenth (great) Tanna killed by the Romans.

Some say that it was R.Yehuda ben Teima, others say it was R.Eliezer ben Dama, and some say that R.Yehuda ben Teima was also called ben Dama. There are yet others who say that R.Chanina ben Chachinay was one of the martyrs, others say R.Yehuda HaNachtum, and others who include R.Tarfon. *[Yuch, Abarbanel, Yal.Reuv., q. Sed.Had.3880].*

It is known that R.Shimon ben Gamliel I (listed above as #1) was no longer living at the time of the destruction of the Second Beit Hamikdash [see below], and that R.Akiva (listed as #4) was alive at the time of the Bar Kochba revolt many years later (see 3887\127). It is therefore assumed that not all ten martyrs were killed during the same period in history (even though the aforementioned prayer allegorically describes them as components of one incident.)

R.Yitzchak HaLevi Rabinowitz (see 5674\1914) raises some important questions (in Dorot HaRishonim *[3.177-181, 199-202, 4.615-20]*) with regard to the previously accepted list of Martyrs. His questions are as follows:

1) If they were killed over an extended period of bloodshed, why have they so often been grouped together?

2) Shmuel HaKatan (see 3836\76), one of the Tanna'im who saw the destruction of the Second Beit Hamikdash, was eulogized by R.Gamliel and R.Elazar ben Azaryah, *[Tal.Smach. 8(47a)]*, (presumably) when they were joint leaders of the Sanhedrin-Academy, long after the destruction of the Beit Hamikdash (see 3844\84). Yet on his deathbed, Shmuel HaKatan predicted the deaths of R.Shimon and R.Yishmael, *[Tal.San.11a, Smach.8(47a)]*, who were certainly the first two martyrs. If so, he could not have been referring to R.Shimon ben Gamliel I, and R.Yishmael ben Elisha (listed above as #3), because R.Shimon died before the destruction, and R.Yishmael immediately after the destruction – long before Shmuel HaKatan was on his deathbed. He must have been referring to another R.Shimon and R.Yishmael.

3). R.Shimon ben Gamliel died (in Yerushalayim) *[Maharsha Sot.49a]* before R.Yochanan ben Zakkai escaped (from the internal siege of Yerushalayim) (see 3827\67, 3828\68) to establish the Sanhedrin-Academy at Yavneh, and it was R.Shimon's son, R.Gamliel II, who presided there. Furthermore, how would he have been killed by the Romans who were still (at that stage) in the northern part of Eretz Yisrael?

4) The Halachot Gedolot *[Hilchot Tisha B'Av and Ta'anit]* mentions R.Shimon ben Gamliel, R.Yishmael, and R.Chanina Sgan HaKohanim, as having been killed on the 25th Sivan. Yet in the various places where the murder of the Martyrs is mentioned *[Tal.Smach.8(47a), Av.Dr.Nat.38.3/ T.D.B.E.30/ Mech. Shmot. 22.22]*, the name of R.Chanina Sgan HaKohanim does not appear. Where then, did the Halachot Gedolot (one of the Ge'onim of around 4500 (740 CE) *[Sed.Had./Shem.Hag.2.61 p.26]*) find the name of R.Chanina Sgan HaKohanim, to include him?

R.Yitzchak HaLevi therefore concludes that the reference to R.Shimon was in fact R.Shimon ben HaSgan (the son of R.Chanina). His name in abbreviated form would have appeared as RShBHS"G, and some scribes, not recognizing the abbreviation, assumed it was a mistake, and copied it as RShBG, the (very common) abbreviation for R.Shimon ben Gamliel. (It was known that R.Shimon ben Gamliel II did not die a violent death, hence it was assumed that it referred to his grandfather, R.Shimon ben Gamliel I. This having been assumed, then the reference to R.Yishmael (with whom he was killed) was taken to refer to R.Yishmael Kohen Gadol who served in the Beit Hamikdash) The Halachot Gedolot, however, could have had a manuscript with a reference to HaSgan, and assumed it to mean R.Chanina Sgan HaKohanim.

R.Yitzchak HaLevi further concludes that it is possible that R.Shimon ben Gamliel I was in fact killed, not by the Romans, but in the civil war that was raging in Yerushalayim during the internal (Jewish) siege (see 3827\67). (The Romans did not even kill Yochanan of Gush Chalav, R.Shimon ben Gamliel's (supposed) ally, even though he was one of the factional *leaders* (see 3827\67) of the rebellion against them (see Chapter 9, 3829\69), why then would they have killed R.Shimon ben Gamliel, who was not a leader of the uprising?)

According to R.Yitzchak HaLevi's explanation, all of the Asara Harugei Malchut would have been killed at the same period in history, during (or after) the Bar Kochba revolt (R.Yishmael refers to R.Yishmael the colleague of R.Akiva), and the incidence of their deaths, all within a short span of time, has lead to the title *Asara Harugei Malchut* (Ten Martyrs).

---

[1] *See Rashi Shab.8b.*

[2]) *R.Akiva was imprisoned for an extended time (see 3894\134), and then he was tortured to death, by having his skin peeled off with hot metals. [Tal.Ber.61b].*

[3]) *When all Jewish religious practice was banned, and an emphasis placed on the ban of Torah study, R.Yehuda ben Bava gathered together R.Meir, R.Yehuda (ben Ila'i), R.Shimon (bar Yochai), R.Yossi, and R.Elazar ben Shamu'a (disciples of R.Akiva, who was already in prison [see Dor.Har.4.641-4]). He met them between two towns, to give them Semichah (ordination) (because the Romans had threatened to annihilate any town in which Semichah was given). He told them to escape (which they did (see 3894\134), except that apparently R.Elazar ben Shamu'a was later captured). R.Yehuda ben Bava was caught on location, and speared (many times) to death. [Tal.San.13b-14a, also San.11a].*

[4]) *R.Yossi ben Kisma was respected by the Romans (apparently others were also, such as R.Yochai (father of R.Shimon) [Tal.Pes.112a]), and when he died, many of them attended his funeral. Upon their return, they found R.Chanina ben Tradyon studying and teaching Torah. They took him, wrapped him in a Sefer Torah scroll, piled up bundles of twigs around him, and before setting him alight, they also placed damp woolen swabs on him, to prolong the agony of being burned to death. [Tal.A.Z.18a].*

Appendix D

The Kov'im. Great Scholars Between Rishonim and Acharonim.

Jewish history has traditionally, over the millenia, been divided into general eras that tend to coincide with developments in Torah, and the scholars of those eras are identified with it, such as the Tanna'im at the time of the Mishna, and the Amora'im at the time of the Gemara.

The beginning of the era of the Rishonim (which included Rashi, the Rif, Rambam and Tosaphot, among others) is clearly defined as the death of R.Hai Gaon, with the subsequent decline in the centrality of the Babylonian Torah centers, and the rise of new centers in France, Germany, and Spain.

After the Rishonim (early Talmud scholars), there followed a Tekufa of Acharonim (later Talmud scholars). There is, however, a blurring of the line drawn between the Rishonim and the Acharonim, with no particular event or date, clearly set, to mark the end of the era of the Rishonim.

In fact, opinions (on the date of the end of the Rishonim and the beginning of the Acharonim) range from as early as the early 1300's (the latest date for the end of the era of Tosaphot) to 1563 (the printing of the Shulchan Aruch).

Such demarkation dates fulfill a role in the study of Torah, in that the scholars of one era treat the opinions of scholars in a preceding era with unquestioning respect. Such demarcations exist in the distinction between the Chumash (Five books of Moses) and the T'nach (Prophets), the Mishna and the Gemara, and the Gemara and Ge'onim. In fact these eras are generally accepted to represent (decreasing) levels of Ru'ach HaKodesh (prophecy, and lower levels of "quasi" prophecy) *[Ramban B.B.12a]*. Acharonim, generally, treat the words of the Rishonim with this deep respect, but the perception of who is classified as a Rishon or not is affected by the (over) 250 year span of doubt.

There is a dilemma, even if we are to accept a clear date for the conclusion of the era of the Acharonim (such as the destruction of European Jewry in 1940). If we then accept an early date for the conclusion of the Rishonim (say 1310), it would lead us to include the Torah scholars and Poskim of our century into the same era of Acharonim (and, by implication, the same level of Ru'ach HaKodesh) as the Tur, the Maggid Mishneh, the Ran, Rivash, Rashbatz, and the Nimukei Yosef — all of whom were before 1492 — as well as the Shulchan Aruch, Radvaz, Eyn Yaakov, Ramak, Ari'zal, Shitta MeKubetzet, R.Moshe Alshich, Maharshal, Maharsha, Maharam, Levush, Sma, Maharal (of Prague), Shaloh HaKadosh, Tosaphot Yom Tov, Bach, Shach, Taz, Chelkat Mechokek, 'Reishis Chochma', Sefer Charedim; plus many others.

Even if we accept a relatively late date for the end of the era of the Rishonim (say 1492), we would still find most of these (aforementioned) scholars co-existing in the same era (Acharonim) as scholars of our era. This possibility is virtually denied by the deep respect the latter scholars display towards the former.

a) Certainly, no Poskim (Halacha authorities) of our era would contradict any of the rulings of the Shulchan Aruch or its commentaries, such as the Shach and Taz.

b) As early as the Ba'al Shem Tov (1698-1760) and his disciples, we find a deep reverence for the words of the Ari'zal (1532-1570) and his contemporary, the 'Reishis Chochma'.

c) R.Shneur Zalman of Lyady, the Ba'al HaTanya VeShulchan Aruch (1745-1813), is quoted as saying, that all the authors (of major works) up until (and including) the Shach and the Taz (printed in 1646) were written with Ru'ach HaKodesh.

The dilemma thus becomes more complex than simply setting a date for the end of the Rishonim, for even the latest date (1563) would leave the Shach and the Taz in the era of Acharonim, together with scholars of our time.

This all compels a conclusion that there needs to be an era between the Rishonim and the Acharonim.

A massive tragedy, such as the expulsion of the Jews from Spain, with the subsequent redistribution of Jewish communities to new locations (in the expanding Ottoman empire) including Turkey, Greece, Eretz Yisrael and North Africa, which all developed vibrant Torah centers, has the hallmarks that signal the end of one era, and the beginning of another. Even more so, when viewed in a broader perspective that the expulsion from Spain was a culmination of other major expulsions from Europe (England (1290), France (1394), Austria (1421), and numerous local expulsions (see index 'expulsions') in the cities and provinces of Germany, Bohemia, Moravia, Switzerland (see 5251\1491) and Italy); and that the Jews from many of these central European expulsions moved eastward to Poland-Lithuania, where a new vibrant Torah center emerged in the 1500's; there is compelling reason to place the end of an era in Jewish history at the Spanish expulsion in 1492.

The printing, in 1646, of the Shach and the Taz (commentaries on the Shulchan Aruch), clearly consolidated the place of Shulchan Aruch as the final word in Halacha. Two years later, the thriving Jewish communities of Poland-Lithuania received a major setback (economically and spiritually) in the devastating massacres of the Cossack uprising under Chmielnitzki, in 1648. Jews in Poland-Lithuania (and later in Russia) never recovered their original status of the pre-1648 era, and were relegated to a miserable second class socio-economic existence.

Remarkably, in the 156 years between 1492 and 1648 we find the following personalities (and works):

The Shulchan Aruch, Radvaz, Eyn Yaakov, Avodat HaKodesh (Kabbala), Ramaz (Remez, Kabbala), Ramak (Pardes), Ari'zal, Shitta MeKubetzet, R.Moshe Alshich, R.Yaakov Pollak, Maharshal, Maharsha, Maharam, Levush, Sma, Maharal (of Prague), Shaloh HaKadosh, Tosaphot Yom Tov, Bach, Shach, Taz, Chelkat Mechokek, 'Reishis Chochma' and Sefer Charedim.

By their names alone, they represent an outstanding era in Jewish history. If, however, we look at the accomplishments of many of these personalities, we find an even more remarkable phenomena.

1) The Shulchan Aruch was, without question, the consolidation of Halacha. The contributions of its author, R.Yosef Karo, its "editor", the Ramo; and its commentaries, the Sma, the Shach, the Taz and the Chelkat Mechokek; all combined to seal yet another phase in the development of Torah. The Shulchan Aruch today is a consolidated work of Halacha, referred to with a similar reverence as the Mishna was referred to in the time of the Gemara, or as the Gemara was referred to by the Ge'onim.

2) The teachings of the Ari'zal (and the Pardes of the Ramak) had a similar profound impact on the study of Kabbala, and rank, with the Zohar, as the major works of Kabbala.

3) The works of the Maharsha, the Maharshal, and the Maharam, (coupled with the Pilpul style introduced into Poland-Lithuania by R.Yaakov Pollak, and the works of the Shitta Mekubetzet), all contributed to the styles and trends of Talmud study that prevail until today.

4) The Bertinura (R.Ovadya) and the Tosaphot Yom Tov have had a basic and lasting impact on the study of the Mishna.

5) The Eyn Yaakov created a concept of its own, with regard to the study of Agada; and the Matanot Kehuna and the Yefei To'ar, both the major commentaries on the Midrash Rabba, have increased the accessibility of the Midrash.

It becomes clear that the era between 1492 and 1648, is more than a period between major upheavals in Jewish life. It was an era of Torah consolidation that left a major impact in the development of Torah.

(The perspective of distance is often necessary before the full impact of the historical contribution of an era can be fully appreciated, and perhaps that distance has now developed that clarity of perspective.)

If we are to say that this era (1492-1648) belongs neither to the Rishonim, nor the Acharonim — representing an era that stands on its own, it would need to be suitably named.

After considering many possibilities, the name Kov'im (consolidation and setting) appears to most appropriately describe the impact of this era in Jewish history.

GLOSSARIES

Glossary 1 — Terminology

Acharon
Literally "last". Refers to Jewish scholar and authority during the period leading into the 20th century (see Appendix D).

Acharonim
plural of Acharon.

Adar
The name of a Jewish month (see glossaries calendar).

Adm.
Used in this book as an abbreviation of the title Admur (see below).

Admur
Abbreviation of the words "Adoneninu (our master) Moreinu (our teacher) veRabeinu (our rabbi)". Leader (or spiritual "master") of a chasidic group. Usually charismatic, and not restricted to scholarly leadership. Also called "Rebbe" or "Tzadik". See 5520\1760, 5575\1814.

Admurim
Plural of Admur.

Agada
Parables, stories, and statements conveying moral lessons. Many pages of the Gemara are devoted to this, and this style forms the body of Midrash.

Akeda
Literally "binding", when Yitzchak was bound up by his father, to be brought as a sacrifice. (See 2084\-1677)

aliya
Emigration to Eretz Yisrael.

Amora'im
Plural of Amora, see below.

Amora
Scholar of the Gemara section of the Talmud (see 3990\230, 4111\351).

Anshei
Literally "people of". Anshei Knesset Hagdola refers to "the people of the Great Assembly", a Sanhedrin type body. (See 3426\-335, 3448\-313.)

Anussim
Literally "forced ones". Used to refer to Jews who accepted other religions under the threat of death, but maintained some religious observance in secret. (See index for Marranos and for secret Jews.)

Av
The name of a Jewish month (see glossaries calendar).

Avoda Zara
Literally "idol worship". Also the name of a section (tractate) of the Talmud dealing with that subject.

Avot
Literally "fathers". A section (tractate) of the Talmud dealing with ethics.

Avot D'Reb Natan
Similar to the Talmud tractate of Avot, see above.

ba'al
Literally "owner" also "author".

Ba'al Shem
Owner of a (good) name. Title used on rare occasions for person reputed to have mystical use of spiritual words and names.

ba'al teshuva
Someone who "owns" teshuva. Refers to a person who has returned to a lifestyle consistent with Halacha.

ba'alei
Plural of ba'al. Ba'alei Tosaphot - authors of the Tosaphot.

Beit Hamikdash
The holy temple in Yerushalayim (Jerusalem).

bnei
Literally "children of". Bnei Yisrael - Children of Israel.

ch'ramim
Plural of cherem.

Chabad
Initials of the Hebrew words Chochma ("wisdom") Bina ("understanding") Da'at ("perception").

Chacham
Wise person. Amongst Sephardi Jews it is used as a title similar to Rabbi.

chachamim
Plural of Chacham. Also used as a general term for sages.

chasid
A pious person. Since the mid 1700's has been used as a noun for followers of the movement started by the Ba'al Shem Tov. (See 5520\1760.)

chasidic
See chasid. Pertaining to the movement.

chasidim
Plural of chasid. Used as a noun for followers of an Admur, see above.

chasidut
The teachings of the movement of the Ba'al Shem Tov. See chasid.

cherem
Excommunication. A Jewish court of law is required to establish this, and a court is required to remove it. Mostly used as a form of punishment and/or socio- religious isolation.

Cheshvan
The name of a Jewish month (see glossaries calendar).

chidushim
Literally "new things". Refers to the scholarly achievement of attaining new interpretations and/or rulings in the study of Torah.

chozeh
Literally "seer". Chozeh of Lublin - the seer from that city, who earned the name by reputation.

Chumash
The "five books of Moses". Chamesh is five.

daf
Page. Daf HaYomi - "The Daily Page" of Talmud study.

dayan
Judge. member of court.

Elul
The name of a Jewish month (see glossaries calendar).

eretz
"The land of". Eretz Yisrael - the land of Israel.

erev
Literally "evening". Usually refers to the day preceding a Holy Day or festival.

Ge'onim
Plural of Gaon, see index.

Gemara
Part of the Talmud - see 4111\351, 4152\392, 4187\427.

ha
A Hebrew prefix meaning "the".

Hagada
The text which is recited on the night of Passover.

Halacha
Jewish law, which includes religious, social and civil law.

Hallel
Literally "praise". Refers to a (small) section of Psalms that is recited (during prayers) on Jewish festivals.

Chol HaMo'ed
The intermediary days of the festivals of Pesach (Passover) and Sukkot (Tabernacles). These days, although part of the festival, manifest a lesser holiness than the first and last days.

HaNagid
A title given to Jewish statesmen.

HaNassi
The president (of the Sanhedrin).

HaNavi
The prophet.

Rosh
HaShana The New Year festival.

Hashem
Literally "the name", meaning The Name. A term used to refer to G-d, without mentioning his name.

Haskala
Literally "pertaining to intellectual scope". A name used for the "intellectual enlightenment movement". See maskil below, and Haskala and maskilim in index.

Heter Iska
A manner of structuring a loan as a joint business venture, whereby interest payments

in fact become profit sharing, and are therefore not forbidden under Jewish law (Halacha).

Hoshana Rabba
The seventh day of the festival of Sukkot (Tabernacles).

Iyar
The name of a Jewish month (see glossaries calendar).

Kabbala
See index.

Kara'ites
See index.

kashrut
As in kosher. Refers to adherence to Jewish (dietary) laws.

Kedusha
Literally "holiness. Refers to a prayer recited by reader and congregation, when all are required to stand.

Kiddush
The prayer and benediction recited over wine, on Shabbat and major festivals.

Kislev
The name of a Jewish month (see glossaries calendar).

kohanim
Plural of kohen.

kohen
Literally "priest". Descendants of Levi (see levi'im, below), and more specifically descendants of Aharon. They performed the major priestly role in the Beit Hamikdash.

Kohen Gadol
High priest, see kohen.

Kov'im
See introduction to chapter 13. Used in this book to refer to major scholars of the era 1492 - 1648, see appendix D.

Kra'im
See index.

Lag B'omer
Literally "the 33rd day of the Omer counting". The Omer counting begins after the first day of Pesach (Passover) and continues for 49 days, until Shavu'ot (Pentecost). Lag B'Omer is a minor Jewish festival, commemorating the end of the death of the disciples of R.Akiva (see 3880\120), and the death of R.Shimon bar Yochai.

levi'im
Descendants of Levi (see 2195\-1566, 2332\-1429) who performed a secondary priestly role in the Beit Hamikdash.

levites
Same as levi'im, above.

maggid
Preacher. A role that was often distinct from the role of rabbi. The rabbi decided matters of Jewish law. The maggid was the preacher.

Mar
A respectful title in Aramaic.

marrano
Secret Jews of Spain and Portugal. See index.

maskil
Persons who identified and followed the Haskala (see above). Many displayed an unintellectual and biased attitude against traditional Jewish values (see maskilim in index).

maskilim
Plural of maskil.

mechutan
A person "connected by marriage".

Megilla
Literally "scroll".

meshumad
Apostate. A Jewish person who has taken the procedure of conversion to another religion.

Midrash
Work of Agada (see above).

Minyan
Shtarot Literally "counting of documents". A system of counting the years on Jewish documents which lasted over 1500 years, see 3449\-313.

Mitnagdim
Those who opposed the movement of chasidim (see above). See index.

motza'ei
The night after.

Mussaf
Additional prayer, recited on Shabbat and festivals.

mussar
Literally "chastisement". Refers to the teaching of discipline and ethics, often in a manner of reproof.

nassi
President. Usually refers to president of the Sanhedrin.

nazir
Literally "special devotion". Refers to a person who takes an oath to refrain from drinking wine, taking haircuts, and coming in contact with items that are ritually impure.

Nissan
The name of a Jewish month (see glossaries calendar).

Nistarim
Plural of nistar - "hidden".

Parshat Chukat
The Torah is divided into weekly readings. The week is often referred to by the name of the upcoming reading. Chukat is the name of one such portion.

Perushim
Literally "separate ones". Refers to the Pharisees, who adhered to Jewish law (Halacha), and thus kept a degree of separateness, in order to refrain from contact with items of spiritual impurity. (See 3570\-191 and index.)

Pesach.
The festival of Passover

piyut
A prayer in poetic form. The author often started every line with the alphabet structure, or with a consecutive letter of his name.

R.
Abbreviation used in this book for "Reb" or "Rabbi".

piyutim
Plural of piyut.

Raban
A title of rabbi with increased reverence.

Rbn.
Abbreviation used in this book for Raban, see above.

Rbnu
Abbreviation used in this book for the title "Rabbenu", which means literally "our teacher/rabbi". Was used only in instance of special reverence.

Rebbe
See Admur, above.

Rishon
Literally "first". Refers to Jewish scholar and authority during the period of 1040 - 1492. (See Appendix D).

Rishonim
Plural of Rishon.

Sanhedrin
The Jewish high court. See 3995\235. (See also index.)

Savurai
See Index.

Sh'elot Uteshuvot
Literally "questions and answers". Local rabbi's addressed their Halacha questions (in writing) to scholars of greater authority. A large collection of written answers were often published (by the author, or his disciples and/or descendants).

Shavu'ot
The festival of Pentecost. Literally means "weeks" because it occurs seven weeks after the first day of Pesach (Passover). (See Lag B'omer, above.)

shi'urim
Literally "measures". Refers to regular sessions of Torah study.

Shma
Shma Yisrael. The most famous passages of the Chumash (Bible) - "Hear O' Israel ...". Recited at least twice daily, as the most important prayer.

shmad
Conversion of a Jew to other religions.

shochet
A person trained to be a ritual slaughterer of kosher meat.

shochtim
Plural of shochet.

Shofet
Literally "judge". A title given to the Jewish rulers at a certain stage in history, see 2533\-1228.

Shoftim
Plural of Shofet.

shtadlan
A Jew who maintained extensive political connections, which were used to assist fellow Jews, particularly in times of need.

Shvat
The name of a Jewish month (see glossaries calendar).

Simchat Torah
Literally "the rejoicing of the Torah". The last day (appended) to the festival of Sukkot (Tabernacles).

Sivan
The name of a Jewish month (see glossaries calendar).

Sukkot
The festival of Tabernacles.

T'nach
Abbreviation for Torah, Nevi'im, Ketuvim. Although this symbolizes the three sections of the Bible: Torah (The Five Books of Moses), Nevi'im (the Prophets), Ketuvim (Hagiographa); it is commonly used to refer to the two latter sections.

tallit
Prayer shawl.

Tammuz
The name of a Jewish month (see glossaries calendar).

Tanna
Scholar of the Mishna section of the Talmud, see 3729\-32, 3949\189.

tanna'im
Plural of Tanna.

Tashlich
Prayers recited on Rosh HaShana, near waters, usually a distance from town.

Tefillin
Phylacteries. Specially prepared black leather boxes (with scriptures on parchment inside), bound on the arm and the head.

tekufa
Era.

tekufot
Plural of tekufa.

teshuva
Refers to a return to a lifestyle consistent with Halacha.

Tevet
The name of a Jewish month (see glossaries calendar).

Tishrei
The name of a Jewish month (see glossaries calendar).

Tish'a B'Av
The ninth day of Av. A day of many tragedies in Jewish history, see 3338\-423, 3829\69.

Torah
Generally refers to the whole body of Jewish religious knowledge.

Tosaphot
Literally "additional". Commentary on the Talmud, see 4865\1105, 5050\1290.

Tosephta
See 3949\189.

Tzadik
Righteous person. Also used to refer to an Admur (see above).

Tzadikim
Plural of Tzadik.

Tzeduki
Sadducee. See index.

Tzedukim
Plural of Tzeduki.

Yudenrat
A form of local Jewish self government under Nazi occupation. The Nazis used these bodies to administer their designs.

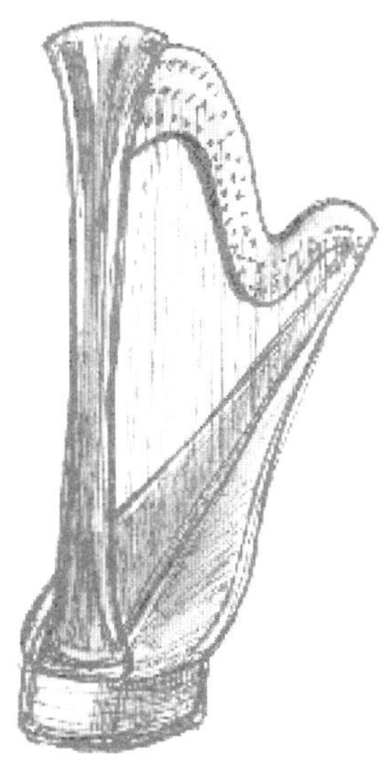

Glossary 2
List Of Abbreviated Reference Names

A.Z. = Avoda Zara
Ant. = Antiquities
Av. = Avot
Av.Dr.Nat. = Avot D'Reb Natan
B.B. = Bava Batra
B.Hab. = Bedek HaBayit
B.HaMa. = Ba'al HaMa'or
B.K. = Bava Kama
B.M. = Bava Metzia
B.Turim = Ba'al HaTurim
B.Y. = Beit Yosef
Bam. = Bamidbar
Bech. = Bechorot
Ber. = Berachot
Bert. = (R.Ovadya) Bertinura
Besh. = Beshalach (Sidra)
Bet. = Betza
Bik. = Bikkurim
Br. = Breishit
C.M. = Choshen Mishpat
Caf.Hachym. = Caf HaChayim
Chab. = Chabakuk
Cha. = Chagai
Chag. = Chagiga
Chan. = Chanuka
Chal. = Challa
Chav.Yair. = Chavat Ya'ir
Ches. = Chesronot HaShas (Hashmatot)
Chosh.Mish. = Choshen Mishpat
Chov.Umaz. = Chovel Umazik
Chul. = Chulin
Cri. = Critot
D.E. = Derech Eretz
D.H. (I or II) = Divrei HaYamim
D.YbY = Dvar Yom BeYomo
Dan. = Daniel
Dev. = Devarim
Dma. = Dmai
Dor.Har. = Dorot HaRishonim
Ed. = Edut (Hil.)
E.H. = Even HaEzer
Encpd.Jud. = Encyclopedia Judaica
Erch. = Erachin
Eruv. = Eruvin
Est. = Esther (Megillat)
Eych. = Eycha
Ez. = Ezra
Gd.Ppl. = Guide for Perplexed (Moreh Nevuchim)
Gevrt.HaSh. = Gevurot HaShem
Gimat. = Gimatriyot
Gir. = Girushin
Git. = Gittin
Hag.Bach = Hagahot HaBach
Hag.M. = Hagahot Maimoniyot
Hag.R.B.Rans. = Hagahot R'Betzalel Ranchburg
Hakd. = Hakdama (Introduction)
Hakd.L'Yad = Hakdama L'Yad (HaChazaka)
Hil. = Hilchot
Hor. = Horiyot
Hosh. = Hoshea
Ibn Ez. = Ibn Ezra
Igg.Mosh. = Iggrot Moshe
Igg.R.Sher.Gaon = Iggeret Rav Sherira Gaon
Igg.Teman = Iggeret Teman
Ish. = Ishut
Kel. = Kelim
Kes.Mish. = Kesef Mishneh
Ket. = Ketuvot
Kid. = Kiddushin
Kid.Hach. = Kiddush HaChodesh
Klly. = Klalei
Koh. = Kohelet
Kol.Mev. = Kol Mevasser
Korb. HaE. = Korban HaEida
Kuz. = Kuzari
Lech.Mish. = Lechem Mishneh
Lik.Sich. = Likutei Sichot
M.K. = Mo'ed Katan
Mach.Vit. = Machzor Vitry
Mag.Av. = Magen Avraham
Mag.Mish. = Maggid Mishneh
Mak. = Makot
Mal.Velov. = Malveh VeLoveh
Mam. = Mamrim
Manscpt.Ed. = recent edition from manuscript
Mas. = Ma'aser
Mas.Hak. = Ma'asei Hakorbanot
Mas.Shen. = Ma'aser Sheni
Mat.Keh. = Matanot Kehuna
Mech. = Mechilta
Meg. = Megilla
Meg.Tan. = Megillat Ta'anit
Me'i. = Me'illa
Mel. (I or II) = Melachim
Metz.Dav. = Metzudat David
Mhrl.MiPrg. = Maharal of Prague
Mhrm. = Maharam
Mhrshl. = Maharshal
Mi.Zer. = Mishnayot Zera'im
Mich. = Michah
Mid. = Midrash
Mido. = Midot
Mik. = Mikva'ot
Mil. = Milchamot
Min. = Minachot
Mish. = Mishna
Mi.Zer. = Mishnayot Zera'im
Mmn. = Maimonides (Rambam)
Mord. = Mordechai
Mrsha. = Maharsha

Naz. = Nazir
Nech. = Nechemyah
Ned. = Nedarim
Nid. = Nida
Nizk.Mam. = Nizkei Mamon
O.C. = Orach Chayim
O.Hat. = Or HaTorah
Onk. = Onkelus
Or.Hach = Or HaChayim
Otz.Hag. = Otzar HaGedolim
Otz. HaMid. = Otzar HaMidrashim (Eznstn)
Otz.Nechm. = Otzar Nechmad
Ovad. = Ovadya
Par. = Para
Pea. = Pe'a
Pek. = Pekudei (Sidra)
Pes. = Pesachim
Pir. Dr.El. = Pirkei D'Reb Elazar
Pir.Mi. = Pirush HaMishna
Pn.Mosh. = Pnei Moshe
Pr.Dr.El. = Pirkei D'Reb Elazar
q. = quoted in (or quoting)
R.H. = Rosh HaShana
Rab. = Rabba
Rab.Tam = Rabbenu Tam
RaN. = Rabbenu Nissim
Re = R'eh (Sidra)
Rut. = Ruth
S.K. = Se'if Katan
SMaG = Sefer Mitzvot (HaGadol)
Saad.G. = Saadya Gaon
San. = Sanhedrin
Sam. = Samchuni
Sed.Had. = Seder HaDorot
Sed.Hat. = Seder HaTanna'im
Sed.Ol. = Seder Olam (Rabba)
Sed.Ol.Zut. = Seder Olam Zuta
Sed.Tan.VeAm. = Seder Tanna'im VeAmora'im
Sef.Hak. = Sefer HaKabbala
Sef.Hay. = Sefer HaYashar
Sef.Mitz. = Sefer HaMitzvot (Maimonides)
Ser.Esh. = Seridey Esh
Sh. = Shmot
Sh.Hsh. = Shir HaShirim
Sh.Mkbtzt. = Shitta Mekubetzet
Sh.Up. = Sh'ela Upikadon
Shab. = Shabbat
Shek. = Shekalim
Shem.Hag. = Shem HaGedolim
Shev. = Shevu'ot
Shilt.Gib. = Shiltei Giborim
Shl. = Shlach (Sidra)
Shluch.Veshut. = Shluchim VeShutfim (Mmn.)
Shm. (I or II) = Shmuel
Shmitt. = Shmitta
Shof. = Shoftim
Shvi. = Shvi'it
Sif. = Sifri
Sif.Chach. = Siftei Chachamim
Smach. = Smachot
Sof. = Sofrim
Sot. = Sota
Suk. = Sukka
T.D.B.E. = Tanna DeBei Eliyahu
TBY. = Tur Beit Yosef
Tal. = Talmud
Tal.Tor. = Talmud Torah
Tan. = Ta'anit
Tan. = Tanchuma
Targ.Yon. = Targum Yonatan
Teh. = Tehilim
Tem. = Temura
Tetz. = Tetzaveh (Sidra)
Tfi. = Tefilla
Tif.Yis.Bo. = Tiferet Yisrael - Bo'az
Tol.Am.Ol. = Toldot Am Olam
Tor.HaOl. = Torat HaOla
Tor.Tem. = Torah Temima
Tos. = Tosaphot
Toseph. = Tosephta
Tos.Y.T. = Tosaphot Yom Tov
Tsh. = Teshuvot
Tsh.Hag. = Teshuvot HaGe'onim,
Tze. = Tzephanya
Tzed.Lad.= Tzeida LaDerech
Tzem.Dav. = Tzemach David
Tzi.El. = Tzitz Eliezer
Vay. = Vayikra
Vayish. = Vayishlach (Sidra)
VeAm. = VeAmora'im
Vik. = Viku'ach
Y.D. = Yoreh De'ah
Yab.Om. = Yabiya Omer
Yad. = Yadayim
Yad. = Yad HaChazaka (Mishneh Torah)
Yad.Mlchi. = Yad Malachi
Yal. = Yalkut
Yal.Reuv. = Yalkut Re'uveni
Yam.Sh.Sh. = Yam Shel Shlomo
Yech. = Yechezk'el
Yef.To. = Yefei To'ar
Yer. = Yerushalmi
Yes.Hat. = Yesodei HaTorah
Yesh. = Yeshayahu (Isaiah)
Yev. = Yevamot
Yir. = Yirmiyahu
Yit. = Yitro (Sidra)
Yom. = Yoma
Ysh. = Yehoshua (Joshua)
Yuch. = Yuchasin
Zech. = Zecharyah
Zev. = Zevachim
Zich.LeRi. = Zichron LeRishonim
Zoh. = Zohar

Glossary 3 — Calendar

How the Jewish (lunar) months co-incide with the secular (solar) months.

Tishrei
A 30 day month which can start as early as September 5, and can end as late as November 3.

The 1st of Tishrei begins the new Jewish year. This results in an overlap until January 1 when the Secular new year begins.

Cheshvan
A 29 or 30 day month (it varies) which starts as early as October 5, and can end as late as December 2.

Kislev
A 29 or 30 day month (it varies) which starts as early as November 4, and can end as late as January 1.

Tevet
A 29 day month which starts as early as December 4, and can end as late as January 30.

Shvat
A 30 day month which starts as early as January 1, and can end as late as March 1.

Adar [**Adar1 Adar2**]
The regular month of Adar is a 29 day month which starts as early as February 1, and can end as late as March 29.

When it occurs at an earlier date there is a 29 day leap year month called Adar2 (the first Adar is then called Adar1, and has 30 days.)

Adar2 begins as early as March 2 and ends as late as April 10. This balances out the 11 days difference between the lunar and the solar calendar (see 1675\-2104).

Nissan
A 30 day month which starts as early as March 12, and can end as late as May 10.

Iyar
A 29 day month which starts as early as April 11, and can end as late as June 8.

Sivan
A 30 day month which starts as early as May 10, and can end as late as July 8.

Tammuz
A 29 day month which starts as early as June 9, and can end as late as August 6.

Av
A 30 day month which starts as early as July 8, and can end as late as September 5.

Elul
A 29 day month which starts as early as August 7, and can end as late as October 4.

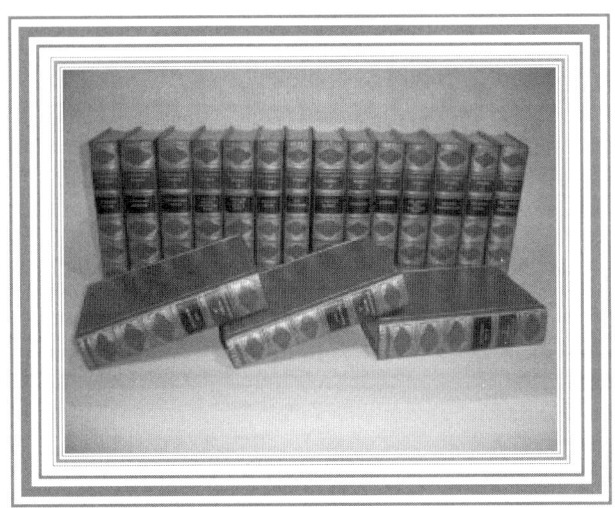

ILLUSTRATIONS

Classic Texts

Biblical, Talmudic , Post-Talmudic
& Halacha Texts

Text A.

327 קסד — יונתן בן עוזיאל

2

ושירין מהווא זמנא עינוי למכהי וקרא ית עשו בריה רבא בארבסר בניסן ואמר ליה ברי הא ליליא
דין עילאי משבחין למארי עלמא ואוצרי טלין מתפתחין ביה ואמר ליה הא נא: ב ואמר הא כדון
סיבת לית אנא ידע יום מותי: ג וכדון סב כדון מאני זינך בית גירך וקשתך ופוק לחקלא וצוד לי
צידא: ד ועיבד לי תבשילין היכמא דרחימית ותיעול לותי ואיכול בגין דתברכינך נפשי עד לא אימות:
ה ורבקה שמעת ברוח קודשא כד מליל יצחק עם עשו בריה ואזל עשו לחקלא למיצד צידא לאיתיאה:
ו ורבקה אמרת ליעקב ברה למימר הא ליליא הדין עלאי משבחין למרי עלמא ואוצרי טלין מתפתחין

פי׳ יונתן

[illegible]

רשב״ם

5

[illegible]

רש״י

4b

כלותה שטינו (כילה כח) אין משחיזין את הסכין אבל מגיהה על גבי חברתה חדד סכינך ושחוט יפה שלא תאכילני נבלה. (כ״ר): וצודה לי. מן ההפקר ולא מן הגזל: (ה) לצוד ציד להביא. מהו להביא אם לא ימצא ציד

[illegible]

שפתי חכמים

11b

[illegible]

דעת זקנים מבעלי התוספות

[illegible]

אבן עזרא

6

מגזרת מרה כלענה כטעם מרירות נפש וכן כתוב כי רעות בנות כנען וכתבה זו הפרשה שישמרו בני ישראל מבנות כנען: (א) הנה נא. כמו עתה: (ג) כליך. יתכן היות שם כלל. והפרט תליך וקשתיך. ותליך האשפה התלויה בעבור החצים או תליך כמו חרב ויחסר וא״ו מן תליך. כאדם עת אנוש: (ה) ורבקה שומעת. היתה שומעת:

רמב״ן

7

כי כן השיבו הארון עם הדורון לאלהים: (ד) בעבור תברכך נפשי. היה בדעתו לברך אותו ברכה שיזכה הוא בברכת אברהם לנחול את הארץ ולהיות הוא בעל הברית לאלהים כי הוא הבכור ונראה שלא הגידה לו רבקה מעולם הנבואה אשר אמר ה׳ לה ורב יעבוד צעיר כי איך היה יצחק עובר את פי ה׳ והיא לא תצלח והנה מתחלה לא הגידה לו דרך מוסר וצניעות כי הלך לדרוש את ה׳ שהלכה בלא רשות יצחק או שאמרה אין אנכי צריכה להגיד נבואה לנביא כי הוא גדול ממני המגיד לי ועתה לא רצתה לאמור

[illegible]

אור החיים

12b

ורבקה שומעת וגו׳. פי׳ מודיע הכתוב כי רבקה כביכול היתה שומעת תמיד לדברי יצחק וגו׳ הנם שלא ידבר בפניה והכן לזה אמר ורבקה שומעת בדבר וגו׳ ולא אמר ותשמע רבקה וגו׳ ולא אמר היתה שומעת וגו׳ ואולי כי דבר אליו יצחק בלט ולזה האמין כבוד יעקב כי הוא עשו כי באוזן עשו דבר והגם כי עיני יצחק כבדו וכו׳ הודיעו כי דברי סתר אליו ואולי כי לזה רמז הכ׳ באו׳ ויקרא את עשו וגו׳ ויאמר אליו בני ויאמר הנני פי׳ נתיחדו לדברים כנמסים:
ורבקה אמרה. אמר תוספת וא״ו כי הסכימה היא לרוח הקודש השרויה עליה: לאמר הנה וגו׳. פי׳ שלא יחשוב כי כבר עבר זמן ארוך מעת דבר יצחק לעשו ויאמר כי לא יספיק הוא לעשות מלוה של רבקה עד שכבר עשו עשה מעשהו לזה אמרה לאמר הנה פי׳ אמרה לו כי באותה שעה שמעה ויש זמן:

כלי יקר

10b

[illegible]

ספורנו

9

[illegible]

אבי עזר

[illegible]

Chumash *(Bible)*
with commentaries
(Mikra'ot Gedolot edition, see 5276\1516)

1. Text of the Chumash (Bible)
2. Yonatan ben Uziel (see 3769\9) *[Some differ – see there].*
3. Onkelus (see 3841\81)
4. Rashi (see 4865\1105) [4^b - Rashi continued.]

326 בראשית כז תולדות

3

אונקלוס

בְּרִי וַאֲמַר לֵיהּ הָא אֲנָא: ב וַאֲמַר הָא כְעַן סֵיבִית לֵית אֲנָא יָדַע יוֹמָא דְאֵימוּת: ג וּכְעַן סַב כְּעַן זֵינָךְ סֵיפָךְ וְקַשְׁתָּךְ וּפוֹק לְחַקְלָא וְצוּד לִי צֵידָא: ד וַעֲבֵיד לִי תַבְשִׁילִין כְּמָא דִי רְחֵימִית וְתָעֵיל לִי וְאֵיכוֹל בְּדִיל דִי תְבָרְכִינָךְ נַפְשִׁי עַד לָא אֵימוּת: ה וְרִבְקָה שְׁמָעַת כַּד מַלֵּיל יִצְחָק עִם עֵשָׂו בְּרֵיהּ וַאֲזַל עֵשָׂו לְחַקְלָא לְמֵיצַד צֵידָא לְאֵיתָאָה: ו וְרִבְקָה אֲמָרַת לְיַעֲקֹב בְּרַהּ לְמֵימַר הָא שְׁמָעִית יָת אֲבוּךְ מְמַלֵּיל עִם עֵשָׂו

עֵינָיו מֵרְאֹת וַיִּקְרָא אֶת־עֵשָׂו | בְּנוֹ
הַגָּדֹל וַיֹּאמֶר אֵלָיו בְּנִי וַיֹּאמֶר אֵלָיו 1
הִנֵּנִי: ב וַיֹּאמֶר הִנֵּה־נָא זָקַנְתִּי לֹא
יָדַעְתִּי יוֹם מוֹתִי: ג וְעַתָּה שָׂא־נָא
כֵלֶיךָ תֶּלְיְךָ וְקַשְׁתֶּךָ וְצֵא הַשָּׂדֶה
וְצוּדָה לִּי צֵידָה: ד וַעֲשֵׂה־לִי
מַטְעַמִּים כַּאֲשֶׁר אָהַבְתִּי וְהָבִיאָה
לִּי וְאֹכֵלָה בַּעֲבוּר תְּבָרֶכְךָ נַפְשִׁי
בְּטֶרֶם אָמוּת: ה וְרִבְקָה שֹׁמַעַת
בְּדַבֵּר יִצְחָק אֶל־עֵשָׂו בְּנוֹ וַיֵּלֶךְ עֵשָׂו
הַשָּׂדֶה לָצוּד צַיִד לְהָבִיא: ו וְרִבְקָה
אָמְרָה אֶל־יַעֲקֹב בְּנָהּ לֵאמֹר הִנֵּה
שָׁמַעְתִּי אֶת־אָבִיךָ מְדַבֵּר אֶל־עֵשָׂו

8

בעל הטורים

[illegible]

רש"י

4

אלו (שהיו מעשנות ומקטירות לע"ז) ד"א כשנעקד ע"ג המזבח והיה אביו רוצה לשחטו באותה שעה נפתחו השמים וראו מלאכי השרת והיו בוכים וירדו דמעותיהם ונפלו על עיניו לפיכך כהו עיניו. ד"א כדי שיטול יעקב את הברכות: (ב) לא ידעתי יום מותי. א"ר יהושע בן קרחה אם מגיע אדם לפרק אבותיו ידאג חמש שנים לפניהם וחמש לאחר כן ויצחק היה בן קכ"ג (כי יעקב בן ס"ג כשנתברך דוק ברש"י סוף הסדר) אמר שמא לפרק אמי אני מגיע והיא בת קכ"ז מתה והריני בן ה' שנים סמוך לפרקה לפיכך לא ידעתי יום מותי שמא לפרק אמי שמא לפרק אבא: (ג) תליך. חרבך שדרך לתלותה: שא נא. ל' השחזה

שפתי חכמים

11

[illegible]

אור החיים

12

ליטול יעקב הברכות ע"י סיבה זו ולא בידיעת יצחק כי מזה סובבו כמה סיבות לבני עמנו:

את עשו. ולא אמר אל עשו כי לא היה רואהו לומר שקראהו אלא קרא את שמו:

בנו הגדול. נתינת טעם למה לא קרא ליעקב כי זה הבכור ואולי שלא ידע מהמכר. וטעם יצחק שהיה חפץ לברך עשו הרשע כי חשב שבאמצעות הברכות יתהפך למדת הטוב וייטיב דרכיו כי הצדיקים יכאבו בעשות בניהם רשע והיה משתדל עמו להטיב ואפשר שהיה מועיל ותמצא שאמרו ז"ל כי נענש יעקב שמנע דיסה מעשו שאפשר שהיתה מחזירתו למוטב הרי שאפשר לו לחזור למוטב:

[illegible]

כלי יקר

10

[illegible]

5. Rashbam (see 4865\1105)
6. ibn Ezra (see 4924\1164)
7. Ramban (see 5030\1270)
8. Ba'al HaTurim (see 5100\1340)
9. Seforno (see 5302\1542)
10. Kli Yakar (see 5379\1619) [10b cont.]
11. Siftei Chachamim (see 5449\1689) [11b cont.]
12. Or HaChayim (see 5501\1741) [12b cont.]

Text B.

שמואל א יז 220

3 רש"י

4 רד"ק

1

ולהבת חניתו שש־מאות שקלים
ברזל ונשא הצנה הלך לפניו:
ח ויעמד ויקרא אל־מערכת ישראל
ויאמר להם למה תצאו לערך
מלחמה הלוא אנכי הפלשתי ואתם
עבדים לשאול ברו־לכם איש וירד
אלי: ט אם־יוכל להלחם אתי והכני
והיינו לכם לעבדים ואם־אני אוכל־
לו והכיתיו והייתם לנו לעבדים
ועבדתם אתנו: י ויאמר
הפלשתי אני חרפתי את־מערכות
ישראל היום הזה תנו־לי איש
ונלחמה יחד: יא וישמע שאול וכל־
ישראל את־דברי הפלשתי האלה
ויחתו ויראו מאד:
יב ודוד בן־איש אפרתי הזה מבית
לחם יהודה ושמו ישי ולו שמנה
בנים והאיש בימי שאול זקן בא
באנשים: יג וילכו שלשת בני־ישי
הגדלים הלכו אחרי־שאול למלחמה
ושם ׀ שלשת בניו אשר הלכו
במלחמה אליאב הבכור ומשנהו
אבינדב והשלשי שמה: יד ודוד הוא
הקטן ושלשה הגדלים הלכו אחרי

5 רלב"ג

2

פי' רבי ישעיה

6 מצודת דוד

7 מצודת ציון

T'nach *(Bible)* with commentaries

1. Text of the T'nach (Bible)
2. Yonatan ben Uziel (see 3769\9)
3. Rashi (see 4865\1105)
4. Radak (see 4951\1191)
5. Ralbag (5098\1338)
6. Metzudat David (see 5530\1770)
7. Metzudat Tzion (see 5530\1770)

Text C.

ר׳ עובדיה מברטנורה | כלאים קרחת פרק ד | תוספות יום טוב | קיט

אם העומד מרובה על הפרוץ (כא) מותר. ואם הפרוץ מרובה על העומד כנגד הפרצה (כב) אסור: ה הנוטע שורה של חמש גפנים. בשא כרם (כג). ובהא אינו כרם (כד) עד שיהו שם שתי שורות (כה). לפיכך הזורע ארבע אמות שבכרם (כו) בית שמאי אומרים קדש שורה אחת (כז). ובית הלל אומרים קדש שתי שורות (כח):

2

3

3

מלאכת שלמה

1

יכין תפארת ישראל בועז

4

משנה ראשונה

Mishna (Talmud) with commentaries

Illustration — a standard classical edition

1. Text of the Mishna (see 3949\189)
2. Bertinura, R.Ovadya (R'av) (see 5248\1488)
3. Tosaphot Yom Tov (see 5377\1616)
4. Tiferet Yisrael (see 5597\1837)

Text D.

אלו מפסיקין פרק שני פאה

1 פרק שלישי

2

3

Mishna (Talmud) with commentaries

Illustration: This appears at the end of Volume One *(Berachot)* of the standard Babylonian Talmud *(known as the Vilna Shas)*. This comprises the Mishna content of the first Talmud-section *Zeraim (laws pertaining to agriculture)* — a section (of the six) which has no Gemara content expounding the Mishna, except for this first tractate Berachot.

1. Text of the Mishna (see 3949\189)
2. Rash (see 4948\1187)
3. Rambam (see 4965\1204)

Illustration: Talmud Bavli (Babylonian Talmud).

Gemara *(Talmud)*
with commentaries

1. Text of the Mishna (Talmud)
2. Text of the Gemara (Talmud)
3. Rashi (see 4865\1105)
4. Tosaphot (see 5050\1290)
5. Bach (see 5400\1640)
6. Mesorat HaShas (see 5449\1689)
7. Hagahot HaGra (see 5558\1797)

Text F.

3

4

2

1

Illustration: Talmud Yerushalmi (Jerusalem Talmud, also called *Talmud Eretz Yisrael*).

1. Text of the Mishna (Talmud)
2. Text of the Gemara (Talmud)
3. Pnei Moshe (see 5541\1780)
4. Korban HaEida (see 5503\1743)

Text G.

נמוקי יוסף חזקת הבתים פרק שלישי בבא בתרא

1

3

4

2

Rif - Halachot
with commentaries

Illustration: Halachot of the Rif, addendum to standard edition of the Talmud (Vilna Shas).

1. Rif (see 4863\1103)
2. HaMaor (see 4910\1150)
3. Nimukei Yosef (see 5153\1393)

Text H.

רבינו נסים שבועות שתים בתרא פרק שלישי שבועות

1

2

Rif - Halachot
with commentaries

Illustration: Halachot of the Rif, addendum to standard edition of the Talmud (Vilna Shas).

1. Rif (see 4863\1103)
2. Ran (see 5104\1344)

215 קח כסף משנה משפטים. הלכות מלוה ולוה פי״א פי״ב מגיד משנה

בין אחר מותו ונמצא טובה על תנאי זה יותר מן התקנה. וסיים גדול עשו בדבר שמא לא ידע הלוה בתקנה זו ונמצא ממון יתומים יוצא שלא כדין שאין כח בתקנת אחרונים לחייב בה יתומים :

1 פרק שנים עשר 2

השגת הראב״ד

א אין נפרעין מן [א] היורשין אלא א״כ היו גדולים אבל יורשין קטנים אין נפרעין מהן שו״ח: ב ואפילו היה בו כל תנאי שבעולם לא יפרע בו המלוה כלום עד שיגדילו היתומים שמא יש להן ראיה ששוברין בו את השטר: ג היתה המלוה רבית של עכו״ם שהרי הרבית אוכלת בנכסיהן מעמידין להם אפוטרופוס ונזקקין לנכסיהן ומוכרין ופורעין החוב. וכן אשה שתבעה כתובתה בין אלמנה בין גרושה מעמידים להם אפוטרופוס ונזקקין משום חן האשה כדי שיהיה לה כלום שתנשא בו האשה לאחר. לפיכך אם קפצה האשה ונשאת ואחר כך באת לתבוע כתובתה מנכסי יתומים אין נזקקין לה עד שיגדילו

5

7

לחם משנה

8

9

משנה למלך

4 מגדל עוז

3 הגהות מיימוניות

Rambam - 'Yad'
Yad HaChazaka
with commentaries

Illustration: Rambam (Maimonides, magnum opus) *Mishneh Torah—Yad HaChazaka*.

1. Text of the Rambam's Halacha (see 4965\1204)
2. Ra'avad's critque (see 4959\1198)

Text I.

62 כסף משנה **שופטים. הלכות עדות פ"א** הרדב"ז

7

6

נפשות או מכות הולך ומעיד שנאמר אין חכמה ואין תבונה לנגד ה'. כל מקום שיש חילול השם אין חולקין כבוד לרב: ג כהן גדול אינו חייב להעיד אלא עדות שהיא למלך ישראל בלבד הולך לבית דין הגדול ומעיד בה אבל בשאר העדויות פטור: ד מצות עשה לדרוש את העדים ולחקרן ולהרבות בשאלתן ומדקדקין עליהן ומסיעין אותן מענין לענין בעת השאלה כדי שישתקו או יחזרו בהן אם יש בעדותן דופי. שנאמר ודרשת וחקרת ושאלת היטב. וצריכין הדיינים להזהר בעת חקירת העדים [שמא מתוכה ילמדו לשקר. ובשבע חקירות בודקין אותם]. באי זו שבוע. באי זו שנה. באי זו חדש. כמה בחדש. באי זה יום מימי השבת. ובכמה שעות ביום. ובאי זה מקום. אפילו אמר היום הרגו או אמש הרגו שואלין לו באי זה שבוע באי זו שנה באי זה חדש בכמה בחדש באי זה יום באי זו שעה. ומכלל החקירות יתר על השבע השוות בכל שאם העידו עליו שעבד

לחם משנה

8

משנה למלך

9

מגדל עוז

4

הגהות מיימוניות

3

3. Hagahot Maymoniyot (see 5059\1298)
4. Migdal Oz (see 5096\1336)
5. Magid Mishneh (see 5104\1344)
6. Radvaz (see 5313\1553)
7. Kesef Mishneh (see 5335\1575)
8. Lechem Mishneh (see 5335\1575)
9. Mishneh LeMelech (see 5487\1727)

Text J.

Shulchan Aruch
ORACH CHAYIM
with commentaries

1. Shulchan Aruch - R.Yosef Karo *(Beit Yosef)* (see 5330\1570)
2. Hagahot of the Ramo *(Mappah)* (see 5330\1570)
3. Taz (see 5406\1646)
4. Magen Avraham (see 5433\1673)
5. Ba'er Heitev (see 5483\1723)
6. Gra (see 5558\1797)
7. Machatzit HaShekel (see 5567\1807)

Text K.

באר הגולה 216 שפתי כהן יורה דעה קעו קעז הלכות רבית טורי זהב

Shulchan Aruch
Yoreh Deya
with commentaries

1. Shulchan Aruch - R.Yosef Karo *(Beit Yosef)* (see 5330\1570)
2. Hagahot of the Ramo *(Mappah)* (see 5330\1570)
3. Taz (see 5406\1646)
4. Shach (see 5406\1646)
5. Ba'er Heitev (see 5483\1723)
6. Gra (see 5558\1797)
7. Pitchei Teshuva (see 5616\1856)

Text L.

Shulchan Aruch
EVEN HAEZER
with commentaries

1. Shulchan Aruch - R.Yosef Karo *(Beit Yosef)* (see 5330\1570)
2. Hagahot of the Ramo *(Mappah)* (see 5330\1570)
3. Taz (see 5406\1646)
4. Chelkat Mechokek (see 5400\1640)
5. Beit Shmuel (see 5449\1689)
6. Ba'er Heitev (see 5483\1723)
7. Gra (see 5558\1797)
8. Pitchei Teshuva (see 5616\1856)

Text M.

Shulchan Aruch
Choshen Mishpat
with commentaries

1. Shulchan Aruch - R.Yosef Karo *(Beit Yosef)* (see 5330\1570)
2. Hagahot of the Ramo *(Mappah)* (see 5330\1570)
4. Sma (see 5374\1614)
5. Shach (see 5406\1646)
6. Ba'er Heitev (see 5483\1723)
9. Ketzot HaChoshen (see 5488\1788)
10. Netivot HaMishpat (see 5569\1809)

חדושי הלכות השותפין פרק ראשון בבא בתרא ואגדות מהרש"א ב

2

חכמת שלמה

1

מהר"ם

3

Commentaries *on the earlier commentaries* of the Talmud

Illustration: Later commentaries of the Talmud — who focused on delving into the commentaries of Rashi and Tosaphot — addendum to standard edition of the Talmud (Vilna Shas).

1. Maharshal (see 5334\1573)
2. Maharsha (see 5374\1614)
3. Maharam (see 5376\1616)

INDEX

(A) = Amora
(E) = Exilarch
(G) = Gaon
(K) = King
(L) = Acharon
(P) = Prophet
(Q) = Queen
(R) = Rishon
(S) = Shofet (Judges)
s. = son of
(T) = Tanna
(V) = Savurai

- *This index gives the* YEAR *as the reference, not the* PAGE.
- *It is advisable to read the whole entry for the year given, because in some instances the reference to a specific year may relate to more than one occurence (and entry) in that year* (see page vi).
- *An asterisk "*" denotes that the* JEWISH CALENDAR YEAR *is used on that listing.*
- *The* JEWISH CALENDAR YEAR *is used until the beginning of Section IV (Chapter 12) "Universal Dispersion", which begins with the year 4800\1040.*
- *Subjects which appear in earlier years — in Sections I to III — as well as also appearing in Section IV, (e.g. Yerushalayim, which appears throughout), are listed in the index twice — in both formats,* JEWISH CALENDAR YEAR *and* SECULAR CALENDAR YEAR, *as separate listings — to retain clarity.*

INDEX

A

B

C

D

L

M

N

S

T

Z

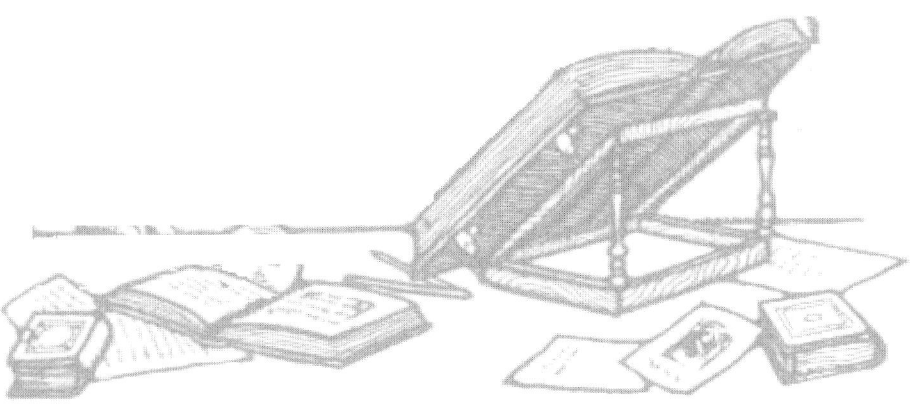

Author of the highly acclaimed
Jewish Time Line Encyclopedia

"A worthy contribution to unadalterated Jewish history."

Rabbi Mordechai Gifter, O.B.M.

"Rabbi Mattis Kantor is blessed with extraordinary skills as an educator. He has prepared an indispensable reference work for every Judaic library. It provides a global perspective on the whole panorama of Jewish history, allowing the researcher and even the casual reader to perceive the patterns of Jewish glory, survival and eternity."

Rabbi J. Fishman, Torah Umesorah, National Society for Hebrew Day Schools

"...the references are most impressive ....Historians who are unfamiliar with the religious literature will be most thankful to Rabbi Kantor for giving them access.... unique among the single volume histories .... user friendly ...."

The Australian Jewish News

"The fine scholarship and painstaking thoroughness reflected in this encyclopedic work are most impressive. The encyclopedia is not only unique in its presentation of Jewish history in light of Jewish tradition, but also—and foremostly—in its directing the reader to the wealth of talmudic and rabbinic sources. For the student of History, it will serve as a key to the treasures of Jewish traditional historical sources to which at present he hardly has any independent access."

Prof. Ezra Shereshevsky, Temple University Dept. of Hebrew & Near Eastern Languages

".....The encyclopedia is constructed in a highly accessible way......"

The Jewish Week, N.Y.

"Kantor's volume has something for everyone ..... no Jewish library should be without."

The Canadian Jewish News

"..... a most important and necessary contribution ....encouraging to see such a comprehensive yet concise documentation....so remarkable in its presentation and style...a valuable asset on the shelf of every Jewish adult and student, teenager and bar mitzvah boy ....."

Rabbi Abraham B. Hecht, President, Rabbinical Alliance of America

"There is no other Jewish history book that provides information in this highly specialized manner ..... The Jewish Time Line Encyclopedia has already become an invaluable reference tool for librarians, scholars, teachers and students."

The Jewish Advocate, Boston

"...there is simply nothing else like it. What the gifted author has done is to examine the broad span of history year-by-year ..... The result is breathtaking.
"Kantor" will not only become a standard reference book; it will also provide hours (perhaps years) of educational enjoyment to the many who will browse, and browse again, through its absolutely fascinating pages."

Arthur Kurzweil,
(then) ***Editor-in-Chief, Jewish Book Club***

"...the volume does provide a very helpful tool ...... a library reference work..."

The Jerusalem Post

"The Jewish Time Line Encyclopedia is a feast for browsers ...... a resoundingly Jewish book...."

The Jewish Post

"There is a uniqueness in the manner ... lends considerable importance to Rabbi Kantor's literary accomplishment."

The Detroit Jewish News

"Rabbi Kantor has written a book of excellent scholarship and great practical value .... the material is based on thorough research of Talmudic and Rabbinic resources............"

Rabbi Berel Wein, Historian, Jerusalem,
formerly - ***Shaarei Torah, N.Y.***

"I am deeply impressed by the grandeur of this book and its usefulness for scholars and students in Jewish history. Its vista comprises the entire panorama of Jewish history. The special value of this volume is its usefulness to the layman and the academic community. It enables potential students and scholars to correlate Jewish history and world history and to understand the significance of Jewish movements in their historical context."

Dr. Bernard Lander
President, Touro College

About the Author

Australian born Rabbi Mattis Kantor studied in Yeshivot in Cleveland, Israel and then New York, where he received Rabbinical ordination from the Yeshiva Tomchei Tmimim in 1966, and a Masters Degree in Educational Administration from Fordham University in 1970.

He is a noted author and lecturer who has held a number of educational positions in the United States and Australia. He has recently retired as the rabbi of Congregation Zichron Moshe in Monsey New York, and is currently writing new works.

He is the author of three major works; all have been featured as a MAIN SELECTION OF THE MONTH *by the Jewish Book Club in the USA.*

A Guide for the Entangled; CHASSIDIC INSIGHTS *was first published in 1978. It is a system of contemporary religious hashkafa philosophy with a mystical Kabala blend.*

A Guide for the Entangled; TEN KEYS FOR UNDERSTANDING HUMAN NATURE *was published in spring of 1994. It is a system of personality analysis based on the Kabala.*

THE JEWISH TIME LINE ENCYCLOPEDIA *was first published in 1989. The exceptional organization of this work and its traditional approach to Jewish history have won it some remarkable acclaim for its brief — yet comprehensive, and simple scholarly, style. It has seen three editions.*

Chumash from Iraq with Targum in Aramaic - from around the year 1,000 just after the period of the Ge'onim there

ISBN 978-0--9670378-3-7
90000>
9 780967 037837